Normal distribution—number of standard deviations away from the mean

$$z = \frac{\bar{x} - \mu}{\sigma} \tag{3-14}$$

Standard error of the mean

$$\sigma_{\bar{x}} = \frac{\sigma}{\sqrt{n}} \tag{4-1}$$

Standard error of the proportion

$$\sigma_{\bar{p}} = \sqrt{\frac{\bar{p}\bar{q}}{n}} \tag{4-2}$$

Confidence interval for the mean

$$\bar{X} \pm z\sigma_{\bar{x}} \tag{p. 105}$$

Confidence interval for a proportion

$$\bar{p} \pm z\sigma_{\bar{p}} \tag{p. 109}$$

Sample size to estimate a mean

$$n = \frac{z^2\sigma^2}{d^2} \tag{4-5}$$

Sample size to estimate a proportion

$$n = \frac{z^2pq}{d^2} \tag{4-6}$$

Finite correction factor

$$cf = \sqrt{1 - \frac{n}{N}} \tag{5-1}$$

Sample size to estimate a mean if the size of the population is known

$$n = \frac{n_o}{1 + (n_o/N)} \tag{5-4}$$

or

$$n = \frac{z^2\sigma^2/d^2}{1 + (z^2\sigma^2/d^2N)} \tag{5-3}$$

Sample size to estimate a proportion if the size of the population is known

$$n = \frac{n_o}{1 + (n_o/N)} \tag{5-4}$$

or

$$n = \frac{z^2pq/d^2}{1 + (z^2pq/d^2N)} \tag{5-5}$$

Estimate confidence size small, and popul

$$t = \frac{\bar{X} - \mu}{s_{\bar{X}}} \qquad \bar{X} \pm ts_{\bar{X}} \tag{p. ...}$$

Sample size estimate when σ is not known

$$n = \frac{t^2s^2}{d^2} \tag{5-8}$$

Sample stratification

$$n_i = n/L \qquad \text{equal allocation} \tag{5-9}$$

$$n_i = \frac{N_i}{N}n \qquad \text{proportional allocation} \tag{5-10}$$

$$n_i = \frac{N_is_i}{\Sigma N_is_i}n \qquad \text{optimal allocation} \tag{5-11}$$

$$n_i = \frac{N_is_i/\sqrt{C_i}}{\Sigma(N_is_i/\sqrt{C_i})}n \qquad \begin{array}{l}\text{least-cost}\\\text{allocation}\end{array} \tag{5-12}$$

Error of a stratified sample

$$s_{\bar{X}_s} = \sqrt{\Sigma\left(\frac{N_i}{N}\right)^2 \frac{s_i^2}{n_i}\left(1 - \frac{n_i}{N_i}\right)} \tag{5-14}$$

Sampling error for a clustered sample

$$\sigma_{\bar{p}_c} = \sqrt{\frac{pq}{n}[1 + r_c(N_s - 1)]}$$

$$r_c = \frac{\Sigma(p_i - p)^2/p_c - \Sigma(p_iq_i/p_c)/(N_s - 1)}{pq} \tag{5-15}$$

Standard error of the difference between two means

$$\sigma_{\bar{X} - \bar{X}_2} = \sqrt{\frac{\sigma_1^2}{n_1} + \frac{\sigma_2^2}{n_2}} \tag{7-1}$$

Standard error of the difference between two means if σ is not known

$$s_{X_1 - \bar{X}_2} = \sqrt{\frac{s_1^2}{n_1} + \frac{s_2^2}{n_2}} \tag{7-2}$$

z value for a test of a difference between means

$$z = \frac{(\bar{X}_1 - \bar{X}_2) - 0}{s_{\bar{X}_1 - \bar{X}_2}} \tag{7-3}$$

(Continued on overleaf)

Overall proportion of successes from the sample proportions

$$\bar{p} = \frac{n_1\bar{p}_1 + n_2\bar{p}_2}{n_1 + n_2} \tag{7-5}$$

Standard error of the difference between proportions

$$s_{\bar{p}_1 - \bar{p}_2} = \sqrt{\bar{p}\bar{q}\left(\frac{1}{n_1} + \frac{1}{n_2}\right)} \tag{7-6}$$

z value for a test of the difference between proportions

$$z = \frac{(\bar{p}_1 - \bar{p}_2) - 0}{s_{p_1 - p_2}} \tag{7-8}$$

Standard error of the difference between means for a small sample with σ unknown

$$s^2 = \frac{(n_1 - 1)s_1^2 + (n_2 - 1)s_2^2}{n_1 + n_2 - 2} \tag{7-9}$$

$$s_{\bar{X}_1 - \bar{X}_2} = s\sqrt{\frac{1}{n_1} + \frac{1}{n_2}} \tag{7-10}$$

t value for a test of a difference between means

$$t = \frac{(\bar{X}_1 - \bar{X}_2) - 0}{s_{X_1 - X_2}} \tag{p. 191}$$

Analysis of variance

$$F = \frac{\text{variation between groups}}{\text{variation within groups}} = \frac{V_B}{V_W} \tag{p. 193}$$

Between column (group) variation (for four groups)

$$V_B = \frac{n_1(\bar{X}_1 - \bar{\bar{X}})^2 + n_2(\bar{X}_2 - \bar{\bar{X}})^2 + n_3(\bar{X}_3 - \bar{\bar{X}})^3 + n_4(\bar{X}_4 - \bar{\bar{X}})^4}{c - 1} \tag{7-11}$$

Within group variation

$$V_W = \frac{\Sigma(X_{rc} - \bar{X}_c)^2}{(n - c)} \tag{7-13}$$

Chi-square test

$$\chi^2 = \Sigma\frac{(O - E)^2}{E} \tag{8-1}$$

Chi-square formula with correction for continuity

$$\chi^2 = \Sigma\frac{(|O - E| - \frac{1}{2})^2}{E} \tag{8-2}$$

Short-cut computation formula without the continuity correction

$$\chi^2 = \frac{N(|AD - BC|)^2}{(A + B)(C + D)(A + C)(B + D)} \tag{8-3}$$

With the correction, the formula would be

$$\chi^2 = \frac{N(|AD - BC| - N/2)^2}{(A + B)(C + D)(A + C)(B + D)} \tag{8-4}$$

Kruskal-Wallis test

$$H = \frac{12}{n(n + 1)}\left[\sum_{i=1}^{K}\frac{T_i^2}{n_i}\right] - [3(n + 1)] \tag{8-5}$$

To correct for ties

$$H_t = \frac{[12/N(N + 1)]\Sigma(R^2/n) - 3(N + 1)}{1 - [\Sigma T/(N_3 - N)]} \tag{9-9}$$

Rank-order correlation

$$r_r = 1 - \frac{6\Sigma d^2}{n(n^2 - 1)} \tag{9-1}$$

To correct for ties

$$r_{r.t} = \frac{[(N^3 - N/12) - \Sigma T_x] + [(N^3 - N/12) - \Sigma T_y] - \Sigma d^2}{2\sqrt{[(N^3 - N/12) - \Sigma T_x][(N^3 - N/12) - \Sigma T_y]}} \tag{9-8}$$

Mann-Whitney test

$$U_1 = n_1 n_2 + \frac{n_1(n_1 + 1)}{2} - R_1 \tag{9-2}$$

$$U_2 = n_1 n_2 + \frac{n_2(n_2 + 1)}{2} - R_2 \tag{9-3}$$

$$\mu_U = \frac{n_1 n_2}{2} \tag{9-4}$$

$$\sigma_U = \sqrt{\frac{n_1 n_2(n_1 + n_2 + 1)}{12}} \tag{9-5}$$

$$z = \frac{U_i - \mu_U}{\sigma_U} = \frac{U - \dfrac{n_1 n_2}{2}}{\sqrt{\dfrac{n_1 n_2(n_1 + n_2 + 1)}{12}}} \tag{9-6}$$

To correct for ties

$$\sigma_{\mu.t} = \sqrt{\left(\frac{n_1 n_2}{N(N - 1)}\right)\left(\frac{N^3 - N}{12} - \Sigma T\right)} \tag{9-7}$$

(*Continued on inside back cover*)

STATISTICS FOR BUSINESS AND ECONOMICS

McGraw-Hill Series in
QUANTITATIVE METHODS FOR MANAGEMENT

Consulting Editor
MARTIN K. STARR, Columbia University

BOWEN and STARR: *Basic Statistics for Business and Economics*

BYRD and MOORE: *Decision Models for Management*

DANNENBRING and STARR: *Management Science: An Introduction*

FITZSIMMONS and SULLIVAN: *Service Operations Management*

GOHAGAN: *Quantitative Analysis for Public Policy*

HEYMAN and SOBEL: *Stochastic Models in Operations Research, Volume I: Stochastic Processes and Operating Characteristics*

McKENNA: *Quantitative Methods for Public Decision Making*

SOBOL and STARR: *Statistics for Business and Economics: An Action Learning Approach*

SWANSON: *Linear Programming: Basic Theory and Applications*

ZELENY: *Multiple Criteria Decision Making*

STATISTICS FOR BUSINESS AND ECONOMICS

An Action Learning Approach

MARION GROSS SOBOL

Edwin L. Cox School of Business
Southern Methodist University

MARTIN K. STARR

Graduate School of Business
Columbia University

McGRAW-HILL BOOK COMPANY

New York / St. Louis / San Francisco / Auckland / Bogotá
Hamburg / Johannesburg / London / Madrid
Mexico / Montreal / New Delhi / Panama / Paris
São Paulo / Singapore / Sydney / Tokyo / Toronto

STATISTICS
FOR BUSINESS
AND
ECONOMICS
An Action Learning
Approach

Copyright © 1983 by McGraw-Hill, Inc.
All rights reserved.
Printed in the United States of America.
Except as permitted under the United States Copyright Act of 1976,
no part of this publication may be reproduced
or distributed in any form or by any means,
or stored in a data base or retrieval system,
without the prior written permission of the publisher.

234567890 DODO 89876543

ISBN 0-07-059571-2

This book was set in Times Roman by University Graphics, Inc.
The editors were Donald G. Mason and Gail Gavert;
the designer was Nicholas Krenitsky;
the production supervisor was John Mancia.
The drawings were done by Danmark & Michaels, Inc.
R. R. Donnelley & Sons Company was printer and binder.

Library of Congress Cataloging in Publication Data

Sobol, Marion Gross.
    Statistics for business and economics.

    (McGraw-Hill series in quantitative methods
for management)
    Includes bibliographies and index.
    1. Commercial statistics. 2. Economics—
Statistical methods. 3. Statistics. I. Starr,
Martin Kenneth, date   . II. Title.
III. Series.
HF1017.S63   519.5   81-19289
ISBN 0-07-059571-2   AACR2

ABOUT
THE AUTHORS

MARION GROSS SOBOL is professor of management science and computers at the Cox School of Business, Southern Methodist University. She received her B.A. in economics from Syracuse University and her M.A. and Ph.D. at the University of Michigan. Currently book review editor for *Interfaces*, an associate editor for *Management Science*, and a member of the Editorial Board of the *Case Research Journal*, Dr. Sobol is also national vice president of Alpha Iota Delta, the decision science honorary society. She has worked at the Survey Research Center, University of Michigan, and in the statistics departments of both the Metropolitan Life Insurance Company and a social service agency. She has contributed articles to such professional journals as *The Journal of the American Statistical Association, Estadistica, The Review of Economics and Statistics, Interfaces, Social Science Quarterly*, and *The Journal of Human Resources*. Her applied articles have appeared in *British Museums Journal, Urban Education, Research in Higher Education, The School Counselor, The Urban Review*, and *Texas Realtor*. She taught at the University of Michigan, Dutchess Community College, the University of Rhode Island, Rutgers, and Rider College before joining the SMU faculty. Besides being a consultant, Dr. Sobol has given seminars on math anxiety and the use of the case method in teaching statistics.

MARTIN K. STARR is professor of management science at the Graduate School of Business, Columbia University. He received his B.S. at M.I.T. and his Ph.D. at Columbia. Professor Starr is editor-in-chief of the journal *Management Science* and a past president of The Institute of Management Sciences. He is consulting editor for the McGraw-Hill Series in Quantitative Methods for Management. In addition, he serves on the editorial board of *Behavioral Science*, the advisory board of the *Nijenrode Studies in Business*, and the academic advisory board of the *Journal of Management Studies*, and he is an editorial adviser to the *Operational Research Quarterly*. Professor Starr has written a number of well-known texts in operations management and management science and has contributed numerous papers in a variety of journals. He is a member of TIMS, ORSA, and the Academy of Management, the Design Methods Group, and the Society of Manufacturing Engineers Management Council, and has served as chairman of professional meetings for IFORS, TIMS, ORSA, and the Society for General Systems Research.

TO

Harold, Diane, Neil, Jessica, and Martin Sobol
—and my parents—with affection.

My father, Harry Starr,
who was the greatest teacher I have known.

CONTENTS

Preface   xv

CHAPTER 1
INTRODUCTION   1

  1-1 Overview of the Book   2
  1-2 Where to Find Information   3
       Almanacs / Regularly Published U.S. Government Documents /
       Financial Firms / Research Organizations / Interest Groups /
       Guides to Periodical Literature / Footnotes and References /
       Bibliographies and Librarians / Computerized Data Bases /
       Card Catalogue
  1-3 Statistics versus Statistical Techniques   7
       What Statistical Analysis Can Do / Causality /
       Representativeness
  1-4 Statistics in Action   9
       Cases / Statistical Experiments or Investigations
  1-5 Bibliography   11

CHAPTER 2
DESCRIPTIVE TECHNIQUES:
FREQUENCY DISTRIBUTIONS, MEASURES OF
CENTRAL TENDENCY, AND VARIATION   13

  2-1 Analysis of Data   14
  2-2 Constructing a Frequency Distribution Table   14
  2-3 Graphic Analysis   16
       Histogram and Frequency Polygon / Cumulative Frequency
       Distribution / Distorted Graphs
  2-4 Measures of Central Tendency: Ungrouped Data   20
       Arithmetic Mean / Weighted Arithmetic Mean
  2-5 Mean for Grouped Data   24

2-6	Computation of the Median for Grouped Data	25
2-7	Percentiles, Deciles, and Quartiles	26
2-8	Measures of Variation: Ungrouped Data	27
	Standard Deviation: Ungrouped Data	
2-9	Standard Deviation: Grouped Data	33
	Problems	
2-10	Chebycheff's Inequality	37
	Problems	
2-11	Coefficient of Variation	38
2-12	Skewness and Kurtosis	40
	Problems	
2-13	Summary	43
2-14	Bibliography	45
2-15	Cases	45

CHAPTER 3
PROBABILITY AND PROBABILITY DISTRIBUTIONS   **55**

3-1	Simple Rules of Probability	57
3-2	Statistical Independence	60
3-3	Mathematical Expectation	63
	Problems	
3-4	Probabilities in Games of Chance	64
3-5	Discrete Probability Distributions	67
	Binomial Distribution / *Computation of Binomial Probabilities* / *Use of Binomial Tables* / *Mean and Standard Deviation of Binomial Distribution* / *Problems* / *Poisson Distribution* / *Relation of Binomial Distribution to Poisson Distribution* / *Use of the Poisson Table* / Problems	
3-6	Continuous Probability Distributions	78
	What Is a Normal Distribution? / Relation of Normal Distribution to Binomial Distribution / Use of the Standard Normal Table / Problems	
3-7	Summary	85
3-8	Bibliography	86
3-9	Cases	87

CHAPTER 4
SAMPLE SELECTION AND SAMPLING THEORY   **95**

4-1	Why Sample?	96
4-2	Common Uses of Sampling	97
4-3	Comparison of Sample Survey Methods	97
4-4	Sample Designs	97
	Probability Samples / Nonprobability Samples	
4-5	Central Limit Theorem	102
4-6	Confidence Intervals	105

4-7   Confidence Intervals When σ Is Not Known   107
       Problems
4-8   Confidence Intervals for a Proportion   108
       Problems
4-9   Sample Size   110
       Problems
4-10   Summary   113
4-11   Bibliography   114
4-12   Cases   114

CHAPTER 5
OPERATIONAL SAMPLE DESIGN   125

5-1   Finite Population Correction Factor   126
       Problems
5-2   Sample Size with Finite Correction Factor   127
       Problems
5-3   Small Samples   130
       The t Distribution
5-4   Sample Size When σ Is Unknown   133
       Problems
5-5   Stratified Sampling   134
       Sample Allocation / Measuring Error / Determination of
       Sample Size for Different Allocation Methods
5-6   Clustered Samples   141
       Measuring Error / Problems / Computer Problems
5-7   Summary   145
5-8   Bibliography   146
5-9   Cases   147

CHAPTER 6
HYPOTHESIS TESTING   153

6-1   Type I and Type II Errors   154
6-2   Null Hypothesis and Scientific Testing Procedure   158
       One-tailed and Two-tailed Tests / Measuring Type II Error /
       How to Lower Type II Error and Retain the Same Type I Error
6-3   Power Curve (Optional Section)   164
6-4   One-Sample Tests   167
       One-tailed Test of a Mean / Two-tailed Test of a Mean / One-
       tailed Test of a Proportion / Two-tailed Test of a Proportion /
       Problems
6-5   Test of a Mean (Small Sample, σ Unknown), t Test 174
       Two-tailed Test of a Mean, σ Unknown, Small Sample / One-tailed
       Test of a Mean, σ Unknown, Small Sample / Problems
6-6   Summary   178
6-7   Bibliography   179

CHAPTER 7
HYPOTHESIS TESTS:
TWO- AND THREE-SAMPLE OR LARGER SAMPLE TESTS   **181**

   7-1 Two-Sample Tests (Large Samples)   182
        Two-tailed Tests of Difference between Means / Problems /
        Two-tailed Tests of Difference between Proportions (Large
        Sample) / Problems / One-tailed Test of Difference between
        Means / One-tailed Test of Difference between Proportions /
        Problems
   7-2 Test of Difference between Means (Small Sample, σ Unknown)   190
        Problems
   7-3 Analysis of Variance   192
        Use of the F Table / Summary of Tests Used in Chapters 6
        and 7 / Problems
   7-4 Summary   199
   7-5 Bibliography   201
   7-6 Cases   201

CHAPTER 8
NONPARAMETRIC METHODS:
CHI-SQUARE TEST AND KRUSKAL-WALLIS TEST   **213**

   8-1 Methods of Data Classification   214
   8-2 Chi-Square Distribution   215
   8-3 Chi-Square Test of Goodness of Fit   215
        Using the Chi-Square Table / *Determining the Number of Degrees
        of Freedom* / *Looking up Values in the Chi-Square Table* /
        Performing a Test of Goodness of Fit
   8-4 Chi-Square Test of Independence   221
        Determining Degrees of Freedom (Independence) / Performing a
        Test of Independence / Conditions for Using Chi-Square Tests
        Properly / Problems / Appendix 8-4A: Correction for Continuity
        and Short-Cut Computation Method
   8-5 Kruskal-Wallis Test: A Test of the Difference between Means   228
        Problems
   8-6 Summary   231
   8-7 Bibliography   232
   8-8 Cases   232

CHAPTER 9
NONPARAMETRIC TESTS OF RANKS, RUNS, AND SIGNS   **239**

   9-1 Rank-Order Correlation   241
        Problems
   9-2 Rank-Sum Test (Mann-Whitney)   247
        Two-tailed Test / One-tailed Test / Problems /
        Appendix A9-2: Correction for Tied Values / *Mann-Whitney
        Test* / *Rank-Order Correlation* / *Kruskal-Wallis Test*

9-3   Kolmogorov-Smirnov Test of Goodness of Fit for Ordinal Data
      (One-Sample Test)   255
9-4   Kolmogorov-Smirnov Test of Independence (Two-Sample Test)   257
      Problems
9-5   One-Sample Runs Test   261
      Problems
9-6   Sign Test   266
      Problems
9-7   Summary   270
9-8   Bibliography   271
9-9   Cases   271

CHAPTER 10
REGRESSION ANALYSIS   **277**

10-1   Scatter Diagrams   278
10-2   Fitting a Line to the Data Points   281
10-3   The Method of Least Squares   284
       Computation of the Least-Squares Regression Line / Using the
       Regression Line for Point Estimates / Appendix 10-3A: Deriving
       the Normal Equations and Formulas for a and b
10-4   Measuring the Standard Error of Estimate   287
10-5   The Meaning of the Standard Error of Estimate   288
10-6   Using the Standard Error of Estimate for a Forecast (Optional) 289
       Appendix 10-6A: Estimating a Conditional Mean
10-7   Conditions for Using Linear Regression Analysis   292
10-8   Coefficient of Determination   293
10-9   Coefficient of Correlation   295
10-10 Significance of the Coefficient of Determination   295
       Problems
10-11 Significance of b, the Regression Coefficient   299
       Problems
10-12 Multiple Regression Analysis   302
10-13 Some Limitations of Regression Analysis   304
       Correlation and Causation / Significance versus Ability to
       Estimate / Curvilinearity / Homoscedasticity / Extrapolation /
       Problems
10-14 Summary   308
10-15 Bibliography   310
10-16 Cases   312

CHAPTER 11
FORECASTING   **327**

11-1   Introduction   328
       Three Types of Forecasts / Data Sources
11-2   Simple Qualitative Forecasts   332
       One-Person Forecasts / Panels / Delphi Method

11-3   Projecting Time Trends from the Past   334
       Short-Range Forecasting / *Arithmetic Mean* / *Moving Average* /
       Exponential Smoothing / *Exponential Smoothing—Short-Cut*
       Technique / Problems / Long-Range Forecasts /
       Decomposition Technique / *Isolating and Studying Seasonal*
       Variations / *Tier Graph* / Problems / *Finding Trend Patterns* /
       Problems / *Studying Cyclical Patterns* / *Recomposition and*
       Forecasting / *Analysis of Forecasts*
11-4   Finding and Projecting Underlying Causes   355
       Regression Analysis / Intention-to-Buy Surveys and Indexes of
       Consumer Sentiment / *Plant and Equipment Expenditure Plans* /
       Consumer Purchase Plans for Durable Goods / *Indexes of*
       Consumer Sentiment / Econometric Models / Input-Output
       Models / Leading Indicators and Diffusion Indexes / Life Cycle
       Analysis / *Consumer Life Cycle* / *Product Life Cycle*
11-5   Summary   367
11-6   Bibliography   368
11-7   Cases   369

CHAPTER 12
DECISION THEORY AND BAYESIAN PROBABILITY   **375**

12-1   Introduction   376
12-2   Payoff Tables   377
12-3   Decision Trees   378
12-4   Expected Value of Perfect Information   380
12-5   Sensitivity Analysis   381
       Problems
12-6   Bayesian Probability   388
       Problems
12-7   Decision Making Using Sample Information (Posterior Probability)   393
12-8   Summary   396
12-9   Bibliography   397
12-10 Cases   398

CHAPTER 13
INDEX NUMBERS   **405**

13-1   Uses and Characteristics of Index Numbers   406
13-2   History of Index Numbers   407
13-3   Unweighted Aggregative Index Numbers   408
       Computation / Dow Jones Index
13-4   Unweighted Index of Price Relatives   409
       Computation / Problems
13-5   Weighted Aggregative Index Numbers   411
       Base-Year Weights: Laspeyres' Index /
       Given-Year Weights: Paasche's Index

13-6   Weighted Index of Price Relatives   412
        Base-Year Weights: Laspeyres' Index /
        Given-Year Weights: Paasche's Index / Problems
13-7   Problems of Index Number Construction   414
        Choice of Base Period / Choice of Items to Include in an Index /
        Choice of Base-Year or Given-Year Weights
13-8   Link Relatives   416
        Construction / Consumer Price Index
13-9   Computation with Index Numbers   420
        Shifting the Base Year / Using an Index to Adjust for Price
        Changes / *Consumer Price Index* / *Gross National Product
        (Implicit) Deflator* / Splicing Two Indexes / *Producer (Wholesale)
        Price Index* / Problems
13-10   Quantity Indexes   426
        Computation / The Index of Industrial Production
13-11   Summary   428
13-12   Bibliography   430
13-13   Cases   431

CHAPTER 14
MULTIVARIATE TECHNIQUES, DATA BASES,
AND COMPUTER SOFTWARE   **439**

14-1   Introduction   439
14-2   Multivariate Analysis   441
        Multiple Regression Analysis / Discriminant Analysis / Factor
        Analysis / Multiple Analysis of Variance
14-3   Data Bases Available for Business and Social Science Research   448
        Inter-University Consortium for Political and Social Research
        (ICPSR) / National Longitudinal Studies (NLS) /
        Census Tapes (1980, 1970) / Compustat Tapes
14-4   Computer Software Statistics Packages   452
        Biomedical Computer Programs (BMD and BMDP) / Statistical
        Package for the Social Sciences (SPSS) / Other Programs
14-5   Interpretation of Computer Printouts   453
        Scattergram and Simple Regression Program /
        Multiple Regression Program
14-6   Statistical Programs for Handheld Calculators   459
14-7   Review Questions   461
14-8   Bibliography   461

Answers to Even-Numbered Problems   **463**
Appendix: Statistical Tables   **493**
Indexes   **505**
   Name Index
   Subject Index

PREFACE

Students in business schools and social science departments seem to view statistics courses as *unintelligible* or *useless* or both. What they don't understand is that most statistical concepts can be *simply explained* using logical, intuitive descriptions and simple high school algebra. And far from being useless, statistical techniques are essential in many fields and becoming ever more important. As the computer enhances our ability to collect data, better estimates help us research, produce, tally, and market our products.

THE ACTION LEARNING APPROACH

Because we believe strongly in the relevance of statistical techniques as they apply to today's world, we have developed our *action learning approach*. By this we mean we want students to experience, as realistically as possible, actual business situations and use their knowledge of techniques and logical processes to set a strategy for handling those situations. Therefore, the cases we offer in this text are based on real-life problems in such areas as marketing, finance, real estate, and education.

Most statistics texts present oversimplified examples to illustrate how specific techniques can be used to answer questions or solve business problems. Such examples are never realistic. Essential training in the diagnosis and the development of a way or possibly several ways of meeting the problem is not possible in these examples and problems.

A case should provide the student with some of the complexity, lack of information, or perhaps excess information characteristic of a real situation. A case should also illustrate the ways in which techniques have been or should not have been employed. Furthermore, a wide variety of cases illustrating many problem areas can greatly enrich learning.

The cases in this text have been written with those assumptions in mind. We offer *several kinds of case material in each chapter*. Each chapter starts with a clear explanation of a statistical technique followed by several *examples* (short cases) which lead students through worked-out answers. Then we offer short *problems* which students can do themselves. At the end of each chapter are several longer, real-life cases. The number and diversity mean that the instructor can assign differ-ent cases each year or can choose cases in areas of greatest interest to the students. Cases can be assigned as written homework and/or used for class discussion. A tra-ditional statistics class provides little opportunity for class discussion because stu-dents don't have enough technical expertise to discuss statistical theory. With our case situations, discussion may center about the appropriate methods to use and the actions one would recommend on the basis of the results.

Thus, through examples, problems, and cases—our action learning approach—we demonstrate how useful and intriguing statistics can be.

ORGANIZATION

The book is divided into 14 chapters. In the *Instructor's Manual* we have suggested possible chapter sequences for one- and two-semester courses. The level of sophisti-cation of the students will determine how much material can be covered in a course. Various chapters can enhance the content for a more sophisticated class. These might include decision trees, forecasting, index numbers, nonparametric tests, more sophis-ticated sampling methods, and multivariate techniques.

Chapter 1 distinguishes between statistics and statistical techniques. It intro-duces the student to practical, up-to-date resources useful in the search for data. The first job experiences of most students usually requires them to find information. This chapter, with its references to standard statistical volumes, periodicals, and comput-erized data bases, will be an invaluable aid.

Chapter 2 provides a discussion of descriptive statistical methods. Measures of central tendency, variation, symmetry, and peakedness are discussed. Computation for grouped and ungrouped data is demonstrated. The application of these measures, so often used and misused, is examined.

Chapter 3 is an introduction to probability theory. Traditionally students have struggled with this area, learning formulations and computations which are then sel-dom applied to estimation in relevant areas. Set notation and Venn diagrams are also often discussed at great length and never used again. We have chosen to present probability theory in a less complicated way, by explaining it in terms of six simple rules, then showing how the rules lead to the binominal distribution. The discussion turns to the use of the Poisson distribution, the relation between the binominal dis-tribution and the normal distribution, and applications of the normal distribution. Bayesian probability theory is not discussed until Chapter 12, but the instructor may introduce it at this point by assigning appropriate pages in Chapter 12.

Chapters 4 and 5 offer one of the most extensive coverages of sampling to be found in an elementary applied statistics text. Chapter 4 begins with a comparison of personal interviews, telephone interviews, and mail questionnaires in terms of such issues as response rate, cost, interviewer bias, timing, and accuracy of data. The chapter covers the Central Limit Theorem and confidence intervals for a mean and a proportion. In Chapter 5, the finite correction factor is covered, and sample size calculations are revised to include the correction factor. The t distribution is explained and confidence intervals are derived for small samples where σ is unknown. Sections on stratified and clustered sampling show how to calculate sample size and how to design a sample for different types of stratification. Sampling error for stratified and clustered samples is presented.

Chapters 6 and 7 are devoted to hypothesis testing using parametric methods. Chapter 6 describes scientific testing procedures, including Type I and Type II errors. An optional section explains the derivation of the related power curve. The latter half of Chapter 6 focuses on one-sample tests—the test of a mean and a proportion. Chapter 7 is devoted to parametric, two-sample, and three- or more sample tests. The test of a difference between means and proportions as well as one-way analysis of variance is also covered.

Chapters 8 and 9 focus on non-parametric hypotheses tests. In Chapter 8, the Chi-Square test and the Kruskal-Wallis test are explained. In Chapter 9, tests of ranks, runs, and signs are included. Rank order correlation and the rank-sum test (Mann-Whitney) are covered. The Kolmogrov-Smirnov tests of goodness of fit and of independence are covered next. The last part of the chapter is devoted to such simple tests as the one-sample runs test and the sign test.

Chapters 10 and 11 furnish the groundwork for economic and business forecasting. Chapter 10, "Regression Analysis," shows the student how to fit a line to data points and how to measure the standard error of estimate, the coefficient of determination, and correlation coefficients. Significance of the regression coefficient and the correlation coefficient are tested. A section on multiple regression analysis discusses the usefulness of the technique and some of the important problems involved in using this method of analysis. Chapter 11, on forecasting, is one of the most thorough in coverage of any elementary text. Short-range forecasting techniques such as moving averages and exponential smoothing are explained. Longer-term forecasting using the decomposition method is illustrated. The student can understand the value of seasonal indexes and deseasonalizing. Trend and cyclical factors are studied. The highlight of the final part of the chapter is the discussion of three important economic forecasting techniques: econometric models, input-output analysis, and leading indicators. The student may apply results of these models to simple forecast analyses.

Decision theory and Bayesian probability are covered in Chapter 12. The student is guided through simple and then more complex decision trees. The expected value of perfect information and sensitivity analyses are both demonstrated. The Bayesian approach is then explained and sample problems are outlined. Finally Bayesian posterior probability is applied to decision tree problems.

The most commonly encountered statistical measures are the various forms of popular index numbers. Dow Jones indexes and Consumer Price Indexes are frequently found in newspapers. Chapter 13 explains how such index numbers are calculated. In addition, the background and history of major indexes used in the United States are discussed.

In the final chapter, several important multivariate techniques are explained. These include analysis of variance, factor analysis, and discriminant analysis. Computer output for cross tabulation and regression programs are provided and explained. Most universities provide some sort of access to statistical packages, but many users have difficulty interpreting the output of these packages. We shed some light on interpreting SPSS programs, which can also apply to similar outputs like BMDP and SAS.

SPECIAL FEATURES OF THE TEXT

1 *Understandability* is the keystone of the text. Each section logically flows from the previous section to build a body of knowledge about a topic. Information is organized to facilitate learning. For example, six different types of areas under a normal curve are pointed out; a table of different types of hypothesis tests outlines parametric and nonparametric tests to be used in different situations; and another table compares different types of surveys according to purpose.

2 *Motivating elements* help to clarify statistical techniques through application. By this we mean students are motivated to learn theories and techniques by seeing how they are used in their most "natural" settings. Most chapters begin with a discussion of the history of a technique or of the reasons why the technique is important. A typical example is then presented. The example is solved using the technique under discussion, and all steps in the solution are pointed out in simple nonmathematical terms. The theory or formula used is also explained in nonmathematical terms. Thus, students experience statistics as a viable, practical course of study—our action-oriented approach.

3 *Applications* illustrate the universality of the techniques and show how they can be used in accounting, marketing, production, economics, finance, real estate, political science, and other fields. Different applications are presented with each new set of techniques. Then, to reinforce our discussion, we generally offer two to four longer cases per chapter—while other texts may have only a few cases scattered throughout the text.

4 There are enough *problems* at the end of each section for instructors to ignore the cases and concentrate on a "traditional" problem-oriented course. Detailed answers are furnished at the end of the text for the even numbered problems. This text does not require the use of the cases; however, since the cases add to the realism of the course, we hope instructors will try to use some of them—and will enjoy the advantages they offer.

5 *Coverage of a wide variety of classical and modern techniques* allows instructors to choose topics that may be covered in various types of courses. The text may be used for a one- or two-semester undergraduate course or an introductory M.B.A. course.

6 *Bibliographies* at the end of the chapter offer supplemental texts and readings. Some of the readings are lower-level and explanatory, while others discuss more advanced examples of the uses of a given technique.

INSTRUCTOR'S MANUAL

A comprehensive *Instructor's Manual* has been specially prepared to help those teaching from this text extract the most out of the material. The manual has a number of useful aids. For example, course outlines are provided for:

(*a*)   One-semester course for a typical undergraduate class

(*b*)   Two-semester course for an undergraduate class

(*c*)   One-semester course for a high-level undergraduate class or MBA class

Also, comprehensive teaching notes are provided for each of the cases. They outline the objectives of the case and then proceed to give very thorough answers to the end-of-case questions. Supplemental questions and topics for discussion are outlined. For instructors who would like to experiment but who have not had experience in this method of teaching, we offer a guidance section on teaching a case in class and on grading cases. A table in the *Instructor's Manual* classifies cases by the fields in which they are applicable. Thus, instructors may concentrate on not-for-profit or production or finance cases according to the needs and interests of their students.

ACKNOWLEDGMENTS

We want to thank our reviewers who gave many excellent and useful suggestions. Whenever possible we have revised the text to include their ideas. Our thanks go to: George A. Collier, Jr., Southeastern Oklahoma State University; Wanzer Drane, Southern Methodist University; Stephen E. Kolitz, Loyola University of Chicago; Michael Liechenstein, St. John's University; Donald Miller, Emporia State University; Don R. Robinson, Illinois State University; Charles R. Scott, Jr., University of Alabama at Tuscaloosa; John T. Sennetti, Texas Tech University; Clifford Sowell, Eastern Kentucky University; Scot A. Stradley, University of North Dakota; and Percy O. Vera, Sinclair Community College.

Special thanks to Don Chatham of McGraw-Hill who started the work on this book and to Don Mason who saw it through to its completion. Marna Santullano kept track of it for many years and Gail Gavert had the editing responsibility. The following graduate and undergraduate students were helpful in the preparation of the cases and problems and in proofreading the text: Rebecca Barr, Jean Stauffer, Tom Sesler, Melinda Snowden, Mike Gaisbauer, Daniel Solis, Lynn Heitmann, Eric Miller, Carl Swanson, Marjorie Hornberger, Jane Fortenberry, and Terrell Potts. Faculty colleagues who were especially helpful are David Springate who introduced us to the Case Research Association, Gene Byrne who laid great emphasis on "action learning" and urged its introduction in statistics classes, and Paul Gray who has actively encouraged the writing of this book. Edith Benham, Mary Kesner, and Bess Vick patiently saw through the revisions of this text.

Marion Gross Sobol
Martin K. Starr

STATISTICS
FOR BUSINESS
AND
ECONOMICS

INTRODUCTION

1-1 OVERVIEW OF THE BOOK

1-2 WHERE TO FIND INFORMATION
Almanacs
Regularly Published U.S. Government Documents
Financial Firms
Research Organizations
Interest Groups
Guides to Periodical Literature
Footnotes and References
Bibliographies and Librarians
Computerized Data Bases
Card Catalogue

1-3 STATISTICS VERSUS STATISTICAL TECHNIQUES
What Statistical Analysis Can Do
Causality
Representativeness

1-4 STATISTICS IN ACTION
Cases
Statistical Experiments or Investigations

1-5 BIBLIOGRAPHY

Social scientists and public and business administrators are constantly faced with decisions. To make these decisions they must gather information and study it. Often the information is numerical and the decision maker must think of a good way to condense and study the "numbers." Alternatively, the information may be insufficient and the decision maker must see if the available information can be used to give an idea about the facts that are not known. Statistics teaches us how to condense and analyze information and how to use incomplete information to make tests and forecasts about the things we do not yet know. There is a certain magic and satisfaction in trying to create order from disorder and in putting together knowledge from uncertainty. This is the excitement of statistics.

1-1

To realize and feel how exciting and interesting statistics can be, we must place ourselves in situations where we need information and answers and then use the techniques we will learn to find solutions for our problems. Traditional applied statistics courses have concentrated on teaching analytical techniques and applying these methods to short, rather uninteresting problems. Problems are excellent ways to review the computations, but they do not provide the realism, the excitement, or the complexity of a "real life" situation. Will this type of study, involving only techniques and very restricted applications, enable the student to "transfer" this training to a real life situation? Moreover, is this type of study designed to arouse the interest of a student in learning statistical techniques?

Recently, it was pointed out in a prominent statistical journal that the formulation of the problem and the subsequent setup of the research design is a very important factor that has been neglected in applied statistics courses. More emphasis on research design and the use of cases and actual statistical experiments was suggested (Federer, 1978). The article went on to point out that there is a dearth of cases available for statistics classes. Indeed, the authors' investigation of the case bibliographies has shown that relatively little has been done in this field.

The purpose of this book is to present materials for an action learning applications-type statistics course. Each chapter develops statistical techniques, illustrates how the techniques are applied, and offers a number of short word problems to test and reinforce student learning. Each chapter also offers *three or more cases* that can be studied using the techniques in that chapter and in the previous ones. Sometimes techniques from later chapters may also be used to analyze these cases and, in a later chapter, the student may be asked to "redo" a case, using a newly learned technique. These cases allow students to immerse themselves in a real life problem having the lack of information in some areas and the surplus of information in others. Many cases acquaint the student with important statistical resource materials.

In addition, class discussion of the cases provides the interest and vitality often lacking in mathematical-type lectures. These discussions may center on such issues as: What is the crucial aspect of the case? How was data collected? How was the test or experiment designed? What was found and what future work might be done? Since the student must organize the data and think about these questions, class discussions become livelier than mere considerations of what someone has done in a statistical study.

This chapter, which is divided into three sections, presents overall introductory information for the study of statistics and the use of this text. First of all, since most statistical studies must use data, a section on where to find information is offered. The average college student may not be aware of some valuable statistical sources, reference works, and computerized reference services. Section 1-2 provides an overview of data sources that will be helpful both for this course and for *future research needs*.

Section 1-3 concisely discusses the scope of statistics in this book. To the layman, statistics may mean data; however, the focus of the statistics course is on how to analyze data in order to reach conclusions and to make action-oriented decisions.

This book introduces the case study method into statistics. Most students reading their first case will say, "I don't know what to do!" To help students use these cases, we have presented significant questions for study after each case. In addition, in Chapter 2, we show a possible solution for the first case (Naro-Shu Case A). In Section 1-4, we present some *general, overall discussion guides* that the teacher and the class can use to analyze and present all cases.

Another method for using statistical techniques in realistic settings is the statistical experiment, which can be presented in the form of a term paper. Each student picks an interesting topic and tries to use newly learned techniques to "solve the problem." Once again a student may say, "I can't think of a problem." In Section 1-4, we offer ways to find a research topic and suggest topics that students have previously used. In fact, some cases in this book reflect "problems" that students decided to study. At the end of the term, many students will say things like "The best part of the course was doing that paper. I'm going to show it to my boss (or my parents or my fraternity)!" One student was fortunate enough to be assigned a similar problem at his first job. His employer was so impressed with the results that he immediately selected the former student for a top executive training program.

Each chapter in this book describes several statistical techniques in individual sections. Each section outlines the situations for the technique's use, and discusses its history. Illustrative examples then show how to use the technique. At the end of each section, a set of problems is given. At the end of each chapter, a summary of the important issues of the chapter is provided. This provides an excellent way to review one's reading and prepare for an examination. The next section in the chapter contains a bibliography, which lists both simple and more complex books that explain the techniques used in the chapter. In addition, articles or books that apply these techniques in special fields—like marketing, real estate, accounting, and public sector uses—are cited. Students may use the references during the course or to supplement other courses. It is hoped that the book provides a "tool kit" of techniques and references that students can take with them after graduation to use in many personal and job-related situations.

At the end of the chapters several short, "real life" cases are offered. These cases span a wide number of fields to show how statistical techniques can be applied to many situations.

The remainder of this chapter focuses on how to find information, what statistical techniques can do, and how to develop case analyses and statistical experiments. Each chapter thereafter discusses a set of statistical techniques and shows how and where they can be used.

WHERE TO FIND INFORMATION

1-2

College graduates' first jobs in most areas usually involve a large amount of "fact finding." The "boss" wants information on the market for a product or a service. A report is due on sales for previous years. Management is considering the possible status of the economy in the near and distant future. A public sector manager needs information relevant to her decision needs.

Sometimes, the first job involves analysis of data available in company or agency files. Subsequent chapters of this book show how this analysis can be handled. Very frequently, the task requires that data be found before anyone can begin an analysis. Suppose one needs information on income levels in a particular city. Many people will suggest a *sample survey*. However, a sample survey is very expensive and time-consuming and should be used only as a *last resort* when no other data source is available. It is often possible to find the results of a sample survey, conducted for another purpose, which can provide the needed answer. The next suggestion will be a trip to the library and a look into the *card catalogue*. Usually, current data is available in government publications, journal articles, or the output of research organizations. These references are difficult to find in the card catalogue.

All analysts should familiarize themselves with sources of data. First, there is *primary* data, which is published by the organization that collects and analyzes it. Then, there is *secondary* data, which has been reprinted from the primary source. A most useful reference work is the *Statistical Abstract of the United States,* which is published annually by the U.S. Department of Commerce and is available in most libraries. The *Statistical Abstract* is a secondary source, since it gathers together data from government and other publications. It contains information on gross national product, tax collections, government welfare programs, business profits, populations and incomes of states, and a myriad of other facts.

Almanacs
Some important almanacs are listed below.

1 *Statistical Abstract of the United States.* Published by the Department of Commerce.
2 *World Almanac.*
3 *Information Please Almanac.*
4 *Economic Almanac.* Published by National Industrial Conference Board.
5 Local almanacs. One example is the *Texas Almanac.* Local almanacs are often published by local newspapers.
6 *Handbook of Labor Statistics.* This statistical handbook is published by the Bureau of Labor Statistics.
7 *Statistical Yearbook of the United Nations.*
8 *HUD Statistical Yearbook.* Published by the Bureau of Housing and Urban Development.
9 *FAA Statistical Handbook.* Published by Federal Aviation Agency, this handbook covers air carriers, aviation facilities, operation, and aeronautical facilities.

Regularly Published U.S. Government Documents
Several regularly published government statistical publications are important sources of data. The list represents only a handful of the many government publications; the *American Statistics Index*, listed below, identifies additional sources.

1 *Census Reports.* Published by the U.S. Department of Commerce.
2 *Survey of Current Business.* Published by the U.S. Department of Commerce, this publication serves as an indicator of business conditions, wholesale and retail commodity prices, and population.
3 *Federal Reserve Bulletin.* Published by the Federal Reserve Board of Governors, this bulletin provides information on finance, deposits, and interest rates.
4 *Monthly Labor Review.* Published by the U.S. Department of Labor, this publication lists unemployment rates, strike data, wholesale prices, and consumer price indexes.

5 *Business Conditions Digest.* This digest, published by the U.S. Department of Commerce, lists 500 economic indicators.

6 *American Statistics Index.* This publication indexes the output of more than 100 government agencies, congressional committees, and statistics-producing programs.

7 *Digest of Education Statistics and Projections of Education Statistics.* Published by the Department of Health, Education, and Welfare.

8 *Monthly Statement of Receipts and Expenditures of the U.S. Government.* Published by the U.S. Department of the Treasury.

9 *Government Finances in (State).* Published annually by the Bureau of the Census, this publication gives information for state and local governments.

10 The Securities and Exchange Commission (SEC) and the U.S. Department of Commerce issue quarterly data on business expenditures for new plant and equipment.

11 *Housing Statistics.* This provides information on the Federal Housing Authority (FHA) mortgages and defaults.

12 *Housing and Urban Development Trends.* Published monthly by the Department of Housing and Urban Development (HUD).

Financial Firms

Stock and financial analysis firms publish data on stock markets, bond markets, and business. Among the regular publications are *Business Week* and the *Wall Street Journal.* Dun and Bradstreet publishes *Monthly New Business Incorporations* and *Monthly Business Failures. Dun's Market Identifiers* lists approximately 4 million businesses. Each listing contains name, address, nature of business, number of employees, sales, and number of locations. Since Dun's is used by lending institutions for credit ratings, businesses that have applied for loans are listed. The only omissions from this record are businesses that do not borrow money, such as banks and very small businesses. *The F&S Index of Corporations and Industries,* published by Predicasts, Inc., is issued weekly and cumulated quarterly. The data published by private financial firms is often very specific and thorough. Stock and bond yields, quality ratings for municipal and corporate bonds, and ratings of individual companies are presented in these reference works. The Standard and Poor's Corporation, located in New York City, publishes the *Standard Corporation Descriptions,* which includes very broad information on many corporations. Data in this semimonthly report includes the corporate debt and capital structures, product background, and audited financial reports. Standard and Poor's also publishes a monthly list of statistics, which includes industrial and cost of living indexes.

Research Organizations

Besides the government, there are a number of reputable research organizations that regularly publish data. These include the National Industrial Conference Board and the National Bureau of Economic Research, which publishes data on business cycles and other economic issues. The Survey Research Center, University of Michigan, studies consumer attitudes and finances. The Brookings Institution in Washington publishes analyses of economic topics. In addition, most large universities have business bureaus that do business and economic research in their local areas.

Interest Groups

Interest groups also publish data. Industry groups and unions publish information for their own particular industry. In using the data, one must be careful. For example, the definition of fringe benefits varies depending on whether one looks at the benefits from a labor or a management standpoint. Trade associations are valuable sources. The Electronics Industries Association, the Aerospace Industries Association, the American Iron and Steel Association, all have information on specific product lines that government agencies do not publish. The reference for finding these organizations is the *Encyclopedia of Associations,* vol. I, (15th ed., 1980), published by the Gale Research Company.

Should you wish to study the income distribution in the local community, Census data is available for each city in the United States. The decennial Census takes samples in order to estimate income in each of the communities. This data is available in the library. One problem with Census material is that since it is gathered every 10 years, by 1988, say, the 1980 information may be obsolete. Local chambers of commerce and boards of education may have more recent income data for their communities.

Guides to Periodical Literature

Much recent data is contained in recent journal articles. While most students are familiar with the *Reader's Guide to Periodical Literature,* there are other indexes that catalogue more useful business, economic, and government periodicals. Some of these are the *Business Periodicals Index, New York Times Index,* and *Public Affairs Information Services Index.*

Footnotes and References

Once articles and tables have been found in journals and abstracts, another useful source of information is the footnotes, bibliographies, and references in these articles. For example, the article by Pearson Hunt, listed at the end of this chapter, contains references on the case method of instruction. You could refer to these articles or books for more information on the case method.

Bibliographies and Librarians

Bibliographies on selected topics are often available. Librarians can help you locate bibliographies and guide you to extensive indexes of government publications. The *Monthly Catalogue,* an index to government publications, may lead you to more current data than decennial statistics. This publication is indexed by author, title, and subject. Librarians, especially research librarians, are an invaluable source of information. Often they can save you much time by directing you to some of the library's latest materials. There are also private companies that search for data for specific problems.

Computerized Data Bases

A recent development, the computerized bibliographic data base, is an excellent tool for rapidly locating references. The researcher gains access to data bases by using a computer terminal. First, the researcher enters the name of the topic being studied and, in a matter of minutes, the computer has searched all data listed in its files and has printed a reference list. Computer-search facilities are now available at most

TABLE 1-1

DATA BASE	DESCRIPTION	START UP DATE
ASI	Statistical publications of the U.S. government	1974
ABI/INFORM	Business and management marketing data	1971
CPI	Consumer Price Index	
PATS	Marketing and statistical data on corporations, industries and products, statistical and bibliographical data	1972
P/E NEWS	Petroleum and energy business news and data by the American Petroleum Institute	1975
SOCIAL SCI SEARCH	Economics, history, business, and sociology	1972

large university and public libraries. There may be a slight charge for searching the files and listing the references and/or an abstract of the article; however, this system is a welcome replacement for hours of file searching. Table 1-1 lists several computerized bibliographies of interest to the business and social science student; there are, of course, other bibliographies for engineering, chemistry, and other disciplines.

Card Catalogue
Finally, you may turn to the card catalogue, which will direct you to books and some government publications. At the end of this chapter is a list of books and articles that describe sources of statistical data.

STATISTICS VERSUS STATISTICAL TECHNIQUES

1-3

In Section 1-2, collection of data or statistics was discussed. Data is collected for study and analysis to solve problems, discover problems, discover opportunities, track performance, and help make policy decisions. How to conduct such analyses is what a statistics course is all about.

What Statistical Analysis Can Do
Two types of statistical analysis are possible: *descriptive* and *inferential* statistics. If we are interested in describing the characteristics of a particular group of people and not in speculating about their characteristics in the future in different situations, we are using descriptive statistics. In a sense, descriptive statistics is a way of "getting it all together," or knowing how a system behaves. If we want to know the income of a small town, for example, we are not interested in a list of 15,000 income figures. We would like to boil it down to, say, average sales, income, production, and output. Chapter 2 discusses some different types of averages that can be used for various situations. Similarly, we might want to know the variation in these incomes or in sales, production, or output. Chapter 2 suggests ways to measure this variation.

Another form of descriptive presentation is the graph. Chapter 2 shows some graphical presentations along with words of caution about how to "spot" misleading graphic presentations. An aim of this book is to make you a careful user of data.

Inferential statistics consists of making and testing assumptions in which we issue probability statements that show how sure (or unsure) we are that a predicted event will occur. For example, if we wish to measure the average income of students' parents, we may take a sample of students. From this sample we can obtain information to estimate the incomes of the parents. If we wish to estimate sales for the next decade, we might relate the advertising expenditures of previous years to the sales of these years. Then we can determine for each level of advertising what types of sales can be predicted. In some cases, we may wish to determine if a certain policy has increased sales or if a new drug has been effective in decreasing colds. Or we may try to decide if the economic status in two communities is significantly different. These statements should be accompanied by an indication of our degree of confidence in these estimates. Methods for drawing inferences are covered in Chapters 3 through 12.

Chapter 3 introduces probability theory. When we do not have complete information, we employ probability theory to help make estimates based on sample data. Methods for making sample estimates and choosing appropriate samples are discussed in Chapters 4 and 5. Inferences about the population, based on samples from the population, are set up in a scientific form so that they can be tested. Chapters 6 and 7 demonstrate how to set up these hypothesis tests and how to perform them. Chapters 8 and 9 show special hypothesis tests for data that are not normally distributed or that can only be ranked or placed in categorical form (such as men or women). Chapter 10 shows how to relate two variables, such as sales and advertising, in order to use one variable to predict the other. In Chapter 11, easy-to-use modern methods for short- and long-range forecasting are presented. Chapter 12 outlines the use of decision trees, which offer a very important way to make an action-oriented decision based on the probabilities of events occurring and the payoffs if they occur. Chapter 13 concentrates on how index numbers are constructed and used. Indexes are probably the most commonly used statistical measures and can be found in the daily newspapers. Chapter 14, the final chapter, provides a brief summary of the chapters, outlines some more advanced statistical techniques not covered in this text, and discusses some important data bases and computer programs designed to perform statistical computation. In the final section of that chapter, a computer printout using regression analysis is presented and explained. A careful study of these chapters is designed to give you the power to locate data, analyze it, and use your analysis to make a decision. The more you exercise this power, the greater it will become! However, you should beware of some problems that may arise in the use of statistical techniques. We now cite two very famous examples: storks' nests and babies' births and the *Literary Digest* poll.

Causality

Very often people use the results of statistical studies to try to discover what causes something to happen. Does cigarette smoking cause cancer? Both descriptive and inferential statistics can give rise to misleading causal interpretations. Just as it is possible to lie with descriptive statistics by drawing misleading graphs, it is possible to make misleading inferences. Just because events or measures seem to be related may not necessarily mean that one causes the other. In Sweden during the 1930s, for example, there was a very high relationship between the number of babies born and the number of storks' nests. One is tempted to conclude that storks deliver babies. Further investigation showed that storks like to build nests near chimneys. During this period, there were many marriages and many new homes were built. Hence, there were more babies and more chimneys available for storks' nests. A related situation, the formation of new households, had led to the increase in babies' births and in storks' nests.

Representativeness

In the 1930s, the magazine *Literary Digest* polled its readers and selected a telephone sample of the general population. Based on this sample, victory was predicted for the Republican candidate. The Democratic candidate won and the subsequent loss of confidence caused the demise of *Literary Digest*. What was wrong? The sample did not represent the country. In the 1930s, only relatively wealthy people owned telephones. Wealthier people at that time were more likely to be Republicans than Democrats. In short, the sample, although it was very large, did not represent the population. Chapters 4 and 5 explain the considerations necessary to obtain representative, adequate samples.

STATISTICS IN ACTION

1-4

Because statistical techniques must be used carefully to provide valid results, student computation of simple, end-of-section classroom examples is not sufficient. These problems demonstrate instances in which the technique may be used, but they do not highlight all the complexities of the problems. Two alternative learning techniques are (1) cases and (2) statistical experiments or investigations.

Cases

A classroom approach that aims at giving a more realistic and applicable approach to the use of statistical techniques can be developed on the foundation of both the case study technique and the term paper. This book carefully explains the statistical techniques, and it also provides cases that can be analyzed. First, a set of short problems is presented to enable the student to practice computation for each of the techniques explained; then, a number of cases are presented. These cases, drawn from business, economics, political science, and sociology, show how applications can be made in more realistic situations.

The cases show the complexity of most problems and the need to sift out and use only the most relevant data, or to obtain more data. They demonstrate how managers have used statistics to solve a problem. They provide the student with opportunities to use case information to solve problems. Most cases that describe what an individual does in a given situation do not provide the ideal solutions. Therefore, these cases can be a challenge for class discussion of what more could be done. Many a statistics class is a "cut and dried" lecture with hardly any class participation. Cases provide a vehicle for active class discussion and a more *democratic* classroom atmosphere. Moreover, these cases show how individual *creativity* can be used to solve problems. Students may find a number of equally good ways to handle the problems involved in these cases. The case method also gives the student a chance to talk in public, to learn how to concede to a peer, and to learn to synthesize arguments. Many employers specify that an important criterion for both hiring and promotion is oral communication ability.

Students who have never used cases, an approach employed in many schools of business and management, will wonder how to handle them. First, several important questions will be included in all cases to guide the student. In addition, a brief discussion of some considerations to be made in the case study follows. Among these considerations are:

1   What is the real problem? What makes you choose this problem?
2   What information is needed to study this problem?
3   Can the available material in the case be used to handle the problem?
　　(*a*)   Was the data collected properly?
　　(*b*)   How do you feel about the method of study used in this case?
4   Is there need for any new factual material? Where could it be obtained? How would you collect it? If necessary, find this material and use it.
5   What statistical techniques should be used? Make the necessary computation. Using the technique chosen, what results do you have?
6   What decision should be made on the basis of these results?
7   How should this decision be communicated to others?
8   What tests could be made at a later date to see if a decision has been effective?

Statistical Experiments or Investigations

Another successful technique for making a statistics course "come to life" is the term paper approach. Many teachers react negatively to this statement. They ask, "How can you write a term paper in statistics? Do you expect students to derive a theorem?" A term paper may be theoretical, but generally the best papers are written when students apply known techniques to problems that interest them.

　　The aim of the term paper is to use a technique studied in the course. Try to analyze a problem that interests you. The data may come from a job, a family business, a study in the dormitory, a sporting event, or reference works.

　　Let us look at some possibilities. Student jobs are often in restaurants, cafeterias, or stores. Excellent papers can be formulated on various topics: What is the best day for tips? Who are the best tippers, men or women, small or large parties? What day should the store close? A family business may furnish data for diverse topics: Does advertising relate to sales? Should there be overtime or two shifts? Can one formulate wage incentive scales based on standard deviations? A colleague reports that "a student who was a preacher showed that he conducted a significantly greater number of funerals in the last quarter of the year than in any other quarter"!

　　In the public sector, there are many interesting issues: Are food stamp purchases seasonal? Do "blockbuster" museum shows like *Pompeii, A.D. 79* attract a different crowd to the museum? Do black parents prefer integrated schools? Do people prefer a state lottery to a sales tax? Do high school counselors read labor market forecasts?

　　Sports are another very popular area of study. One student tested whether tennis balls stored in the open, in regular cans, or in special vacuum cans had more "bounce." Other topics include: Does one brand of golf ball travel significantly farther than another brand? Is there really an advantage in playing on the home court, swimming in the home pool, playing on the home field? Does height or weight relate to performance? Is attendance better when the team is winning? One student developed a method to measure a band's performance by comparing its sound level to that of other bands.

　　Dormitories furnish sites for surveys of the relation of grade point average to hours of study or sleep, the relation of allowance to parental income, and the relation of contributions to a sorority to the unemployment index or the Dow Jones Index. Enterprising young men may survey the date preferences of young women. Or vice versa.

An experiment can be designed and its results studied. A group of students tried popping a given number of kernels of corn with different amounts of oil at different temperature levels. As an interesting byproduct, they had enough popcorn for the whole floor of a dormitory to eat at the next football game. An experiment was used in a fast food restaurant to see if there were more sales for a particular item when it occupied a different place on the menu board. A woman student used a decision tree to figure out whether she should move in with her boyfriend! A survey in a local shopping center provided data on distance traveled to stores.

Library research can furnish data for studying the relation of unemployment indexes to enrollment in various welfare programs or to the success of different types of businesses. One student, using data gathered in the library, related Dow Jones Index numbers to pledges to her church and found that contributions went down six months after the Dow did. Differences in foreign exchange rates were related to wholesale price indexes, but little relationship was found. Finding no relation between two things may prove just as interesting as finding that relationships do exist.

Some guidelines for the setup of these term papers follow:

1   State the problem you are investigating.
2   Why is this problem important to the firm or society (or you)?
3   Where will you obtain your data?
4   What techniques will you employ to solve this problem?
5   What difficulties have arisen when you tried to apply these techniques? How have you resolved these difficulties?
6   What does your analysis show? Include tables. If you have used a computer program to solve your problem, the actual computer output is not needed if it is summarized in tables, which can be placed in appendixes at the end of the paper.
7   What policy would you recommend on the basis of your study?
8   What additional information and analysis might have been useful in studying the problem?

The term paper requirement should be discussed early in the term in order to have enough time to think of a problem, or to consult with teachers, friends, relatives, coaches, and employers about interesting topics. This will also allow sufficient time for data collection. Your instructor and use of this text will help you choose appropriate statistical techniques for the analysis. We now begin our study of how to use statistical techniques to formulate, analyze, and solve problems.

BIBLIOGRAPHY

1.5

Coman, E. T.: *Sources of Business Information,* rev. ed. Englewood Cliffs, N.J.: Prentice-Hall, 1964.

Federer, Walter T.: "Some Remarks on Statistical Education," *The American Statistician,* vol. 32, no. 4, Nov. 1978, pp. 119–121.

Hunt, Pearson: "The Case Method of Instruction," *Harvard Educational Review,* vol. XXI, no. 3, Summer 1951.

Kavesh, Robert, William F. Butler, and Robert Platt (eds.): *Methods and Techniques of Business Forecasting.* Englewood Cliffs, N.J.: Prentice-Hall, 1974. See J. F. Rodriquez, "Sources of Data," chap. 2, pp. 124–159—a thorough review article broken down into categories for output and income, components of demand, industry statistics, and finance.

Morton, J. E.: "A Student's Guide to American Federal Government Statistics," *Journal of Economic Literature,* vol. X, no. 2, June 1972, pp. 371–397.

Sheehy, E. P.: *Guide to Reference Books,* 9th ed., Chicago: American Library Association, 1976. Note the section on statistics.

Silk, L. S., and M. L. Curly: *A Primer on Business Forecasting with a Guide to Sources of Business Data.* New York: Random House, 1970. Paperback volume containing a thorough list of data sources as well as information on methods of forecasting.

Wasserman, P., and J. O'Brien: *Statistics Sources,* 6th ed. Detroit: Gale, 1980. Cites annuals, yearbooks, directories, and other publications. Emphasis is on data in published form. Agencies, associations, and other organizations valuable as sources of information in fast-changing fields are also identified.

Other sources are mentioned in the chapter.

DESCRIPTIVE TECHNIQUES:
Frequency Distributions, Measures of Central Tendency, and Variation

2-1 ANALYSIS OF DATA

2-2 CONSTRUCTING A FREQUENCY DISTRIBUTION TABLE

2-3 GRAPHIC ANALYSIS
Histogram and Frequency Polygon
Cumulative Frequency Distribution
Distorted Graphs

2-4 MEASURES OF CENTRAL TENDENCY: UNGROUPED DATA
Arithmetic Mean
Weighted Arithmetic Mean

2-5 MEAN FOR GROUPED DATA

2-6 COMPUTATION OF THE MEDIAN FOR GROUPED DATA

2-7 PERCENTILES, DECILES, AND QUARTILES

2-8 MEASURES OF VARIATION: UNGROUPED DATA
Standard Deviation: Ungrouped Data

2-9 STANDARD DEVIATION: GROUPED DATA
Problems

2-10 CHEBYCHEFF'S INEQUALITY
Problems

2-11 COEFFICIENT OF VARIATION

2-12 SKEWNESS AND KURTOSIS
Problems

2-13 SUMMARY

2-14 BIBLIOGRAPHY

2-15 CASES
Case 2-1: Naro-Shu Company (A)
Case 2-2: The Lite-Bite
Case 2-3: Northeast National Bank

2-1   Frequently, we have numerical information on the whole population and need a method to summarize it in a meaningful way. For example, there may be a list of the salaries of 1000 workers in a factory. The list may read $10,000, $12,000, $17,000, $13,000, $9,000, and so forth. Or we may have a test of the sale prices of 20,000 houses sold in a given city, or the scores of 4000 freshmen on the Scholastic Aptitude Test.

No one is particularly interested in looking at a list of thousands of numbers, since it is difficult to form any conclusions from such a long data string. This chapter offers three *descriptive techniques* for studying lists of data. They are:

1   Grouping the data into useful categories, which may be presented in a table, graph, or chart.

2   Finding a measure of central tendency. The "average," which you have calculated for many years, is a measure of this type. Alternately, we may wish to know where the middle point in the data is. (Measures of this type are called measures of central tendency.)

3   Looking at and measuring the degree to which the numbers vary above and below the average.

CONSTRUCTING A FREQUENCY DISTRIBUTION TABLE

2-2   Let us say we have information on the ages of 2000 people in a certain town, obtained perhaps from a study done by the local chamber of commerce. One of the many ways to divide this data into age-group categories is shown in Table 2-1. If you know your statistics, you should be able to spot five errors in this table. How many can you spot? To begin with, in what category would we place a 10-year-old? As it stands, the categories have overlapping boundaries. This first error could be rectified by setting up categories as (*a*) 0 and under 10, 10 and under 20, and so forth. Another way to set up mutually exclusive bounds would be (*b*) 0 to 9.9 years, 10 to 19.9 years, and so forth, or (*c*) 0 to 9.99 years, 10 to 19.99 years, etc.

If we use methods (*b*) or (*c*), we must set up a rule for rounding. Thus, where would we place 9.95? In category (*b*)? In this book, we will "round up" when the number to the left of the last digit is even and "round down" when the number to the left is odd. Thus, 9.95 becomes 9.9 and is placed in category (*b*) (0 to 9.9 years). If we have 9.995 and are using the categories in (*c*), this becomes 9.99. Rounding

TABLE 2-1

CATEGORY	AGE GROUP	NUMBER OF PEOPLE
1	0 to 10	215
2	10 to 20	235
3	20 to 30	300
4	30 to 50	625
5	50 to 80	560
6	Over 80	65
		2000

15

DESCRIPTIVE
TECHNIQUES:
FREQUENCY
DISTRIBUTIONS,
MEASURES OF
CENTRAL TENDENCY
AND VARIATION

9.985 to two places would give us 9.99, since 8, the number immediately preceding the 5, is even. If there are more digits after the 5 and we wish to round to two places, we will "round up." Thus, 9.9852 would become 9.99 and 9.9952 would become 10.00.

The number of people or objects in each category is called the *frequency*. Generally, people compare the frequencies in the various categories to form a notion of how large each category is. For the groupings in Table 2-1, such comparison is difficult. The fourth category has 625 people and the third category only 300. However, a closer look shows that the fourth category, 30 to 50, covers 20 years whereas the third category only covers 10 years. Generally, all categories should be the same size. This is the second error in our table.

Sometimes, at the end of a series, we find that there are only a few people in each category. Thus, in Table 2-1, we might have had one person 105 years old. To handle this problem, we can make wider categories (let us say 30-year age groups) or set up an "open-ended" category. The category "over 80" is "open-ended." However, an open-ended category is difficult to use for computation. Later on, when we try to compute the average age from this frequency distribution, we will see that it is necessary to know the midpoint of each category. If the category goes from 0 to less than 10, we may assume that the midpoint is 5. What is the midpoint of a category that reads "over 80"? To overcome this problem, it is customary to place an asterisk at the title of the category and provide an informative footnote. For example, we might say, "Of these 65 people who are 80 years of age or older, 40 are at least 80 but less than 90, 24 are at least 90 but less than 99; the remaining 1 is 105 years old." Now a researcher can do further work on these numbers.

The number of categories used generally varies between 5 and 12 depending on the number of items to be classified and on the range (distance from the highest to the lowest number) of the data. More than 12 categories make it difficult to compare so many groups. If there are very few categories, a great deal of information can be lost by forcing people into a small number of groups. For example, we could have two groups in this problem:

Under 30	750
30 and over	1250
	2000

Now if we want other information at some later date, such as the number of people over age 60, we are forced to go back to the original data and make a new table with more categories. The user's strategic needs may also help determine the ideal number of categories. A study of what age groups read different magazines or use different brands may require special categories.

A third problem with the table is that there is no title. A good table should contain at least the three W's (where, when, and what). Thus, the table could be titled "Age of Residents of Wixiewatchie, Washington, July 1977."

Fourth, a good table should always have a footnote that tells where the information was obtained (who collected the numbers). Lastly, the category number shown in the first column in Table 2-1 is unnecessary since it is understood. Putting it all together, the revision should look like Table 2-2.

TABLE 2-2

AGE OF RESIDENTS OF WIXIEWATCHIE,
WASHINGTON, JULY 1977

AGE	NUMBER OF PEOPLE
0 but under 10	215
10 but under 20	235
20 but under 30	300
30 but under 40	315
40 but under 50	310
50 but under 60	240
60 but under 70	190
70 but under 80	130
80 and over*	65
Total	2000

*Of the 65 people who are 80 years of age or over, 40 are
at least 80 but less than 90, and 24 are at least 90 but less
than 100; the 1 remaining person is 105 years old.
Source: Wixiewatchie Chamber of Commerce, July 1977.

GRAPHIC ANALYSIS

2-3

Histogram and Frequency Polygon

The results of Table 2-2 can also be presented in graphic form, which makes it easier to compare the relative size of each of the categories. Frequency distributions may be presented as a histogram (bar chart) or a frequency polygon. For these graphs, the number of people (frequencies) in each class are presented on the vertical (Y) axis, the category quantity measured (in this case, age) on the horizontal (X) axis.

Generally, both axes begin at 0, although sometimes either one will not. If the X or the Y value doesn't start at 0, a wavy line cutting the axes [see Figure 2-3(b)] should be used to show that the graph is only part of a regular graph. Be careful with graphs that do not start at 0—they can be misinterpreted. An example, the Trimgym Company, will be shown after the data on the ages of families in Wixiewatchie is plotted.

We have plotted a bar for each age class. The information on the open-ended class provided in the footnote of Table 2-2 helps us prepare a more accurate plot, as shown in Figure 2-1. To make a frequency polygon, connect the midpoints of each of the bars with a dotted line (as shown).

Cumulative Frequency Distribution

Sometimes we may want to know the percentage of the population under 30 years of age or the percentage earning more than $10,000. While this information can be read from a graph or computed from a table, it can also be plotted in cumulative form. Using the data in Table 2-2, for example, we can develop a cumulative distribution, as shown in Table 2-3. The cumulative percent column enables us to tell what percent of the people in the table are below a certain age. For example, 37.5% of the people are younger than 30. Note that this figure is computed by adding the percent

17

DESCRIPTIVE
TECHNIQUES:
FREQUENCY
DISTRIBUTIONS,
MEASURES OF
CENTRAL TENDENCY
AND VARIATION

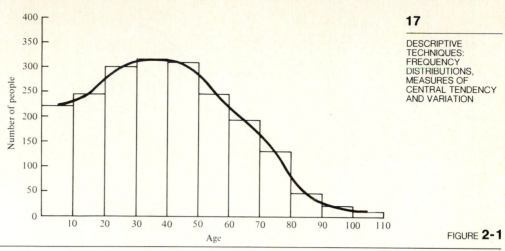

FIGURE **2-1**

Age of residents of Wixiewatchie, Washington, July 1977. Note that we show both a histogram (bar chart) and the corresponding frequency polygon (smooth curve). **Source:** Wixiewatchie Chamber of Commerce, 1977.

for less than 10 (10.7), the percent between 10 and 20 (11.8), and the percent between 20 and 30 (15.0).

The frequency polygon for Table 2-3 is called an *ogive* curve. It is shown in Figure 2-2. Now if you wanted to know how many people are 65 years of age or less, you could draw a line from 65 and read the graph (point *A*), which indicates that about 1700 people are 65 or less.

Distorted Graphs

The "gee whiz" graph is frequently seen in newspapers, company reports, and other types of graphic presentations. The watchful student can easily develop a system for

TABLE 2-3

LESS THAN CUMULATIVE DISTRIBUTION OF AGES OF RESIDENTS,
WIXIEWATCHIE, WASHINGTON, JULY 1977

AGE OF RESIDENTS	FREQUENCY	CUMULATIVE PERCENT
Less than 10	215	10.7
Less than 20	450	22.5
Less than 30	750	37.5
Less than 40	1065	53.3
Less than 50	1375	68.7
Less than 60	1615	80.7
Less than 70	1805	90.3
Less than 80	1935	96.7
Less than 90	1975	98.7
Less than 100	1999	99.9
Less than 110	2000	100.0

Source: Wixiewatchie Chamber of Commerce, July 1977.

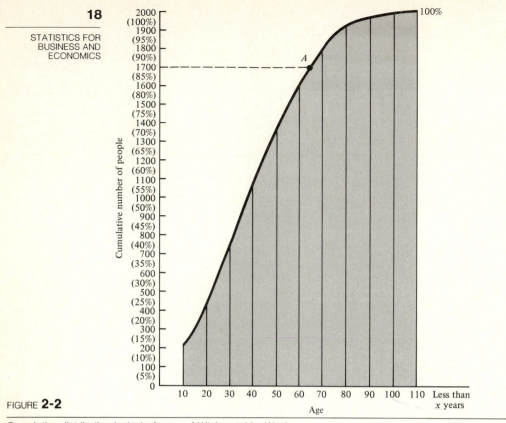

FIGURE **2-2**

Cumulative distribution (ogive) of ages of Wixiewatchie, Washington, residents in July 1977. **Source:** Wixiewatchie Chamber
of Commerce, 1977.

spotting these graphs (note the axes on the graph). Let us illustrate. Henry Jones
became the sales manager for Trimgym Reducing Products Co. in January 1974.
The following table shows sales figures for 1970–1977.

ANNUAL SALES	THOUSANDS OF DOLLARS
1970	400
1971	410
1972	420
1973	430
1974	435
1975	437
1976	439
1977	441

If we were to plot this on a graph where we started at zero sales (Y axis), it would
look like Figure 2-3(a). This graph does not look good for Jones. In fact, if we look
at the numbers, his predecessors' sales increased $10,000 per year while Henry's
annual increases have been more modest. To show himself in a better light, Jones

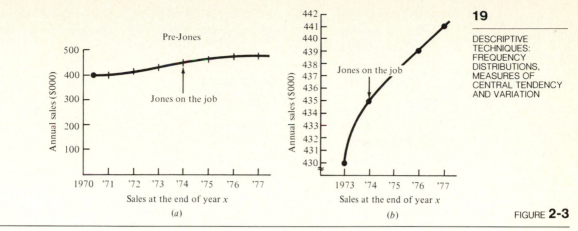

19

DESCRIPTIVE
TECHNIQUES:
FREQUENCY
DISTRIBUTIONS,
MEASURES OF
CENTRAL TENDENCY
AND VARIATION

FIGURE **2-3**

(a) Graph with regular Y axis. (b) Graph with extended Y axis.

stretches out the Y axis [Figure 2-3(b)] and only includes the sales for one year before his arrival. Looking at Figure 2-3(b), Jones now appears to be a successful sales manager. The combination of dropping the data from the previous years and the expansion of the scale of the Y axis makes Jones look good. Notice that Jones has appropriately used a serrated line on the Y axis to show the reader that he is using only a part of the axis. [See Figure 2-3(b).]

Other distortions are possible using two-dimensional pictures. For example, let us compare the production of watches in Japan from 1973 to 1977. Production doubled from 22 million to 44 million units. If we use a pictorial diagram [Figure 2-4(a)] to represent the number of watches, we would draw one bar twice as large as the other.

In Figure 2-4(a) we have *doubled both the height and width,* giving an impression of much greater growth; in effect, we have quadrupled the area. In Figure 2-4(b), width has been kept the same, so that area doubles just as output does. *Conclusion:* There are many ways to present erroneous impressions. It is important to know how to present honest information and how to recognize distortions.

We have now discussed ways of grouping and displaying information in the

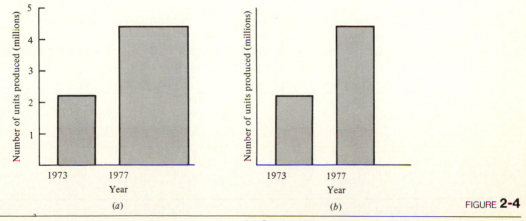

FIGURE **2-4**

(a) Graph with incorrect areas. (b) Graph with correct areas.

form of tables, graphs, and pictorial diagrams. Often a summary offering an average of some type is needed. The next section discusses ways to find the averages (central tendency) of a group of numbers.

MEASURES OF CENTRAL TENDENCY: UNGROUPED DATA

2-4

Arithmetic Mean

After data has been presented in graphic form, it is still necessary to provide measures of central tendency that describe where the middle or the midpoint of the data tends to fall. The best known measure of *central tendency* is the *arithmetic mean* or the *average*. If you wanted the average grade for your five (3 credit) courses, you would add the five grades and divide by 5 (the number of courses). In mathematical terms, let the five grades be denoted.

$$X_1 = 95$$

$$X_2 = 90$$

$$X_3 = 85$$

$$X_4 = 82$$

$$X_5 = 70$$

Ungrouped Data   You will notice that these five observations are not grouped in a frequency distribution (we have only individual numbers and not categories); therefore, we call this *ungrouped data*. If we wish to add these five numbers, we give each one a name in terms of X. Thus, for any series of numbers, we can use subscripted numbers as the names. The first number is X_1 (read it as X sub-one), the second is X_2 (X sub-two), and so forth. Now, to tell someone to add them and divide by the number of observations (N) for all the items in the population, we can say

$$\frac{X_1 + X_2 + X_3 + X_4 + X_5}{N} = \mu \qquad \text{mean of a population} \qquad (2\text{-}1)$$

A population consists of all the possible units (places, people, things) from which information can be obtained that is relevant to the problem being studied. Thus, if we want to know the average allowance of full-time U.S. college students, all full-time college students in this country are the population.

The greek letter μ (mu) stands for the mean of a population. This is called a population *parameter*. If we wish to find the mean of a sample taken from the population, we call it $\overline{X}$ (X bar). A number computed from a sample is called a *statistic*.

If we wish to know the grade point average of students in the freshman class for an elementary mathematics course, we could add the grades for all students and divide by the number of students. This would be the *population mean* μ, because we have calculated the mean for *all* students, the entire population in this grade. Another method to find a grade point average would be to take the grades of a *sample* of students, such as every tenth student, and average these grades. This estimate would be called $\overline{X}$, the mean of a sample, and we would use it to estimate the population mean. It is easier to use every tenth number to estimate the population mean, but one must be very careful about choosing a good sample. Chapters 4 and 5 discuss sampling techniques.

21

DESCRIPTIVE
TECHNIQUES:
FREQUENCY
DISTRIBUTIONS,
MEASURES OF
CENTRAL TENDENCY
AND VARIATION

Obviously, if we add many numbers together, the formula becomes very long. In order to shorten Equation 2-2, the Greek letter Σ (read capital sigma) is used to indicate summation.

Subscript notation, in which each observation is given a number, is used in many texts. To simplify notation, it has been omitted in this book. Using subscript notation, the formula for the mean of the population would be

$$\mu = \frac{X_1 + X_2 + X_3 + \cdots + X_N}{N} = \frac{\sum_{i=1}^{N} X_i}{N} \tag{2-2}$$

This equation is read, "the sum of the X_i values as i goes from 1 to N, divided by N." Equation 2-2 can be expressed in simplified form as

$$\mu = \frac{\Sigma X}{N} \qquad \text{mean of a population} \tag{2-3}$$

This equation can be read, "the mean is equal to the sum of all the X_i values divided by the number of X_i values." Now, if we wish to calculate the *mean of a sample*, we call it $\overline{X}$ and let n equal the number of observations in the sample. The formula for the mean of a sample is, in subscript notation,

$$\overline{X} = \frac{\sum_{i=1}^{n} X_i}{n}$$

In simplified form, it is

$$\overline{X} = \frac{\Sigma X}{n} \qquad \text{mean of a sample} \tag{2-4}$$

Let us say we have a sample of 10 house values in a given area and wish to calculate the mean price of houses for this sample.

(1) 15,000	(5) 14,000	(9) 49,000
(2) 18,000	(6) 42,000	(10) 42,000
(3) 25,000	(7) 63,000	
(4) 30,000	(8) 220,000	

$$\overline{X} = \text{mean house price} = \frac{\$518,000}{10} = \$51,800$$

The arithmetic mean seems rather high when we look at the original house prices. Actually, there are only two houses that are worth \$51,800 or more. This illustrates one of the problems of the arithmetic mean; it tends to be pulled up or down by extreme values, such as \$220,000. How can this problem be avoided?

Another measure of central tendency, the median, may be more representative for this type of information. In order to find the median, arrange the numbers from highest to lowest (or lowest to highest); this is called an ordered *array*. Pick the middle number. To find the position of the middle number, use the formula $(n + 1)/2$. If we have 10 numbers, the middle number will be between 5 and 6, or the 5.5th number. Ranking the house prices in order from lowest to highest we have:

(1)   14,000

(2)   15,000

(3)   18,000

(4)   25,000

(5)   30,000   } add 2 middle numbers and divide by 2: 72,000/2
                 = $36,000 = median
(6)   42,000

(7)   42,000

(8)   49,000

(9)   63,000   If we omitted the tenth number, the median would be the fifth number ($30,000).

(10) 220,000

Since there are 10 numbers, the median will be half way between the fifth and the sixth numbers, or $36,000. Looking at the data $36,000 seems more like a representative value than $51,800. Government statistics on average income are always expressed in terms of medians. This offsets the influence of several billionaires. In 1975, for example, median family income in the United States was *$13,772,* while the estimated mean family income was *$17,146.*[1] Similarly, statistics on wealth, such as liquid assets (cash and checking accounts, U.S. savings bonds, and savings accounts), are usually presented in terms of medians, since negative assets (debt) do not usually offset very high asset holdings. If you were an attorney for a union, what measure of central tendency of wages would you present as evidence of the need for a pay raise? What information might the attorney for the company present?

There is another measure of central tendency—*the mode.* You are acquainted with the mode in fashion; it is the style worn by most women or men. The mode is the most common event (number). For our 10 figures, $42,000 is the mode because it appears twice while all the other numbers appear only once. One of the problems with the mode is that it is not unique. There can be only one mean and only one median, but there can be several modes. For example, if the first two numbers were 14,000, there would be two modes—$14,000 and $42,000. This would be called a *bimodal distribution.* Modes have meaning only for very large samples where information that a distribution is bimodal can be seen on a histogram. For Table 2-2, the *modal class* goes from 30 to 40 and the mode is 35 (the midpoint of the class). If a large distribution has a mode or modes that differ significantly from the mean and median, this information should be presented in a statistical report. The mode should be viewed with suspicion if we have a small number of data points.

---

[1]This is estimated by multiplying mean per capita income $5,832 by average family size (2.94).

Weighted Arithmetic Mean

23

DESCRIPTIVE
TECHNIQUES:
FREQUENCY
DISTRIBUTIONS,
MEASURES OF
CENTRAL TENDENCY
AND VARIATION

Frequently, it is necessary to compute averages for a total population where we have information on the mean value for each group. Let us say we know that average income for men under 30 years of age is $15,000; for men at least 30 years of age but less than 65, it is $22,000; and for men 65 years of age and over, it is $5,000. If we add the three figures and divide by 3, we have

$$\begin{array}{r} X \\ \hline \$15,000 \\ 22,000 \\ 5,000 \\ \hline 3\overline{)42,000} \\ \overline{X} = \$14,000 \end{array}$$

The mean would be $14,000, which would provide an underestimate of income *because* this type of average assumes that there are an equal number of people in each group. Instead, we should multiply the value of income in each group by the number of people in each group (W) to arrive at the average income. Suppose that there are 25,000,000 men under 30 years of age, 60,000,000 men at least 30 years of age but under 65, and 15,000,000 men 65 years of age and over. We can weight each average as shown in Table 2-4; $17,700 is a more accurate estimate of average income because there are more people in the middle-income category than in the other two groups.

TABLE 2-4

AGE	AVERAGE INCOME X	NUMBER IN GROUP W (in millions)	WEIGHTED TOTAL WX
Under 30	$15,000	25	375,000
30 but under 65	22,000	60	1,320,000
65 and over	5,000	15	75,000
		$\Sigma W = 100$	$\Sigma WX = 1,770,000$

$$\overline{X}_w = \frac{\Sigma WX}{\Sigma W} \qquad \text{Weighted Mean} \qquad (2\text{-}5)$$

$$\overline{X}_w = \frac{1,770,000}{100} = \$17,700$$

The weighted arithmetic mean is used every time a grade point average is computed. (See Table 2-5.)

Suppose A = 4 points, B = 3 points, C = 2 points, D = 1 point, F = 0.

$$\overline{X}_w = \frac{\Sigma WX}{\Sigma W} = \frac{47}{15} = 3.13$$

Frequently, the weighted mean is used to average ratios or percentages. For example, if we know that 90% of women workers and 70% of male workers retire at

	CREDITS W	GRADE X	WEIGHTED TOTAL WX
Russian	5	A (4)	20
Chemistry	4	B (3)	12
Calculus	3	C (2)	6
English	3	B (3)	9
	$\Sigma W = 15$		$\Sigma WX = 47$

65 years of age, this does not mean that 80% of all workers retire at 65. Women constitute 35% of the labor force. Therefore, 77% of the labor force will retire at 65.

	W in labor force		X % that retire	WX
Women	.35	×	90% =	31.50%
Men	.65	×	70% =	45.50
	1.00			ΣWX 77.00%

$$\bar{X}_w = \frac{77.00}{1} = 77\%$$

MEAN FOR GROUPED DATA

2-5   Computation of the mean for ungrouped data is a relatively simple matter. How can the mean be computed when the data is in the form of a frequency distribution like Table 2-6?

For each of the salary groups in Table 2-6, we do not know where any particular individual is located. Therefore, if we wish to use a value to represent a group, we must use the midpoint (or *class mark*) of that group. This technique is thus an approximation. Let us set up a column called X (column 3) for the midpoint of each class. To get each midpoint, we add the upper and lower value and divide by 2. For 65 to under 75, the class mark is 70; for 65.0 to 74.9, it would be 69.95 or 70.

Now, the classes with more people or observations should have more influence than the other classes. Therefore, in column 4, weight each class mark or class midpoint X by the number of people (f) in each class. The total of column 4 is $11,060. If this total is divided by the total number of observations (110 people), we find that the mean weekly salary is approximately equal to $100.545 = \$100.55$.

The formula for the mean of a frequency distribution of the population is

$$\mu = \frac{\Sigma fX}{N} \tag{2-6}$$

where N is the number of people in the population; for a sample, it would be

$$\bar{X} = \frac{\Sigma fX}{n} \tag{2-7}$$

where n is the number of people in the sample. Equations 2-6 and 2-7, which are approximations, are comparable to Equation 2-3 and 2-4.

WEEKLY SALARY, PACKAGING DEPARTMENT, FRISKIE KRUNCHEES, JUNE 1977

DESCRIPTIVE
TECHNIQUES:
FREQUENCY
DISTRIBUTIONS,
MEASURES OF
CENTRAL TENDENCY
AND VARIATION

(1) WEEKLY SALARY	(2) NUMBER OF EMPLOYEES f	(3) CLASS MIDPOINT X	(4) fX	(5) CUMULATIVE FREQUENCY cf
$65 under 75	5	70	350	5
75 under 85	10	80	800	15
85 under 95	20	90	1,800	35
95 under 105	36	100	3,600	71
105 under 115	22	110	2,420	93
115 under 125	12	120	1,440	105
125 under 135	5	130	650	110
	110		11,060	

$$\bar{X} = \frac{11,060}{110} = \$100.545$$

This computation reveals that the construction of classes is important. Generally, the people in each class should be equally distributed throughout the class or else concentrated in the middle of the class, since the midpoint of the class is used to represent the class. Incomes usually are concentrated near a zero figure—$100, $200, or $150. Therefore, if we set up classes from $100 to under $110, most people falling in this category would have an income of $100, yet we would use $105 to represent the category. Therefore, our average income figure would be too high. It would be wiser to have the class go from $95 to under $105.

When classes are constructed, it is important to look at the distribution of the data in the categories. However, once the data is presented to you in a tabular form, there is nothing you can do but use the midpoint of each class. Thus, information is lost when data is grouped, and the results are less accurate than they would be if each data item was considered in the calculation.

Another problem in computing the mean for grouped data arises when there is an open-ended class. For example, in the data in Table 2-2 on the ages of people in Wixiewatchie, Washington, what can be used as the midpoint of the class "80 and over"? Since the footnote provides additional information, it is possible to estimate the midpoint of the class. If no additional data was provided, the mean could not be computed and one would have to rely on the computation of the median as a measure of central tendency.

COMPUTATION OF THE MEDIAN FOR GROUPED DATA

2-6

To compute the median for ungrouped data, we arranged all the numbers in order from lowest to highest and found the middle number. For grouped data, we see that the classes are already in order; however, the median will be somewhere within the middle class—the class in which the middle person falls. We use a process of interpolation, which is a way to find intermediate values of a quantity between two given values (beginning and end of the class) to find the median. Since there is generally a large amount of data in a frequency distribution, we treat the data as if it comes from a continuum, and the position of the middle number can be found by dividing the total frequency (N or n) in half. For the data in Table 2-6, we have $N/2 = 110/2 = 55$. We are therefore looking for the 55th person in this salary continuum. Where is that person?

To locate the 55th person's class, we form a cumulative frequency distribution cf (Table 2-6, column 5) by adding the frequencies in column 2. In the class "from $85 but under $95," we have 35 people. In the next class (95 to 105), we have 36 people. If we want the 55th person we will have to go 20/36 into this class, since we have included 35 people in all three of the previous classes. Because each income class is $10 wide, we would add (20/36) ($10) to the income at the beginning of the class $95. We are thus assuming an even spread of incomes through the classes.

$$\$95 + \frac{20}{36}(\$10) = \$95 + \$5.555 = \$100.555$$

Now, to write this in terms of a formula, let

Md = median

L_{md} = lower limit of median class

n = number of observations

cf_{md} = cumulative frequency up to median class

i = width of each class (class interval)

f_{md} = frequency in median class (number of people in median class)

$$Md = L_{md} + \frac{(n/2) - cf_{md}}{f_{md}}\,i \qquad \text{median for grouped data} \qquad (2\text{-}8)$$

Now try to compute the median for the ages of people in Wixiewatchie (Table 2-2).

PERCENTILES, DECILES, AND QUARTILES

2-7

The median divides the distribution into two equal parts. Other useful divisions are *deciles,* which divide the distribution into 10 equal parts; *quartiles,* which divide the group into four equal parts; and *percentiles,* which divide the group into 100 equal parts. These measures may be calculated for grouped or ungrouped data.

The median is the 5th decile, the 50th percentile, or the 2d quartile. A technique similar to that used for calculating the median is used to calculate these other measures. Suppose, for example, that we would like to find the 3d quartile for worker incomes in Table 2-6. This would be the income above which we would find the top 25% of the workers. Therefore, we are looking for the income of the $3n/4$ worker, $\frac{3}{4}$ (110) = 82.5. Looking at the cumulative frequency table, we see that this worker is in the class "$105 and under $115." Starting with the lower limit of this class, we have

$$\$105 + \frac{(82.5 - 71.0)}{22}(\$10) = \$110.23$$

These measures are frequently used for grades or test scores. Thus, some exclusive universities consider admitting only students who are in the top decile of their high school graduation class. Other schools may stipulate that a student must be in the top quartile on the Scholastic Aptitude Test.

We have seen that if we have a large set of numbers to describe, some measure of central tendency gives the reader an idea of the magnitude of these numbers. For example, look at these four sets of numbers.

(a) 10, 10, 10, 10, 20, 30, 30, 30, 30

(b) 20, 22, 21, 20, 20, 19, 18, 20, 20

(c)   1, 4, 6, 8, 20, 32, 34, 36, 39

(d) 10, 12, 14, 16, 20, 24, 26, 28, 30

Lo and behold, they all have the same mean (20) and the same median (20), yet the four sets are quite different. What can be done to indicate their differences?

Another look at the sets of numbers reveals that they differ in how scattered they are about the mean. In group (b), most of the numbers are close to the mean. In group (c), there is a large amount of variation between the numbers and the mean. To have a more complete description of this numerical data, we should provide a measure of this variation.

One possible variation measure is the *range*—the distance between the highest and lowest number.

For group (a), the distance is 10 → 30, for a range of 20.

For group (b), the distance is 18 → 22, for a range of 4.

For group (c), the distance is   1 → 39, for a range of 38.

For group (d), the distance is 10 → 30, for a range of 20.

Looking at (a) and (d), we see that the range is 20, yet all but one of the numbers in group (a) are at the extreme values of 10 and 30, however, the numbers in group (d) are nearly uniformly spaced throughout the range.

Another useful measure is the *average deviation*. For each number in a set, we can subtract the mean and then sum these deviations. Now, if you computed the mean properly, this figure should *always* be 0. (This is derived from the definition of the mean, since it is the arithmetic midpoint of the numbers.) Let's try a new example

$$
\begin{array}{ll}
3 & 3 - 5 = -2 \\
4 & 4 - 5 = -1 \\
5 & 5 - 5 = 0 \\
6 & 6 - 5 = +1 \\
\underline{7} & 7 - 5 = \underline{+2} \\
\bar{X} = \dfrac{25}{5} = 5 & 0
\end{array}
$$

You might suggest, "Well, forget the signs and use the absolute deviations." This would lead us to MAD (mean absolute deviation), which in this case would be $\frac{6}{5}$ = 1.2.

The next measure to be discussed dispenses with the sign problem by squaring the deviations, adding up the squared deviations and dividing this sum by the number of observations, and then taking the square root of this number. This measure, called the *standard deviation,* is used to overcome the sign problem and also has useful statistical prediction properties.

First, let us spend some time learning how to compute the standard deviation. Then, we will discuss at length how it can be used. The standard deviation is a universally known and a highly useful measure. In fact, if only one measure could be taught in a statistics course, the standard deviation would probably be the best one to choose. (The mean is important, but it is easy to teach and most students already know how to compute it.)

Let us express the method of computing the standard deviation in terms of a formula. If we were computing the standard deviation for a sample, it would be

$$s = \sqrt{\frac{\Sigma(X - \bar{X})^2}{n - 1}} \qquad \text{sample standard deviation} \qquad (2\text{-}9)$$

If we square this expression, we have the *sample variance s^2.*

The population parameter would be σ (σ is the Greek letter sigma)

$$\sigma = \sqrt{\frac{\Sigma(X - \mu)^2}{N}} \qquad \text{population standard deviation} \qquad (2\text{-}10)$$

This expression, without the square root sign, is called the *population variance σ^2* (sigma squared).

You will notice that in computing the sample standard deviation, we divide by $n - 1$ rather than by n; N = population size, n = sample size. Estimates from a sample, particularly a small one, may not be near the population value because the population may be scattered more widely than a sample. The use of the denominator $n - 1$ tends to increase the size of the standard deviation, particularly for a small sample.[2] Now, let us compute s for our small sample.

X	$X - \bar{X}$	$(X - \bar{X})^2$
3	-2	4
4	-1	1
5	0	0
6	$+1$	1
7	$+2$	4
$\Sigma X = 25$		$\Sigma(X - \bar{X})^2 = 10$

$$\bar{X} = \frac{25}{5} = 5$$

---

[2]This statistic ($s^2 = \Sigma(X - \bar{X})^2/n{-}1$, is called an *unbiased estimator* of the population parameter σ^2. If all possible samples of a given size n were drawn from the population with replacement and s^2 were computed for each of these samples, the average value of s^2 would be equal to σ^2.

$$s^2 = \sqrt{\frac{\Sigma(X - \bar{X})^2}{n - 1}}$$

$$s = \sqrt{\frac{10}{4}} = \sqrt{2.5} = 1.58$$

29

DESCRIPTIVE
TECHNIQUES:
FREQUENCY
DISTRIBUTIONS,
MEASURES OF
CENTRAL TENDENCY
AND VARIATION

If we compute s for each of the four distributions on page 27, we find that they are (*a*) $s = 10$, (*b*) $s = 1.12$, (*c*) $s = 15.47$, and (*d*) $s = 7.35$, respectively.

Now that we have computed the standard deviation, what does it mean? If all the numbers in a group were the same as the mean, σ or s would be 0. If the numbers are close to the mean, σ or s would be lower than if the numbers were widely spread about the mean. Thus, σ or s measures *dispersion* or *scatter* about the mean.

The standard deviation takes on special significance when we talk of it in terms of the *normal distribution.* You may have heard the normal distribution described as a *bell-shaped curve.* Generally, when we have a large population, most of the observations will be near the mean; however, there will be some that are spread out far away from the mean. If we study such things as height, weight, intelligence, grade point average, delivery times, we find a distribution that looks like the one shown in Figure 2-5. First, the distribution is symmetric: you can fold the curve in half at the mean, and both sides match. Secondly, there is only one mode. Thirdly, most measurements are near the mean. Lastly, there are some measurements, the unusual ones, scattered far away from the mean; however, the farther you go from the mean, the fewer observations you find. The tails or ends of this distribution never quite touch the x axis. They go from $-\infty$ to $+\infty$ (asymptotic); this is called a normal distribution. The area under the curve in Figure 2-5 is 1, and once we know μ and σ we can tell what percent of the observations are within a given number of standard deviations about the mean. We discuss this probability distribution in greater detail in Chapter 3.

If we have a set of observations that are normally distributed and we take 1 standard deviation on either side of the mean (see Figure 2-5), 68.26% of the area

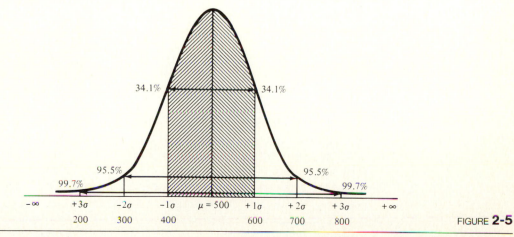

FIGURE **2-5**

Graph of a normal curve.

under the curve will be in the area from $(\mu - 1\sigma)$ to $(\mu + 1\sigma)$ (shaded area). If we take the mean $\pm 2\sigma$, then we find 95.5% of our observations and the mean $\pm 3\sigma$ = 99.7% of all observations. If we think that in an actual situation the distribution will be normal (for example, heights, weights, temperature), then we can approximate the actual distributions with information from the theoretical distributions. For example, if the mean weight of male college students is 160 pounds and the standard deviation is 10 pounds, we would expect the middle 68% of the male college students to weigh between 150 and 170 pounds. Thus we can make estimates of actual weights by using the theoretical normal curve.

The standard deviation and the assumption of a normal distribution is commonly used in test scoring. For example, on the Scholastic Aptitude Test (SAT), 500 is generally regarded as the mean and 100 points is considered to be 1 standard deviation.[3] Let's approximate the distribution of these scores by laying them out on a normal curve.

We know that below 500, the mean, we have 50% of the area under the theoretical curve. We also know that between the mean plus 1 standard deviation and the mean minus 1 standard deviation, we have 68% of the area under the theoretical curve (68% of the area is between scores of 400 and 600). Therefore, since the theoretical curve is symmetric, 34% are between 500 and 600 and 34% are between 400 and 500. Now, we can look at the graph and see that if you scored 600 on the test, only 16% of the students in this country (50% $-$ 34%) have better scores than you do, given that the actual curve is very similar to the theoretical normal curve. Similarly, if you scored 400, only 16% of the students in the country scored below you.

Let us examine some uses for the standard deviation.

EXAMPLE 2-1   Suppose you needed to sell some stock in order to have money for a down payment on a house. You own two stocks, Standard Coal and Northwest Coal. Here are the facts that can be obtained from averaging prices from the stock page and computing the standard deviations around these averages. Which one should you sell? Assume that prices are normally distributed.

	MEAN PRICE	STANDARD DEVIATION	CURRENT PRICE
Standard Coal	55	5	60
Northwest Coal	48	4	60

Standard Coal is 1 standard deviation above its mean; Northwest Coal is now 3 standard deviations above its mean [Figure 2-6(*a*) and (*b*)].We said before that in a normal distribution 99.7% of all observations are included between the mean $\pm$ 3 standard deviations. This leaves .3% of the area under the curve for Northwest Coal to be divided between the two tails. Since the area under each half of the curve is .5, this means .0015 is the area to the right of 60; thus, only 1.5 tenths of 1 percent of the time can the stock price be expected to be 60 or higher.

---

[3]Lately, mean SAT scores have been declining and 450 is now closer to the mean.

31

DESCRIPTIVE
TECHNIQUES:
FREQUENCY
DISTRIBUTIONS,
MEASURES OF
CENTRAL TENDENCY
AND VARIATION

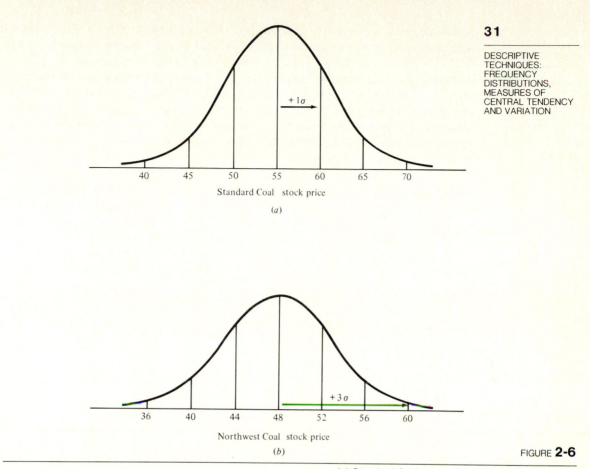

FIGURE **2-6**

(*a*) Standard Coal prices. (*b*) Northwest Coal prices.

The best decision—provided you have no other information on the firms, such as new coal discoveries by one of the firms—would be to sell Northwest Coal because it is unusually high. Only .15% of the time has it ever been higher than 60, whereas Standard Coal has been above 60 about 16% of the time.

We will learn more about areas under the normal curve in the following chapters.

EXAMPLE 2-2   You are seeking a salesperson for Wispie Widgets, a new product for teenagers. They are shoe lifts that make a person seem taller. Two people apply for the job and supply you with information on their previous experience and average weekly sales. Jones says she typically sold $2000 of merchandise per week, while Blackwell says he sold $20,000 per week.

At first glance it would seem that Blackwell is the person to hire. His average sales exceed those of Jones. But wait! What is Blackwell selling? If Blackwell sells Rolls Royce cars and Jones sells pencils, perhaps this could account for the tremendous difference in average weekly sales. If we look in trade journals for average industry sales per week, we would be in a better position to judge if Jones and Blackwell were above average salespersons. Let us say that average sales were $1200 in Jones's field and $16,000 in Blackwell's field. Now, we see that both salespersons are above average. Still, it is difficult to decide which is the better one. If we have industry figures showing sales, it is possible to compute a measure of variation around average sales (standard deviation). For Jones's business, the standard deviation is $300; for Blackwell's, it is $4000. Assume that what both Jones and Blackwell sold previously does not relate to our product.

	JONES	BLACKWELL
Average weekly sales (for each salesperson) $\bar{X}$	$2,000	$20,000
Industrywide average weekly sales μ (for industry in which salesperson worked)	$1,200	$16,000
Standard deviation for sales σ (for industry in which salesperson worked)	$ 300	$ 4,000

Now, we are in a position to make a decision. Both salespersons are above average, but Blackwell's sales are 1 standard deviation above the sales of the average salesperson in his field, while Jones's sales are $2\frac{2}{3}$ standard deviations above the average salesperson. So we prefer Jones because only a small percentage of salespersons in her field equaled her sales. We wish to devise a formula to compute the number of standard deviations from the mean. This formula is

$$z = \frac{x - \mu}{\sigma} \qquad \text{for population data} \qquad (2\text{-}11)$$

$$z = \frac{X - \bar{X}}{s} \qquad \text{for sample data} \qquad (2\text{-}12)$$

These are called z scores or standard scores, and we study them in greater detail in Chapter 3.

Using the formula (for Jones $z = 2\frac{2}{3}$, and for Blackwell $z = 1$),

Jones	Blackwell
$z = \dfrac{2000 - 1200}{300} = 2\frac{2}{3}$	$z = \dfrac{20,000 - 16,000}{4000} = 1$

EXAMPLE 2-3 Ken Coates, an angry employee, approaches the personnel director to complain about his wage rate. He claims that he produces far more units than the other workers in his division, but that his pay does not reflect his productivity. The personnel director looks at the wage records and finds that the average worker in Coates's division earns $5.00 per hour, while Coates earns $6.00 per hour. Then, the director consults the factory foreman. Coates produces 700 Wispie Widgets per hour while the average worker produces 550 per hour. Obviously, Coates is above average in both wage rate and productivity. A colleague suggests that the personnel director compute how much Coates exceeds

average productivity, and reward Coates in terms of the number of standard deviations he is above the mean. Computation, using the payroll records of Coates's division, reveals that the mean pay is $5.00 per hour and the standard deviation is $1.00 per hour. Computation, using factory output records for the division, reveals that the mean output is 550 units per hour and the standard deviation is 60 units per hour. The manager computes the z scores for wages and productivity.

$$\text{Productivity (units)} \qquad\qquad \text{Wages (\$)}$$

$$Z_p = \frac{X - \bar{X}}{s} = \frac{700 - 550}{60} = \frac{150}{60} = 2.5 \qquad Z_w = \frac{\$6.00 - \$5.00}{\$1.00} = \frac{1.00}{1.00} = 1$$

Coates is 2.5 standard deviations above average in productivity and 1 standard deviation above average in wages. He should be 2.5 standard deviations above average in wages, or at least somewhat better than 1. The personnel director multiplies the 2.5 standard deviations by $1.00, the size of a standard deviation in wages, to compute a bonus of $2.50 per hour.

$$(2.5)(1.00) = 2.50 \text{ bonus}$$

$$+ \underline{\;5.00\;} \text{ average wage}$$

$$\$7.50$$

The personnel director decides to raise Coates's hourly wage to $7.50 to make it conform with his productivity. The compensation for piecework in many factories is based on the average output and an average wage. Workers producing above average will earn more. Often these systems are based on standard deviations, but such systems are not primarily associated with pay on an hourly basis, but rather with a base wage plus a per piece incentive.

STANDARD DEVIATION: GROUPED DATA

2-9

In order to measure variation around the mean (standard deviation), we have subtracted the mean from each observation, squared this difference, summed all the squared differences, divided by the number of observations, and taken the square root of this result. Computation for grouped data is similar:

1 Subtract the mean from the midpoint of each class category (class mark): $X - \bar{X}$.
2 Square this difference: $(X - \bar{X})^2$.
3 Multiply by the frequency in the class: $f(X - \bar{X})^2$.
4 Sum all of these weighted squared deviations: $\Sigma f(X - \bar{X})^2$.
5 Divide by the total number of observations minus 1 if you are working with sample data; otherwise, divide by the total number in the population.
6 Take the square root of this expression:

$$s = \sqrt{\frac{\Sigma f(X - \bar{X})^2}{n - 1}} \qquad \begin{array}{l}\text{standard deviation—} \\ \text{grouped data, sample}\end{array} \qquad (2\text{-}13)$$

TABLE 2-7

WEEKLY SALARY, PACKAGING DEPARTMENT, FRISKIE KRUNCHEES, JUNE 1977

(1) WEEKLY SALARY($)	(2) NUMBER OF EMPLOYEES f	(3) CLASS MIDPOINT X	(4) $(X - \bar{X})$	(5) $(X - \bar{X})^2$	(6) $f(X - \bar{X})^2$
65 under 75	5	70	−30.545	932.997	4,664.985
75 under 85	10	80	−20.545	422.097	4,220.970
85 under 95	20	90	−10.545	111.197	2,223.940
95 under 105	36	100	− 0.545	.297	10 .692
105 under 115	22	110	+ 9.455	89.397	1,966.734
115 under 125	12	120	+19.455	378.497	4,541.964
125 under 135	5	130	+29.455	867.597	4,337.985
	110				21,967.270

$$\bar{X} = 100.545 \text{ (see Table 2-4)}$$

$$s = \sqrt{\frac{\Sigma f(X - \bar{X})^2}{n - 1}} = \sqrt{\frac{21{,}967.270}{109}} = \sqrt{201.535}$$

$$s = 14.196$$

$$\text{or } \sigma = \sqrt{\frac{\Sigma f(X - \mu)^2}{N}} \qquad \begin{array}{l}\text{standard deviation—}\\ \text{grouped data, population}\end{array} \qquad (2\text{-}14)$$

If we take the information from Table 2-6 (found on p. 25), we can calculate the standard deviation for our grouped data on workers' wages and set up Table 2-7.

If we can assume that this distribution is approximately normal, we would expect approximately 68% of the workers to have incomes between $100.545 − $14.196 ($\mu - 1\sigma$) and $100.545 + $14.196 ($\mu + 1\sigma$), from $86.35 to $114.74.

Problems

1 Assume the following data on charge purchases made by students at a college bookstore for one day:

$40.36	$67.50	$79.98
43.68	69.60	83.00
46.70	69.60	84.20
49.80	72.25	87.79
53.60	73.80	88.80
58.00	74.40	89.64
59.60	75.42	90.03
62.00	75.42	91.60
64.69	75.42	95.50
65.73	79.20	98.00

Assume the following classes:

35

DESCRIPTIVE
TECHNIQUES:
FREQUENCY
DISTRIBUTIONS,
MEASURES OF
CENTRAL TENDENCY
AND VARIATION

$40.00 and under $50.00

$50.00 and under $60.00

$60.00 and under $70.00

$70.00 and under $80.00

$80.00 and under $90.00

$90.00 and under $100.00

Now construct a frequency distribution and calculate the mean, median, and standard deviation for the frequency distribution.

2 Suppose you have just been hired to work in the advertising department of a large manufacturing company. Your supervisor has just given you the following list of one-year advertising expenditures of a sample of firms in the industry (in thousands of dollars). She tells you to give her some meaningful statistics from it. Complete your assignment and show all work done so that your supervisor can see what you have done. (*Hint:* Group the data into eight equal classes starting with $160.0)

$163.2	$184.0	$205.7	$219.9
169.5	185.2	209.8	220.0
169.8	185.2	211.1	222.4
175.4	189.7	212.6	222.7
177.6	192.3	212.9	225.6
177.6	192.3	213.4	229.8
178.8	192.4	214.5	231.4
180.4	194.8	218.7	236.8
183.7	197.6	218.7	238.6
183.9	200.3	218.7	239.0

3 It has been reported that last July was the hottest July in Arizona in several years. Arizona meteorologist John Coleman says that this is ridiculous; just the summer before, he remembers, July temperatures exceeded 110° whereas this July's high was only 109°. Based upon the following July temperature highs for the four weeks in each of the two years, who is right, Coleman or the reports? What must the reports have meant by hottest as opposed to Coleman's definition?

	HIGH TEMPERATURE			
	WEEK 1	WEEK 2	WEEK 3	WEEK 4
July 1980	97	95	111	97
July 1981	101	109	103	103

4   A yogurt producer has decided to capitalize on a recent boom in the demand for flavored yogurt. He markets his product under several brand names (A, B, C, D) now and wants to step up his advertising to include emphasis on flavors, while at the same time, keeping his brand names distinct. He realizes that if he deviates too much from the price expectations of his different brands' customers, they will be cautious about trying the flavors. Therefore, the producer decides to test market his product at three different price levels for each of his four brands (A, B, C, D).

   (*a*)   Find a weighted average price for each brand based upon how much was purchased by each brand's customers at each of the three test prices. (Round to the nearest penny.)

   (*b*)   What would be the total sales income for each brand in this test market situation if the producer priced at the weighted average levels and the same quantities of each brand were purchased?

   (*c*)   To aid the producer in his budgeting for next year, we assume that the test market frequencies are $\frac{1}{512}$ of expected monthly sales and that the demand for flavored yogurt will not be seasonal. Assume that average prices are used for each brand, and that amounts sold for brands in the sample will be bought at this price. What can the producer expect in yearly flavored yogurt sales?

BRAND	PRICE	FREQUENCY OF PURCHASES
	$.20	33
A	.25	42
	.29	30
	$.35	40
B	.37	47
	.40	23
	$.41	28
C	.43	31
	.45	34
	$.47	47
D	.49	27
	.51	17

5   Sheila Coker decided to survey the number of hours undergraduate student assistants worked each week while they attended Claymore College. She had the following results:

HOURS WORKED	NUMBER OF STUDENTS
0 but less than 5	8
5 but less than 10	24
10 but less than 15	48
15 but less than 20	120
20 but less than 25	90
25 but less than 30	20
30 but less than 35	10

   (*a*)   Graph this distribution.

   (*b*)   Compute the mean, median, and standard deviation.

   (*c*)   If student assistants are paid $3.10 per hour, what is the weekly payroll cost to the university? (Show your work.)

6   **37**

DESCRIPTIVE
TECHNIQUES:
FREQUENCY
DISTRIBUTIONS,
MEASURES OF
CENTRAL TENDENCY
AND VARIATION

6   The U.S. Department of Labor issued the following information on the number of people of white, black, and Hispanic origin in the civilian labor force in March 1979.

(*a*)   For each group, calculate the mean age, median age, and standard deviation for age of people in the labor force.

(*b*)   Above what age would the top 30% of the labor force in each of these groups be?

(*c*)   Which group shows the most variation in age?

(*d*)   Which group is the youngest?

AGE GROUP	NUMBER OF WHITES (000)	NUMBER OF BLACKS (000)	NUMBER OF HISPANICS (000)
15 to 24*	2093	2513	2207
25 to 34	2317	2818	1926
35 to 44	1694	1983	1368
45 to 54	1509	1620	960
55 to 64	1066	908	574
65 to 74*	273	305	539
	8952	10,147	7574

*Actual data slightly revised to simplify computation by providing for equal-sized classes.
Source: U.S. Department of Labor, *Marital and Family Characteristics of the Labor Force,* March 1979.

CHEBYCHEFF'S INEQUALITY

2-10

In the previous section, we assumed that the populations studied were normally distributed. In this situation, the area under the curve enclosed by 1 standard deviation on either side of the mean ($\mu \pm 1\sigma$) is 68.3%. The area enclosed by 2 standard deviations on either side of the mean ($\mu \pm 2\sigma$) is 95.5%; the area enclosed by three standard deviations ($\mu \pm 3\sigma$) is 99.7%.

If we don't know what the distribution is, Chebycheff's inequality can be used to determine the *minimum amount* of area that will be enclosed between the mean and a given number of standard deviations. The inequality states

$$\text{Area} \geq 1 - \frac{1}{K^2}$$

K is the number of standard deviations. Using this formula, a table can be derived for areas under a normal curve and for areas of a distribution about which we are uncertain. Because of the method used in the computation of the standard deviation, this inequality holds true for almost any distribution. Notice that if we are sure we have a normal distribution, our area is expected to fall between the mean and a given number of standard deviations.

K NUMBER OF STANDARD DEVIATIONS AROUND THE MEAN	NORMAL DISTRIBUTION	CHEBYCHEFF'S INEQUALITY
1	68.3	—
2	95.5	75.0
3	99.7	88.9

EXAMPLE 2-4   A real estate developer hopes to build a housing development in a small community. The development should appeal to middle-class home owners. The chamber of commerce indicates that the mean income for this town is $9,876 and the standard deviation is $2,015. Within what limits would we find the middle 60% of the incomes in this town?

Since we are uncertain whether incomes in this community are normally distributed, use Chebycheff's inequality

$$1 - \frac{1}{K^2} = .60$$

$$-\frac{1}{K^2} = -.40$$

$$\frac{1}{K^2} = .40$$

$$K^2 = 2.5$$

$$K = 1.58$$

The middle 60% of the population should be within $\pm$ 1.58 standard deviations of the mean, 9,876 $\pm$ 3,183.7. The range within which at least 60% of the incomes will fall is $6,690.30 to $13,061.70.

Chebycheff's inequality is an example of a method that can be used when we are not sure of the nature of the distribution. In Chapters 8 and 9, more examples of distribution-free statistics are covered.

Problems

1   A doctor's office usually receives many calls early in the morning. Between 9 a.m. and 10 a.m., the average number of calls is 48 and the standard deviation is 8.74. The doctor wants to know at least how many calls he will receive 75% of the time. He feels that if the top of this range exceeds 60 he should hire another receptionist. The doctor is not sure that these calls are normally distributed.

2   The Varsity Bookstore sells books on Friday evenings. The number of customers is a random variable with $\mu = 112$ and $\sigma = 12$. According to Chebycheff's inequality, what is the probability they will serve between 52 and 172 customers?

COEFFICIENT OF VARIATION

2-11   The standard deviation measures scatter or variability around the mean. Often it is useful to compare the variability of two sets of numbers. For example, is there more variation in the income of college students' parents than in college students' allowances? Generally, simple comparison of the standard deviations is possible. However, there are two cases in which this comparison is not recommended: (1) when one compares the variability of two measures that are expressed in different units, such as dollars and inches or wages and productivity; and (2) when we compare the variability of two measures expressed in the same units but of completely different magnitudes, such as monthly mortgage payments on a home and monthly expenditure on electricity.

In order to put these two comparisons into perspective, the coefficient of variation (CV) is used to measure relative variation. The coefficient of variation is equal to the standard deviation divided by the mean times 100. For each comparison, the standard deviation is related to the mean so that variation in numbers with small means and with large means can be made comparable.

Symbolically,

39

DESCRIPTIVE
TECHNIQUES:
FREQUENCY
DISTRIBUTIONS,
MEASURES OF
CENTRAL TENDENCY
AND VARIATION

$$CV = \frac{\sigma}{\mu}(100) \qquad \text{coefficient of variation—population} \qquad (2\text{-}15)$$

$$CV = \frac{s}{\bar{X}}(100) \qquad \text{coefficient of variation—sample} \qquad (2\text{-}16)$$

Thus, to compare wages and productivity,

$$CV_W = \frac{s_W}{\bar{X}_W} \qquad CV_p = \frac{s_p}{\bar{X}_p}$$

Let us explore two examples using the coefficient of variation.

EXAMPLE 2-5 We might wish to see if the IQ (intelligence quotient) of workers varies more than their work output. If the two tended to vary to the same degree, we might infer that there is a close relationship between IQ and productivity. Using a sample of workers, we obtain the following information:

IQ	*Output*
$\bar{X} = 100$ points	$\bar{X} = 7000$ units
$s = 20$ points	$s = 3000$ units

Comparison of the two standard deviations is meaningless since they are in different units. Now, compute the coefficients of variation:

$$CV_{IQ} = \frac{20}{100}(100) = 20 \qquad CV_{output} = \frac{3000}{7000}(100) = 42.9$$

Output varies more than twice as much as IQ. Thus, output may not be strongly related to intelligence as measured by IQ.

EXAMPLE 2-6 Are doctors' salaries more scattered than those of accountants?

	DOCTORS	ACCOUNTANTS
$\bar{X}$	$55,000	$30,000
s	15,000	10,000
CV	$\frac{15}{55}(100) = 27.3$	$\frac{10}{30}(100) = 33.3$

At first glance, it would seem that doctors' salaries tend to vary more than accountants because s is larger. The coefficient of variation shows that accountants' salaries are relatively more variable.

2-12   In order to describe data, we have used measures of central tendency (mean, median, and mode) and measures of variation (range and standard deviation). Two sets of data may have similar means and yet still not be the same. Look at the graphs in Figure 2-7. The graph on the left-hand side is symmetric and unimodal; hence, the mean, median, and mode will coincide. The second graph is not symmetric and the longer tail of the distribution is on the left-hand side (skewed to the left). The mode is located at the peak of the distribution (note that this is a unimodal distribution). This means there are more observations on the left-hand side of the mode than on the right-hand side. Because the extreme values are concentrated on the left-hand side, the mean, which is more influenced by extremes, lies to the left of the median.

If the concentration of extreme values is on the right-hand side, the mean and median lie to the right of the mode, with the mean being farther to the right than the mode [Figure 2-8(*a*)]. Thus, if the mean is to the right of the median, the distribution is skewed to the right. If the mean is less than the median, the distribution is skewed to the left. Generally, an income distribution is skewed to the right because several extremely high incomes raise the mean.

Another descriptive measure of a distribution is a measure of *peakedness* (kurtosis). If we look at the three curves in Figure 2-9, we see that all are symmetric yet have different shapes.

The normal curve in (*a*) is called *mesokurtic* (standing for an intermediate amount of peakedness). The curve in (*b*) is very peaked; almost every value is concentrated near the mean. This curve is called *leptokurtic*. Finally, the curve in (*c*) is flat and the values are equally "stretched out" over a long range. This curve is called *platykurtic*. A teacher faced with a class grade distribution like graph (*b*) for a test would have a difficult time distinguishing between A, B, C, D, and F papers, since all papers would be very similar. A distribution like graph (*c*) indicates great variation in scores on the exam.

Problems

1   Clara Brown is a young graphic designer working for a large advertising firm on Michigan Avenue in Chicago. In the 3 years since she's been out of school and working, she's noticed that when purchasing pen points for her lettering purposes, cost was a major factor in determining her purchase decision. She decided that on her lunch breaks this week, she'd observe how many pen point purchases made by fellow graphic designers fell into each cost category; then, she'd compare these purchases

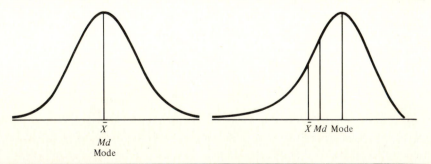

FIGURE **2-7**

Comparison of normal and skewed distributions.

41

DESCRIPTIVE
TECHNIQUES:
FREQUENCY
DISTRIBUTIONS,
MEASURES OF
CENTRAL TENDENCY
AND VARIATION

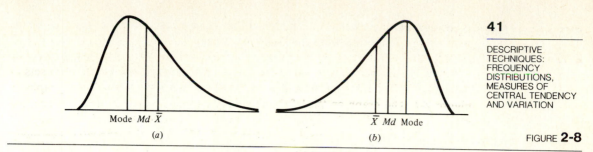

Mode Md $\bar{X}$
(a)

$\bar{X}$ Md Mode
(b)

FIGURE **2-8**

(a) Distribution skewed to the right. (b) Distribution skewed to the left.

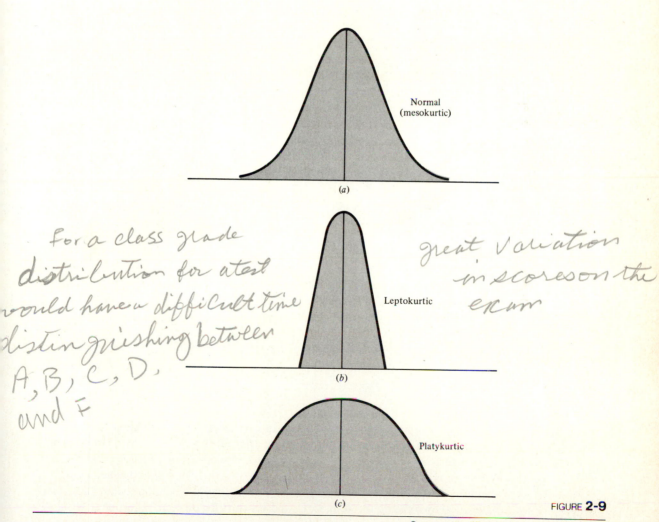

Normal
(mesokurtic)

(a)

Leptokurtic

(b)

Platykurtic

(c)

FIGURE **2-9**

Curves with different levels of peakedness.

For a class grade distribution for a test would have a difficult time distinguishing between A, B, C, D, and F

great variation in scores on the exam

to her own purchase behavior. She found that the average price she spent for a pen point was $1.75. Here's what she found in 1 week:

PEN POINT COST GROUPS ($)	NUMBER OF PURCHASES IN THE WEEK
From 0.70 and under 1.00	4
From 1.00 and under 1.30	48
From 1.30 and under 1.60	100
From 1.60 and under 1.90	128
From 1.90 and under 2.20	92
From 2.20 and under 2.50	52
From 2.50 and under 2.80	6

(*a*) Compute the mean and coefficient of variation for the distribution. Does Clara Brown spend more or less than the average spender?

(*b*) Compute the median.

(*c*) In a normal distribution, the mean plus or minus 1 standard deviation includes the middle 68.3% of the data values. Calculate the 68.3% price range for this data.

2 Stanley Rougham just finished discussing the results of a tough math test with some fellow unfortunate classmates. Stanley thought that it was unfair for a professor to adhere to a normal distribution in awarding grades on a test as difficult as this one. One of Stanley's friends, Marcus, said that he thought the grades were pretty skewed, so Stanley and Marcus took a poll of their classmates to check the distribution.

CLASSMATE	SCORE
1	53
2	63
3	77
4	68
5	75
Stan	68
6	59
7	81
8	84
9	79
Marc	75
10	82
11	76
12	52
13	76
Total 15	

(*a*) Compute the *mean, median,* and *standard deviation* for the class scores.

(*b*) The professor has decided that the interval from 1 standard deviation above and 1 below the mean is the C range for grades. From 1 to 2 deviations above the mean is a B; more than 2, an A. A D is awarded for falling between 1 and 2 standard deviations below the mean, an F, more than 2 deviations below the mean. At what grades should the A, B, C, D, and F's start for this test? How many students fall into each interval groups? Does this distribution seem to be skewed? If so, which way?

    (c) Do you agree with Stanley? How would you grade the 15 students?

3 In problem 6, Section 2-9, calculate the coefficient of variation for whites, blacks, and Hispanics. Which group shows the highest relative variation? How does this compare to the standard deviation?

43

DESCRIPTIVE
TECHNIQUES:
FREQUENCY
DISTRIBUTIONS,
MEASURES OF
CENTRAL TENDENCY
AND VARIATION

SUMMARY

2-13

1 In this chapter, ways to describe and condense a large amount of information have been presented. First, the grouping of data into *classes* that form a *frequency distribution* has been discussed. For convenient display, 5 to 12 classes are ideal; *class boundaries* should not overlap and classes should be equal in range. If open-ended classes are used, a footnote describing the items that have been placed in the class should be given. Generally, the distribution of values within a class should be uniform, or the values should at least be centered in the middle of the class *(class mark).*

2 Frequency distributions can be presented in graphic form by using a *histogram* (bar graph) or a *frequency polygon,* in which the class mark is plotted for each class and then all of these observations are connected. A cumulative graph "less than" or "more than" distribution *(ogive)* can be plotted. All tables, graphs, and charts should have a title that describes the "what, where, and when" facts about the table or chart. In addition, tables, charts, and graphs should contain a footnote to tell the sources.

3 Three measures of central tendency for ungrouped data are the *mean,*

$$\mu = \frac{\Sigma X}{N} \quad \text{or} \quad \bar{X} = \frac{\Sigma X}{n}$$

the *median,* and the *mode.* To find the median, we group the data in order from lowest to highest and choose the middle number $(n + 1)/2$. To find the mode, we pick the value that occurs most frequently. The median is often used to represent data when there are extreme values that "distort" the mean. The mode is seldom used, since it is not a unique measure.

4 For grouped data, the same three measures may be computed. To compute the mean for grouped data, we multiply the frequency (number in each class) by the class midpoint (class mark), sum all these numbers, and divide by the total number of frequencies.

$$\mu = \frac{\Sigma fx}{N} \quad \text{or} \quad \bar{X} = \frac{\Sigma fx}{n}$$

Computing the median involves finding the class in which the median (middle number $n/2$) occurs and then interpolating to find where in this class the number falls. The formula is

$$Md = L_{md} + \frac{(n/2) - cf_{md}}{f_{md}} i$$

5   *Quartiles* divide the distribution into four equal parts; *deciles* divide it into 10 equal parts; *percentiles* divide into 100 equal parts. For grouped data, a method similar to that used for the calculation of the median can be used to calculate quartiles, deciles, and percentiles.

6   Measures of variation, or scatter about the mean, include the *range* and the *variance,* or *standard deviation.* The range is obtained by subtracting the lowest from the highest value in the population. The variance for ungrouped data is obtained by squaring the deviations from the mean, adding the sum of the squared deviations, and dividing by N for the population or by $n - 1$ for a sample. If we take the square root of the variance, we have the standard deviation.

$$\sigma = \sqrt{\frac{\Sigma(x - \mu)^2}{N}} \qquad \text{population standard deviation}$$

$$s = \sqrt{\frac{\Sigma(X - \bar{X})^2}{n - 1}} \qquad \text{sample standard deviation}$$

7   Computation of the *variance* (σ^2) for grouped data involves finding the deviation of each class mark (midpoint) from the mean for the distribution, squaring this deviation, multiplying the squared deviations by the number of observations (frequency) of each class, and then dividing the number by N for the population or by $n - 1$ for the sample. The square root of the variance is called the standard deviation (σ).

$$\sigma = \sqrt{\frac{\Sigma f(X - \mu)^2}{N}}$$

$$s = \sqrt{\frac{\Sigma f(X - \bar{X})^2}{n - 1}}$$

8   When it is not known if a distribution is normal, *Chebycheff's inequality* may be used to determine the *minimum* amount of area between the mean and a given number of standard deviations. The formula is

$$\text{Area} \geq 1 - \frac{1}{K^2}$$

where K is the number of standard deviations to the left and right of the mean.

9   Relative scatter or variation for two or more groups that are expressed in different units (such as money, IQ, and age) can still be compared by using the *coefficient of variation.*

$$CV = \frac{s}{\bar{X}}(100) \qquad \text{or} \qquad CV = \frac{\sigma}{\mu}(100)$$

If the groups are measured in the same units but their mean values are not of the same order of magnitude, it is also advisable to use the coefficient of variation to compare relative variation.

45

DESCRIPTIVE
TECHNIQUES:
FREQUENCY
DISTRIBUTIONS,
MEASURES OF
CENTRAL TENDENCY
AND VARIATION

10 Other measures of a distribution are *skewness* and *kurtosis*. If the mean is to the right of the median, the distribution is skewed to the right. Another way to determine the direction of skewness is to look at the side having the longer tail. The distribution is skewed in this direction. Conversely, if the mean is to the left of the median, the distribution is skewed to the left. Incomes and savings are most often skewed to the right as large positive values are not counterbalanced by large negative ones.

Kurtosis refers to the peakedness of the curve. A very peaked curve, in which every value is concentrated near the mean, is called *leptokurtic*. A flat curve is called *platykurtic*. This is an indication that even though curves may be a symmetric, some distributions may show considerable spread while others remain very concentrated about the mean.

BIBLIOGRAPHY

2-14

Two humorous approaches to descriptive statistics are:

Huff, Darrel: *How to Lie with Statistics*. New York: Norton, 1954.
Runyon, Richard: *Winning with Statistics*. Reading, Mass.: Addison-Wesley, 1977.

Two basic texts containing good expository chapters on descriptive statistics are:

Freund, John E: *Modern Elementary Statistics,* 5th ed., Englewood Cliffs, N.J.: Prentice-Hall, 1979. See Chapters 2, 3, and 4.
Hamburg, Morris: *Basic Statistics*. New York: Harcourt, 1979. See chapter 3.

CASES

2-15

Case 2-1   Naro-Shu Company (A): Feasibility of Establishing a Specialty Retail Store, Choosing a City

Charles Dart, a native Texan, graduated from Southern Methodist University Business School in 1975 and decided to open a specialty retail shoe store catering to women wearing narrow widths. He had worked in shoe stores before his Army service. After his return from the Army, he continued selling shoes on a part-time basis while completing his college education. While working in these shoe stores he had noticed that a large percentage of his women customers wore narrow widths, yet most stores stocked chiefly average widths. Therefore, he felt that a store specializing in narrow widths would have a good chance for success. He decided to establish his store in a large metropolitan area in Texas, because he was a native Texan and felt that the Southwest had excellent growth opportunities.

Consultation with the *Texas Almanac,* published by the *Dallas Morning News,* revealed that in 1973 Texas had 24 Standard Metropolitan Statistical Areas (SMSAs), more than any other state. These areas are designated by the U.S. Office of Management and Budget (OMB) based on criteria that include population, economic, and social requirements. After studying the SMSAs, Dart decided to further explore six of the largest SMSAs (listed in Table 1), since he felt a specialty shoe store would need a large market. These were Dallas, Ft. Worth, Houston, San Antonio, El Paso, and Austin. He didn't explore the fourth-largest SMSA as it contained three smaller cities—Beaumont, Port Arthur, and Orange.

TABLE 1

CHARACTERISTICS OF SIX LARGE TEXAS SMSAs, 1973

CHARACTERISTIC	DALLAS	FT. WORTH	HOUSTON	SAN ANTONIO	EL PASO	AUSTIN
Owner-occupied housing	60.0%	66.7%	60.1%	63.9%	58.7%	54.9%
Median age	26.5	26.9	25.9	24.1	22.4	24.2
Age 65 or over (in December 1972)	7.3%	7.6%	6.1%	7.7%	5.8%	7.1%
Population	1,675,200	806,800	2,140,900	912,700	372,200	336,100
Per capita personal income	$4,408	$3,918	$4,393	$3,561	$3,172	$3,585
Households with air conditioning	81.2%	81.9%	77.5%	63.5%	70.9%	76.3%
Median value of owner-occupied housing	$16,784	$13,399	$14,664	$12,565	$13,629	$16,660
Effective buying income (million $)*	$7,213	$3,173	$8,687	$2,884	$1,074	$1,208
Households owning autos	89.0%	90.9%	88.4%	85.4%	84.2%	90.3%
Households with telephone	86.4%	88.5%	86.2%	85.8%	80.1%	88.1%
Percent employed by private industry	81.4%	80.2%	81.9%	66.8%	72.0%	57.9%

* According to *Sales Management* (May, 1973), effective buying incomes provide a bulk measurement of market potential "ability to buy." They are generally equivalent to disposable personal income, as measured for the National Income Accounts. They are personal income (wages, salaries, interest, dividends, profits, and property incomes) minus state and local taxes. Income includes net cash income, income in kind, and imputed income. An example of income in kind is the value of produce that the farmer consumes from his own farm. Imputed income includes allowances for goods and services that do not go through the marketplace, such as free child-care clinics at work.
Source: *Texas Almanac,* 1975, *Dallas Morning News;* and *Sales Management,* May 1973.

When Charles looked over the data in Table 1, he found that he had considerable trouble coming to a decision. He thought, "Effective buying income is higher in Houston, but median per capita income is higher in Dallas. Moreover, I have reason to believe from my own experience that wealthier ladies are more likely to prefer narrow widths, since the expensive shoe stores are more likely to stock narrow widths."

A Note on Cases
In order to show how cases are used, the initial cases in this book offer a number of questions that direct attention to some of the more important issues in the case. In addition, a sample solution for this first case is given. This is not to suggest that this is the only possible solution. Part of the realistic and useful nature of cases is that there are a number of possible solutions and decisions that can be made using the same data depending on the original assumptions. In fact, very often the sign of a successful manager is creativity and the ability to find new solutions. Remember that all solutions suggested may not be equally good, but we can at least sort out the inconsistent ones.

Questions
1 Discuss the premise on which Dart's decision about the best city in which to locate his store will be based? Do you think wealthier women are more likely to have narrow feet?

2 Why is median age and median value of owner-occupied housing used in place of mean age and mean value of owner-occupied housing?

3 What other kinds of information should Dart collect before he makes his decision?

4 What information presented in this case is irrelevant?

5 On the basis of the information contained in this case, which city would you pick? Why?

6 What is a Standard Metropolitan Statistical Area? What data can be obtained for such an area? How often is this information collected? (Data of this sort is available in almanacs for other states. *Sales Management* and the U.S. Department of Commerce publish this information for all states.)

47

DESCRIPTIVE
TECHNIQUES:
FREQUENCY
DISTRIBUTIONS,
MEASURES OF
CENTRAL TENDENCY
AND VARIATION

Sample Solution

1 Does the fact that more expensive stores stock narrow widths indicate that wealthier women are more likely to have narrow feet? It seems more reasonable to believe that it is expensive to stock a wide range of widths; hence only high-price shoe stores that make a large amount of money on each purchase can afford to stock widths that they are not sure that they can sell. Possibly women with narrow feet who must buy their shoes in low- and medium-priced stores "settle" for an average width shoe because that is all they can afford. This thought might lead to first an assessment of what percentage of women can actually use a narrow shoe—this might be done by a survey (see Naro-Shu Case C in Chapter 7). Secondly, if there is a sizable proportion of women with narrow feet, a store in the middle- or low-price range that catered to narrow shoes might be very successful.

2 Medians are preferable to means because medians are not as likely to be influenced by extreme values. Several million-dollar houses would noticeably increase the mean value of all housing. You might be interested in how many high-priced houses exist, if this information were available, if you felt that women who bought narrow shoes tended to be wealthy. We have seen that this may not be so. In fact, this type of thinking may lead to incorrect strategy (see solution 1).

3 In question 1, it was decided that it would be important to know what percent of the population would need narrow shoes. A survey of women might be obtained from manufacturers' information or possibly from a discussion or a survey with retailers or shoe sellers. Charles might undertake a survey to estimate potential demand for narrow widths. Once some potential cities and store sites were selected, it would be worthwhile to see whether they contained any stores that specialized in narrow width shoes.

4 Quite a bit of information can be obtained, but not all information is relevant. Would TV ownership, auto ownership, or the number of people employed in private industry relate to women's shoe sales? Possibly one might say that if fewer autos were owned more shoes might be needed. Examination of the table indicates very little variation in the percent of families owning cars among the six cities. Why should age and TV ownership influence shoe purchases? Not all data is useful.

5 Information in the case would lead to the choice of two possible cities, Houston or Dallas, if made only on the basis of population size. One would expect that a larger city would contain a larger number of people with narrow feet. Of course, the final choice should examine whether there are any specialty stores in this city offering shoes in narrow widths.

Although the population of Dallas was smaller than that of Houston, Charles

Dart chose the city because per capita personal income and median value of owner-occupied housing were higher. Houston had higher effective buying income, but Dart had better contacts in the Dallas area since he had worked there. He felt that wealthier people would be more likely to demand and pay for proper fitting.

6 The Standard Metropolitan Statistical Area is an important concept used for statistical studies of incomes, unemployment, price indexes, and spending behavior. Data on these areas is available in most libraries in government publications.

(*a*) What are the criteria for SMSAs? How many are there?

A SMSA always includes a city (cities) of specified population that constitutes the central city and the county (counties) in which it is located. An SMSA also includes contiguous counties when the economic and social relationships between the central and contiguous counties meet specified criteria of metropolitan character and integration. An SMSA may cross state lines. In New England, SMSAs are composed of cities and towns instead of counties.

Each SMSA must include at least: (1) one city with 50,000 or more inhabitants or (2) one city having a population of at least 25,000 which, with the addition of the population of contiguous regions, incorporated or unincorporated, has a population density of at least 1000 persons per square mile. These together constitute, for general economic and social purposes, a single community with a combined population of at least 50,000, provided that the county or counties in which the city and contiguous regions are located has a total population of at least 75,000.

The Office of Statistical Standards in the Office of Management and Budget (OMB), with the advice of representatives of the major federal statistical agencies, defines the SMSAs. As of April 1980, the OMB had defined 318 SMSAs in the United States and Puerto Rico.

(*b*) What data is collected by the government in each of these areas?

Information on population (age, nativity, mobility)

Health and vital statistics

Climate and physical environment

Construction and housing

Labor and equipment

The Statistical Abstract of the United States and Department of Commerce and Department of Labor publications contain information for each SMSA.

(*c*) How frequently does the government collect this information? Economic censuses are done on a complete basis every 5 years (1977, 1982, 1987, etc.). On an annual basis, less-detailed surveys of manufacturers are conducted and data is published on key measures of manufacturing activity. An annual survey is made of county business patterns.

Case 2-2   The Lite Bite: Overhead Cost Analysis

Speedy Food Marts, a chain of more than 200 convenience food stores with fast service, late hours, and a limited variety of goods (similar to 7-11 stores) located in Kentucky, Tennessee, Indiana, Illinois, and New England, was interested in performing a cost study to predict the overhead costs for different size stores. A study of utility costs was assigned to Bill Jones of the firm's finance and accounting department.

Bill's report read as follows:

My original hypothesis was that a store doing a higher volume of business would run up a higher electrical bill, and I have attempted to prove that hypothesis in this project.

49

DESCRIPTIVE
TECHNIQUES:
FREQUENCY
DISTRIBUTIONS,
MEASURES OF
CENTRAL TENDENCY
AND VARIATION

Obviously, many factors had to be considered in doing this project. First of all, to eliminate any variations due to seasonality, the utility costs are based on the full fiscal year ending on June 30, 1975. Also, after examining the data, it was very obvious that electrical and gas costs varied so much by region—the Boston region being more than twice as expensive as the others—that for the data to be meaningful, I would have to concentrate on one region. Therefore, to avoid the differences in electrical costs, and the differences involving the length of seasons between the northern and southern regions, I decided to limit my project to the first region, the Louisville, Kentucky, area.

I felt this region would be suitable since it is the largest single region, containing 65 stores. After looking over the data for Louisville, I decided that because of the good distribution in the categories of the frequency distribution using this one region would be acceptable.

The frequencies were established with $50,000 intervals ranging from annual sales of $250,000 through $600,000. The yearly total of gas and electrical costs for each store was placed in the appropriate category at the time of the data collection. The average (mean and median) and standard deviation of each frequency group was calculated. Then, in the final table, all the averages and standard deviations are shown for comparison.

I tried to see if there was much relationship between price and sales. Secondly, I tried to make some estimates of the cost of utilities 95% of the time so that I could predict the costs for stores of different sizes.

Questions

1   Compute means, medians, and standard deviations for frequency classes 6 and 7 and write them in on the table. Now add them to Table 8.

2   How would you recommend that the manager of the 200 convenience stores use this data?

3   Describe the relationship between total sales and utility costs. What advice would you give to a store about optimal size with respect to utility cost? What other information might be useful for the calculation of utility cost?

4   If a manager opened a store with an approximately $325,000 annual business, make an estimate of the utility costs.

5   How could Table 8 estimates of the mean and standard deviations be used as guidelines for store performance?

6   If utility costs rose by a constant percentage (20%) for each frequency class, how would these affect optimal size?

Data

Tables 1–7 give the utility costs for *each* of the stores in the yearly sales category. Mean, median, and standard deviations are also given for Tables 1–5. Table 8 summarizes the other seven tables.

TABLE 1

FREQUENCY CLASS 1

Sales: At least $250,000 but less than $300,000

STORE NUMBER	UTILITY COST	DEVIATION $(X - \bar{X})$	DEVIATION SQUARED $(X - \bar{X})^2$
1	$ 4,564	$-51	$ 2,601
2	4,564	-51	2,601
3	4,638	23	529
4	4,443	-172	29,584
5	4,753	138	19,044
6	4,725	110	12,100
	$27,687		$66,459

Mean = $4,615   Median = $4,601   Standard deviation = $\sqrt{\dfrac{\$66,459}{5}}$ = $115

TABLE 2

FREQUENCY CLASS 2

Sales: At least $300,000 but less than $350,000

STORE NUMBER	UTILITY COST	DEVIATION $(X - \bar{X})$	DEVIATION SQUARED $(X - \bar{X})^2$
1	$ 3,791	$-748	$ 599,504
2	4,749	210	44,100
3	3,923	-616	379,456
4	4,647	108	11,664
5	4,943	404	163,216
6	4,885	346	119,716
7	4,814	275	75,625
8	4,561	22	484
	$36,313		$1,353,765

Mean = $4,539   Median = $4,698   Standard deviation = $\sqrt{\dfrac{\$1,353,765}{7}}$ = $440

TABLE 3

FREQUENCY CLASS 3

Sales: At least $350,000 but less than $400,000

STORE NUMBER	UTILITY COST	DEVIATION $(X - \bar{X})$	DEVIATION SQUARED $(X - \bar{X})^2$
1	$ 4,298	$-402	$ 161,604
2	4,621	-79	6,241
3	4,015	-685	469,225
4	5,206	506	256,036
5	4,830	130	16,900
6	5,030	330	108,900
7	4,899	199	39,601
	$32,899		$1,058,507

Mean = $4,699.85   Median = $4,830   Standard deviation = $\sqrt{\dfrac{\$1,058,512}{6}}$ = $420

TABLE 4

FREQUENCY CLASS 4

Sales: At least $400,000 but less than $450,000

51

DESCRIPTIVE
TECHNIQUES:
FREQUENCY
DISTRIBUTIONS,
MEASURES OF
CENTRAL TENDENCY
AND VARIATION

STORE NUMBER	UTILITY COST	DEVIATION $(X - \bar{X})$	DEVIATION SQUARED $(X - \bar{X})^2$
1	$ 4,546	$-201	$ 40,401
2	4,720	-27	729
3	4,274	-473	223,729
4	4,814	67	4,489
5	5,161	414	171,396
6	4,588	-159	25,281
7	4,497	-250	62,500
8	4,849	102	10,404
9	5,035	288	82,944
10	4,543	-204	41,616
11	4,989	242	58,564
12	5,278	531	281,961
13	4,754	7	49
14	4,184	-563	316,969
15	4,904	157	24,649
16	4,510	-237	56,169
17	5,179	432	186,624
18	4,618	-129	16,641
	$85,443		$1,605,115

Mean = $4,747   Median = $4,737   Standard deviation = $\sqrt{\dfrac{\$1,605,115}{17}}$ = $307

TABLE 5

FREQUENCY CLASS 5

Sales: At least $450,000 but less than $500,000

STORE NUMBER	UTILITY COST	DEVIATION $(X - \bar{X})$	DEVIATION SQUARED $(X - \bar{X})^2$
1	$ 4,837	$-236	$ 55,696
2	5,286	213	45,369
3	5,393	320	102,400
4	5,190	117	13,689
5	4,462	-611	373,321
6	5,258	185	34,225
7	4,842	-231	53,361
8	5,481	408	100,464
9	4,995	-78	6,084
10	4,990	-83	6,889
	$50,734		$791,489

Mean = $5,073   Median = $5,092.50   Standard deviation = $\sqrt{\dfrac{\$791,498}{9}}$ = $297

TABLE 6

FREQUENCY CLASS 6

Sales: At least $500,000 but less than $550,000

STORE NUMBER	UTILITY COST	DEVIATION $(X - \bar{X})$	DEVIATION SQUARED $(X - \bar{X})^2$
1	$ 4,691		
2	4,567		
3	5,674		
4	4,896		
5	5,196		
	$25,024		

TABLE 7

FREQUENCY CLASS 7

Sales: At least $550,000 but less than $600,000

STORE NUMBER	UTILITY COST	DEVIATION $(X - \bar{X})$	DEVIATION SQUARED $(X - \bar{X})^2$
1	$ 4,802		
2	5,533		
3	5,462		
4	5,013		
5	5,235		
6	5,041		
7	4,864		
8	4,236		
9	5,151		
10	5,367		
11	4,659		
	$55,363		

TABLE 8

COMPARISON BY CLASS (Summary)

SALES VOLUME	MEAN	MEDIAN	STANDARD DEVIATION
$250,000 but less than $300,000	$4,615	$4,601	$115
$300,000 but less than $350,000	4,539	4,698	430
$350,000 but less than $400,000	4,699	4,830	412
$400,000 but less than $450,000	4,747	4,737	307
$450,000 but less than $500,000	5,073	5.093	309
$500,000 but less than $550,000			
$550,000 but less than $600,000			

TABLE 1

WEEKLY TRANSACTIONS PER TELLER, JANUARY 1980

53

DESCRIPTIVE
TECHNIQUES:
FREQUENCY
DISTRIBUTIONS,
MEASURES OF
CENTRAL TENDENCY
AND VARIATION

TELLERS	JAN. 2–4	JAN. 7–11	JAN. 14–18	JAN. 21–25	JAN. 28–31	MONTHLY TRANSACTIONS	YEARS OF SERVICE	HOURLY WAGE RATE
1	340	821	774	758	635	3,328	5	$6.00
2	300	865	866	845	685	3,561	4	5.75
3	318	972	880	903	763	3,836	2	4.75
4	362	999	1,025	1,060	932	4,378	1	4.00
						15,103		

$$\text{Average monthly transactions per teller} = \frac{15,103}{4} = 3775.75$$

Case 2-3   Northeast National Bank: Computation of Wage Rates

The Northeast National Bank decided to review its expenses and output in an attempt to raise productivity. Henry Johnson, who had just been appointed head cashier of the suburban branch, decided to study the number of transactions completed each day by each of his tellers to see if they related to the wages his tellers earned. If the pay scale didn't conform to the productivity of the tellers, he would work out a system of incentive wages to reward more productive tellers and thus increase productivity. Each deposit or withdrawal was considered a transaction. In addition, each check cashed or drawn was considered a transaction. Assume each teller's window is equally likely to be chosen by customers.

The bank employed four tellers whose wages depended on the number of years of service. Teller 1, for example, earned $6.00 an hour and had worked for the bank for 5 years. Teller 2 earned $5.75 an hour and had worked 4 years. Teller 3 earned $4.75 an hour and had 2 years of experience. Finally, Teller 4 earned $4.00 per hour and had worked for 1 year.

During January 1980, Mr. Johnson kept records on the transactions completed by each teller each day. Then, he made weekly summaries of the transactions for each teller. Table 1 presents the results of his study.

Mr. Johnson decided that the primary reason for higher wage rates should be productivity. He therefore worked out a formula whereby each teller who produced an average amount (measured in terms of transactions) would earn $4.50 per hour. For each standard deviation above the mean, the teller would earn an additional 50 cents per hour. For each standard deviation below the mean, the teller would earn 50 cents less per hour.

His colleagues and superiors suggested that this was too severe and gave no rewards for seniority. Johnson therefore decided he would pay 20 cents per hour more for each additional year of service. He finally combined the whole system into this formula.

Hourly pay

$$= \$4.50 \pm .50 \left(\begin{array}{c} \text{number of standard deviations} \\ \text{above or below mean} \end{array} \right) + .20 \left(\begin{array}{c} \text{number of years} \\ \text{on the job} \end{array} \right)$$

Questions

1 Work out the hourly pay for each of the four tellers. (First compute the standard deviation; use the sample formula since these four tellers were only a sample of tellers employed at any one time.)

2 What seems to be the relationship between years of work and the number of transactions completed? How do you think a relationship like this might come about?

3 Would you recommend that Northeast National Bank institute this incentive plan?

4 Would you modify this system? How?

5 In what types of business would a wage incentive system like this be most effective?

PROBABILITY AND PROBABILITY DISTRIBUTIONS

3

3-1   SIMPLE RULES OF PROBABILITY

3-2   STATISTICAL INDEPENDENCE

3-3   MATHEMATICAL EXPECTATION
Problems

3-4   PROBABILITIES IN GAMES OF CHANCE

3-5   DISCRETE PROBABILITY DISTRIBUTIONS
Binomial Distribution
Computation of Binomial Probabilities
Use of Binomial Tables
Mean and Standard Deviation of Binomial Distribution
Problems
Poisson Distribution
Relation of Binomial Distribution to Poisson Distribution
Use of the Poisson Table
Problems

3-6   CONTINUOUS PROBABILITY DISTRIBUTIONS
What Is a Normal Distribution?
Relation of Normal Distribution to Binomial Distribution
Use of the Standard Normal Table
Problems

3-7   SUMMARY

3-8   BIBLIOGRAPHY

3-9   CASES
Case 3-1: Does Fate Relate?
Case 3-2: DRC Limousine Insurance
Case 3-3: Naro-Shu Company (B)
Case 3-4: People *vs.* Collins

In the two preceding chapters, we have been fortunate enough to have full information on any of the populations we wished to study. We therefore concentrated on ways of summarizing and analyzing this information. It is more common that we do not have complete information and need to make an estimate of what we think might happen.

Probability theory, which focuses on the chances of particular events happening, is very useful for the solution of these problems. Current thought seems to point to Girolamo Cardano (1501–1576), an Italian doctor who published a gamblers' manual called the *Book on Games of Chance,* as the founder of probability theory. The book showed the number of ways in which two dice could be thrown and went on to explore the ways in which three dice could be thrown. According to historians, Cardano predicted the day of his death. When he found that he was still alive on the selected day, he committed suicide to preserve his reputation as a forecaster.[1]

Modern-day statisticians don't seem to take things so seriously. In accordance with probability theory, we hope to be right most of the time but not every single time. Conceptually, there are three ways of determining the probability of an occurrence:

1 Objective (classical) probability
2 Relative frequency of occurrence
3 Subjective probability

Objective probability depends on the physical characteristics of the object studied. For example, if we toss a coin (assume it isn't warped), the chance of a head is 1/2. Similarly, if we use a true die, the chance of rolling a 6 is 1/6. If we take a card from a full deck, the chances of getting an ace are 4/52, since there are 4 aces and 52 cards.

Objective probability is very good for solving problems that involve the use of physical objects; however, for business situations, this is not very useful. How can the insurance company predict the percentage of cars that will be involved in accidents in the coming year? How can manufacturers determine what percent of their product will be defective? How can retailers predict demand in order to stock the proper number of washing machines? The statistician who tries to make these forecasts must focus on *relative frequency of occurrence* in the past. The statistician must look at the proportion of time that the event has occurred over a long time period. Thus, if the rate for minor accidents has been 1 out of 50 cars (relative frequency) in the past, 1/50 will be used to compute the probability of a minor accident in the future.

$$P = \frac{1}{50} = .02 = 2\%$$

This long-run relative frequency approach assumes that we have repeated examples of the same situation, and that it stays the same over time. In business, this is often not possible—for example, when business must try to predict new situations.

A third type of probability is *subjective probability.* This determination of

---

[1]Amy King and Cecil R. Read, *Pathways to Probability,* Holt, Rinehart and Winston, New York, 1963, p. 14.

probabilities is based on personal beliefs. Even if a person has no previous experience with an event, he or she may try to place a probability upon the likelihood of occurrence of that event. Frequently, in business situations, this may be the only way to assign probability to an occurrence.

In this chapter we will discuss prior, or classical, probability theory. In Chapter 12, we will discuss posterior probability—where we have some previous information and we use it to make predictions about the future.

SIMPLE RULES OF PROBABILITY

Simple probability computations can be generally expressed in terms of one or more of these six rules.

3-1

Rule 1 All probabilities will vary between 0 and 1. Thus, $P(A)$, or the probability that event A will occur is $0 \leq P(A) \leq 1$. A probability near 0 means that we are almost completely certain something will not happen. A probability near 1 means we are almost completely positive that the event will take place. Now, if someone tells you that the probability that he will inherit \$1 million is 5.0, something is wrong.

Rule 2 If there are only two events that can happen, one and only one must occur. For example, you inherit \$1 million or you don't. This can be expressed in the following manner:

$$P(A) \qquad \text{probability that you inherit \$1 million} \tag{3-1}$$

$$P(\sim A) \qquad \text{probability of not } A; \text{ that is, } A \text{ doesn't happen}$$

Now, if there are only two possibilities, their probabilities must add to 1.

$$P(A) + P(\sim A) = 1 \tag{3-2}$$

By simple algebraic manipulation we can say that the probability an event will occur is 1 minus the probability that the event won't occur.

$$P(A) = 1 - P(\sim A)$$

For example, if the probability that you will not inherit \$1 million is .999, the probability that you will inherit a million is .001. Conversely,

$$P(\sim A) = 1 - P(A)$$

Rule 3 The following rule holds for *mutually exclusive events*. Mutually exclusive events are those that cannot occur simultaneously. For example, one is overweight, underweight, or of normal weight; one cannot have both a surplus and a deficit on the balance sheet.

Computation of the probability for these events follows the addition rule.

$$P(A \text{ or } B) = P(A) + (B) \tag{3-3}$$

$$P(A \text{ or } B \text{ or } C) = P(A) + P(B) + P(C)$$

In a class, the following grades and numbers of students were observed.

GRADE	NUMBER OF STUDENTS
A	10
B	20
C	40
D	20
F	10
	100

If we now pick students at random from this class so that each student has the same chance of being chosen, event A occurs if the grade for the student chosen is an A. There are 10 outcomes in event A. The probability of picking a student with a grade of A or B will be

$$P(A) + P(B) = \frac{10}{100} + \frac{20}{100} = \frac{30}{100} \qquad \text{or 30 percent}$$

The probability of getting a grade of C or better would be

$$P(A) + P(B) + P(C) = \frac{10}{100} + \frac{20}{100} + \frac{40}{100} = \frac{70}{100}$$

Rule 4 The following rule holds for events that are *not mutually exclusive*. For example, one could be a teacher and a woman; a card could be an ace and a diamond. Now, if we wanted to compute the probability of drawing an ace or a diamond from the deck, we could begin by adding together the probability of finding an ace $P(A)$ and the probability of finding a diamond $P(D)$.

$$P(A \text{ or } D) = P(A) + P(D)$$
$$= \frac{4}{52} + \frac{13}{52}$$

There is one card here that has been counted twice, and that is the ace of diamonds. If we drew a picture of all the cards in the deck, we would see something like Figure 3-1. Now, we have circled all the diamonds, then all the aces in Figure 3-1. As you

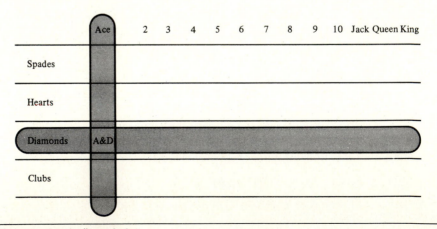

FIGURE **3-1**

Probability of events that are not mutually exclusive.

can see, the ace of diamonds has been circled twice. To compute the correct probability, we subtract the overlapping area. The final formula becomes

$$P(A \text{ or } D) = P(A) + P(D) - P(A \text{ and } D) \qquad (3\text{-}4)$$

$$P(A \text{ or } D) = \frac{4}{52} + \frac{13}{52} - \frac{1}{52} = \frac{16}{52}$$

Rule 5 This rule computes the probability for events that are *independent*. An independent event is one where the outcome of the event does not affect a subsequent event. For example, if we toss a coin twice in a row, the result of the first toss does not affect the second toss; if we win on this week's lottery, it does not affect who wins next week.

Let us calculate the probability of getting two heads in a row when we toss a coin twice. We could define A as getting a head on the first throw and B as getting a head on the second.

$$P(A \text{ and } B) = P(A) \times P(B)$$

$$\text{Probability of a head} = \frac{1}{2} \qquad (3\text{-}5)$$

$$P(A \text{ and } B) = \left(\frac{1}{2}\right)\left(\frac{1}{2}\right) = \frac{1}{4}$$

Another problem of this type concerns the chances of having three male children in a row.

$$P(A \text{ and } B \text{ and } C) = \left(\frac{1}{2}\right)\left(\frac{1}{2}\right)\left(\frac{1}{2}\right) = \frac{1}{8}$$

Actually, we are not so certain that these events are independent. In recent years, there has been some evidence that parents with a large family of children of one sex have a probability greater than 1/2 of having another child of the same sex.

Rule 6 Now, we come to events that are *not independent*. In this case, what happens the first time affects what happens the second time. Let us say that we have a table on which there are 20 boxes. Five of these boxes contain $10 bills. What is the probability of picking two boxes in a row that contain $10 bills?

In order to pick a $10 bill twice in a row, we must pick one each time. Once we have picked a box that contains a $10 bill, the chance of picking a second box with a $10 bill changes, because there are now 19 boxes and only 4 contain $10 bills. If we express this as a formula, we have

$$P(A \text{ and } B) = P(A) \times P(B/A) \qquad (3\text{-}6)$$

$P(B/A)$ is read as "the probability of B given that A has occurred." For our example, the probability of picking a $10 bill on the first try (A) and again on the second try (B) is equal to the probability of picking a $10 bill the first time, multiplied by the probability of picking a $10 bill the second time, given that we picked one the first time, so that there are fewer $10 boxes available.

Numerically, we have

$$P(A \text{ and } B) = \left(\frac{5}{20}\right)\left(\frac{4}{19}\right) = \frac{20}{380} = \frac{1}{19} = .0526$$

Now if we *replace* the boxes and shuffle them around after the first pick, the probabilities will be independent. On the second trial, we would also have 5 chances in 20 of finding the $10 bill.

$$P(A \text{ and } B) = P(A) \, P(B)$$

$$= \frac{5}{20} \times \frac{5}{20} = \frac{25}{400} = \frac{1}{16} = .0625$$

Some practice with this notation may help. Assume B is the chance that someone is a banker and A is the probability that someone earns over $100,000 a year. Then, $P(B/A)$ would mean the chance that one is a banker, given that one earns more than $100,000 a year. $P(A/B)$ would be the probability that one earns more than $100,000, given that one is a banker.

Often Rule 6 can be transposed. Thus, if we have picked a box with the bills the first time (A), we may want to calculate the probability of picking a box with the bills the second time (B).

$$P(B/A) = \frac{P(A \text{ and } B)}{P(A)} \tag{3-7}$$

STATISTICAL INDEPENDENCE

3-2

Two events, A and B, are independent if and only if $P(A \text{ and } B) = P(A) \cdot P(B)$. Another way to say this is, If $P(B/A) = P(B)$, then A and B are independent of each other. For example, if a club is drawn from the deck, what is the probability that it is a king?

$$P(K) = \frac{4}{52} = \frac{1}{13}$$

$$P(K/C) = \frac{P(K \text{ and } C)}{P(C)} = \frac{1/52}{1/4} = \frac{1}{52} \times \frac{4}{1} = \frac{1}{13}$$

Both probabilities are the same; therefore, they are *independent*. Independent means that knowledge of one event has no predictive value for the occurrence of another event. We can do this the other way, too. For example, suppose a king is drawn. What is the probability that it is a club?

$$P(C) = \frac{13}{52} = \frac{1}{4}$$

$$P(C/K) = \frac{P(K \text{ and } C)}{P(K)} = \frac{1/52}{4/52} = \frac{1}{4}$$

Once again, both probabilities are the same. Thus, the chances of choosing a king from the whole deck are the same (1/13) as for choosing a king from among the clubs. Now, if there were more kings in the club suit (let us say 2) and if we knew we had drawn a club, the card would more likely be a king (2/13) than if we had just drawn a card from the whole deck. In this latter case, suit and choice of kings are not statistically independent.

Let us try another example of this type.

EXAMPLE 3-1   In a recent election, the pollsters took a sample of public opinion toward the Equal Rights Amendment. Table 3-1 (shown below), which outlines opinions of 5000 male and females, was published.

1   Given that the person selected is a female, what is the chance that she will be opposed?
2   What is the chance that a given individual will be either a male or opposed?
3   Are opinion and sex independent for this sample?

First, let us express each of these terms in letters.

A_1: Male B_1: In favor

A_2: Female B_2: Opposed

1   $P(B_2/A_2)$ is the formulation for this problem. According to Equation 3-7,

$$P(B_2/A_2) = \frac{P(B_2 \text{ and } A_2)}{P(A_2)} = \frac{500/5000}{2500/5000} = \frac{1}{5}$$

2   Using *Rule 4* $P(A \text{ or } B) = P(A) + P(B) - P(A \text{ and } B)$

$P(A_1 \text{ or } B_2) = P(A_1) + P(B_2) - P(A_1 \text{ and } B_2)$

$$= \frac{2500}{5000} + \frac{2000}{5000} - \frac{1500}{5000} = \frac{3000}{5000} = \frac{3}{5}$$

3   To be independent, we would really have to say that the same proportion of males and females were opposed to the bill. Thus, if we drew a male from the population, the chance of his being opposed should be equal to the overall proportion opposed. The probability that given that someone is a male, he will be opposed, should equal the overall probability that someone will be opposed.

If $P(B_2/A_1) = P(B_2)$, sex and opinion are independent.

$$P(B_2/A_1) = \frac{P(A_1 \text{ and } B_2)}{P(A_1)} = \frac{1500/5000}{2500/5000} = \frac{1500}{2500}$$

TABLE 3-1

MALE AND FEMALE OPINIONS OF ERA

	IN FAVOR (B_1)	OPPOSED (B_2)	TOTAL
Men (A_1)	1000	1500	2500
Women (A_2)	2000	500	2500
	3000	2000	5000

The overall probability of being opposed to the bill is 2000/5000.

$$\frac{1500}{2500} \neq \frac{2000}{5000} \quad \text{or} \quad \frac{3}{5} \neq \frac{2}{5}$$

Therefore, sex and opinion are not independent.

EXAMPLE 3-2 Suppose local auto dealers advertise in the following manner:

TV alone	5%
Radio alone	15
Newspapers alone	20
None of the above	10
TV and radio	15
Newspapers and radio	5
TV and newspapers	10
All three	20
	100%

1   What proportion of local auto dealers advertise on the radio? P(radio) = P(radio alone, or TV and radio, or newspapers and radio, or all three)

$$15\% + 15\% + 5\% + 20\% = 55\%$$

2   If an advertiser places ads on both TV and radio, what is the probability that he also places ads in newspapers?

$$\text{(All three)}$$

$$P(N/(R \& TV)) = \frac{P(N \& R \& TV)}{P(R \& TV)} = \frac{20\%}{(15\% + 20\%)} = \frac{20\%}{35\%} = 57.1\%$$

$$\text{(TV \& R + all three)}$$

3   Are the events placing ads on TV and placing them on the radio independent?

$$P(TV) = \quad 5\% + 15\% + 10\% + 20\% = 50\%$$

$$P(R) = \quad 15\% + 15\% + 5\% + 20\% = 55\%$$

$$P(TV/R) = \frac{P(TV \& R)}{P(R)} = \frac{TV \& R(15\%) + \text{all three } (20\%)}{R(15\%) + TV \& R(15\%) + N \& R(5\%) + \text{all three}(20\%)} =$$

$$\frac{35}{65} = 53.8\%, P(TV) \neq P(TV/R), \text{ as } 50\% \neq 53.8\%$$

Therefore, the events are not independent.

4   Are the events placing ads in newspapers and placing them on radio independent?

$$P(N) = 20\% + 5\% + 10\% + 20\% = 55\%$$

$$P(R) = 15\% + 15\% + 5\% + 20\% = 55\%$$

$$P(N/R) = \frac{P(N \& R)}{P(R)} = \frac{N \& R(5\%) + \text{all three}(20\%)}{R(15\%) + TV \& R(15\%) + N \& R(5\%) + \text{all three}(20\%)} = \frac{25\%}{55\%}$$

$$= 45.4\%$$

The events are not independent since

$$P(N) \neq P(N/R) \qquad 55\% \neq 45.4\%$$

MATHEMATICAL EXPECTATION

3-3

Expected value or mathematical expectation is a basic use of probability to predict what would happen in the *long run* if we had repeated opportunities in a similar situation. Expected value is obtained by multiplying the probability of an event occurring by the payoff (if the event should occur) and summing over all events. If the prize in a lottery is $1000 and 100 tickets are sold, we have 1 chance in 100 of winning if we purchase 1 ticket ($P = 1/100$). The payoff is $1000, so the expected winnings are equal to $\Sigma[X \cdot P(X)]$ or $1/100(1000) + 99/100(0) = \$10$. The expected value of a ticket, or the mathematical expectation, is $10. Now, if we can purchase a ticket for $10 or less, we would be taking a good risk. If the tickets are exactly $10, this is called a *fair game* since the total payoff is equal to the amount of money taken in.

Often these mathematical expectation problems are more complex. For example, suppose you are asked to join in a game where you roll one die. If you roll a 1 you win $100; if a 2, you win $200; if a 3, you win $250; if a 4, you lose 75; if a 5, you lose 250; and if a 6, you lose 100. What is the expected value of this game? For each of the outcomes, multiply the probability by the payoff and add the amounts together: $\Sigma[X \cdot P(X)]$, so the sum of the probabilities is 1.

$\frac{1}{6}(\$100) + \frac{1}{6}(\$200) + \frac{1}{6}(\$250) - \frac{1}{6}(\$75) - \frac{1}{6}(\$250) - \frac{1}{6}(\$100)$

$= 16.667 + \$33.333 + \$41.667 - \$12.500 - \$41.667 - \$16.667 = \$20.833$

According to the mathematical expectation, you would expect to make an average of $20.83 per game in the long run. If it costs less than $20.83 to play, you would have expectation of winning in the long run.

Mathematical expectation is the cornerstone of the insurance industry since companies can figure the probability of certain risks and then multiply by the amount that they will have to pay to determine if it pays in the long run to insure certain risk. (See Case 3-2.) Mathematical expectation is also the foundation for decision theory, which is covered in Chapter 12.

Problems

1 There are two adjacent apartment housing developments, Brookwood and Nash-moor, which contain middle- and upper-income tenants in the following porportions:

	MIDDLE	UPPER	TOTAL
Brookwood	20	10	30
Nashmoor	30	40	70
	50	50	100

Tenants complain that one tenant must be a "ham radio operator," because there is a tremendous disturbance in nightly broadcasts.

(a)   What is the probability that the ham operator lives in Brookwood? In Nashmoor? Is upper income? Is middle income?

(b)   If the ham operator is from Brookwood, what is the probability of his being middle income?

(c)   If the ham operator is of middle income, what is the probability that he is from Nashmoor?

(d)   What is the probability of the person being either middle income or living in Nashmoor?

2   Is a state lottery that is used to raise tax money a fair game? Why?

3   An insurance company offers a 50-year-old woman a $5000 one-year term insurance policy for an annual premium of $100. Suppose the number of deaths in this age group is 4 per 1000? What is the expected gain or loss for the insurance company?

4   A builder is bidding on a construction job that promises a profit of $40,000 with a probability of 3/5, and a loss (from late performance penalties) of $10,000 with a probability of 2/5.

(a)   What is the builder's expected profit if he gets the job?

(b)   Would he be better off bidding on a job that promised a profit of $30,000 with a probability of 4/5, and a loss of $10,500 with a probability of 1/5?

PROBABILITIES IN GAMES OF CHANCE

3-4

We have now outlined rules for computing simple probabilities. The same rules can be used for more complex situations, but often the same event can occur in a number of ways and we must combine estimates of the number of possible combinations with the probabilities of their occurrence. Let us look at different outcomes when we throw a pair of dice. As you know, a die has six faces. The die can land with a 1, 2, 3, 4, 5, 6 showing on the top. Thus, if we throw two dice, the highest possible total score is 12, and the lowest is 2. We assume that there is independence between the throws of the dice. Thus, what happens on the first throw does not affect what happens on the second. Let us make a diagram of what can happen (see Figure 3-2). To get a 2, we must throw a 1 on each die. Therefore, using rule 5, the probability is $1/6 \times 1/6 = 1/36$. Now, if we want the probability of throwing a 3, if we get a 1 on the first throw we need a 2 on the second.

$$P(1) \times P(2)$$

$$1/6 \times 1/6 = 1/36$$

However, if we get a 2 on the first throw, we can still get a 3 by throwing a 1 on the second.

$$P(2) \times P(1)$$

$$1/6 \times 1/6 = 1/36$$

There are two ways of obtaining a 3, and each has a probability of 1/36; therefore, the chance of obtaining a 3 is 2/36.

First throw   Second throw   Probability (1/36)
for two throws (1/6)(1/6)

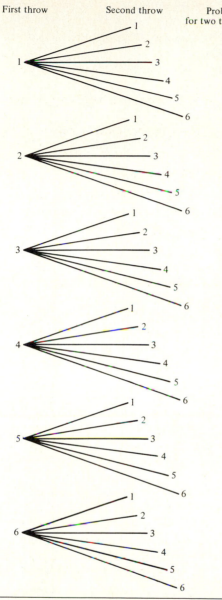

FIGURE **3-2**

Outcomes of throwing 2 dice.

There are three ways to get a 4: 1 and 3, 2 and 2, and 3 and 1. Therefore, the probability is 3/36. The probabilities for all outcomes in Figure 3-2 are shown in Table 3-2.

If winning combinations are a 7 or 11, then by rule 3, since these possibilities are mutually exclusive,

$$P(7 \text{ or } 11) = P(7) + P(11) = 6/36 + 2/36 = 8/36 = 2/9$$

Thus, 2/9 is the probability of obtaining a 7 or an 11. When we add all the probabilities together for all events that could happen, they add to 1. If we list all the

TABLE 3-2

OUTCOMES FOR THROWING TWO DICE

OUTCOME	PROBABILITY DISTRIBUTION
2	1/36
3	2/36
4	3/36
5	4/36
6	5/36
7	6/36
8	5/36
9	4/36
10	3/36
11	2/36
12	1/36
	36/36 = 1

probabilities of the events that could happen, this is called a *probability distribution*. The previous list of all the possibilities involved in throwing two dice is a probability distribution.

Discussions of chance events sometimes center about *odds*. The odds in favor of an event are the ratio of the chances for the event to the chances against the event.

The odds for getting a 7 or 11 are

$$\frac{8/36}{28/36} = 2/7 \quad \text{or} \quad 2 \text{ to } 7$$

The odds for not getting a 7 or an 11 are 7 to 2.

To continue with simple probability, let us suppose we throw a coin three times. Let us write down all of the possibilities.

$$
\begin{array}{cc}
\text{H H H} & \text{T T T} \\
2 \text{ heads, 1 tail} \rightarrow \left\{ \begin{array}{cc} \text{H T H} & \text{T T H} \\ \text{H H T} & \text{H T T} \\ \text{T H H} & \text{T H T} \end{array} \right\} \leftarrow 1 \text{ head, 2 tails}
\end{array}
$$

There are eight outcomes.[2] The probability of 3 heads is 1/8 since there is only one way to obtain 3 heads. Thus, we have $1/2 \times 1/2 \times 1/2 = 1/8$. Now, if we look at the probability of 2 heads, there are 3 ways to obtain this result; $3 \times 1/8 = 3/8$ is the probability of obtaining 2 heads. The probability distribution for heads (and for tails) is

3 heads	1/8
2 heads (1 tail)	3/8
1 head (2 tails)	3/8
no heads (3 tails)	1/8
	8/8 = 1

---

[2]The first throw has two possibilities, the second two, and the third two: $2 \times 2 \times 2 = 8$.

What if a coin is tossed 4 times? Now, there are 16 possibilities: $2 \times 2 \times 2 \times 2 = 16$, $(2^4 = 16)$.

```
H H H H        H H T T ⎤     T T T T
HTTT           TTHH   |     THHH
THTT           THTH   |     HTHH
TTHT           HTHT   ⎬     HHTH
TTTH           THHT   |     HHHT
               HTTH ⎦
```

The chances of getting 2 heads and 2 tails would be 6/16.

These problems refer to possibilities with throwing coins and dice; however, the same principles apply to many business situations.

EXAMPLE 3-3   Suppose a sales rep makes 4 calls per morning. The chances of making a sale are 50/50. What is the probability that she will make (1) 4 sales, (2) at least 3 sales, (3) no sales?

Answers

1.   This is similar to the coin toss problem. If getting a head is determined a success (no pun intended), the chance of 4 heads (4 sales) is 1/16: $1/2 \times 1/2 \times 1/2 \times 1/2$.
2.   At least 3 sales means 3 or more sales. Therefore, we must add the probability of 4 sales plus the probability of 3 sales: 1/16 + 4/16 = 5/16.
3.   Getting no sales would be similar to tossing no heads, and the probability would be 1/16.

DISCRETE PROBABILITY DISTRIBUTIONS

3-5

A *probability distribution* is a mutually exclusive list of all the events that can result from a chance process and the corresponding probability of each event occurring. Thus, if we tossed a coin twice and wished to find the probability distribution for the number of heads obtained, we would list the probability of obtaining no heads, 1 head, and 2 heads. This is called a *discrete* distribution because there are distinct, discrete possibilities—no heads, 1 head, or 2 heads. A *discrete random variable* assumes a countable number of values, while a *continuous random variable* assumes an infinite number of values. One cannot obtain, for example, 1.2 heads. Tossing coins yields discrete possibilities. There are many applications in business of this type. For example, what are the exact number of defective TV tubes? How many automobiles does the average family possess? In this section, we will learn to use two distributions to help solve problems for discrete random variables. These distributions are the *binomial distribution* and the *Poisson distribution*. In Section 3-6, we will study how continuous distributions can be analyzed. Continuous random variables are those that can take on an unlimited number of values. For example, we could measure weight accurately to kilograms, to grams, or to an even finer degree of accuracy. Thus, if our variable could be graphed as a *continuous (smooth) curve instead of as a polygon* that can only have a set number of values, we will call it a continuous variable. In Section 3-6, we will use a normal curve to analyze these probabilities. In addition, we will show how it is often possible to use normal curve information to study a discrete probability distribution.

Binomial Distribution

Computation of Binomial Probabilities   We have written all the possibilities for throwing a coin 4 times. Now, if we were to throw a coin 7 times, there would be 128 possibilities. Writing out all these possibilities would be difficult and tedious. We would like a formula to compute the probabilities of such events.

Before we start to find a formula for binomial probabilities, there are three specifications that must be met. When we toss a coin, we have a binary situation—either a head or a tail may appear. This formula refers to the *binomial distribution,* where there are *two possible alternatives* for each event. What about computation for problems that use dice? These can be converted to binary decisions, for example, by studying the chance of throwing a 6 or not throwing a 6. In this case, even though there are two alternatives, the chances for obtaining a 6 or some other result are not 50/50. Since there are 6 faces on the die, the chance of obtaining a 6 on a given throw are 1/6, and the chance that a 6 will not be obtained is 5/6. Our formula will provide for the *probability* of an event occurring as well as for the number of ways in which it can occur.

The second specification for the binomial distribution is that our *events must be independent of each other.* That is, what happens on the first trial cannot affect what happens on subsequent trials. The third specification is that the probability of a success is p and the probability of a failure is $q = (1 - p)$, and *that they remain constant from trial to trial.*

Let us say we want to compute the probability of having 1 head and 3 tails when we flip a coin 4 times. How many ways can this event occur? The possible outcomes satisfying our criterion (1 head, 3 tails) are

$$HTTT \qquad THTT \qquad TTHT \qquad TTTH$$

The laws of permutations and combinations provide an answer to this problem.

Let us assume that from 10 students we want to elect 3 officers: president, vice president, and secretary. There are 10 choices for president. Once we choose a president, there are 9 choices for vice president. Thus, there are $10 \times 9 = 90$ ways of choosing a president and vice president. Now, if we wish to choose 3 officers, we have 10 choices for president, 9 for vice president, and 8 for secretary (since we have already designated 2 for president and vice president); in all, $10 \times 9 \times 8 = 720$ choices. How can this be written? 10! (read "10 factorial") is $10 \times 9 \times 8 \times 7 \times 6 \times 5 \times 4 \times 3 \times 2 \times 1$. We wish to stop this multiplication after 3 numbers. If n is the number of candidates and x is the number of offices (or trials), we can write this as

$$\frac{n!}{(n - x)!}$$

$$= \frac{10 \times 9 \times 8 \times 7 \times 6 \times 5 \times 4 \times 3 \times 2 \times 1}{7 \times 6 \times 5 \times 4 \times 3 \times 2 \times 1} = 10 \times 9 \times 8 = 720$$

If the order did not count because, for example, we were trying to form a 3-person committee rather than to fill the jobs of president, vice president, and secretary, there would be fewer arrangements. Any three persons from the 10 people on the list (for example, A, B, and C), could make 6 different committees if order counted. However, a committee of ABC is the same as CBA; therefore, to eliminate these duplications we should divide by $x!$. (In this case $x! = 3!$.)

ABC
CBA
BAC   The number of permutations or different orders for a slate of 3
ACB   candidates is equal to 3!, or $3 \times 2 \times 1 = 6$. If we are making
CAB   committees, these 3 people A, B, C can form only 1 committee.
BCA

Since we are constituting 3-person committees, we are not concerned about order and wish to eliminate the number of orders; therefore, we divide by $x!$. In this case $x = 3$. The number of 3-person committees using 10 different people would be

$$\frac{n!}{x!(n-x)!} = \frac{10 \times 9 \times 8 \times 7 \times 6 \times 5 \times 4 \times 3 \times 2 \times 1}{(3 \times 2 \times 1)(7 \times 6 \times 5 \times 4 \times 3 \times 2 \times 1)} = 120$$

Let's use this formula to determine the number of ways of throwing 1 head and 3 tails with 4 coin tosses:

$$n = 4 \quad \text{number of trials}$$

$$x = 1 \quad \text{number of heads}$$

$$\frac{4!}{1!\,3!} = \frac{4 \times 3 \times 2 \times 1}{1 \times 3 \times 2 \times 1} = 4$$

The ways of throwing two heads and two tails are

$$\frac{4!}{2!\,2!} = \frac{4 \times 3 \times 2 \times 1}{2 \times 1 \times 2 \times 1} = 6$$

Now that we know the way to figure the number of combinations, we need a second part of the formula to compute the probability that the 1 head and 3 tails, for example, will occur. If we toss a coin 4 times, the chance of 1 head and 3 tails is computed by multiplying the probability of 1 head and 3 tails by the number of ways that one could obtain 1 head and 3 tails. See Table 3-3.

TABLE 3-3
PROBABILITIES OF OBTAINING 1 HEAD AND 3 TAILS IN 4 COIN TOSSES

DEFINITIONS	WAYS TO GET 1 HEAD AND 3 TAILS	PROBABILITY OF OBTAINING 1 HEAD AND 3 TAILS
$p = 1/2$, $q = 1/2$	H T T T	$1/2 \times 1/2 \times 1/2 \times 1/2 = 1/16$
p = probability of tossing a head	T H T T	$1/2 \times 1/2 \times 1/2 \times 1/2 = 1/16$
$q = (1 - p)$ = probability of tossing a tail	T T H T	$1/2 \times 1/2 \times 1/2 \times 1/2 = 1/16$
x = number of heads	T T T H	$1/2 \times 1/2 \times 1/2 \times 1/2 = \dfrac{1/16}{4/16}$
n = number of trials		

Thus, for 1 head and 3 tails, (where p is the probability of tossing a head and q is the probability of tossing a tail), the probability is

$$(p)^1(q)^3 = \text{probability of 1 head times the probability of 3 tails}$$

$$p^x\, q^{n-x} = (1/2)^1\, (1/2)^3 = 1/16$$

We have calculated 4 ways to get 1 head and 3 tails. Thus, the probability for obtaining 1 head and 3 tails is $4 \times 1/16 = 1/4$.

Putting the two parts of the formula together, we have a formula for the probability of a given number of successes (in this case heads) $P(X)$.

$$P(X) = \frac{n!}{x!\,(n-x)!}\, p^x q^{n-x} \tag{3-8}$$

where n = number of trials
      x = number of successes
      p = probability of a success
      q = probability of a failure

Let us use the formula to compute some simple coin toss and dice problems and then go on to apply it to some business situations. (Remember that $0! = 1$, and any number raised to the zero power equals 1.)

EXAMPLE 3-4   If we toss a coin 6 times, what is the probability of obtaining 4 heads and 2 tails?

$$P(X) = \frac{n!}{x!\,(n-x)!}\, p^x q^{n-x} \qquad n = 6$$

$$x = 4 \qquad \text{number of heads desired}$$

$$p = 1/2$$

$$q = 1/2$$

TABLE 3-4

OUTCOMES FOR TOSSING A COIN 6 TIMES

	NUMBER OF HEADS	PROBABILITY	COMPUTATION OF PROBABILITY
$P(0)$	0	1/64	$\dfrac{6!}{0!\,6!}\,(1/2)^0(1/2)^6 = 1/64$
$P(1)$	1	6/64	$\dfrac{6!}{1!\,5!}\,(1/2)^1(1/2)^5 = 6/64$
$P(2)$	2	15/64	$\dfrac{6!}{2!\,4!}\,(1/2)^2(1/2)^4 = 15/64$
$P(3)$	3	20/64	$\dfrac{6!}{3!\,3!}\,(1/2)^3(1/2)^3 = 20/64$
$P(4)$	4	15/64	$\dfrac{6!}{4!\,2!}\,(1/2)^4(1/2)^2 = 15/64$
$P(5)$	5	6/64	$\dfrac{6!}{1!\,5!}\,(1/2)^5(1/2)^1 = 6/64$
$P(6)$	6	1/64 64/64	$\dfrac{6!}{6!\,0!}\,(1/2)^6(1/2)^0 = 1/64$

$$P(4) = \frac{6!}{4! \; 2!} (1/2)^4 (1/2)^2$$

$$= \frac{6 \times 5 \times 4!}{4! \times 2 \times 1} (1/16)(1/4)$$

$$= 15/64 = 23\%$$

Show all the possibilities and graph them. The possible outcomes if a coin is tossed 6 times are shown in Table 3-4. (Note that we did not write out the 4! since we had a 4! in both the numerator and denominator and we could cancel them.)

EXAMPLE 3-5   If we toss a die 5 times, what is the chance of obtaining 3 ones?

$$P(3) = \frac{5!}{3! \; 2!} (1/6)^3 (5/6)^2 \qquad n = 5$$

$$x = 3$$

$$P(3) = \frac{5 \times 4 \times 3!}{3! \times 2 \times 1} (1/216)(25/36) \qquad p = 1/6 \text{ (probability of obtaining 1)}$$

$$= \frac{250}{7776} = 3.2\% \qquad q = 5/6 \text{ (probability of obtaining any other number)}$$

EXAMPLE 3-6   A firm finds that 10% of the transistors that it produces are defective. This firm ships packages of 5 transistors to be used in a radio kit. In order to complete a radio, 5 transistors must be used. What is the probability that there will be no defective transistors in a package of 5?

$$P(0) = \frac{5!}{0! \; 5!} (1/10)^0 (9/10)^5 \qquad n = 5$$

$$x = 0$$

$$p = 1/10$$

$$P(0) = (1)(1) \frac{59,049}{100,000} = 59\% \qquad q = 9/10$$

We have used the fact that any number or fraction raised to the zero power is 1, $(5^0 = 1, (1/5)^0 = 1)$. Also, note again that $0! = 1$.

Use of Binomial Tables   When n becomes large, it becomes difficult to compute probabilities because p and q must be raised to high powers. For example, if $p = .2$, $q = .8$, $n = 12$, and we want to compute the probability of 2 successes, we have the following equation:

$$P(2) = \frac{12!}{2!10!}(.2)^2(.8)^{10}$$

$$= \frac{12 \times 11}{2}(.04)(.1074)$$

$$= .2835$$

Table A-1 (in Appendix A at the back of the book) lists for trials (n) from 1 to 20 in the left-hand column and probabilities from .10 to .5. The $P(X)$ values that we might like to have are listed for each value of n in the left-hand column. The probabilities go across the top of the page. Thus, if we look for $n = 12$, $p = .2$, $x = 2$, we find that $p(2) = .2835$. Note that the table cannot be used if the p value is not on the table, such as .33 or .67.

Mean and Standard Deviation of Binomial Distribution   We have computed the probability of various outcomes using the binomial distribution. If we compute all possible outcomes with a given level of probability of a success (p) and a given number of trials (n), the sum of all possible outcomes is 1. In Table 3-5, we compute the probabilities of obtaining sixes if we toss a die 4 times.

If we wished to compute the expected value or the mean of a probability distribution μ, we would compute it like the mean of a frequency distribution. The mean outcome μ tells us the average outcome for the distribution. For the mean of a frequency distribution, we have the formula $\mu = \Sigma fX/n$ (see Chapter 2). Now, each of the probabilities we have computed for column 3 in Table 3-5 is the relative frequency of the occurrence $f/n = P(X)$. To obtain the mean, we must multiply this relative frequency $P(X)$ by the corresponding value of the random variable X, giving us $XP(X)$, and then sum over all the values of the random variable X.

Since we are dealing with a discrete distribution, the class midpoint X, which we used in our computation for the frequency distribution, would be the outcome X (in this case the different outcomes are 0, 1, 2, 3, 4). The formula is

$$\mu = \Sigma[X \, P(X)] \tag{3-9}$$

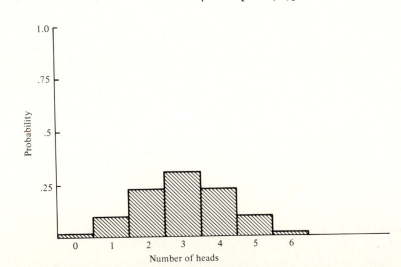

FIGURE **3-3**

Outcomes for tossing a coin 6 times.

TABLE 3-5

CALCULATION OF EXPECTED VALUE AND STANDARD DEVIATION FOR A BINOMIAL DISTRIBUTION
(Number of sixes tossed in 4 throws of a die)

(1) OUTCOME (X) (NUMBER OF SIXES)	(2) SUBSTITUTING IN BINOMIAL FORMULA	(3) PROBABILITY $P(X)$	(4) COL. 1 × COL. 3 $XP(X)$	(5) $(X - \mu)$	(6) $(X - \mu)^2$	(7) $P(X)(X - \mu)^2$
0	$\frac{4!}{0!\,4!}\left(\frac{1}{6}\right)^0\left(\frac{5}{6}\right)^4$	625/1296	0	$-2/3$	4/9	2500/11,664
1	$\frac{4!}{1!\,3!}\left(\frac{1}{6}\right)^1\left(\frac{5}{6}\right)^3$	500/1296	500/1296	1/3	1/9	500/11,664
2	$\frac{4!}{2!\,2!}\left(\frac{1}{6}\right)^2\left(\frac{5}{6}\right)^2$	150/1296	300/1296	4/3	16/9	2400/11,664
3	$\frac{4!}{3!\,1!}\left(\frac{1}{6}\right)^3\left(\frac{5}{6}\right)^1$	20/1296	60/1296	7/3	49/9	980/11,664
4	$\frac{4!}{4!\,0!}\left(\frac{1}{6}\right)^4\left(\frac{5}{6}\right)^0$	1/1296	4/1296	10/3	100/9	100/11,664
		1296/1296	$\Sigma XP(X) = 864/1296$			6480/11,664

$\Sigma[X\,P(X)]$ in Table 3-5 is $864/1296 = 2/3$. Thus, the most likely outcome if we tossed a die 4 times, for many, many turns and recorded our results on each set of 4 tosses, would be somewhere between 0 and 1 (no 6 in 4 tosses; or one 6 in the 4 tosses). A shortcut method for computing the mean is given by

$$\mu = np \qquad (3\text{-}10)$$

For this problem $n = 4$, $p = 1/6$, and $np = 4/6 = 2/3$.

In similar fashion, we can compute the standard deviation of this distribution. To compute the standard deviation, we subtract the mean of the probability distribution from the midpoint of each category $(X - \mu)$, then square this value $(X - \mu)^2$. Now, multiply each squared value by the corresponding relative frequency $P(X)$ and sum the values $\Sigma P(X)(x - \mu)^2$. Now take the square root. The formula is

$$\sigma = \sqrt{\Sigma P(X)(x - \mu)^2} \qquad (3\text{-}11)$$

$$\sigma = \sqrt{6480/11664} = \sqrt{.5555} = .745$$

The shortcut formula for this is

$$\sigma = \sqrt{npq} = \sqrt{4(1/6)(5/6)} = \sqrt{20/36} = \sqrt{.555} = .745 \qquad (3\text{-}12)$$

In Example 3-11, we will use both the mean and the standard deviation to fit the same information with a binomial and a normal distribution to see if there is much difference in the probabilities predicted.

Problems

1 Past surveys of the graduates of a very large liberal arts college show that 40% of the students continue their education at the graduate level. If 8 graduating students are selected at random,

(a) What is the probability that exactly 6 students will go to graduate school?

(*b*)   What is the probability that at least 5 students will go to graduate school?

2 A large corporation requires all new employees to go through a 1-year training program. Personnel files show that 3 out of every 5 trainees complete the program and stay with the company for at least 3 years. If the company hires 6 new employees and the dropout rate remains unchanged,

(*a*)   What is the probability that at least 3 trainees will be with the company after 3 years?

(*b*)   What is the probability that exactly 4 will remain after 3 years?

3 Before marketing a new drug invented to prevent the common cold, the medical laboratory tested it on 15 people for a 1-year period. Assume that the probability of catching a cold is .4 without this medication and that there are no other factors influencing a person's susceptibility to the common cold. Test results showed that 11 people did not catch a cold. Assuming that the medication is ineffective, what is the probability that at least this many people would not catch a cold? (Note in this problem that we have a very small sample for a medical test. Because we are using the binomial distribution, it is difficult to compute the probability for very large samples. In the next section of this chapter, some ways of converting to a normal distribution, which can be easily applied to large samples, will be shown.)

4 A local hamburger franchise observes that 40% of its business comes from students at a nearby college. If 8 independent orders are placed,

(*a*)   Find the probability that exactly 4 are from students at the college.

(*b*)   Find the probability that more than 5 are from students at the college.

5 A car mechanic figures that 1 out of 4 cars comes into the shop for a tuneup. If 8 cars come in during a certain hour, and x is the number of customers who want a tuneup,

(*a*)   Determine the probability of 0, 1, 2, or 3 customers wanting a tuneup.

(*b*)   Draw a probability distribution for 0 to 8 cars. (You may use the table.)

(*c*)   Determine the average or expected value and the standard deviation.

(*d*)   Use the probability distribution just constructed to determine the population measurements lying within 1 standard deviation of the mean. (*Hint:* Take the mean $\pm 1\sigma$.)

Poisson Distribution

Relation of Binomial Distribution to Poisson Distribution   We have now discussed the binomial distribution, which is a *discrete* distribution. A discrete distribution is one where the variables take on only a countable number of values. For example, we have discussed the number of heads tossed with a coin, the number of sixes rolled with a die, and the number of defects in a sample.

There is another important discrete distribution that can be arrived at by starting with the binomial distribution and allowing n (the number of trials) to approach infinity and p (the probability of a success) to approach 0.

$$P(x) = \frac{\mu^x e^{-\mu}}{x!} \tag{3-13}$$

This formula was derived by the French mathematician Simeon Denis Poisson in the early 1800s. As a result, the distribution is called the *Poisson distribution*. This distribution has two virtues:

1 To use the binomial distribution, you must know both n and p. (This means you must know the number of trials and the probability of a success.) There are many situations where we know what has happened on the average (μ) in the past but don't know the number of trials or the probability of a success in any given trial. How can you predict deaths in auto accidents without knowing how many auto trips people take, how long they last, and what the risks are? With the Poisson distribution, you can know only the mean number of accidents in the past and can compute the probability of X over a range of values.

2 In the next section, we show one of the original problems used to test the Poisson distribution. In recent years, the Poisson distribution has been used to explore the number of atoms in a radioactive sample that will disintegrate in a given time period. In the 1930s, the telephone company developed a series of Poisson distribution tables that we will use. The telephone company uses the distribution to calculate the probability that a busy signal results from equipment malfunction. Thus, the Poisson distribution helps compute the probabilities of *rare* events ($p \rightarrow 0$).

In summary, there are two situations for which the Poisson distribution is useful: (1) to compute the probability distribution when p is very low (*rule of thumb:* use the Poisson if $p \leq .05$); and (2) to compute probabilities when only the mean (μ) is known.

Use of the Poisson Table

Let us look at the formula $P(x) = (\mu^x e^{-x})/x!$; x is the number of successes, μ is the mean (which is np if you know n and p), and e is a constant (which is the base of natural logarithms, approximately 2.718).

The mean μ is the average number of occurrences in a given time or space interval. The standard deviation of the Poisson distribution is equal to the square root of μ ($\sigma = \sqrt{\mu}$). Since we have to compute μ^x and $e^{-\mu}$, we need a log table or a suitable calculator to use this formula. Therefore, we use the tables in Appendix A to compute Poisson probabilities. Note that values for μ go across the top and the probabilities for each value of x go down the columns under the corresponding μ value. Example 3-7 uses a Poisson table (Table A-2) to solve an inventory problem.

EXAMPLE 3-7 Kelsey Nurseries finds that it sells an average of 5 Colorado blue spruce trees per week. Since it buys its shrubs and trees on Friday for the entire week, it would like to know how many to stock. Kelsey is an exclusive nursery and it does not like to turn away, and possibly lose, customers. Therefore, Kelsey buys 7 trees at the beginning of the week. What is the proportion of weeks that Kelsey will turn away customers?

Refer to Table A-2, under $\mu = 5$.

$P(0) = .0067$

$P(1) = .0337$

$P(2) = .0842$

$P(3) = .1404$　　　Sum = .8666

$P(4) = .1755$　　　(Probability that Kelsey

$P(5) = .1755$　　　can satisfy its customers

$P(6) = .1462$　　　if it stocks 7 trees)

$P(7) = .1044$

$P(8) = .0653$

$P(9) = .0363$

$P(10) = .0181$

$P(11) = .0082$

$P(12) = .0034$

$P(13) = .0013$

$P(14) = .0005$

$P(15) = .0002$

If Kelsey stocks 7 trees, it will be able to satisfy all its customers in 86.66% of the weeks; add $P(0)$ through $P(7)$. Now, if it stocked 8 trees, it would satisfy 93.19% of its customers; if it stocked 9 trees, 96.82%. The company is now in the position of balancing the cost of holding extra stock against the risks of antagonizing or losing its customers.

EXAMPLE 3-8　The number of passenger ships arriving in New York harbor each day is Poisson-distributed, with a mean of 5. What is the probability that in 2 days exactly 15 ships will arrive? What are the chances that more than 15 ships will arrive?

If the mean for one day is 5, the mean for 2 days is 10. For $\mu = 10$, $p(15) = .0347$ or 3.47%. (See Table A-2.) For $\mu = 10$,

$P(16 + 17 + 18 + 19 + 20 + 21 + 22 + 23 + 24)$

$= (.0217 + .0128 + .0071 + .0037 + .0019 + .0009 + .0004 + .0002 + .0001)$

$= .0484.$

This is the chance that more than 15 ships will arrive in 2 days.

EXAMPLE 3-9　A famous case in which the Poisson distribution was applied was the prediction of the number of Prussian cavalrymen who were killed by their horses. This is a very good example of the use of the Poisson distribution, because it is a case of an event that rarely occurred, and it is a case where we do not know n and p separately, but do know the mean ($\mu = np$).

In 1898, Ladislaus von Bortkewitsch published the book *The Law of Small Numbers,* describing his study of 14 corps of cavalry over the 20-year period from 1875 to 1894.[3] This made a total of 280 experiments (14 × 20). The experience of each corps for one year was considered an experiment. The results follow:

(1) DEATHS PER YEAR	(2) NUMBER OF CORPS YEARS	(3) ACTUAL NUMBER OF DEATHS (COL. 2 × COL. 1)	(4) PROBABILITY (TABLE A-2)	(5) THEORETICAL (280 × COL. 4)
0	144	0	.4966	139.0
1	91	91	.3476	97.3
2	32	64	.1217	34.1
3	11	33	.0284	8.0
4	2	8	.0050	1.4
5 or more	0	0	.0007	.2
	280	196	1.0000	

$$\mu = \frac{196}{280} = 0.7$$

Using the Poisson table, we can now figure, with a mean of 0.7, the probability of 0, 1, 2, 3, 4, and 5 or more deaths. These probabilities are listed in column 4. Now, if we wish to find the number of deaths that would be forecast for each category, multiply the probability by 280, the number of corps years (no pun intended). This gives column 5, the theoretical predictions for deaths. Comparison of the theoretical and actual (columns 2 and 5) yields results that are very close. In Chapter 7, when we have learned the chi-square test, we will test whether there is a significant difference between the actual and theoretical distributions.

Problems

1 The $6 million man's bionic body contains 500 components. The probability that any single component will malfunction is .002. Using the Poisson distribution, find the probability that the bionic man will not malfunction at all. (If any part is broken, he will not work.)

2 An automated pretzel twister twists pretzels from long strips of dough. On the average, 1 in 250 pretzels is twisted incorrectly. If the pretzels are boxed in packages of 150, find the probability that any given box will contain no abnormal pretzels.

3 The number of trees that fall per year due to natural causes in a 5-acre plot in a large forest is 3. These must be cut and shipped away. Find the probability that there will be no trees cut, and that there will be less than 5 trees cut.

4 Out of 1000 golf balls hit daily at a driving range, the average number to reach the trees is 4. If a random sampling of 100 balls is taken, what is the probability that 1 will reach the trees? That exactly 3 will reach the trees?

[3]Warren Weaver, *Lady Luck*, Doubleday-Anchor, New York, 1963, pp. 264–270.

5 A 300-page book is bound by a machine that occasionally slips and ruins a page. If the machine ruins 2 pages in 500 on the average, what is the probability that a given book contains no defects?

6 A novelty store has determined that the demand for pet rocks averages 6 per month. Determine the probability distribution of the monthly demand for pet rocks (up to 10). If the store stocks 5 rocks during a certain month, what is the probability of demand exceeding supply?

7 Suppose a large lumberyard has 20 automatic saws for cutting trees into 25-foot boards. These saws are in constant operation, and the probability that an individual machine breaks down on any given day is .05. By use of the Poisson distribution, determine the probability that exactly two saws will break down.

8 Landings at a small airport occur randomly and independently of one another at the average rate of 1 every 5 minutes. The present landing capacity is 25 airplanes per hour, and the airport commissioner feels the airport should be expanded. If you were on the budgeting committee, would you vote for or against expansion?

9 If the chance of finding diamonds in an acre of mine field in Arkansas is found to be 7 diamonds per acre, what is the probability of finding exactly 5? Assume independence.

10 Because of the great demand for pocket calculators, a local manufacturer stepped up production. However, 1 out of 50 calculators now has some kind of defect that will be detected before the unit is sold. If 700 are produced on a certain day, find the probability that (*a*) more than 15 will have to be thrown out, (*b*) less than 8 will be defective, and (*c*) none will be defective.

11 Drilling for oil on a platform in the ocean is a hazardous job; a serious accident happens on the average of 2 times every 15 days. What is the probability of more than 4 serious accidents happening over a 60-day period?

CONTINUOUS PROBABILITY DISTRIBUTIONS

3-6

What Is a Normal Distribution?

The German astronomer Karl Frederick Gauss (1777–1855) was the first to publicize the normal distribution. When he was calculating the paths of stars, he reasoned that errors of measurement could occur. He developed the idea of a *normal curve of error* to describe how measurement errors were distributed. If one were cutting out coins on a machine, not all coins would be exactly the same size. If we found the average (mean) size, most coins would be very near the mean. However, some coins might be a bit too large and some a bit too small. Relatively few would be exceedingly large or small. The curve would be smooth, symmetric, and bell-shaped. The tails of the curve would come increasingly close to the *x* axis but never quite touch it (asymptotic to the *x* axis). As you will remember, we discussed the normal distribution in Chapter 2. We will now discuss its use for estimating probabilities.

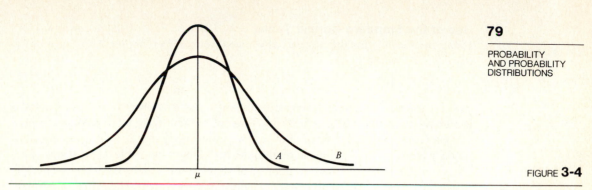

FIGURE **3-4**

The normal curve.

If we know the mean and the standard deviation for this normal curve, we can compute probabilities for any event (or error). Some of the many things that can be studied by use of a normal curve are heights and weights for a population, scores on SAT tests, and temperatures over the course of a year. In Chapter 4, we see that sampling theory relies on the normal curve. The normal distribution, in fact, is the most important distribution studied in statistics.

In Figure 3-4, both curves A and B are normally distributed with the same mean. But we can see that the numbers in B are not as closely concentrated near the mean; thus, curve B has a larger standard deviation. Knowledge of the mean and standard deviation allows us to plot any normal curve. The area under the curve is 1, with .5 on either side of the mean.

Relation of Normal Distribution to Binomial Distribution

When we worked with the binomial distribution in Section 3-5, we saw that the computation of probabilities became increasingly difficult when the number of trials (n) was greater than 10. Even the binomial tables in Appendix A compute only probabilities up to $n = 20$. (See Table A-1.)

If we examine probability distributions for $n = 2, 5, 10$, $p = .5$, and $p = .1$, and plot them in Figure 3-5, we observe the following behavior. When $p = .5$, we note that by the time $n = 10$ the distribution is close to the normal distribution. When $p < .5$, the probability distribution approaches the normal distribution more slowly. In fact, for small n, the probability distribution doesn't even seem symmetric, but as n approaches infinity the probability distribution approaches normality. A general rule of thumb suggests that when $np \geq 5$ (where p goes from 0 to .5), one can use the normal distribution instead of the binomial. Thus, if $p = .5$, $n = 10$, and if $p = .1$, $n = 50$, the normal distribution can be used. If p is greater than .5, use $n(1 - p) > 5$. Thus if $p = .7$, $n = 10$ we would have $n(1 - p) = .3(10) = 3$. Hence we should not use the normal distribution.

Now, if we know that a distribution can be approximated by the normal distribution, we are in a position to use the normal table to make estimates of probabilities for this distribution. To use the normal distribution, we must know the mean and standard deviation of the population. The mean and standard deviation are known as the *parameters* of the distribution. Parameters characterize a distribution. Thus, two distributions may be normal and have the same mean, but they may differ in spread because one has a larger standard deviation than the other. (See Figure 3-4.) If we know the mean and standard deviation for a distribution that is thought to be normal, we can make estimates of the probabilities of certain events by using the standard normal tables.

Using the formula for the z score, which we discussed in Chapter 2, we have

$$z = \frac{X - \mu}{\sigma} \tag{3-14}$$

The z score measures the number of standard deviations away from the mean. We can convert all values of X (which is a value of an item from a frequency or probability distribution) to the number of standard deviations that it is from the mean of its distribution. The standard normal table, or z table (see Table A-3), displays the area from the mean to a certain number of standard deviations from the mean. The left-hand column tells the number of standard deviations from the mean, to one decimal place. Going along the top of the table, we see a second decimal place. Thus, we could look up 1.25 standard deviations by looking under 1.2 and then under .05. Where they come together we read the area .3944. This is the area from the mean to 1.25 standard deviations to the right of the mean. Thus, all the numbers inside the table are areas from the mean to a designated number of standard deviations from the mean. There are basically six types of probabilities that can be found using the standard normal distribution. (See Figure 3-6.)

One of the problems of the transitions from the binomial distribution to the normal distribution is that the normal distribution is *continuous* but the binomial distribution is *discrete*. If we wish to apply the normal distribution to approximate the probabilities for the binomial distribution problem, we can adjust our data slightly. Example 3-10 shows a simple method of adjustment.

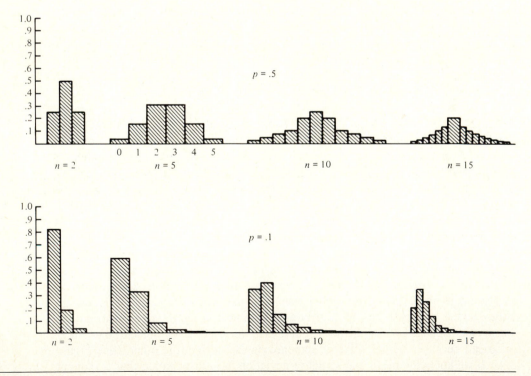

FIGURE **3-5**

Binomial probability distributions (varying n and p).

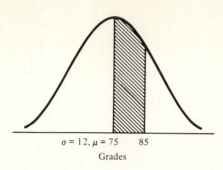

$\sigma = 12, \mu = 75 \quad 85$
Grades

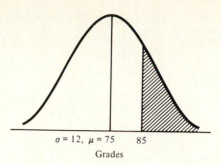

$\sigma = 12, \; \mu = 75 \quad 85$
Grades

1 Area from the mean to a point. If class grades are normally distributed and the mean grade is 75 and $\sigma = 12$, what percent of students have grades between 75 and 85?

$$z = \frac{85 - 75}{12} = \frac{10}{12} = .83$$

When you are .83 standard deviations from the mean, the area between this point and the mean is .2967; therefore, 29.67% of students will have grades between 75 and 85.

2 Area from a point to the end of the curve. What percent of students will have grades of 85 and higher?

$$z = \frac{85 - 75}{12} = \frac{10}{12} = .83$$

Area from 75 to 85 = .2967. Total area under this half of curve = .5000; therefore, the percent above 85 is .5000 – .2967 = .2033, or 20.33%. The tail goes to infinity, but the total area from 85 to the end is .2033.

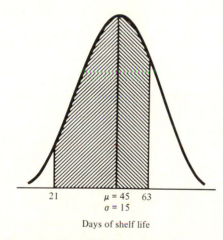

$21 \qquad \mu = 45 \quad 63$
$\sigma = 15$

Days of shelf life

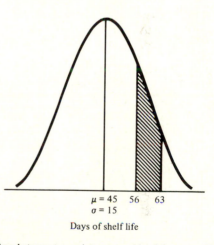

$\mu = 45 \quad 56 \quad 63$
$\sigma = 15$

Days of shelf life

3 Area to the right and left of the mean. The average shelf life of Doodle Krispies is 45 days, with a standard deviation of 15 days. What percent of the time will Doodle Krispies last between 3 and 9 weeks? Converting weeks to days, we have 21 to 63 days.

$$z = \frac{21 - 45}{15} = -1.6 \quad \begin{array}{l} \text{corresponding area} \\ .4452 \end{array}$$

$$z = \frac{63 - 45}{15} = 1.2 \quad \begin{array}{l} .3849 \\ \overline{.8301} \end{array}$$

Now, do not add the z values 1.2 and 1.6, as the area between 1 and 2 standard deviations is not equal. Instead, find the percentage of area under the curve and add. (If we had added 1.2 and 1.6, we would have 2.8. Looking this up in the table, the area would be less than .5000).

4 Area between two points on one side of the mean. What percent of Doodle Krispies will last from 8 to 9 weeks? Converting weeks to days, we have 56 to 63 days.

$$z = \frac{56 - 45}{15} = .73 \quad \begin{array}{l} \text{corresponding area} \\ .2673 \end{array}$$

$$z = \frac{63 - 45}{15} = 1.2 = .3849 \quad \begin{array}{r} .3849 \\ -.2673 \\ \hline .1176 \end{array}$$

11.76% of the time the cereal will last from 8 to 9 weeks.

FIGURE **3-6**

Computation of 6 types of areas under the normal curve.

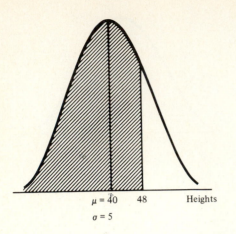

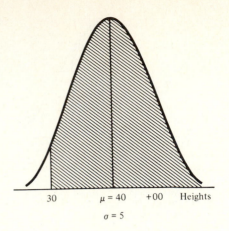

5 Area below a point that is greater than the mean. Heights of 5-year-old children are normally distributed, with a mean of 40 inches and a standard deviation of 5 inches. What percent of 5-year-olds stand less than 48 inches tall?

$$z = \frac{48 - 40}{5} = \frac{8}{5} = 1.6 \qquad \text{corresponding area} \\ .4452$$

We must add .5000 to .4452 to find the area below 48. This is .9452 or 94.52%. Note: Lower tail goes to –infinity, but the area under this half of curve is .5000.

6 Area above a point that is less than the mean. In the previous problem, we wish to estimate the percent of children who are taller than 30 inches.

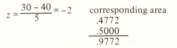

$$z = \frac{30 - 40}{5} = -2 \qquad \begin{array}{l} \text{corresponding area} \\ .4772 \\ \underline{.5000} \\ .9772 \end{array}$$

FIGURE **3-6** (*Continued*)

EXAMPLE 3-10 The telephone company estimates that an average of 448 calls are made between 4 and 5 p.m. on a given line. The standard deviation is 30 calls. What percent of the time will there be between 429 and 490 calls? Assume we can use the normal distribution to analyze this data. In order to approximate probabilities for this discrete data (that is, the number of telephone calls), we try to assume that it is continuous. Any number of calls between 428.5 and 490.5 will be classified in these bounds. (Of course, fractional phone calls don't exist. But if phone calls were continuous, everything from 428.5 on would be considered 429 and every value up to 490.5 would be treated as 490.) Now, we place this on a normal curve, shown in Figure 3-7.

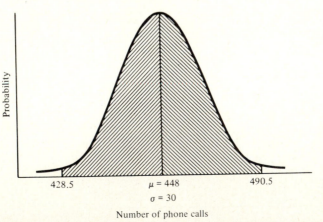

FIGURE **3-7**

Telephone calls made from 4 to 5 p.m.

$$z = \frac{X - \mu}{\sigma}$$

$$z = \frac{428.5 - 448}{30} = \frac{-19.5}{30} = -.65$$

$$z = \frac{490.5 - 448}{30} = \frac{42.5}{30} = 1.42$$

Looking at the normal table, the probability on the left side of the mean is .2422. On the right side of the mean, the area is .4222. Adding the two probabilities, we have

	Corresponding area
$z = $ .65	.2422
	.4222
$z = $ 1.42	.6644 = 66.44%

EXAMPLE 3-11   We now show an example that compares the probabilities using the binomial and the normal distributions.

Using the binomial and the normal distributions, compute the probability of tossing 9 heads when you toss a coin 15 times. Using the binomial distribution,

$$P(9) = \frac{15!}{9!\ 6!}(1/2)^9\ (1/2)^6$$

$$= \frac{15!\,14!\,13!\,12!\,11!\,10!\ 9!}{9!\ 6!\ 5!\ 4!\ 3!\ 2!\ 1!} = 5005$$

$$P(9) = 5005 \left(\frac{1}{512}\right)\left(\frac{1}{64}\right)$$

Since 1/512 converts to .0020, and 1/64 to .0156, $P(9) = .1527$. Now, to convert to the normal distribution, we must know the *mean* and the *standard deviation,* because we have said that the mean and standard deviation single out a unique normal distribution. Using our shortcut formulas from page 73, we have

$$\mu = np = 15 \times 1/2 = 7.5 \qquad \sigma = \sqrt{npq} = \sqrt{15(1/2)(1/2)} = 1.936$$

Secondly, we must convert a discrete to a continuous distribution. Thus, the probability of 9 heads becomes the probability of 8.5 to 9.5 heads.

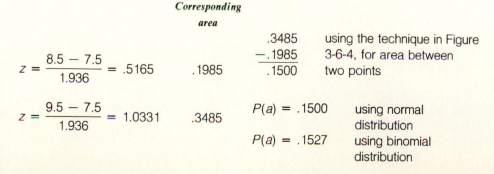

	Corresponding area		
		.3485	using the technique in Figure
		−.1985	3-6-4, for area between
$z = \dfrac{8.5 - 7.5}{1.936} = .5165$	.1985	.1500	two points
$z = \dfrac{9.5 - 7.5}{1.936} = 1.0331$	.3485	$P(a) = .1500$	using normal distribution
		$P(a) = .1527$	using binomial distribution

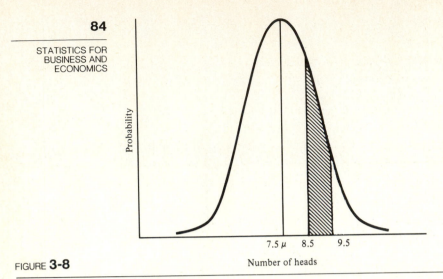

FIGURE **3-8**

Probabilities of tossing 9 heads in 15 tosses.

The probabilities computed by the normal and binomial distributions are very close. This corresponds well with our rule of thumb, which allowed the use of the normal distribution when $np > 5$. In this case, $np = 15\ (\frac{1}{2}) = 7.5$.

Problems

1 The "Widow-Maker" is the name of a particularly obstinate bull ridden by cowboys in a rodeo. The time to ride the bull is normally distributed, with a mean of 6.5 seconds and a standard deviation of 1.2 seconds. What is the probability that a cowboy will ride Widow-Maker for (*a*) more than 8 seconds and (*b*) less than 3 seconds?

2 The rock promoters for The Group are trying to decide between two facilities for Friday night's concert. One building holds 8000 people and one holds 10,500. If the audience for The Group is normally distributed, with a mean of 7000 and a standard deviation of 700 people, which stadium should they reserve? (Assume that the larger stadium is more expensive to reserve.)

3 Flash Goodyear is competing at the Indy 500 this year in a new car. The speed for the car is normally distributed, with a mean of 182 mph and a standard deviation of 6 mph. Flash estimates that the winning car in the race should make the final lap at 190 mph or more. What is the probability that Flash will win the race?

4 The amount of mail handled daily by a small post office in Connecticut is normally distributed, with a mean of 1200 and a standard deviation of 35. The postmaster would like to know the probability that the volume of mail will exceed 1300. What is the probability that the volume will not reach 1000? Will be between 1100 and 1250?

5 On the college track team, the weight of women standing 5-ft 6-in is normally distributed, with a mean weight of 125 pounds and a standard deviation of 1.8 pounds.
    (*a*) What is the probability that a certain woman weighs over 130 pounds?
    (*b*) The probability is 25% that she weighs how much?

(c) What is the probability that she weighs between 120 and 126?

(d) Above what weight will the heaviest 10% of the women be?

6 A Chevrolet dealer wishes to know how many Citations to order for the coming month. Estimated demand for Citations in May is normally distributed, with a *standard deviation of 25 and a mean of 150.*

(a) What is the probability that he will need more than 170?

(b) What is the probability that he will need less than 100?

7 The number of telephone calls in Giventown at noon is normally distributed, with a mean of 525 and a standard deviation of 45. The maximum number of calls that can be handled simultaneouly by the phone company for the town is 650. What is the probability of an overload?

8 A client wishes to know what price he might be able to get for a business property. The realtor estimates that a sale price for that property of $100,000 would be exceeded no more than 5% of the time. A price of at least $70,000 should be obtained at least 90% of the time. Assuming the distribution of sales prices to be normal, answer the following questions.

(a) What are μ and σ for this distribution?

(b) What is the probability of a sale price greater than $90,000, less than $80,000, and between $90,000 and $100,000?

SUMMARY

3-7

1 There are three ways of arriving at probability estimates: (1) *objective probability,* (2) *relative frequency of occurrence,* and (3) *subjective probability.*

2 There are six simple rules of probability:

$$0 \leq P(A) \leq 1$$

$P(A) = 1 - P(\sim A)$	mutually exclusive events
$P(A \text{ or } B) = P(A) + P(B)$	mutually exclusive events
$P(A \text{ or } B) = P(A) + P(B) - P(A \text{ and } B)$	non–mutually exclusive events
$P(A \text{ and } B) = P(A)P(B)$	independent events
$P(A \text{ and } B) = P(A)P(B/A)$	nonindependent events

$$\text{or } P(B/A) = \frac{P(A \text{ and } B)}{P(A)}$$

3 If $P(B/A) = P(B)$, then A and B are independent.

4 The expected value of a set of alternatives is equal to $\Sigma[P(X) \times \text{payoff of } X]$.

5 *Discrete probability distributions* can be made when there are distinct probabilities; for example, 1 head, 2 heads, or 3 heads. The probability distribution lists the probability of all alternatives. The sum of the probability of all the alternatives is 1.

6 The *binomial distribution* can be used when there are exactly two possible alternatives: when each event is independent of each other and when the probability of a success remains constant from trial to trial. The formula for the computation is:

$$P(x) = \frac{n!}{x!(n - x)!}\, p^x q^{n-x}$$

Table A-1 may also be used to find binomial probabilities. The mean of a binomial distribution is

$$\mu = np$$

and the standard deviation is

$$\sigma = \sqrt{npq}$$

7 The Poisson distribution is another discrete distribution. It should be used as $n \to \infty$ and p is very low ($p \to 0$), or when only μ is known. The formula is

$$P(x) = \frac{\mu^x e^{-\mu}}{x!}$$

Table A-2 may be used to find Poisson probabilities.

8 *Continuous probability distributions* study variables that can be measured to any degree of fineness, such as height, or the size of machine parts.

9 The most important continuous probability distribution is the *normal distribution*. There are many such curves, and each is defined by its *mean* and *standard deviation*. The curve formed by this distribution is smooth, symmetric, and bell-shaped. The tails of the curve come increasingly close to the X axis but never quite touch it.

10 Areas under the normal curve can be found by using Table A-3 and computing the number of standard deviations away from the mean using the formula

$$z = \frac{X - \mu}{\sigma}$$

BIBLIOGRAPHY

3–8

Three simple paperback histories of probability are:

King, Amy C., and Cecil B. Read: *Pathways to Probability.* New York: Holt, 1963.
Levinson, Horace C.: *Chance, Luck and Statistics.* New York: Dover, 1963.
Weaver, Warren: *Lady Luck.* New York: Doubleday-Anchor, 1963.

General explanations of probability can be found in:

Freund, John E., and F. J. Williams, *Elementary Business Statistics: The Modern Approach*, 3d ed. Englewood Cliffs, N.J.: Prentice-Hall, 1977.
Neter, Wasserman, and Whitmore: *Fundamental Statistics for Business and Economics*, 4th ed. Boston: Allyn and Bacon, 1973. See chapters 6, 7, and 8.

Theoretical discussion can be found in:

Feller, William: *An Introduction to Probability Theory and Its Applications,* volume I, 2d ed. New York: Wiley, 1957.

Case 3-1   Does Fate Relate?

The personnel department of Biranca Computer Company has found that personal interviews and study of résumés generally have not provided adequate information for predicting who will be effective salespersons. Salespersons must spend a month in special training at company headquarters in San Diego and work for six months with an experienced salesperson before going out on their own. During this time, they are paid by the company; in addition, the company must pay living expenses at the San Diego Hilton for the new employees and their instructors.

Deborah Bleeker, manager of the personnel department, wanted to develop a better method of screening applicants so that she could be assured of hiring people who would successfully complete the training period and go on to be good salespersons. When she reflected on the qualities that are essential to a good salesperson, such attributes as aggressive, persistent, self-reliant, forceful, confident, and outgoing came to her mind.

A study of psychological tests indicated that several easy-to-give tests might prove helpful in determining success in the training and the sales work. One of these was an 11-question version of Rotter's test for internal and external control.[1] "*Internal control* refers to the perception of positive and/or negative events as a consequence of one's own action, and that events are under personal control; *external control* refers to the perception of positive and/or negative events as being unrelated to one's own behavior in certain situations and therefore beyond personal control."[2] To summarize, the test studies whether one considers that his or her *own behavior* (internal control) determines the outcomes in his or her life, or whether he or she feels that fate (external control) is responsible for his or her successes and failures. For example, a question on this test would give applicants a chance to choose between these two statements: (1) "In my case, getting what I want has little or nothing to do with luck." Or, (2) "Many times we might just as well decide what to do by flipping a coin."

Applicants must choose the statement closest to their own opinion, and must rank it as to how close it is to their opinion. Each of the 11 responses is assigned a score from 1 to 4 in order of increasing external control. A score near 11 indicates a strong feeling of personal control; a score near 44 indicates a belief that events are not related to behavior and that fate is very important in determining what happens.

Since this test was easy to administer, Bleeker decided to give the test to all new applicants and relate the results to the success in finishing the course and the 6-month training period. The test was administered to the 110 accepted applicants

[1]H. M. Lefcourt, "Internal vs. External Control of Reinforcement: A Review," *Psychological Bulletin,* vol. 65, 1966, p. 206.
[2]*Ibid.*

TABLE 1

	(1) APPLICANTS' SCORE	(2) NUMBER OF APPLICANTS ACCEPTED	(3) NUMBER PASSING COURSE	(4) NUMBER PASSING COURSE WHO COMPLETED TRAINING
Strong personal control	11–17	20	19	10
↓	18–24	15	13	10
	25–31	35	30	27
↓	32–38	30	20	18
Weak personal control	39–44	10	5	5
		110	87	70

in the following year, and the results are shown in Table 1. Then, she computed the probability of passing the course for applicants within each of the five categories. (See Table 2.) It seemed quite clear to her that preference in hiring should be accorded to people who had scores between 11 and 17, a very internal orientation that indicated a great deal of self reliance. People with scores higher than 31 should be excluded, since they don't have a very good chance of passing.

Questions

1 Would you recommend the use of this test and its conclusions to management?

2 The case furnishes information on success in the course and success in completing the training period which involves traveling with an experienced salesperson. What other measures of success might be used?

3 Plot the data on two graphs: one for the probability of passing the course and one for the probability of completing training, using probability on the Y axis.

4 Can you suggest any improvements in the analysis using the data furnished in the case? What results do you get? (*Hint:* Find probabilities of passing the course *and* completing the apprenticeship and try to explain your results.)

5 As a result of your analysis, what recommendations do you make now?

Case 3-2   DRC Limousine Insurance

Digital Recording Company, a large conglomerate consisting of electronics concerns, large household appliance manufacturing, home furnishings, and a radio station, has its corporate offices in New York City. DRC's appliance manufacturing and design departments and the electronics manufacturing and design facilities are

TABLE 2

APPLICANTS' SCORE	NUMBER ACCEPTED	NUMBER PASSING COURSE	PROBABILITY OF PASSING COURSE $P(A)$
11–17	20	19	19/20 = .95
18–24	15	13	13/15 = .87
25–31	35	30	30/35 = .86
32–38	30	20	20/30 = .67
39–44	10	5	5/10 = .50
	110	87	

scattered throughout cities and towns of northern and central New Jersey. The New Jersey site farthest from the city is approximately 55 miles south of New York, close to the Philadelphia area. In order to keep in contact with the managerial staff of the plants, the company maintains a fleet of cars and a number of chauffeurs at each location. The cars are used to transport important personnel to and from Kennedy and La Guardia airports in New York and Newark and Philadelphia airports. In addition, trips with two or more executives going to New York headquarters are generally driven in these company limousines.

Roger Kerin, the business manager, is in charge of the expenses for these cars at all the New Jersey locations. Each year he must buy insurance for the whole fleet. While it is mandatory that he purchase liability insurance, collision insurance that will pay for the nonreimbursed damages on DRC cars can be a self-insured risk.

A canvass of local insurance companies reveals that the lowest bid for coverage up to $4000 per car is for an annual fee of $2000 for all 20 cars. Kerin feels that this seems rather high because the cars are driven by professional chauffeurs who tend to have fewer accidents than other drivers.

A study of the accident record for company cars during the past 10 years indicates that there were 12 accidents in which collision insurance was needed. A study of the cost for each accident reveals the information shown in Table 1 below.

Using the information in Table 1, Kerin computed the top cost per accident by multiplying each cost by the probability of its occurrence and summing all the values. In order to make a cautious estimate, he multiplied each probability by the maximum cost for that category.

$$\Sigma \text{ Cost } [P(X)] = \text{expected cost}$$
$$\$100(.417) + \$500(.250) + \$1000(.167) + \$2000(.083) + \$3000(.000)$$
$$+ \$4000(.083) = 41.7 + 125 + 167 + 166 + 0 + 332 = \$831.7$$

Kerin wondered how he could use this information to make a reasonable estimate of the expected annual cost to the company if it insured for its own risk.

Questions

1 Would you self-insure?

2 What probability distribution would be useful here? Why?

3 Compute the expected loss using the information supplied in the case.

TABLE 1

COSTS PER ACCIDENT, $	NUMBER OF ACCIDENTS	PROBABILITY
100 or less	5	5/12 = .417
100–500	3	3/12 = .250
501–1000	2	2/12 = .167
1001–2000	1	1/12 = .083
2001–3000	0	0 = .000
3001–4000	1	1/12 = .083
	12	1.000

4 What choice should Kerin make? Why? What would his chance of losing (paying more than $2000) in a given year be?

5 What other considerations might be studied? For example, how would inflation affect the results of the computation?
Optional: How could one adjust for inflation?

6 How does the fact that the information is based on 12 accidents affect the outcome? What alternative data sources could be used?

7 Would it pay to buy $100 deductible (first $100 of damages not reimbursed) insurance at a cost of $1000?

Case 3-3 Naro-Shu Company (B): Feasibility of Establishing a Specialty Retail Store, Choosing a Site

In the Naro-Shu Company (A) case, Charles Dart selected Dallas as a site for a new shoe store catering to women wearing narrow widths. Dallas was a large city that boasted of many shopping centers. The largest center, Northpark, had a total retail volume of $100 million in 1972. This was almost as large as the $174 million volume of the Central Business District during the same period. In addition, there were seven other shopping centers in the city and its environs that had a total sales volume ranging from $40 million to $60 million during the period.[1]

Using the publication *Dollars & Cents of Shopping Centers: 1975,* published by the Urban Land Institute, Dart compiled the figures in Table 1. This table lists the median dollar sales per square foot for different types of women's shoes in different types of shopping centers. Dart decided that he didn't want to be tied to a chain or franchise store since he liked to do things "on his own." Comparisons of independent shoe stores showed the highest dollar sales per square foot to be in the superregional shopping centers (see Table 1). Charles Dart, however, felt this was not sufficient evidence for a decision since shopping centers with higher sales may often have much higher rental costs. When median total charges per square foot were subtracted from median total sales per square foot to compute the median net return (column 7), the slight superiority of the superregional centers appeared improved. Regional centers, however, were also close behind with median net return of $64.39 per square foot as compared to $66.12 per square foot for the superregional centers. The community and neighborhood centers lagged far behind these figures.

From the standpoint of net returns, Charles Dart felt that either a superregional center or a regional center was obviously preferable. However, he was a bit worried about variations. While average income in a given type of center might be very high, there were often extreme variations in sales and hence average income for different stores. Thus, a new small store might do very poorly in a relatively prosperous shopping community. On the other hand, if the variation were very large, a new store had the possibility of making an extremely high profit.

Dart knew what the sales per square foot were for the top decile as well as the median. The *Dollars & Cents of Shopping Centers: 1975* had presented this information. He decided to assume that sales per square foot were normally dis-

---

[1]*Dallas Morning News,* August 17, 1975.

TABLE 1

COMPARISON OF SALES PER SQUARE FOOT AND TOTAL CHARGES PER SQUARE FOOT FOR WOMEN'S SHOE STORES IN DIFFERENT TYPES OF SHOPPING CENTERS

TYPE OF CENTER AND STORE	SALES PER SQUARE FOOT, $		TOTAL CHARGES PER SQUARE FOOT, $		
	(1) MEDIAN	(2) TOP 10%*	(3) MEDIAN	(4) TOP 10%*	(5) MEDIAN NET RETURN (SALES MINUS TOTAL CHARGES)
Superregional centers†					
All stores (112)	68.21	130.51	6.32	11.59	61.89
National chain (76)	68.11	127.34	6.51	11.65	61.60
Local chain (22)	69.37	120.61	6.02	8.82	63.35
Independent (14)	71.89	207.97	5.77	14.56	66.12
Regional centers‡					
All stores (139)	67.46	129.02	6.36	9.45	61.10
National chain (102)	58.34	123.58	5.59	9.27	52.75
Local chain (25)	91.20	136.25	7.39	11.39	83.81
Independent (12)	71.16	98.04	6.77	8.79	64.39
Community centers §					
All stores (32)	35.44	84.80	3.82	6.28	31.62
National chain (15)	33.89	74.79	2.71	6.01	31.18
Local chain (9)	50.93	91.50	4.03	5.23	46.90
Independent (8)	56.67	105.37	4.82	6.42	51.85
Neighborhood centers (only family shoes)¶					
All stores (30)	35.63	108.70	3.01	5.10	32.62
National chain (10)	32.31	76.30	3.46	4.15	28.85
Local chain (10)	32.63	39.44	2.62	2.94	30.01
Independent (10)	51.43	144.67	3.74	7.03	47.69

*The top 10% of the stores, the upper decile, would have higher charges or higher incomes than this.
†*Superregional centers* have at least 750,000 square feet of gross leasable area and a minimum of three department stores of generally not less than 100,000 square feet.
‡*Regional centers* provide a variety and depth of "shopping goods" comparable to a central business district of a small city. One or two major department stores of generally not less than 100,000 square feet are the principal tenants of this type of center.
§*Community centers* provide "convenience goods" and a wide range of facilities selling "shopping goods" such as apparel and furniture; these centers may include banking, professional services, and recreational facilities. A junior department store or variety store is the principal tenant in this type of center.
¶*Neighborhood centers* provide daily living needs: food, drugs, hardware, personal services, etc. A supermarket is the principal tenant of this type of center. Only family shoe stores were included in the studies of neighborhood shopping centers.
Source: *Dollars & Cents of Shopping Centers: 1975.* Urban Land Institute.

tributed for most samples studied. He thought he should try to formulate measures of variation in income in an attempt to arrive at a decision.

Questions

1 You are especially interested in variations at the extreme ends of the distribution, particularly variations below and above the median. Does this data offer these results?

2 If you assume the distributions are normal, can you use what happens in the top percentile to approximate what happens in the lower decile?

3 Using the information for the 90th percentile, compute net returns for this percentile, then calculate the standard deviation. (Use the median net return to approximate the mean, and assume that the mean is not known.)

4 What conclusions do you draw about the best location when you compare superregional and regional shopping centers?

5 If Dart is a risk-averter, which of these two centers should he choose? Why?

6 If Dart likes to take a risk, which should he choose? Why?

7 Which would you choose? Why?

Case 3-4   People *vs.* Collins

This is an actual legal case as described in the *Harvard Law Review.*[1] In the *People vs. Collins,* the California Supreme Court overturned the conviction of a lower court and held that mathematical testimony was inadmissible. The case follows:

> An elderly woman walking home in an alley in a western city was assaulted from behind and robbed. Mrs. Miller caught only a glimpse of her assailant, enough to describe her as a young woman with blond hair, but nothing more. A witness who happened to be near the entrance to the alleyway stated that a white woman with dark-blond hair tied back in a ponytail ran out of the alleyway and entered a yellow automobile driven by a black male with a mustache and beard. A few days after the incident, police officers investigating the robbery arrested a couple who fit this description and charged them with the crime.

At the trial, the district attorney called as the key witness a mathematics professor who introduced into evidence probability statistics showing that the probability that the accused were guilty was overwhelming. This mathematician used the "product rule" of elementary probability theory, which states that the probability of the joint occurrence of a number of mutually independent events equals the product of the individual probabilities of each of the events.

The prosecution then had the witness give the following individual probabilities of the relevant characteristics of the guilty couple in this case:

Young woman with blond hair	1/3
Young woman with ponytail	1/10
Man with mustache	1/4
Black man with beard	1/10
Yellow automobile	1/10
Interracial couple	1/1000

Applying the product rule to these assumed values, the prosecutor concluded that there was only 1 chance in 12 million that a couple selected at random would possess the incriminatory characteristics. Since the total population of the city was

---

[1]See Michael O. Finkelstein and William B. Farley, "A Bayesian Approach to Identification Evidence," *Harvard Law Review,* vol. 83, Jan. 1970; and Lawrence H. Tribe, "Trial by Mathematics: Precision and Ritual," vol. 84, Apr. 1971.

less than 12 million, the jury convicted the accused on the basis of this testimony and the prosecutor's conclusion.

Questions

1   Work out the probabilities that the mathematician presented. Is there 1 chance in 12 million for this event to occur?

2   If this case were brought up on appeal, how would you dispute the use of this statistical approach in the lower court?

3   What might have been a good way to present statistical evidence for the prosecution?

SAMPLE SELECTION AND SAMPLING THEORY

4-1   WHY SAMPLE?

4-2   COMMON USES OF SAMPLING

4-3   COMPARISON OF SAMPLE SURVEY METHODS

4-4   SAMPLE DESIGNS
      Probability Samples
      Nonprobability Samples

4-5   CENTRAL LIMIT THEOREM

4-6   CONFIDENCE INTERVALS

4-7   CONFIDENCE INTERVALS WHEN σ IS NOT KNOWN
      Problems

4-8   CONFIDENCE INTERVALS FOR A PROPORTION
      Problems

4-9   SAMPLE SIZE
      Problems

4-10 SUMMARY

4-11 BIBLIOGRAPHY

4-12 CASES
      Case 4-1: Southern California Savings Bank
      Case 4-2: Desegregation in Dallas

Previous chapters have been directed at condensing and analyzing data when we have information for the whole population. Often, however, one studies a population for which it is not possible to obtain complete information. Sampling, in which one tests a small portion of the population and uses the laws of probability to make an estimate of the entire population, is an excellent way to handle this problem.

Finding a good sample is often not easy. For example, if we sample the fruit at the top of a basket we may have no idea if there is rotten fruit in the middle of the basket. If we are studying college students' attitudes and we interview students on the steps of the business school, we may never encounter an engineering student. Determining the right size for a sample, selecting the right sampling method so that the sample represents the population, and making estimates for the population from which the sample comes is the theme of this chapter. Before we start, it is important to convince ourselves that we really need to take a sample. Wouldn't it be better to study the entire population?

WHY SAMPLE?

4-1

1 Time and cost are probably the two most important reasons for sampling. If one wants to determine if customers in a given market will buy a product, one doesn't usually have the time or funds to interview all potential customers. For example, try interviewing everyone who uses dentrifice in the United States.

2 Testing may prove destructive. A commonly misquoted joke in statistical literature tells of the general who suggested testing all bombs by trying to detonate them before they were loaded on bombers. Obviously, if you wish to test the durability of your product, stress tests on the entire output may leave you with no product to sell.

3 Accuracy is another reason for sampling. At first glance, this seems incongruous. One would think that a study of the entire population would be more accurate than a study of a sample. If one has a very large population and wishes to take a complete count, then one must hire a large number of inventory takers who must work at a very rapid pace. As more personnel are hired, it is likely that they may be less efficient than the original employees. Thus, a limited number of skilled workers, studying a well-defined sample, may provide more accurate results than a sloppy survey of the entire population.

A number of years ago, under the leadership of United Airlines, a study was made to see if one airline could compensate another for portions of airline tickets on the basis of sampling rather than on full accounting. United Airlines found that there were more than 100,000 fares each month on portions of tickets due other airlines. For example, if a traveler uses two airlines for a given trip he pays only the first airline, which later reimburses the second airline. For a 4-month period, United Airlines used a sampling plan and also examined all its accounts. It found that for three pairs of carriers for the 4-month period, sampling errors amounted to $\pm \$700$ per $1 million of tickets. The cost of completely calculating $600,000 of billings was $1500. It would be cheaper to pay for the sampling errors than to pay for complete billing. Thus, the airlines found it possible to make accurate settlements by sampling about 10%, or 10,000, of these 100,000 monthly fares. This sample method of payment is called *inductive accounting*. The typical annual interairline billings between two companies exceed $20,000,000. Sample errors have been found to be less than one-tenth of 1 percent by comparing full billing and sample billing. Savings for any one of the large carriers have been estimated at over $75,000 annually, and the industry has saved more than $500,000 a year.[1]

[1] Mark Slonem, *Sampling in a Nutshell*, Simon and Schuster, New York, 1960, pp. 113–116.

Sampling can be used to gather a wide variety of business, government, industrial, economic, sociologic, and psychologic data. Some common examples follow:

1 The U.S. Bureau of the Census samples to obtain information on education, income distribution, and other population characteristics.

2 Industrial firms sample to check product quality.

3 Accounting firms use sampling to audit accounts. In fact, many large firms publish sampling manuals.

4 Survey research centers use sample data to study savings, income, fertility, labor market behavior, and workers' attitudes.

5 Opinion survey organizations (Gallup and Roper) use samples to study political issues and public opinion.

6 Medical and pharmaceutical researchers use statistical techniques to study the effects of drugs and cures for disease.

7 Market research companies evaluate listener samples for TV ratings (Neilsen).

8 Marketing research companies use samples to investigate the effectiveness of advertisements, consumer preferences, and potential markets.

In recent years the sample survey has grown in importance. The public is aware of the Gallup and Roper studies as well as many other polls available in the media. The "pollsters" have gained much publicity by forecasting election results. In fact, some people have suggested that we could use sample surveys instead of elections, provided we have good samples. In the 1976 presidential election, the public was very surprised because the forecasters would make no prediction at the last minute. They stated that the vote was so close that the margin was "within sampling error." In a later section of this chapter, we discuss what is a good sample and why it is sometimes not possible to make a forecast.

A sample survey can be made by using a mail questionnaire, telephone interview, or a personal interview. Each technique involves different problems of cost, response rate, time, bias, and accuracy. Table 4-1 summarizes these features for each survey technique.

Probability Samples

Taking a sample to use for the study of a population means that one must make sure that the sample really represents the population. The first problem is to decide what is the population that should be sampled. If we are studying political preferences of students at a university, we must decide if this includes both graduate and under-

TABLE 4-1

COMPARISON OF THREE SAMPLE SURVEY METHODS

	PERSONAL INTERVIEW	MAIL QUESTIONNAIRE	TELEPHONE INTERVIEW
Cost	Very expensive: $10–100 per interview	Relatively inexpensive	Relatively inexpensive
Time required	Repeated callbacks plus travel	Returns on mailings may take 4–6 weeks	Call time and call back time
Length of interview	Allows for in-depth interviews, good rapport	Long questionnaires not returned: 1–2 pages ideal	Limited for in-depth interview: 5–20 minutes
Accuracy of data	Ability to develop rapport and obtain data	Fair ability to obtain data	Hard to obtain personal data—suspicious of phone interview
Response rate	85–92% possible for a good survey with callbacks; some information on who is not responding	10–20% response rate; bad response rate bias; interested people tend to return questionnaire; no idea of who is not responding	Fair response, but no idea of nonresponse; problems of unlisted numbers and people with no phones
Interviewer bias	Possible bias due to manner and appearance of interviewer as well as method of asking questions	Possible bias due to style of letter, person signing letter	Some bias, possibly because of voice or attitude, but not as great as for personal interview

graduate students, full-time students and part-time students. Deciding on these elements in the population studied is called the development of a *frame*. The frame lists all elements in the population to be sampled.

Once we have decided upon the frame, we must decide on the elementary units to be sampled. In this case it is individual students. Now, we come to the problem of choosing the people for inclusion in the sample. This is not always easy. For example, if we wanted to study the student population at a university and we took a sample outside the women's dormitory, we would probably have too many women who lived in dormitories to have a representative sample. *A random sampling* procedure yielding a representative sample requires *that everyone in the population has an equal chance of being chosen.*

Back to our study of the university students. If we stand on the steps of the student union, we are apt to oversample residential students as opposed to commuters. Perhaps we could try *a list of students*. The student directory is such a list and it could provide a ready-made frame. The registrar's office may even provide you with a list, provided that it violates no federal security laws. Are there any problems with a list? Yes! Students who have registered *late* may not be on it, and so they have no chance of being chosen for your sample. Your study will therefore be representative of university students who have registered in time to be in the student directory or on the registrar's list. However, the list is probably your best bet for a campus study. You will still need to contact students once you have selected them from a list.

Choosing people from a list may be done using a table of *random* numbers. If

TABLE 4-2
RANDOM NUMBERS

4318	8048	5949	2731	3670	745
368	9883	2203	6310	2748	416
679	2665	93	600	7920	873
1798	4032	1329	1125	1862	1070
1278	1580	4243	2291	1833	9604
1889	3695	667	603	5587	1102
1869	3829	1513	362	1957	5297
5216	4727	2964	1306	347	2600
2167	3671	6187	383	2544	4683
2467	21	26	435	5414	941
3897	347	1306	853	1965	2008
3395	2607	200	1876	1544	3321
351	4924	87	16	7844	3397
2325	527	5449	397	3172	2480
2162	5096	9865	443	802	1089
2224	27	7294	502	211	22
4019	433	24	4135	1007	6522
856	5675	2318	2751	1905	5148
99	924	5850	4990	4291	132
435	1956	3407	3354	83	641
1328	2500	2195	755	659	388
1912	1262	1625	53	3362	971
697	4220	786	6806	2205	135
771	790	1590	3155	1778	604
3176	431	738	8105	1259	2328
538	2291	3532	2662	2996	3164
3298	1910	100	996	443	304
1726	1024	2618	1511	270	2110
2769	1932	3966	3813	3482	2522
1552	510	636	1822	1701	1907
11409	1751	137	3071	1009	4924
1813	1169	507	651	1532	5995
471	1144	661	764	4229	164
2428	81	1611	1746	4983	2061
27	5630	7520	1157	361	2602

we were interested in sampling from a group of 10 people, for example, we could number 10 pieces of paper from 0 through 9 and put them in a container. Then, we could mix the slips of paper and draw out a number. This is essentially what has been done when a random number table is constructed. Such a table uses numbers of one, two, three, four or more digits, and a computer picks a number at random. These numbers are then recorded on a table, such as Table 4-2.

Table 4-2 shows a list of 210 randomly selected numbers. Let us say that we wanted to select a sample of 30 people from a list of 1000. First, we would number everyone on the list from 1 to 1000. Now, we might decide which number to choose as the start of our sample. Assume we close our eyes and put our pencil down upon a number, say 679, the third number in column 1. Now, assume that we continue reading down this column from this point on and then start at the top of the next column. We discard numbers that are too large for our list (that is, greater than 1000). (We could just as easily read across the rows. Any procedure is acceptable as long as we follow it consistently.)

Now, let us pick 30 numbers and underline them. In the first column, we choose 679, 351, 856, 99, 435, 697, 771, 538, 471, 27; in the second column, 21, 347, 527, discard 27 (since we selected it previously), 433, 924, 790, 431, 510, 81; in the third column, 93, 667, 26, 200, 87, 24, 786, 738, 100, 636, 137. We now look up these numbers on our numbered list and interview the appropriate persons.

You may wonder at this point why you can't make up numbers from your head. Tests have shown that people have a bias toward certain numbers and tend to keep repeating them. Thus, a computer-generated random number table ensures that each number has an equal chance of being chosen. Many hand calculators nowadays have random number programs that can be used to generate a set of random numbers.

To use the random number table for our study of university students, we number each person on the list of students and then, if we need a sample of 100, for example, we choose 100 random numbers from a table (See Table 4-2). This is *simple random sampling*. Another method consists of starting with a random number from the random number table and counting down to this number on our list. Then, if the list consists of 5000 names and we want a sample of 100, we chose every 50th name after the random start. This is called *systematic random sampling*. If the list follows some numerical pattern, this latter method can't be used. An example of this error was a sample drawn from a list of army platoons. For each platoon, the leader was listed first, then the two sergeants, and then the men in the companies. Since there are 40 men in a platoon, if one chooses every 43d man and had started with the leader, everyone in the sample would be a platoon leader!

Another random sampling technique is called *stratified random sampling*, in which we divide our population into groups and take a selected sample size in each of the groups. This technique is used for two reasons: (1) it can lead to reduced sampling error; and (2) it ensures a large enough sample in each stratum (class) for the study of the particular strata. For example, if one wanted to study freshmen, sophomores, juniors, and seniors, instead of picking a sample of 100 from the entire directory, it might be safer to list all the seniors and randomly select 25 from the list. Freshmen, sophomores, and juniors could be picked in a similar manner. A number proportionate to the size of each group in the population could be chosen. However, let us say one group is a small proportion of the population and yet one would like to study the group intensively. Then, it is possible to oversample, that is, to take a disproportionately large sample from this group.

Assume that we have estimates that minority people constitute approximately 15% of the U.S. population. If we were to take a sample of 500 people throughout the country, this would mean that we would have approximately 75 minority people to study. Perhaps we would like a larger group of minority people in our sample so that we could make an extensive study of their shopping habits. We can divide our population to be sampled into two groups (strata) and choose 250 whites and 250 minority people. Now, if average income was $15,000 for whites and $10,000 for minority people, we could *not* add the two together directly to find national average income. Instead, we can weight each by its proportion in the population and sum them:

$$\bar{X} = 15{,}000(.85) + 10{,}000(.15) = \bar{X} = \$14{,}250$$

Another technique used in sampling is *clustering*. Thus far we have been discussing the selection of a sample from a list. Often a list doesn't exist. For example, to study residents of a particular area of a city, telephone directories may be inadequate since some residents have unlisted numbers or do not own a telephone. It is common in these situations to use *area sampling*. Census tracts showing all the blocks and the number of residences on each block are available for most parts of the United States, particularly for the Standard Metropolitan Statistical Areas. (See Cases 2-1 and 4-2.)

Now, since all the residences can be numbered, a random sampling technique can be used to choose 100 homes. These homes may even be stratified and chosen separately for high-, middle- and low-income groups. If 100 homes are chosen at random, however, they may be scattered throughout the city. This makes it very expensive to do the interviewing. It is possible to group interviews closer together by choosing several census tracts and taking several interviews in a particular geographical area, for example, the same block. This is called *clustering* groups of sample elements selected together. Generally, while stratification may reduce sampling error, clustering tends to decrease costs and increase sampling error for the same size sample, because people who live close together are more likely to be similar than others. Chapter 5 discusses stratification and clustering in more detail. Today, samples for the major government agencies and university research studies, as well as marketing research, use a combination of clustering and stratification to control cost and error and to provide adequate size groups for intensive study.

Nonprobability Samples

These samples do not rely on the laws of probability for selection, but depend on the judgment of interviewers or their supervisors.

1 *Convenience samples* consist of studies of people who happen to be available or who call in their results.

For example, let us say you proposed on a TV program that tuition at the state university be reduced. If the program were open for public reaction, no doubt groups of college students would respond in the affirmative. Yet even if 10,000 people responded, we are not sure this represents the feelings of the public since only interested people will call.

2 *Quota samples* attempt to ensure that the sample represents the characteristics of the population. For example, if we knew that 53% of the population were female, that 20% were more than 65 years old, and that 50% owned homes, then we might instruct an interviewer that in a sample of 100, 53 must be women, 20 must be older than 65, and 50 must own their home.

There are two big problems here. Since the interviewer is free to select anyone who meets these specifications, he or she may choose in a nonrandom fashion. It is easier to interview the retired, the sick, unemployed people, and mothers at home with their children because these people are most likely to be at home. Everyone doesn't have an equal chance of selection. Furthermore, if an interviewer is told to take one house per block he or she might be more likely to pick the best-looking house or one without a dog; thus, everyone doesn't have an equal chance of selection. We cannot make good estimates of sampling error because we haven't used a random sampling procedure.

Secondly, perhaps the sample is representative in terms of age, sex, and home ownership, but not representative of different income groups since the interviewer was not advised to use this criterion for respondent selection. Furthermore, if the original estimates of the population subgroups are wrong or out of date (for example, if 60% of people really own homes), the quotas will not accurately reflect the characteristics of the current population.

3 *Judgment samples,* selected by the personal judgment of the sampler, are cheaper than probability samples. It is sometimes stated that these may be more accurate for very small scale surveys, but they provide no way to estimate sampling error. A company may try out a new product in a specific city because they feel that this city is representative of an area. Interviewers may be asked to study "typical" students or business persons. Different interviewers may vary in what they consider to be typical, and it is not clear that everyone in the population has an equal chance of being chosen. Results from these nonprobability samples generally should not be analyzed using statistical techniques, since probabilities of selection aren't known.

CENTRAL LIMIT THEOREM

4-5

Now that we have discussed some of the problems in choosing a sample, we should look into the mathematical theory that enables us to use a sample to make an estimate for the population. The cornerstone of all sampling theory is the *Central Limit Theorem.* The theorem states that if we take the average or mean of each of many samples of sufficient size from a given population, then the mean of these samples' means approaches the population mean. Also, the sample means are *normally* distributed around the population mean. This tells us that if we have sufficiently large samples, even though the original population is not normally distributed, the sample means will be normally distributed. For most population distributions, sample means are normally distributed and we can use areas under the normal curve to test whether these samples can be used to make reasonable estimates of population means. Let us express this in terms of a set of diagrams (see Figure 4-1).

In Figure 4-1(*a*), we note that the population distribution is skewed to the right. In Figure 4-1(*b*), the distribution of sample means is normally distributed with a *much smaller range* (5-ft 2-in to 5-ft 10-in) than the population range (4-ft 8-in to

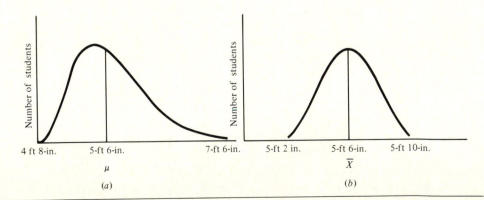

FIGURE **4-1**

(*a*) Original population distribution of heights of all college entrants at Eastern State College in 1980. (*b*) Distribution of means of *samples* (size of 50) of heights of college entrants at Eastern State College.

7-ft 6-in). Figure 4-1(*b*) is the *distribution of sample means* so that each point is an *average* of 50 heights. Even if one selects a 4-ft 8-in person for the sample, this will probably be counterbalanced by the heights of the other 49 people in the sample.

Since the sample means are normally distributed, we can use normal table probabilities (*z* values) to determine the likelihood of obtaining sample means of a given size from a population with given characteristics. However, to use this table, we must have some idea of the variation of sample means. What affects variation? In Figure 4-2, we can see that means of samples from the group in the chart on the left, which is the original population in Figure 4-1(*a*) (Eastern State College), probably will vary more than those from the population in Figure 4-2(*b*) (Northern State University). Eastern State has a larger standard deviation than Northern State. The distribution of sample means depends *directly* on the *standard deviation,* or the variance of the population from which these means are derived.

Secondly, if we take a very small size sample (say, 2 people), we could get a mean of 4-ft 8-in or 7-ft 6-in from the Eastern State population. However, if the sample size is increased to 50, we are more likely to get a scattering of high and low values in each sample, and the sample mean will be closer to the population mean. The larger the sample size, the closer the sample means. Thus, the variation in sample means is *inversely* related to sample size.

To review briefly, let us look at three diagrams. In Figure 4-2, we see the height distribution of the two *populations:* Eastern State College and Northern State University. Neither distribution is normal; they are both skewed to the right. The standard deviation for Northern State is smaller than for Eastern. In Figure 4-3, we plot the results of *one sample of 50* from each of the two populations. Thus, we plot each of the 50 values for a sample from both Eastern and Northern. Typical plots might look like Figure 4-3. Since the variation in population values for Eastern State is greater than for Northern State, the sample values are more likely to be "spread out" for Eastern State.

Now, if we take samples of 100, 200, and 500 from each group and plot their means, we see that the means are normally distributed, that the width of the distribution decreases as sample size increases, and that the width of the sample mean distributions is larger for Eastern State, whose population has a larger standard

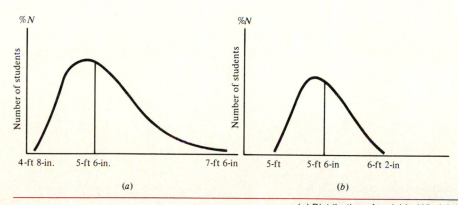

(*a*)   (*b*)   FIGURE **4-2**

(*a*) Distribution of variable *X* (height) in the population at Eastern State College. (*b*) Distribution of variable *X* (height) in the population at Northern State University.

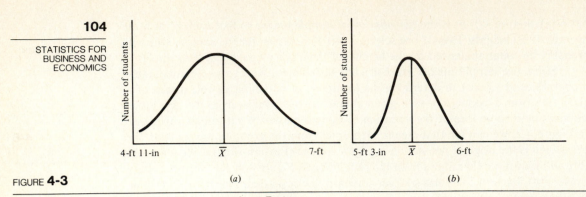

FIGURE **4-3**

(a)

(a) Distribution of variable X (height) in a sample at Eastern
State College. (b) Distribution of variable X (height) in a sample
at Northern State University.

deviation. Note that each curve on these graphs is obtained by finding the means for
many samples of a given size and plotting them.

Putting these two factors together we arrive at the *standard error of the mean,*
the standard deviation of sample means

$$\sigma_{\bar{x}} = \frac{\sigma}{\sqrt{n}} \tag{4-1}$$

where σ is the standard deviation in the original population and n is the sample size.
This standard error of the mean is the standard deviation of the means of samples
which are taken from the population.

Similarly, assume we are sampling to estimate a proportion. For example, do
55% of consumers like the blue dandruff shampoo? We will assume, provided that
we use a large enough sample, that because of the Central Limit Theorem, sample
proportions are normally distributed around the population proportion. The standard
deviation of sample proportions is called the *standard error of a proportion* and is
given by the formula

$$\sigma_{\bar{p}} = \sqrt{\frac{pq}{n}} \tag{4-2}[1]$$

[1]This is really the same as Equation 4-1 if the reader realizes that proportionate variation is pq, and
thus its standard deviation is $\sqrt{pq}$.

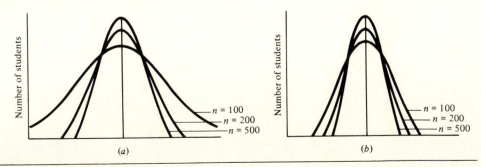

FIGURE **4-4**

(a)

(b)

Distribution of $\bar{X}$ for three sample sizes: (a) Eastern State College, (b) Northern State University.

From these two formulas we can compute the sample size needed for a given level of accuracy and confidence limits for many types of probability samples. In Equations 4-1 and 4-2 note that the use of the bar in the subscripts $\sigma_{\bar{x}}$ and $\sigma_{\bar{p}}$ denotes that we are discussing sample means and proportions.

CONFIDENCE INTERVALS

If we have chosen a good sample and have calculated the mean or a proportion from this sample for the effect we wish to study, we may offer this estimate to the public or a company as an estimate for the population mean or proportion. This is called a *point estimate*. The only problem is that we offer evidence from one sample about the nature of the population, and the reader has no idea how reliable this estimate is. Another sample will produce a different result.

Reliability depends on sample size n and the amount of variability in the original population σ. Thus, we could offer the mean and the *standard error of the mean* $\sigma_{\bar{x}} = \sigma/\sqrt{n}$. (Remember that when we discussed the Central Limit Theorem we said that if the sample size were sufficiently large, the sample means would be normally distributed and their standard error would be $\sigma_{\bar{x}} = \sigma/\sqrt{n}$.) Even more helpful would be a combination of the estimate, the standard error of the estimate and some notion of the probability of being correct. This information can all be combined in what is called a *confidence interval*.

Since sample means are normally distributed, we can use normal curve probabilities to describe our estimates. For a 95% confidence interval, we would take our estimate of the mean ($\bar{X}$) and add 1.96 standard errors $\sigma_{\bar{x}}$, because in the normal distribution 95% of the area under the curve is within ± 1.96 standard deviations of the mean. Similarly, if we wanted a 90% confidence interval, we would take our sample mean ± 1.65 standard errors.

$$\bar{X} \pm 1.96\sigma_{\bar{x}} = 95\% \text{ confidence interval}$$

$$\bar{X} \pm 1.65\sigma_{\bar{x}} = 90\% \text{ confidence interval}$$

Let us reflect for a moment on the interpretation of the confidence interval. Assume we have a population with mean μ. In Figure 4-5, we take 4 samples from this population, compute the means, and find the 95% confidence intervals for each. Then, we would expect that 95 out of 100 of these intervals will include the population mean. We see in Figure 4-5 that 3 out of the 4 sample intervals (1, 3, 4) include the population mean. Only sample interval 2 does not encompass the population mean.

Suppose your sample mean is $\bar{X} = 50$, your population standard deviation is $\sigma = 10$, and your sample size is 100 people. Find the 99%, 98%, 95%, and 90% confidence intervals for the mean.

INTERVALS FORMED IN
THIS WAY WILL INCLUDE:

Confidence interval $= \bar{X} \pm Z\,\sigma_{\bar{x}}$

| 99% confidence interval | $50 \pm 2.58 \dfrac{10}{\sqrt{100}}$ ($z = 2.58$) | $= 50 \pm 2.58(1)$ $= 47.42$ to 52.58 | The population mean 99% of the time |

98%	$50 \pm 2.33 \dfrac{10}{\sqrt{100}} = 50 \pm 2.33(1)$ $= 47.67$ to 52.33	The population mean 98% of the time
95%	$50 \pm 1.96 \dfrac{10}{\sqrt{100}} = 50 \pm 1.96(1)$ $= 48.04$ to 51.96	The population mean 95% of the time
90%	$50 \pm 1.65 \dfrac{10}{\sqrt{100}} = 50 \pm 1.65(1)$ $= 48.35$ to 51.65	The population mean 90% of the time

We can see that as the level of confidence rises, the width of the confidence interval increases. This has been referred to as "knowing more and more about less and less." In any event, the confidence interval is preferable to the point estimate, since it allows the reader to speculate on how trustworthy an estimate of the population characteristic from a sample actually is.

Let us now see how a confidence interval can give a sample-based estimate of a population mean. This interval gives a range of values within which we expect to find the population mean. The width of the range depends on the amount of variation in the original population σ, and is inversely related to the square root of the sample size. The larger the sample, the smaller the confidence interval.

Example 4-1 A study of a sample of 400 bank accounts is made to estimate the average size of a bank account. The sample mean is calculated to be $7542. From previous studies of bank accounts, it is known that the standard deviation is $1020. Set up a 95% confidence estimate for the mean size of bank accounts.

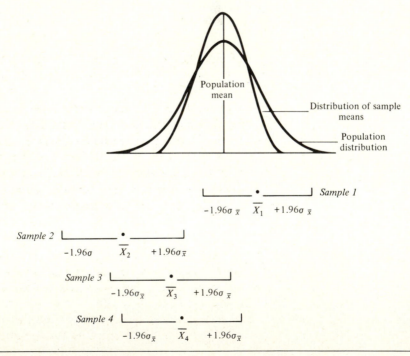

FIGURE **4-5**

Comparison of confidence intervals and population mean.

Using the z table, if we go 1.96 standard errors to the right and left of the mean, we include 95% of the observations. Our confidence interval is

$$\bar{X} \pm z\sigma_{\bar{x}} = \$7542 \pm 1.96 \frac{(1020)}{\sqrt{400}}$$

$$= \$7442.04 \text{ to } \$7641.96$$

Thus, we estimate that the true value of the population mean is between these two numbers.

CONFIDENCE INTERVALS WHEN σ IS NOT KNOWN

4-7

In previous examples, we assumed knowledge of the standard deviation of the population when we estimated the standard error of the mean. Unless we have repeatedly studied the same population, it is quite unlikely that we would know the standard deviation of the population, especially if this were the population for which we were trying to estimate a mean or a proportion.

In this case, we can estimate the population σ by taking the standard deviation of the items in the sample using Equation 4-3. We used this equation in Chapter 2 to find the standard deviation for sample data.

$$s = \sqrt{\frac{\Sigma(X - \bar{X})^2}{n - 1}} \qquad (4\text{-}3)$$

The *standard deviation of the sample* measures the deviation of each item in the sample around the sample mean. Remember that $\sigma_{\bar{x}}$, *the standard error of the mean,* shows the *variation of sample means* around the population mean; it measures how wrong or right a given sample might be. Now, compute the standard error of the mean $s_{\bar{x}}$ using s.

$$s_{\bar{x}} = \frac{s}{\sqrt{n}} \qquad (4\text{-}4)$$

Let us try an example where we do not know the population σ. If the sample is small (generally, we define small as less than 30) and the population is normally distributed, we use the t table (see Chapter 5); with a larger sample, we generally use the z table.

Example 4-2 An ice cream factory wishes to know the average number of children per block in a given neighborhood. A sample of 64 blocks within the neighborhood indicates that the average number of children is 50. When the standard deviation is estimated for these 64 blocks, it is found to be $s = (8)$, using Equation 4-3. Calculate a 90% confidence interval for the number of children.

For a 90% confidence interval, we must look up an area of .4500 in the z table (divide .90 by 2, as the z table shows area on one side of the mean); this gives us a z value of 1.65. Now use s in place of σ to calculate s .

$$s_{\bar{x}} = \frac{s}{\sqrt{n}} = \frac{8}{8} = 1$$

$$\bar{X} \pm z\, s_{\bar{x}} = 50 \pm 1.65\, \frac{8}{\sqrt{64}}$$

48.35 to 51.65

Now, we have estimated with 90% confidence that the average number of children per block falls between 48.35 and 51.65.

Problems

1 A simple random sample of 144 electronic calculators was taken to determine the length of time a full charge would last if the calculator was left on and no operation was performed. The results of the tests on the sample were:

$$\bar{X} = 14 \text{ hours}$$

$$s = 1 \text{ hour}$$

Estimate with a 96% confidence interval the mean length of time a calculator will last on a full charge.

2 In a management study of workers' wages, a simple random sample of 196 employees was taken from a production line workforce. The mean of the sample was found to be $10,000; the standard deviation, $760. Determine a 95% confidence interval for the workforce.

3 Assume that 220 tennis balls were selected at random from a production run. These balls were found to have a mean life of 26 games and a standard deviation of 4 games. Obtain a 95% confidence interval.

CONFIDENCE INTERVALS FOR A PROPORTION

4-8

The Central Limit Theorem can also be applied to the distribution of sample proportions. As we stated on p. 104, sample proportions are normally distributed around the population proportion when n is sufficiently large. The standard deviation of sample proportions is called the *standard error of a proportion* and is measured by the formula

$$\sigma_{\bar{p}} = \sqrt{\frac{pq}{n}}$$

Now, let us obtain confidence intervals for proportions.

EXAMPLE 4-3 Assume that Balfour Polls wants to find out what percent of the population will vote for the Republican candidate. A sample of 100 voters reveals that 55 will vote Republican. Should we predict that the Republican candidate will win (assuming that there are just two parties)?

If Balfour wishes to have a 95.5% confidence interval that the Republican will win, we can set up their interval as $\bar{p} \pm zs_{\bar{p}}$ First, compute $\bar{p}$. The ratio of Republicans to total voters is 55/100; the sample proportion, $\bar{p}$ = .55. Now, one cannot find $\sigma_{\bar{p}}$ since we don't know the population proportion voting for the Republican; in fact, this is what one is trying to estimate. Therefore, use $\bar{p}$, the estimate of p from the sample, to calculate $s_{\bar{p}}$:

$$s_{\bar{p}} = \sqrt{\frac{\overline{pq}}{n}} \qquad (4\text{-}5)$$

The 95.5% confidence interval uses a z value of 2.0. Thus,

$$s_p = \sqrt{\frac{(.55)(.45)}{100}} = .0497; \ \bar{p} \pm zs_{\bar{p}} = .55 \pm 2(.0497)$$

$$= .4506 \text{ to } .6494$$

Thus, Balfour estimates that between 45% and 65% of the population will vote for the Republican candidate. Since there is the possibility that 45% may vote for the Republican candidate, giving the Democrat the win, it would be very risky for Balfour Polls to predict a Republican victory. Essentially, this is what happened to the pollsters on the eve of the 1976 presidential election. Many firms said the results "were within sampling error" and refused to offer a prediction. In order to make a prediction of victory, the confidence interval must be decreased in size. The best way to do this would be to increase the sample size. How much should the sample size be increased? In the next section, we discuss how to calculate sample size so that we can estimate within specified bounds and maintain a given level of confidence.

Problems

1 A study of a sample of 100 customers at the university bookstore indicated that 40% preferred new books while 60% wanted used ones.

(*a*) Estimate the standard error of a proportion for those favoring new books. What is the standard error of a proportion for those favoring old books?

(*b*) Construct a 98% confidence interval for the proportion of the population favoring new books.

(*c*) Construct a 95% confidence interval for the proportion of the population favoring new books.

2 A fancy food store wants to be sure that they will not run out of their customers' favorite wine. A survey of 100 customers indicates that 20% of the customers buy this wine. Next week the store expects 4000 customers to shop for their goods. Would they be safe in stocking 800 bottles of this wine? (What percent of the time would they be unable to serve customers?) What stock policy would you recommend so that there would be only 3 chances in 100 that they run out of wine?

3 A random sample of 81 shipments from Puerto Rico to New York on steamers shows that there is an average gross weight of 48,000 pounds, with a standard deviation of 3600 pounds.

(*a*) Find a 95% confidence interval for the average gross weight of all shipments by steamer from Puerto Rico to New York.

(*b*) Find a 90% confidence interval for these shipments.

4   A study of 49 overdue accounts at a physician's office indicates that the average amount outstanding is $58.00, with a standard deviation of $3.20.

(*a*)   Construct a 99% confidence interval for average amount due.

(*b*)   What can we say with a probability of .99 about the possible size of our error if we estimate this average as $58.00?

SAMPLE SIZE

4-9

Let us suppose that we wish to estimate the mean height of a population, and want to have a 95% confidence interval that is no wider than ± 2 inches. Assume we know from previous studies that the standard deviation for height is 6 inches. What size sample should we take?

Let us put this information in terms of an equation. We want our confidence interval to be no wider than 2 inches to the right and the left of the mean; thus, the total width of the confidence interval will be 4 inches.

$$(1.96)\,\frac{\sigma}{\sqrt{n}} = \pm 2 \qquad \text{confidence interval desired on each side of the mean}$$

This means that 1.96 standard errors (needed for 95% confidence; $z = 1.96$) must equal 2. Now substitute 6 for σ and solve for n.

$$(1.96)\,\frac{(6)}{\sqrt{n}} = 2$$

$$\frac{(1.96)(6)}{2} = \sqrt{n}$$

$$\frac{(1.96)^2(6)^2}{2^2} = n \qquad \text{squaring both sides of the equation}$$

$$\underset{z^2}{}\quad\underset{\sigma^2}{}$$

$$\underset{d^2}{\frac{(3.84)(36)}{(4)}} = 34.57 \text{ (or 35)} \qquad \text{always round } up \text{ as we can't take .56 of a person}$$

If we name each item—z is the number of standard errors needed for a given level of confidence, σ is the standard deviation of the original population, and d is the precision (one-half the desired width of the confidence interval)—the formula for sample size to estimate a mean is

$$n = \frac{z^2\sigma^2}{d^2} \tag{4-6}$$

Let us try an example to compute sample size for the estimation of a mean. Note that we can specify the levels of z and d, but σ must be known before taking the sample.

EXAMPLE 4-4   A social service agency wants to study food stamp recipients among its clients to estimate the average amount of food stamps received per month. They want to estimate the average with 95.5% confidence and within ±$3.

Previous food stamp studies show that the standard deviation is $20. How big a sample should they choose?

$$z = 2.00$$

$$d = 3.00$$

$$\sigma = 20$$

$$n = \frac{z^2\sigma^2}{d^2} = \frac{4(400)}{9} = \frac{1600}{9} = 177.8$$

$$n = 178$$

For the estimation of a proportion, the formula to compute sample size is

$$n = \frac{z^2pq}{d^2} \qquad (4\text{-}7)$$

EXAMPLE 4-5 Let us assume that we wish to estimate the vote for a particular candidate within ±2% (precision of 2%) with a 95% confidence level, and have reason to think that the vote will be very close (50/50). This could be the election case that we discussed previously. Then, substituting in Equation (4-7), we have

$$n = \frac{(1.96)^2(.5)(.5)}{(.02)^2}$$

$$n = \frac{(3.84)(.25)}{.0004} = 2400$$

If we wish to be even more precise, or correct within ±1%, then

$$n = \frac{(1.96)^2(.5)(.5)}{(.01)^2} = \frac{3.84(.25)}{.0001} = 9600$$

We can see that we must have a sample of almost 10,000 people if we desire to make a very precise (±1%) prediction for closely contested elections. This is a very large, expensive sample to obtain at the last minute on the eve of an election. Most commercial pollsters rely on samples of 1000. (This is why many forecasters refused to make predictions on the eve of the 1976 presidential election. They claimed that they could make no prediction because the differences were "within sampling error.") The results of their surveys may have shown a sample proportion $\bar{p} = 51\%$ for one candidate, but since the sampling error was about .016, with a sample of 1000, a 95% confidence interval for the vote for president would go from .479 to .541; thus, one could not be certain of victory if a sample survey of 1000 respondents found $\bar{p} = .51$.

   If one does not know the proportion in the population p, the most conservative estimate of sample size assumes that p is .5, since pq is a maximum for this value. (Do you see why?) If we are sure, for example, that the population proportion is near .9, we can take a smaller sample. Let us assume that we want to estimate the proportion of people who prefer a cinnamon-flavored cereal to the plain variety. If we assume 50/50 and want to have a 95.5% confidence interval of no more than $\pm.02$, our sample size is

$$n = \frac{z^2 pq}{d^2}$$

$$n = \frac{4(.5)(.5)}{(.02)^2} = \frac{1}{.0004} = 2500$$

We need 2500 subjects. If we think our proportion is near .9,

$$n = \frac{4(.9)(.1)}{(.02)^2} = 900$$

Thus, for estimates near 50/50, you need a much larger sample for a given level of accuracy. Once again, if one is not sure of the value of the population proportion, the safest course is to assume that $p = .5$. It is the largest estimate that can be made.

In Chapter 5, we study confidence intervals for small samples and the relation of sample size and population size. In addition, we study stratified and clustered sampling in greater depth.

Problems

1 A local yogurt store wants to estimate the mean number of ounces that their machine uses to fill each carton. It is known from past experience that the standard deviation is approximately 0.4 ounces. How large a sample should be taken to estimate with 95% confidence the mean fill within $\pm.1$ ounces?

2 A large company wishes to estimate the mean words per minute (wpm) that the secretarial staff can type. Past employment records indicate that the standard deviation of typing skills is 12 wpm. How many secretaries should be tested to estimate with 95.5% confidence the mean skill within ± 5 wpm?

3 The New York Subway, a submarine sandwich shop, wants to estimate the mean thickness of meat from their slicing machine. From past experience, the standard deviation is known to be .02 inches. How many slices should they check to be 95% confident that the mean thickness is within $\pm.005$ inches?

4 Assume you are doing a research project for a statistics class, in which you wish to take a poll of the students at your university to determine the percentage who have a car at school. You know from past experience that somewhere between 35 and 40 percent of the student body have cars. Estimate how many students should be polled to obtain a 95.5% confidence interval that estimates the percentage having cars within ± 4 percentage points.

5 In making plans for the number of classes to hold for summer school, an admissions administrator wishes to take a sample to see what proportion of the student body stays for the summer session. Past records indicate that no more than 15% of the students stay for summer school. What size sample should be taken for him to be 95% confident that his estimate is within ± 2 percentage points of the true proportion?

1 Sampling can be used to obtain a wide variety of information. It may save *time* and *money* and *improve accuracy*.

2 Common sample survey methods employ *mail questionnaires, telephone interviews,* or *personal interviews*. Comparison of cost, time, accuracy, response rate, and interviewer rules are summarized in Table 4-1.

3 Sample designs include probability samples where a *frame* is defined and each sample in the *population* has an equal chance of being chosen. *Simple random sampling* usually employs random numbers that are assigned to different members of the population. *Systematic random sampling* uses a random start and then draws *sample units* from the population at set intervals. Stratified random sampling involves dividing the population into relevant groups, or *strata,* and choosing a set number within each strata. *Cluster samples,* in which a number of interviews are taken within a given area, lower costs but tend to increase sampling error.

4 Nonprobability samples include *convenience samples, quota samples,* and *judgment samples*.

5 Sampling theory is based on the *Central Limit Theorem,* which states that if repeated samples of sufficiently large size are taken from a population, the sample means will be *normally distributed* about the population mean. The standard deviation of these sample means, called the *standard error of the mean,* is equal to

$$\sigma_{\bar{x}} = \frac{\sigma}{\sqrt{n}}$$

6 Similarly, the Central Limit Theorem states that if samples of sufficiently large size are taken to estimate a *proportion,* the mean of the proportions will approach the population proportion and the sample proportions will be normally distributed around the population proportion. The standard deviation of the population proportion, called the *standard error of the proportion,* is given by

$$\sigma_{\bar{p}} = \sqrt{\frac{pq}{n}}$$

7 Using samples, estimates of a mean or a proportion can be made as *point* estimates or *confidence intervals*. The confidence interval offers a level of confidence and a notion of the sampling error. Thus, an interval for the mean equals

$$\bar{X} \pm z\sigma_{\bar{x}}$$

An interval for a proportion equals

$$\bar{p} \pm z\sigma_{\bar{p}}$$

8 If σ is not known, an estimate may be used by taking the standard deviation of the sample itself.

$$s = \sqrt{\frac{\Sigma(x - \overline{x})^2}{n - 1}}$$

9 The sample size required to estimate a mean with specified precision is given by the formula

$$n = \frac{z^2\sigma^2}{d^2}$$

where d is one-half the width of the total confidence interval desired; that is, the total interval is $\pm d$.

10 The sample size to estimate a proportion is given by the formula

$$n = \frac{z^2pq}{d^2}$$

d is defined previously.

BIBLIOGRAPHY

4-11

Cochran, William G.: *Sampling Techniques,* 2d ed. New York: Wiley, 1958.

Groves, Robert M., and Robert L. Kahn: *Surveys by Telephone.* New York: Academic Press, 1979. Comparison of telephone and personal interview surveys.

Mendenhall, Ott Schaeffer: *Elementary Survey Sampling.* Belmont, Calif.: Wadsworth, 1971. Simple, thorough discussion of sampling theory.

Slonem, Mark: *Sampling in a Nutshell.* New York: Simon and Schuster, 1960. Simple, humorous discussion of sampling in this paperback.

Stephan, Frederick F., and Philip McCarthy: *Sampling Opinions—An Analysis of Survey Procedures.* New York: Wiley, 1958.

Stuart, Alan: *Basic Ideas of Scientific Sampling.* London: Griffen, 1964. Simple, concise discussion of simple random sampling and stratified sampling in this paperback.

CASES

4-12

Case 4-1 Southern California Savings Bank

Lee Breeden, vice president for public relations of the Southern California Savings Bank, had been entrusted with the job of attracting new accounts to the bank. The bank was first established in downtown Los Angeles in 1946, and this branch had 27,495 accounts in spring, 1978. Starting in 1957, new branches were established throughout the Los Angeles area. None of the new branches had as many accounts as the oldest one, and Breeden was interested in finding ways to attract newer, younger depositors to the 17 remaining branches.

After some reflection and in consultation with a marketing research firm, she decided to survey the bank's customers and to specifically study the characteristics and feelings of the newer account holders. She drew up a questionnaire to study the bank's image and the services its customers desired to find out how customers felt about bank services and if newer customers were banking close to home or close to work. The latter information would help the bank decide where to locate new branches.

The questionnaire also contained a number of questions about demographic and financial factors. For example, it asked average balance at Southern California Savings Bank, income, family size, age, marital status, the number of people in the household, number of employed adults, and education level.

Using the computer files and a random sampling procedure, mail questionnaires were sent to 8000 of the 86,272 accounts. Of these 8000 questionnaires, 2524 questionnaires were returned. This was a response rate of 32% (2524/8000), which is quite good for a mail survey. The total accounts and questionnaires returned for each of the branches are shown in Table 1 (on p. 116). Forty-three percent of the respondents said they had more than one account with Southern California Savings Bank.

Ms. Breeden realized that there is a certain amount of selectivity among the people who return mail questionnaires. Often, people who are very angry or very pleased with the service are more likely to respond. Thus, even though the response rate is high, the final response may not be a representative sample of the original population. Before using her results, she decided to check for representativeness.

1 How could she check for representativeness? Perform a check of this sort and discuss your results.

2 The planning analyst of the bank found that the average (mean) account size was $4930 in 1975 and $5704 in 1978, but the median *average balance* for respondents to the questionnaire was $10,984. It seemed to the analyst that there had been a very selective response to the mail questionnaire. Discuss.

3 Examine the data on the percentage of customers banking close to home and the services desired by each of the branches. What do your findings mean?

4 What recommendation would you give to the chairman of Southern California Savings Bank?

Case 4-2: Desegregation in Dallas

In 1964, when Congress passed the Civil Rights Act, 98% of black students in the South attended all-black or mostly black schools. As early as 1955, the first school desegregation case, *Albert Bell vs. Robert S. Rippy,* was filed in Dallas. In December 1956, Federal District Judge William H. Atwell, ruled against the plaintiff. He felt that the courts should not take note of the work of the social scientists. In 1957, this ruling was reversed by the Fifth Circuit Court of Appeals. Judge Atwell had ordered *complete* desegregation of all Dallas schools for the 1957–58 school year, but that order was found too drastic by the Fifth Circuit. In 1959, the school district was ordered to prepare a realistic desegregation plan within 30 days.

The plan submitted was a "stairstep plan" that maintained neighborhood zones and integrated the schools one grade per year beginning with the first grade. The plan to integrate the schools was begun in 1961; a plan to desegregate faculty was started in 1968. However, in October 1970, Eddie Tasby filed a suit in Federal District Court charging that the school district continued to maintain a dual school system through use of neighborhood assignment plans, choice of school building sites, and the staffing of teaching and administrative positions. On June 6, 1971,

TABLE 1

SOUTHERN CALIFORNIA SAVINGS BANK BRANCH DATA

(As of Feb. 28, 1978)

BRANCH CODE	OPENING DATE	BASED ON BANK DATA			% BANKING CLOSE TO HOME RATHER THAN CLOSE TO WORK	BASED ON SURVEY DATA, % DESIRING:		
		NUMBER OF ACCOUNTS	DOLLAR VOLUME	NUMBER OF RESPONDENTS FROM EACH BRANCH*		EVENING HOURS	SATURDAY HOURS	TRAVEL CLUB†
01	1946	27,495	$165,364,000	697	71%	15.6%	16.2%	19.4%
02	1956	9,383	44,471,000	249	90	29.0	11.6	16.1
03	1956	6,473	35,503,000	185	73	19.9	27.0	15.6
04	1956	8,429	42,736,000	195	85	26.7	28.9	14.1
05	1956	8,568	67,295,000	226	78	13.3	19.7	22.0
06	1964	6,778	48,024,000	199	82	19.2	17.8	14.4
07	1965	3,544	16,262,000	93	80	25.6	40.7	15.1
08	1966	2,622	11,166,000	65	79	27.8	40.7	7.4
09	1967	2,790	14,914,000	95	74	24.7	27.3	18.2
10	1971	2,341	11,397,000	61	70	29.2	41.7	25.0
11	1974	845	2,368,000	25	89	28.6	35.7	21.4
12	1974	1,037	3,723,000	34	88	36.0	44.0	20.0
13	1972	1,620	10,413,000	48	70	28.9	50.0	23.7
14	1973	1,429	7,710,000	48	74	29.7	51.4	10.8
15	1974	921	4,709,000	54	88	26.2	42.3	28.6
16	1976	655	2,101,000	26	93	44.4	52.3	22.2
17	1976	474	1,348,000	33	90	43.3	55.6	11.1
18	1976	868	2,499,000	41	92	35.9	56.4	17.9
		86,272	$492,003,000	2374				

*The total survey response was 2524, but 150 respondents didn't indicate at what branch they banked.
†In the travel club, the depositor saves specified amounts each week for trips, much like one would in a Christmas club.

Federal District Judge William Taylor returned a finding that "all vestiges of the dual school system still remain in Dallas." He instructed the School Board to eradicate the dual system. The case continued to be argued in circuit court and no decision was made until July 23, 1975, when the case was remanded to Judge Taylor. Judge Taylor asked the business leaders of Dallas to formulate a workable plan. He felt that a plan by influential business leaders would be most likely to gain acceptance. The Dallas Alliance—a business community service organization— devised a plan that eventually (March 10, 1976) was adopted by the court.

The plan provided for integration in grades 4–8 in four areas of the city. South Oak Cliff, a predominantly black community in the southern portion of the city, was excluded. Students in all other areas were bused to other schools to improve the black-white ratios. The desegregation plan also called for curriculum innovations; magnet schools offering special arts, business, science, or vocational programs at the junior high school and high school levels were also established and made available to all students to provide special academic and interest orientations. Minority ratios for teachers and administrators were also instituted.

In spring 1976 the Lichten Foundation for Human Rights, a group of concerned citizens, decided to institute a study to see how the predominantly black parents in South Oak Cliff, where there was no integration, felt about busing and integrated schools. Would they approve of busing to integrate schools? Would they approve of busing to magnet schools? Did they feel that their children had anything to gain by attending integrated schools? Were they satisfied with the schools their children were attending?

Four professors at a local university, representing the disciplines of sociology, psychology, education, and statistics, were asked to study these attitudes. They decided to take a sample of 300 parents of children in grades 4–8 in South Oak Cliff to find out what these parents felt. The number of students in each grade in the South Oak Cliff subdistrict was as follows:

GRADE	WHITES	BLACKS	MEXICAN-AMERICANS	TOTAL
4	19	1,908	46	1,973
5	10	1,999	39	2,048
6	15	2,129	40	2,184
7	24	2,328	35	2,387
8	16	2,278	34	2,328
	84	10,642	194	10,920

It was hoped that this sample of 300 families would yield 250 completed interviews, since not everyone contacted might agree to be interviewed.

The Dallas Independent School District at first agreed to provide lists of names and addresses of students who were attending the 15 schools in the area having classes in grades 4–8. The district had done extensive research in order to characterize the incomes, housing, deprivation index, parents' education, index of student mobility, dropout rate, attendance, and academic achievement in each of these 15 schools.

It was decided to use a two-stage sampling procedure. In stage 1, four representative schools would be chosen from the 15 schools in the district, using the academic and socioeconomic characteristics for each school provided by the research department of the school district. This stratification would ensure an adequate number of students in various socioeconomic classes, and would reduce interviewing cost since it would involve interviews in only four school areas. After the four schools were chosen, lists of students attending these schools would be obtained. The enrollment at each school would be calculated and a number proportionate to the enrollment would be chosen from each school's list in order to obtain 300 listings. For example,

SCHOOL	ENROLLMENT	NUMBER CHOSEN FROM LIST
A	900	$\frac{900}{2800} \cdot 300 = 96$
B	1000	$\frac{1000}{2800} \cdot 300 = 107$
C	500	$\frac{500}{2800} \cdot 300 = 54$
D	$\frac{400}{2800}$	$\frac{400}{2800} \cdot 300 = \frac{43}{300}$

This method would provide the names of 300 families who would be interviewed.

In July 1976, the Dallas Independent School District decided that it could not provide the sample from school district lists unless it had some control over the survey. The Lichten Foundation felt that the survey should be independent of the school district. A new sampling procedure was needed!

When lists are unobtainable, *area sampling* can be used. This is a procedure in which the ultimate sampling units are households. Every 10 years the U.S. Census Bureau maps and lists the census tracts used for the decennial census. A city is divided into tracts. A tract usually consists of a number of blocks and can contain up to 4000 households. The number of households on each block is listed, and other characteristics for the tracts, such as average income and housing conditions, are provided.

The South Oak Cliff district was composed of 17 tracts containing 30,445 households in the 1970 Census. A map of the area is shown in Figure 1, with Census tracts numbered; tract 87.01 is outlined in dark pencil. In Figure 2, we see a larger map of tract 87.01, where all the blocks are named and numbered. Using Census information (obtained from the documents section of larger libraries[1]), the block numbers corresponding to those on the map are listed in Table 1, column 1; the number of households per block is listed in column 2; and the cumulated sequence number is given in column 3. We can see that the households in this tract go from 1 to 1463. Block 211 seems to be an area with apartments, since there are 214 houses on this block.

It was decided that since there were 10,920 children in South Oak Cliff schools, about 30,445 residences in these tracts, and some households probably

---

[1]Most city and college libraries have Census reports for their city and state. Larger libraries have tract information for the United States. To purchase Census tract data, one can go to a federal government bookstore (usually in the Federal Building) or write to the Superintendent of Documents, U.S. Government Printing Office, Washington, D.C. 20402.

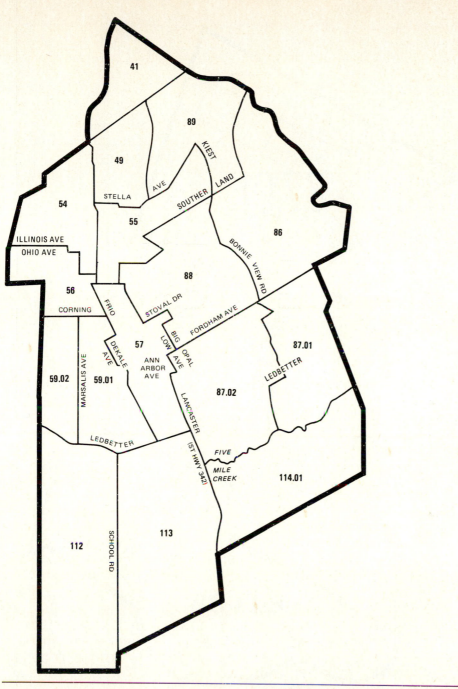

FIGURE **1**

Section of a map of Census tracts; area marked off is South
Oak Cliff.

had 2 children in grades 4–8, approximately 1 house in 4 would contain a child in
grades 4–8. It was hoped that a total of 250 interviews with parents would be
completed from these 1049 house numbers. If one house in 3.5 contained a child
in the proper grade, this would mean about 300 eligible households would be
located. Assuming that ⅙ wouldn't respond, this would give approximately 250

FIGURE **2**

Map of Census tract 87.01.

interviews. Using a program to generate random numbers, 1049 numbers from 1 through 30,449 were generated; these numbers were arranged in order of magnitude and then the corresponding house numbers were picked from the 30,449 houses in the tracts.

Let us look again at tract 87.01. If we consider that all the tracts contain a total of 30,449 housing units, the 1463 numbers in this tract fall between 16,033 and 17,495 (since this was not the first tract counted). Now, the computer converted these random numbers between 16,033 and 17,495 to a number in the tract. Thus, if the random number picked was 16,033, it was 1 in the tract. If the next random number picked was 16,079, it was 46 in the tract. Looking at Table 1, we see that 46 would be on block 102 in 87.01. Since we had already passed 5 houses by the end of block 101, this would be the 41st house on block 102. (See

TABLE 1

LISTING OF BLOCKS AND NUMBER OF HOUSEHOLD UNITS IN CENSUS TRACT 87.01

(1) BLOCK	(2) TOTAL NUMBER OF UNITS	(3) CUMULATED SEQUENCE NUMBER*
101	5	1–5
102	88	6–93
103	16	94–109
104	12	110–121
105	21	122–142
106	99	143–241
107	6	242–247
108	23	248–270
109	18	271–288
110	17	289–305
111	13	306–318
112	11	319–329
113	12	330–341
114	16	342–357
115	17	358–374
116	7	375–381
201	2	382–383
202	22	384–405
203	29	406–434
204	30	435–464
205	23	465–487
206	8	488–495
207	16	496–511
208	13	512–524
209	8	525–532
210	30	533–562
211	214	563–776
212	9	777–785
213	9	786–794
214	29	795–823
215	125	824–948
301	34	949–982
302	23	983–1005
303	19	1006–1024
304	39	1025–1063
305	31	1064–1094
306	30	1095–1124
307	26	1125–1150
308	21	1151–1171
309	17	1172–1188
310	106	1189–1294
312	35	1295–1329
313	42	1330–1371
314	36	1372–1407
315	39	1408–1446
317	17	1447–1463

*These 1463 housing units are actual numbers 16,033 to 17,495 in South Oak Cliff.

TABLE 2

CONVERSION OF RANDOM NUMBERS CHOSEN FOR THE TRACT TO
HOUSE NUMBERS IN TRACT 87.01

(1) NUMBER	(2) CONVERTED RANDOM NUMBER CHOSEN IN TRACT	(3) BLOCK NUMBER/ HOUSE NUMBER
1	1	101/1
2	46	102/41
3	51	102/46
4	58	102/53
5	118	104/9
6	139	105/18
7	166	106/24
8	180	106/38
9	202	106/60
10	205	106/63
11	207	106/65
12	277	109/7
13	305	110/17
14	323	112/5
15	325	112/7
16	438	204/4
17	452	204/18
18	466	205/2
19	526	209/2
20	568	211/7
21	614	211/52
22	615	211/53
23	621	211/59
24	625	211/63
25	664	211/102
26	669	211/107
27	685	211/122
28	730	211/168
29	756	211/194
30	839	215/16
31	855	215/32
32	872	215/49
33	933	215/110
34	948	215/125
35	984	302/2
36	1037	304/13
37	1057	304/33
38	1098	306/4
39	1137	307/13
40	1233	310/45
41	1241	310/53
42	1250	310/62
43	1251	310/63
44	1261	310/73
45	1290	310/102
46	1322	312/28
47	1351	313/22
48	1370	313/41

Table 2, column 3.) Thus, the first two units sampled are 1 and 46, which are house 1 on block 101 and house 41 on block 102, respectively.

We now show a magnified picture of blocks 101 and 102 to show how an interviewer chooses the appropriate housing unit. Look at the map on Figure 3. Household 1 is always in the southwest corner of the block; from there on, the

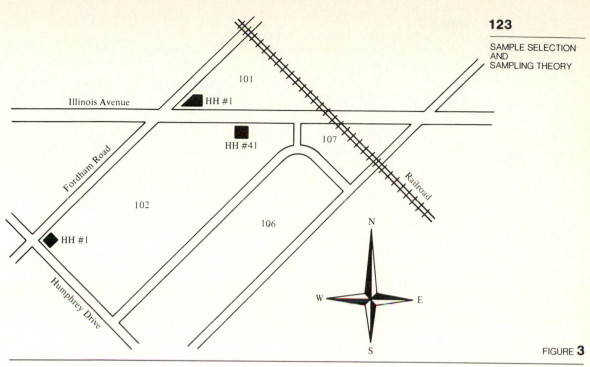

FIGURE **3**

Interviewers' selection diagram.

interviewer must number going clockwise around the block. Household 41 on block 102, on which there are 88 households, is probably somewhere midway around the block, depending on whether there are any apartment houses.

In Table 3, we summarize the number of households the Census records (column 2) and the number of households the random number generating process chose for each tract (column 3). In column 4, percent of households chosen in each tract is shown. As you can see, approximately 3–4% of each tract has been chosen, and overall 1049/30,445, or .034 of all houses, have been chosen. Thus, our sample is about equally representative of all tracts.

It was obvious to the group performing the study that this new sampling plan would be far more difficult to implement than the original plan, where the school district would have provided them with a listing of names and addresses of parents of students in the 4th to 8th grades in the Dallas Independent School District. On the other hand, this plan might have some advantages that the other sample didn't. The group, who were primarily novices in the use of survey research methods, also reflected upon the instructions it should provide its interviewers. The interviewers were university students who needed information on dress, manner of interviewing, and number of callbacks at a given address. The students would be paid $3 for a completed interview, compared to the $10–$15 per interview paid for professional interviewers.

Questions

1 Discuss the advantages and disadvantages of using a sample from the school lists of parents of students in the 4th to 8th grades in the Dallas Independent School District as compared to using Census listings of housing units in the

TABLE 3

LIST OF 17 CENSUS TRACTS IN SOUTH OAK CLIFF

(Number of households and number of households chosen in each tract)

(1) TRACT NUMBER	(2) NUMBER OF HOUSEHOLDS	(3) NUMBER OF CHOSEN HOUSEHOLDS	(4) PERCENT OF CHOSEN HOUSEHOLDS
41	1280	53	.041
49	2132	86	.040
54	2568	79	.031
55	1380	37	.027
56	1800	59	.033
57	2053	70	.034
59.01	2089	61	.029
59.02	987	37	.037
60.01	415	11	.027
86	1328	38	.029
87.01	1463	48	.033
87.02	3558	139	.039
88	3620	134	.037
89	2576	89	.035
112	996	34	.034
113	1143	35	.031
114.01	1057	39	.037
17 tracts	30,455 units	1049	Overall % = $\dfrac{1049}{30,445}$ = .034

area. Include such topics as cost, time required to find the correct families, and representativeness.

2 What kind of instructions would you write for the interviewers who will have to find the correct housing units? What topics should the instructions cover?

3 How would you formulate the questions on busing so that the answers will be unbiased and useful? Remember that time, distance, and availability are variables. Remember the education level of the interviewees.

4 *Optional:* (Use after Chapter 5 has been covered.) How might area sampling be made less costly?

OPERATIONAL SAMPLE DESIGN

5

5-1   FINITE POPULATION CORRECTION FACTOR
Problems

5-2   SAMPLE SIZE WITH FINITE CORRECTION FACTOR
Problems

5-3   SMALL SAMPLES
The t Distribution

5-4   SAMPLE SIZE WHEN σ IS UNKNOWN
Problems

5-5   STRATIFIED SAMPLING
Sample Allocation
Measuring Error
Determination of Sample Size for Different Allocation Methods

5-6   CLUSTERED SAMPLES
Measuring Error
Problems
Computer Problems

5-7   SUMMARY

5-8   BIBLIOGRAPHY

5-9   CASES
Case 5-1: Sampling to Determine Educators' Priorities
Case 5-2: PRIDEPAK Fertilizer

Chapter 4 outlined the fundamentals of sample selection and sampling theory. In this chapter we discuss some refinements that enable us to decrease sample size for a fixed level of precision, to work with data from small (limited) samples, and to formulate sample designs that lower cost and increase precision.

You probably noted at the end of Chapter 4, when we discussed estimates of sample size, that we used the population standard deviation, the desired confidence level, and the desired degree of precision as the criteria for our estimates. Perhaps you were thinking, "Shouldn't we take a smaller sample from a small population and a larger sample from a large population?" In other words, doesn't population size make a difference? The answer is that to some extent population size does matter.

FINITE POPULATION CORRECTION FACTOR

5-1 If we took a sample that was equal to the entire population, we would have no sampling error. If we took a sample from an infinite population, the sample size would never reach the population size. However, in most practical situations, our population is of finite size and our sample may constitute a large part of this population.

The really important issue to consider is the *relation between sample size and population size.* If a sample constitutes a large proportion of a population, it usually yields a better estimate of a population parameter than a sample that is a small proportion of the population. If N is population size and n is sample size, the ratio of sample size to population size n/N, called the *sampling fraction,* is the crucial factor. We can use the finite population correction factor cf, which is

$$cf = \sqrt{1 - \frac{n}{N}} \tag{5-1}$$

to reduce our standard errors and, hence, to reduce our confidence intervals or our sample size. We multiply this fraction by $\sigma_{\bar{X}}$ and z to find the reduced width of the confidence interval. The larger the sampling fraction n/N, the more we can reduce the confidence interval or the sample size. Before we illustrate this, let us compare correction factors for different values of n and N. For example, if we have a sample of 100 from a population of 1000, then

$$cf = \sqrt{1 - \frac{100}{1000}} = \sqrt{.9} = .95$$

If we take a sample of 500 from a population of 1000, then

$$cf = \sqrt{1 - \frac{500}{1000}} = \sqrt{.5} = .71$$

Our correction factor is .71.

This correction factor can be used to improve our interval estimates. Suppose we estimate the mean income of parents from a sample of 500 students in a school with a population of 1000 students, and we wish to make a 95% confidence interval. We know that the population standard deviation is $5000. Our sample mean $\bar{X}$ is $20,000.

We now show how the use of the finite correction factor can reduce the width of our confidence intervals.

Confidence interval without
finite population correction

$$\bar{X} \pm z\sigma_{\bar{x}}$$

$$\$20{,}000 \pm 1.96 \frac{5000}{\sqrt{500}}$$

$$20{,}000 \pm 1.96 \,(223.61)$$
$$20{,}000 \pm 438.28$$

Confidence interval with
finite population correction

$$\bar{X} \pm z\sigma_{\bar{x}}cf$$

$$\$20{,}000 + 1.96 \frac{5000}{\sqrt{500}} \sqrt{1 - \frac{500}{1000}} \qquad (5\text{-}2)$$

$$20{,}000 \pm 1.96 \,(223.61)(.71)$$
$$20{,}000 \pm 311.18$$

The correction factor can also be used to reduce the width of confidence intervals for a proportion. We multiply the correction factor by the z value and the standard error of the proportion $\sigma_{\bar{p}}$.

We can see that the width of the confidence interval in Equation 5-2 was reduced by approximately 29% [$(438.28 - 311.18)/438.28 = .29$] when the sample was one-half the size of the population.

If our sample is, or promises to be, a large proportion of the population, we may find that we can use a smaller sample size to obtain the same level of precision and degree of confidence. In the next section, we derive formulas for sample size that allow for the correction factor.

Problems

1 College President Trueblood was convinced that students at Canoli College were deficient in mathematics. He had the math department administer a test to 200 students, out of a total college population of 2000. The average grade on the test was 73. According to national statistics, the mean grade for this test is 78 and the standard deviation 2.

(*a*) Construct a 95% confidence interval for the mean grade for Canoli College students.

(*b*) Now, construct a 90% confidence interval.

(*c*) Does it look like Canoli College students are deficient?

2 In a town of 900 families, a poll asks 162 families to state their annual contribution to the church. The sample mean is $450. Previous studies indicate a population standard deviation of $160. Construct a 95% confidence interval for church contributions.

3 In the same town, a poll of 100 families reveals that 54 attend church regularly. Compute a 95% confidence interval for the percent of the population attending church regularly.

SAMPLE SIZE WITH FINITE CORRECTION FACTOR

5-2

Let us start by building a formula for a confidence interval where we want a certain level of precision d to be equal to the number z of standard errors $\sigma_{\bar{x}}$ needed for a given confidence level. First let

$$d = z\sigma_{\bar{x}}$$

We used this relationship to derive the formula for sample size in Chapter 4. Now we can include the finite correction factor on the right-hand side, which reduces the size of the confidence interval needed for a certain confidence level. Using simple algebra, we can now obtain a new sample size formula.[1]

$$n = \frac{z^2\sigma^2/d^2}{1 + (z^2\sigma^2/d^2N)} \tag{5-3}$$

Another shorter method could be used if we have already computed sample size (n_o) without using the correction factor. Recall that

$$n_o = \frac{z^2\sigma^2}{d^2}$$

where n_o = sample size without correction factor. Then substituting in Equation 5-3 above, since $[1 + (n_o/N)]$ is greater than 1, the sample size using the correction factor is always smaller than the sample size without the correction factor

$$n = \frac{n_o}{1 + (n_o/N)} \tag{5-4}$$

In similar fashion, the formula to obtain the sample size for a proportion using the correction factor is

$$n = \frac{(z^2pq/d^2)}{1 + (z^2pq/d^2N)} \tag{5-5}$$

---

[1] We derive this formula as follows:

$$d = z\sigma_{\bar{x}} \sqrt{1 - \frac{n}{N}}$$

Square both sides:
$$d^2 = z^2\sigma_{\bar{x}}^2 \left(1 - \frac{n}{N}\right)$$

Substitute $\frac{\sigma}{\sqrt{n}}$ for $\sigma_{\bar{x}}$:
$$d^2 = z^2 \frac{\sigma^2}{n} \left(1 - \frac{n}{N}\right)$$

Combine:
$$d^2 = \frac{z^2\sigma^2}{n} \left(1 - \frac{n}{N}\right)$$

Multiply:
$$d^2 = \frac{z^2\sigma^2}{n} - \frac{z^2\sigma^2 n}{nN}$$

Rearrange:
$$\frac{z^2\sigma^2}{n} = d^2 + \frac{z^2\sigma^2}{N}$$

Multiply each side by n:
$$z^2\sigma^2 = n\left(d^2 + \frac{z^2\sigma^2}{N}\right)$$

Solve for n:
$$n = \frac{z^2\sigma^2}{d^2 + (z^2\sigma^2/N)}$$

Combine terms:
$$n = \frac{z^2\sigma^2}{(Nd^2 + z^2\sigma^2)/N}$$

Now, dividing both top and bottom by d^2, we obtain

$$n = \frac{z^2\sigma^2/d^2}{1 + (z^2\sigma^2/d^2N)}$$

or

$$n = \frac{n_o}{1 + (n_o/N)}$$

You may use this Equation 5-6 if you have already obtained sample size without the correction factor.

Equations 5-3 and 5-5 provide estimates of sample size when we expect that the sample is a large proportion of the population. Let us compare the sample size with and without the use of the correction factor. Assume we have a school population of 1000 students and we wish to estimate parental incomes within ± $1000, with a 95% confidence level. We know from previous studies that the standard deviation for incomes is $6000.

$$N = 1000$$

$$d = \text{desired precision} = \pm \$1000$$

$$\text{population } \sigma = \$6000$$

$$\text{confidence level} = 95\%, \ z = 1.96$$

Sample size without correction   *Sample size with correction (using Equation 5-4)*

$$n_o = \frac{z^2 \sigma^2}{d^2} \quad \text{Equation 4-4}$$

$$n_o = 138.2$$

$$n_o = \frac{(3.84)(6000)^2}{(1000)^2}$$

$$n = \frac{138.2}{1 + (138.2/1000)} = \frac{138.2}{1.1382}$$

$$= 121.4$$

$$n_o = \frac{(3.84)(36,000,000)}{1,000,000} = 138.24 \qquad n = 122$$

$$n_o = 139$$

Since we can't interview a fraction of a person, always raise sample size to the next integer. Knowledge of the population size has enabled us to reduce our sample size by approximately 12%!

Problems

1 An auditor wishes to study a population of 100 accounts by sampling. He knows that the standard deviation for the population is $60. He wants to find the mean and have a 95% confidence interval that would be no larger than ± 16. How large a sample should he take?

2 Zippy Air Conditioners purchases 300 compressors from a salvage dealer who assures them that the equipment is in good order. A sample of 40 air conditioners is chosen and 30 are found to be in working order. Zippy wishes to predict, with a 95% level of confidence and a confidence interval of ± 10%, what percent of the equipment will work. What size sample should they choose?

3 Estimate the sample size you would need to estimate the percentage of the business school population (there are 1000 students) who would prefer the case method of teaching to lecture classes. You would like a 98% confidence level and an error of no more than ± 5%. What if you reduced the confidence level to 95%?

SMALL SAMPLES

5-3

Perhaps you noted that every time we mention the Central Limit Theorem, the caveat "if the sample size is sufficiently large" precedes or follows it. It is rather like reading the "fine print" in a contract. What is sufficiently large?

In Figure 4-4, we pointed out that the variation of the means of samples of small size is greater than that of the means from samples of large size. Small sample means may vary more than large sample means because if, in the course of sampling, a selection of unusual values at the upper or lower tails of the distribution occurs, they may not be counterbalanced by other values in the middle or other extreme of the population. Assume that in our study of college students in the previous chapter, we selected a sample of two students 4-ft 8-in and 4-ft 9-in; then our sample mean is 4-ft 8.5-in. If we plotted the distributions of means of different size samples, there would be a slightly different shaped curve for each sample size.

As a visual example, look at Figure 5-1. What if the sample size is 30 or less?

In the early 1900s at the Guinness brewery in Dublin, a man named Gosset was carrying on experiments with small samples. He developed a set of curves for the distribution of $t = (\overline{X} - \mu)/s_{\overline{X}}$. There was one curve for each sample size. In addition, for each of these curves he measured the areas between the means and a given number of standard errors $t = (\overline{X} - \mu)/s_{\overline{X}}$. When he tried to publish his results, he did not wish to be identified as an employee of the brewery. Nevertheless, Gosset submitted his article, which plotted t values for different size samples, and signed it "a student." His table, which presents the results for curves for each sample size, is called the *Student's t distribution*.

In order to compute the z statistic, the population standard deviation must be known. Often, we have to estimate the standard error of the mean $s_{\overline{X}}$, which is the

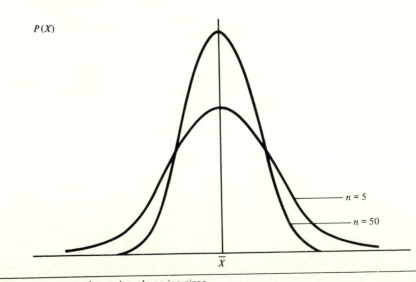

$P(X)$

$n = 5$

$n = 50$

$\overline{X}$

FIGURE **5-1**

Probability distributions for means of samples of varying sizes.

standard deviation of sample means. When we know the population standard deviation σ, the standard error of the mean is $\sigma_{\bar{x}}$. If we use an estimate of the population standard deviation obtained by calculating the standard deviation within the sample, s, we will call our standard error the mean $s_{\bar{x}}$. Similarly, we have to estimate the standard error of a proportion from the sample. In this case, the t statistic is used.

$$ t = \frac{(\overline{X} - \mu)}{s/\sqrt{n}} $$

where s is the estimate of standard deviation from sample and n is the size of sample used to estimate standard deviation.

This t statistic is not normally distributed. It is symmetrical and approaches normality as the sample size becomes large. (See Figure 5-2.) We see that as n increases, our curve in Figure 5-1 for the sample distributions of the mean $\overline{X}$ starts to take on normal characteristics. Therefore, if the sample size is greater than the t table can handle, we may use normal curve statistics (the z table) to estimate the distribution of sample means.

There are three conditions that would lead us to use this t distribution. First, we must assume that the population is normal or approximately normally distributed. Secondly, the population standard deviation is unknown and, finally, the sample size is 30 or less.

The t Distribution

If we plot the t distribution, it varies for different size samples. (See Figure 5-2.) Thus, the t distribution starts to approach the z distribution as n increases. Often, if the sample size is larger than 30, the z distribution is used even when σ is unknown. However, recent studies by the American Institute of Certified Public Accountants have demonstrated that if σ must be estimated from a sample, it is sometimes unwise to use normal curve statistics z before the sample from which s is estimated approaches 120.

The t distribution shows that for very small sample sizes the distribution is lower at the mean and higher at the tails than the normal distribution. Thus, if we wish to include 68% of our population (area under the curve), we wish to move *more*

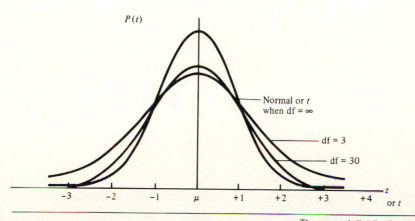

FIGURE **5-2**

The normal distribution and the t distribution for varying degrees of freedom.

than 1 standard deviation to the right and left of the mean as we did in the normal distribution. The *t* distribution is characterized by *degrees of freedom* that are one less than sample size $(n - 1)$, when we are trying to estimate a mean.

Degrees of freedom are the number of measures that can vary freely. For example, if we have a set of 5 numbers and want to be sure that they add to 25, we can pick the first 4 numbers at random, but we must be able to choose the last number ourself. Thus, for 5 numbers that always add to 25, we have 4 degrees of freedom. For example, if the first 4 numbers randomly chosen are 6, 3, 8, and 12, the last number must be -4 or the numbers will not add to 25. Thus, we lose 1 degree of freedom in choosing our numbers at random that must add to a given sum.

The *z* table shows values for areas under the normal curve. If we were to make a table like this for the *t* distribution, we would need a table for each number of degrees of freedom. Thus, we would have more than 30 tables. Instead, the table has been condensed so that each horizontal line represents a given level of degrees of freedom, and *t* values given are those that leave 10%, 5%, 2%, and 1% in both tails combined (area between $\pm t$ equals .90, .95, .98, and .99, respectively). See Table A-4. We'll also use this table to solve the following problem.

EXAMPLE 5-1 Let us assume that we took a sample of 25 students and want to set up a 95% confidence interval for parental income. The sample mean is $20,000 and the sample standard deviation $5000. Then, instead of using the *z* value of 1.96 (appropriate for a large sample), we look up $P = .05$ and 24 degrees of freedom in the table, giving us a *t* value of 2.064. Now, proceed to formulate the confidence interval as we have done previously, using *t* instead of *z* values.

The confidence interval is

$$\mu = \bar{X} \pm ts_{\bar{x}}$$

$$= 20,000 \pm (2.064) \frac{5000}{\sqrt{25}}$$

$$= 20,000 + (2.064)(1000)$$

$$= 20,000 \pm 2,064$$

$$= \$17,936 \text{ to } \$22,064$$

Our confidence interval is now larger than it would have been using the *z* value, because we are less certain of the results from a small sample when σ is unknown than we would have been with the results of a large sample.

The standard deviation for a sample is found by using the following formula, given in Chapter 2,

$$s = \sqrt{\frac{\Sigma (X - \bar{X})^2}{n - 1}}$$

Using this value for the standard deviation, the formula for the standard error of the mean when using the standard deviation calculated from the sample is

$$s_{\bar{x}} = \frac{s}{\sqrt{n}} \tag{5-7}$$

In fact, since we generally don't know σ, it is more likely that we will use $s_{\bar{x}}$ than $\sigma_{\bar{x}}$.

Since the t distribution approaches the normal distribution as n increases, we may use z values if n exceeds 30, even if we use s as an estimate of σ (except for the cases mentioned above). To review, we can always use the z table if we know σ, when the population is normally distributed. If we must calculate s from a sample and know that the population is normally distributed, we can use the t distribution when the sample size is less than 30. As the sample size becomes larger, we may use the normal distribution to make confidence interval estimates. In certain situations, it may be useful to continue to use the t statistic even when sample size is greater than 30.

SAMPLE SIZE WHEN σ IS UNKNOWN

We have raised the question about what to do when we don't know the population standard deviation. This is especially important when we are trying to determine sample size, since the sample size formulas require that we know σ and p

$$n = \frac{z^2 \sigma^2}{d^2} \qquad n = \frac{z^2 pq}{d^2}$$

If we are trying to estimate a proportion, we do not have to know the population proportion; we may take our most conservative estimate of sample size by assuming $p = .5$ and $q = .5$. Let us look at some different estimates of sample size using different values of p and assuming z and d are the same. Let $z = 1.96$ and let precision $d = \pm.05$.

$$\text{If } p = .5, \quad n = \frac{1.96^2(.5)(.5)}{.05^2} = \frac{3.84(.25)}{.0025} = 384$$

$$\text{If } p = .3, \quad n = \frac{1.96^2(.3)(.7)}{.05^2} = \frac{3.84(.21)}{.0025} = 323$$

$$\text{If } p = .1, \quad n = \frac{1.96^2(.1)(.9)}{.05^2} = \frac{3.84(.09)}{.0025} = 139$$

Allowing p to equal .5 requires the largest sample size. If we had information that p is significantly lower or higher, we could probably reduce our sample size.

Now, we might want to estimate a sample size where the precision d was a given percent of the population proportion. For example, we would like d to be 5% of the population proportion ($d = .05p$). If $p = .5$,

$$n = \frac{1.96^2(.5)(.5)}{[.05(.5)]^2} = \frac{1.96^2(.5)(.5)}{.000625} = 1536$$

Let us assume that we are trying to estimate a mean, and the population standard deviation is not known. The most expeditious approach is to take a sample, use the t distribution, and estimate the standard deviation from the sample. This gives us the following formula:

$$n = \frac{t^2 s^2}{d^2} \qquad \qquad (5-8)$$

Let us say we are making a survey of downpayments on a house in a certain area. Assume that we take a sample of 25 and have a mean of $20,000. Using the sample, we compute the standard deviation:

$$s = \sqrt{\frac{\Sigma(X - \bar{X})^2}{n - 1}} = \$1980$$

Now, assume we wish to estimate downpayments within $\pm$ $500 with a confidence level of 95%.

$$n = \frac{2.064^2(1980)^2}{500^2} = \frac{4.26(3,920,400)}{250,000} = 66.8 \qquad \text{raise to 67}$$

The required sample size is 67; therefore, since we have already sampled 25 people, we must sample 42 more. Now, new computations of the sample mean should be made that take into account all 67 people in the sample. Of course, the first 25 people and the subsequent 42 should have been chosen by an appropriate probability sampling method.

Problems

1 Assume a scuba diving school buys 16 air tanks for student use from a large production run of a wholesaler. On the average, these tanks last 30 minutes, and this duration is normally distributed. The population standard deviation is unknown, but an estimate was calculated as $s = 3$ minutes. Form a 95% confidence interval for the mean.

2 A jewelry store owner purchases 9 solar-powered wristwatches from a large sample. The average length of time these watches stay charged on a 1-hour exposure to light is 24 hours, and it is normally distributed. The sample standard deviation is found to be 30 minutes. Form a 98% confidence interval of the mean.

3 An accountant wishes to compute the value of inventory for the Baxter Automotive warehouse, which stocks air filters and sparkplugs. He decides to determine stock from a sample but wonders how large a sample to take. He takes a sample of 25 air filters and finds that the average price is $12.00, with a standard deviation of $.80. How large a sample should he take to estimate value with a 95% confidence interval with a confidence interval width of $\pm$ $.10?

4 A study of wages sampled 196 of 625 workers. The mean wage was $12,000 and the standard deviation was $760. Estimate a 95% confidence interval for the workforce.

STRATIFIED SAMPLING

5-5

In Chapter 4 we found that a sample may be stratified to ensure that we have a large enough group to study in each stratification category and/or to reduce sampling error. There are a number of ways in which a sample of a given size can be divided or allocated among strata. These include equal allocation, proportional allocation, optimum allocation, and least-cost allocation.

Let us examine the meaning of each method of dividing the total sample size among the categories and the implications of each type of allocation in terms of sampling error. Assume that we have the following information on the value of stocks

TABLE 5-1

135

(1)	(2)	(3)	(4)	(5)	(6)
STRATUM	COST PER INTERVIEW	ITEMS IN STRATA IN POPULATION N_i	STANDARD DEVIATION OF ITEMS IN STRATA* s_i	$N_i s_i$	$\dfrac{N_i s_i}{\sqrt{C_i}}$
1. Large cities and suburbs	$25	1000	$1000	$1,000,000	200,000
2. Medium-size and small cities	16	3000	500	1,500,000	375,000
3. Rural communities	9	2000	700	1,400,000	466,667
		$N = 6000$		$3,900,000	1,041,667
				$\Sigma N_i s_i$	$\Sigma \dfrac{N_i s_i}{\sqrt{C_i}}$

*May be calculated by computing standard deviation of items in samples from each strata.

purchased for a stock brokerage firm that caters to wealthy clients. The geographical distribution (area of residents) for their clients is given in Table 5-1, column 3.

Sample Allocation

Let us say that we have a sample size of 600 that we wish to allocate to the three strata (large cities, medium-size and small cities, and rural communities). The number of items in the population in each stratum must be known (N_i), and the standard deviation of the item studied in each stratum (s_i) should be known from previous studies or from an estimate of the population made from some small initial pilot study. If we use *equal allocation*, the same number of people will be chosen in each stratum. In this problem we will have 200, 200, 200.

Proportional allocation is a very popular method of sample stratification. The sample is divided in the same proportions as the original population. This is called a *self-weighting sample* because everyone in the sample is selected in proportion to the total population so that the mean of the total sample is used to estimate the total population, without adjusting for each stratum. The formula to select each stratum is

$$n_i = \frac{N_i}{N} n \qquad \text{or} \qquad n_i = \frac{n}{N} N_i$$

As we remember, n/N is the sampling fraction. Thus, we multiply a constant sampling fraction f, in this case .1, by the population in each stratum to find the sample size for each stratum. For example, in strata 1, 2, and 3 we have

$$n_1 = \frac{600}{6000} (1000) = 100$$

$$n_2 = \frac{600}{6000} (3000) = 300$$

$$n_3 = \frac{600}{6000} (2000) = 200$$

In stratum 3 we have 200; in stratum 2, 300; and in stratum 1, 100.

A third variation is *optimum allocation* (Neyman), which divides the sample so that we can get the *smallest amount of sampling error* for a sample of a given size. Here we take a larger proportion of our sample from the stratum with the largest amount of variation. Since our sampling error is $s_{\bar{x}} = s/\sqrt{n}$, enlarging n for the category with greatest s tends to cut down overall sampling error.

Let us look at a simple example if we have a sample of 400 to divide in two categories; category 1 has a standard deviation of 100, while category 2 has a standard deviation of 10. If we divide the sample equally, we get

$$s_{\bar{x}_1} = \frac{100}{\sqrt{200}} = 7.07 \qquad s_{\bar{x}_2} = \frac{10}{\sqrt{200}} = .71$$

$$s_{\bar{x}_1}^2 = 49.98 \qquad s_{\bar{x}_2}^2 = .50$$

Now, if we put 360 in category 1 and 40 in category 2, we have

$$s_{\bar{x}_1} = \frac{100}{\sqrt{360}} = 5.27 \qquad s_{\bar{x}_2} = \frac{10}{\sqrt{40}} = 1.58$$

$$s_{\bar{x}_1}^2 = 27.77 \qquad s_{\bar{x}_2}^2 = 2.50$$

We can see that the sum of the standard errors has been reduced and that the sum of the standard errors squared (the variances) has fallen considerably. In addition, this optimal formula also depends on stratum size. The larger the difference between stratum sizes and between stratum variances, the greater the increase in efficiency by using the optimal allocation. Samples of electronic firms, stores, or farms where there are large differences in strata size can be made more efficient by using optimal rather than proportional allocation methods. The allocation formula is

$$n_i = \frac{N_i s_i}{\Sigma N_i s_i} n$$

Table 5-2 shows the results for each stratum.

$$n_1 = \frac{1000(1000)}{[1000(1000)] + [3000(500)] + [2000(700)]} (600)$$

$$= \frac{1,000,000}{1,000,000 + 1,500,000 + 1,400,000} (600) = \frac{1,000,000}{3,900,000} (600)$$

$$= 153.8 = 154$$

$$n_2 = \frac{1,500,000}{3,900,000} (600) = 230.7 = 231$$

$$n_3 = \frac{1,400,000}{3,900,000} (600) = 215.4 = 215$$

We can see that this technique increases the sample size in stratum 1, which had the highest standard deviation, and lowers the sample in the second category, which had the smallest variation.

There is one very important consideration in doing sample research—cost. Interviewer cost is usually one of the largest parts of a sample survey budget. A recent study by the National Opinion Research Center showed that only 25% of

TABLE 5-2

137

ALLOCATING A GIVEN SIZE SAMPLE TO DIFFERENT STRATA

Equal allocation	$n_i = \dfrac{n}{L}$	$\begin{aligned} n_1 &= 200 \\ n_2 &= 200 \\ n_3 &= 200 \end{aligned}$	(5-9)
Proportional allocation	$n_i = \dfrac{N_i}{N} n$	$\begin{aligned} n_1 &= 100 \\ n_2 &= 300 \\ n_3 &= 200 \end{aligned}$	(5-10)
Optimum allocation (Neyman)	$n_i = \dfrac{N_i s_i}{\Sigma N_i s_i} n$	$\begin{aligned} n_1 &= 154 \\ n_2 &= 231 \\ n_3 &= 215 \end{aligned}$	(5-11)
Least-cost allocation	$n_i = \dfrac{(N_i s_i)/\sqrt{C_i}}{\Sigma[(N_i s_i)/\sqrt{C_i}]} n$	$\begin{aligned} n_1 &= 115 \\ n_2 &= 216 \\ n_3 &= 269 \end{aligned}$	(5-12)

N_i = number in population
     in stratum i
N = total population
C_i = cost per interview
     in stratum i

n_i = sample in stratum i

n = total sample size
L = number of strata

s_i = standard deviation of sample
     in stratum i

interviewer costs resulted directly from interviewing; 40% were due to travel time and related expenses, and the remaining 35% covered study, editing of question-naires, and other clerical tasks.[2] The cost breakdown also showed that "interviewers in metropolitan areas spend a greater proportion of their time in traveling than do interviewers in non-metropolitan areas, since they have more difficulty in finding respondents at home, although non-metropolitan interviewers travel longer distances."[3]

Since our basic example divides the strata into rural areas, smaller cities, and metropolitan areas, let us assume different interviewing costs in each of these strata. We assume that because of all the callbacks involved (for a good random sample we should keep calling back to obtain the interview to ensure that working people have proportional representation in the sample), interviews cost $25 in large cities, $16 in small cities, and $9 in rural areas. Our allocation formula takes into account stratum size, standard deviation, and cost. It ensures that for a given total sample size we have the least cost.

$$n_i = \frac{N_i s_i / \sqrt{C_i}}{\Sigma (N_i s_i / \sqrt{C_i})} n$$

For stratum 1, we have

[2]S. Sudman, *Reducing the Cost of Surveys*, Aldine, Chicago, 1967, pp. 633–634.
[3]Ibid., p. 633.

$$n_1 = \frac{1000(1000)/\sqrt{25}}{[1000(1000)/\sqrt{25}] + [3000(500)/\sqrt{16}] + [2000(700)/\sqrt{9}]}$$

$$= \frac{200,000}{200,000 + 375,000 + 466,667} = \frac{200,000}{1,041,667} = 115$$

Similarly, for stratum 2, we have $n_2 = 216$; for stratum 3, $n_3 = 269$.

Measuring Error

We have now divided the strata into groups according to the principles of equal, proportional, optimal, and least-cost allocation. Since one purpose of stratification is to reduce sampling error, we now calculate and compare the relative sampling error of samples chosen by the different methods.

The formula for variance for each strata, with modifications for the fact that the sample may be a large proportion of the population (finite correction factor), is obtained by squaring the formula

$$s_{\bar{x}} = \frac{s}{\sqrt{n}} \sqrt{1 - \frac{n}{N}}$$

Doing so, we obtain the variance

$$V_{\bar{x}} = \frac{s^2}{n} \left(1 - \frac{n}{N} \right) \tag{5-13}$$

To get the total variance for all strata combined, we weight each variance by the importance of that stratum in the population $(N_i/N)^2$. Taking the square root, we get the standard error of the mean for all the strata combined.

$$s_{\bar{x},s} = \sqrt{\Sigma \left[\left(\frac{N_i}{N} \right)^2 \frac{s^2}{n_i} \left(1 - \frac{n_i}{Ni} \right) \right]} \tag{5-14}$$

For *equal allocation,* sample size in each group is 200; therefore, the formula is*

$$s_{\bar{x},se} = \left[\left(\frac{1000}{6000} \right)^2 \frac{1000^2}{200} \left(1 - \frac{200}{1000} \right) + \left(\frac{3000}{6000} \right)^2 \frac{500^2}{200} \left(1 - \frac{200}{3000} \right) \right.$$

$$\left. + \left(\frac{2000}{6000} \right)^2 \frac{700^2}{200} \left(1 - \frac{200}{2000} \right) \right] 1/2$$

$$= \sqrt{(.028)(.5000)(.8) + (.25)(1250)(.93) + (.111)(2540)(.9)}$$

$$= \sqrt{112.000 + 291.563 + 244.755}$$

$$= \sqrt{648.318}$$

$$= 25.46$$

For *proportional allocation,* the sample size in each group is 100, 300, and 200, respectively; therefore, the formula is

---

*Exponent notation has been used instead of radical signs when equations are too long to fit on one line.

$$s_{\bar{x},sp} = \left[\left(\frac{1000}{6000} \right)^2 \frac{1000^2}{100} \left(1 - \frac{100}{1000} \right) + \left(\frac{300}{6000} \right)^2 \frac{500^2}{300} \left(1 - \frac{300}{3000} \right) \right.$$
$$\left. + \left(\frac{2000}{6000} \right)^2 \frac{700^2}{200} \left(1 - \frac{200}{2000} \right) \right]^{1/2}$$

$$= \sqrt{(.028)(10,000)(.9) + (.25)(833.333)(.9) + (.111)(2450)(.9)}$$

$$= \sqrt{252 + 187.500 + 244.755}$$

$$= \sqrt{684.255}$$

$$= 26.16$$

For *optimal (Neyman) allocation,* the sample size in each group is 154, 231, and 215. Therefore, the error formula is

$$s_{\bar{x},so} = \left[\left(\frac{1000}{6000} \right)^2 \frac{1000^2}{154} \left(1 - \frac{154}{1000} \right) + \left(\frac{3000}{6000} \right)^2 \frac{500^2}{231} \left(1 - \frac{231}{3000} \right) \right.$$
$$\left. + \left(\frac{2000}{6000} \right)^2 \frac{700^2}{215} \left(1 - \frac{215}{2000} \right) \right]^{1/2}$$

$$= \sqrt{(.028)(6493.506(.846) + (.25)(1082.251)(.923) + (.111)(2279.070)(.8925)}$$

$$= \sqrt{153.818 + 249.729 + 225.782}$$

$$= \sqrt{629.329}$$

$$= 25.10$$

For *least-cost allocation,* the sample size in each group should be 115, 216, and 269, respectively.

$$s_{\bar{x},SLC} = \left[\left(\frac{1000}{6000} \right)^2 \frac{1000^2}{115} \left(1 - \frac{115}{1000} \right) + \left(\frac{3000}{6000} \right)^2 \frac{500^2}{216} \left(1 - \frac{216}{3000} \right) \right.$$
$$\left. + \left(\frac{2000}{6000} \right)^2 \frac{700^2}{269} \left(1 - \frac{269}{2000} \right) \right]^{1/2}$$

$$= \sqrt{(.028)(8695.652)(.885) + (.25)(1157.407)(.928) + (.111)(1821.561)(.8655)}$$

$$= \sqrt{215.478 + 268.518 + 174.998}$$

$$= \sqrt{658.994}$$

$$= 25.67$$

As we have stated previously, the error is smallest for optimal allocation. Let us look at costs. From Table 5-3 we can see that a savings of $1248 can be obtained by using least-cost instead of equal allocation; $729 can be saved using least-cost allocation rather than optimal allocation. The increase in error in using least-cost rather than optimal allocation will be .57 (.57/25.10), or 2.3%. Cost and accuracy

TABLE 5-3

COMPARISON OF SAMPLING ERROR AND COST FOR DIFFERENT SAMPLE ALLOCATIONS

STRATA	PER INTERVIEW COST	NUMBER OF INTERVIEWS			
		EQUAL ALLOCATION	PROPORTIONAL ALLOCATION	OPTIMAL ALLOCATION	LEAST-COST ALLOCATION
1	$25	200	100	154	115
2	16	200	300	231	216
3	9	200	200	215	269
Total cost		$10,000	$9100	$9481	$8752
Error		25.46	26.16	25.10	25.67

considerations can then be used to decide on the best study design. In the next section, we show how the original sample size (in this case, we just assumed it would be 600) can be determined for the four different methods of sample allocation.

Determination of Sample Size for Different Allocation Methods

In all previous cases, we assumed a given sample size (600) and allocated this sample among the strata. Now, however, we can assume a given level of precision d, given confidence limits (z values), and given standard deviations and actually compute the ideal sample size by using the equations shown in Table 5-4. These equations give us the overall sample size. We can allocate this sample among the strata. Note that if n_i/N_i is small, the second terms in the denominator may be eliminated, leaving only N^2d^2/z^2 in the denominator.

Now, assume you want a 99.7% confidence interval ($z = 3$) and a level of precision of ± 75. Calculate sample size for each type of allocation in the problem we have been using.

	COST	N_i	s_i	$N_i s_i$	$N_i s_i^2$	$N_i^2 s_i^2$
1	25	1000	1000	1,000,000	1,000,000,000	1,000,000,000,000
2	16	3000	500	1,500,000	750,000,000	2,250,000,000,000
3	9	2000	700	1,400,000	980,000,000	1,960,000,000,000
				3,900,000	2,730,000,000	5,210,000,000,000

$d = 75$ $L = 3$ $z = 3$ $N = 6000$

TABLE 5-4

EQUATIONS FOR COMPUTATION OF SAMPLE SIZE FOR VARIOUS TYPES OF ALLOCATION

TYPE OF ALLOCATION	EQUATION	
Equal stratification	$n = \dfrac{L \Sigma N_i^2 s_i^2}{(N^2 d^2/z^2) + \Sigma N_i s_i^2}$	L = Number of strata d = desired width of confidence interval on each side of mean z = confidence level desired N = population size
Proportional stratification	$n = \dfrac{N \Sigma N_i s_i^2}{(N^2 d^2/z^2) + \Sigma N_i s_i^2}$	
Optimal	$n = \dfrac{(\Sigma N_i s_i)^2}{(N^2 d^2/z^2) + \Sigma N_i s_i^2}$	
Least cost	$n = \dfrac{(\Sigma N_i s_i \sqrt{C_i})(\Sigma N_i s_i/\sqrt{C_i})}{(N^2 d^2/z^2) + \Sigma N_i s_i^2}$	

For equal stratification:

$$\frac{3(5,210,000,000,000)}{6000^2(75^2/3^2) + 2,730,000,000} = \frac{3(5,210,000,000,000)}{25,230,000,000} = 619.5 = 620$$

For proportional stratification:

$$\frac{6,000(2,730,000,000)}{25,230,000,000} = 1,638,000 = 649.23 = 650$$

For optimal stratification:

$$\frac{3,900,000^2}{25,230,000,000} = \frac{15,210,000,000,000}{25,230,000,000} = 602.85 = 603$$

For least-cost stratification:

$$\frac{(5,000,000 + 6,000,000 + 4,200,000)(200,000 + 375,000 + 466,666.67)}{25,230,000,000}$$

$$= 626.96 = 627$$

CLUSTERED SAMPLES

5-6

Frequently, random sampling must be done on an area basis because adequate lists do not exist or are inaccessible. (See Case 4-2.) Many important government surveys (Survey of Consumer Finances and Current Population Surveys) sample by studying maps and selecting houses throughout an area. If one chooses houses at random throughout the city, the costs of visiting these widely scattered dwellings can be prohibitive. An alternative way of sampling is to group blocks or areas into clusters of approximately equal population. Then, a number of these clusters are chosen at random. Within each cluster, all households may be interviewed or, if a *multistage sampling technique* is used, a random choice of households can be made.

Comparing this cluster sample to a random choice of households throughout the city, for example, the cost is lower per element (a household) because of lower listing cost (it is necessary to list only the houses on the blocks selected) and lower location cost. It is easier for an interviewer to talk to several people on one block than to several people scattered throughout the city.

The problem encountered in using this type of analysis is that people who live on the same block are more likely to be similar than people who are scattered throughout the city. If enough clusters are sampled, however, this problem of increased error due to homogeneity within the clusters can be alleviated.

Besides area sampling, there are other ways that cluster samples can be used. For example, if one wishes to interview departing passengers in an airport, a cluster might be a plane load. If one were searching through files of land holdings for tax information, pages in a ledger would be clusters.

The theory of cluster sampling is rather complex, depending on whether one takes equal- or unequal-sized clusters. A general formula for the standard error of cluster estimates has two terms. The first relates to variability *between* cluster means or proportions; the second, to the variability *within* clusters.

Measuring Error

Thus far, we have discussed examples where one is trying to estimate a mean. These formulas can be altered to make estimates when one tries to estimate a sample proportion. For a simple random sample, when one is trying to estimate a proportion, the standard error of a proportion is

$$\sigma_{\bar{p}} = \sqrt{\frac{pq}{n}}$$

If the sample is taken from clusters, the formula becomes (if clusters are equal size)

$$\sigma_{\bar{p}_c} = \sqrt{\frac{pq}{n}\,[1 + r_c(N_s - 1)]} \qquad (5\text{-}14)$$

N_s is the size of each cluster and r_c is the intercorrelation between the sample members averaged over all the clusters. The formula for r_c is

$$r_c = \frac{\Sigma(p_i - p)^2/p_c - \Sigma(p_iq_i/p_c)/(N_s - 1)}{pq} \qquad (5\text{-}15)$$

where $\sigma_{\bar{p}_c}$ = standard error of a clustered sample
   p_c = number of clusters
   p_i = value of p in the ith cluster
   N_s = size of each cluster
   p = population proportion
   n = total members in the sample

If r_c is greater than 0, there is correlation within the clusters and the error will increase. If N_s approaches 1, so that there are relatively few people in each cluster, the error will not be appreciably larger than the error with simple random sampling.

The first example shows the effects of the use of a cluster sample on the standard error of estimate. Assume that one takes a sample of 400 in four clusters of 100 each. For this sample, assume that the overall population proportion is $p = .6$ and $q = .4$. For a simple random sample, the standard error of a proportion would be

$$p = .6$$

$$q = .4$$

$$\sigma_{\bar{p}} = \sqrt{\frac{.6(.4)}{400}} = .024$$

(Assume that one finds the following proportions in each of the clusters.)

Four clusters

$p_1 = .6,\ q_1 = .4$	$n_1 = 100$	$(p_1 - p)^2 = 0$	$\dfrac{p_1q_1}{p_c} = \dfrac{.24}{4}$
$p_2 = .5,\ q_2 = .5$	$n_2 = 100$	$(p_2 - p)^2 = .01$	$\dfrac{p_2q_2}{p_c} = \dfrac{.25}{4}$
$p_3 = .7,\ q_3 = .3$	$n_3 = 100$	$(p_3 - p)^2 = .01$	$\dfrac{p_3q_3}{p_c} = \dfrac{.21}{4}$
$p_4 = .6,\ q_4 = .4$	$n_4 = 100$	$(p_4 - p)^2 = 0$	$\dfrac{p_4q_4}{p_c} = \dfrac{.24}{4}$
		$\Sigma(p_i - p)^2 = .02$	$\Sigma\dfrac{p_iq_i}{p_c} = \dfrac{.94}{4}$

The estimate of p is $(.6 + .5 + .7 + .6)/4 = .6$. (Note that all clusters are the same size.) To find the intercorrelation between samples, we substitute in Equation 5-15.

$$0 + \frac{(.5 - .6)^2}{4} + \frac{(.7 - .6)^2}{4} + 0 = \frac{.02}{4} = \Sigma \frac{(p_i - p)^2}{p_c}$$

$$\frac{.6(.4)}{4}(99) + \frac{.5(.5)}{4}(99) + \frac{.7(.3)}{4}(99) + \frac{.6(.4)}{4}(99) = \frac{.94}{4}(99)$$

$$= \Sigma p_i q_i / p_c / (Ns - 1)$$

$$r_c = \frac{(.02/4) - [(.94/4)/(99)]}{.6(.4)}$$

$$= \frac{.005 - .00237}{.24} = .01096$$

$$\sigma_{\bar{p}_c} = \frac{.6(.4)}{400}[1 + 0.01096(99)]$$

$$\sigma_{\bar{p}_c} = .0006(1.08504)$$

$$\sigma_{\bar{p}_c} = .0255$$

for the simple random sample $\sigma_{\bar{p}} = .024$.

Since the error is now greater, it may be worthwhile to use this error estimate in determining the appropriate sample size for a given level of confidence and degree of precision. A pilot study could be used to determine the approximate proportions in each cluster.

Formulas for unequal cluster size are available in a number of sampling references.[4]

Problems

1 The university staff and faculty form two strata of people working at the university. A sample is taken from each group to determine the average income of all university employees.

	FACULTY	STAFF
Number of elements in stratum	1,000	2,000
Number in sample	100	225
Stratum sample mean	$18,900	$12,000
Standard deviation in stratum	2,000	1,000

(*a*) Estimate the mean for the whole population.
(*b*) Estimate the standard error of the mean for the whole population.

2 Johnson's Jewelry was introducing a new set of men's jewelry. The product line included bracelets and neck chains. The sales manager wondered if the proportion preferring the jewelry varied by social class. Therefore, he decided to sample customers in three types of income areas. City statistics gave the following number of people in the population in various income groups.

[4]See Kish; Cochran; and Hansen, Hurwitz, and Madow.

INCOME CLASS	APPROXIMATE NUMBER OF PEOPLE	NUMBER SAMPLED	NUMBER WHO WOULD BUY JEWELRY
Over $35,000	40,000	160	40
$20,000–$34,999	240,000	300	100
Under $20,000	420,000	500	250
	700,000		

(a)   Make an estimate of the overall percentage of customers who would buy men's jewelry.

(b)   Compute a 95% confidence level about the estimate. *Hint:* The standard error of a proportion in each stratum is

$$s_{\bar{p}} = \sqrt{\frac{p_i q_i}{n_c}}$$

Use $(s_{\bar{p}})^2$ in place of $s_i^2 / n_i = s_{\bar{x}}^2$.

(c)   Does preference for jewelry seem to relate to income class?

(d)   If you were to design a survey to study this problem in another city with a similar population distribution, how would you allocate a sample of 700 among the three income groups? Let $s_i = \sqrt{p_i q_i}$.

3   For the following data, how would you allocate a sample of 600?

WOMEN IN REAL ESTATE IN PONCA CITY

EDUCATIONAL LEVEL	NUMBER OF WOMEN	ESTIMATED STANDARD DEVIATION OF INCOME
High school	2000	$ 250
Some college	3000	500
College graduate	1000	1000

(a)   If you were doing a study of income, how would you allocate the sample by (1) proportional allocation and by (2) optimal allocation?

(b)   What information would you need for least-cost allocation?

Computer Problems

1   Write a program to compute sample size. (The user should be able to enter different z, d, and σ values.)

2   Write a program to compute sample size using the finite correction factor.

3   Write a program to compute confidence intervals. (The user should be able to enter z and $\sigma_{\bar{x}}$ values.)

4   Write a program to compute confidence intervals using the finite correction factor.

5   Develop a program to allocate a given sample to different strata using proportional, optimal, and least-cost allocation.

6   Set up a program to calculate errors for different types of (a) stratified and (b) clustered samples.

7 Study differences in clustered samples when there are 20 clusters, as opposed to 4 clusters, by using a computer program.

1 The relation between population size and sample size can be used to reduce the size of confidence limits or to allow for a smaller sample size. The confidence interval can be multiplied by the *finite correction factor*.

$$cf = \sqrt{1 - \frac{n}{N}}$$

This is especially effective if the sample is a large proportion of the population.

2 Required sample size may be reduced if the size of the population is known. The formula for the sample needed to estimate a mean is

$$n = \frac{n_o}{1 + (n_o/N)} \quad \text{or} \quad n = \frac{z^2\sigma^2/d^2}{1 + (z^2\sigma^2/d^2N)}$$

where n_o is the sample size needed without the correction factor.

3 Similarly, the formula to determine the required sample size to estimate a proportion when the correction factor is used is

$$n = \frac{n_o}{1 + (n_o/N)} \quad \text{or} \quad n = \frac{z^2pq/d^2}{1 + (z^2pq/d^2N)}$$

4 If σ is unknown, sample size is small, and the population is normally distributed, the t table may be used to estimate confidence intervals and sample size.

$$t = \frac{\bar{X} - \mu}{s_{\bar{X}}}$$

The confidence interval for a mean is

$$\bar{X} \pm ts_{\bar{X}}$$

5 When σ is not known, a sample estimate s can be used to compute sample size. The formula becomes

$$n = \frac{t^2s^2}{d^2}$$

6 A sample can be stratified to ensure that there is a large enough sample from each group to make a study of that group or stratum, or to reduce sample error. There are four ways to divide a given size sample among various strata.

$$n_i = n/L \quad \text{equal allocation}$$

$$n_i = \frac{N_i}{N}n \quad \text{proportional allocation}$$

$$n_i = \frac{N_i s_i}{\Sigma N_i s_i}\, n \qquad \text{optimal allocation}$$

$$n_i = \frac{N_i s_i / \sqrt{C_i}}{\Sigma(N_i s_i / \sqrt{C_i})}\, n \qquad \text{least-cost allocation}$$

Proportional allocation results in a *self-weighting* sample; optimal allocation provides the *smallest* amount of sampling error; and least-cost allocation provides the lowest cost for a given sample size.

7 The formula to measure the error of a stratified sample is

$$s_{\bar{X},s} = \sqrt{\Sigma\left(\frac{N_i}{N}\right)^2 \frac{s_i^2}{n_i}\left(1 - \frac{n_i}{N_i}\right)}$$

8 Cluster samples reduce interviewing costs because a number of interviews are taken in the same neighborhood. The homogeneity within the clusters increases sampling error. The sampling error for a clustered sample is

$$\sigma_{\bar{p}_c} = \sqrt{\frac{pq}{n}\,[1 + r_c(N_s - 1)]}$$

$$r_c = \frac{\Sigma(p_i - p)^2/p_c - \Sigma(p_i q_i/p_c)/(N_s - 1)}{pq}$$

BIBLIOGRAPHY

5-8

Cochran, William G.: *Sampling Techniques,* 2d ed. New York: Wiley, 1963. A thorough presentation of sampling theory.

Ferber, Robert, and P. J. Verdoorn: *Research Methods in Economics and Business.* New York: Macmillan, 1967. See chapters 5 and 6 for an excellent explanation and comparison of sampling methods.

Hansen, Morris, William Hurwitz, and William Madow: *Sample Survey Methods and Theory,* vol. I. New York: Wiley, 1953. Thorough explanation of sampling theory.

Kish, Leslie: *Survey Sampling.* New York: Wiley, 1967. A thorough analysis of survey sampling with formulas for all varieties of sampling problems.

Neter, John, and James K. Loebbecke: *Behavior of Major Statistical Estimators in Sampling Accounting Populations.* New York: American Institute of Certified Public Accountants, 1975. An empirical study comparing standard errors for sample sizes 100 and 200 from moderately and more highly skewed populations indicates that the larger sample size may often be necessary to use normal curve statistics.

Robertson, Jack C.: *Auditing.* Dallas: Business Publications, 1979. See chapter 10 on statistical decision and estimates, and the appendix on stratified random sampling for estimation of amounts.

Spurr, William A., and Charles P. Bonini: *Statistical Analyses for Business Decisions,* revised ed. Homewood, Ill.: Irwin, 1973. See chapter 12 for a clear, concise explanation of survey sampling. Good section on ratio estimation.

Sudman, S.: *Reducing the Cost of Surveys.* Chicago: Aldine, 1967.

Summers, George W., William S. Peters, and Charles P. Armstrong: *Basic Statistics: An Introduction.* Belmont, Calif.: Wadsworth, 1977. See chapter 13 for a concise summary of sampling theory.

Warwick, Donald, and Charles Lininger: *The Sample Survey: Theory and Practice.* New York: McGraw-Hill, 1975. Simple "how to take a sample" information.

Yamane, Taro: *Elementary Sampling Theory*. Englewood Cliffs, N.J.: Prentice-Hall, 1967. Thorough analysis of sampling theory with simple mathematical derivations of important formulas.

CASES

5-9

Case 5-1 Sampling to Determine Educators' Priorities[1]

The South Texas Multi-Regional Processing Center serves eight education regions: 1–3, 13–15, 18, and 20. Each year the state provides each Regional Processing Center (RPC) and Multi-Regional Processing Center (MRPC) with a computer tape of all the professional-level educators within the areas they serve. This tape (the professional personnel tape) contains a great deal of information on each educator, including name, school, county, region, grade level taught, and subject taught. The school districts and education service centers have access to the information within their particular area.

For several years, the Education Service Center, Region 20, of the San Antonio Independent School District, has been determining educational needs by collecting responses from a random sample of all educators in the region. This information provided an accurate picture of what educators generally saw as the primary educational needs. However, because ESC-20 services such a large number and a diversity of educators, the service center was also interested in determining the needs for subgroups of educators (special education teachers, principals, counselors, etc.). To do this, questionnaires are sent to educators in all subgroups. A random sample of all educators, even if it was quite large, could not be counted on to select enough persons in a subgroup to provide reliable information on their needs. For example, principals make up 1.8% of all educators in Region 20. It would be expected that in a random sample of 2000 educators, 36 principals would be included. Assuming a return rate of 50% for questionnaires in this sample, there would be only 18 principals responding. Research indicates that there is reason to question the results from such a small sample (Borg, 1973; Hays, 1973), and that there are certainly too few responses to allow any conclusions to be made about principals at different grade levels (elementary, junior high, and high school).

To avoid sending questionnaires to all educators in Region 20 while still collecting the desired information, the evaluation component of ESC-20 decided to use a stratified random sampling technique. This approach consists of selecting an independent and random sample from each of several identified subgroups. This type of sampling is "particularly appropriate in studies where part of the research analysis is likely to be concerned with comparisons between various subgroups" (Borg, 1973).

The following steps were taken by ESC-20 in selecting the sample for the 1977 needs assessment:

---

[1]This case is based on consultation with John E. Andrews and Alan L. Roecks of the Educational Service Center, Region 20, of the San Antonio Independent School District. Much of the information was presented in a paper at the Southwest Educational Research Association, Austin, Texas, January 1978.

1   The professional personnel tape was reviewed to determine the type of information available. This included names, addresses, ages, and years of service. In designing the questionnaire, information already available on the tapes could be omitted and new information could be collected. If questionnaires are not personally identified so that one could match the people on the tape with those in the questionnaires, overall statistics for the tape and the sample returning questionnaires could be studied to see if the sample is representative. Thus, were newer teachers more likely to return questionnaires?

2   The subgroups of interest were identified. Twelve subgroups within Region 20 were determined from the job classifications and grade levels. These are listed below.

Elementary teachers	Teachers' aides
Junior high teachers	Special education teachers
High school teachers	Learning resource personnel
Elementary school principals	Superintendents
Junior high principals	Supervisors
High school principals	Counselors

Each subgroup was further divided into three parts based on geographical location. The three geographical groupings were (1) suburban school districts, (2) urban districts in San Antonio having a high percentage of minority students, and (3) rural districts. This brought the total to 36 subgroups.

3   The percentage of persons to be sampled from each subgroup was determined. Sampling theory indicates that a minimum of 30 respondents from each subgroup is necessary to produce reliable results. Since it was anticipated that the response rate would be about 50%, 60 persons must be sampled from each subgroup to ensure the response of 30 persons. The percentage to be sampled from each subgroup was easily determined by the formula

$$\text{Percentage to be sampled} = \frac{60}{\text{number in subgroup}}$$

In the few cases where the subgroup population was less than 60, 100% of that subgroup was included in the sample. The total population of educators was 17,111 in 1976–1977.

4   Before questionnaires were mailed, a special code was placed on each questionnaire to indicate to which subgroup it was being sent. Then, it was possible to make studies of each subgroup and various combinations of subgroups.

The following studies were conducted from the survey:

1   The ranking of needs was determined for each of the 36 subgroups.

2   The rankings of additional subgroups were determined. For example, three of the subgroups are the elementary school teachers in three different geographical locations. By combining the results from these three groups in the proper proportions, the needs of a new subgroup (elementary school teachers regionwide) could be determined.

3   The rankings for the region as a whole were determined. Since the 36 subgroups comprised virtually all educators in the region, the results for each

TABLE 1
NUMBER OF EDUCATORS IN SELECTED GROUPS, EIGHT REGIONS, SOUTH TEXAS, 1977

	SUBURBAN DISTRICTS	URBAN DISTRICTS IN SAN ANTONIO (PRIMARILY MINORITY)	RURAL DISTRICTS
Elementary school teachers	1441	2499	1029
Junior high school teachers	825	1141	337
High school teachers	1281	1523	831
Elementary school principals	72	109	51
Junior high school principals	20	26	20
High school principals	16	14	27
Teachers' aides	833	1689	805
Special education teachers	523	767	164
Learning resource personnel	82	83	48
Superintendents	11	4	31
Supervisors	56	164	27
Counselors	189	298	75
	5349	8317	3445

subgroup could be combined in the correct proportion to produce the regionwide totals.

A discussion with the South Texas Processing Center revealed the number of people in each of the 36 groups. (See Table 1.)

Questions

1 Find the percentage sampled in each of the 36 groups.

2 What will the total sample size be?

3 Is this a proportional sample? Explain.

4 If you wanted to sum the number of the educators to get an overall estimate of the percentage with a favorable attitude toward the school, how would you weight the responses of each group?

5 Suppose 50% of the elementary school teachers in rural districts, 65% of the elementary school teachers in urban districts of San Antonio, and 60% of elementary school teachers in suburban districts opposed the "open classroom system." What percentage of elementary school teachers opposes the "open classroom system"?

6 Do you recommend that ESC continue to use this system? Would you qualify your recommendations in any way?

References
Borg, W. R., and M. D. Gall: *Educational Research.* New York: McKay, 1973.
Hays, W. L.: *Statistics for the Social Sciences.* New York: Holt, 1973.
Isaac, S.: *Handbook in Research and Evaluation.* San Diego: Knapp, 1971.

Case 5-2 PRIDEPAK Fertilizer
The PRIDEPAK Fertilizer Company wishes to build a new plant to manufacture a granular urea fertilizer. Granular fertilizers are in pellets and prove easier to apply

than the older prilled products, which are of a flourlike consistency. PRIDEPAK feels that the new product will be preferred to the prilled in the future, since it is slow to release and thus has a longer lasting effect.

In order to build the new factory, PRIDEPAK needs a sizable loan. The Nutmeg National Bank of Connecticut has agreed to a loan of $5 million to start construction in January 1982, another $5 million by July 1982, and an additional $3 million by the end of 1982, for a total of $13,000,000. PRIDEPAK, though, must show that it has at least $20 million of collectible accounts receivable as of November 1981 for loan collateral.

Although there are records of the total amount of the accounts receivable, there are no summaries relating billing dates and amounts of accounts receivable. Collectibility of an account decreases with the amount of time for which the account is outstanding. The company estimates the following collection expectations based on their previous experience.

TIME OUTSTANDING, DAYS	PROBABILITY OF COLLECTION, %
121 or more	10
91–120	33
61–90	67
60 or less	100

Since accounts receivable is a very important component of the assets of PRIDEPAK, the bank demands an audit of the records. A complete audit of all accounts receivable to record the amount and billing date for each account would be very time consuming, so accountants often use statistical sampling to obtain this type of information.

PRIDEPAK hires an independent CPA, Rebecca Barr, to report to the bank. Ms. Barr was pressed for time and could not examine all the accounts in time to make the needed statements. She remembered from her auditing classes that stratified sampling was a cheaper, more accurate way of making auditing estimates than sampling from the total population. For example, the virtue of this method is that high-value or highly variable items can be audited completely if necessary, thus reducing sampling error for that stratum to 0. Sample sizes in the other strata can be reduced since the variation in these strata is smaller. Thus, the overall dollar estimate can be made with fewer total sample items.

Using the previous year's study of the relative number and variation of accounts in each time-outstanding group, Rebecca felt that she could set up a stratified sample and estimate the total amount collectible from accounts receivable.

STRATA	NUMBER OF ACCOUNTS	STANDARD DEVIATION
1. More than 120 days	16	$5000
2. 91–120 days	84	1000
3. 61–90 days	200	500
4. 60 days or less	700	300
	1000	

Questions

1 Compute the total sample size for optimal allocation in which your desired error is no more than ± $20 for a 95.5% confidence level.

2 What size samples should be taken in each stratum? What should you do in stratum 1?

3 Suppose that after taking samples the accountant for PRIDEPAK found that total audited value for the samples in each strata was $2,600,000 for strata 1, $3,750,000 for strata 2, $2,040,000 for strata 3, and $1,440,000 for strata 4. Make an estimate of average account size. Will PRIDEPAK be able to obtain the loan?

4 Find the standard error of this estimate.

HYPOTHESIS TESTING

6

6-1 TYPE I AND TYPE II ERRORS

6-2 NULL HYPOTHESIS AND SCIENTIFIC TESTING PROCEDURE
One-tailed and Two-tailed Tests
Measuring Type II Error
How to Lower Type II Error and Retain the Same Type I Error

6-3 POWER CURVE (OPTIONAL SECTION)

6-4 ONE-SAMPLE TESTS
One-tailed Test of a Mean
Two-tailed Test of a Mean
One-tailed Test of a Proportion
Two-tailed Test of a Proportion
Problems

6-5 TEST OF A MEAN (SMALL SAMPLE, σ UNKNOWN), t TEST
Two-tailed Test of a Mean, σ Unknown, Small Sample
One-tailed Test of a Mean, σ Unknown, Small Sample
Problems

6-6 SUMMARY

6-7 BIBLIOGRAPHY

In Chapters 4 and 5 we used probability theory to make estimates about populations on the basis of information from a sample of that population. We have made *point* and *interval* estimates of the mean and proportions in these populations. We continue with this type of statistical analysis, but now try to frame these inferences so that they lead to a decision. For example, we will try to answer such questions as: Shall we accept or reject a shipment of goods? Does a certain drug provide relief for headaches? Does an advertising campaign lead to increased sales? Have voting preferences changed in a certain city?

6-1

In order to make these decisions, we will set up a theory about the population we wish to study. Then, we will take a sample from that population and test, on the basis of the characteristics of the sample, if it is likely that the population has the characteristics described in the theory. Thus, if we were testing a certain shipment of bolts to see if the average width was 1 inch and our sample from this shipment showed that the average width was 1.25 inches, we would be worried that the average bolt width in the shipment might not meet the 1-inch specification.

In the course of using a sample to make an estimate about the population, there are two types of errors that may arise. First, we may reject a true hypothesis. This is called a *Type I error*. In the example with the bolts, the hypothesis is that the average bolt width in the shipment is 1 inch. Perhaps it is true that the average width *is* 1 inch, yet somehow in our sample we encountered many larger bolts and so found an average size of 1.25 inches. If we had set up a rule that says reject when $\overline{X}$ (the mean of our sample) is greater than 1.1 inch or less than .9 inch, we would reject a good shipment and send it back to the producer. This would be a Type I error; we have rejected a good shipment. This error is sometimes called the *producer's risk*, because the buyer has tested the sample and the producer who has shipped the goods to the buyer must accept the returned merchandise even though the shipment was good. (Many times, instead of returning such a rejected shipment, the buyer and producer agree to detail the entire lot, which is equivalent to 100% inspection. Only the rejects are then replaced.)

Now, there is another way we can make an error, and that is if we *accept* a false hypothesis. Let us assume in this case that we receive a shipment of bolts. We test a sample and find that the average width is close to 1 inch. We therefore accept the shipment. Later, we find that the sample was unusual and the size of most bolts is actually more than 1 inch. This is a *Type II error*. We have accepted a false hypothesis, namely that the average bolt measures 1 inch. This is sometimes referred to as the *consumer's risk*, because the consumer has accepted a bad shipment.

We could express the types of error that could result from our study of a sample of bolts in the form of a table (see Table 6-1). This procedure of trying to decide what a population looks like by studying a sample from it means that we must know about the error of samples from this population. In Chapter 4, when we were studying the Central Limit Theorem, we said that if we took many samples of sufficient

TABLE 6-1

HYPOTHESIS: AVERAGE WIDTH OF BOLTS IN POPULATION EQUALS 1 INCH

ACTION	TRUE HYPOTHESIS (AVERAGE WIDTH OF BOLTS = 1 INCH)	FALSE HYPOTHESIS (AVERAGE WIDTH OF BOLTS ≠ 1 INCH)
Accept H_0	OK	Type II error—accept bad bolts (consumer's risk)
Reject H_0	Type I error— reject good bolts (producer's risk)	OK

size from a given population, sample means would be normally distributed and the
standard error of these sample means would be proportional to the standard deviation
of the population from which the samples were chosen, and inversely proportional to
the square root of sample size. Thus, the standard error of the mean is

$$\sigma_x = \frac{\sigma}{\sqrt{n}}$$

In the problem about accepting a shipment of bolts, let us assume that the
population standard deviation for the bolt manufacturer is $\sigma = .2$ inch. W also have
decided to take a sample of 64 bolts from the shipment sent to us. The standard error
of the sample mean is $\sigma_{\bar{x}} = .2/\sqrt{64} = .2/8 = .025$ inch.

Let us illustrate how sample means are distributed for this example. Figure
6-1(a) shows the normal distribution of the sample means for this example. If the
true population mean is 1.000, 68% of the sample means should fall between .975
and 1.025 ($\mu \pm 1\sigma_x$). Similarly, if the true population mean is 1.000, 95.5% of the
sample means should fall between $\mu \pm 2\sigma_{\bar{x}}$ (from .950 to 1.050).

Now, assume that the mean of our sample of 64 bolts is 1.060. We are interested in knowing the likelihood that a sample with this size mean could come from
a population with a mean of 1.000. Since sample means are normally distributed,
the z table can give us the probability of finding a mean of 1.060 for a sample of 64
from a population with a standard deviation of .200.

If we put this number on Figure 6-1(b), we see that it is far out on the right-

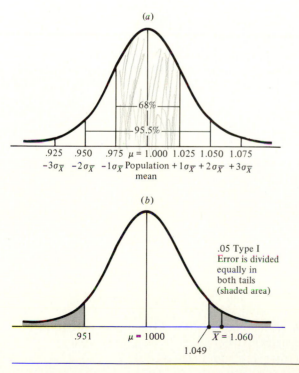

FIGURE **6-1**

(a) Distribution of sample means. (b) Plot of one sample mean.

hand tail. We plot this same sample mean on Figure 6-1(b) to find out how many standard errors from the assumed population mean it is; we get

$$z = \frac{\bar{X} - \mu}{\sigma_{\bar{X}}} = \frac{1.060 - 1.000}{.025} = \frac{.060}{.025} = 2.4$$

Looking up $z = 2.4$ in the z table, we find that the area between the mean and z is .4918; thus the area from 1.060 to the end of the distribution is .5000 − .4918, or .0082. This is the probability that, given a population mean of 1, a sample of 64 would have a mean value of 1.060 or higher. It seems unlikely that our sample came from a population with a mean of 1.000, but there is a .0082 probability that it might have. To phrase this another way, the probability of observing a sample mean of 1.060 or greater in a random sample of 64 drawn from a shipment of bolts with a mean width of 1.000 and a standard deviation of .020 is .0082. Since there is a very low probability that this shipment could have a mean of 1.000, we reject it and return it to the manufacturer. Generally, when these problems are studied, the reject criterion is set so that an acceptable amount of Type I error is allowed. Customary levels of Type I error for some types of business decision problems are 5 in 100 (.05) and 1 in 100 (.01). For example, if the allowance had been .05 in this problem, we would have put .025 on each tail. We have darkened an area equal to .025 of the area under curve A on each tail of the curve. This is our rejection area. If a sample mean falls in this area, we are unsure that the population it came from really has a mean of 1.000; therefore, we reject the corresponding shipment.

We now figure out the boundaries of this rejection area in terms of the number of standard errors of the mean (z value) and the numerical values for the sample means that tell us when to reject a sample mean. We enter these values in Figure 6-1(b).

Assume we had picked .05 Type I error, and decided to divide it evenly on each side of the curve because we were just as worried that the bolts might be too small (and hence not fit the nuts). If we wish to exclude 5% of the means (.05 Type I error), we then exclude 2½% of the sample means on each side of the curve. Looking up the z value that corresponds to .4750 (area from the mean to the cutoff point on each side of the curve), we find that our z value is +1.96 and −1.96. Now, if we wish to convert these z values (standard normal probabilities) to numerical values (inches in this case) to indicate the range of sizes within which we accept our shipment, we multiply z by the standard error of the mean $\sigma_{\bar{X}}$ and add and subtract this from the population mean $\mu = 1.000$.

$$1.000 \pm (1.96)(.025) = 1 \pm .049$$

Thus the cutoff points are .951 inch and 1.049 inches. Every sample mean that falls between these two measurements would lead us to accept the shipment. Every sample mean greater than 1.049 inches or less than .951 inch would lead us to reject the shipment. In this way, 5% of all perfectly good shipments would be rejected. This seems like a pretty strict rule. What if we lowered the Type I error and decided to be more liberal about accepting shipments? For example, assume we used $3\sigma_{\bar{X}}$ as our cutoff point. Then, the acceptance range would be between

$$\bar{X} + 3\sigma_{\bar{X}} = 1.075 \text{ inches}$$

and

$$\overline{X} - 3\sigma_{\bar{x}} = .925 \text{ inch}$$

Now, hardly any good shipments would be rejected. What is the danger? If we accept almost all shipments and thus cut down Type I error (rejecting good bolts), we have a very high chance of Type II error (accepting a false hypothesis) by accepting bolts that are too large or too small. An example shows how this works.

Assume that if bolts are not 1 inch in diameter on the average, they are 1.1 inches. If we draw a curve for μ of 1.100 inches [see Figure 6-2(b)] and assume that the standard deviation for this population is also .2, we can find out how far 1.075 inches, our new cutoff point, is from the mean of this alternative population.

$$\frac{1.075 - 1.1000}{.025} = -\frac{.025}{.025} = -1$$

If the cutoff point is $\pm 3\sigma_{\bar{x}}$, 99.7% of the area of curve A is included between the mean $\mu = 1.000$ and the two cutoff points 1.075 and .925; *Type I error is 1 − .997 = .003* (shaded area). The probability that the sample might have come from a population with a much higher or much lower mean is *greatly* increased. In this case, since 1.075 is 1 standard error from the mean of an alternate population with a mean of 1.100 (curve B), there is .5000 − .3413 or .1587 Type II error—the part of curve B that could have been accepted as coming from curve A. This is the area of curve B to the left of 1.075. Thus, there is a 16% chance that a sample with a mean of 1.075 might have come from a population with a mean of 1.100 inches. (See the shaded area.) There is a very large probability of a Type II error, namely of accepting a false hypothesis (that the bolts are really good) because we have assumed that the true population mean is 1.0. Every time we set up a test, we must decide which type of error is more serious, for unless we change sample size, we increase Type II error if we decrease Type I error. Conversely, if we decrease Type II error, we increase Type I error. Try moving the cutoff point to the right and to the left, and watch what happens to the Type I and Type II errors.

Type I error means we reject good merchandise. Since this is the producer's risk, we may want to set very high Type I error, and hence smaller Type II error.

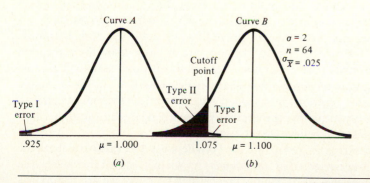

FIGURE **6-2**

(a) Distribution of sample means from population where $\mu = 1.000$. (b) Distribution of sample means from population where $\mu = 1.100$.

But this may antagonize our suppliers, who will not wish to take back good shipments or agree to 100% inspection for a large number of shipments. Furthermore, it causes us to lose time as we must reorder and await new shipments. On the other hand, accepting a false hypothesis (Type II error) can also have serious consequences. In a subsequent section of this chapter we will work on a problem for testing parachute cord. Obviously, we would not want to accept shipments of weak parachute cord. Consequently, Type II error becomes more important than Type I error. Similarly, for medical experiments, if too much of a given chemical is included in a pill it might prove dangerous to patients. Hence, we would be very worried about accepting medications that might in reality have too much of a given drug. The amount of allowable Type I error is referred to as the *level of significance or the α (alpha) error;* the level of allowable Type II error is often called the *β (beta) error.* Thus α and β are the probabilities of Type I and Type II errors, respectively. Both errors must be considered in determining the conditions for making a decision about the population based on a sample from that population.

NULL HYPOTHESIS AND SCIENTIFIC TESTING PROCEDURE

6-2

Let us assume that you are president of the local parachute club. An important part of your job is to order parachute cord for the members. You want to be sure that the cord supports at least 1500 pounds. You order 1000 cartons of cord, and decide that you will test the cord before accepting the shipment.

We will set up a scientific test procedure that consists of three steps. First, decide on a null hypothesis. A *null hypothesis* is generally set up so that you assume that whatever you are testing (for example, the effects of a given medication) has had *no effect*. It is then up to you to disprove the hypothesis that the thing you are testing has no effect. To show it has an effect, you must exceed the critical value specified in the test. For example, in a case in Chapter 7 we study whether taking aspirin leads to a decrease in blood clots. The null hypothesis H_0 is that aspirin has no effect on the number of blood clots. The alternative hypothesis H_1 is that aspirin does decrease the number of clots.

If sample results don't support the null hypothesis, we reject the null hypothesis. Rejecting a null hypothesis when it is true is a Type I error; accepting the null hypothesis when it is false is a Type II error. If the null hypothesis were true, the Type I error is the percentage of sample means from the hypothesized population that falls within the rejection area (significance level). If our sample statistic falls within the acceptance area, this does not prove that the null hypothesis is true. It just doesn't give any evidence to reject it. The only sure way is to know the population parameter, and that is what we are trying to estimate with our sample. Thus, we accept the null hypothesis because we don't have evidence to reject it. If our sample statistic falls within the rejection area (shaded area), we reject the null hypothesis. This does not necessarily mean that the alternative hypothesis is true, but rather that we have statistical reason to believe that it might be true.

The null hypothesis in the parachute cord problem is set so that we assume the *population mean exceeds or equals 1500 pounds.* As we have stated previously, the null hypothesis assumes that everything is fine or that whatever we are testing has no effect. In this illustration, we would be glad to find that we can accept the null hypothesis that the cord is good so that we do not have to send the shipment back.

We now set up a null hypothesis H_0 and an alternate hypothesis H_1. We are not worried that the parachute cord is too strong, but rather that it is too weak. Therefore, we put all chance for error on the weak side.

$$H_0: \mu \geq 1500 \qquad \text{null hypothesis}$$

$$H_1: \mu < 1500 \qquad \text{alternate hypothesis}$$

Now, we must specify the amount of allowable Type I error (the α error). This is the chance that we reject perfectly good parachute cord. We could let this be 1% or 5%, both commonly used levels of Type I error. In Figures 6-2 and 6-3, we can see that every time we decrease Type I error, we increase Type II error (the chance that we accept a false null hypothesis—in this case, assuming the cord is good when actually it isn't).

Table 6-1 showed Type I and Type II errors for the bolts problem. Table 6-2 shows Type I and Type II errors for the parachute cord problem. We let μ be the true population mean.

This hypothesis testing technique will now be applied to the test of parachute cord. When we test parachute cord, we are particularly worried about Type II error (the chance that we accept weak cord), so we select the larger Type I, .05. We might even take .10, .15, or larger to minimize Type II error, because we are so worried that the cord may be too weak. The determinant is what values of Type II error exist and what do we think can be tolerated. For example, however, let us choose .05 as our Type I error. In addition, we set a design for testing the cord.

There are 1000 boxes in the shipment. We take a sample of one piece of rope from 100 boxes at random. Some samples are from the ends, other from the middle portions of the cord. Therefore, n is 100. From previous studies of parachute cord, we know that the standard deviation of this type of cord is 300 pounds. Since n is large and σ is known, we pick the z test.

In our second step—the z test with .05 level of significance or α error (a one-tailed test)—we put all 5% of the Type I error on the left-hand side of the curve to make it hard for a low sample mean to pass the test, since we are only worried about alternatives less than 1500 pounds. Thus, the sample mean must be closer to the assumed population mean than it would be if the 5% were divided evenly between both tails of the distribution (see Figure 6-3). This is a one-tailed test. If the .05 were divided evenly on the tails, the cutoff points would be A and B. On the lower side,

TABLE 6-2

ACTION	H_0 IS TRUE: μ FOR PARACHUTE CORD $\geq$ 1500 POUNDS	H_0 IS FALSE: μ FOR PARACHUTE CORD $<$ 1500 POUNDS
Accept H_0	$1 - \alpha$ confidence level Correct decision	β Type II error (accept bad cord)
Reject H_0	Type I error (reject good cord) α significance level	Correct decision Power of test (explained in Section 6-3) $1 - \beta$

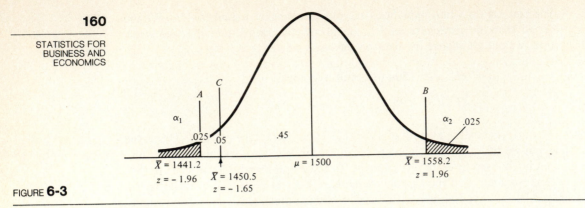

FIGURE **6-3**

One-tailed and two-tailed tests.

any mean greater than A would lead us to accept H_0. By putting the 5% on the left side only, our cutoff point is C. This makes it harder to accept H_0.

The final step of our scientific procedure consists of setting up a critical area. If the value of the sample mean X falls below this critical value, we reject H_0. This is shown in Figure 6-3. If a sample mean falls below $z = -1.65$ or $\bar{X}$ is less than 1450.5, we reject H_0. (*Note:* $-1.65(300/\sqrt{100}) = -49.5$ and $1500 - 49.5 = 1450.5$. This is the value at cutoff point C.) Both A and B are cutoff points for the two-tailed test where $\alpha_1 = \alpha_2 = .025$ (everything less than A or greater than B is rejected); C is the cutoff point for a one-tailed test where $\alpha = .05$. Everything less than C is rejected.

One-tailed and Two-tailed Tests

If we have chosen an α of .05 or any other value (.10, .15, or .02), we may divide it on two sides of the curve so that we reject a shipment where the sample mean is too large or too small, as in the case of the shipment of bolts that might be too *small* or too *large*. This is a *two-tailed test*. On the other hand, we may only be worried about one set of alternatives. For example, when we study parachute cord, we are not worried that it is too strong; we are worried that it is too weak. Thus, we put all Type I error on the side of the distribution about which we are most worried. This is a *one-tailed test*.

Looking at Figure 6-3, we could have cutoff points A and B, which represent .025 on each side of the distribution, or point C, which cuts off .05 on the left-hand side of the curve. In terms of z values, A and B are 1.96 standard errors from the assumed population mean ($1500 \pm 1.96\,\sigma_{\bar{x}}$). Thus, the upper and lower cutoff points are 1441.2 and 1558.8. If we found a sample mean that was more than 1441.2 (or less than 1558), we would accept the hypothesis that the mean strength of the cord was 1500 pounds. Using the one-tailed test, we now find the cutoff point or critical value. If we put our 5% Type I error on the left-hand side of the curve, the area from the mean to .05 would be .4500; this corresponds to a z value of -1.65. The cutoff is

$$1500 - 1.65\,\sigma_{\bar{x}} = 1500 - 1.65\left(\frac{300}{\sqrt{100}}\right)$$

$$= 1500 - 49.50 = 1450.50$$

If we look at Figure 6-3, we see that with all the error on the left tail, the cutoff point is 1450.5 (C); with the error split evenly, the cutoff point on the left tail is 1441.2 (A). Thus, by putting all the error on one side, the test of H_0 becomes more difficult to pass; a sample mean must have a larger value to infer that it really comes from a population with a mean strength of 1500 pounds.

Now that we have explained the difference between a one- and a two-tailed test, we proceed to set up the third step of the *hypothesis test procedure* for the parachute cord problem, which is a one-tailed test. We repeat our computation to set up our cutoff points in terms of either the z value or an $\bar{X}$ value.

Using cutoff point C and the normal table, we find that $z = -1.65$ at the point where we are .4500 of the area away from the mean. So we can set up the test in this way: If $z < -1.65$, reject H_0.

We can also figure out a value for $\bar{X}$ corresponding to $z = -1.65$, since we know σ, μ, and n.

$$z = \frac{\bar{X} - \mu}{s_{\bar{X}}}$$

$$-1.65 = \frac{\bar{X} - 1500}{300/\sqrt{100}}$$

$$-1.65 = \frac{\bar{X} - 1500}{30}$$

$$30(-1.65) + 1500 = \bar{X}$$

$$1450.5 = \bar{X}$$

We can set up our hypothesis test by saying the following: If $\bar{X} < 1450.5$, reject H_0.

The decision rule gives the same results whether we use z or $\bar{X}$; it is *not necessary* to use *both values* in performing a hypothesis test. Let's now look back upon the procedure. A scientific test should be set up *before* one examines the sample data. The steps are:

1 Set up the null hypothesis and the alternate hypothesis.
2 Set the level of significance (the amount of Type I error) and decide on the type of test (z or t or others) and whether you will use a one- or two-tailed test.
3 Set up the critical area either in terms of the z value, t value, or other test value. (We cover the t test in Chapter 7, and Chapter 9 provides a table to help you decide what kind of test to use.) Or, set up the critical area in terms of a value for a sample mean or sample proportion that the sample statistic cannot exceed without being rejected, or a value below which $\bar{X}$ or $\bar{p}$ cannot fall without being rejected. Thus, we set up a critical region that can be on one or both sides of the distribution. If $\bar{X}$ or $\bar{p}$ falls within this region, the null hypothesis is rejected.

For the parachute cord example (hypothesis test),

1 $H_0: \mu \geq 1500$
   $H_1: \mu < 1500$

2 z test, .05 level of significance, one-tailed test

3 If $z < -1.65$, reject H_0; or, if $\bar{X} < 1450.5$, reject H_0.

Measuring Type II Error

Let us return to the parachute cord example. Examine the Type I error (rejecting good cord) and the Type II error (accepting bad cord). To compute the magnitude of the Type II error, we must know the *specific value of the alternate* μ *if it were* lower than 1500. Let us assume it is 1400. We are assuming that if the manufacturer cannot make parachute cord with a strength of 1500 pounds, the cord will have a strength of 1400 pounds. This is a difficult assumption to make, but in *order to calculate Type II error we must have an alternate value for* μ. The reader may contend that the alternate could be 1450, 1475, or almost any value. This is usually true. The power curve used in Section 6-3 is designed to compute the Type II error using alternative values of μ. Now, looking at Figure 6-4(a) and (b), we see a population with mean of 1500 and, alternatively, of 1400. Obviously, from a given sample, the sample mean might be somewhere between 1400 and 1500 or even less than 1400 or more than 1500, and we would not be sure from which of the two populations the sample had come. In our parachute cord example, we said $z = -1.65$ and Type I error $= .05$. Therefore, our cutoff point was $1500 - (1.65)(30) = 1500 - 49.50 = 1450.50$. Now, to find the Type II error chance of accepting a false hypothesis (that the cord is strong when in reality it is weak), we measure that part of our curve with a mean of 1400—curve B (alternate hypothesis), which is to the right of 1450.5. [The blackened area in Figure 6-4(b) is Type II error.] It is the area from a population with a mean of 1400 that would be accepted as having come from a population with a mean of 1500. We use the z formula:

$$z = \frac{1450.5 - 1400}{30} = \frac{50.5}{30} = 1.68$$

If we look up $z = 1.68$ in the table of areas under the normal curve, the area equals .4535. Therefore, the area to the right of 1450.5 in curve B is $.5000 - .4535 = .0465$, or approximately 4.7%. Thus, if the alternative to having a mean of 1500 is having a mean of 1400, and we have a cutoff point of 1450.5, we have allowed a

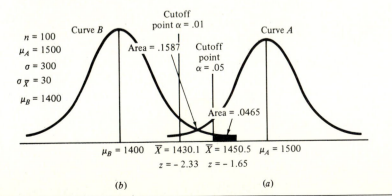

FIGURE **6-4**   (b)   (a)

Comparison of Type I and Type II error: (a) hypothesized mean; (b) alternate mean.

Type I error of 5% and a Type II error of 4.7%. Suppose we wish to have a Type I error of 1%. Let us trace what would happen to the Type II error.

If we cut off an area of 1% on our curve that has a mean of 1500, the area between the mean and the cutoff point is .4900, which corresponds to a z value of -2.33. (We are on the left-hand side of the mean; therefore, we use -2.33.) The cutoff point is $1500 - (2.33)(30) = 1500 - 69.90 = 1430.10$.

To find the Type II error, we use the mean of the curve on the left-hand side of Figure 6-4; $(1430.1 - 1400)/30 = 30.1/30 = 1.003$. The area from the mean to 1.003 standard deviation (1.00 on our z table) is .3413; therefore, the area to the right of 1430.1 in curve B is .1587, or 16% (the blackened area plus the white area under curve B between 1430.1 and 1450.5). Which is preferable?

$$\alpha = .05, \beta = .047 \qquad \text{or} \qquad \alpha = .01, \beta = .159$$

Type I (α) error in this case means that we reject perfectly good parachute cord. Type II (β) error means that we accept bad parachute cord. Obviously, it is far more dangerous to accept bad cord than to reject good cord, and we should try for the smallest amount of Type II error.[1] If we wish to lower Type II error below 4.7% without raising Type I error because our suppliers will not accept a higher rejection rate, our only alternative is to *increase our sample size.*

How to Lower Type II Error and Retain the Same Type I Error

In the parachute cord problem, we have a sample size of 100 (since we have assumed that testing is destructive, all of the cord can't be tested), a Type I error of 5%, and a Type II error of 4.7%. If we wish to maintain the Type I error at 5% and reduce the Type II error to 1%, we could set up one equation for each of our two curves ($\mu = 1400$; $\mu = 1500$). Look at Figure 6-5. Let $\overline{X}$ be the cutoff point where $\beta = .01$ and $\alpha = .05$. Working from the right-hand curve, where Type I error (curve A) equals .05, we have

$$-1.65 = \frac{\overline{X} - 1500}{\sigma_{\overline{X}}}$$

Therefore, we have

$$1500 - 1.65\,(\sigma_{\overline{X}}) = \overline{X} \tag{6-1}$$

Working from the left-hand curve, Type II error (curve B) equals .01, we have

$$+2.33 = \frac{\overline{X} - 1400}{\sigma_{\overline{X}}}$$

Therefore, we have

$$1400 + 2.33\,(\sigma_{\overline{X}}) = \overline{X} \tag{6-2}$$

---

[1] We might consider whether we are willing to have 1400-pound average breaking strength (note, it is the mean)—about 5 in 100 jumps. First, in the population, an actual jump cord may have *only* 1200-pound protection—the cord is bound to break. Secondly, we might be willing to accept $\beta = .047$ if H_1 has $\overline{\mu}$ equal to 1450 rather than to 1400.

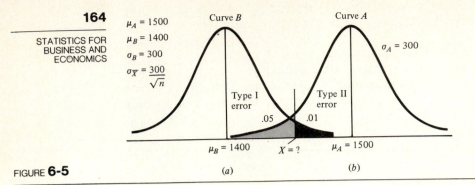

$\mu_A = 1500$
$\mu_B = 1400$
$\sigma_B = 300$
$\sigma_{\overline{X}} = \dfrac{300}{\sqrt{n}}$

FIGURE **6-5**

Lowering Type II error while retaining same Type I error: (a) alternate mean; (b) hypothesized mean.

Set Equation 6-1 equal to 6-2. Since both equations equal $\overline{X}$, we can set the two equations equal to each other.

$$1500 - 1.65\,\frac{300}{\sqrt{n}} = 1400 + 2.33\,\frac{300}{\sqrt{n}}$$

Simplifying, we have

$$2.33\,\frac{300}{\sqrt{n}} + 1.65\,\frac{300}{\sqrt{n}} = 100$$

$$3.98\,\frac{300}{\sqrt{n}} = 100$$

$$3.98(300) = 100\sqrt{n}$$

$$1194.00 = 100\sqrt{n}$$

$$11.94 = \sqrt{n}$$

$$142.56 = n$$

$$143 = n$$

Thus, if sample size were increased from 100 to 143, it would be possible to control Type I and Type II error at 5% and 1%, respectively. This is because the variation in the distribution of sample means decreases as sample size increases.

You will notice in this problem that we assumed that the population μ would be 1400 if it were not 1500. Usually, this information isn't known and it's necessary to compare estimates where μ is set at varying levels. When Type II error is particularly important, a power curve may be set up. In Section 6-3, we show how Type II error varies for different alternate population means. Without an alternate hypothesis, it is impossible to specify a Type II (β) error. Most hypothesis tests deal with Type I error and minimize Type II error by keeping Type I error reasonably high.

POWER CURVE (OPTIONAL SECTION)

6-3

One way to estimate both Type I and Type II errors over a continuum of alternative H_1's is to set up a power curve. This curve shows $1 - \beta$ ($1 -$ probability of a Type

II error), or the chance that *we won't make a Type II error*. For each of a number (or continuum) of alternate hypotheses, it shows the *power of the test to reject a false null hypothesis*. In Figure 6-5, for our parachute cord example, we show Type I error (α) and Type II error for the true population means of 1400 and 1500 pounds. Using the parachute cord problem, let us set up a power curve. The heights on the Y axis in Figure 6-6 below the curve show the probability of rejecting a false null hypothesis called the *power of the test*. The distance from the curve to 1.00 shows the probability of a Type II error. On the X axis, we have different alternative assumptions (H_1, H_2, H_3, ...) for the value of the mean (μ_1, μ_2, μ_3, ...). As before, we assume $\sigma = 300$ and $n = 100$; then $\sigma_{\bar{x}} = 30$. Now, we have already computed that if $\alpha = .05$ using a one-tailed test, the cutoff point is $1500 - 1.65(30)$, or 1450.5. *For the remaining computations needed to complete this curve, we continue to use this cutoff point, which keeps α at .05.* If the alternative mean were 1400 (keeping σ and n the same; see Figure 6-7), the Type II error would be computed by finding z:

$$z = \frac{1450.5 - 1400}{30} = \frac{50.5}{30} = 1.68$$

Using the z table, we can look up the area between 1450.5 and 1400. It is equal to .4535, as we calculated in our original problem. If $z = 1.68$, area $= .4535$. Then, $.5000 - .4535 = .0465$, which is our Type II error; $1 - \beta = .9535$. The power curve illustrates all the possibilities of Type II error as we use different ideas of what the alternative hypothesis might be. It also tells the *probability of not making a Type*

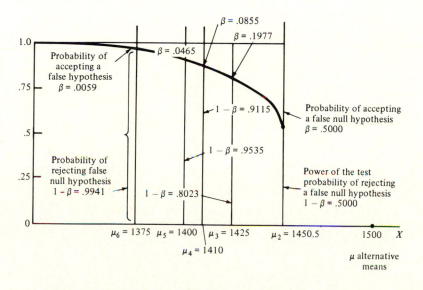

Valves for Power Curve where $\mu = 1500$

Alternate μ	Cutoff point	α	β	Power of the test
1375	1450.5	.05	.0059	.9941
1400	1450.5	.05	.0465	.9535
1425	1450.5	.05	.1977	.8023
1450	1450.5	.05	.4920	.5080
1450.5	1450.5	.05	.5000	.5000

FIGURE **6-6**

Power curve for parachute cord problem.

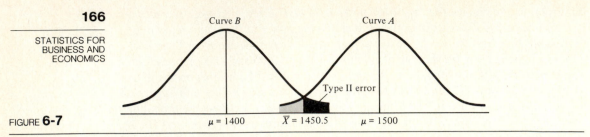

FIGURE **6-7**

Computation of Type II error when $\mu_B = 1400$.

II error which is the power of the test (the probability of rejecting the null hypothesis given that it is not true by an amount shown along the X axis). Now, let us try a different mean value for the alternative hypothesis (curve B), again keeping n and σ the same. Assume $\mu_B = 1425$ (Figure 6-8). Notice that curves A and B are now closer together than when μ_B equaled 1400. If our cutoff point for acceptance on curve A is still 1450.5, notice that now we accept more of the area under curve B as having come from curve A. Let us compute the Type II error for (Figure 6-8)

$$z = \frac{1450.5 - 1425}{30} = \frac{25.5}{30} = .85$$

If $z = .85$, the area between this value and the mean equals .3023 (z table). There-fore, the area of curve B that may be accepted as having come from curve A is .5000 $-$ .3023, or .1977. This is the type II error when $\mu_B = 1425$. The power of the test is $1 - \beta = .8023$.

When $\mu = 1450.5$ (see Figure 6-9) and our cutoff point is also $\bar{X} = 1450.5$, 50% of the time samples from the alternate distribution would be accepted as having come from a population with a mean of 1500. Now, if we draw a diagram of the two distributions with means of 1450.5 and 1500, respectively (curves B and A, Figure 6-9), we can see that 50% of the samples from population B (shaded area) are accepted as having come from curve A (population A). Thus, we have a 50% Type II error and a 5% Type I error (blackened area). Since the chance of a Type II error is 50%, the chance of *not* making a Type II error is $1 - \beta$, or $1 - .50$—50%. The *power of the test* is .50; on Figure 6-6, this would be our observation on the X axis at $\mu = 1450.5$. Similarly, we could compute the power for any number of hypotheses. For example, if the alternate hypothesis were $\mu = 1410$, then

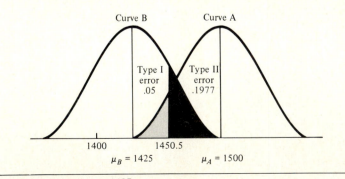

FIGURE **6-8**

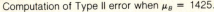

Computation of Type II error when $\mu_B = 1425$.

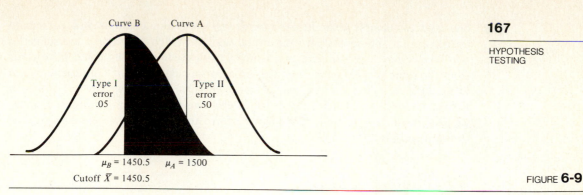

Cutoff $\bar{X} = 1450.5$

FIGURE **6-9**

Computation of Type II error when $\mu_B = 1450.5$.

$$z = \frac{1450.5 - 1410}{30} = 1.35 \qquad area = .4115$$

$$\beta = .5000 - .4115 = .0885$$

$$1 - \beta = 1.000 - .0885 = .9115$$

This value is shown in Figure 6-6 for $\mu = 1410$. Now, assume the alternate mean is 1375.

$$z = \frac{1450.5 - 1375}{30} = \frac{75.5}{30} = 2.52 \qquad area = .4941$$

This value is shown in Figure 6-6 for $\mu = 1375$.

$$\beta = .5000 - .4941 = .0059$$

$$1 - \beta = .9941$$

From Figure 6-6, we can see that the power of a test $(1 - \beta)$, or the chance of not making a Type II error, is lowest when the alternate hypothesis is very close to the cutoff point. It becomes higher as the alternate hypothesis moves farther away from the cutoff point.

Combining what we have learned in these two sections we can try, in a situation in which we do not know the alternate hypothesis, to create power curves for various alternative hypotheses and sample sizes and to determine the most appropriate sample size. Notice that in all cases we have assumed a .05 Type I error, a one-tailed test, and hence a critical value of 1450.5. We could recompute the power curve for all the different alternative means and assume a .10 Type I error. This curve would show more power for each alternative hypothesis because the critical test is much harder to pass; the cutoff point is greater than 1450.5. We could also compute power curves for two-tailed tests.

Now that we have pointed out the types of errors that can occur, we concentrate on the different types of hypothesis tests.

ONE-SAMPLE TESTS

In the remainder of this chapter, we learn how to perform one-sample hypothesis tests that use the normal distribution and z or t tables. First, we distinguish between

6-4

one- and two-sample tests. In *one-sample tests,* we take a sample and attempt to estimate what the population from which we have taken the sample looks like; in *two-sample tests,* we compare two samples to determine if they could have come from the same population or from two different populations. For both the one- and two-sample tests, we can test a *mean* and a *proportion.* Also, we can use a one- or a two-tailed test. In the parachute cord and the bolts problems earlier in this chapter, we performed a test of a mean. We now perform another test of a mean and proceed to test a proportion.

One-tailed Test of a Mean

Now, let's do a problem that tests a mean.

EXAMPLE 6-1   A government agency recently found that an artificial sweetener used in diet soft drinks may have harmful side effects. Therefore, it set limits on the amount that each can may contain at .1 ounce. The manager of a local soft drink company, thinking that the mixing machine may not be staying within the tolerable limit, runs a test on 100 cans. The test shows the cans to have an average of .13 ounces of artificial sweetener. The population standard deviation is .06.

1   Should the manager adjust the machine if $\alpha = .05$? (*Hint:* Set up the hypothesis test.)
2   If $\alpha = .02$, should the manager adjust the machine?
3   Which value of α would you pick for this problem?
4   What if $\bar{X} = .12$ ($\alpha = .02$)?
5   At what value of $\bar{X}$ should he keep the machine ($\alpha = .02$) as it is?

1 (*a*)   Null hypothesis $H_0: \mu \leq .1$.
            Alternate hypothesis $H_1: \mu > .1$
   (*b*)   z test, $\alpha = .05$, one-tailed test
   (*c*)   Decision rule: If $z > 1.645$, reject H_0.

$$z = \frac{.13 - .1}{.06/\sqrt{100}} = \frac{.03}{.06/10} = \frac{.03}{.006} = 5 \qquad \text{reject } H_0; \ 5 > 1.645$$

2 (*a*) $H_0: \mu \leq .1$
            $H_1: \mu > .1$
   (*b*)   z test, $\alpha = .02$, one-tailed test
   (*c*)   If $z > 2.05$, reject H_0; $z = 5$, $5 > 2.05$, so reject H_0.
3   .05 would be better as it would allow for less Type II error.
4 (*a*) $H_0: \mu \leq .1$
            $H_1: \mu > .1$
   (*b*)   z test, $\alpha = .02$, one-tailed test
   (*c*)   If $z > 2.05$, reject H_0.

$$z = \frac{.12 - .1}{.06/\sqrt{100}} = \frac{.02}{.06/10} = \frac{.02}{.006} = 3.33 \qquad \text{reject } H_0; \ 3.33 > 2.05$$

$$2.05 = \frac{\bar{X} - .1}{.06/10}$$

$$.0123 = \bar{X} - .1$$

$$\bar{X} = .1123$$

Note that in **1, 2,** and **4** when we reject the null hypothesis we are saying that we believe that the amount of sweetener is *not* less than or equal to government requirements. As a result of our tests, we have some reason to believe that there is more than the specified amount of sweetener in the beverages.

In the parachute cord problem, as well as the sweetener problem, we illustrated a one-tailed or one-sided test, where we put all the Type I error on one side (cord too weak) because we didn't care if the population cord strength was excessive. Let us assume that we are worried about something that may be too big or too small, such as the bolt shipment problem. This was a two-tailed test: if the bolts are too small, they will not secure the parts of the machine; if they are too large, they will not fit into the holes. We now show how a two-tailed test is set up.

Two-tailed Test of a Mean

EXAMPLE 6-2   Assume we are filling boxes with cereal. We do not wish to have too little in a box because the government will penalize us. We do not wish to overfill the box since it wastes cereal and is costly. Say that we need to put 16 ounces in each box. Previous studies have shown that the standard deviation for the filling machine for the boxes is $\sigma = 1$ ounce. Let us set up a two-tailed hypothesis test that will be used with a sample of 100 boxes.

1 H_0: $\mu = 16$ ounces
H_1: $\mu \neq 16$ ounces
2   Level of significance of .05 required by law, z test, two-tailed test. (Now, we assume that on each side of the mean we have an area of .4750. This leaves an area of .025 on each tail of the distribution. Our acceptance area on each side of the mean is .4750, leaving .05 in both tails combined.)
3   (*a*)   If $z > 1.96$ or < -1.96, reject H_0. (Looking up .4750 in the standard normal table, we find that it corresponds to a z value of 1.96.)
      or

(*b*) $16 + 1.96 \dfrac{1}{\sqrt{100}} = 16 + .196 = 16.20$

$16 - 1.96 \dfrac{1}{\sqrt{100}} = 16 - .196 = 15.80$

      If $\bar{X} < 15.80$ or > 16.20, reject H_0

If our sample of 100 boxes reveals that $\bar{X}$ is less than 15.8 or greater than 16.2, we reject H_0 and try to reset our machines so they fill the boxes more accurately.

Note that without an alternate hypothesis it is impossible to specify a β error. Most hypothesis tests deal with the α error and tend to minimize β error by keeping α at a reasonably high level. If β error is particularly important, a power curve may be set up.

One-tailed Test of a Proportion

We have tested means using one- and two-tailed tests. Now, we perform a similar test on proportions.

EXAMPLE 6-3   The local Republican candidate hired a market research agency to test his popularity. He felt that if he could be assured that at least 60% of the city would vote for him, he would be safe in the next election. The research firm agreed to poll a random sample of 400 city voters and report the results. Set up a test of the results and draw a diagram. (Note that α wasn't specified. In this case, use a common level (.05 or .01) depending on how much Type II error you are willing to accept.)

1 H_0: $p \geq .60$
    H_1: $p < .60$
2   .05 level of significance, z test, one-tailed test
3   If $z < -1.65$, reject H_0. (Now if we put all the error on one tail, the area between the mean and the cutoff point is $-.4500$. The corresponding z value is -1.65. See Figure 6-10.) Or

$$\sigma_{\bar{p}} = \sqrt{\frac{.60(.40)}{400}}$$

$$\sigma_{\bar{p}} = .0245$$

$$1.65\,(.0245) = .040$$

$$.60 - .04 = .56$$

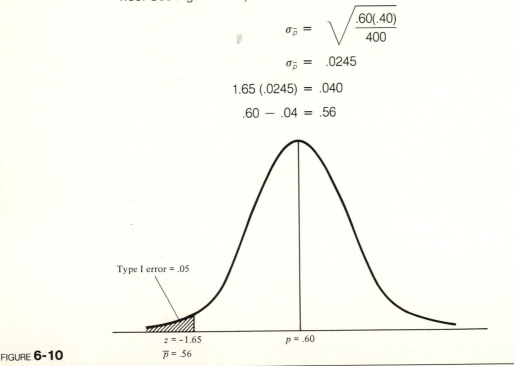

Type I error = .05

$z = -1.65$
$\bar{p} = .56$

$p = .60$

FIGURE **6-10**

Rejection area for voting analysis problem.

Therefore, another way to word the critical test on step 3 is to say "Reject H_0 if $\bar{p} < .56$."

Now, when the sample is taken, 55% say they will vote for the candidate.

$$z = \frac{.55 - .60}{.0245} = -2.041$$

Since z is less than -1.65, we reject H_0; we do not believe that the true population proportion is .60 or, using the other criteria, since $.55 < .56$ we reject H_0.

We may also wish to make a two-sided test of a proportion, and the method is similar to that used for a two-sided test of a mean.

Two-tailed Test of a Proportion

EXAMPLE 6-4   The advertising manager of a savings bank claimed that 70% of its customers were in the age group 25–45, and consequently 70% of the advertising appeals should be directed at people in this group. Furthermore, he felt it would be wise to establish all new branches in the northern suburbs, where young business couples were buying new homes. The advertising manager took a sample of 200 accounts and found the sample proportion in this age group to be 65%. Is the manager's claim valid if the level of significance is 0.05?

1 H_0: $P = .70$ (P refers to the population proportion)
     H_1: $P \neq .70$
2   Level of significance $= .05$, z test, two-tailed test
3   If $z > 1.96$ or < -1.96, reject H_0.
     The standard error of a proportion, developed in Chapter 4, is

$$\sigma_{\bar{p}} = \sqrt{\frac{pq}{n}} = \sqrt{\frac{.7(.3)}{200}} = \sqrt{0.00105} = .0324$$

$$z = \frac{\bar{p} - P}{\sigma_{\bar{p}}} = \frac{.65 - .70}{.0324} = \frac{-.05}{.0324} = -1.54$$

Accept H_0 since -1.54 is larger than -1.96.

Now, what if the sample proportion turned out to be .85? Then, $z = (.85 - .70)/.0324 = 4.6296$. Now reject H_0. It would seem that the proportion in this age group is even larger than we had thought. (See Figure 6-11.)

An alternate solution is to determine a cutoff point by translating our z values into actual percentages. For a .05 α level, split equally on the two tails, our z value is 1.96. Now, multiply this by the size of the standard error and add and subtract this from the population proportion. We can now put these percentage cutoff points on Figure 6-11.

$$z\sigma_{\bar{p}} = 1.96(.0324)$$

$$.70 \pm (1.96)(.0324)$$

$$.6365 \text{ to } .7635$$

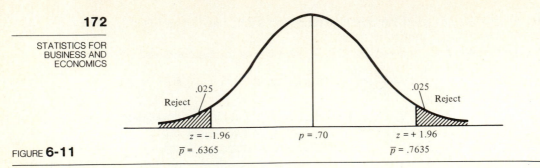

FIGURE **6-11**

Rejection areas for a two-tailed test.

If the sample proportion $\bar{p}$ is anywhere between 63.65% and 76.35%, we must assume that the population proportion could be 70%. In this case, p is .85 and exceeded the .7635 cutoff point. Therefore, we reject H_0.

Problems

1 In the parachute cord problem described in this chapter, which type of error was more important: Type I or Type II? Should the significance level be set high or low for this problem? Discuss.

2 A recent bill submitted to Congress calls for the inspection of used cars and issuance of a report to the prospective buyer. If the report is good and the car turns out to be in bad shape, the buyer could sue the used car dealer. What type of error is more important for the dealer?

3 (a) For Example 6-1, compute the power of the test and sketch a power curve for the hypothesis that $\mu = .10$ and $\mu = .11$. Use α of .05 and a one-tailed test.
   (b) *Optional:* Now, compute the power of the test and sketch the power curve using $\alpha = .10$.
   (c) If the sweetener was really dangerous, what would you recommend?

4 A local bicycle store specializing in lightweight racing bikes was experiencing what seemed to be an unusual number of complaints about spokes breaking on a certain model. Because of this, the owner took 64 spokes out of the shipment and ran a test on them. Since it was a destructive test, he did not wish to use too large a sample. According to the manufacturer's specifications, the average tensile spoke strength should be at least 200 pounds, with a known standard deviation of 20 pounds.
   (a) If the owner found the tensile strength to be 190 pounds per spoke, should he send the shipment back, use detailing, or accept the shipment? Use $\alpha = .05$ since the supplier would not accept more than 5% in rejects of good merchandise.
   (b) What is the minimum $\bar{X}$ possible for the owner to keep the shipment of spokes?

5 A certain type of solar energy cell requires a special crystal in its construction. Since this crystal is very expensive, producers of solar energy cells want to keep it as small as possible but still large enough to work efficiently. The crystals average .4 grams in weight and are known to have a standard deviation of .02 ($\alpha = .05$).

(*a*)   If 100 crystals are selected at random from a production process, lot, or shipment and have an average weight of .42, should these be used in solar cells?

(*b*)   If 100 crystals are selected, what is the largest average that could be acceptable?

(*c*)   If we want $\alpha = .05$ and error no larger than $\pm .006$, what size sample should we use?

6   An advertising agency working for a large fast-food company had prepared an advertising campaign based on the assumption that 40% of the customers were over age 25. The company wanted the advertisements changed if the percentage was greater than or less than 40%. Assume that the company only wants a 5% chance of incurring a Type I error and the survey shows that 300 of the customers are over age 25 and that 300 are age 25 or below in a sample of 600. Should the advertising campaign be changed?

7   Concern has been mounting recently about declining Scholastic Aptitude Test scores among future college entrants. Over a current 3-year period, scores fell from 955 to 948 for a sample group of 200 graduating high school students. Tests have shown the standard deviation on SAT tests to be 100 points. At a .05 level of significance, determine if there is sufficient evidence to suspect a change in students' ability.

8   Last month an area retailer found that its average sale per customer amounted to $35 with a standard deviation of $8. After a significant increase in promotional advertising for this month, the average sale per customer increased to $37 (with the same standard deviation) for a random sample of 40 receipt tickets. Determine the effectiveness of the advertising campaign on the amount of average sales at a .05 level of significance.

9   A quality control supervisor at a local manufacturing plant wanted to spot-check production of the small appliance durability from the assembly line. On previous tests, the average life of a particular model blender was 1500 hours with a standard deviation of 150 hours. After testing 50 units, average appliance life was found to be only 1440 hours.

(*a*)   At a .02 level of significance, is there sufficient evidence that these blenders may be substandard?

(*b*)   What level of α would you need to accept H_0?

10   A large aircraft manufacturer accepts many shipments of components that have been subcontracted to other firms. One particular subcontracter supplies a set of 1-inch-diameter mechanical linkages for hydraulic control systems. Previous tests have shown that the standard deviation of these finely machined rods was only .005 inch. Construct a decision rule for accepting parts if the plane manufacturer plans to measure only 50 items in each shipment. The measurement is very expensive and takes considerable time. The manufacturer will not have time to investigate more than 50 items. Use a .05 level of significance.

11   A manufacturer of auto mufflers claims that distributors find that no more than 6% of the parts in any shipment are defective. Red's Guaranteed Mufflers decided to test this claim using a .05 probability of rejecting the claim when it is true, since the manufacturer would accept only a 5% return rate or detailing on "good" merchandise. The manager selected 125 parts at random and found 11 to be defective. What conclusion should be reached concerning the manufacturer?

12 One of the nation's leading breweries is marketing a new light beer aimed especially at calorie-conscious younger Americans. In fact, the brewery based its entire advertising strategy on the assumption that 50% of its consumers were 28 years old or less. To test this assumption, the company interviewed 500 consumers randomly chosen at various types of outlets and found that 238 were 28 years old or less and that the remaining 262 were older. If the company desired to allow only a .05 probability of rejecting the ad agency's claim that 50% of the customers are under 28 when it is true, should they change their advertising policy?

13 In a recent congressional election, a well-known pollster took a sample of 200 registered voters on the eve of the contest. Only 79 respondents favored candidate X, who had held 47% of the vote a week earlier.

(*a*) If the pollster wished to allow only a .02 level of error that candidate X has slipped in the ratings, should their earlier prediction be allowed to stand?

(*b*) What if α were raised to .05?

14 The President's 1980 energy program called for at least 75% of all adult Americans to cut their gasoline consumption by 10% next year. A national survey of 1000 people revealed that only 705 thought that they could possibly achieve savings in that range. Is the President's goal realistic? Since the Energy Council wanted to present a favorable answer to the media, they debated whether to use an α level of .01 or .05. Which one leads to a more optimistic test? Use the one you have chosen to determine if the goal seems realistic.

15 The curator at the New York Museum of Fine Arts feels that Impressionists are the favorite artists of the museum-going public. She goes so far as to state that 90% of the public would like to see an exhibit of Gauguin, Matisse, Seurat, and Degas. The director challenges her to take a survey on a Sunday afternoon. A random sample of 97 museum goers indicates that 75% would like to see this type of show. Is the curator's statement still justified?

TEST OF A MEAN (SMALL SAMPLE, σ UNKNOWN), t TEST

6-5

In the previous discussion of the distribution of sample means, we gave a conditional statement that *if the samples were large enough* the sample means would be normally distributed about the population mean and the standard error of the mean would be $\sigma/\sqrt{n}$. Thus, we also assumed that we knew the population standard deviation σ. Frequently, we do not know the population standard deviation and have to estimate it using s, the standard deviation within the sample itself. If the sample is large, s may be a fairly accurate estimate of σ (the population) standard deviation, and the z table is often used. If the sample is small (the rule of thumb for many business and social science applications is $n < 30$), we use the t distribution—as we did to formulate the confidence interval for a small sample when σ was not known. Note that in order to use the t distribution we must have reason to believe that the population from which our sample comes is normally distributed. If we have a small sample and do not think the parent population is normally distributed, we may use nonparametric statistical tests, which will be explained in Chapters 8 and 9. Table 9-10 outlines tests for different types of assumptions.

We now show how the t table is used in one- and two-tailed tests of means when σ is not known.

Two-tailed Test of a Mean, σ Unknown, Small Sample

The testing procedure using the t table is very similar to that used for the z test, except that we must specify the degrees of freedom $(n - 1)$ and must have reason to believe that the population from which the sample is taken is approximately normally distributed and therefore not highly skewed. Let us do an example.

EXAMPLE 6-5 A small calculator manufacturing firm buys chargers for its calculators from an electronics firm. In order for the charger to fit the calculator, its prongs must measure 2 millimeters. The calculator manufacturing firm has not dealt with the electronics firm before and they, therefore, have no idea what the production standard deviation will be, although usually the dimensions are normally distributed. They decide to take a sample of 25 chargers, since the extensive tests destroy the chargers, and estimate the value of s. This value turns out to be .18 millimeters. They also find from this sample that the average diameter of the prongs of the chargers is 2.3 millimeters. Test at the .05 level of significance and determine if the company should accept the chargers.

1 H_0: $\mu = 2$ millimeters
H_1: $\mu \neq 2$ millimeters
2 $\alpha = .05$, t test, 24 df, two-tailed test

$$s_{\bar{x}} = .18/\sqrt{25} = .036$$

To find the t value look in the t table; when df is 24 and the level of significance is .05 divided equally on the two tails, the t value is 2.064. The critical values are 2 $\pm$ 2.064(.036). Thus, our acceptance range goes from 1.9266 to 2.074.

3 Decision rule:

(a) If $\bar{X} < 1.926$ or $\bar{X} > 2.074$, reject H_0.
          Or, alternately,
(b) If $t < -2.064$ or $t > 2.064$, reject H_0.

Now, if we look at the sample, we find using our first decision rule.
(a) $\bar{X} = 2.3$, so reject H_0 using rule 3(a).
If we calculate a t value,

(b) $$t = \frac{\bar{X} - \mu}{s/\sqrt{n}} = \frac{2.3 - 2.0}{.18/\sqrt{25}} = \frac{0.3}{.036} = 8.333$$

reject H_0 using rule 3(b), since $8.333 > 2.064$.

In this problem we were equally worried that the prongs were too small or too large and therefore used a two-tailed test. In the next section, we discuss a one-tailed test of a mean.

One-tailed Test of a Mean, σ Unknown, Small Sample

The one-tailed test is often used when we are interested or worried about whether something is too large or too small, but are not worried about both sides of the distribution. Thus, we may wish to know if rural families earn *at least* $10,000 a year or if *more than* 500 students need university loans for the coming semester. Let us try an example of a one-tailed test of a mean where σ is unknown and sample size small.

EXAMPLE 6-6   A survey of dormitory students on the campus of Rutgers, the State University of New Jersey, was taken by the student council to determine if the average allowance for student necessities (snacks, entertainment, transportation, school supplies, and other items) was at least $100 a week. A local bank had promised special student accounts if students would deposit a minimum of $400 a month in a checking account. The council was trying to show that at least half of the students received $400 or more, so they interviewed a random sample of 28 students. Then they called in a student who had taken a statistics course to analyze their data. The student was upset that only 28 students had been interviewed, but he decided that by using the *t* distribution (since he felt that at a state school allowances would be normally distributed) he could perform the test. The sample gave a mean weekly allowance of $90 and the standard deviation within the sample was $10. Would there be a reason to believe that the average allowance is $100 or more? Use $\alpha = .05$.

1 $H_0: \mu \geq \$100$
   $H_1: \mu < \$100$
2 $\alpha = .05$, *t* test, df $= 27$, one-tailed test

$$s_{\bar{x}} = \frac{10}{\sqrt{28}} = 1.890$$

Now, if we look at the *t* table, we find that the cutoff points or the values suggested are for the given α level divided *equally* on the two tails. With $\alpha = .05$ and a two-tailed test with 27 degrees of freedom, the *t* value is ± 2.052. These are points *A* and *B* on Figure 6-12.

If we choose to put all Type I error on the left-hand side so that we accept as few low allowances as possible as having come from a population where μ

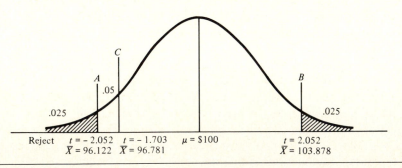

Reject $t = -2.052$ $t = -1.703$ $\mu = \$100$ $t = 2.052$
$\bar{X} = 96.122$ $\bar{X} = 96.781$ $\bar{X} = 103.878$

FIGURE **6-12**

Comparison of one- and two-tailed *t* tests.

= \$100, our cutoff point C is on the left-hand side of the curve but is to the right of the two-tail cutoff point on that side of curve A. To find this in our table, look under 27 degrees of freedom and the .10 column (since this point would cut off 5% on each tail). The value for the one-tailed test, where $\alpha = .05$, is -1.703. Thus, any t value calculated to be less than -1.703 would mean we should reject the null hypothesis. Let us now continue setting up our hypothesis test.

The *critical value* is $\$100 - (1.703)(1.890) = 100 - 3.219 = 96.781$

3 Decision rule:
(a) If $\bar{X} < 96.781$, reject H_0, or
(b) If $t < -1.703$, reject H_0.
   Using rule 3(a), $\bar{X} = 90$, so we reject H_0.
   Using rule 3(b), $t = (90 - 100)/1.890 = -5.291$.

Since $-5.291 < -1.703$, we reject H_0. We don't have good enough evidence to assume that the average allowance is at least \$100. It might be advisable to redo this study using a larger sample.

In Chapter 5 when we studied confidence intervals, we pointed out that in many cases it may be advisable to use the t distribution when σ is unknown, particularly if the sample size is less than 30. Accountants particularly may use the t distribution for samples up to a size of 200 since accuracy is very important for their estimates. Look at your t table and you will see that as n becomes larger the values in the t table begin to approach those in the z table.

When *tests of a proportion* for a large sample are considered, it is assumed that the sampling distribution of a proportion approximates a normal distribution as n becomes large. Therefore, the z table is used for hypothesis testing. You will remember from Chapter 3 that as n approaches infinity, the binomial distribution begins to look like the normal distribution. Therefore, if we are testing a proportion and n is large (>30), the z table may be used to set up a critical value for a hypothesis test. If a test of proportions is used and the sample size is small, the binomial distribution may be used. We do not consider any of these tests in this text.

In this chapter, we introduced a very important set of statistical ideas. The Type I and Type II errors are present in every decision-making situation. The hypothesis testing procedure and the power curve provide ways for estimating and trying to control these types of errors. We then showed how to take a sample and to make an estimate about the population from which this sample came. These tests are called *one-sample tests*. We have shown one- and two-tailed tests of a mean and a proportion. These tests use the z distribution. In addition, we have shown one- and two-tailed tests of a mean when σ is unknown and the sample size is small. These tests use the t distributions. In Chapter 7, we continue with hypothesis testing procedures for two or more samples. As an example of a two-sample test, we might be interested in testing whether the cost of housing in two cities is different. We will take two samples of housing costs and try to decide if they have come from the same or different populations. Tests of difference between means and tests of difference between proportions will be explained.

One multisample test might study several textbooks to see if the books have different effects on students' test scores. Analysis of variance is used to study this type of problem.

Problems

1 Tubby Toots special reeds for clarinets are said to last for 100 hours of use. A study of 15 clarinet players hired by the Boston Symphony indicated that the musicians had to replace their reeds after an average of 85 hours with a standard deviation of 10 hours. At the .01 level of significance, would the claims of Tubby Toots be considered justifiable?

2 Disaster Charge, a new form of charge account, is initiated for people who have bad credit ratings and cannot qualify for other charge accounts. In Disaster Charge, the client must pay a 5% monthly fee on any payments delinquent for more than a month. If the charge is not fully paid in 3 months, the account is suspended. The company president claims that the average delinquent balance is usually equal to or less than $200. A sample of 20 delinquent accounts reveals that the average balance is $210 with a standard deviation of $25.

(*a*) Is the president justified in his claim? Use an α level of .05.

(*b*) If 200 accounts were sampled and gave $\bar{X} = 210$ and $s = \$25$, what would your conclusions be?

3 Chicago Power and Light Company (CPL Co.) finds that its customers are dissatisfied with street lights. They complain that one or more lights are out per block in the residential areas, and that the lights are not repaired for at least 2 months. The problem seems to be that CPL Co. must wait for customer complaints because workers do not check the lights at night. Lights are repaired as soon as they are reported. The company set up an experiment in which 30 lights chosen at random throughout the residential areas were shut off; records were kept of how quickly complaints were received to see if the average reporting time was 60 days. At the end of 3 months, the company found that 2 of the 30 lights studied were never reported. The remaining 28 lights were reported after an average of 58 days with a standard deviation of 10 days. Are the customers' complaints justified? Would you recommend that the company find another way to monitor street lights? Use a two-tailed test with $\alpha = .05$. (Ignore the two lights that were never reported.)

SUMMARY

6-6

1 A Type I error occurs when a *true* hypothesis is rejected. This type of error is sometimes called the *producer's risk* because perfectly good shipments may be returned to the producer.

2 A Type II error occurs when a *false* hypothesis is accepted. This is sometimes referred to as the *consumer's risk* because the consumer has accepted a bad shipment.

3 In setting up the hypothesis test, a *null hypothesis* and an *alternate hypothesis* are stated. If the null hypothesis is rejected, there is statistical reason to believe that the alternate hypothesis may be true.

4 A test of an hypothesis should involve three steps: (*a*) specification of the null hypothesis and the alternate hypothesis; (*b*) type of test (such as *t* or *z*), the level of significance, one- or two-tailed specification; and (*c*) critical value expressed in terms of z or t, or expressed as a numerical value that must be compared to the sample statistic.

5 In order to calculate Type II error, it is necessary to know a *specific value* for the alternative hypothesis. To lower Type II error and retain the same level of Type I error, sample size must be increased.

6 A *power curve* assumes a given sample size, σ value, level of α, and a set cutoff point. It shows the ability of the test to reject a false null hypothesis for a number of different alternative population means or proportions.

7 Use of a one- or a two-tailed test depends on the nature of the problem. For example, if the penalties are very bad if something is too small, all Type I error should be placed on the small side. If we are worried that something may be either too small or too large, the error should be divided evenly on both sides of the distribution.

8 In one-sample tests, we test a mean or a proportion. For both tests, we look to see if, on the basis of a given sample statistic (mean or proportion), we can make a conclusion about the true population mean or the true population proportion. To make this test, a cutoff point is calculated by specifying a z value or using the z value to give a specific numerical value that must be exceeded by the sample mean or the sample proportion in order to reject the null hypothesis. To test the mean, $\sigma_{\bar{x}} = \sigma/\sqrt{n}$ or $s_{\bar{x}} = s/\sqrt{n}$ is used. For a proportion, $\sigma_{\bar{p}} = \sqrt{\overline{pq}/n}$ is used, where $\overline{p}$ is the sample proportion.

9 The t table is used to determine critical values for a test of a mean when σ is not known, the sample size is small, and the underlying population distribution is thought to be normal. Generally, as a rule of thumb, a small sample has been defined as $n < 30$, although in some situations sample sizes up to 200 warrant the use of the t table.

BIBLIOGRAPHY

6-7

Levin, Richard I.: *Statistics for Management.* Englewood Cliffs, N.J.: Prentice-Hall, 1978, chapter 9, pp. 240–283. Excellent simple exposition of hypothesis testing.

Plane, Donald R., and Edward B. Opperman: *Statistics for Management Decisions.* Dallas: Business Publications, 1977, chapter 9, pp. 177–208. Good technical explanation of hypothesis testing.

Richards, Larry E., and Jerry J. LaCava: *Business Statistics: Why and When.* New York: McGraw-Hill, 1978, chapter 8, pp. 152–187. Another simple explanation of hypothesis testing.

HYPOTHESIS TESTS:
Two- and Three-Sample or Larger Sample Tests

7

7-1   TWO-SAMPLE TESTS (LARGE SAMPLES)
Two-tailed Tests of Difference between Means
Problems
Two-tailed Tests of Difference between Proportions (Large Sample)
Problems
One-tailed Test of Difference between Means
One-tailed Test of Difference between Proportions
Problems

7-2   TEST OF DIFFERENCE BETWEEN MEANS (SMALL SAMPLE, σ UNKNOWN)
Problems

7-3   ANALYSIS OF VARIANCE
Use of the F Table
Summary of Tests Used in Chapters 6 and 7
Problems

7-4   SUMMARY

7-5   BIBLIOGRAPHY

7-6   CASES
Case 7-1: Beta Blockers
Case 7-2: Southwestern Optical Prices
Case 7-3: The NARO-SHU Company (C)

In Chapter 6, we introduced the concepts of Type I and Type II error, and the scientific hypothesis testing procedure. We then went on to demonstrate a one- and two-tailed test of a mean and a proportion. A power curve was introduced to show the interaction of different alternate hypotheses and Type II error. We then showed a method for handling a hypothesis test where the population standard deviation was unknown and the sample size was small. These tests were all *one-sample* tests, where we were studying whether a sample mean or a sample proportion could have come from a population with a given mean or a given proportion. We now introduce *two-sample* tests, where we study whether two sample means or proportions might have come from the same population or populations with the same means, or whether it is likely that they represent two different populations. Later on in this chapter we discuss analysis of variance, which enables us to compare three or more sample means.

TWO-SAMPLE TESTS (LARGE SAMPLES)

7-1

In the previous chapter, when we discussed the test of a mean or a proportion, we were trying to determine the chances that a sample could have come from a population with a specified mean or proportion. Thus, we were trying to base an estimate of a population mean or proportion on a sample mean or proportion. Now, we are studying two sample means or proportions and trying to determine whether these means or proportions could have come from the same population. If the samples have different means, these differences might be a result of sampling error. Thus, even though we have taken a random sample, occasionally we may find that most items in the sample have come from one tail of the population distribution. You will remember that sample means and proportions were normally distributed and that some were high and some were low. If we obtain two different sample means, is it because of sampling error or because the populations from which these samples were drawn really have different means? We will study how to test the difference between sample means and then the difference between sample proportions. These tests are useful in answering such questions as: Do wage rates differ in two communities? Is there a difference in the longevity of two types of products? Do the political preferences of two cities vary?

Two-tailed Tests of Difference between Means

If we look at two sample means and they differ, is it because they have come from two different populations or is it that they have come from the same population and the difference is due to sampling error? We are now going to set up tests for differences between means.

First, using the Central Limit Theorem, the sampling distribution of the differences between sample means $\bar{X}_1 - \bar{X}_2$ is approximately normal for the means of two large independent samples. The mean of this distribution of sample means is $\mu_1 - \mu_2$ (the difference between population means). We assume that this difference between population means is 0. Thus, the null hypothesis will always be that the samples came from two populations with equal means. We then have to reject this hypothesis to infer from the sample information that two populations have different means. If the two samples studied are independently chosen, the standard deviation of the sampling distribution is

$$\sigma_{\bar{X}_1 - \bar{X}_2} = \sqrt{\frac{\sigma_1^2}{n_1} + \frac{\sigma_2^2}{n_2}} \qquad (7\text{-}1)$$

where σ_1^2 and σ_2^2 are the variances of the two populations, and n_1 and n_2 are the sample sizes drawn from each of these populations. If we do not know population variances and our two samples are large enough, we may substitute the variances for each of the samples s_1^2 and s_2^2, respectively. Thus, the formula becomes

$$s_{\bar{x}_1 - \bar{x}_2} = \sqrt{\frac{s_1^2}{n_1} + \frac{s_2^2}{n_2}} \qquad (7\text{-}2)$$

Now if we diagram the sampling distribution of the differences between two means, it will look like Figure 7-1. When we start from $\mu_1 - \mu_2 = 0$ and measure one standard error of the difference between means ($\sigma_{\bar{x}_1 - \bar{x}_2}$) to the right and left of $\mu_1 - \mu_2 = 0$, we enclose 68.3% of the difference between means, if the samples have come from the same populations. Similarly, if we move two standard errors to the right and left of $\mu_1 - \mu_2 = 0$, we would enclose 95.5% of the sample difference between means. On this diagram we can set up cutoff points beyond which we reject the null hypothesis. First assume that the samples have been independently chosen. This means that the selection of items in the first sample is not affected by the selection of items in the second sample. If $\bar{X}_1$ and $\bar{X}_2$ are independent random variables, and if we assume that $\mu_1 = \mu_2$ and sample size is sufficiently large, the sampling distribution of $\bar{X}_1 - \bar{X}_2$ is approximately normal with mean $\mu_1 - \mu_2 = 0$ and standard deviation $\sigma_{\bar{x}_1 - \bar{x}_2}$ (or, if the sample size is large, we may use $s_{\bar{x}_1 - \bar{x}_2}$). If the standard deviations are unknown and the sample sizes are small, we use the t distribution, as explained in Section 7-2.

Once we have found the standard error of the difference between two means, we may calculate z and compare it to the critical value of z that we have chosen for our hypothesis test. We choose the critical value of z by deciding on the size of the Type I error (level of significance) and whether we desire a one- or a two-tailed test.

To calculate z, we use the equation

$$z = \frac{(\bar{X}_1 - \bar{X}_2) - (\mu_1 - \mu_2)}{s_{\bar{x}_1 - \bar{x}_2}} \qquad (7\text{-}3)$$

Since we start with the assumption that $\mu_1 - \mu_2 = 0$, we can make this term 0 in Equation 7-3. We therefore use the equation

$$z = \frac{(\bar{X}_1 - \bar{X}_2)}{s_{\bar{x}_1 - \bar{x}_2}} \qquad (7\text{-}4)$$

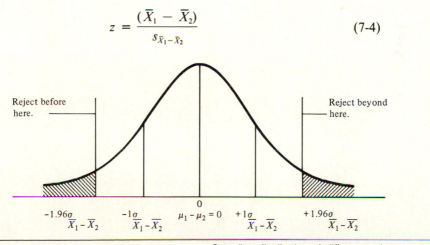

FIGURE **7-1**

Sampling distribution of differences between means for two-tailed test. For a two-tailed test, $\alpha = .05$; the shaded areas are the rejection areas. If $\bar{x}_1 - \bar{x}_2 > 1.96$ or < -1.96, reject H_0.

We can mark off our cutoff points in terms of z values on Figure 7-1 and then compare the calculated z value. Let us use an example.

EXAMPLE 7-1 A manufacturing company wants to locate in a city with low labor costs. Two cities have been suggested, Queenston and Kingston. A survey of salaries of laborers in the two cities published by the chambers of commerce reveals that the average salary of 300 factory workers studied in Queenston is $4.20 per hour; the average salary of 400 factory workers studied in Kingston is $4.00 per hour. The standard deviation for Queenston is 30 cents; for Kingston, 20 cents. Is there a significant difference in wages in the two cities, or can the two cities be considered to be the same?

1 $H_0: \mu_1 - \mu_2 = 0$
$H_1: \mu_1 - \mu_2 \neq 0$

2 z test, two-tailed test, $\alpha = .05$

$$s_{\bar{X}_1 - \bar{X}_2} = \sqrt{\frac{s_1^2}{n_1} + \frac{s_2^2}{n_2}}$$

$$s_{\bar{X}_1 - \bar{X}_2} = \sqrt{\frac{.30^2}{300} + \frac{.20^2}{400}}$$

$$s_{\bar{X}_1 - \bar{X}_2} = \sqrt{.0003 + .0001} = .02$$

The critical difference is .02 (1.96), or .0392.

3 Decision rule:

(a) If $(\bar{X}_1 - \bar{X}_2) > .0392$ or $< -.0392$, reject H_0.

or

(b) If $z > 1.96$ or < -1.96, reject H_0.

$$(\bar{X}_1 - \bar{X}_2) = \$4.20 - \$4.00 = .20$$

Since .20 > .0392, reject H_0 (using decision rule 3(a) above). Or

$$z = \frac{(\bar{X}_1 - \bar{X}_2)}{s_{\bar{X}_1 - \bar{X}_2}} = \frac{4.20 - 4.00}{.02} = \frac{.20}{.02} = 10$$

Since 10 > 1.96, reject H_0 (using decision rule 3(b) above). There is statistical reason to believe that there is an average wage rate difference. Now the original data must be examined to see which city has the lower wage rates. In this problem, it is Kingston.

Problems

1 The graduating class of two prestigious business schools were surveyed about their average starting salary with the following results:

SCHOOL	AVERAGE STARTING SALARY ($)	STANDARD DEVIATION ($)	SAMPLE SIZE
A	17,500	400	175
B	17,700	300	120

At a .05 confidence level, do we have adequate reason to believe that graduates of school B have equal starting salaries?

2 A calculator company was trying to decide between two brands of batteries to recommend in its calculators. If the batteries were of equal life, the company preferred brand 1 because of its better distribution network. Based on the following data and using a .04 confidence level, which battery should the quality control engineer recommend?

BATTERY	MEAN LIFE (HR)	STANDARD DEVIATION (HRS)	SAMPLE SIZE
Brand 1	107	12	100
Brand 2	112	15	100

Two-tailed Tests of Difference between Proportions (Large Sample)

Frequently, we wish to test if two sample proportions have come from a population with a given proportion or from two different populations. If the two sample proportions are statistically different, we could assume that the two samples come from different populations. Just as we computed an estimate for s in the previous section, we now compute an estimate of the overall proportion of successes for the two samples combined.

$$\bar{p} = \frac{n_1\bar{p}_1 + n_2\bar{p}_2}{n_1 + n_2} \tag{7-5}$$

In this equation $\bar{p}_1$ is the proportion in sample 1 and $\bar{p}_2$ is the proportion in sample 2. Now compute the standard error of the difference between proportions, assuming that $(\bar{q} = 1 - \bar{p})$.

$$s_{\bar{p}_1 - \bar{p}_2} = \sqrt{\bar{p}\bar{q}\left(\frac{1}{n_1} + \frac{1}{n_2}\right)} \tag{7-6}$$

Now, we can compute the critical z value using the formula

$$z = \frac{(\bar{p}_1 - \bar{p}_2) - (p_1 - p_2)}{s_{\bar{p}_1 - \bar{p}_2}} \tag{7-7}$$

Since $p_1 - p_2$ is assumed to be 0, our formula becomes

$$z = \frac{\bar{p}_1 - \bar{p}_2}{s_{\bar{p}_1 - \bar{p}_2}} \tag{7-8}$$

Remember that the two samples must be independently chosen and the individual sample sizes should be relatively large (rule of thumb: n_1 and n_2 should each exceed 30) to use this hypothesis testing procedure.

EXAMPLE 7-2 A manufacturer of razor blades wishes to test if women and men are equally appreciative of its new Zippy snipper serrated blade. He picks 100 women and 200 men who currently use razor blades and, after a 2-week trial period, asks them whether they prefer the Zippy snipper to their current blade. To encourage response, the manufacturer pays a premium of $2.00 for each response. The results are as follows: 38% of the women and 44% of the men prefer the blade.

WOMEN	MEN
$n_1 = 100$	$n_2 = 200$
$p_1 = 38$	$p_2 = 44$

The manufacturer wishes to test at the .10 level of significance. Setting up the test procedure:

1 $H_0: p_1 - p_2 = 0$
   $H_1: p_1 - p_2 \neq 0$
2 z test, level of significance = .10, two-tailed test, $z = 1.65$

$$\bar{p} = \frac{100(.38) + 200(.44)}{300} = \frac{38 + 88}{300} = .42$$

$$s_{\bar{p}_1 - \bar{p}_2} = \sqrt{(.42)(.58)\left(\frac{1}{100} + \frac{1}{200}\right)}$$

$$= \sqrt{.2436(.015)} = .0604$$

The critical value (.604)(1.65) = .0997
3 Decision rule:
(a) If $z > 1.65$, reject H_0; or if $z < -1.65$, reject H_0.
   or
(b) If $\bar{p}_1 - \bar{p}_2 > .0997$ or $< -.0997$, reject H_0.

$$z = \frac{(.38 - .44) - 0}{.0604} = \frac{.06}{.0604} = -.99$$

Since $z > -1.65$, do not reject H_0; there is no statistically significant difference between men's and women's opinions of Zippy, using decision rule 3(a). Using decision rule 3(b), $|.38 - .44| = .06$, $.06 < .0997$; therefore, we cannot reject H_0.

The test of a difference between means and proportions is a very useful one for studying differences between two groups. Differences between male and female freshmen and seniors, blue collar and white collar workers, tennis scores on clay courts and scores on grass courts, two different types of treatments, and two prices may all be studied using this type of analysis.

Problems
1 A company preparing to make job offers to recent college graduates was interested in student attitudes about employment. During the spring, the company made surveys at two large universities to determine if students considered starting salaries or working conditions more important in accepting a job. At a .05 level of significance, could the company judge the stated attitudes of the students at schools 1 and 2 to be the same?

SCHOOL 1		SCHOOL 2	
Salary most important	314	Salary most important	239
Working conditions most important	186	Working conditions most important	161
	$n_1 = 500$		$n_2 = 400$

2 The election date was fast approaching and Charmarc, a national pollster, wished to have the best estimate to offer to the local media. Having formulated a prediction on data from 5 days before the election, the pollster found that 50.3% said they would vote for Harper. The head pollster examined data from a random survey taken 3 days before the election. This sample was slightly smaller because it was difficult to get as many people on a Sunday night before the Tuesday election. Based on a .05 level of significance, should the firm alter its original prediction? Should the firm make a prediction of which candidate will win?

FIVE DAYS BEFORE ELECTION			THREE DAYS BEFORE ELECTION		
Harper	553	50.3%	Harper	451	47.5%
Clutts	547	49.7%	Clutts	499	52.5%
Number polled	1100	100.0%		950	100.0%

3 A carousel purchaser was testing the timers for a new set of carousels, spinning spiders, and other amusement rides. Two types of timers were tested for 100 trials per group, and the average times then recorded for each timer. Timplex timers were cheaper, but a timer that gave a shorter time was preferred as it would allow for more rides per day.

TIMER	MEAN LENGTH OF TIME (MIN)	STANDARD DEVIATION (MIN)
Timplex	2.40	.30
Clocker	2.26	.40

At a 2% level of significance, is there a substantial difference between the timers?

One-tailed Test of Difference between Means

If we are worried whether one drug is better than another, or whether one firm pays more than another, we may choose to put our Type I error on one tail of the distribution. Revising Figure 7-1, we get Figure 7-2. Let us illustrate with an example.

EXAMPLE 7-3 Carbon Bread has decided to market a new product. It is their regular bread, but it is enriched with iron. Choosing stores at random they send regular Carbon bread to some stores and the Carbon plus Iron bread to others. Stores are supplied with as much bread as they need, and weekly sales are tallied at the end of the week. The stores chosen for each group had bread sales during the first 6 months of 1980. Carbon bread will switch to the new bread only if there is evidence that sales are significantly higher for the new iron-enriched bread. Type

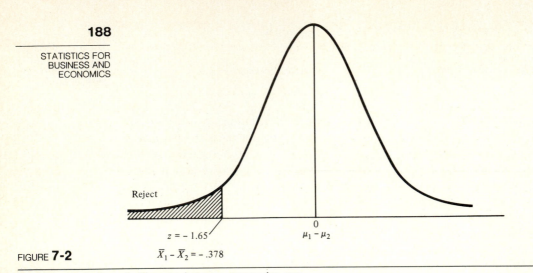

Reject

$z = -1.65$

0

$\mu_1 - \mu_2$

FIGURE **7-2**

$\bar{X}_1 - \bar{X}_2 = -.378$

Sampling distribution of difference between means for one-tailed test. For a one-tailed test, $\alpha = 0.5$; the shaded area is the rejection area on the left.

I error is set at .05 for this test. The sales (in tens) are as follows. Plain Carbon is sent to 50 stores, Carbon plus Iron to 60 stores.

PLAIN CARBON	CARBON PLUS IRON
$\bar{X}_1 = 50$	$\bar{X}_2 = 53$
$s_1 = 1.0$	$s_2 = 1.4$
$n_1 = 50$	$n_2 = 60$

1 $H_0: \mu_1 - \mu_2 \geq 0$
   $H_1: \mu_1 - \mu_2 < 0$
2 $\alpha = .05$, one-tailed test

$$s_{\bar{X}_1 - \bar{X}_2} = \sqrt{\frac{1.0^2}{50} + \frac{1.4^2}{60}} = .229$$

If we want the mean of sample 2 (Carbon plus Iron) to be larger than the mean of 1 (plain Carbon), our critical value for $z = -1.65$. If $\bar{X}_1 - \bar{X}_2 < 1.65(.229)$, or $\bar{X}_1 - \bar{X}_2 < -.378$, reject H_0.
3 Decision rule:
(a) If $z < -1.65$, reject H_0.

or

(b) if $\bar{X}_1 - \bar{X}_2 < .378$, reject H_0.

$$z = \frac{50 - 53}{.229} = \frac{-3}{.229} = 13.100$$

Therefore, reject H_0. Or,

$$50 - 53 = -3, \qquad -3 < -.378$$

Therefore, reject H_0. The 300 per week sales difference is significant.

One-tailed Test of Difference between Proportions

189

HYPOTHESIS TESTS:
TWO- AND THREE-
SAMPLE OR LARGER
SAMPLE TESTS

A test of difference between proportions can be performed as a one-tailed test. Let us try an example of this test.

EXAMPLE 7-4 The grade inflation committee wishes to know if the proportion of students who received A grades was decreasing as a result of the committee's recent report to the faculty that showed that grades had risen since 1967 and that the New York College of Fine Arts' grades had risen faster than grades in other art academies in the state. A sample of grades in 1979 and in 1980, after the committee's report was given, were studied to see if the proportion of A grades had fallen significantly.

	1979	1980
Proportion of A grades	$p_{79} = .60$	$p_{80} = .40$
Number of students	$n_{79} = 100$	$n_{80} = 90$

1 $H_0: p_{80} - p_{79} \geq 0$
      $H_1: p_{80} - p_{79} < 0$
2 z test, one-tailed test, .05 level of significance

$$\bar{p} = \frac{100(.6) + 90(.4)}{100 + 90} = .505$$

$$S_{\bar{p}_{80} - \bar{p}_{79}} = \sqrt{(.505)(495)\left(\frac{1}{100} + \frac{1}{90}\right)} = \sqrt{(.505)(.495)(0.21)} = .072$$

The critical value is $(.072)(1.65) = .119$

3   Decision rule: If $z < -1.65$, reject H_0. Or, if $\bar{p}_{80} - \bar{p}_{79} < -.119$, reject H_0.

$$z = \frac{.40 - .60}{.072} = -2.78$$

Since $-2.78 < -1.65$, reject H_0.

$$p_{80} - p_{79} = .40 - .60 = -.20$$

Since $-.20 < -.119$, reject H_0. We therefore have reason to believe that grades have gone down since the grade inflation committee report was issued.

Problems

1   A company is considering two competing drugs that treat the same ailment, a skin disease. Drug 1 has been long-established and has a good reputation in the medical industry; however, preliminary results indicate that the cure rate with new drug 2 may be higher. The company wishes to develop drug 2 only if the cure rate is significantly higher, because the cost of advertising a new drug is quite high. They use a .01 level of significance, because if the drugs are the same they do not wish to discard the old one. Presented with the additional data gathered by its research lab, what should the company do?

PATIENTS	DRUG 1	DRUG 2
Cured	104	132
Not cured	76	38
Total	180	170

2 Fashion designer Alexander Lemeani is interested in the type of audience most eager to buy his "high-style creations." The women must be wealthy to afford his outfits; however, he also suspects that tall women would be more likely to prefer his creations. At the fall fashion show he distributes a questionnaire asking women to list their height and their impression of his creations. He finds that 70 of 145 short women (5-ft 4-in and under) and 143 of 215 tall women (over 5-ft 4-in) liked the outfits. Does this data support his idea that tall women are more likely to buy his high-style creations? Use a .05 significance level. Then, test at .01 level. Do the results differ?

TEST OF DIFFERENCE BETWEEN MEANS (SMALL SAMPLE, σ UNKNOWN)

7-2

The t test should be used when σ is not known for the two distributions, sample size is small, and we can assume that our samples come from normally distributed populations. In the previous case, since the sample size was quite large, even though the standard deviation was unknown, we used the z test because as we have seen in Chapter 5 the t tables begin to approximate the z tables as sample size increases. If we can assume that the population distribution approximates the normal distribution, we can use t tables for small sample approximations when σ is not known. To use the t table, we must set a significance level and know the number of degrees of freedom. In each sample, we lose 1 degree of freedom; therefore, the number of degrees of freedom is $n_1 + n_2 - 2$. In order to calculate the standard error of the difference between two means, we must know the standard deviation for each population (σ_1 and σ_2). If these parameters are unknown, we can use the standard deviations from the two samples in Equation 7-9 to compute s, which is a weighted standard deviation for the two groups.

The formula for s is

$$s = \sqrt{\frac{(n_1 - 1)s_1^2 + (n_2 - 1)s_2^2}{n_1 + n_2 - 2}} \qquad (7-9)$$

This expression or value for s that pools the different standard deviations can then be used in Equation 7-10 to find the standard error of the difference between two means. (Note that we are assuming that $\sigma_1^2 = \sigma_2^2$ for the pooling.)

$$s_{\bar{x}_1 - \bar{x}_2} = \sqrt{\frac{s^2}{n_1} + \frac{s^2}{n_2}} = s\sqrt{\frac{1}{n_1} + \frac{1}{n_2}} \qquad (7-10)$$

EXAMPLE 7-5 Women in Communications, Inc. wanted to see if there was a significant difference in the incomes of local women in public relations and in magazine writing. A study of women in these fields yielded the following results. There were 15 women in public relations and 10 women in magazine writing in the local organization. A test was set up as follows:

	PUBLIC RELATIONS	MAGAZINE WRITING
	$n_1 = 15$	$n_2 = 10$
	$\bar{X}_1 = \$13{,}500$	$\bar{X}_2 = \$11{,}900$
	$s_1 = \$2{,}000$	$s_2 = \$500$

1 $H_0: \mu_1 - \mu_2 = 0$
$H_1: \mu_1 - \mu_2 \neq 0$

2 $\alpha = .05$; two-tailed test; t test; for .05 and 23 degrees of freedom, $t = 2.069$.

$$df = n_1 + n_2 - 2 = 15 + 10 - 2 = 23$$

$$s = \sqrt{\frac{(n_1 - 1)s_1^2 + (n_2 - 1)s_2^2}{n_1 + n_2 - 2}}$$

$$= \sqrt{\frac{14(2000)^2 + 9(500)^2}{15 + 10 - 2}} = \$1591.42$$

$$s_{\bar{X}_1 - \bar{X}_2} = 1591.42 \sqrt{\frac{1}{15} + \frac{1}{10}} = 1591.42(.408) = 649.30$$

The critical value is $(2.069)(649.30) = 1343.40$

3 Decision rule:

(a) If $t > 2.069$ or $t < -2.069$, reject H_0.

or

(b) If $\bar{X}_1 - \bar{X}_2 > 1343.40$, reject H_0. Or if $\bar{X}_1 - \bar{X}_2 < -1343.40$, reject H_0.

$$t = \frac{13{,}500 - 11{,}900}{649.30} = 2.464$$

Since $2.464 > 2.069$, reject H_0. Or, $13{,}500 - 11{,}900 = 1600$; since $\$1600 > \$1343.40$, reject H_0. The statistical evidence leads to the belief that salaries are higher in public relations than in magazines.

Problems

1 A manufacturer issued two types of test tires, one containing steel belts and the other using plutonium particles, and decided to use a real life test. Sets of tires were given to a sample of users and tire wear was measured at regular intervals. Relying on consumer feedback and measures of tire wear, the following data was received on the sets of tires.

TIRE	MEAN LIFE OF SET (MILES)	STANDARD DEVIATION	NUMBER OF CONSUMERS
Steel	43,000	3500	11
Plutonium	40,800	2100	12

At a .05 level of significance, would you conclude that there is a difference between the two types of tires? If so, which one should be manufactured if it is cheaper to make the steel tires?

2 A local association of doctors concerned with the rise in malpractice insurance rates decided to record the average malpractice settlement for two 2-year periods in their town. Taking a sample of one out of five cases settled in 1970–1971 and 1979–1980, could the doctors conclude that the value of settlements had risen? Use a .05 level of significance.

YEAR	MEAN SETTLEMENT	STANDARD DEVIATION	NUMBER OF CASES
1970–1971	$12,050	$1050	14
1979–1980	13,000	875	12

ANALYSIS OF VARIANCE

7-3

In the previous problems, we have tested the difference between two means using a z or a t test. If there are more than two means to be compared, numerous tests will be needed. For example, if there are four groups—A, B, C, D—we would have to test A and B, A and C, A and D, B and C, B and D, and C and D. This would mean six tests.

A simpler method of comparing means of different groups to determine if all groups could have come from populations with the same mean is called *analysis of variance*. This technique assumes that the populations are normally distributed and that, since all these groups have come from the same population or populations with the same means, they have the same variance.[1] If we cannot assume that each population is normally distributed, the Kruskal-Wallis test, described in the next chapter, may be used.

The analysis of variance is really a technique to study whether means for the same variable (such as test scores, wage rates, output) differ from one group to another. The technique uses the *variation within each group* and the *variation between groups* to study whether means differ. If we look at Figure 7-3, we have some idea of the nature of the test. In Figure 7-3(a), we have three different means $\overline{Y}_1$, $\overline{Y}_2$, and $\overline{Y}_3$ in a study of test grades obtained by students using three different texts: alpha, beta, and zeta. Note that test score means are the same for the three texts in Figures 7-3(a) and 7-3(b), but that the variation of test scores within groups is much less in Figure 7-3(a) than in Figure 7-3(b). The X's represent different student grades. Note that the groups are small, 5 to 6 students. In Figure 7-3(a), note that the sample means (large dots) vary and the sample test grade values (crosses on the graph) are concentrated about the means. Thus, the variation within groups is small. In Figure 7-3(b), the means are the same as those in (a), but there is a much larger amount of variation of test grades in each group (look at the range

---

[1]This is called *homoscedasticity*.

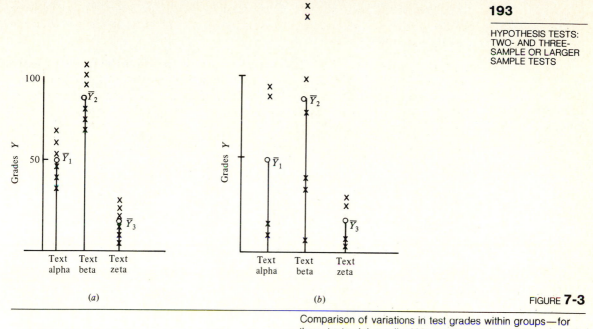

FIGURE **7-3**

Comparison of variations in test grades within groups—for three texts: (*a*) small within group variation; (*b*) large within group variation.

of the crosses for each text). In Figure 7-3(*a*), it is more likely that the difference in average test scores is due to the different texts than in Figure 7-3(*b*), where *within* each sample there is a tremendous amount of variation. The analysis of variance technique essentially uses this method to determine if there is a significant difference between groups. It sets up a ratio, called the *F* ratio, that compares the variation between groups means to the variations within groups.

$$F = \frac{\text{variation between groups}}{\text{variation within groups}}$$

If the ratio is greater than 1, we have reason to believe that our differences are due to the different conditions (in this case, texts) used by each of the groups.[2] Thus, we are looking at the variances between and within groups to decide if the means differ. The name analysis of variance is often abbreviated ANOVA, and many computer software packages have programs to compute this test. The test is frequently used, and some students have even assumed that ANOVA was the name of an important Italian statistician! We now explain how the test is performed in terms of an example.

Suppose four texts are to be considered for a computer course. The department chairperson decides to randomly divide a class of 20 students into 4 groups and to give each group a different text. As a control, the class will be taught in one group of 20 students by the same teacher. At the end of the term the same final test is administered to all 20 students. In order to show that this problems can be done fo. unequal-size as well as equal-size groups, the four groups will consist of 4, 5, 6, 5

---

[2]The exact value needed for a given level of significance is by a table for the *F* distribution.

students, respectively. The final test grade for each student is listed in the table below.

	Text name			
STUDENT NUMBER	(1) JOHNSON	(2) McCARTHY	(3) JONES	(4) RILEY
1	60	93	80	90
2	80	92	79	82
3	66	78	68	79
4	70	95	75	60
5	—	87	74	69
6			92	—
ΣX_i	276	445	468	380
n_i	4	5	6	5
$\bar{X}_i$	69	89	78	76
$\bar{\bar{X}} = 78.45$				

Now the *grand mean* $\bar{\bar{X}}$, the mean for all 20 students, is computed by adding all 20 numbers and dividing by 20. For each column, a mean is computed by adding the numbers in the column and dividing by the number of students in each column.

If the tests were equally good in influencing final test grades, the mean test grades for each text (column) would be about the same. If the means differed and the variation within each of the textbook groups (the variation about the mean test score for each textbook) was about the same or greater than the variation of the group means (the mean test score for each textbook) about the overall mean ($\bar{\bar{X}}$), we would not be able to infer any influence due to the texts. However, if the differences *between* groups are greater than the variations within groups, we say that our groups show significantly different results and hence the different texts may have had an influence on student performance. After we have finished our computation, if there is a significant difference between texts then in order to choose the best text, we must look at the original data to determine the textbook having the highest mean test score.

Before we go ahead, let us set up the hypothesis test. Assume we allow a 5% Type I error. (Even though there is no real difference in the books, we say there is.)

1 $H_0: \mu_1 = \mu_2 = \mu_3 = \mu_4$
  $H_1: \mu_1, \mu_2, \mu_3,$ and μ_4 are not all equal.
2   Analysis of variance, $\alpha = .05$, F test, df $= 3/16$ (see Table A-5).

To compute the degrees of freedom, we must figure out the degrees of freedom between groups (numerator) and within (denominator) groups. There are four groups $\bar{X}_1, \bar{X}_2, \bar{X}_3,$ and $\bar{X}_4$ that are used to calculate the grand mean $\bar{\bar{X}}$. Three numbers could be chosen freely at random if we wished to obtain a certain $\bar{\bar{X}}$, but the last is determined so that we can obtain a specified total. Thus, our degrees of freedom between columns is the number of columns c minus 1 ($c - 1$). Since there are four columns, we have 3 degrees of freedom in the numerator. To make our column totals produce the column means $\bar{X}_1, \bar{X}_2, \bar{X}_3, \bar{X}_4$, we must be able to determine one number in each column. Thus, we have lost 1 degree of freedom in each column. Therefore, our degree of freedom for the within group variation is the total number of observations n minus the number of columns c since we lose 1 degree of freedom for each column. Therefore, the degrees of freedom for the denominator of the F ratio, the within group variation in this problem, is df $= n - c$ or $20 - 4 = 16$. Degrees of freedom $(c - 1)/(n - c)$ for this problem is 3/16. We now compare the between group and within group variation. In order for there to be a significant difference between the groups, the variation between groups should exceed the variation within groups. How much larger should the variation between groups be? We can obtain this criterion by using the F distribution (Table A-5). We use this combination of degrees of freedom between and within groups to look up levels for the F distribution for given levels of significance.

Use of the *F* Table

We have discussed the ratio of between group variations to within group variation. The higher this ratio, the more likely that the different samples (groups using texts) do not come from the same population. This ratio of the two estimates of the population variance is called the *F statistic*. The distribution is named after R. A. Fisher, a famous statistician who first studied its form in 1924.

$$F = \frac{\text{estimate of variation between groups}}{\text{estimate of variation within groups}}$$

Looking at Figure 7-4(a), we see that the F distribution is a family of distributions like the t distribution. For each level of significance and for each number of degrees of freedom in the numerator (variation between means) and in the denominator (variation within columns), there is a different value of F. Thus, the degrees of freedom in the numerator in our text problem are the number of samples (4) minus 1 or $(c - 1) = 3$. The degrees of freedom in the denominator are the number of observations (20) minus the number of columns (4), or 16. Using the F table, $\alpha = .05$, df $= 3$ for the numerator (we call this V_1) and df $= 16$ for the denominator (we call this V_2), trace 3 (degrees of freedom between the groups) across the top and go down to 20 (degrees of freedom within the groups) on the vertical column. (We go to the nearest number to 16, namely 20, since the table omits 16.) We see that the .05 level of significance for F is 3.10. (The number in boldface type is for the .01 level of significance with this combination of degrees of freedom.) Thus, if the ratio of F exceeds 3.10, there is a significant difference between the columns, and we reject the null hypothesis that there is no difference between texts. Figure 7-4(b) illustrates this curve and shows the cutoff points for $\alpha = .05$ and $\alpha = .01$. Step 3 of the hypothesis test reads

3 If $F > 3.10$, reject H_0.

We see that the greater the variation between the means of columns as compared to the variation within the columns, the more likely it is that the F ratio is high and the null hypothesis $\mu_1 = \mu_2 = \mu_3 = \mu_4$ is rejected. First, let us compute the *between column variation* V_B. This is the variation of the column means around the grand mean, divided by the number of columns minus 1. We must weight the differences of column means about the grand mean by the number of observations in each column. The formula is

$$V_B = \frac{n_1(\overline{X}_1 - \overline{\overline{X}})^2 + n_2(\overline{X}_2 - \overline{\overline{X}})^2 + n_3(\overline{X}_3 - \overline{\overline{X}})^2 + n_4(\overline{X}_4 - \overline{\overline{X}})^2}{(c - 1)} \quad (7\text{-}11)$$

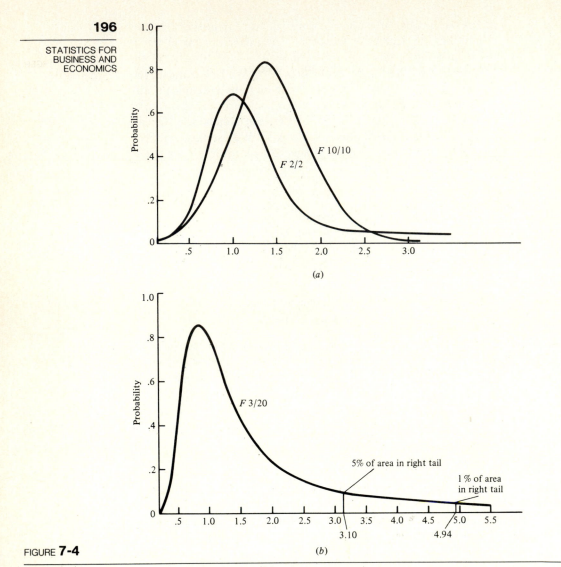

FIGURE **7-4**

(a) F distribution curves: curves for varying degrees of freedom.
(b) F distribution curves: curves for $V_1 = 3$, $V_2 = 20$ (textbook problem).

$\overline{X}_1$ is the mean of column 1, $\overline{\overline{X}}$ the overall mean, n_1 the number of items in column 1, and so on. Using the four column means 69, 89, 78, and 76, respectively, and the overall mean $\overline{\overline{X}} = 78.45$, we obtain:

(1) $\overline{X}_i - \overline{\overline{X}}$	(2) $(\overline{X}_i - \overline{\overline{X}})$	(3) $(\overline{X}_i - \overline{\overline{X}})^2$	(4) $n_i(\overline{X}_i - \overline{\overline{X}})^2$
69–78.45	−9.45	89.3	357.2
89–78.45	10.55	111.3	556.5
78–78.45	−0.45	0.2	1.2
76–78.45	−2.45	6.0	30.0
			944.9

In column 1 we subtract the grand mean from each column mean. In column 2 we record the result of the subtraction. Column 3 consists of the squared value for each item in column 2. In column 4 we weight each squared deviation by the number of people in the column. V_B is found by dividing the total in column 4 by the number of columns minus 1.

$$V_B = \frac{\Sigma n_i(\bar{X}_i - \bar{\bar{X}})^2}{c - 1} = \text{between column variation} \qquad (7\text{-}12)$$

$$V_B = \frac{944.9}{3} = 314.967$$

To compute the variation within groups, we take the variation of each of the numbers in each column around the column mean. Note that in our subscript notation, the first subscript is row and the second is column; therefore X_{12} is the number in the first row and second column. In this problem, X_{12} would be 93. (See p. 198.) Adding 212, 186, 326, and 546, we get 1270. The formula for within column variation is

$$V_W = \frac{\Sigma(X_{rc} - \bar{X}_c)^2}{n - c} \qquad (7\text{-}13)$$

Therefore, variation within columns is

$$V_W = \frac{1270}{16} = 79.375$$

Since F is the ratio of V_B/V_W,

$$F = \frac{V_B}{V_W} = \frac{314.967}{79.375} = 3.968$$

Since $3.968 > 3.10$, we reject H_0. We have reason to believe that the books do make a difference in test scores. Note that the analysis of variance does not directly tell what the best book is. To find this out, we must examine the original data. The data shows that the McCarthy text (2) provides the highest mean grades (89). Books 3 and 4 have almost the same mean.

Summary of Tests Used in Chapters 6 and 7

We have now developed 5 basic tests. We can test:

1 Sample mean: Could a sample mean have come from a population with a given mean?
2 Sample proportion: Could a sample proportion have come from a population with a given proportion?
3 Difference between two means: Could two sample means have come from two populations with the same means?
4 Difference between two proportions: Could two sample proportions have come from two populations with the same proportions?
5 Difference between several means: Could several sample means have come from populations with the same means?

	(1)		(2)		(3)		(4)	
	$(X_{rc} - \bar{X}_c)$	$(X_{rc} - \bar{X}_c)^2$	$(X_{rc} - \bar{X}_c)$	$(X_{rc} - \bar{X}_c)^2$	$(X_{rc} - \bar{X}_c)$	$(X_{rc} - \bar{X}_c)^2$	$(X_{rc} - \bar{X}_c)$	$(X_{rc} - \bar{X}_c)^2$
	$X_{11} - \bar{X}_1 = 60 - 69$	81	$X_{12} - \bar{X}_2 = 93 - 89$	16	$X_{13} - \bar{X}_3 = 80 - 78$	4	$X_{14} - \bar{X}_4 = 90 - 76$	196
	$X_{21} - \bar{X}_1 = 80 - 69$	121	$X_{22} - \bar{X}_2 = 92 - 89$	9	$X_{23} - \bar{X}_3 = 79 - 78$	1	$X_{24} - \bar{X}_4 = 82 - 76$	36
	$X_{31} - \bar{X}_1 = 66 - 69$	9	$X_{32} - \bar{X}_2 = 78 - 89$	121	$X_{33} - \bar{X}_3 = 68 - 78$	100	$X_{34} - \bar{X}_4 = 79 - 76$	9
	$X_{41} - \bar{X}_1 = 70 - 69$	1	$X_{42} - \bar{X}_2 = 95 - 89$	36	$X_{43} - \bar{X}_3 = 75 - 78$	9	$X_{44} - \bar{X}_4 = 60 - 76$	256
			$X_{52} - \bar{X}_2 = 87 - 89$	4	$X_{53} - \bar{X}_3 = 74 - 78$	16	$X_{54} - \bar{X}_4 = 69 - 76$	49
		212		186	$X_{63} - \bar{X}_3 = 92 - 78$	196		546
						326		

Problems

199

HYPOTHESIS TESTS:
TWO- AND THREE-
SAMPLE OR LARGER
SAMPLE TESTS

1 The Gardner Ferry Nursery grows its African violets under special ultraviolet lights. They test three brands—Normalite, Grow-lite, and Luxor—to see whether they differ in terms of average hours of light provided. In terms of hundreds of hours, the results are listed below. Is there a significant difference between bulbs? If there is a difference, which bulbs should be purchased?

NORMALITE	GROW-LITE	LUXOR
90	97	88
85	85	96
105	102	86
88	95	91
92	101	79
460	480	440

(*a*) Use a .01 level of significance.
(*b*) Would a .05 level of significance change the answer?

2 Greengold Glue is testing four types of epoxy glue to see if there is any variation in hardening time. Five samples showing the results for each type of glue are taken. The following results are given. Is there a significant difference between glues at the .05 level?

STICKUM	QWIKSTICK	TITEBOND	STICKWIKET
4.5	4.7	3.9	5.4
3.7	5.1	4.2	3.3
4.6	4.8	4.3	4.0
4.1	4.3	3.8	3.8
4.6	4.1	3.4	4.6

SUMMARY

7-4

1 Two sample tests may be either a test of a difference between means or a difference between proportions. In these tests, the null hypothesis is that there is no difference between means or proportions. To test the difference between means, we calculate the standard error of the difference between two means.

$$\sigma_{\bar{X}-\bar{X}_2} = \sqrt{\frac{\sigma_1^2}{n_1} + \frac{\sigma_2^2}{n_2}}$$

If σ is not known, s_1 and s_2 are calculated within the samples and used to find the standard error of the difference between two means.

$$s_{\bar{X}_1-\bar{X}_2} = \sqrt{\frac{s_1^2}{n_1} + \frac{s_2^2}{n_2}}$$

The z value is then computed using the formula

$$z = \frac{(\bar{X}_1 - \bar{X}_2) - 0}{s_{\bar{X}_1-\bar{X}_2}}$$

since $\mu_1 - \mu_2$ is assumed to be 0.

2 To test the difference between proportions, we estimate the overall proportion of successes from the sample proportions.

$$\bar{p} = \frac{n_1\bar{p}_1 + n_2\bar{p}_2}{n_1 + n_2}$$

$$s_{\bar{p}_1-\bar{p}_2} = \sqrt{\bar{p}\bar{q}\left(\frac{1}{n_1} + \frac{1}{n_2}\right)}$$

The z value is then computed using the formula

$$z = \frac{(\bar{p}_1 - \bar{p}_2) - 0}{s_{\bar{p}_1-\bar{p}_2}}$$

since $p_1 - p_2$ is assumed to be 0.

3 To test the difference between means for a small sample with σ unknown, we calculate s_1 and s_2 from the samples and then calculate s^2 for the two samples combined.

$$s^2 = \frac{(n_1 - 1)s_1^2 + (n_2 - 1)s_2^2}{n_1 + n_2 - 2}$$

$$s_{\bar{X}_1-\bar{X}_2} = s\sqrt{\frac{1}{n_1} + \frac{1}{n_2}}$$

The t value is then computed as

$$t = \frac{(\bar{X}_1 - \bar{X}_2) - 0}{s_{\bar{X}_1 - \bar{X}_2}}$$

$\mu_1 - \mu_2$ is assumed to be 0, and the degrees of freedom are $n_1 + n_2 - 2$.

4 Analysis of variance is used to test for differences among several means. If the difference between groups is significantly greater than the differences within groups, we can say that there is a difference in the effects of alternate treatments tested. The F test (Table A-5) examines

$$F = \frac{\text{variation between groups}}{\text{variation within groups}} = \frac{V_B}{V_W}$$

Between column (group) variation (for four groups) is computed using the formula

$$V_B = \frac{n_1(\bar{X}_1 - \bar{\bar{X}})^2 + n_2(\bar{X}_2 - \bar{\bar{X}})^2 + n_3(\bar{X}_3 - \bar{\bar{X}})^3 + n_4(\bar{X}_4 - \bar{\bar{X}})^4}{c - 1}$$

Within group variation is computed using the formula

$$V_W = \frac{\Sigma(X_{rc} - \bar{X}_c)^2}{(n - c)} \qquad F = \frac{V_B}{V_W}$$

Now compare this value to the value for the level of significance desired. Use the F table, where the degrees of freedom is $c - 1$ for the numerator and $n - c$ for the denominator.

Hays, William L.: *Statistics for the Social Sciences,* 2d ed. New York: Holt, 1973, chapters 12 and 13. An in-depth discussion of analysis of variance.

Iversen, Gudmund R., and Helmut Norpoth: *Analysis of Variance.* Beverly Hills, Calif.: Sage, 1976. Good thorough explanation of one- and two-way analysis of variance.

McClave, James T., and P. George Benson: *Statistics for Business and Economics,* rev. ed. San Francisco: Dellen, 1979. See Chapter 10 for an excellent simple discussion of two-sample estimation.

Neter, John, William Wasserman, and G. A. Whitmore: *Fundamental Statistics for Business and Economics,* 4th ed. Boston: Allyn and Bacon, chapter 18. Explanation of power curve and testing difference between means and proportions.

Spurr, William, A., and Charles P. Bonini: *Statistical Analysis for Business Decisions,* rev. ed. Homewood, Ill.: Irwin, 1973, chapter 11, pp. 308–319. Excellent description of analysis of variance assuming equal-size groups.

Case 7-1   Beta Blockers

A group of Swedish researchers at Sahlgren's Hospital at the University of Goteborg were testing a new set of drugs, called beta blockers, to see if these drugs provided early treatment of high blood pressure to reduce the risk of a heart attack. Early computations indicated that there was no significant difference in fatal heart attacks between the groups treated with beta blockers and those not treated with these drugs.

"The beta blockers" are so named because they block the impulses in a nerve system known as the beta-adrenergic system, which helps control the heart as well as certain glands. Although several such drugs have been available and long-used in Europe, only one is available in the U.S. at the moment. The U.S. drug, propanalol, wasn't approved by the U.S. Food and Drug Administration for treatment of high blood pressure until late 1976 although it has been approved for other uses for several years previously. Propanalol is sold under the trade name Inderal by the Ayerst division of American Home Products Corp.

In the Swedish study, researchers recruited 1026 men, aged 47 to 54, who had high blood pressure. Of these, 635 were treated for their hypertension while 391 were left untreated as a control group. The men were recruited for the study in 1970 through 1973.

The treatment consisted of care at a special hypertension clinic with a "beta blocker" drug being the treatment of first choice. If that failed to lower pressure a diuretic was added followed by other drugs to lower blood pressure in various ways. By the end of four years of treatment, 78% of the treated group was still using a "beta blocker."

At the end of four years and four months, 0.8% of the treated group had fatal heart attacks or died of coronary artery disease, the clogging of the arteries that underlies the heart attack. By contrast, 1.5% of the untreated control group had died of such causes. In addition, 2.8% of the treated men had had nonfatal heart attacks compared with 5.4% of the untreated controls.[1]

Questions

1 Test the results of the Goteborg group.

2 Would there be any other way to test the effects of propanalol? What does this show?

3 What suggestions would you make to improve the Goteborg research?

4 What was the purpose of the control group? How could the concept of a control group be used in a business study?

Case 7-2 Southwestern Optical Prices[2]

In 1975, the Dallas regional office of the Federal Trade Commission conducted a survey of prescription eyeglass firms in three cities in each of the following states—Texas, Oklahoma, and Louisiana—to see if prices were lower in the states that permitted advertising of prices. It was expected that prices would be lower in Texas, because both Oklahoma and Louisiana had legal restrictions against disseminating information to consumers.

According to the theory of free competition, both the entrepreneurs and the consumers should possess information on prices. In this way, consumer pressure will force prices to their lowest possible point consistent with normal return for enterprise.

Separate data was collected in each of the nine cities for opticians, optometrists, and ophthalmologists. Ophthalmologists and optometrists examine the eyes and prescribe and dispense eyeglasses; opticians only dispense eyeglasses. Part of the original data collected for this survey is presented in Tables 3, 4, and 5. Three major cities were selected in each state and a number of opticians, optometrists, and ophthalmologists were randomly selected from the classified Yellow Pages of the telephone directory. Interviewers priced three standard frames and lens prescriptions in each of the establishments selected. Data for the three was similar; therefore, data is presented for only one frame and lens prescription.

Ophthalmologists specialize in the diagnosis and treatment of eye disease and abnormal conditions, including refractive errors. As physicians, they are authorized to prescribe drugs, lenses, or other treatment or to perform surgery to remedy these conditions. A survey by the American Association of Ophthalmology in 1967 indicated that approximately 40% of the ophthalmologists responding to their questionnaires actually dispensed eyeglasses.[3] The Public Health Service and

---

[1] *Wall Street Journal* Jan. 24, 1978, p. 1.

[2] This case was prepared by Associate Professor Marion G. Sobol of Southern Methodist University with the help of Carl Swanson, regional director of the Federal Trade Commission, as a basis for classroom discussion. It was presented at a case workshop and distributed by the Intercollegiate Case Clearing House, Soldiers Field, Boston, Mass.

[3] The descriptions, legal references, and the results of the FTC price survey are published in "Advertising of Ophthalmic Goods and Services," *Staff Report to the Federal Trade Commission and Proposed Trade Regulation Rule,* Jan. 1976, pp. 5–20. Tables 1, 2, and 3 are original unpublished data, collected here for this study.

other experts have estimated that ophthalmologists account for 36% of all prescriptions written and 15% of all eyeglasses dispensed.

Optometrists examine the eye and related structures to determine the presence of vision problems, eye disease, or other abnormalities. They prescribe and adapt corrective lenses and/or other optical aids and may use visual training aids when indicated to preserve or restore maximum visual activity. Optometrists do not prescribe drugs, definitively diagnose or treat eye disease, or perform surgery. Optometrists as a whole account for 60% of all prescriptions written and 60% of all eyeglasses dispensed.

Dispensing opticians or ophthalmic dispensers make, fit, supply, and adjust eyeglasses according to prescriptions written by ophthalmologists and optometrists. Dispensing opticians dispense about 23% of all eyeglasses sold at retail.

Advertising laws for each of these three groups differ. Since ophthalmologists are part of the medical profession, they are universally barred from any commercial practices, including advertising, under state laws and the AMA Code of Ethics covering physicians and surgeons. Price advertising by optometrists is prohibited in any form by 40 states. Among these states are *Louisiana* and *Oklahoma*. Texas allows an optometrist to advertise only in the name of any dispensing optical company that he or she owns or operates, and then only after burdensome filing and disclosure requirements have been met. Opticians are also enjoined from price advertising in 13 states that do not license the profession. These states include *Louisiana* and *Oklahoma,* where the optometry laws apply prohibitions to all persons or similar all-inclusive designations.

To summarize, ophthalmologists may not advertise in any of the three states. In Louisiana and Oklahoma, opticians and optometrists may not advertise prices. In Texas, price advertising is permitted to these two groups if they meet filing and disclosure requirements.

As a result of this study of 144 firms by the FTC in 1975 (the basic data for which is presented in Tables 3, 4, and 5), *the following information was published* by the Federal Trade Commission. The following section is a *direct quotation* from the report.

Results of the FTC Price Survey

We expected to find that the average price of lenses and frames would be lower in Texas than in Oklahoma and Louisiana because of the legal restrictions against disseminating information to consumers in the latter two states. Table 1 indicates some partial results of the price survey.

TABLE 1
AVERAGE COST OF EYEGLASSES AND
STANDARD DEVIATION
(DSA frame and medium-strength lens)

	$\bar{X}$	s_i	
Texas	$38.93	$7.48	($N = 30$)
Oklahoma	41.21	7.59	($N = 57$)
Louisiana	43.09	8.29	($N = 57$)

In order to determine the cost of an average eyeglass transaction, I added, for each sample, the cost of the *DSA* frame to the cost of a medium-strength lens made of glass. For example, if Texas Optical charged $20 for the *DSA* frame and $35 for the medium-strength lens, I took the total of $55 as the cost of purchasing from Texas Optical. I then added for each state the cost from all sources (optometrists, ophthalmologists, and opticians) and took an average and the standard deviation from the average in each state.

A *t* statistic was calculated to determine if the difference in average prices between states was statistically significant. The results of this test generally are consistent with the hypothesis developed earlier. The price of eyeglasses in Texas is significantly lower than in Louisiana and Oklahoma. However, the Oklahoma-Texas relationship is not as strong as the Texas-Louisiana relationship. The price of eyeglasses is not signficantly different between Oklahoma and Louisiana, as we expected.

The results of the statistical tests [shown in Table 2] generally support our hypothesis that prices would be lower in Texas. Also, since information restrictions of various sorts exist in Oklahoma and Louisiana, we would not expect prices to be different in these two states, as indicated by the results. Although the results of the Dallas survey were generally consistent with our expected findings, there are some problems connected with the conduct of the survey which limit its usefulness.

Since many government hearings were to be held subsequent to the publication of this report, the regional director reflected upon the feasibility of using other measures on these data. Even the original report had implied that there were some aspects of the study that limited its usefulness.

Further study of the data was needed. The director tested differences in prices of frames and lenses separately, assuming that the frames were standard items whereas grinding of the lenses was a more skilled operation; hence, prices might be expected to show more differences in the latter case. He noted little difference in the variation between these prices for each of the states and overall prices for each of the states.

He then tried to relate eyeglass prices in each state to the cost of living. Here he encountered some difficulty because the Consumer Price Index was not available for each of the nine cities studied. Furthermore, since index numbers were not available for any cities in Oklahoma, it was difficult to make estimates of price indices for each of the three states.

The director, Carl Swanson, still had the feeling that he had not used the

TABLE 2

t TEST RESULTS

	t STATISTIC	LEVEL OF SIGNIFICANCE*
Texas vs. Oklahoma	1.33	.100
Texas vs. Louisiana	2.28	.025
Oklahoma vs. Louisiana	1.25	.300

*The higher the level of significance, the greater the probability that there is no significant difference between means. The highest acceptable level is usually .10, or 10%. Texas vs. Oklahoma is on the borderline.

survey data to its fullest extent and he reflected upon other methods of studying the effects of advertising restrictions in the three states.

Questions

1 Examine Tables 3, 4, and 5 on pp. 206–208 to see what other breakdown of the data might show a stronger contrast between the states. Perform this analysis.

2 What statistical technique would enable you to compare all three states at the same time? Perform this analysis.

3 What legislative recommendations should the FTC make with regard to the advertising of optical goods?

Case 7-3 Naro-Shu Company (C): Feasibility of Establishing a Specialty Retail Store (Is a Store Needed?)

In the Naro-Shu Company (A) case in Chapter 2, Charles Dart, a native Texan who had served in the Armed Forces and then graduated from business school, had decided to open a shoe store specializing in women's shoes in narrow widths. He wished to open the store in a large metropolitan area of Texas. He had reason to believe that wealthier women were more likely to purchase shoes in narrow widths since his experience as a shoe salesman had indicated that the more expensive stores were more likely to offer a line of shoes in narrow widths. After considering the financial figures for the six largest cities in Texas, he decided upon Dallas because per capita income and the median value of owner-occupied housing were highest in that city.

Once he had chosen the city, he decided to look at the various shopping centers in that city. After visiting a local real estate company and comparing data that the realtor furnished with overall data from the Southwest that he gleaned from *Dollars & Cents of Shopping Centers: 1975,* he chose Northpark Shopping Center. It offered highest profit per square foot of space and least variability in profits for all the centers studied. Details are given in Naro-Shu Company (B) in Chapter 3.

Now that he had chosen a shopping center, he decided upon a two-faceted study of the shoe market in this area to find out what widths customers preferred to wear. First, he would examine the distribution of widths stocked by the existing stores and then he would interview a sample of customers in the shopping center.

The managers of each of the fourteen shoe stores in the shopping center (this included shoe departments in department stores and specialized stores like booteries) were asked to approximate the percentage of widths in their stock.

The codes used by Charles are as follows:

W (wide)	= C width	
M (medium)	= B width	
N (narrow)	= AA width	N and S and Q are all
S (slim)	= AAA width	considered to be
Q (quad)	= AAAA width	narrow widths T

$$T = N + S + Q$$

(*Text continues on p. 209.*)

TABLE 3
OKLAHOMA OPTICAL COSTS, 1975

OKLAHOMA CITY OPTICIANS

FIRM	FRAMES	LENSES	TOTAL
A	14.50	21.50	36.00
B	18.90	21.90	40.80
C	17.00	26.00	43.00
D	13.90	17.90	31.80
E	22.00	27.00	49.00
F	23.00	28.00	51.00
G	12.50	29.50	42.00
H	17.50	28.70	46.20
I	15.00	24.00	39.00
J	15.00	35.80	50.80
K	16.50	31.80	48.30
L	16.00	32.50	48.50
	$N = 12$	$N = 12$	$N = 12$
	$\Sigma X = 201.8$	$\Sigma X = 324.60$	$\Sigma X = 526.4$
	$\bar{X} = 16.82$	$\bar{X} = 27.05$	$\bar{X} = 43.87$

OKLAHOMA CITY OPTOMETRISTS

FIRM	FRAMES	LENSES	TOTAL
A	12.00	20.00	32.00
B	14.00	27.00	41.00
C	12.00	20.00	32.00
D	15.00	35.00	50.00
E	14.00	26.00	40.00
F	18.00	27.00	45.00
G	18.00	26.00	44.00
H	14.00	30.00	44.00
I	12.50	15.00	27.50
J	17.00	22.00	39.00
	$N = 10$	$N = 10$	$N = 10$
	$\Sigma X = 146.50$	$\Sigma X = 248.00$	$\Sigma X = 394.50$
	$\bar{X} = 14.65$	$\bar{X} = 24.80$	$\bar{X} = 39.45$

OKLAHOMA CITY OPTHAMOLOGISTS

FIRM	FRAMES	LENSES	TOTAL
A	18.00	31.00	49.00
B	18.00	28.00	46.00
C	15.00	22.60	37.60
	$N = 3$	$N = 3$	$N = 3$
	$\Sigma X = 51.00$	$\Sigma X = 81.6$	$\Sigma X = 132.6$
	$\bar{X} = 17.00$	$\bar{X} = 27.20$	$\bar{X} = 44.20$

TULSA OPTICIANS

FIRM	FRAMES	LENSES	TOTAL
A	17.50	37.50	55.00
B	17.95	28.50	46.45
C	18.00	28.00	46.00
D	14.00	22.00	36.00
E	16.00	28.50	44.50
F	12.00	15.00	27.00
G	15.00	24.50	39.50
H	8.50	27.00	35.50
I	21.75	29.75	51.50
J	15.00	25.00	40.00
	$N = 10$	$N = 10$	$N = 10$
	$\Sigma X = 155.70$	$\Sigma X = 265.75$	$\Sigma X = 421.45$
	$\bar{X} = 15.57$	$\bar{X} = 26.58$	$\bar{X} = 42.15$

TULSA OPTOMETRISTS

FIRM	FRAMES	LENSES	TOTAL
A	20.00	26.00	46.00
B	12.00	17.00	29.00
C	18.00	31.00	49.00
D	18.00	25.00	43.00
E	16.00	26.00	42.00
F	14.00	32.00	46.00
G	8.95	14.00	22.95
H	22.00	21.00	43.00
I	16.00	26.00	42.00
J	15.00	28.00	43.00
	$N = 10$	$N = 10$	$N = 10$
	$\Sigma X = 159.95$	$\Sigma X = 246.00$	$\Sigma X = 405.95$
	$\bar{X} = 16.00$	$\bar{X} = 24.60$	$\bar{X} = 40.60$

TULSA OPTHAMOLOGISTS

FIRM	FRAMES	LENSES	TOTAL
A	15.00	25.00	40.00
B	22.50	33.00	55.50
	$N = 2$	$N = 2$	$N = 2$
	$\Sigma X = 37.50$	$\Sigma X = 58.00$	$\Sigma X = 95.50$
	$\bar{X} = 18.75$	$\bar{X} = 29.00$	$\bar{X} = 47.75$

LAWTON OPTICIANS

FIRM	FRAMES	LENSES	TOTAL
A	10.00	15.00	25.00
B	12.00	23.00	35.00
C	16.00	30.00	46.00
	$N = 3$	$N = 3$	$N = 3$
	$\Sigma X = 38.00$	$\Sigma X = 68.00$	$\Sigma X = 106.00$
	$\bar{X} = 12.67$	$\bar{X} = 22.67$	$\bar{X} = 35.33$

LAWTON OPTOMETRISTS

FIRM	FRAMES	LENSES	TOTAL
A	18.00	22.00	40.00
B	17.00	32.00	49.00
C	18.00	24.00	42.00
D	10.00	12.00	22.00
E	12.00	22.00	34.00
	$N = 5$	$N = 5$	$N = 5$
	$\Sigma X = 75.00$	$\Sigma X = 112.00$	$\Sigma X = 187.00$
	$\bar{X} = 15.00$	$\bar{X} = 22.40$	$\bar{X} = 37.40$

LAWTON OPTHAMOLOGISTS

FIRM	FRAMES	LENSES	TOTAL
A	14.00	23.00	37.00
B	16.00	25.00	41.00
	$N = 2$	$N = 2$	$N = 2$
	$\Sigma X = 30.00$	$\Sigma X = 48.00$	$\Sigma X = 78.00$
	$\bar{X} = 15.00$	$\bar{X} = 24.00$	$\bar{X} = 39.00$

TABLE 4

TEXAS OPTICAL COSTS, 1975

DALLAS OPTICIANS

	FRAMES	LENSES	TOTAL
A	22.00	22.00	44.00
B	8.50	22.00	30.50
C	12.50	22.00	34.50
D	18.50	24.00	42.50
E	14.00	18.00	32.00
F	15.00	23.00	38.00
G	15.50	23.50	39.00
H	15.00	18.00	33.00
	$N = 8$	$N = 8$	$N = 8$
	$\Sigma X = 121.00$	$\Sigma X = 172.50$	$\Sigma X = 293.50$
	$\overline{X} = 15.12$	$\overline{X} = 21.56$	$\overline{X} = 36.69$

DALLAS OPTOMETRISTS

	FRAMES	LENSES	TOTAL
A	15.00	20.00	35.00
B	16.00	20.00	36.00
C	8.50	22.00	30.50
D	15.00	28.00	43.00
E	14.00	16.00	30.00
F	8.00	30.00	38.00
G	5.60	12.00	17.60
H	15.00	23.00	38.00
	$N = 8$	$N = 8$	$N = 8$
	$\Sigma X = 97.10$	$\Sigma X = 171.00$	$\Sigma X = 268.10$
	$\overline{X} = 12.14$	$\overline{X} = 21.38$	$\overline{X} = 33.51$

DALLAS OPHTHALMOLOGISTS

	FRAMES	LENSES	TOTAL
A	15.00	20.00	35.00
B	12.00	26.00	38.00
C	10.00	32.00	42.00
D	12.00	22.00	34.00
E	12.00	22.00	34.00
	$N = 5$	$N = 5$	$N = 5$
	$\Sigma X = 61.00$	$\Sigma X = 122.00$	$\Sigma X = 183.00$
	$\overline{X} = 12.20$	$\overline{X} = 24.40$	$\overline{X} = 36.60$

HOUSTON OPTICIANS

FRAMES	LENSES	TOTAL
	No comparable frames	

HOUSTON OPTOMETRISTS

FRAMES	LENSES	TOTAL
	No comparable frames	

HOUSTON OPHTHALMOLOGISTS

	FRAMES	LENSES	TOTAL
A	18.00	42.00	60.00
B	20.00	40.00	60.00
C	15.00	28.00	43.00
	$N = 3$	$N = 3$	$N = 3$
	$\Sigma X = 53.00$	$\Sigma X = 110.00$	$\Sigma X = 163.00$
	$\overline{X} = 17.67$	$\overline{X} = 36.66$	$\overline{X} = 54.33$

SAN ANTONIO OPTICIANS

	FRAMES	LENSES	TOTAL
A	9.90	24.90	34.80
B	12.00	27.00	39.00
C	15.00	23.00	38.00
	$N = 3$	$N = 3$	$N = 3$
	$\Sigma X = 36.90$	$\Sigma X = 74.90$	$\Sigma X = 111.80$
	$\overline{X} = 12.30$	$\overline{X} = 24.97$	$\overline{X} = 37.27$

SAN ANTONIO OPTOMETRISTS

	FRAMES	LENSES	TOTAL
A	15.00	30.00	45.00
B	14.00	20.00	34.00
C	15.00	25.00	40.00
D	14.00	22.00	36.00
	$N = 4$	$N = 4$	$N = 4$
	$\Sigma X = 58.00$	$\Sigma X = 97.00$	$\Sigma X = 155.00$
	$\overline{X} = 14.50$	$\overline{X} = 24.25$	$\overline{X} = 38.75$

SAN ANTONIO OPHTHALMOLOGISTS

None studied

TABLE 5
LOUISIANA OPTICAL COSTS, 1975

NEW ORLEANS OPTICIANS

FIRM	FRAMES	LENSES	TOTAL
A	19.00	38.00	57.00
B	16.00	24.00	40.00
C	18.00	26.00	44.00
D	15.00	29.00	44.00
E	18.50	32.50	51.00
F	15.00	37.50	52.50
G	20.00	35.00	55.00
	$N = 7$	$N = 7$	$N = 7$
	$\Sigma X = 121.50$	$\Sigma X = 222.00$	$\Sigma X = 343.50$
	$\bar{X} = 17.36$	$\bar{X} = 31.71$	$\bar{X} = 49.07$

SHREVEPORT OPTICIANS

FIRM	FRAMES	LENSES	TOTAL
A	19.00	28.00	47.00
B	8.00	16.00	24.00
C	18.50	24.00	42.50
D	12.50	24.00	36.50
E	15.00	28.00	43.00
F	15.00	27.00	42.00
	$N = 6$	$N = 6$	$N = 6$
	$\Sigma X = 88.00$	$\Sigma X = 147.00$	$\Sigma X = 235.00$
	$\bar{X} = 14.67$	$\bar{X} = 24.50$	$\bar{X} = 39.17$

BATON ROUGE OPTICIANS

FIRM	FRAMES	LENSES	TOTAL
A	18.95	27.95	46.90
B	14.00	28.00	42.00
C	14.95	26.95	41.90
D	21.20	27.56	48.76
E	18.00	28.00	46.00
F	22.00	24.00	46.00
G	10.00	30.00	40.00
	$N = 7$	$N = 7$	$N = 7$
	$\Sigma X = 119.10$	$\Sigma X = 192.46$	$\Sigma X = 311.56$
	$\bar{X} = 17.01$	$\bar{X} = 27.49$	$\bar{X} = 44.51$

NEW ORLEANS OPTOMETRISTS

FIRM	FRAMES	LENSES	TOTAL
A	16.00	34.00	50.00
B	14.00	30.00	44.00
C	17.00	26.00	43.00
D	14.50	14.00	28.50
	$N = 4$	$N = 4$	$N = 4$
	$\Sigma X = 61.50$	$\Sigma X = 104.00$	$\Sigma X = 165.40$
	$\bar{X} = 15.38$	$\bar{X} = 26.00$	$\bar{X} = 41.38$

SHREVEPORT OPTOMETRISTS

FIRM	FRAMES	LENSES	TOTAL
A	25.00	35.00	60.00
B	15.00	23.00	38.00
C	18.00	29.00	47.00
D	14.00	22.00	36.00
E	14.00	22.00	36.00
F	18.00	20.00	38.00
G	25.00	35.00	60.00
	$N = 7$	$N = 7$	$N = 7$
	$\Sigma X = 129.00$	$\Sigma X = 186.00$	$\Sigma X = 315.00$
	$\bar{X} = 18.43$	$\bar{X} = 26.57$	$\bar{X} = 45.00$

BATON ROUGE OPTOMETRISTS

FIRM	FRAMES	LENSES	TOTAL
A	20.00	30.00	50.00
B	13.00	36.00	49.00
C	16.00	29.00	45.00
D	10.00	30.00	40.00
E	5.95	9.10	15.05
F	15.00	40.00	55.00
G	12.00	22.00	34.00
H	16.00	24.00	40.00
I	17.00	25.00	42.00
J	10.00	14.00	24.00
K	10.50	18.00	28.50
	$N = 11$	$N = 11$	$N = 11$
	$\Sigma X = 145.45$	$\Sigma X = 277.10$	$\Sigma X = 422.55$
	$\bar{X} = 13.22$	$\bar{X} = 25.19$	$\bar{X} = 38.41$

NEW ORLEANS OPHTHALMOLOGISTS

FIRM	FRAMES	LENSES	TOTAL
A	10.00	28.00	38.00
B	20.00	28.00	48.00
C	20.00	28.00	48.00
D	15.00	30.00	45.00
E	12.00	28.00	40.00
F	18.00	29.00	47.00
G	12.00	40.00	52.00
	$N = 7$	$N = 7$	$N = 7$
	$\Sigma X = 107.00$	$\Sigma X = 211.00$	$\Sigma X = 318.00$
	$\bar{X} = 15.28$	$\bar{X} = 30.14$	$\bar{X} = 45.43$

SHREVEPORT OPHTHALMOLOGISTS

FIRM	FRAMES	LENSES	TOTAL
A	18.00	31.00	49.00
B	14.00	24.00	38.00
C	16.00	22.00	38.00
D	14.00	27.00	41.00
E	15.00	25.00	40.00
F	18.50	24.00	42.50
G	15.00	27.00	42.00
H	12.50	24.00	36.50
	$N = 8$	$N = 8$	$N = 8$
	$\Sigma X = 123.00$	$\Sigma X = 204.00$	$\Sigma X = 327.00$
	$\bar{X} = 15.38$	$\bar{X} = 25.50$	$\bar{X} = 40.88$

BATON ROUGE OPHTHALMOLOGISTS

FIRM	FRAMES	LENSES	TOTAL
A	28.00	24.50	52.50
	$N = 1$	$N = 1$	$N = 1$
	$\Sigma X = 28.00$	$\Sigma X = 24.50$	$\Sigma X = 52.50$
	$\bar{X} = 28.00$	$\bar{X} = 24.50$	$\bar{X} = 52.50$

Each of the stores gave him percentage figures for the widths they stocked. He also found that A widths were steadily being phased out by many shoe manufacturers. (For the purpose of his study, where A's did exist, they were grouped with M widths.)

Dart's information took a week to collect. Although the stores had given him the average price of shoes sold, he also felt he should have some information on volume of sales of each store. Store managers would not give him these facts. However, he did manage to make rough estimates of volume of sales by counting the number of women buying shoes in each store for a sampling of hours. This information is also included in Table 1 (see p. 210). He also noted that the more expensive stores were more likely to stock the highest proportion of narrow widths.

Charles felt that the information collected on proportion of widths and price was fairly accurate. Since managers were reluctant to offer sales volume figures, he was not as sure of his sales volume data. Using his information, Charles computed the mean proportions of each of the narrow widths (N, S, Q). He did this by adding the proportion for the 14 shops and dividing by 14. His findings are shown in Table 1.

He then concluded if the experience of each of the stores were weighted equally, the proportion of narrow widths stocked to all shoes stocked, by the shoe store sample, could be said to be 33.7%. As a second approach to his problem, and since he had taken a part-time salesman's job in the shoe department of a large medium-priced department store in the shopping center, Dart decided to record the foot widths of the women whom he waited on for a period of 2 weeks. By then, he had records of 397 women which are given in Table 2. The proportion of narrow widths (p_T) needed to the sample population (n) is

$$p_T = \frac{T}{n} = \frac{200}{397} = 50.4\%$$

Using hypothesis testing techniques he had learned in his basic statistics class, Charles Dart then tried to ascertain if the population width distribution he found could have come from a population width distribution similar to that of the shoe store's inventory proportions. He did this by setting up a hypothesis test to see if the percentage widths in the consumer population conformed to the percentage of widths stocked by these stores in the chosen shopping center. Since the stores stocked 33.7% narrow widths, Charles Dart decided to see if the sample of consumer widths obtained was appreciably larger than 33.7%. If it were smaller

TABLE 2

SHOE WIDTHS OF WOMEN MEASURED IN
A STORE IN A 2-WEEK PERIOD

SIZE	NUMBER OF PEOPLE
N	120
S	63
Q	17
T	200 Narrow widths
M + W	197 Other
Total (n)	397

TABLE 1

PERCENTAGE OF STOCK DEVOTED TO DIFFERENT WIDTHS

(14 shoe departments in Northpark Shopping Center)

| STORE CODE | WIDTHS, % | | NARROW | | | | AVERAGE PRICE ($) | AVERAGE NUMBER OF PAIRS OF SHOES SOLD PER WEEK | TYPE OF STORE |
	WIDE	MEDIUM	N	S	Q	TOTAL			
1	25	65	10	—	—	10	14	1800	National chain
2	5	80	15	—	—	15	16	1500	NC department store
3	10	80	10	—	—	10	18	1300	National chain
4	—	80	20	—	—	20	18	1600	National chain
5	—	80	20	—	—	20	20	500	National chain
6	1	79	19	1	—	20	20	400	Independent
7	—	75	25	—	—	25	22	300	Independent
8	5	60	25	8	2	35	24	400	National chain
9	2	53	30	15	—	45	25	800	NC department store
10	3	62	20	13	2	35	26	200	National chain
11	—	40	40	20	—	60	28	200	Local chain
12	—	44	27	15	14	56	38	300	NC department store
13	—	40	35	15	10	60	40	600	NC department store
14	—	40	30	15	15	60	50	400	National chain
			326	102	43			10,300	
			14	14	14				
			23.3%	7.3%	3.1%*				

$p_N = 23.3\%$

$p_S = 7.3\%$

$p_Q = 3.1\%$

$p_T = 33.7\%$

*These average percentages are calculated by adding the percentage for all 14 stores and dividing by 14. They are *not weighted* by the number of shoes sold per store, since the latter estimates are rough approximations.

than or equal to 33.7%, he felt there would be no need for another store that emphasized narrow widths.

211 HYPOTHESIS TESTS: TWO- AND THREE- SAMPLE OR LARGER SAMPLE TESTS

He specified the hypothesis:

1 $H_0: p_n \leq .337$
   $H_1: p_n > .337$
2 Level of significance = .05, one-tailed test, z test

Dart felt that he would allow a 5% chance of a Type I error so that he could minimize the chances of a Type II error. Since his sample was 397, he used the z distribution to estimate the number of standard errors in the determination of the critical point for his decision.

$$z = 1.65$$

3 Decision criteria:
(a) If $z > +1.65$, reject H_0.

$$\sigma_{\bar{p}} = \sqrt{\frac{(.337)(.663)}{397}} = \sqrt{\frac{.223431}{397}} = .0237$$

$$z = \frac{.504 - .337}{.0237} = 7.05 \quad \text{reject } H_0$$

Or,
(b) Critical value

$$(1.65)(.0237) = .039$$

$$.337 + .039 = .376$$

If $\bar{p} > .376$, reject H_0; since $\bar{p} = .504$ reject H_0. This means that if the proportion of narrow widths in the consumer population sample is greater than 37.6, there would be 5 chances in 100 that this sample could have come from a population whose average proportion of narrow widths was 33.7%. Since the consumer sample proportion of narrow widths was 50.4%, it was quite unlikely that it had come from a population with an average of 33.7% narrow widths.

At this point, Charles Dart wondered what he had proved.

Questions

1 How do you find out about traffic and profitability of shopping centers?

2 (a) What approach was used in this case to determine feasibility for a Naro-Shu Store?

(b) What are some of the problems in using this approach?

(c) What alternative approach(es) could have been used?

3 Using the information in Table 1, compute a weighted percentage of narrow shoes sold using sales volume for each store. Test this figure.

4 Comment on the sampling procedure used here. Could you suggest a better alternative?

5 What other hypothesis test might have been used here? Why was a one-tailed test used?

6 What should Dart consider in deciding what sales volume is needed to be profitable?

7 Four stores now sell over 50% of their sales in larger widths. What are the characteristics of these stores? What might be a good marketing strategy for Dart?

NONPARAMETRIC METHODS:
Chi-Square Test and Kruskal-Wallis Test

8-1   METHODS OF DATA CLASSIFICATION

8-2   CHI-SQUARE DISTRIBUTION

8-3   CHI-SQUARE TEST OF GOODNESS OF FIT
Using the Chi-Square Table
Determining the Number of Degrees of Freedom
Looking up Values in the Chi-Square Table
Performing a Test of Goodness of Fit

8-4   CHI-SQUARE TEST OF INDEPENDENCE
Determining Degrees of Freedom (Independence)
Performing a Test of Independence
Conditions for Using Chi-Square Tests Properly
Problems
Appendix 8-4A: Correction for Continuity and Short-Cut Computation
    Method

8-5   KRUSKAL-WALLIS TEST: A TEST OF THE DIFFERENCE BETWEEN
MEANS
Problems

8-6   SUMMARY

8-7   BIBLIOGRAPHY

8-8   CASES
Case 8-1: Aspirin and Sex Differences
Case 8-2: Bonanza International
Case 8-3: Durell Country Club

In Chapters 6 and 7, we tested hypotheses using the t or z table. Use of these distributions generally means that we have assumed that the original population is normally distributed and can make some estimates of population parameters. To use the z table, we should know the parameters (defining characteristics of the original distribution). The standard deviation and the mean are the parameters of the normal distribution. If we know these two measures for a normally distributed population, we have defined a unique population.[1] If we are trying to estimate a mean for a normal population, we must know the standard deviation in order to use the z table. If we calculate the standard deviation *on the basis of a sample,* we use the t distribution unless the *sample becomes very large,* in which case the distribution approaches the z distribution.

If we can make no assumptions about the population or if the data used is in classifications that are nominal or ordinal (see below), *distribution-free* or *nonparametric tests* are advisable. These names have been used interchangeably in statistics texts. We call the tests *nonparametric,* as it assumes that the distribution form is unknown. These nonparametric tests are often very simple to compute and are applicable to a wide variety of situations.

The chief disadvantage of nonparametric measures is that they are less efficient than normal curve or Poisson statistics. For example, for the same population size, when we didn't know whether the normal curve applied, Chebychev's inequality required a much wider interval for inclusion of 90% of the data than did the z table (see Section 2-10). Similarly, in hypothesis testing problems, we may need a larger difference between two means to prove that there is a significant difference in population means than we need with normal curve statistics. The same applies to other well-known distributions. Thus, nonparametric methods are easy to use and require little information about the population parameters, but they are less precise and efficient than normal curve statistics or statistics of other well-known distributions when the data has actually come from these types of populations.

METHODS OF DATA CLASSIFICATION

8-1

Nonparametric techniques are especially useful when one or more of the variables studied is nominal or ordinal. Scales of measurement may be of four types—nominal, ordinal, interval, and ratio.

A nominal variable is one where order has no meaning. For example, groups such as male or female, or black, white, or Chicano are considered nominal variables. They are descriptive and have no quantitative properties.

Ordinal data ranks categories from highest to lowest or lowest to highest. Even though the categories are in order, we do not know if rank 1 is just as far from rank 2 as rank 2 is from rank 3. Order has meaning but the distance between ranks isn't clear. Thus, we may rank job applicants 1, 2, and 3. This does not mean that the difference between 1 and 2 is the same as the difference between 2 and 3. All we are saying is that 1 is better than 2, 2 better than 3.

An *interval scale* has a constant unit of measurement, but its zero point or origin is arbitrary. The most common example of an interval scale is temperature. We can say that *differences between values* on a temperature scale are multiples of each other. Thus, the difference between 20°F and 0°F is *twice* as much as between 10°F and 0°F. We *cannot* say that 20°F is *twice as warm* as 10°F. We convert 20°F and 10°F to Centigrade using the formula

---

[1]To define a unique population we must also make other measures, such as skewness and peakedness (see Chapter 2). We know for a normally distributed population that the distribution is symmetric and mesokurtic.

$$T_c = \frac{5}{9}(T_f - 32)$$

$$T_c = \frac{5}{9}(20 - 32) = \frac{5(-12)}{93} = -\frac{20}{3} = -6.67 \qquad \text{for } 20°\text{F}$$

$$T_c = \frac{5}{9}(10 - 32) = \frac{5(-22)}{9} = \frac{-110}{9} = -12.2 \qquad \text{for } 10°\text{F}$$

215

NONPARAMETRIC
METHODS:
CHI-SQUARE TEST
AND KRUSKAL-
WALLIS TEST

The Centigrade readings are not in the ratio of 2/1. Many statistical measures can be performed on data that uses an interval scale.

Ratio scales are the highest-level scales in that all arithmetic operations are possible on these scales. These scales have a unique zero point and constant units of measurement. Measures of weight and length are scales of this type. Six inches is 6 inches away from 12 inches, and something that is 12 inches long is twice as long as something that is 6 inches long. Monetary amounts are scales of this type. Ten dollars is twice as much as $5. Generally, most business and social science data is not in the form of ratio scales. Often, it is not in the form of interval scales. The ratio and interval scales are sometimes called *cardinal* scales. Often, business and social science data is estimated in the form of ordinal or nominal scales. Nonparametric tests *must be used* with nominal and ordinal scales. They may be used with interval and ratio scales when the distribution of the population is unknown or nonnormal and when important parameters, such as σ, must be estimated. The first, very useful, and well-known nonparametric test to be studied in this chapter involves the *chi-square distribution*.

CHI-SQUARE DISTRIBUTION

8-2

The chi-square distribution, developed by Karl Pearson in 1899, was explained in one of a series of 18 papers titled "Mathematical Contributions to the Theory of Evaluation." The tests that use this distribution make no assumptions of normality about the underlying distribution of the population. Like the *t* distribution, the shape varies with the number of degrees of freedom, which are the number of observations or sets of observations that are free to vary. We can see in Figure 8-1 that there is a different-shaped probability distribution for each level of degrees of freedom. The *t* distribution is always symmetric, while the chi square (χ^2) curves are positively skewed (skewed to the right; see Chapter 2). As the degrees of freedom increase, the shape of the χ^2 curves approaches the normal distribution. The chi-square table (Table A-6) can be used to find—for each level of the degrees of freedom and for each level of α (Type I error)—how large the computed value of χ^2 must be to infer that there is little chance that the sample tested could have come from a population with certain specified characteristics.

CHI-SQUARE TEST OF GOODNESS OF FIT

8-3

The chi square will be used to test *goodness of fit* and *independence* (see Section 8-4). The tests for goodness of fit show whether a given data distribution looks like a normal distribution, a Poisson distribution, a uniform distribution, or any other kind of distribution that one might like to specify. Too large a computed value of χ^2

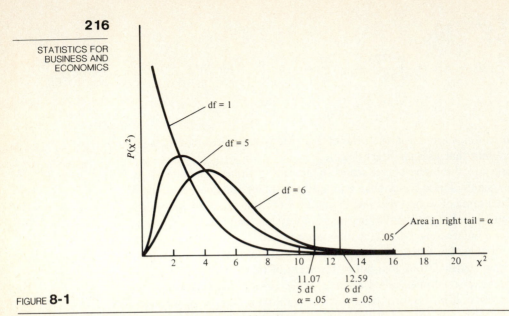

FIGURE **8-1**

Chi-square distribution for 1, 2, 5, and 6 degrees of freedom.

implies the fit is not good; that is, the observed data does not conform to the hypothesized distribution.

The computation of values for χ^2 is really very simple. You might have developed a test like this on your own if you had a chance to think about it. We start with a simple example, develop a formula, and discuss how we could test our results. Then, we set up the regular three-step hypothesis test procedure that we used in Chapters 6 and 7.

If you were tossing a coin, you would expect to have a 50/50 chance of heads or tails. Thus, if you tossed a coin 20 times, you would expect to get 10 heads and 10 tails. Now suppose you tossed the coin 20 times and found you had 6 heads and 14 tails. Would you infer that the coin isn't fair? How could you test it? Naturally, you would look at the difference between what you expected—10 heads and 10 tails—and what you found—6 and 14. To calculate the chi-square test, we subtract what we obtained from what we expected, square this value, and divide this squared difference by our expected value. Then, we sum all squared variations. If there is little difference between what we expected and what we obtained, we would assume that our coin is fair. However, if there was a large difference and the value of our summed squared variations was large, we would be worried. The chi-square table will be used as a guide to when we can infer that the coin is defective. Now, let us write this as a computation formula

$$\chi^2 = \Sigma \frac{(\text{observed frequency} - \text{expected frequency})^2}{\text{expected frequency}}$$

Let O be the observed frequency and E the expected frequency.

$$\chi^2 = \Sigma \frac{(O - E)^2}{E} \tag{8-1}$$

For our coin tossing example, we now compute

$$\chi^2 = \frac{(6 - 10)^2}{10} + \frac{(14 - 10)^2}{10} = 1.6 + 1.6 = 3.2$$

217

NONPARAMETRIC
METHODS:
CHI-SQUARE TEST
AND KRUSKAL-
WALLIS TEST

Now, we need to know whether this value is large enough to infer that the coin is defective, so we consult Table A-6.

Using the Chi-Square Table

To use the chi-square table, we must have an α level and the number of degrees of freedom. Like the table for the t distribution, each horizontal line in the χ^2 table represents the distribution for that number of degrees of freedom.

Determining the Number of Degrees of Freedom The number of degrees of free-dom does *not* depend on sample size but on the number of cells or frequency classi-fications that we compare. There should be *at least 5 items* in each theoretical fre-quency class. In the coin tossing problem, where we tossed the coin 20 times, there were 10 theoretical heads and 10 theoretical (expected) tails. If there are not at least 5 items the value of chi square is inflated because squared differences are divided by a very small size expected frequency $(O - E)^2/E$. Often, when the categories are too small, they can be combined for an effective test.

To fit a distribution, the number of categories to be compared and the number of parameters needed to define the distribution help determine the degrees of free-dom. Generally, the formula is the number of categories K minus the number of parameters and minus 1 for the totals, which must be kept the same for the theoret-ical and the actual observations.

1 To fit a *uniform distribution* (where all the categories have the same probability as in a coin or dice problem), we lost 1 degree of freedom since the total degrees of freedom equals the number of categories minus 1 $(K - 1)$.
2 To fit a *binomial distribution* where n and p are the parameters, the degrees of freedom are $K - 2$. Since n is also the total number of trials, we do not have to subtract a degree of freedom for the total.
3 In the *normal distribution,* the parameters are μ and σ. We lose 1 additional degree of freedom for n (the total number of observations, which must be equal). Therefore, degrees of freedom equal $K - 3$.
4 In the *Poisson distribution,* μ is the parameter. We lose 1 additional degree of freedom for n (the total number of observations for the actual and theoretical data, which must be equal). Therefore, degrees of freedom equal $K - 2$.

Thus, for a goodness of fit test, the number of degrees of freedom depends not on sample size but on the number of frequency classifications or cells that we compare.

Looking up Values in the Chi-Square Table To look up a value in the table, we note that degrees of freedom go down the left-hand column and that the α level in the right tail goes across the top of the table. Thus, for $\alpha = .05$ and 7 degrees of freedom, the χ^2 value is 14.067. If we keep the same degrees of freedom and change α to .01, the χ^2 value is 18.475. In our coin toss problem, we had two categories—heads and tails. The degree of freedom is 1. If $\alpha = .05$, $\chi^2 = 3.841$.

We note that the computed value of χ^2 is very small if the theoretical (expected) and actual (observed) are very similar. If the chi-square value calculated from the data is greater than the value in the table, we have evidence to reject a null hypothesis. The null hypothesis is our usual hypothesis that there is no difference between sample observations and presumed population values. If our calculated χ^2 is greater than the value given in the table for our chosen level of α, we can reject the idea that there is "no significant difference." Thus, we may infer that a difference exists.

For example, in Figure 8-1 with 6 degrees of freedom and $\alpha = .05$, the computed χ^2 value must exceed 12.59 to prove that there is a significant difference. Thus, we are saying that there are only 5 chances in 100 that the sum of the squared difference between the population and the sample values divided by the theoretical value gives a χ^2 value as high as 12.59 or higher when the sample comes from a population with given characteristics (that is, normal, binomial, or Poisson distribution, or whatever we are testing).

Performing a Test of Goodness of Fit

We illustrate this testing technique using a simple example of what should be a uniform distribution.

EXAMPLE 8-1   Assume that we want to test if a die is biased. If we throw it many times, the frequency of appearance of 1, 2, 3, 4, 5, and 6 should be equal. This is called a *uniform distribution*. First, set up the hypothesis test and suppose we toss the die 150 times.

1 H_0: The die is unbiased (tosses of the dice form a uniform distribution).
   H_1: The die is biased.
The null hypothesis is that the difference between the sample observations and the presumed population value is due to random fluctuation only and not that the population is different from that presumed.
2   Chi-square test, .05 level of significance, 5 degrees of freedom.
   In this step we specify that we use the chi-square test and the .05 level of significance. We choose an α level of .05; common levels are .05 and .01. The degrees of freedom depend on the number of categories we have. For the uniform distribution of the dice, we have six categories (1−6) for which we match observed frequencies and theoretical expectations. If the die is unbiased, we would expect 25 in each category (theoretical frequency) in 150 throws. Assume the observed frequencies come out as shown in Table 8-1.

TABLE 8-1
ACTUAL AND EXPECTED FREQUENCIES IN DIE-THROWING PROBLEM

FREQUENCY	NUMBER ON DIE						TOTAL
	1	2	3	4	5	6	
Observed	27	35	35	10	25	18	150
Theoretical	25	25	25	25	25	25	150

219

NONPARAMETRIC
METHODS:
CHI-SQUARE TEST
AND KRUSKAL-
WALLIS TEST

If we hold the observed and theoretical totals the same (150), we subtract 1 degree of freedom because there are 6 categories to match and we must be able to choose the number of people in the last category to keep equal totals for our observed and theoretical data. Therefore, we have 5 degrees of freedom; the first five numbers can be of any level (≤ 150), but we are not free to choose the sixth because the total must be 150.

Now, step 3 sets up the *critical value* that x^2 must exceed to infer that the die is biased.

3 If $x^2 > 11.070$, then reject H_0.

Using 5 degrees of freedom and .05 level of significance, Table A-6 gives a value of 11.070 (see Figure 8-2). As we compute the x^2 value, we see that if the actual values are very close to the theoretical values, then the number we compute for x^2 is small because $\Sigma[(O - E)^2/E]$ is small. If the actual values are quite different from the theoretical, our computed x^2 value is large and exceeds the value in the table. Note that since our values are always squared, x^2 is always positive. In this case, 5% of the time (Type I error, level of significance) x^2 could be greater than 11.070 and the die would be judged biased even though it isn't. This sample of 150 throws is seldom evenly distributed even if the die is perfectly good, because there are sampling errors. Essentially, the chi-square test gives us a cutoff point that suggests how large a reasonable sampling error might be. Once the error appears too large, we have to say that it is unlikely that a sample of this sort could have come from (in this case) a population (of dice) with a uniform distribution.

Since we have set a Type I (α) error of .05, it is possible that 5% of the time x^2 will be 11.070 or higher, even though the population actually has a uniform distribution. If we wanted only a .01 Type I error (chance of rejecting a true hypothesis), x^2 for 5 degrees of freedom will be 15.086. Thus, it will be more difficult to say that the die is biased, when it isn't. We have set a Type I error of .05 rather than .01 because .05 gives a smaller Type II error (chance of accepting a bad die). If we are very worried about accepting a bad die, we might use a .10 Type I error.

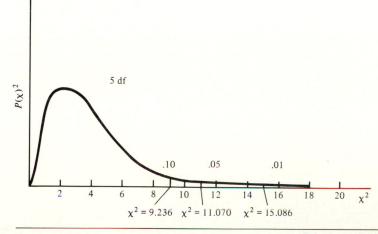

FIGURE **8-2**

Chi-square distribution for 5 degrees of freedom, with α equal to .10, .05, and .01.

Then, if $x^2 > 9.236$, we would reject the die. Thus, we would have less chance of accepting a bad die, and more chance of rejecting a good one. To compute x^2,

$$x^2 = \frac{(27 - 25)^2}{25} + \frac{(35 - 25)^2}{25} + \frac{(35 - 25)^2}{25} + \frac{(10 - 25)^2}{25}$$

$$+ \frac{(25 - 25)^2}{25} + \frac{(18 - 25)^2}{25}$$

$$= \frac{4}{25} + \frac{100}{25} + \frac{100}{25} + \frac{225}{25} + 0 + \frac{49}{25} = \frac{478}{25}$$

$$= 19.12$$

Since $19.12 > 11.070$, reject H_0; we have reason to believe the die isn't fair.

Distributions that can be fitted include the normal, binomial, Poisson, or any other (even those with irregular shapes).

In Chapter 3 we developed theoretical values for the Prussian cavalry officers who would be kicked to death by their horses. It seemed from the data that actual and theoretical values from a Poisson distribution were very close. We are now in a position to test if there is a significant difference between actual and theoretical values.

EXAMPLE 8-2 See Table 8-2. We note that in the last two rows, the theoretical values are less than 5. Combining the last three rows in Table 8-2, we present a shortened table showing columns 1, 2, and 5 (Table 8-3).

1 H_0: Data fits a Poisson distribution with $\mu = .7$.
H_1: Data does not fit a Poisson distribution with $\mu = .7$.

TABLE 8-2

COMPARISON OF THEORETICAL (POISSON) AND ACTUAL DEATHS: PRUSSIAN CAVALRY, 1875–1894

(1) DEATHS PER YEAR	(2) NUMBER OF CORPS	(3) NUMBER OF DEATHS	(4) PROBABILITY	(5) THEORETICAL	
0	144	0	.4966	139.0	
1	91	91	.3476	97.3	
2	32	64	.1217	34.1	Combine these
3	11	33	.0284	8.0	categories to ensure
4	2	8	.0050	1.4	a theoretical value of
5 or more	0	0	.0007	.2	at least 5 in each
	280	196	1.000	280	cell.

$n = 280$

$$\mu = \frac{196 \text{ number of deaths}}{280 \text{ number of corps}} = .7$$

Source: Warren Weaver, *Lady Luck: The Theory of Probability*, Doubleday: Anchor, New York, 1963, pp. 264–270.

TABLE 8-3 　　　　　　　　　　　　　　　　　　　　　　　　　　　**221**

NONPARAMETRIC
METHODS:
CHI-SQUARE TEST
AND KRUSKAL-
WALLIS TEST

(1) NUMBER OF DEATHS	NUMBER OF CORPS	
	(2) ACTUAL	(5) THEORETICAL
0	144	139.0
1	91	97.3
2	32	34.1
3 or more	13	9.6
	280	280.0

2 Chi-square test, .05 level of significance, 2 df (we lost 1 for μ and 1 for n).
3 If $\chi^2 > 5.991$, reject H_0.

$$\chi^2 = \frac{25}{139} + \frac{39.7}{97.3} + \frac{4.41}{34.1} + \frac{11.6}{9.6} = 1.921$$

Since $\chi^2 < 5.991$, accept the null hypothesis. The Poisson distribution provides a good fit for this problem.

CHI-SQUARE TEST OF INDEPENDENCE

8-4

When we study groups of people, we are frequently interested in seeing if different proportions in each group favor a given candidate, prefer a particular product, or vary on any dimension that we wish to study. Since we often have nominal or at most ordinal data, the chi-square test is ideally suited to determine if two variables are related to each other or are independent.

Let us say that we wish to relate education to political preference. If there is *no* relation between education and political preference for each educational group, the same proportion in each educational group favors a given candidate. Thus, we can say that political preference is independent of education. Table 8-4 shows four educational categories and three candidates. We test the data to see if political preference is related to or is independent of level of education. For example, if it were related, we could make such statements as "Educated people are more likely to vote for Hartz." The chi-square test only tells us if there appears to be a significant difference in the preferences of different educational groups. To determine *what* the difference is, we must consult the data from which we computed the χ^2 values.

If *education were not related* to political preference, the proportion voting for

TABLE 8-4
RELATION OF EDUCATION TO POLITICAL PREFERENCE
ACTUAL NUMBERS VOTING FOR EACH CANDIDATE

CANDIDATE	DIDN'T COMPLETE HIGH SCHOOL	COMPLETED HIGH SCHOOL	SOME COLLEGE	COMPLETED COLLEGE	TOTAL DISTRIBUTION
Jones	50	80	60	30	220
Kenner	20	60	80	20	180
Hartz	30	60	60	50	200
	100	200	200	100	600

each candidate would be about the *same* for each educational group. Rapid inspection of the table indicates that this is not so. Thirty percent of those people who completed college prefer Jones as compared to 50% of those who didn't complete high school. We now test if these differences could result from sampling error or if they are so large that one cannot reasonably say they result from sampling error. Once again we set up our three-step analysis.

1   H_0: Education is not related to political preference.
    H_1: Education is related to political preference.
2   Chi-square test, .05 level of significance, and df $= (r - 1)(c - 1) = 2(3) = 6$. (In computing degrees of freedom, ignore the totals column and use the remaining number of rows r and columns c. We explain this step shortly.
3   If $\chi^2 > 12.592$, reject H_0.

The second step tells the analyst that the chi-square test will be used with an .05 level of significance. The most commonly used levels of significance are .01 and .05. We have explained above that if we wish to lower Type II error we could use a $\alpha = .10$.

Determining Degrees of Freedom (Independence)

We determine the degrees of freedom by using the formula df $= (r - 1)(c - 1)$. This works because if we want the totals on the right-hand side to equal those in the theoretical distribution, we must lose 1 degree of freedom in each row. Now, if we want the theoretical totals to equal the actual totals, we lose 1 degree of freedom in each column. If we count the remaining numbers, we have 6. As one can see, we have eliminated one row and one column of numbers, hence $(r - 1)(c - 1)$. Looking at the actual numbers voting for each candidate, if we cross out one number in each row and one in each column (see numbers in circles), 6 numbers (degrees of freedom) remain. (See Table 8-4.) Now, using 6 degrees of freedom and an $\alpha = .05$, look up the χ^2 value in the table. If our computed χ^2 exceeds this value, we have reason to believe (at the .05 level) that education does influence political preference.

Performing a Test of Independence

In order to compute χ^2, we must have theoretical values. The values in the table are our actual values. If education didn't affect candidate preference rating, we would have the same proportion voting for Jones, Kenner, and Hartz in each category as we have in the total's column.

Jones	220	36.67%
Kenner	180	30.00
Hartz	200	33.33
	600	100.00%

We use these figures to compute theoretical totals. For row 1, we multiply .3667 times the sum of each column to find what number should be placed in each column. Going across the first row we have .3667 × 100 = 36.67; .3667 × 200 = 73.34; .3667 × 200 = 73.34; and .3667 × 100 = 36.67. Rounding off, we get the theoretical values for row 1 (numbers in brackets beside original numbers) in Table 8-5. To calculate theoretical values for row 2, 180/600 = .3. For row 2, we have .3(100)

TABLE 8-5
RELATION OF EDUCATION AND POLITICAL PREFERENCE

CANDIDATE	SOME HIGH SCHOOL		COMPLETED HIGH SCHOOL		SOME COLLEGE		COMPLETED COLLEGE		TOTAL
	ACTUAL	THEORETICAL	ACTUAL	THEORETICAL	ACTUAL	THEORETICAL	ACTUAL	THEORETICAL	
Jones	50	(36.7)	80	(73.3)	60	(73.3)	30	(36.7)	220
Kenner	20	(30.0)	60	(60.0)	80	(60.0)	20	(30.0)	180
Hartz	30	(33.3)	60	(66.7)	60	(66.7)	50	(33.3)	200
	100	100.0	200	200.0	200	200.0	100	100.0	600

= 30; .3(200) = 60; .3(200) = 60; and .3(100) = 30. For row 3, we have 200/600 = .3333. Rounding off, .3333(100) = 33.3; .3333(200) = 66.7; .3333(200) = 66.7; and .3333(100) = 33.3. We must be sure the theoretical column totals equal the column totals (100, 200, 200, and 100, respectively) as the actual columns, and that the theoretical row totals equal the actual row totals (220, 180, and 200, respectively).[2]

Let us compute χ^2:

$$\chi^2 = \Sigma \frac{(O - E)^2}{E}$$

Working across the rows we have,

$$\frac{(50 - 36.7)^2}{36.7} = 4.82 \qquad \frac{(80 - 73.3)^2}{73.3} = 0.61 \qquad \text{for Jones}$$

$$\frac{(60 - 73.3)^2}{73.3} = 2.41 \qquad \frac{(30 - 36.7)^2}{36.7} = 1.22$$

$$\frac{(20 - 30)^2}{30} = 3.33 \qquad \frac{(60 - 60)^2}{60} = 0 \qquad \text{for Kenner}$$

$$\frac{(80 - 60)^2}{60} = 6.67 \qquad \frac{(20 - 30)}{30} = 3.33$$

$$\frac{(30 - 33.3)^2}{33.3} = 0.33 \qquad \frac{(60 - 66.7)^2}{66.7} = 0.67 \qquad \text{for Hartz}$$

$$\frac{(60 - 66.7)^2}{66.7} = 0.67 \qquad \frac{(50 - 33.3)^2}{33.3} = 8.38$$

Adding these numbers, $\chi^2 = 32.44$. Since 32.44 exceeds 12.592, we reject H_0 and conclude that there is a significant relationship between political preference and education. If we wish to examine which voters will select each type of candidate, we must go back to the original table. Here, we see that 50% of college graduates (50/100) will vote for Hartz, while 30% of the other three educational groups will vote for him. On the other hand 50% of those who didn't complete high school will vote for Jones. Thus, it would seem that Hartz appeals to the well-educated and Jones to the less-educated. Further examination of the data may reveal other interesting differences.

This type of analysis may be useful for many economic- and business-oriented problems. For example: Does brand preference relate to education, to age, to income level, or to different combinations of age and income levels? Do TV viewing habits relate to age, income, or education? Does consumer spending in durable goods relate to psychologic attitudes or unemployment levels?

Conditions for Using Chi-Square Tests Properly

First, we should note that chi-square tests cannot be used on data in percentage form. They must be used on raw data. Thus, if numbers are given in percentage form they should be converted to actual numerical values (see the problems section below).

---

[2]Another way to calculate these values is to multiply the marginal totals by each other and divide by the grand total. Thus, for people with some high school training who would vote for Jones, we have [220(total voting for Jones) $\times$ 100(total with some high school)]/600(grand total) = (220 $\times$ 100)/600 = 36.7.

Another problem in using the chi-square test is encountered when the sample size used for the test is very large. This usually leads to a very large value for χ^2, which gives significant results. Thus, in our coin-tossing problem, if we tossed the coin 2000 times and found 600 heads and 1400 tails, our computed value for χ^2 would be

$$\chi^2 = \frac{(600 - 1000)^2}{1000} + \frac{(1400 - 1000)^2}{1000} = 320$$

When we had only 20 tosses our corresponding χ^2 value was 3.1! More advanced texts, such as *Nonparametric Statistics* (see the bibliography), provide methods of handling these problems. Generally, however, the chi-square test should be used for smaller sample sizes.

In addition, always remember that for *both* tests of *goodness of fit* and *independence* the theoretical value in each cell should be at least 5. Combining rows or columns in some logical fashion is a way of ensuring the desired theoretical frequency in each cell.

Finally, we consider the case of the 2 × 2 contingency table, which is used when there are two categories for each variable. For example, if we were studying the differences in opinion of men and women on the Equal Rights Amendment, we would have a 2 × 2 table.

	MEN	WOMEN
Pro	A	C
Con	B	D

In order to use the chi-square test, we must be sure all expected frequencies are 5 or more. Thus, our sample size must be at least 20. It is advisable to use the continuity correction for this computation for a 2 × 2 table. Appendix 8-4A shows some short-cut computation methods for a 2 × 2 table, and also discusses the continuity correction.

Problems

1 An accounting professor at a local college wanted to see if grades in her class were independent of the students' socioeconomic standing. She took the grades of all students in the class and obtained the following results. Test the hypothesis that good performance is independent of a student's socioeconomic standing using 0.05 significance level.

ACTUAL OBSERVED FREQUENCIES

SOCIOECONOMIC STANDING	GRADE			TOTAL
	C	B	A	
Lower	16	24	10	50
Middle	16	30	14	60
Upper	10	20	10	40
Total	42	74	34	150

2 A car dealer feels that accessories ordered on new cars are dependent on the buyer's age. To determine the validity of this theory, he looked at statistics of last year's car sales and found the following:

OBSERVED FREQUENCIES
(Amount spent on accessories)

AGE GROUP	0	$1–$500	MORE THAN $500	TOTAL
18–22	12	20	8	40
23–27	25	15	20	60
28–32	10	15	20	45
Total	47	50	48	145

Test this hypothesis at the 0.05 level of significance.

3 A department store sells $25 or $100 gift certificates each year during the Christmas season. The store manager wants to determine if the price of the certificate has anything to do with what a customer purchases with it. Given the following data from store records of gift certificate purchases for January, determine if types of items purchased are independent of the value of the gift certificate.

OBSERVED FREQUENCIES
(Type of purchases)

VALUE OF CERTIFICATE	CLOTHING	HARDWARE	APPLIANCES	SPORTING GOODS	TOTAL
$ 25	60	30	25	35	150
$100	90	30	20	35	175
Total	150	60	45	70	325

4 International Trucking determined that last year they sold 20% of their large tractor trailer trucks in the Far East, 40% in Europe, 20% in South America, 10% in Canada, and 10% in the United States. This year they sold 50 trucks in the Far East, 75 in Europe, 40 in South America, 10 in Canada, and 25 in the United States. Does the sales distribution in the current year differ significantly from that of the previous year at the .01 level?

5 The president of a college appoints a committee to study whether there has been a tendency toward grade inflation from 1965 to 1979. The committee goes to the registrar's office and finds grades for all the undergraduate colleges in 1965. A sample of 80 grades for 1979 is taken from school records. The grades were distributed as follows (assume these are all for 3-credit courses):

	1965 GRADES	1979 GRADES
A	1020	20
B	1000	16
C	2500	16
D	900	5
F	400	3
Withdrew	300	20
	6120	80

Use the chi-square test to determine whether there has been a significant change in grade distribution from 1965 to 1979. (*Hint:* Interpret what 1965 grades would have been for 80 people and compare to 1979 grades.)

6 *Optional* (involves fitting a normal distribution). A combined test of verbal and mathematical ability is administered to a class of economics majors. The department wishes to study whether the scores are normally distributed. The following data is collected.

TEST SCORE INTERVAL	NUMBER OF STUDENTS
30 but < 40	7
40 but < 50	23
50 but < 60	43
60 but < 70	55
70 but < 80	38
80 but < 90	26
90 but < 100	13
	205

Test at the .05 level to see if this distribution conforms to a normal distribution. (*Hint:* First compute $\overline{X}$ and s for the sample. Now, using the z table, compute the area under the curve for each interval; that is, for the first interval, find the area from 30 to 39.9, etc. Multiply this probability by 205 to determine the number of students one would expect to find in each category.)

Appendix 8-4A: Correction for Continuity and Short-Cut Computation Method

As the number of degrees of freedom increases, the chi-square distribution approaches a normal distribution. For very small numbers of degrees of freedom, the chi-square distribution is a good approximation if the correction for continuity is used. To correct for continuity, we assume that the observed frequency O of the formula occupies an interval, the lower limit of which is half a unit below the observed frequency and the upper limit of which is a half unit above the observed frequency. Thus, the correction for continuity reduces by .5 the difference between the observed value of χ^2 and the expected value. We used a similar type of correction in Chapter 3 when we went from the discrete binomial distribution to the continuous normal distribution. The formula with the correction factor is

$$\chi^2 = \Sigma \frac{(|O - E| - \frac{1}{2})^2}{E} \tag{8-2}$$

There are some short-cut formulas that enable us to compute χ^2 more rapidly for a 2×2 table. If the student doesn't have a computer program available, this technique can enable him or her to make rapid computation of χ^2 values. Let us label the cells of a typical 2×2 table as follows:

	Male	*Female*	
Republican	A	B	A + B
Democrat	C	D	C + D
	A + C	B + D	N

Without the continuity correction, the computation formula would be

$$\chi^2 = \frac{N(|AD - BC|)^2}{(A + B)(C + D)(A + C)(B + D)} \qquad (8\text{-}3)$$

With the correction, the formula would be

$$\chi^2 = \frac{N(|AD - BC| - N/2)^2}{(A + B)(C + D)(A + C)(B + D)} \qquad (8\text{-}4)$$

The hypothesis test remains the same as described in this chapter; the only difference is in the method of computing χ^2. Let us assume that we wish to test whether males and females feel differently about pension plans. Previous studies have indicated that females may be more interested in current work benefits, since they may not work until retirement age. A study of the Starr Electronics Company reveals the following:

	Females	Males	
Favor pension	10	11	21
Against pension	46	13	59
	56	24	80

We set up our usual hypothesis test.

1 H_0: Men and women are equally in favor of pensions.
   H_1: Men and women are not equally in favor of pensions.
2 Chi-square test, df $= 1$, $\alpha = .05$.
3 If $\chi^2 > 3.84$, reject H_0.

Using Equation 8-2,

$$\chi^2 = \frac{80(|130 - 506| - 80/2)^2}{(21)(59)(56)(24)} = \frac{80(336)^2}{1,665,216} = 5.42$$

Note that by using the formula you avoid computation of theoretical values. Since $5.42 > 3.84$, reject H_0. Looking at the table, we see that 18% of women are in favor of the plan while 46% of men favor it. On the basis of this chi-square test, it is hard to attribute this difference to chance or sampling variation. It seems to represent a true difference in opinion.

KRUSKAL-WALLIS TEST: A TEST OF THE DIFFERENCE BETWEEN MEANS

8-5

In the section on analysis of variance in Chapter 7, we pointed out that the Kruskal-Wallis test determined whether there was a difference between sample means. However, the test assumed that the samples would come from populations that are normally distributed. Often, for economic and sociologic data, it is not clear whether the underlying population distribution is normal. There are other situations where analysis of variance cannot be used—for example, if the data is not based on an interval or ratio scale but is ordinal data, then analysis of variance may not be used. Thus, when we have (1) ordinal data or (2) data based on an interval or ratio scale but for which the underlying distribution may not be normal, the data can still be put into rank order and the Kruskal-Wallis test used.

Let us start with the example we used for analysis of variance in the preceding chapter. In this example, we studied whether the use of different texts had different effects on students' test scores. First, we must rank-order all observations from lowest to highest (or from highest to lowest). If two grades are the same and should be ranked in the fourth and fifth places, for example, then give each one a rank of 4.5.

We have ranked all of these test scores from highest (1) to lowest (20) in Table 8-6. (Note that since there was a two-way tie for the 19th position, we gave both texts ranks of 19.5.) Ranks are in parentheses beside the original numbers. Sum the ranks for each group. The test statistic calculated is H, which is defined as

$$H = \frac{12}{n(n+1)} \left[\sum_{i=1}^{K} \frac{T_i^2}{n_i} \right] - [3(n+1)] \qquad (8\text{-}5)$$

where n_i = size of sample in ith group
$n = \Sigma n_i$ = sample size for all groups combined
T_i^2 = sum of the ranks, squared for each of the groups

This test uses the chi-square table with degrees of freedom equal to the number of columns minus 1 ($c - 1$). Thus, degrees of freedom depend on the number of groups rather than on sample size. Each group should have at least three observations in it.

Now, substituting into the formula to compute H,

$$H = \frac{12}{20(21)} \left[\frac{61^2}{4} + \frac{24.5^2}{5} + \frac{66.5^2}{6} + \frac{58^2}{5} \right] - [3(21)]$$

$$H = .029(930.250 + 120.050 + 737.042 + 672.800) - 63$$

$$H = .029(2460.142) - 63 = 71.344 - 63 = 8.344$$

Looking at the formula and at this particular problem, we see that the total for all the ranks from 1 to 20 is 210. If all the groups had the same total (that is, 52.5) and the same number of people (5), the size of H that would be computed (63.945 − 63

TABLE 8-6

TEST GRADES FOR STUDENTS USING DIFFERENT TEXTS
(Ranks are in parentheses)

OBSERVATION NUMBER	TEXTS			
	JOHNSON	McCARTHY	JONES	RILEY
1	60 (19.5)	93 (2)	80 (8.5)	90 (5)
2	80 (8.5)	92 (3.5)	79 (10.5)	82 (7)
3	66 (18)	78 (12)	68 (17)	79 (10.5)
4	70 (15)	95 (1)	75 (13)	60 (19.5)
5	—	87 (6)	74 (14)	69 (16)
6	—	—	92 (3.5)	—
Σx_i	276 (61)	445 (24.5)	468 (66.5)	380 (58)
n_i	4	5	6	5
$\bar{X}_i$	69	89	78	76

$\bar{\bar{X}} = 78.45$

= .945) would be less than if each group had unequal sums of ranks. If we squared 50 and 50, for example, we would get 2500 + 2500, or 5000; if we square 25 and 75, we get 625 + 5625, or 6350. Thus, *the more unequal the rank sums of the groups and hence the more different the groups, the larger the value of H*. In order to determine the critical value of H, we use the chi-square table, with degrees of freedom equal to the number of columns minus 1 ($c - 1$), and the level of significance that we have established. In this problem, there are 4 columns (books), hence 3 degrees of freedom. The chi-square table gives a value of 7.815 for $\alpha = .05$ (the Type I error specified in the original problem) and 3 degrees of freedom.

Setting up our usual hypothesis test, we have:

1   $H_0: \mu_1 = \mu_2 = \mu_3 = \mu_4$
    H_1: The means are not equal.
2   Kruskal-Wallis test, .05 level of significance, 3 df
3   If $H > 7.815$, reject H_0 (Look up the value of H in the chi-square table with 3 degrees of freedom and a .05 level of significance.)

We have ranked our test scores and calculated a value of $H = 8.344$.

Since 8.344 exceeds 7.815, reject H_0; there is a significant difference between test scores obtained by students using different books. This result is similar to the result obtained using analysis of variance in Chapter 6. Note how much easier it is to calculate this test than to use analysis of variance. We would have had to use this test if we had a normality problem or if we were dealing with ordinal data. Often, when conditions for analysis of variance are fulfilled, the Kruskal-Wallis test is used first because it provides an easy way to test for differences. We discuss additional nonparametric techniques in Chapter 9.

Problems

1   A college alumni association wishes to test whether alumni from different areas of the country have different income levels. If they do, they will concentrate their fund-raising efforts in the richer areas, since they feel that the bulk of college contributions come from large donations. They take a sample of 10 families in each of three areas of the country to obtain the following results. Test at the .05 level of significance.

NORTHEAST FAMILY INCOME	SOUTHWEST FAMILY INCOME	WEST COAST FAMILY INCOME
20,000	21,000	28,000
4,000,000	30,000	29,000
15,000	32,000	27,400
30,000	21,600	14,000
40,000	34,000	26,500
25,000	42,000	31,500
22,000	46,000	41,000
18,000	50,000	28,500
19,000	17,000	63,000
26,000	43,000	19,500

2   A student who works in a restaurant has a theory that the larger the party, the smaller the percentage of the check to be left as tip. He takes samples of 5 parties

for each size group and finds that the following percentage is tipped. Is there a significant difference at the .01 level?

231

NONPARAMETRIC
METHODS:
CHI-SQUARE TEST
AND KRUSKAL-
WALLIS TEST

| | PERCENTAGE OF BILL TIPPED | | |
PARTY OF 1	PARTY OF 2	PARTY OF 3 AND 4	PARTY OF 5 OR MORE
25 %	20 %	15 %	4 %
20	16	16	13
15	22	8	17
14	11	7	0
10	5	0	0

SUMMARY

8-6

1 Four types or scales of measurement may be used to classify variables. A *nominal* variable is one for which order has no meaning. Examples are categories like male or female, or white, black, or Chicano. For *ordinal* data, the information can be placed in rank order but item 1 is not necessarily as far from item 2 as 2 is from 3. An interval *scale* has a constant unit of measurement, but has an arbitrary zero point. *Ratio* scales have a unique zero point and constant units of measurement.

2 *Nonparametric, or distribution-free, statistics* are used for data classified in ordinal or nominal scales. In addition, these techniques are used where the underlying distributions are not normal or where the parameters of these distributions cannot be calculated.

3 The *chi-square* test is a nonparametric test that can be used to study goodness of fit or independence.

$$\chi^2 = \Sigma \frac{(O - E)^2}{E}$$

where O is the observed, or actual, frequency and E is the expected, or theoretical, frequency. For tests of goodness of fit, the theoretical frequency is calculated. To do this, we multiply the probabilities for each of the elements (or classes) of these distributions by the total number of people in the sample. The degrees of freedom are equal to the number of classes minus the number of parameters held constant. The degrees of freedom lost must also include 1 for the total of the sample size and 1 for each parameter of the distribution.

4 For tests of independence or the relationship between two variables, a table is set up having one variable distributed down the columns and another distributed across the rows. Theoretical values are computed by assuming that if one variable did not affect the other, the distribution of the sample in each class would be the same as it is for the total sample. Degrees of freedom are calculated by using the formula

$$df = (rows - 1)(columns - 1)$$

If the computed value of χ^2 exceeds the value obtained from the table for a given α level and for a specified number of degrees of freedom, the null hypothesis is rejected.

5 The *Kruskal-Wallis test* is used to test the difference between means when the data is in rank order or we are uncertain that the underlying population is normally distributed. All data must be ranked; then, the sums of the ranks for each of the columns (conditions) is compared using the chi-square distribution and the formula for H:

$$H = \frac{12}{n(n + 1)} \left[\sum_{i=1}^{K} \frac{T_i^2}{n_i} \right] - [3(n + 1)]$$

The degrees of freedom equal the number of columns minus 1. If the value calculated for H exceeds the χ^2 value for a given level α and for a given number of degrees of freedom, the null hypothesis is rejected and we assume that there is a significant difference between means.

BIBLIOGRAPHY

8-7

Statistics
Mosteller, Frederick, and Robert E. K. Rourke: *Sturdy Statistics: Nonparametrics and Order Statistics.* Reading, Mass.: Addison-Wesley, 1973. Chapters 8, 9, 10, and 11 focus on the chi-square test, and chapter 12 discusses the Kruskal-Wallis statistic.
Siegel, S.: *Nonparametric Statistics.* New York: McGraw-Hill, 1956. This book was a landmark in the introduction of nonparametric statistics for applied statisticians. Gives a very clear explanation of the use of each technique.
Spurr, William A., and Charles P. Bonini: *Statistical Analysis for Business Decisions.* Homewood, Ill.: Irwin, 1973. See chapter 11.

Marketing
Green, Paul Z., and Donald S. Tull: *Research for Marketing Decisions,* 3d ed. Englewood Cliffs, N.J.: Prentice-Hall, 1975. See chapter 10.

Social Sciences
Senter, R. J.: *Analysis of Data.* Glenview, Ill.: Scott, Foresman, 1969. See chapter 13.

Measurement Scales
Torgerson, Warren S.: *Theory and Methods of Scaling.* New York: Wiley, 1958. A classic in the area of scaling techniques.

CASES

8-8

Case 8-1 Aspirin and Sex Differences
A group of Harvard Medical School surgeons conducted a controlled study to help resolve a controversy over whether aspirin is effective in preventing or reducing blood clotting problems that occur after major surgery.

It's estimated that between 50,000 and 150,000 Americans die annually from blood clots that develop after surgery. Such clots are the most common complication in hip-replacement surgery. The clots form in patients' calves or thighs, where they are called thrombi. If untreated, they often break loose and travel to the lungs. Then known as pulmonary emboli, they can be fatal.

Some scientists disputed earlier studies on the anti-clotting benefits of aspirin because the clot incidence in patients receiving aspirin wasn't compared with incidence in an untreated control group.

In the Harvard study, about half of a group of 95 patients undergoing total hip-replacement surgery were given four aspirin tablets daily, from the day prior to surgery to several weeks after the operation. The rest were given placebos. Neither the doctors nor the patients involved knew who took aspirin. New diagnostic methods allowed doctors to detect and treat leg thrombi before they could go to the lungs.

Four of the 23 men on aspirin developed thrombi, as compared with 14 of the 25 men who took placebos. Yet the tablets failed to give significant measure of protection to the female patients. Thrombi occurred in seven of the 21 women given aspirin, and nine of the 26 women who received placebos, the report said. Both the men and women were over 40 years old, and most of the women were postmenopausal.[1]

The doctors in a previous study had not used a placebo (a harmless substance given to humor a patient rather than to act as a remedy). The placebo is used to control the psychologic state of patients and for psychosomatic effects. In the previous study only 7 of 38 men, as compared to 22 of 48 women, developed thrombi. Since some scientists had disputed this earlier study because the clot incidence in patients receiving aspirin wasn't compared with incidence in an untreated control group, it was decided to conduct the controlled experiment. The controlled experiment, reported in *The Wall Street Journal,* was more complex; it involved a separate study of men and women, with groups who did and did not take the aspirin. For example, the study for women could be set up in a 2 by 2 matrix and then tested for significance.

	Women	
	Aspirin	*Placebo*
Thrombi	7	9
No thrombi	14	17
	21	26

Questions

1 Using statistical techniques, evaluate each of these studies (that is, the one for men and the one for women) to see if there are any sex-linked differences.

2 How would you present your findings to the surgeons? Be specific in your recommendations.

3 Why did good scientific procedure call for the use of a placebo?

4 How might a device similar to a placebo be used in market research experiments? Suggest a design for a market research experiment that would use this technique.

Case 8-2 Bonanza International

Bonanza International, Inc., is a publicly held company based in Dallas, Texas, that operates and franchises family restaurants in 40 states and Canada. Currently, Bonanza has 631 stores in operation, 255 of which are company-owned. The res-

[1] *The Wall Street Journal,* Dec. 8, 1977.

taurants, projecting a Western theme, have a serving line, interior seating, and on-site parking facilities. The restaurant features a limited menu, emphasizing 12 luncheon and dinner entrees. The Bonanza menu consists of a backlit, photographic board with interchangeable positions for pictures and listings of each entree. Since there is no printed menu for the customer to read, all purchase decisions must be made from the visual images projected on the menu board.

The pictures of entrees are arranged randomly on the menu board. The placement of pictures varies between stores, and in some stores the arrangement varies from day to day. Bonanza asserts that a relationship exists between the position of entrees on the menu board and the entrees customers order most frequently. Bonanza has made no previous study to determine the influence of entree position on the sales of the entree.

This project, as proposed by Bonanza to a team of MBA students,[1] involved the implementation of marketing research to measure consumer behavior patterns in making purchasing decisions. In studying the reactions of consumers to entree position on the menu board, Bonanza hopes to develop a criterion for designing an entree arrangement on the board that maximizes profits. By determining the impact the positions on the menu board have on entrees ordered most frequently, Bonanza may effectively use this relationship to promote and/or control the sale of a particular item.

Methodology   The project team conducted a pretest in the Bonanza restaurant located on Meadow Road. During a 90-minute period, the team members observed customers as they read the menu board. Noting customer eye movement and recording subsequent entree decisions, the team members collected the following data that aided in drawing assumptions for positions on the menu board. The menu board was arranged in the following design; the numbers below the entree denote the sales volume of that item during the test period.

Fish	Great Bonanza burger	Top sirloin	Chicken fried steak	Sirloin strip	Chopped steak
1	2	0	3	4	3
Steak sandwich	Bonanza burger	Child's plate	T-bone	Filet mignon	Rib eye
0	3	1	3	0	4

The total customer count or sample size during this time period was 24: 20 adults and 4 children. The entry aisle was on the right-hand side of the store. From the project team's observations, customers initially viewed the board from the right-hand corners. Customer eye movement then flowed across the top row to the left-hand corner, down to the bottom left-hand corner, and across to the right-hand side. The eye flow generalized by the project team is illustrated by the following pattern:

---

[1]This case resulted from a research project performed by Jane Fortenberry and Terrell Potts under the supervision of Professors Marion Sobol and Thomas Barry.

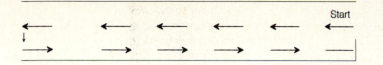

235

NONPARAMETRIC
METHODS:
CHI-SQUARE TEST
AND KRUSKAL-
WALLIS TEST

Due to the observation that the initial and final customers' glances focused upon items on the right-hand side, and the fact that the items on the right-hand side yielded greater sales volume, the project team assumed that the right-hand side had more of an impact on customer buying decisions than the left-hand side. This assumption is contingent upon where the customer stands to place his or her order. When a right-hand entry aisle to the store is present, the upper right-hand corner position offers greater visibility to the customer than the lower left-hand corner. Thus, these two corners, upper right and lower left, were chosen for study for the pilot projects.

For the pilot study, team members visited all Bonanza stores in the Dallas area to select 10 stores with controllable characteristics—an identical menu board constructed in two horizontal rows with six entree positions in each row and a right-hand aisle for customer entry.

The project team designed a standard for determining the two entree items to be altered in each of the test stores. First, the sales history of each store's entree items was recorded for the past 6 weeks. Based on this record, team members assigned a numerical ranking to each entree according to the volume of units sold. The items with the largest sales volume were ranked number one; the items with the second largest sales volume ranked number two, and so forth.

Second, the project team decided to vary the position on the menu board for the fourth and fifth most popular items in each store due to the fact that three entrees—chicken fried steak, chopped steak, and rib eye steak—constitute 62.1% of the total sales in all stores. Choosing the less-popular items would create a greater variance in weekly sales, showing that the favored position rather than the popularity of the item affects sales volume. The team members placed the fourth-ranked item in the top right-hand corner of the menu board for the first week, and placed the item ranked fifth in the lower left-hand corner for the first week. Items ranked 1–3 and 6–12 remained in the same positions throughout the study.

Third, all the stores exhibited the same design in weeks 1 and 3 and the same alternate design in weeks 2 and 4. Altering the menu at the end of a 1-week period allowed for any fluctuation in customer attendance on individual days of each week. Using 2 weeks for each position allowed more observation than 1 week would have offered. An illustration of the design for weeks 1 and 3 appears below. Here, item 1 is most popular and item 12 least popular.

7	6	3	2	1	4
5	8	9	10	11	12

The alternate design for weeks 2 and 4 appears on the next page. Items 4 and 5 differed in the 10 stores. Top sirloin, Bonanza burger, child's plate, and chicken fried steak were in these positions in some stores:

7	6	3	2	1	5
4	8	9	10	11	12

During the initial contact with the 10 store managers, the team members explained the project, gathered sales history, and specified the arrangement of entrees on the menu board for the first week. At this time, the manager received a detailed instruction letter and the tally sheet for the first week.

Throughout the study a project team member called each participating store manager on Tuesday evening to remind him of the changes on the menu board that would occur the following morning. Before each store opened on Wednesday morning, the project team collected the tally sheets on which the number of each entree sold for the 7-day period had been recorded. The project team distributed new tally sheets and also rearranged menu boards at this time. Thus, the project week went from Wednesday morning through Tuesday evening.

Team members totaled the entree sales at the end of each week and at the end of the 4-week period. The combined results are summarized in Table 1 below.

Case 8-3 Durrell Country Club

Alice Murray is a University of Louistown graduate student who works during Christmas and spring break in the pro shop of the Durell Country Club. Alice has always enjoyed golf and, during her undergraduate days at Oregon State University, she was captain of the women's golf team. However, she was surprised to find that the University of Louistown had no women's golf team, even though Alice was able to find several capable players who would be interested in participating. Alice talked to the coach of the men's golf team about the possibility of a women's

TABLE 1

TOTAL WEEKLY SALES (10 STORES) OF 4TH AND 5TH RANK ITEMS
(1-month period)

SALES RANKING	UPPER RIGHT POSITION	LOWER LEFT POSITION
4th item	5440	4514
5th item	3566	3251
Total sales for all items		
Week 1 = 22,214		
Week 2 = 18,963		
Week 3 = 21,397		
Week 4 = 19,166		

Questions

1 Is there any indication that position on the signboard affects sales? Analyze.

2 Based on your examination of the research design, what are some of the limitations of this analysis?

3 Why did the research team vary the positions of the 4th and 5th items instead of the 1st and 2d items?

4 From a profit maximization standpoint, what recommendations would you make to management?

team. Coach Caufield showed Alice the expense sheet for the men's team and explained that no money was available for a women's team in the school's budget. Alice took a copy of the expense sheet, studied each major category, and decided that she could reduce expenses significantly to obtain funds for her team.

Alice drew up a proposed expense sheet and presented it to the budget council. They studied her proposals and decided that they would use the money promised to the cheerleaders for new pom-poms and uniforms for a women's golf team if Alice could actually purchase equipment and transportation in accordance with her proposed expense sheet. Alice got to work trying to find the best quality equipment at the lowest price.

Alice began her testing procedure by comparing four different brands of golf balls (Harper, Topnotch, Marksman, and Proball) to find out if the difference in performance among the brands justified the price differences. All four had a psi (pounds per square inch) rating of 90. The higher the psi rating, the harder the ball—and hence the farther it travels. Alice suspected that some brands were more consistent than others in that rating. To test this theory, she took 10 golf balls from each of the four brands and tested their psi using a compression device. The compression device is used by many professional golfers and is sold in almost all pro shops. The scale rates from 60 to 105 psi.

Alice recorded the following data on the four brands. She couldn't decide whether the differences in psi's justified price differences because the psi's were so varied. She was not sure if the psi for the balls was normally distributed.

PRESSURE			
HARPER ($13.60/DOZEN)	TOPNOTCH ($13.60/DOZEN)	MARKSMAN ($12.60/DOZEN)	PROBALL ($14.40/DOZEN)
78	76	82	79
83	80	83	86
85	86	84	87
86	87	85	87
87	88	86	88
88	89	88	90
90	90	88	90
91	91	89	94
92	92	90	97
95	93	96	98

Questions

1 What is the first measure Alice should make? What results will she obtain?

2 Suggest and perform a test to determine if the pressure of the four brands is significantly different.

3 What parametric test would be similar to this? What would we have to assume to use this test?

4 What benefits might be derived by presenting these findings to the coach? Disadvantages?

NONPARAMETRIC TESTS OF RANKS, RUNS, AND SIGNS

9

9-1   RANK-ORDER CORRELATION
Problems

9-2   RANK-SUM TEST (MANN-WHITNEY)
Two-tailed Test
One-tailed Test
Problems
Appendix A9-2: Correction for Tied Values
Mann-Whitney Test
Rank-Order Correlation
Kruskal-Wallis Test

9-3   KOLMOGOROV-SMIRNOV TEST OF GOODNESS OF FIT FOR ORDINAL DATA (ONE-SAMPLE TEST)

9-4   KOLMOGOROV-SMIRNOV TEST OF INDEPENDENCE (TWO-SAMPLE TEST)
Problems

9-5   ONE-SAMPLE RUNS TEST
Problems

9-6   SIGN TEST
Problems

9-7   SUMMARY

9-8   BIBLIOGRAPHY

9-9   CASES
Case 9-1: Earned Run Average and Baseball Strategy
Case 9-2: Larker Pen Refills
Case 9-3: National Personnel Association

In Chapter 8, we discussed nonparametric tests that were used to prove or disprove hypotheses about goodness of fit (chi-square test), independence of two variables (chi-square test), and differences between means (Kruskal-Wallis test). We also defined four types of scales of measurement that may be used to classify variables. A *nominal* variable is one for which order has no meaning. Examples are categories like male or female; white, black, or Mexican-American. For the *ordinal* scale, the information can be placed in rank order, but item 1 is not necessarily as far from item 2 as 2 is from 3. An *interval* scale has a constant unit of measurement, but the zero point is arbitrary. *Ratio* scales have a unique zero point and constant units of measurement. *Nonparametric* or *distribution-free statistics* are used for data classified in ordinal or nominal scales. In addition, these techniques are used where the underlying distributions are not normal or where the parameters of these distributions cannot be calculated. In this chapter, we introduce additional nonparametric techniques that can be used in the above-mentioned situations. We also provide a very useful table that can help you decide *when* to use a particular parametric or nonparametric technqiue.

First, we will discuss a technique for computing the correlation coefficient for ranked data. Using this technique for ranked data we can estimate whether two variables are related. This technique is called *rank-order correlation.*

Another measure that can be used with ranked data is the *rank-sum test* (Mann-Whitney or Wilcoxon test), which is used to test whether two independent groups have been drawn from the same population. It is used instead of the parametric test of a difference between means or proportions, when we can make no assumptions about the underlying population distributions or when our data, for the two populations to be compared, can only be ranked. Next, we introduce the Kolmogorov-Smirnov test, which can be used when we have ordinal data and independent samples to determine whether two samples come from different populations or the same population or to test for goodness of fit.

Rank-order correlation, the rank-sum test, and the Kolmogorov-Smirnov are used for *ordinal data* (data that can be ranked). Nonparametric statistics also offer techniques for analyzing data that can only be classified into categories without ranks—*nominal data.* We have discussed the chi-square test in Chapter 8. Another useful measure for nominal data is the *runs test,* which evaluates the randomness of a sample chosen for interview or from a productive process. A run is a succession of similar events or observations (many products wider than normal) preceded and followed by a different event or sequence of events, or by no event (many products narrower than normal, or none at all). Thus, if in a production process our first 20 products were too wide, the next 20 too narrow, and the succeeding 20 too wide again, we have three runs—first wide, then narrow, then wide. We might begin to suspect that we were having a cyclical problem with our production equipment. Similarly, if we had picked a sample of 60 people for a taste test and the first 30 liked product A and the next 30 liked product B, we might be inclined to think there was something nonrandom about these choices since we have many consecutive choices of A followed by many consecutive choices of B. The *runs test* is used to study randomness.

When we have situations in which the same people are used in two experiments so that we have related samples rather than independent ones, we can test for a difference between the groups before and after the test by using a nonparametric technique called the *sign test*. The parametric test that could be used here is the paired *t* test, which is available in more advanced statistics texts. Marketing and medical research often use these techniques to set up an experimental group and a control group that are studied before and after treatment.

The sign test may also be used to determine if there are differences about the median. Normally, we would expect that 50% of our sample values would be above the population median and 50% below it. Using the sign test for these differences from a hypothesized median, we can determine whether a hypothesized median is likely to be the true population median.

There are many nonparametric analyses that can be used in different situations when we have different data classifications and different types and numbers of samples. (Table 9-10 classifies the tests studied so far.) If these tests do not seem to apply to your problem, look at the books listed in the bibliography at the end of this chapter and Chapter 8. We now introduce the techniques that we have described above.

RANK-ORDER CORRELATION

In Chapter 10 we will perform regression analyses on *continuous interval* or *ratio* data. This analysis is very valuable because it yields a prediction line $\hat{Y} = a + bX$ and an estimate of the amount of variation of the dependent variable that could be explained by use of the independent variable.

9-1

Now, if we have ordinal data where one or more of our variables is ranked, we should not fit a line to the data because we cannot make the same inferences that we made previously when we assumed normal distributions and continuous errors. However, we can compute r and R^2 which measures the degree of relationship between two variables. If $R^2 = 1$, we can use one variable to predict the other (i.e., using the amount of advertising we can predict sales). If $R^2 = 0$, we cannot use advertising to predict sales. If our data is interval-scaled, this nonparametric technique called rank-order correlation technique could provide a rapid estimate of the degree of relationship between the two variables. This coefficient or rank-order correlation is called r_r, and the computation formula is

$$r_r = 1 - \frac{6 \, \Sigma d^2}{n(n^2 - 1)} \tag{9-1}$$

where d is the difference between the ranks of the two corresponding values. If we square r we have r^2, which is the percentage of variation in the dependent variable explained by the independent variable. Thus, it is an indicator of the degree of relationship between the two variables we are studying. A very effective use of this measure often arises when we compare two r_r values to see which sets of variables seem to show the most relationship. Thus, we could compare the rankings of residents of the North to that of residents of the West versus that of residents of the North and residents of the South on certain quality of life features. From this we could tell if the views of Northerners were closer to those of Westerners or Southerners.

We now give an example of how r_r is computed and used.

EXAMPLE 9-1 Ms. Rebecca Barr, once the personnel manager, has been promoted to a position on the corporate staff and would like to find a replacement to
fill her old job as personnel manager. She has two assistant managers who are
hard workers and seem to be equally capable. Finally, she decides to choose her
replacement on the basis of ability to evelute new applicants. Obviously (to her
anyway), the one with the best judgment is the one who agrees the most closely
with her on the evaluation of job applicants. Choosing 10 applicants, she interviews
them for a secretarial position; then, she sends each applicant to the two assistant
managers and asks them to rank them. The rankings are as follows (1 = highly
favorable, 10 = least favorable):

APPLICANT	MS. BARR'S RANKING	ASSISTANT MANAGER R'S RANKING	ASSISTANT MANAGER S'S RANKING
A	1	2	1
B	10	5	10
C	2	1	2
D	3	3	9
E	8	6	3
F	9	7	8
G	7	8.5	4
H	4	4	7
I	5	10	5
J	6	8.5	6

We see here that assistant manager R could not decide whether applicant G was
better than J. Since they were competing for places 8 and 9, she handled this *tie*
by giving both applicants the rank 8.5.[1] If three applicants had been tied for positions that could otherwise have been ranked 8, 9, 10, the average rank 9 should
be assigned to all three.

Now, each manager's ratings should be compared with Ms. Barr's. It is hard
to tell who is closest by comparing the rankings; hence, we compute r_r for Ms. Barr
and each manager in Tables 9-1 and 9-2. The manager with the highest r_r is in
closest agreement with Ms. Barr. Note that several wide differences in ranks have
a large effect on results since differences in rank are squared.

We can see that Manager R shows a somewhat higher relationship with Ms.
Barr than does Manager S. In this problem, if all the ranks matched exactly, all
values of d would be 0 and $r_r = 1 - 0 = 1$. Similarly, if all values were reversed,
total disagreement $r_r = -1$. In this example, in which all ranks are reversed
between Manager R and Ms. Barr, we have Table 9-3.

Often we have data that is expressed in *interval* or *ratio terms,* but where
rank-order correlation can provide a quick measure to test if there is a linear relationship between the two variables. This is particularly true if there are not many
data points and it is difficult to determine if the variables are normally distributed.

---

[1]If there are many tied ranks in the problem, this tends to decrease the amount of correlation. See
Appendix A9-2 for a correction formula.

TABLE 9-1

COMPARISON OF RANKINGS BY MS. BARR AND MANAGER R

APPLICANT	MS. BARR'S RANKING	ASSISTANT MANAGER R'S RANKING	DIFFERENCES BETWEEN RANKS	
			d	d^2
A	1	2	−1	1
B	10	5	5	25
C	2	1	1	1
D	3	3	0	0
E	8	6	2	4
F	9	7	2	4
G	7	8.5	−1.5	2.25
H	4	4	0	0
I	5	10	−5	25
J	6	8.5	−2.5	6.25
				68.5

$$r_r = 1 - \frac{6(68.5)}{10(99)} = .585$$

TABLE 9-2

COMPARISON OF RANKINGS BY MS. BARR AND MANAGER S

APPLICANT	MS. BARR'S RANKINGS	ASSISTANT MANAGER S'S RANKING	DIFFERENCES BETWEEN RANKS*	
			d	d^2
A	1	1	0	0
B	10	10	0	0
C	2	2	0	0
D	3	9	−6	36
E	8	3	5	25
F	9	8	1	1
G	7	4	3	9
H	4	7	−3	9
I	5	5	0	0
J	6	6	0	0
				80

$$r_r = 1 - \frac{6(80)}{10(99)} = .52$$

*Note that it does not matter which variable you subtract from which to calculate d, since the squared amount of d^2 is used. Therefore, the signs are not a problem.

TABLE 9-3

COMPARISON OF TWO SETS OF RANKS THAT ARE EXACTLY OPPOSITE

APPLICANT	MS. BARR	MANAGER R	d	d^2
A	1	10	-9	81
B	2	9	-7	49
C	3	8	-5	25
D	4	7	-3	9
E	5	6	-1	1
F	6	5	1	1
G	7	4	3	9
H	8	3	5	25
I	9	2	7	49
J	10	1	9	81
				330

$$r_r = 1 - \frac{6(330)}{10(99)} = 1 - 2 = -1$$

TABLE 9-4

WHERE SALOMON BROTHERS RANKS ON WALL STREET

INVESTMENT BANKER	FISCAL YEAR ENDS	TOTAL CAPITAL IN MILLIONS OF DOLLARS FISCAL 1977*	PRETAX PROFITS IN MILLIONS OF DOLLARS
Merrill Lynch	December 31	645.9	71.3
Salomon Bros.	September 30	191.7	55.0
E. F. Hutton	December 31	174.3	33.5
Dean Witter Reynolds	August 31	162.9	34.5
Bache	July 31	152.3	7.2
Paine Webber	September 30	117.6	18.3
Goldman Sachs	November 25	117.6	Not available
First Boston	December 31	84.2	6.8
Shearson Hayden Stone	June 30	84.1	18.8

*Includes subordinated debt (debt that doesn't have a first claim on assets).
Source: *Business Week,* Apr. 3, 1978 p. 78.

TABLE 9-5

COMPARISON OF RANKS ON CAPITAL HOLDINGS AND PRETAX PROFITS FOR INVESTMENT
BANKERS, FISCAL 1977

INVESTMENT BANKER	TOTAL CAPITAL*	PRETAX PROFITS*	d	d^2
Merrill Lynch	1	1	0	0
Salomon Bros.	2	2	0	0
E. F. Hutton	3	4	-1	1
Dean Witter Reynolds	4	3	1	1
Bache	5	7	-2	4
Paine Webber	6	6	0	0
First Boston	7	8	-1	1
Shearson Hayden Stone	8	5	3	9
				16

*Ranked from highest to lowest.

EXAMPLE 9-2   We wish to determine if there is a relationship between the profits of investment bankers and their total capital using data from the *Business Week;* see Table 9-4. In this case, we must first rank each bank in terms of total capital and pretax profits; see Table 9-5.

We have omitted Goldman Sachs since profit data was not available, and we would not be able to compare the two variables.

$$r_r = 1 - \frac{6\Sigma d^2}{n(n^2 - 1)} = 1 - \frac{6(16)}{8(63)} = .81$$

(To continue with this problem, please read Chapter 10, "Regression Analysis," first.)

In this problem we would like to test if there is a relationship between total capital and pretax profits. We can test if ρ is significant by using the t test, just as we test r in regression analysis.

1 H_0: There is no relation between total capital and pretax profits ($\rho = 0$). Note that ρ is the population parameter.
   H_1: There is a relationship ($\rho \neq 0$).
2 t test, 6 degrees of freedom, .05 level of significance.
3   If $t > 2.447$, reject H_0.

$$t = \frac{\rho \sqrt{n - 2}}{\sqrt{1 - \rho^2}} = \frac{.81 \sqrt{6}}{\sqrt{1 - .6561}} = \frac{1.9841}{.5864} = 3.384 \qquad 3.384 > 2.447$$

We reject H_0; there is a relationship between total capital and pretax profits. As capital rises, pretax profits also rise.

Problems

1   In 1978, the following 12 cities received ratings (100 was the highest) as a place to live and work.

CITY	(1) EMPLOYMENT OPPORTUNITIES	(2) PROFESSIONAL STIMULATION	(3) CULTURAL OPPORTUNITIES	(4) OVERALL, AS A PLACE TO LIVE
Atlanta	44	73	76	87
Boston	38	85	78	77
Chicago	80	79	89	70
Dallas	67	72	68	93
Denver	14	56	62	87
Detroit	37	49	40	35
Houston	89	82	85	94
Los Angeles	60	78	66	56
New York	78	87	92	51
Philadelphia	34	56	64	58
San Francisco	44	80	88	76
Washington	46	68	93	59

Source: *The Wall Street Journal.*

Calculate the rank correlation coefficient for each pair of ratings for the above data: columns 1 and 2, 1 and 3, 1 and 4, 2 and 3, 2 and 4, 3 and 4. (Rank the ratings.)

(*a*) Which pair of rankings shows the best relationship?
(*b*) Which pair of rankings shows the least relationship?

2 A random survey was conducted in an attempt to show the degree of relation between grade point average and starting salaries of recent graduates. After contacting 10 students at random who had entered the job market, the following figures were collected.

STUDENT	GRADE POINT (4.0 SCALE)	STARTING SALARY (YEARLY)
1	2.8	$15,500
2	3.4	18,700
3	2.7	16,000
4	2.3	14,300
5	3.2	19,000
6	3.8	20,300
7	2.75	16,800
8	3.0	16,500
9	2.1	13,700
10	2.85	14,850

Calculate the rank-correlation coefficient for the above data.

3 The following are the ratings given to the performance of 10 college musical groups by two judges.

GROUP	RATING, JUDGE A	RATING, JUDGE B
1	4.58	6.46
2	8.02	9.21
3	7.44	6.84
4	9.31	8.72
5	2.41	3.58
6	4.77	3.49
7	6.85	6.75
8	7.83	5.47
9	3.69	2.91
10	6.26	7.03

Calculate the rank-correlation coefficient as a measure of consistency between the judges. Assume that 10 is the best ranking and 1 the worst.

4 Both the AP and UPI wire services rank the top 20 football teams in the country during the season. On two consecutive Tuesdays when the polls were released, the same 20 teams were found in both listings but in different order. (Assume that 1 is the highest ranking and 20 the lowest.)

	RANKING			
	OCTOBER 7		OCTOBER 14	
TEAM	AP	UPI	AP	UPI
A	1	2	1	2
B	3	3	3	1
C	2	1	2	3
D	4	5	5	5
E	5	4	4	4
F	7	7	6	8
G	6	8	8	6
H	8	6	7	7
I	9	9	10	9
J	11	10	9	10
K	10	11	11	12
L	12	13	12	15
M	13	12	15	11
N	14	14	13	13
O	17	15	14	16
P	15	17	18	14
Q	16	16	16	18
R	18	19	17	17
S	20	18	19	20
T	19	20	20	19

Determine the rank-correlation coefficient for each week and determine on which date the ratings are most consistent.

RANK-SUM TEST (MANN-WHITNEY)

The rank-sum test, sometimes called the *U test,* is used to test whether two independent samples could have come from the same population. It is similar to a *z* or a *t* test of a difference between means and is used when data is ordinal (can only be ranked) or when no assumptions can be made that a variable is normally distributed. To perform this test, we must rank all observations of both groups in order of increasing size. We then sum the ranks for each group. If the two groups are the same and of the same size, the sums of ranks for each will be the same or similar. In this test, the sum of the ranks of each of the two groups is calculated in a statistic called U. Then, the theoretical mean μ_U and standard deviation σ_U of the sampling distribution is computed. If the sample is large enough (the groups we are interested in proving different add to at least 20), the normal curve areas can be used to test whether the rank sums of the two groups are significantly different. The U statistic is compared to the mean using the usual z test, and the null hypothesis is proved or disproved. We illustrate by using an example.

9-2

Two-tailed Test

EXAMPLE 9-3   Let us try using the Mann-Whitney technique to compare the life of different brands of car batteries. A consumer testing group wishes to compare batteries with 24-month guarantees offered by two large mail order department

TABLE 9-6

MONTHS OF LIFE FOR WARP AND WOOFS BATTERIES

	WARPS	RANK	WOOFS	RANK
1	24	23	19	32
2	23	25.5	20	30
3	21	28.5	18	34.5
4	18	34.5	32	5
5	30	8.5	32	5
6	36	3	13	39
7	37	2	12	40
8	38	1	21	28.5
9	25	20.5	22	27
10	25	20.5	23	25.5
11	19	32	24	23
12	27	15.5	26	18
13	28	13	27	15.5
14	30	8.5	28	13
15	31	7	29	10.5
16	32	5	19	32
17	17	36	26	18
18	16	37	24	23
19	28	13	15	38
20	26	18	29	10.5
		$R_1 = 352$		$R_2 = 468$

stores, Warps and Woofs. The testing group picks a random sample of 20 batteries from Warps and 20 batteries from Woofs and tests them in similar models of cars in similar ways. The figures on battery life appear in Table 9-6.

To begin, rank the battery life from highest (longest life = 1) to lowest (shortest life = 40). If there are two numbers competing for the 6th and 7th place, let each one be the average value, 6.5. Thus, we have three batteries that lasted 32 months, and these would be in ranks 4, 5, and 6. Since the three batteries have the same numerical value, we give them the average of 4, 5, and 6, which is rank 5. Notice that all the batteries are ranked in order despite whether they are sold by Warps or Woofs. Later, we compare the sum of the ranks for each of the two stores.

We now calculate the U statistic, which was developed by Wilcoxon and also by Mann and Whitney. It is usually called the *Mann-Whitney test,* since Mann and Whitney were responsible for popularizing it. It depends only on the sizes of the two samples n_1 and n_2 and the sum of the ranks for either of the groups (R_1 = sum of ranks for Warps, R_2 = sum of ranks for Woofs).

$$U_1 = n_1 n_2 + \frac{n_1(n_1 + 1)}{2} - R_1 \tag{9-2}$$

or

$$U_2 = n_1 n_2 + \frac{n_2(n_2 + 1)}{2} - R_2 \tag{9-3}$$

We set up a hypothesis test to determine whether the sum of the ranks for one brand is significantly different from the sum of the ranks for the other. If the two

groups have come from the same or similar populations, we would expect R_1 and R_2
to be similar if there were the same number of observations in each group. However,
since we can use this test for comparison of two samples of different size, we must
make adjustments for different sample sizes. The formula for the U statistic takes
into account sample size differences. Note that in Equation 9-2 n_1 (sample size in
the first group) is used in the second term, whereas in Equation 9-3 n_2 is used in the
second term.

The sampling distribution of U for large sample sizes has a mean μ_U of

$$\mu_U = \frac{n_1 n_2}{2} \tag{9-4}$$

when the two samples can be assumed to come from the same population. Thus, we
subtract the population mean μ_U from the calculated value of μ (U_i) and divide by
the standard deviation of U which is

$$\sigma_U = \sqrt{\frac{n_1 n_2 (n_1 + n_2 + 1)}{12}} \tag{9-5}$$

This gives a value for z which may be compared to the z value for the desired level
of significance. The z table may be used to set the desired value for a certain level
of significance as long as $n_1 \geq 10$ and $n_2 \geq 10$. It is not necessary that n_1 and n_2 be
the same size. If n_1 and n_2 are small, tables are available to estimate probabilities.[2]
z tables may be used if either n_1 or n_2 exceeds the small sample table values.

$$z = \frac{U_i - \mu_U}{\sigma_U} = \frac{U - \dfrac{n_1 n_2}{2}}{\sqrt{\dfrac{n_1 n_2 (n_1 + n_2 + 1)}{12}}} \tag{9-6}$$

If our calculated value of z exceeds the value of z needed for a given level of significance, we can reject the null hypothesis. We will be stating that we do not think the
two samples have come from the same population. We now analyze this problem
about the average life of Warps and Woofs (Example 9-3).

1   H_0: $\mu_1 = \mu_2$. There is no difference between two brands.
    H_1: $\mu_1 \neq \mu_2$. There is a difference between the two brands.
2   U test, .05 level of significance, two-tailed, z table.
3   If $z > 1.96$ or < -1.96, reject H_0.

The U statistic has a rank mean of $\mu_U = n_1 n_2 / 2$ under H_0; n_1 is the number of
items in sample 1 (Warps $= 20$) and n_2 is the number of items in sample 2 (Woofs
$= 20$).

$$\mu_U = \frac{20(20)}{2} = 200$$

---

[2] See Mosteller and Rourk, *Sturdy Statistics,* Reading, Mass., Addison Wesley, 1973, pp. 337–340.

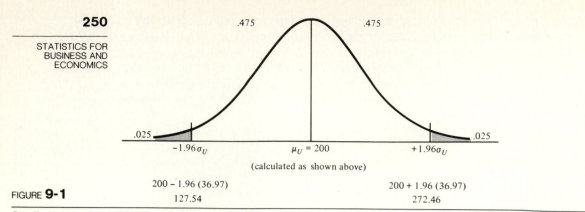

FIGURE **9-1**

Cutoff points for two-tailed Mann-Whitney test.

The standard error of the U statistic under H_0 is

$$\sigma_U = \sqrt{\frac{n_1 n_2(n_1 + n_2 + 1)}{12}}$$

$$= \sqrt{\frac{20(20)(41)}{12}}$$

$$= \sqrt{\frac{16400}{12}} = \sqrt{1366.67} = 36.97$$

As we see, the standard error and the mean of the distribution depend solely on sample sizes. Now we compute U using the formulas.

$$U_1 = n_1 n_2 + \frac{n_1(n_1 + 1)}{2} - R_1 \quad \text{or} \quad U_2 = n_1 n_2 + \frac{n_2(n_2 + 1)}{2} - R_2$$

where R_1 is the sum of ranks in sample 1 and R_2 the sum of ranks in sample 2.

The value of U_1 or U_2 can be tested with a z test since the sample size is greater than 20 for Example 9-3. (Adding n_1 and n_2, we obtain a sample size of 40.) As you can see in Figure 9-1, since $\alpha = .05$, our cutoff points are $\pm 1.96 \, \sigma_U$ (1.96 (36.97) $= \pm 72.46$). Thus, if our values of U_1 or U_2 are less than 127.54 or greater than 272.46, we reject the null hypothesis and infer that there is a significant difference in the brands.

Now we compute U for this sample and compare it to the critical values.

$$U_1 = n_1 n_2 + \frac{n_1(n_1 + 1)}{2} - R_1$$

$$U = (20)(20) + \frac{(20)(21)}{2} - 352 \quad \text{(based on ranks for Warps)}$$

$$U = 400 + 210 - 352 = 258$$

Since 258 is less than 272.46, we accept H_0 or using criterion 3,

$$z = \frac{258 - 200}{36.97} = 1.57$$

Therefore, we accept H_0 because $+1.57 < +1.96$.

Computation of U using the other formula and the ranks sum for Woofs's yields

$$U_2 = n_1 n_2 + \frac{n_2(n_2 + 1)}{2} - R_2$$

$$U_2 = 400 + 210 - 468 = 142$$

Looking at the right side of the distribution, $142 > 127.54$, our upper cutoff point. Therefore, we accept H_0 or, computing z, we have $142 - 200/36.97 = -1.57$; we accept H_0 since $-1.57 > -1.96$.

Thus the rank-sum test indicates that there is no significant difference between Warps's and Woofs's batteries. If there had been a significant difference, we would have had to examine the original data and see if the ranks for Warps are higher and thus on the average Warps batteries appear to last longer. If there are many tied ranks for the original data there are correction formulas available (see Appendix A9-2).

One-tailed Test

It is also possible to use the Mann-Whitney Test for a one-tailed test. Suppose we hope that a new disinfectant proves more effective than our previous one. In Example 9-4 we show how to test this.

EXAMPLE 9-4   The maternity ward of Framingham Lying In Hospital is testing a new disinfectant for its nurseries. The chief nurse decides to use the new disinfectant in nursery A and the old one in nursery B. There is some opposition to this by the hospital board, since they know nothing of the new disinfectant; however, the journals indicate that it is good. Finally, the chief nurse is allowed to implement the experiment. This experimental treatment is used for 16 weeks and the following infection rates are noted for each nursery for each of the weeks (Table 9-7). Should the hospital change its disinfectant? Use $\alpha = .10$.

Setting up our hypothesis test, we have:

1 H_0: $\mu_B \leq \mu_A$. Infection rates in B are less than or equal to those in A.
   H_1: $\mu_B > \mu_A$. Infection rates in B are greater than those in A.

TABLE 9-7
INFECTION RATES USING NEW AND OLD DISINFECTANT

WEEK	(NEW) NURSERY A	(OLD) NURSERY B	WEEK	(NEW) NURSERY A	(OLD) NURSERY B
1	.112	.336	9	.021	.332
2	.321	.221	10	.300	.243
3	.129	.212	11	.254	.263
4	.161	.121	12	.242	.232
5	.010	.012	13	.014	.093
6	.002	.210	14	.003	.207
7	.003	.310	15	.009	.182
8	.012	.013	16	.102	.257

2 Mann-Whitney U test, .10 level of significance, one-tailed test, z table.
3 If $z > 1.28$, reject H_0.

Now, we rank the infection rates for both nurseries from lowest (.002, ranked 1) to highest (.336, ranked 32).

A		B	
RATE	RANK	RATE	RANK
.112	13	.336	32
.321	30	.221	21
.129	15	.212	20
.161	16	.121	14
.010	5	.012	6.5
.002	1	.210	19
.003	2.5	.310	29
.012	6.5	.013	8
.021	10	.332	31
.300	28	.243	24
.254	25	.263	27
.242	23	.232	22
.014	9	.093	11
.003	2.5	.207	18
.009	4	.182	17
.102	12	.257	26
	$R_A = 202.5$		$R_B = 325.5$
	$n_A = 16$	$n_B = 16$	
	$R_A = 202.5$	$R_B = 325.5$	

Note that the sum of the ranks for A (new disinfectant) is $R_A = 202.5$, and the sum of the ranks for B (old disinfectant) is $R_B = 325.5$; thus, it seems that the new disinfectant might be better. Let us test this difference for significance.

$$\mu_U = \frac{(16)(16)}{2} = 128$$

$$\sigma_\mu = \sqrt{\frac{16(16)(33)}{12}} = 26.53$$

$$U_A = (16)(16) + \frac{272}{2} - 202.5 = 189.5$$

$$U_B = (16)(16) + \frac{272}{2} - 325.5 = 66.5$$

$$Z_A = \frac{189.5 - 128}{26.53} = 2.318$$

Since $2.318 > 1.28$, we reject H_0. Infection rates in B (old disinfectant) seem to be higher than those in A. There seems to be reason to switch to the new disinfectant.

Problems

1 The Johnson Bar review course claimed to offer its students a significant advantage in the bar exams. Professors at Utopia City Law College felt that outside reivew was unnecessary because a student who had recently completed law school could do equally well without a review course. The dean decided to compare the grades of recent law school graduates who had and had not taken the review course. The grades were as shown below. Would you advise students to take the review course?

Johnson: 76, 88, 72, 49, 74, 63, 91, 89, 82, 77, 79, 84, 48, 90, 70

Utopia City: 88, 82, 75, 91, 63, 48, 79, 99, 70, 83, 74, 92, 86, 95, 93

2   A random sample of 15 students in a math class showed the following differences in scores between the midterm and the final.

STUDENT	SCORE AT MIDTERM	SCORE ON FINAL
1	78	85
2	84	88
3	87	83
4	65	79
5	94	92
6	72	80
7	76	82
8	90	90
9	88	81
10	75	77
11	78	83
12	91	97
13	85	89
14	82	83
15	69	70

Determine at a .05 level of significance in a one-tailed test if the scores on the final were significantly higher than those on the midterm.

3   Management at a local assembly plant was checking the effects of a new incentive plan on production. After a trial period, a random sample of 12 workers revealed the following.

WORKER	HOURLY PRODUCTION BEFORE NEW PLAN	HOURLY PRODUCTION AFTER NEW PLAN
A	20	26
B	19	21
C	17	17
D	22	25
E	18	17
F	16	20
G	26	28
H	24	29
I	32	30
J	21	22
K	15	18
L	28	25
M	25	29
N	23	24
O	27	28

Using a .05 level of significance in a one-tailed test, determine if the new incentive plan was effective in increasing production.

4 A series of automated production lines had been suffering a rash of breakdowns until the new plant engineer instituted a more frequent maintenance schedule for the machines. The engineer took two production plants, instituted a new maintenance system in one, and left the other with the old maintenance system. Comparing the incidence of malfunction in the plant with the new maintenance system (Plant 2) to the plant with the old maintenance (Plant 1) yielded the following data.

	BREAKDOWNS PER MONTH	
	PLANT 2	PLANT 1
PRODUCTION LINE	NEW MAINTENANCE SYSTEM	OLD MAINTENANCE SYSTEM
A	2	1
B	4	0
C	7	5
D	5	6
E	0	2
F	3	1
G	4	1
H	1	2
I	2	5
J	6	2
K	9	4
L	3	3
M	5	1
N	6	3
O	8	2

Was the accelerated maintenance plan effective using the statistical criterion of a one-tailed test at a .05 level of significance?

Appendix A9-2: Correction for Tied Values

Mann-Whitney Test   This test assumes that scores come from a continuous distribution. If we could measure to any level of precision, we would not have ties. Business and social science data cannot be measured this accurately, and tied ranks often occur. When ties do occur, the mean of the tied ranks is assigned to all values. The effect of correcting for ties is to *increase* the value of the statistic computed, and hence to make it easier to reject the null hypothesis. For the Mann-Whitney test, the correction for ties is made in the standard deviation of the sampling distribution. Formerly, the standard deviation was

$$\sigma_\mu = \sqrt{\frac{(n_1)(n_2)(n_1 + n_2 + 1)}{12}}$$

If there are many ties, we substitute

$$\sigma_{\mu,t} = \sqrt{\left(\frac{n_1 n_2}{N(N-1)}\right)\left(\frac{N^3 - N}{12} - \Sigma T\right)} \tag{9-7}$$

Note that if there are no ties Equation 9-7 reduces to the preceding formula. In this equation,

$$N = n_1 + n_2$$

$$T = \frac{t^3 - t}{12}$$

where t is the number of observations tied for a given rank; to get ΣT, sum for all groups of tied ranks. Now, use this value for σ_{μ_t} in place of σ_μ in Equation 9-6.

The value of σ_{μ_t} will be somewhat smaller than the value for σ_μ; thus z will be somewhat larger than when the correction was not used. When we correct for ties z is larger, making it more significant, but the correction is only effective when there is a large proportion of ties.

Rank-Order Correlation   Similarly, if there are a large proportion of ties when one is using the rank-order correlation formula, an alternative formula should be used. The effect of the tied ranks will be to lower the sum of squared deviations for the variables. Thus $r_{r,t}$ is somewhat larger than r_r.

$$r_{r,t} = \frac{[(N^3 - N)/12 \ - (\Sigma T_x)] + [(N^3 - N)/12 \ - (\Sigma T_y)] - \Sigma d^2}{2\ \sqrt{[(N^3 - N)/12 - (\Sigma T_x)]\ [(N^3 - N)/12 - (\Sigma T_y)]}} \qquad (9\text{-}8)$$

where N is the total number of *pairs* of observations and $T = (t^3 - t)/12$; t is number of observations tied at a given rank. These T values are then summed for the ties in variable x to get T_x, and for the variable y to get T_y.[3]

Kruskal-Wallis Test   To correct for ties, we compute H by the regular formula in Chapter 8 and divide by $1 - [\Sigma T/(N_3 - N)]$ giving the formula for H_t:

$$H_t = \frac{[12/N(N + 1)]\ \Sigma\ (R^2/n) - 3(N + 1)}{1 - [\Sigma T/(N_3 - N)]} \qquad (9\text{-}9)$$

where $T = t^3 - t$ (when t is the number of tied observations in a tied group of scores) and N is the number of observations in all K samples together.[4]

KOLMOGOROV-SMIRNOV TEST OF GOODNESS OF FIT FOR ORDINAL DATA (ONE- SAMPLE TEST)

Previously, we have used the chi-square test to test for goodness of fit. In this test we compare sample data to a known distribution, for example, the Poisson, uniform, or normal distribution. The Kolmogorov-Smirnov test can also be used for goodness of fit, and it proves especially useful for comparing categories that can at least be ranked in order. This test is generally more powerful than the chi-square test, and it does not require a minimum expected frequency in each cell of 5 (see Chapter 8), as the chi-square test does.

9-3

---

[3]Additional information on these formulas may be found in Siegel, *Nonparametric Statistics*, New York, McGraw-Hill, 1956, pp. 123–126, 206–210.
[4]*Ibid*, pp. 188–193.

TABLE 9-8

HOW WILL YOUR ECONOMIC SITUATION BE NEXT YEAR?

OPINION		(1) OBSERVED NUMBER	(2) OBSERVED PROPORTION	(3) OBSERVED CUMULATIVE PROPORTION cF_O	(4) THEORETICAL PROPORTION (UNIFORM DISTRIBUTION)	(5) THEORETICAL EXPECTED CUMULATIVE PROPORTION cF_E	(6) COLUMN 5 MINUS COLUMN 3 (D_C)
Much better	(1)	40	.40	.40	.20	.20	.20
Better	(2)	20	.20	.60	.20	.40	.20
Same	(3)	15	.15	.75	.20	.60	.15
Worse	(4)	10	.10	.85	.20	.80	.05
Much worse	(5)	15	.15	1.00	.20	1.00	.00
		100					

Let us say we were trying to study a distribution with five categories ranging from high to low to see whether it was equally likely that someone would fall in any of the categories (uniform distribution). In order to use this test, we calculate the cumulative probability distribution for our theoretical distribution and compare it to the cumulative probabilities for our observed sample distribution. If we had five categories and were testing to see if they fitted a uniform distribution, our theoretical cumulative probability distribution would be .20, .40, .60, .80, and 1.00, because in a uniform distribution with 5 categories we would expect 20 percent of the values to fall in each category. We then perform a cumulative probability distribution for our actual sample data. The category with the maximum deviation between the two cumulative distributions (actual and theoretical) is found and tested.

We will show how this test is used for attitudinal preferences that may be ranked in five categories ranging from much better through same to much worse (e.g., tastes better to tastes worse). Similar five-category (five-point) scales are used in attitudinal surveys in which categories may range from strongly agree through undecided to strongly disagree. These scales were developed by Rensis Likert at the Institute of Social Research and are often called *Likert scales*.

Suppose we ask 100 people what they expect their economic situation will be next year, and wish to compare their answers to a uniform distribution to determine if attitudes tended to be found more often in optimistic rather than pessimistic categories. In Table 9-8, answers to attitudinal questions have been ranked on a five-point Likert-type scale: much better (1), better (2), same (3), worse (4), much worse (5).[5]

We now cumulate the proportions of people in each attitudinal group. If the opinions were evenly divided, there would be 20% in each group (column 4). When the point of largest divergence for the cumulative distributions is found, the sampling distribution can be consulted to see if such a large divergence could have come about by chance if the observations are really a random sample from the theoretical distribution we are testing. Kolmogorov and Smirnov have calculated tables for the distribution of the maximum deviation D under the assumption that both distributions (theoretical and actual) are the same.

[5]Likert attitude scales are discussed in Reynolds and Wells, *Consumer Behavior,* New York, McGraw-Hill, 1976, pp. 233–235.

The Kolmogorov-Smirnov D statistic tests the absolute value of the maximum deviation between the cumulative theoretical proportions (column 5) and the actual cumulative proportions (column 3). D_C is the largest cumulative difference between the two frequencies. For an α level of .05, for example, for large samples, the critical difference D_C is calculated by finding the maximum absolute difference between theoretical and actual cumulative frequencies.

$$D_C = \max \, |cF_E(X) - cF_O(X)| \qquad (9\text{-}10)$$

where $cF_E(X)$ is the proportion of cases *expected* to have scores equal to or less than X, and $cF_O(X)$ is the proportion of sample observations that have scores equal to or less than X.

According to Kolmogorov and Smirnov's calculations if the sample size n is over 35 any D_C value equal to or greater than $D_i = 1.36/\sqrt{n}$ will be significant at the .05 level (two-tailed test). For sample sizes smaller than 35, a table is available.[6] This formula is used with a goodness of fit test where one sample is compared to a theoretical proportion. If the calculated difference D_C is larger than this value of D, there is a significant difference.

$$D = \frac{1.36}{\sqrt{n}} = \frac{1.36}{\sqrt{100}} = .136 \qquad (9\text{-}11)$$

For $\alpha = .01$, the corresponding formula is $D = 1.63/\sqrt{n}$. For $\alpha = .10$, the value is $D = 1.22/\sqrt{n}$. Note that these are critical values for a two-tailed test.

1 We set up the hypothesis test. H_0: There is no difference between proportions in different opinion categories.
H_1: There is a difference in proportions in different opinion categories.
2 Kolmogorov-Smirnov test, $\alpha = .05$, two-tailed test.
3 If the largest difference of cumulative sums exceeds .136, reject H_0.

The largest difference between the theoretical and actual cumulative proportions is .20 (see row 1 or 2); thus, the hypothesis of no difference between proportions in each opinion category is rejected. This same test could have been performed using the chi-square test of goodness of fit for a uniform distribution, but the Kolmogorov-Smirnov test is more likely to spot differences. It is a *more powerful* test because it treats the data as if it were ordinal; the chi-square test treats the data as if it were nominal. The chi-square test, however, must be used for nominal data.

KOLMOGOROV-SMIRNOV TEST OF INDEPENDENCE (TWO-SAMPLE TEST)

In the one-sample test we studied whether sample values have come from some specified theoretical distribution. We can also use the Kolmogorov-Smirnov test to infer whether two samples have been taken from the same population, or from populations with the same distribution. The two-tailed test studies differences in central tendency or variance or skewness. The one-tailed test can be used to help decide whether the

---

[6]See Siegel, *Nonparametric Statistics*, New York, McGraw-Hill, 1956, p. 251.

values of the populations from which the sample is chosen are larger ("better") than those of a control group. This two-sample test uses the cumulative distribution in the same way as the one-sample test. If the two samples have come from the same population, their cumulative distributions should be very similar. A large deviation between the cumulative distributions of the two samples leads us to reject H_0, that both samples come from the same population, and infer that they represent two separate populations.

There are four possible variations of the two-sample test:

1 Small sample (either n_1 or n_2 is less than 40 or both n_1 and n_2 are less than 40), two-tailed test.
2 Small sample (either n_1 or n_2 is less than 40 or both n_1 and n_2 are less than 40), one-tailed test.
3 Large samples (both n_1 and n_2 are greater than 40), two-tailed test.
4 Large samples (both n_1 and n_2 are greater than 40), one-tailed test.

We will study the *large-sample, one-tailed test* because it is particularly useful for analyzing whether one treatment is better than another, or whether one product is better than another. Tests for the other three variations may be found in a more advanced text or in Siegel (pp. 127–136). These tests use special Kolmogorov-Smirnov two-sample tables. The test for the large-sample, one-tailed test calculates the differences between cumulative frequencies but uses a chi-square test for significance.

We now test the difference in proportions for two large samples. If the sample is large enough and a one-tailed test is used, a chi-square table, using 2 degrees of freedom, can be used to test differences in opinions between two groups. The chi-square value is computed using the following equation.

$$\chi^2 = 4D_C^2 \frac{n_1 n_2}{n_1 + n_2} \tag{9-12}$$

Assume we wish to compare attitudes toward the economy of college graduates and non–college graduates. We have reason to believe college graduates tend to be more optimistic than less educated people. Using a five-point attitudinal scale as outlined above, the results shown in Table 9-9 are obtained. Note that cumulative fre-

TABLE 9-9

OPINION OF BUSINESS CONDITIONS FOR HIGH SCHOOL VERSUS COLLEGE GRADUATES

OPINION OF BUSINESS CONDITIONS NEXT YEAR	(1) COLLEGE GRADUATES	(2) NON-COLLEGE GRADUATES	CUMULATIVE FREQUENCIES				ABSOLUTE DIFFERENCE
			COLLEGE		NON-COLLEGE		
			FRACTION	DECIMAL	FRACTION	DECIMAL	
Much better	30	15	30/55	.545	15/50	.300	.245
Better	15	15	45/55	.818	30/50	.600	.218
Same	3	6	48/55	.872	36/50	.720	.152
Worse	6	8	54/55	.982	44/50	.880	.102
Much worse	1	6	55/55	1.000	50/50	1.000	—
	55	50					

quencies must be calculated in terms of the proportion of the total number of people in the sample. Thus, sample sizes in the two groups studied may differ.

1   H_0: College graduates are less optimistic or equally as optimistic as non-college graduates.
   H_1: College graduates are more optimistic than non-college graduates.
2   Kolmogorov-Smirnov test, chi-square table, one-tailed test, 2 df, $\alpha = .05$.
3   If $\chi^2 > 5.991$, reject H_0.

D_C is the largest cumulative difference between two frequencies. (In this problem, the largest cumulative percentage difference between college graduates and non-college graduates is $.545 - .300 = .245$, row 1. The formula to compute χ^2 is:

$$\chi^2 = 4D_C^2 \frac{n_1 n_2}{n_1 + n_2}$$

$$= 4(.245)^2 \frac{55(50)}{105} \qquad (9\text{-}13)$$

$$= .2401 \left(\frac{2750}{105} \right) = 6.288$$

Since $6.288 > 5.999$, reject H_0. Therefore, college graduates are not less likely or equally likely to be optimistic. College graduates are more optimistic with respect to economic attitudes than non-college graduates.

Problems

1   A pen point company is considering the manufacturing of ballpoint pens with tips of different thicknesses ranging from very fine to wide. The company will manufacture four widths: very fine, fine, medium, and wide. By talking to 100 office supply salespersons, they assume that 10% will prefer very fine, 20% wide, 30% fine, and 40% medium. A month of sales testing at Weller Office Products indicated that 50 very fine, 50 fine, 70 medium, and 40 wide points were sold. Does the company have reason to belive that their original percentages were incorrect?

2   What other parametric and nonparametric tests could have been used in problem 1? Use the tests and compare results. Do they all lead to the same conclusions? For this problem, why is the Kolmogorov-Smirnov test preferable?

3   Fancyfree Hair Coloring offers a new line of blond hair dyes. There are six shades ranging from very light (platinum) to dark reddish blonde (auburn accent). Fancyfree manager, Bonnie Campion, believes that the lighter shades will sell better than the darker ones. Gray-haired women would use the light shades since they would not have to bleach their original hair shade. Younger women might also prefer the very light shades, since these would give a striking color to their hair. Thus, Fancyfree decided to manufacture 75% of its product between shades 1, 2, 3 (25% each); the other 3 shades were produced in quantities of 10%, 10%, and 5% of the total batch.
   After a year's experience in local beauty parlors, the following sales (in number of bottles) were noted.

BLONDE DYE SHADES		NUMBER OF BOTTLES SOLD
1	Light platinum blonde	2,000
2	Light golden blonde	3,000
3	Light natural ash blonde	3,000
4	Darker ash blonde	1,000
5	Light blonde, auburn accent	700
6	Dark blonde, dark auburn accent	300
		10,000

(*a*)   Should Fancyfree change the relative quantities it produces of each dye?

(*b*)   If the sample were 1000 and the same relative proportions were sold, would your answer change?

(*c*)   What if the sample size were 100 with the same relative proportions?

4   Dr. Janet Healey, a sociologist, thinks that women are more likely to be promoted in the profit-making sector of the economy than in the government and nonprofit sectors. She thinks that this should hold true since profit-making businesses can use market performance to test how well an employee has done. In the government sector, there is generally no marketplace test of performance. A sample of 100 employees from business firms and 50 people from government agencies and the nonprofit sector were asked the following question at an economic conference sponsored by the University of California, Los Angeles: In the past 10 years, for equally qualified people, what do you think the pattern for promotion has been?

1   Men have been promoted much more readily than women.
2   Men have been promoted more readily than women.
3   Men and women have been promoted at the same rate.
4   Women have been promoted more readily than men.
5   Women have been promoted much more readily than men.

The answers for each sector were as follows:

CHOICE	GOVERNMENT/NONPROFIT	PROFIT-MAKING
1	20	10
2	20	25
3	8	50
4	2	10
5	0	5
	50	100

Test at the .01 level of significance.

5   Using the Kolmogorov-Smirnov test and the data from the example about the number of soldiers in the Prussian cavalry who died from being kicked by their horses (see Chapters 3 and 8), test to see if the actual distribution of deaths can be fitted by the Poisson distribution. Test at the .05 level.

DEATHS	ACTUAL NUMBER	THEORETICAL (POISSON)
0	144	139.0
1	91	97.3
2	32	34.1
3	11	8.0
4	2	1.4
5 or more	0	0.2
	280	280.0

ONE-SAMPLE RUNS TEST

9-5

Random samples are a basic requirement for using statistical tests. As we stated in Chapter 4, everyone within the population must have an equal chance of being chosen in order to have a random sample. If samples are not chosen in this fashion, the answers they give might not provide an accurate picture of the population. We now discuss kinds of bias or nonrandomness that can be found by analyzing the *internal structure* of our sample. This technique determines whether there is constant alteration in the pattern of responses (yes, no, yes, no), patterns of the same reponse followed by long patterns of a different response (yes, yes, yes, yes, no, no, no, no), or a seemingly random alternation of responses (yes, yes, no, yes, no, no, yes, no). If a researcher were sent to a high school to interview a random sample of teenage boys and girls to determine if they would be interested in a new magazine and the following pattern of results was observed (I = interested; N = not interested), we might be suspicious that the order in which these teenagers were chosen was not random.

Sample *A*:   I I I I I I I I I I   N N N N N N N N N N N

In this case it was found that 10 girls were interviewed first, and all were senior cheerleaders emerging from practice. The group of 11 boys that followed were all football players also emerging from practice sessions. While it would be satisfactory to interview all the girls first and then the boys, since these were special types of girls and boys, namely all cheerleaders and all football players, their opinions of the magazine might not reflect the ideas of the entire high school population. On the other hand, if we received the results in following pattern, we might be suspicious that the choice of respondents was a bit too orderly.

Sample *B*:   N I N I N I N I N I N I N I N I N I N I N

A technique that can be used to analyze the order of returns and test them for randomness is a *runs test. A run is a set of identical (or similar) events that is preceded and followed by different events or by none at all.* For example, if we had the following order in the results of our interviews of 21 teenagers, we would have 12 runs.

Sample *C*:	I	NNN	III	NN	I	NN	II	N	I	N	II	NN	Answers
	1	2	3	4	5	6	7	8	9	10	11	12	Number of run

If there are too few runs, we might suspect some nonrandom grouping of elements; if there are too many runs, perhaps there is a special pattern or cycle occurring in the data. (For example, sample A has 2 runs, sample B has 21, and sample C has 12.) The number of people interested (I) is equal to $n_1 = 10$ in these samples, and the number of people not interested (N) is $n_2 = 11$.

Market research agencies can use these tests to see if opinions or the sex and age of respondents in a sample survey tend to exhibit any patterns that indicate an inaccurate sampling technique. In a factory, quality control inspectors who constantly test products to determine whether they conform to set standards can use this test to detect a problem in the production process. Thus, if there is a cyclical pattern in which all products are too heavy first and then too light, this may indicate that certain types of adjustment should be made in the machinery.

If our sample size is small (both n_1 and n_2 are less than 10), there are tables that indicate both the lowest and highest number of runs consistent with the null hypothesis that the answers occur in a random order. For the example above, where $n_1 = 10$ and $n_2 = 11$, the tables indicate that between 6 and 17 runs are indicative of a random sample at the .05 level.[7] Less than 6 runs and more than 17 indicate a pattern of nonrandomness. Thus, sample A (2 runs) and sample C (21 runs) indicate nonrandomness, while sample B (12 runs) leads us to accept the null hypothesis that the answers occurrred in random order.

If either n_1 or n_2 is greater than 20, we find that the normal distribution may be used to approximate the distribution of r (the number of runs). With a mean of μ_r and a standard deviation of σ_r, let n_1 be the number of objects of one kind and n_2 the number of objects of another kind.

$$\mu_r = \frac{2n_1 n_2}{n_1 + n_2} + 1 \qquad (9\text{-}14)$$

and the standard deviation is

$$\sigma_r = \sqrt{\frac{2n_1 n_2 (2n_1 n_2 - n_1 - n_2)}{(n_1 + n_2)^2 (n_1 + n_2 - 1)}} \qquad (9\text{-}15)$$

If n_1 and n_2 are sufficiently large (either n_1 or n_2 is greater than 20), the sampling distribution of r can be approximated by a normal curve and the values of z yielded in Equation 9-16 are approximately normally distributed with zero mean and unit variance. We use the z test as we did in our previous hypothesis testing chapters. Let r be the number of runs in the data we are studying.

$$z = \frac{r - \mu_r}{\sigma_r}$$

If we are testing the null hypothesis that the runs are a random sample, with a two-tailed test and a .05 level of significance, we can test whether z is greater than or less than -1.96.

Using the problem of choosing high school students to study preference for a magazine, and assuming we now have a sample where $n_1 = 20$ and $n_2 = 21$, we find

---

[7]Ibid, pp. 252–253, Table F.

the following pattern where D stands for the student who likes the magazine and N stands for the student who does *not* like the magazine.

DD NNN DDDD N D N D NNN DDDDD

NN DD NNN D N D N D N DD NNNNN

We now compute μ_r, r, σ_r, and z. Let n_1 be the number of students who do like the magazine (D), $n_1 = 20$; n_2 be the number of people not interested in magazine (N), $n_2 = 21$; and r be the number of runs (20).

$$\mu_r = \frac{2n_1n_2}{n_1 + n_2} + 1$$

$$= \frac{2(20)(21)}{41} + 1 = 21.488 \qquad \text{mean of sampling distribution of } r \text{ statistic}$$

$$\sigma_r = \sqrt{\frac{2(20)(21)[\,2(20)(21) - 20 - 21\,]}{(20 + 21)^2(20 + 21 - 1)}} = \sqrt{\frac{671,160}{(1681)(40)}}$$

$$= \sqrt{9.9816} = 3.159 \qquad \text{standard error of the } r \text{ statistic}$$

Now, set up the hypothesis test.

1 H_0: The interview responses are randomly mixed.
  H_1: The interview responses are not randomly mixed.
2 $\alpha = .05$, two-tailed test, runs test, z table.
3 Critical value: If z is greater than 1.96 or less than -1.96, reject H_0.

In this set of interviews $r = 20$; therefore,

$$z = \frac{20 - 21.488}{3.159} = .471$$

Since $-.471$ is greater than -1.96, accept H_0. The order of interview responses appears to be randomly distributed.

This technique for studying runs is particularly useful in detecting cyclical patterns. There can be a trend, that is, one long-run pattern or a cyclical pattern of alternating trends [for example, there will first be many L's (too large) and then many S's (too small)]. Both patterns might indicate that there is trouble or that there is a potential for trouble with a production process.

EXAMPLE 9-5   A quality control inspector could test runs above and below the median to see if machinery is consistently defective in one direction or shows a cyclical pattern. Both results might indicate some problem with the machinery. A random pattern of direction above and below the median, on the other hand, would lead the inspector to believe that the machinery is functioning well. Assume that samples of 100 are tested each day for proper product width for a month and the following daily median widths of samples are presented.

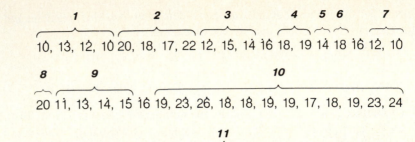

If we arrange these 43 numbers in order from lowest to highest, 16 is the median. Now, rank each number as below or above the median (omit all 16s). Numbers with dots above them are *below the median* (*b*). Those without dots are *above the median* (*a*). The runs from left to right are:

b,b,b,b	a,a,a,a	b,b,b	16	a,a	b	a	16	b,b	a	b,b,b,b	16
1	2	3	Omit	4	5	6	Omit	7	8	9	Omit

Below   Above

a,a,a,a,a,a,a,a,a,a,a,a	b,b,b,b,b,b
10	11

Note that the first four numbers—10, 13, 12, and 10—constitute a run below the median; the fifth number (20) is above the median and starts the next run—20, 18, 17, 22. This is a run above the median. There are 11 runs in this sequence of 43 numbers. We now test to see if these numbers fall randomly above or below the median. Let n_1 be the number of observations below median (20), n_2 be the number of observations above median (20), and r be the number of runs (11).

$$\mu_r = \frac{2(20)(20)}{40} + 1 = 21$$

$$\sigma_r = \sqrt{\frac{2(20)20[\,2(20)(20) - 20 - 20\,]}{(20 + 20)^2 (20 + 20 - 1)}}$$

$$= \sqrt{\frac{800(760)}{1600\,(39)}} = \sqrt{\frac{608,000}{62,400}} = \sqrt{9.7436}$$

$$= 3.12$$

$$z = \frac{11 - 21}{3.12} = -3.205$$

1 H_0: Numbers above and below the mean are randomly distributed.
  H_1: Numbers above and below the mean are not randomly distributed.
2 $\alpha = .05$, two-tailed test, runs test, z table.
3 Critical value: If z is greater than 1.96 or less than -1.96, reject H_0.

Since $z = -3.205$, reject H_0. There is evidence of two few runs above or below the median in distribution of parts produced. Thus, there seems to be cyclical patterns of output that are too large and then too small. The same test may also be used for runs above and below the mean.

Problems

1 A coin was tossed 35 times with the following results:

H T T H T H H H T H T T T H T H H
T H H T H T T H T T T H H T T T T

Test for randomness at a .05 level of significance.

2 The Critikas Marketing Research Company hired a set of interviewers to study whether the teenagers in Baltimore preferred Popsi Cola or Cooler Cola. Interviewers were instructed to take a random sample of 45 to 50 students at each junior high school and to record their preferences. The company would compute the percentages. Jessica Winnie, an interviewer, presented the following interview chart for one school. The results are listed in the order in which they were given: P = prefers Popsi Cola, C = prefers Cooler Cola, N = likes neither. Does the company have reason to question Jessica's results? *Hint:* Ignore N responses.

P P P P P P P N C C C C C C C C C N N N P P P
P C C C C C C C N N P P N P P P N C C C C C C C

3 Rolling a die 37 times produced the following order of numbers:

3 5 2 6 1 2 4 5 1 6 1 3 2 6 5 3 4 1 5 2
6 4 3 4 6 1 2 4 6 5 2 2 5 1 4 6 2

Test for randomness at a .10 level of significance for:
(*a*) An even-odd distribution.
(*b*) A high-low (4,5,6–1,2,3) distribution.

4 During day-by-day trading on the stock market in February and early March, the Dow Jones industrial average closed either up (U) or down (D) in the following order:

U U D U D D D U U D D U D
U U U D U D D U U D U D U U D

At a .05 level of significance, would this market exhibit a random trend, or would a particular pattern be indicated?

5 A market research group studied the randomness of the sequence of patrons' sex at a local shopping mall. On a typical Wednesday morning, they observed the following group of 30 people (by sex) entering the mall during a particular 5-minute interval:

F F F M F F M F F F M M F M F F
F M F M F F F F M M F M M F

Would the sex of shoppers be regarded as random at a .10 level of significance?

6 Allenby Auto Repairs believes that repairs are seasonal. The chief mechanic thinks that there are more repairs in the North in the winter because of the cold, and that repairs in the South are not seasonal since the detrimental effects of the winter are just as bad as those of an exceedingly hot summer. The following figures on the number of engine repairs are collected for Chicago and Dallas by Allenby Auto Repairs.

NUMBER OF REPAIRS

YEAR	DALLAS, BY QUARTER				CHICAGO, BY QUARTER			
	I	II	III	IV	I	II	III	IV
1975	76	72	69	77	113	94	118	118
1976	68	49	80	75	122	90	117	116
1977	70	58	63	67	115	85	116	117
1978	72	76	68	65	117	86	120	119
1979	70	66	69	73	122	80	124	123
1980	74	59	64	75	125	81	125	126
1981	78				130			

Find the median number of repairs per quarter for each city. If there is a cyclical effect, the number of runs above and below the median will follow a pattern. There may be fewer runs when the pattern is not random. Test Chicago and Dallas for randomness at the .20 level of significance.

SIGN TEST

9-6 The *sign test* can be used when very little data is available. It compares the number of plus and minus signs based on the signs of the differences between pairs of observations. For example, if we wish to see if dormitory living causes weight loss or weight gain we can compare the weight of a student before entering the dorm with the weight of the same student after living in the dorm for a period of time. If the student's weight increased we would have a plus; if it stayed the same, a 0; and if it fell, a minus. This technique can also be used when asking a group of consumers to evaluate two products to see if one product consistently rates higher than another. As we saw in the study of weight change, the sign test is particularly useful for studying two samples that are not independent. Here, we were looking at weight changes over time for the *same* group of people. We now continue with the analysis of weight change using the sign test.

The university health director wished to ascertain if first-year female students who were not trying to diet gained or lost weight during the year they lived in a dormitory. Some students said the bad food in the dorm discouraged eating; thus, most students lost weight. Others felt that the food was so starchy that it caused them to gain weight. Since weight is a personal topic, the director felt that accurate answers could not be obtained by asking the students to tell how much weight they had gained or lost. Therefore, the director took a sample of 150 students at the beginning of the year and asked them if they planned to diet while in college. At the end of a semester, the director asked 120 girls who had not planned to diet if they had in fact dieted and had gained or lost weight. Twenty students indicated they had dieted and were eliminated from the sample. Of the remaining 100, 50 gained weight

(+), 10 stayed the same, and 40 lost weight (−). By means of a sign test we can determine if losses and gains are equally likely. They seem to be similar, but it is necessary to make a specific test to tell whether the differences are significant. Often, with large samples, apparently small differences may prove quite significant.

Let p be the probability of gaining weight and $1 − p$ be the probability of losing weight, since we have eliminated those students whose weight stayed the same. This is a binomial problem but, as we have seen in Chapter 3, when $np > 10$ we can use the normal tables. Since $n = 90$ here and $p = .5$, $np = 45$ and the normal table can be used. If there were no difference in the weight gainers and losers, we would expect an equal number of people to lose weight and to gain weight.

1   H_0: $p = .50$.
    H_1: $p \neq .50$.
2   $\alpha = .05$, z test, two-tailed test.
3   If z is greater than 1.96 or less than $−1.96$, reject H_0.

Eliminate the 10 whose weight stayed the same since they can't be included in either group (+ or −) and compare the 50 who gained weight to the 40 who lost weight.

$$\bar{p} = \frac{50}{90} = .556$$

$$\sigma_p = \sqrt{\frac{pq}{n}} = \sqrt{\frac{.50(.50)}{90}} = .053$$

$$z = \frac{\bar{p} − p}{\sigma_{\bar{p}}} = \frac{.556 − .50}{.053} = 1.057$$

Since $1.057 < 1.96$, do not reject H_0. It seems that weight loss and weight gain are equally likely for students who aren't consciously dieting.

One feature of the sign test is that the samples used do not have to be independent. For example, we could compare the evaluations of the *same* people for two different household products. In studies where *matched pairs* are used, the samples are carefully matched to each other. This type of sample may be used because if, for example, a group is asked to taste two drinks consecutively, the flavor of the second drink may be affected by that of the first drink. Thus, it may be necessary to have two completely different samples with similar characteristics taste the drinks. Age, sex, and previous experience may be the characteristics matched for a worker's sample. Similarly, even though more high-powered tests, such as the rank-sum test may be used, the sign test can rapidly test the difference between two population distributions.

EXAMPLE 9-6   A consumer test organization compared two types of bathroom tile cleaner, Scratchy and Skrapey, by taking a sample of 30 homemakers. Each homemaker was given a bottle of each cleaner and was instructed to try out each one on a 3-foot-square tile wall and rate each cleaner on a scale of 1 to 3: 1 = poor, 2 = good, and 3 = excellent. For the purpose of these tests, it does not matter in which direction the ranks are made (1 = excellent or 1 = poor) as long as the ratings for both products are done consistently. Similarly, for all tests involving ordinal data in this chapter, the choice of 1 for the best or the worst rank will not matter in the evaluation of the results. The ratings looked like this.

HOMEMAKER	RATING FOR SCRATCHY	RATING FOR SKRAPEY	SCRATCHY SCORE — SKRAPEY SCORE
1	3	3	0
2	2	1	+
3	1	1	0
4	1	2	−
5	2	1	+
6	1	2	−
7	3	3	0
8	2	1	+
9	2	1	+
10	2	2	0
11	2	1	+
12	1	1	0
13	3	2	+
14	2	2	0
15	1	2	−
16	2	1	+
17	3	1	+
18	1	3	−
19	3	2	+
20	3	2	+
21	1	1	0
22	3	1	+
23	3	1	+
24	2	2	0
25	2	1	+
26	2	1	+
27	1	2	−
28	1	2	−
29	3	2	+
30	3	2	+

If we try to use the rank-sum test to determine if Scratchy is better than Skrapey, there will be too many ties and hardly any differentiation of ranks since the ranks can go only from 1 to 3. Therefore, we use the sign test. First, subtract Skrapey ratings from Scratchy ratings for each homemaker to get a plus or minus value.

We have 8 ties; thus there are 22 cases to compare because we have eliminated the 8 tied scores. When we compare Scratchy and Skrapey, there are 16 pluses and 6 minuses. (In 16 cases Scratchy is judged better; in 6 cases Skrapey is judged better.)

Now, set up the hypothesis test $np = 22(.5) = 11.0$; since np is greater than 10, we can use the normal distribution to approximate this binomial problem.

1 H_0: $p = .5$ that an equal-size group of the population feels the product is equal. H_1: $p \neq .5$ that an equal-size group of the population does not feel the product is equal.
2 $\alpha = .05$, sign test, z table, two-tailed test.
3 If z is greater than 1.96 or less than -1.96, reject H_0.

$$\sigma_{\bar{p}} = \sqrt{\frac{.5(.5)}{22}} = .1068$$

$$z = \frac{(16/22) - .5}{.1068} = 2.130$$

Since z is greater than 1.96, we reject H_0. It seems that significantly more people prefer Scratchy cleaner. We could work the other way too:

$$z = \frac{6/22 - .5}{.1068} = -2.130$$

Since -2.130 is less than -1.96, reject H_0.

Problems

1 During an open house tour for new homes, the prospective owners were questioned on how they felt about two different floor plans. The costs and square footage were the same. Ratings from 1 to 3 were assumed, with 3 being "better suited to their needs," 2 being "no specific preference," and 1 being "not suitable." Use a .02 level of significance and a two-tailed test. The ratings were:

PROSPECTIVE OWNER	PLAN A	PLAN B	PLAN (A — B)
1	3	1	+
2	2	1	+
3	1	3	—
4	3	3	0
5	3	2	+
6	2	2	0
7	2	1	+
8	3	2	+
9	1	2	—
10	2	3	—
11	3	2	+
12	2	1	+
13	1	3	—
14	2	3	—
15	3	1	+
16	2	2	0
17	1	2	—
18	3	2	+
19	3	1	+
20	2	1	+
21	2	3	—
22	3	3	0
23	2	1	+
24	3	2	+

Was one plan preferred over the other?

2 A group of 80 elementary school students visited two museums on a field trip: the Museum of Natural History and then the Health and Science Museum, which presented a program for the students. When the students returned to school, the teachers asked them which was their favorite museum. Five students liked both museums equally, 45 preferred the Health and Science Museum, and 30 preferred the Museum of Natural History. Is there a difference? Use $\alpha = .05$ and two-tailed test.

3   A sample of college students in a finance course was exposed to an experiment for the first half of the year. The first part of the course was taught with the lecture technique, the second part with the case method. After the course was over, the students were given a survey. One question asked them to rank the method of presentation of course materials. In all, 125 students returned questionnaires, and 75 of these students preferred the lecture method; 50 students preferred the case method.

(a) Is there a difference? Use $\alpha = .01$ and a two-tailed test.
(b) What would happen if you use $\alpha = .05$ and a two-tailed test?

SUMMARY

9-7

We have now developed an extensive list of hypothesis testing techniques for use under a wide variation of assumptions, for varied purposes, and with differing levels of information.

Nonparametric tests are advantageous in that they are *easy to compute;* compare the ease of computing the rank-order correlation coefficient (p. 241) to that of the correlation coefficient in the next chapter. Furthermore, these tests are not based on an assumption as to whether the populations are normally distributed. Finally, it is not necessary to have continuous or even interval data. These tests may be used on ranked data and many may be used for simple (less than, more than) comparisons. Frequently, business and social science data is hard to quantify and, at best, we can only rank measures, for example, in personnel evaluations. These nonparametric tests provide a good way to study such information.

On the other hand, when we use nonparametric techniques we very often "lose information." Thus, in the rank-order comparison of the investment firms, we didn't use the actual dollar values of the assets of each firm, and there was a large difference in the amounts of assets. Similarly, in the sign test when we evaluated bathroom tile cleaners, we did not make use of the 1, 2, and 3 ratings; thus, the difference between 3 and 1 was considered as a plus, and the difference between 2 and 1 received the same plus rating. Nonparametric tests provide quick estimates, but one should choose a test that uses as much data as possible, depending upon the need for a correct decision and the cost of obtaining greater accuracy.

Because nonparametric tests generally may not capitalize on all available information, they are not always very efficient. The confidence interval using this type of test will be larger than one that uses a parametric test. To put this another way, it becomes more difficult to reject our null hypothesis when we use a nonparametric test.

For example, when we tried to determine if opinion categories were uniformly distributed (Kolmogorov-Smirnov) with $\alpha = .05$, we needed a difference of $D = .136$ between our theoretical proportions and our cumulative sample proportions to prove that the theoretical value for each of the five proportion categories was not .20. With a parametric test of proportions, we would have $1.96 \sqrt{(.2)(.8)/100} = .0784$ needed for a significant difference at the .05 level.

TABLE 9-10
SUMMARY OF TYPES OF TESTS USED FOR STATISTICAL INFERENCE

TYPE OF DATA	TYPE OF TEST	SINGLE SAMPLE	TWO SAMPLES	THREE OR MORE SAMPLES
Nominal	Nonparametric	Chi-square	Chi-square	Chi-square
		Runs test (randomness)		
		Sign test (direction)		
Ordinal	Nonparametric	Chi-square	Mann-Whitney (rank-sum test)	Kruskal-Wallis (one-way analysis of variance)
		Kolmogorov-Smirnov	Rank-order correlation (relationship)	
Interval or ratio	Parametric	z test of mean and proportion	Simple correlation (relationship)*	Analysis of variance
		t test of mean and proportion (small sample, σ not known)	z test of difference between means and proportions	
			t test of difference between means and proportions	

*See Chapter 10.

Thus, a difference of .136 is needed for the nonparametric test, while a difference of .0784 is sufficient for the parametric test.

In Table 9-10, we have classified the tests and techniques learned in Chapters 6 to 9. Similar parametric and nonparametric tests for ranked and nonranked data are found in the same columns.

BIBLIOGRAPHY

Hamburg, Morris: *Basic Statistics*. New York: Harcourt, 2d ed., 1979, chapter 11.
Levin, Richard L.: *Statistics for Management*. Englewood Cliffs, N.J.: Prentice-Hall, 1978, chapter 12.
Mendenhall, William, and James E. Reinmuth: *Statistics for Management and Economics*. North Scituate, Mass.: Duxbury Press, 1978, chapter 18.

See the bibliography for Chapter 8, which covers such nonparametric tests as the chi-square and Kruskal-Wallis.

9-8

CASES

9-9

Case 9-1   Earned Run Average and Baseball Strategy

As a new assistant baseball coach in the Southwest Conference (SWC), Bob Jackson was active in all phases of the baseball team. When the head coach asked Bob for advice on recruiting for new positions on next year's team, Bob decided to look at other teams in the league. After compiling several sets of statistics, he then went to the business school at Texas Tech for some help. In talking with the faculty, Bob said he was trying to determine if strong hitters or pitchers were more effective in the Southwest Conference in moving to the number 1 spot. If pitching was more effective, Bob also wished to know if a good left-handed pitcher would be better than a good right-handed pitcher, given that 80% of the batters in the league were right-handed.

So far Bob had compiled the following data from actual SWC statistics:

TEAM	1978 SWC RANKING	1978 BATTING AVERAGE	1978 EARNED RUN AVERAGE (ERA)
Arkansas	2	.266	3.34
Baylor	3	.267	5.25
Houston	4	.307	3.94
Rice	9	.241	3.64
Southern Methodist	6	.245	5.31
Texas	5	.242	3.39
Texas A&M	1	.265	2.43
Texas Christian	8	.252	5.80
Texas Tech	7	.244	4.49

Batting average is the percentage of time that a batter gets a hit. So, the higher the average, the higher the batting strength of the team (calculated by hits divided by the number of times at bat). Earned run average (ERA) is the average number of earned runs per 9 innings given up by the pitchers of a team; so, the lower the average, the higher the pitching strength of the team. In addition, the following data was gathered on the 1978 Texas A&M baseball team (ranked number 1) to see if right- or left-handed pitchers were more effective:

	HITS	AT BATS
Left-handed pitcher vs. right-handed batter	56	209
Right-handed pitcher vs. right-handed batter	187	647
Left-handed pitcher vs. left-handed batter	12	42
Right-handed pitcher vs. left-handed batter	51	196

Questions

1   (a)   Should the statistics teacher recommend recruitment of strong hitters or pitchers to raise the standing of the team? Use $\alpha = .05$.

(b)   If pitchers are selected, should they be right- or left-handed?

2   Can you prove or disprove the old coaches' adage: Pitchers are always less effective against batters of opposite "handedness."

3   What other data might be useful to Bob? How should it be used? Write a report for the head coach. Remember that he is not a statistician.

4   *Optional:* Using multiple regression analysis (explained in Chapter 10), predict SWC rank by including both pitching and batting scores in the equation. Does this improve R^2? Why?

TABLE 1
CONTROL CHART, WALTERS REFILLS

	Stop (out of control) – fix machinery		
$+2\sigma_x$			10.10 cm
$+1\sigma_x$			10.05 cm
$U = 10$ cm			10.00 cm
$-1\sigma_x$			9.95 cm
$-2\sigma_x$			9.90 cm
	Stop (out of control) – fix machinery		

Case 9-2 Larker Pen Refills

Willie Walters Manufacturing Company produces refills for ballpoint pens. These refills are made to fill Larker pens, quality ballpoint pens. The refills may also be used in other pens, but Walters figures that its primary customers are Larker pen owners. In order for the refill to fit properly, it must be 10 centimeters long. Because of manufacturing variations, it is not possible to produce refills that measure exactly 10 centimeters, so a tolerance limit of $\pm$ .10 centimeters is allowed. If the refill is longer than 10.1 centimeters, it is too long and will not fit in the refill chamber; if it is too short, it will move around in the pen case and not provide the writing accuracy for which Larker pens are famous.

To control the quality of Walters Company refills, Neil Leon, the president, decides on a quality control system. The company will monitor average length of refills as they come off the system. It will set up a control table (see Table 1). Using sampling theory (see Chapter 4), it feels that if a sample mean is more than 2 standard errors above or below the desired population mean (in this case the 10 centimeters desired), it will stop the production line and examine the machinery. Let us examine the control chart in Table 1. The standard deviation for the length of refills is .5 centimeters. Samples of 100 will be taken every 10 minutes from noon to 4 p.m.

The standard error of the mean is

$$\sigma_{\bar{x}} = \frac{.5}{\sqrt{100}} = \frac{.5}{10} = .05 \qquad \text{(see Chapter 4)}$$

Plus and minus 2 standard errors are drawn on the chart.

Now, it occurs to Neil that even though the refills may not deviate enough to stop the machinery, it may be possible to detect future problems with the machinery because there are certain patterns in the samples. Thus, a series of samples that are too large (yet not large enough to stop the machinery) may be a sign that things are going wrong. In addition, if one set of refills is too long and the next set too short and there is constant alternation, it may be a sign that the machine is subject to some type of vibration that consistently oscillates, which may signal an impending breakdown.

Using a sample of 100 taken every 10 minutes, Neil examines results to see if they are random or periodical. Some sample results are listed below.

TIME	AVERAGE LENGTH OF REFILLS	
12:00	10.02	
12:10	10.01	
12:20	10.03	
12:30	10.05	
12:40	10.06	1
12:50	10.08	
1:00	10.09	
1:10	10.08	
1:20	9.98	2
1:30	9.99	
1:40	10.00	
1:50	10.01	
2:00	10.03	
2:10	10.04	
2:20	10.05	
2:30	10.06	
2:40	10.04	3
2:50	10.03	
3:00	10.01	
3:10	10.02	
3:20	10.03	
3:30	10.00	
3:40	9.93	4
3:50	9.98	

Questions

1 Do all the sample means fall within the control bands ($\pm 2\sigma_{\bar{x}}$) on the chart? (Plot them.) Does the data indicate a lack of control due to unusually large variation in sample means? Now use $\alpha = .10$ to avoid large Type II error, since accepting bad samples may lead to future production difficulties. Do all sample means fall within these bounds?

2 Do the results show any sign of periodicity? What sort of problems could arise from periodicity?

3 What can Neil Leon say to management about the process?

Case 9-3 National Personnel Association

National Personnel Association undertook a study to see if the average graduate business student of two U.S. universities performed equally well in their first year of employment. Random samples of alumni were drawn from school A and school B, both private colleges in the northeastern part of the United States. The personnel association contacted personnel directors of large corporations where graduates from both schools were employed. The directors cooperated by following the explicit instructions included with the survey. In rating the first-year performance of the selected employees, they used a scale ranging from 1 to 100, with a score of 100 given to the "ideal employee."

Table 1 shows the scores given to 18 students from school A and 20 from school B.

TABLE 1

PERSONNEL DIRECTORS' RATINGS OF
GRADUATES OF TWO U.S. UNIVERSITIES

(After 1 year of work experience)

SCHOOL A	SCHOOL B
96	98
86	50
89	95
75	70
61	80
48	92
81	54
60	88
62	67
54	94
51	97
68	84
93	74
73	92
71	82
83	85
53	79
50	91
	90
	83

Questions

1 Is there a difference in the average performance rating of an alumnus of school A compared to that of an alumnus of school B? (Use $\alpha = .05$.)

2 How might this type of analysis be used for other sorts of information that a personnel office might wish to study? Give some examples.

REGRESSION ANALYSIS

10

10-1 SCATTER DIAGRAMS

10-2 FITTING A LINE TO THE DATA POINTS

10-3 THE METHOD OF LEAST SQUARES
Computation of the Least-Squares Regression Line
Using the Regression Line for Point Estimates
Appendix 10-3A: Deriving the Normal Equations and Formulas for *a* and *b*

10-4 MEASURING THE STANDARD ERROR OF ESTIMATE

10-5 THE MEANING OF THE STANDARD ERROR OF ESTIMATE

10-6 USING THE STANDARD ERROR OF ESTIMATE FOR A FORECAST
(OPTIONAL)
Appendix 10-6A: Estimating a Conditional Mean

10-7 CONDITIONS FOR USING LINEAR REGRESSION ANALYSIS

10-8 COEFFICIENT OF DETERMINATION

10-9 COEFFICIENT OF CORRELATION

10-10 SIGNIFICANCE OF THE COEFFICIENT OF DETERMINATION
Problems

10-11 SIGNIFICANCE OF *b*, THE REGRESSION COEFFICIENT
Problems

10-12 MULTIPLE REGRESSION ANALYSIS

10-13 SOME LIMITATIONS OF REGRESSION ANALYSIS
Correlation and Causation
Significance versus Ability to Estimate
Curvilinearity
Homoscedasticity
Extrapolation
Problems

10-14 SUMMARY

10-15 BIBLIOGRAPHY

10-16   CASES

Case 10-1: Lester Real Estate Appraisal

Case 10-2: Corporate Research and Development (R&D) and Corporate
          Success

Case 10-3: Strategies to Achieve Growth Objectives for a Collegiate
          Basketball Program

Case 10-4: International Harvester Truck Sales Forecasts

Case 10-5: Lemando Computer Appraisal

In a sense the statistician is a mathematical detective, going from the known to the unknown. In Chapters 6, 7, 8, and 9 we examined sample characteristics and tried to infer what were the characteristics of the population from which they came. Now we undertake a potentially more fruitful type of study. If we can find two related variables, such as sales and advertising, eating and gaining weight, or hours of study and grade point average, we may be able to use our knowledge of one variable to predict the other. Thus, if we knew how much we would spend on advertising, we might be able to obtain a good estimate of future sales. If we knew how many calories an individual ate per week, we could predict weekly weight gain. If we knew how many hours a student studied, we might be able to estimate grade point average. Of course, not all things depend on one variable alone; thus, grade point average might also depend on the intensity of study and course difficulty, but often we can find one variable that can lead us to very good estimates of another variable. This chapter discusses how such related variables can be identified and how estimates of the unknown can be made using the knowledge that we have, a process not very different from that used by detectives.

The variable that we forecast is called the *dependent variable*. The variable we use to make the forecast is the *independent variable*. Thus, in one model, sales are the dependent variable and advertising is the independent variable. We would say that the more we advertise the more we will sell. Similarly, in another model, unemployment is the independent variable and food stamp enrollments is the dependent variable. This may arise because as people become unemployed they register for food stamps. There can be several independent variables; for example, economic conditions as well as advertising may influence sales. But first, we consider relationships between one dependent variable and one independent variable.

SCATTER DIAGRAMS

10-1   Before we employ mathematical techniques to use our knowledge of one variable to predict another, we will try to plot some observations for the two sets of variables on a graph to see if there is a relationship. If there is no relationship between sales and advertising, we can say that sales (dependent variable) doesn't depend on advertising and won't bother to do any further calculation. How can we tell this from a graph?

We must be careful also of our time patterns. Relationships could go two ways. Sales this month might depend on last month's advertising. In this case, sales is the dependent variable and advertising is the independent variable. In another situation,

TABLE 10-1

RELATION OF MAIL ORDER SALES AND ADVERTISING EXPENDITURES

DATE OF ADVERTISING	AMOUNT SPENT ON ADVERTISING X	DOLLAR AMOUNT OF SALES IN THE FOLLOWING MONTH Y
Sept. 1	$1700	$ 50,000
Oct. 1	3000	100,000
Nov. 1	2000	75,000
Dec. 1	1500	45,000
Jan. 1	600	20,000
Feb. 1	1500	50,000

a firm that has had good sales may determine its future advertising budget on the basis of previous sales. In this situation, advertising is the *independent* variable and sales is the *dependent* variable.

Now let us examine some plots of data to see how we can determine whether there is a relationship. These graphs are called *scatter diagrams* because we are looking at how the points are scattered on our graph. Traditionally, the independent variable is plotted on the X axis and the dependent variable (the variable you are trying to predict) is plotted on the Y axis. As an example, let us use data relating advertising for mail order gifts with gift sales in the next month for a series of months (Table 10-1), and plot them in Figure 10-1.

Plotting the data can be informative if it gives some idea whether the relationship is a straight line or a curved line (curvilinear), whether the relationship is neg-

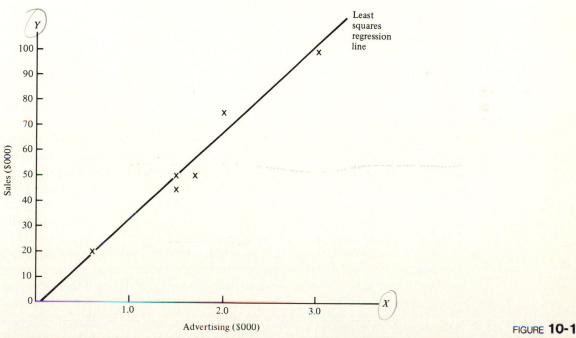

FIGURE **10-1**

Relation of mail order sales and advertising expenditure.

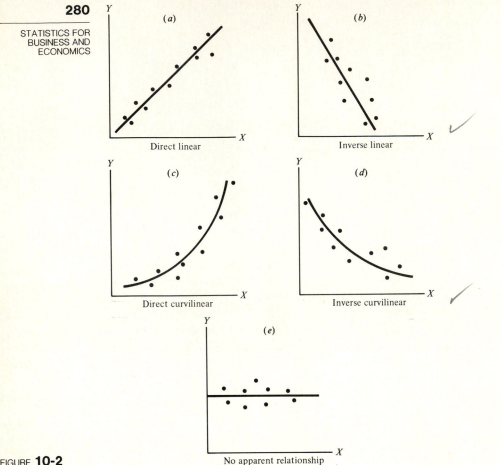

FIGURE **10-2**

Linear and curvilinear relationships.

ative or positive, or whether there is no apparent relationship between the two quantities studied. If Y increases as X increases (for example, as advertising increases, sales increases, as in Figure 10-1), we have a direct or positive relationship. Figure 10-2(a) and (c) provides examples of direct or positive relationships. If Y decreases as X increases, we have a negative or inverse relationship.[1] For example, if we are relating defects in a production process to the amount of inspection time per piece, we may find that the longer the inspection time the fewer the errors. This is an inverse relationship; see Figure 10-2(b) and (d). Figure 10-2(a)–(e) presents graphs of various types of linear and curvilinear relationship.

In Figure 10-2(e), we see that no matter what the value of X is, Y is always approximately the same. In this case, we would say there is no apparent relationship between X and Y, or Y does not seem to depend upon X. At times, if there seems to

[1]The equation of the straight line is $Y = a + bx$, where a is the value of the Y intercept (value of Y when $X = 0$) and b is the slope (see Section 10-2). For the line shown in Figure 10-2(a), the value of b is positive. For Figure 10-2(b), the value of b is negative. Thus, a curve with the equation $Y = 4 - 2X$ would have a negative slope; a curve with the equation $Y = 4 + 2X$ would have a positive slope.

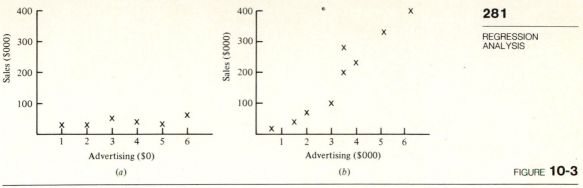

(a) Scatter diagram for sales with X axis in $10 units. *(b)* Scatter diagram for sales with X axis in $1000 units.

FIGURE **10-3**

be no apparent relationship, it may be because of the scale of the measurements that we are using for X and Y. For example, look at Figure 10-3(a) and (b).

When sales in hundreds of thousands of dollars are related to ads in 10 dollar units [Figure 10-3(a)], the X scale is so long that it is difficult to trace a relationship between sales and advertising. When sales in hundreds of thousands of dollars are related to advertising in thousands of dollars [Figure 10-3(b)], there does seem to be a relationship. It is important to find meaningful units for the measurement of X and Y in order to use a scatter diagram to its full advantage.

FITTING A LINE TO THE DATA POINTS

10-2

Once the data points have been plotted, a line can be fitted by "eye" or by mathematical techniques to the data. Later, we will use the equation for this line to make forecasts. The problem with fitting a line to the data is that if we fit the line by eye, by drawing what we think is the best-fitting line, the line may not be *unique*. Someone else may draw another line that seems to fit equally well. Four persons A, B, C, and D may draw the lines shown in Figure 10-4. We are looking for the one best-

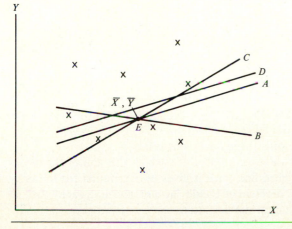

FIGURE **10-4**

Four lines that might "fit" a scatter diagram.

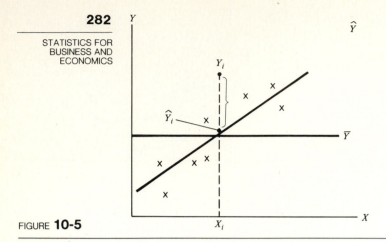

FIGURE **10-5**

Least-squares regression line—the best-fitting line.

fitting line upon which all analysts agree. In Figure 10-4, there are four lines (*A, B, C,* and *D*) that might fit the bill equally well.

Another method for fitting a curve would specify that the line should go through the mean of *X,* $\overline{X}$ and *Y,* $\overline{Y}$. In Figure 10-4, this would be point *E.* It can be seen that there are at least three different lines (*A, B, C*) that can go through point *E.* Actually, there are an infinite number of lines that can go through any point.

Besides the fact that we feel that the line should go through the mean of both *X* and *Y,* we are particularly interested that the line fit as closely as possible to all data points. We could specify that we want the total error (deviations of each point from the line) to be very small.

In Figure 10-5, we fit the line $\hat{Y}$ (the estimating line for *Y*) to a set of data points. The error or deviation is measured vertically from the data point to the line because we are interested in how wrong our estimate of the *Y* variable (dependent variable) is. Thus, our error here would be $Y_i - \hat{Y}_i$, the distance in brackets in Figure 10-5. Now, we could take all of these errors and add them.

$$\sum_{i=1}^{n} (Y_i - \hat{Y}_i) \qquad (10\text{-}1)$$

(Y_i is the actual value of *Y* where *X* = X_i; Y_i's are our original data points. $\hat{Y}_i$ is the value of *Y* on the estimating line where *X* = X_i. Thus, if we take the X_i value for each of our data points and substitute it in the equation for $\hat{Y}$, we find the $\hat{Y}_i$ values.) We can now specify that the best-fitting line is the one about which the sum of these errors is a minimum. However, if this line goes through the point ($\overline{X}, \overline{Y}$), the mean of *X* and *Y,* then the negative and the positive errors will cancel (for this is the definition of the mean) and we will find that we can draw an infinite number of lines through ($\overline{X}, \overline{Y}$) about which the sum of the deviations is 0.

Nevertheless, the idea that we want a line about which the sum of the deviations is as small as possible is a good one since it gives us a criterion for the best-fitting line. We can eliminate the problem of the deviations canceling each other by using the sum of the absolute values of the deviations

$$\Sigma |Y_i - \hat{Y}_i| \qquad\qquad (10\text{-}2)$$

just as we calculated the mean absolute deviations around the mean in Chapter 2. However, an easier solution is available by minimizing the sum of the errors squared.

$$\Sigma(Y_i - \hat{Y}_i)^2 \qquad\qquad (10\text{-}3)$$

This is called the *least-squares criterion* because the sum of the squared deviations about the estimating line $\hat{Y}_i$ will be the smallest amount possible.

Minimizing the sum of the errors squared overcomes the sign problem since all errors are squared. The technique also puts emphasis on large errors. Secondly, if we can assume our data points are normally distributed around the estimating line for each value of X, we will be able to make tests using our errors of estimation.

Using calculus (see Appendix 10-3A), two formulas are derived that enable us to calculate the equation for our least-squares estimating line

$$\hat{Y} = a + bX \qquad\qquad (10\text{-}4)$$

In this linear equation, a is the Y intercept (the value of Y when $X = 0$); b is the slope of the line. The slope of a straight line is the change in Y that corresponds to a one-unit change in X. Thus, if we have an equation

$$Y = 3 + 2X$$
$$\uparrow \quad \uparrow$$
$$(a) \quad (b)$$

We can plot this line as shown in Figure 10-6.

1 First if $X = 0$, $Y = 3$; therefore, the Y *intercept* is called $a = 3$.
2 Secondly, if X increases by 1 unit, Y increases by 2 units ($b = 2$). Therefore, if X moves from 0 to 1, Y goes from 3 to 5, and we can draw our line $Y = 3 + 2X$ because we have two points D and E; $D = (0, 3)$, $E = (1, 5)$. In our notation every point on a graph must have two values; the X value is mentioned first and the Y value second. $D = (X, Y) = (0, 3)$.

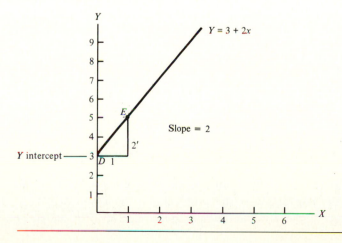

FIGURE **10-6**

Slope and intercept for a straight line.

Using mathematical principles we now fit a line of this type to the points on our scatter diagram. This will be our least-squares line because it minimizes the squared deviations of the data points from the line.

THE METHOD OF LEAST SQUARES

10-3

When we solve for the values of b (slope) and a (Y intercept), we obtain the equation for the line about which the sum of the deviations squared is a minimum. $\Sigma(Y - \hat{Y})^2$ is a minimum; also, $\Sigma(Y - \hat{Y})$ is 0. The values of a and b are computed using the following formulas (see Appendix 10-3A for derivations).

$$a = \bar{Y} - b\bar{X} \qquad (10\text{-}5)$$

$$b = \frac{\Sigma XY - n\bar{X}\,\bar{Y}}{\Sigma X^2 - n\bar{X}^2} \qquad (10\text{-}6)$$

Thus, $(\bar{X}, \bar{Y})$ lies on the line as we have said previously. We now use these equations to find a and b for our sales and advertising data.

Computation of the Least-Squares Regression Line

The line that will now fit is frequently called the *least-squares regression* line. The regression phenomenon was first observed by Francis Galton (1822–1911) when he related the heights of sons to the heights of their fathers. He found that if a father is above average height, his sons tend to be above average in height; however, if the father is extremely tall, his sons do not exceed the average as much as he does. Similarly, short fathers tend to have short sons, but the height of the sons is not likely to be as much below the average as the father's height. Thus, the heights seem to *regress* toward the average. Many phenomena exhibit this movement toward the average.

Using these formulas for a and b, let us find the equation for the least-squares regression line for Figure 10-1 (mail order sales) and plot the line on Figure 10-1. You will note that we have expressed both X and Y in thousands to shorten computation. At the end, when we use X and Y, we must add three zeros to get the proper answer. If you would like, try to plot a straight line "by eye" to fit these data points; then, you may compare it to the one you have fitted using the least-squares regression line.

For Table 10-2, complete the following steps:

1 Compute ΣX by adding all the values in the X column. $\Sigma X = 10.3$.
2 Compute ΣY by adding all the values in the Y column. $\Sigma Y = 340$.
3 Compute ΣXY by multiplying each value in the X column by each value in the Y column and then adding all of the XY values. $\Sigma XY = 689.50$.
4 Compute ΣX^2 by squaring each value of X and adding them all together. $\Sigma X^2 = 20.75$.
5 Compute $\bar{X}$, the mean of the X values, which equals $\Sigma X/n = 10.3/6 = 1.717$; n is the number of pairs of observations. In this problem, $n = 6$. $\bar{X} = 1.717$.
6 Compute $\bar{Y}$, the mean of the Y values, which equals $\Sigma Y/n$, $\bar{Y} = 340/6 = 56.667$.

TABLE 10-2

285

REGRESSION
ANALYSIS

RELATION OF MAIL ORDER SALES AND ADVERTISING EXPENDITURE

(1) AMOUNT SPENT ON ADVERTISING X (000)	(2) DOLLAR AMOUNT OF SALES Y (000)	(3) (COL. 2 × COL. 1) XY	(4) (COL. 1 SQUARED) X^2	(5) (COL. 2 SQUARED) y^2
1.7	50	85.00	2.89	2,500
3.0	100	300.00	9.00	10,000
2.0	75	150.00	4.00	5,625
1.5	45	67.50	2.25	2,025
.6	20	12.00	.36	400
1.5	50	75.00	2.25	2,500
$\Sigma X = 10.3$	$\Sigma Y = 340$	$\Sigma XY = 689.50$	$\Sigma X^2 = 20.75$	$\Sigma Y^2 = 23,050$

Now, substituting in Equations 10-5 and 10-6, we find

$$b = \frac{689.500 - 6(1.717)(56.667)}{20.750 - 6(1.717)^2}$$

$$= \frac{689.500 - 583.783}{20.750 - 17.689}$$

$$= \frac{105.717}{3.061}$$

$$= 34.537$$

$$a = \bar{Y} - b\bar{X}$$

$$= 56.667 - b(1.717)$$

$$= 56.667 - 34.537(1.717)$$

$$= -2.633$$

Note that we must solve for b before we can solve for a. Therefore, we have the equation

$$\hat{Y} = -2.633 + 34.537X$$

We have used a consistent number of decimal places (three) in all calculations.

Now, draw this line on the graph where we have plotted our original six points. (An easy way to plot is to allow X to equal 0 and solve the equation for Y; then, allow the maximum Y within its data range (20–100) and solve for X. We then have two points: $(0, -2.633)$ and $(2.972, 100)$. If we plot and connect them with a straight line, we have the estimating line for this data (see Figure 10-1).

Using the Regression Line for Point Estimates

We now have the estimating equation $\hat{Y} = -2.633 + 34.537X$. Suppose we wish to know how much business to expect when we invest $1800 in advertising. Substitute 1.8 for X (since we have moved the decimal three places) in the estimating equation. Our forecast value of Y is 59.534. Multiplying by 1000, we forecast that there will be $59,534 in sales for $1800 spent on ads. We now have an estimate of Y. We should be careful that we do not try to estimate the effects of advertising too far out of the range of the advertising in the sample from which the regression line was calculated ($600–$3000). This type of estimation, called *extrapolation,* can be dangerous since the relationship between advertising and sales may change when we have levels of advertising very much higher than $3000 or lower than $600. Thus, extreme extrapolation is dangerous; extrapolation not too far from our original values may be useful.

Let us look again at the estimating equation. Multiplying the value of a (-2.633) by 1000 (because we are using units of 1000; see top of table) gives us $a = -2633$. This tells us how much sales would be if there were no advertising. This equation can't be used where $X = 0$. Nevertheless, for various reasonable ranges of X (advertising), the equation proves very useful.

The b value, which is the slope of the line, is called the *regression coefficient.* It tells us that for every $100 increase in advertising, sales will increase by $3453.70. Thus, if we place $1000 advertising in a month, we expect the next month's sales of $34,537 - $2,633 = $31,904. If we increase our advertising to $1100, we expect sales to be $3453.70 higher, or $35,357.70.

Appendix 10-3A: Deriving the Normal Equations and Formulas for a and b

To derive the least-squares equations (sometimes called normal equations), we must minimize the sum of the squared deviations as a function of a and b.

$$\text{Min } F(a, b) = \text{Min } \Sigma(Y - \hat{Y})^2$$

This is the sum of all the squared deviations from the regression line $\hat{Y}$. Substituting $\hat{Y} = a + bX$,

$$\text{Min } F(a, b) = \text{Min } \Sigma(Y - a - bX)^2$$

To obtain a minimum, we take the partial derivatives with respect to a and b and set them equal to 0. Using the rule for an implicit function (those that contain an item in parenthesis where it may not be possible to solve for Y except in numerical terms), the partial derivative with respect to a is

$$\frac{\partial F(a, b)}{\partial a} = -2\Sigma(Y - a - bX) = 0$$

The partial derivative with respect to b is

$$\frac{\partial F(a, b)}{\partial b} = -2\Sigma(Y - a - bX)(X) = 0$$

Expanding the partial derivative with respect to a,

$$-2\Sigma Y + 2na + 2b\Sigma X = 0$$

$$-\Sigma Y + na + b\Sigma X = 0 \qquad \text{divide by 2}$$

$$\Sigma Y = na + b\Sigma X \qquad \text{regroup}$$

Expanding the partial derivative with respect to b,

$$-2\Sigma XY + 2a\Sigma X + 2b\Sigma X^2 = 0$$

$$-\Sigma XY + a\Sigma X + b\Sigma X^2 = 0 \qquad \text{divide by 2}$$

$$\Sigma XY = a\Sigma X + b\Sigma X^2 \qquad \text{regroup}$$

The second derivatives are positive, indicating that a minimum is obtained. These equations are now solved for a and b to give

$$a = \frac{\Sigma Y}{n} - b\frac{\Sigma X}{n} = \bar{Y} - b\bar{X}$$

$$b = \frac{\Sigma XY - n\bar{X}\bar{Y}}{\Sigma X^2 - n\bar{X}^2}$$

Similar derivations of normal equations for multiple regression analysis using X_1, X_2, and Y may be found in advanced statistics texts.

MEASURING THE STANDARD ERROR OF ESTIMATE

If we look at Figure 10-7, we see two sets of data points and the straight lines (least-squares regression lines) that have been fitted to these points. In Figure 10-7(a), the points are close to the line, while in Figure 10-7(b) there is more scatter about the regression line. We know which line provides the better estimate of gift sales. Obviously, we would find estimates from (a) more accurate than those from (b), but by how much? Therefore, we now wish to develop a measure of variation about the regression line, to tell us how well the line fits the points. This measure is similar to the standard deviation that measures variation around the mean.

The measure of variation around the estimating equation is called the *standard error of estimate*. To get it we must take each data point Y_i and subtract from it the estimate that would have been made from the regression line $\hat{Y}_i$ for that value of X_i. Having done this for each data point, we then square these deviations and add them. This sum is divided by $n - 2$ and the square root is taken. This is the definitional formula for the standard error of estimate. We also provide a computation formulation that will be easier to use.

$$s_{y.x} = \sqrt{\frac{\Sigma(Y_i - \hat{Y}_i)^2}{n - 2}} \qquad (10\text{-}7)$$

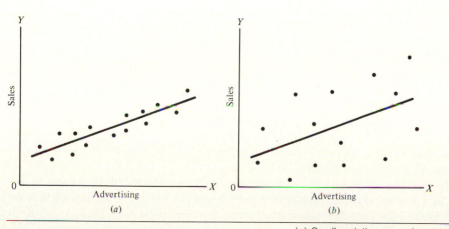

(a)   (b)

FIGURE **10-7**

(a) Small variation around regression line. (b) Large variation around regression line.

Previously, s represented the standard deviation computed from a sample. If we computed the standard deviation of a sample of observations around the mean of the Y values, we would call it s_y. If we had calculated the standard deviation around the mean of the x values, we would call it s_x. The use of $s_{y.x}$ indicates that we are taking the standard deviation of a sample around the regression line where y (the number to the left of the period) is the dependent variable and x (the number to the right of the period) is the independent variable. Similarly, $s_{y.x}$ denotes the standard error of a regression line, computed from a sample where Y is the dependent variable. The sum of the deviations squared is divided by $n - 2$, because we wish to make it an unbiased estimate of the variation around the *true* population regression line. Why do we use $n - 2$? For each parameter that we estimate, we lose 1 *degree of freedom*. In this case, we estimate a and b; therefore, we lose 2 degrees of freedom. A general formula for the denominator is $n - k$ where k is the number of parameters estimated. Later on in this chapter, we study multiple regression, which relates several variables to one dependent variable. Thus, if we have 5 independent variables, we must estimate the Y intercept and 5 regression coefficients. Therefore, we have a denominator of $n - 6$.

According to the definitional formula we take each data point, find the X_i value, and substitute it in the estimating equation to find $\hat{Y}_i$. Then, we subtract $\hat{Y}_i$ from Y_i, the original value at this value of X_i, and then square these deviations. Finally we sum these squared deviations, divide by $n - 2$, and take the square root. This is quite a long process. A short-cut formula can be derived to calculate $s_{y.x}$ without all of this computation; it is:

$$s_{y.x} = \sqrt{\frac{\Sigma Y^2 - a\Sigma Y - b\Sigma XY}{n - 2}} \qquad (10\text{-}8)$$

Now let us compute these values for the sales advertising problem. The only value that we haven't calculated previously when we found a and b is ΣY^2. We do this by taking each Y value, squaring it, and summing all of the squared Y values. We have entered this as column 5 in Table 10-2.

$$s_{y.x} = \sqrt{\frac{23,050 - [-2.633(340)] - 34.537(689.5)}{4}}$$

$$= \sqrt{\frac{131.96}{4}} = 5.744$$

Now, multiply this by $1000, since all our figures are in thousands, and we obtain $5744.

THE MEANING OF THE STANDARD ERROR OF ESTIMATE

10-5

Now that we have computed the standard error of the regression line, let us discuss its use. If we return to Figure 10-7, we can see that $s_{y.x}$ will be much smaller for graph (a) than for graph (b); $s_{y.x}$ measures the dispersion around the regression line just as s_x measures the dispersion of values around the mean. Let us assume that the data points are normally distributed about the regression line. Then, if we draw bands about the regression line at a distance of $1s_{y.x}$ above and below the line, this

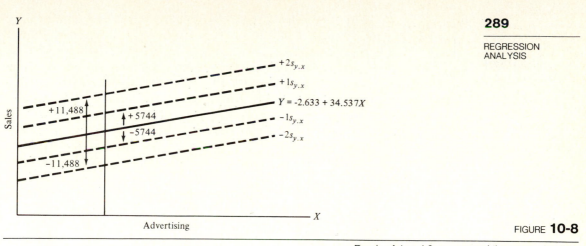

FIGURE **10-8**

Bands of 1 and 2 $s_{y \cdot x}$ around the regression line.

zone, $\hat{Y} \pm 1s_{y.x}$, should include 68% of the data points for this sample. Similarly, if we draw bands $2s_{y.x}$ above and below, 95.5% of the sample data points will be included; see Figure 10-8. We assume in this figure that for each X value the Y values form a normal distribution, with $\hat{Y}$ as the mean of the distribution and $s_{y.x}$ as the standard deviation. We also assume that for every value of X in this range, no matter how far from the mean, the Y values have the same distribution and standard deviation ($s_{y.x}$). If our sample size were large, we would expect to find 95.5% of our sample points within ± 2 standard errors around the regression line ($\pm 11,488$). In this case, we have only six sample points; hence, we would have to use the t table. To include 95% of the sample points with $n - 2$ degrees of freedom (4 degrees of freedom) for this example, we have a t value of 2.776. Multiplying this by 5744, we obtain 15,945.34. We would expect 95% of our sample points to be between $\hat{Y}$ $\pm\$15,945.34$.

Thus, if we wish to estimate the region within which a certain percentage of sample points lies, we use

$$\hat{Y} \pm ts_{y \cdot x} \tag{10-9}$$

USING THE STANDARD ERROR OF ESTIMATE FOR A FORECAST (OPTIONAL)

10-6

Our primary reason for using the regression analysis has been to make forecasts for our dependent variable Y. By substituting in the regression equation, we can make a *point* estimate. We have seen that a *confidence interval* is a preferable form of estimate.

If we try to estimate a *mean* value when, for example, we say that if we repeatedly invest a certain amount in advertising what would our sales be on the average, we would have a narrower confidence limit than if we tried to make a *one-time* forecast of sales (a prediction of an individual value of Y) based on the level of advertising. We will discuss the formula used to predict an *individual* value of Y. The for-

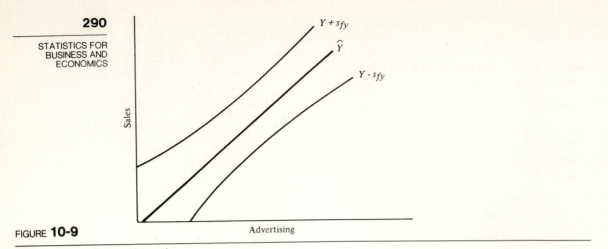

FIGURE **10-9**

Upper and lower forecast intervals.

mula to estimate the mean value of Y for a given level of X is given in Appendix 10-6A. First, we must use our formula for $s_{y \cdot x}$ and multiply it by

$$\sqrt{1 + \frac{1}{n} + \frac{(X - \bar{X})^2}{\Sigma X^2 - n\bar{X}^2}}$$

to get $s_{f \cdot y}$, the standard error of a forecast of Y. Thus, we have

$$s_{f_y} = s_{y \cdot x} \sqrt{1 + \frac{1}{n} + \frac{(X_f - \bar{X})^2}{\Sigma X^2 - n\bar{X}^2}} \qquad (10\text{-}10)$$

Note that as n increases the size of the forecast error decreases. Looking at the third term under the square root sign, we see if we are trying to forecast Y for the mean value of X $(\bar{X})$, this third term will cancel. Thus, the farther the value of X used to forecast is from the mean of X, the wider our confidence interval. The confidence bands curve out from the mean (see Figure 10-9).

To compute the forecast interval for an individual forecast, we substitute our value for X in the regression equation to obtain a value for $\hat{Y}$. We then multiply the appropriate t value for the level of confidence desired by s_{f_y} and add and subtract this from the $\hat{Y}$ value that we calculated. The confidence interval for an individual forecast would be

$$\hat{Y} \pm t s_{f \cdot y} \qquad (10\text{-}11)$$

or

$$Y \pm t s_{y \cdot x} \sqrt{1 + \frac{1}{n} + \frac{(x_f - \bar{X})^2}{\Sigma X^2 - N\bar{X}^2}} \qquad (10\text{-}12)$$

We now calculate a confidence interval for a forecast of sales. We call it a 95% forecast interval. Now, let us take the regression line used in Section 10-3

$$\hat{Y} = a + BX = -2.633 + 34.537X$$

and make an interval forecast for sales when advertising is $1800. Substituting $1.8 for X, $\hat{Y} = -2.633 + 34.537(1.8) = 59.534$. Now, multiply by 1000. Then, if we wanted a 95.5% confidence interval, we take our forecast value $59,539 and build a confidence interval around it. Actually, this is a small sample and we have estimated the parameters of the equation; therefore, the t distribution should be used. For 4 degrees of freedom and a 95% confidence interval, $t = 2.776$. Now, the forecast confidence interval is

$$59,534 \pm 2.776(5744) \sqrt{1 + \tfrac{1}{6} + \frac{(1.8 - 1.717)^2}{20.75 - 6(1.717)^2}}$$

$$= 59,534 \pm 2.776(5744) \sqrt{1 + \tfrac{1}{6} + \frac{.006883}{20.75 - 17.6885}}$$

$$= 59,534 \pm 2.776(5744)(1.081)$$

$$= 59,534 \pm 17,236.92$$

$$42,297.08 - 76,770.92$$

Note that the smaller the sample the wider the confidence interval, because the t value and the term under the square root sign $(1/n)$ will be larger. If the interval is wide, realize that the estimating equation may not be very accurate; that is, the data points are widely scattered about the estimating line. See Appendix 10-6A for discussion of the standard error of a forecast mean.

In Chapter 4, when we gave estimates of the mean of a population based on a sample from that population, we found that it was not good to offer a *point estimate* since this type of estimate did not give the reader a chance to judge the accuracy of the estimate. Instead of a point estimate, an interval estimate was offered that provided a confidence level.

The idea of forecasts that feature a confidence interval is now widely approved. The Securities and Exchange Commission has been considering a ruling that companies issuing stock to the public should provide forecasts of their profits for the coming year. Companies are encouraged to issue forecasts in the form of interval forecasts. This enables the public to gain some notion of the accuracy of the forecasts.

Appendix 10-6A: Estimating a Conditional Mean
If we were trying to predict *mean* sales at a given level of advertising (1.8) for repeated trials, our confidence interval would be narrower than if we were making an individual forecast. Our formula would now be

$$\hat{Y} \pm t s_{y.x} \sqrt{\frac{1}{n} + \frac{(X - \bar{X})^2}{\Sigma X^2 - n\bar{X}^2}}$$

Our interval would be

$$59,534 \pm 2.776(5744) \sqrt{\tfrac{1}{6} + \frac{.006883}{20.75 - 17.6885}}$$

$$= 59,534 \pm 2.776(5744)(.411)$$

$$= 59,534 \pm 6553.54$$

$$\$52,980.46 - \$66,087.54$$

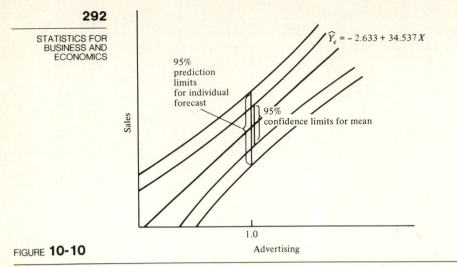

$$\widehat{Y}_e = -2.633 + 34.537X$$

95%
prediction
limits
for individual
forecast

95%
confidence limits for mean

Sales

1.0

Advertising

FIGURE **10-10**

Confidence interval for estimate of a mean compared to individual forecast interval.

Therefore, the desired 95% confidence limits are approximately from $53,000 to $66,000 for *mean* sales where advertising is $1800 per period. Figure 10-10 shows the difference between the confidence limits for a mean and the confidence intervals for an individual estimate.

CONDITIONS FOR USING LINEAR REGRESSION ANALYSIS

10-7

In order to use linear regression analysis, we have first assumed that there is a linear relationship that we can determine from the scatter diagram. Another assumption that must be made in order to make forecasts is that the Y values are independent of each other, so that if we obtain a large value of Y on our first observation, the result of the second observation will not necessarily provide a large value. If these Y values are related by other than the regression line, we can say they are *autocorrelated*. A standard test for *autocorrelation* is the Durbin-Watson test, which is presented in econometrics texts.[2]

Third, we must assume that for each value of X the corresponding Y values are normally distributed and that the standard deviations of the Y values for each value of X are the same. This latter assumption, that for each value of X the standard deviation of the Y values are the same, is called *homoscedasticity*. If the standard deviation of Y values varies for different values of X, it is called *heteroscedastic*. Figure 10-11 shows two distributions to which the same line has been fitted. Figure 10-11(a) is homoscedastic, (b) heteroscedastic.

[2]See J. Johnston, *Econometric Methods,* McGraw-Hill, New York, 1972.

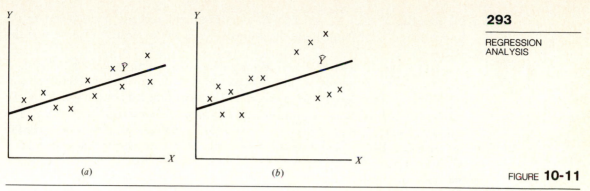

FIGURE **10-11**

(*a*) Homoscedastic distribution. (*b*) Heteroscedastic distribution.

COEFFICIENT OF DETERMINATION

The *standard error of estimate* measured how poor our forecast was. Actually, we are more seriously concerned with how *good* a forecast we can make. We now develop a measure to be used in studying how the use of the least-squares regression line improves our forecasting ability.

10-8

    If we have no data upon which to base our estimates and wish to estimate sales (for next year, for example), the best estimate is probably an average of sales in the previous years (the mean) $\overline{Y}$. Since we have concluded that sales is related to advertising, we fit a line to the relationship, estimate advertising for next year, and use this as a basis for estimating next year's sales (see Figure 10-12).

    In the example we have been using, $\overline{Y}$ (the mean) for the 6 months of data is 56.667. Multiplying by 1000 because our sales are in units of $1000, we have a sales estimate of $56,667. We can use our equation $\hat{Y} = -2.633 + 34.537X$, which relates sales and advertising, to make a forecast. Assuming that we think we will spend $2000 on advertising next year; substitute 2.0 into the equation and our value $\hat{Y}$ that we forecast for Y is $66,441. Now, if we look at the graph for this sample, we see point Y (the actual sales) was $75,000 when advertising was $2000. Thus,

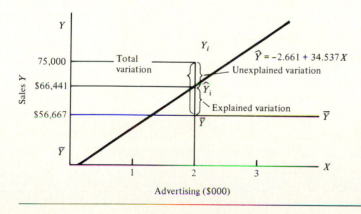

FIGURE **10-12**

Explained, unexplained, and total variation.

the estimate of sales $\hat{Y}_i$, which took advertising into account, came closer to the actual sales of \$75,000 than did the estimate based on the mean $\bar{Y}$ of previous sales (\$56,667).

If we look at these relationships for every sample point, we can figure out how much the use of the regression line to make an estimate has improved our forecasts over estimates that use only the mean of Y. Let us call the sum of the squares of the difference between the mean and our actual values *total variation* $\Sigma(Y - \bar{Y})^2$. The sum of the squares of the differences between what the regression line would predict and the mean $\Sigma(\hat{Y} - \bar{Y})^2$ is what we have been able to explain by using the regression line. This is the improvement of the forecast over what the mean would have predicted; hence, it is called the *explained variation*. Even though we have improved upon the prediction that the mean would have provided, we have not been able to predict exactly what sales would be. The sum of the squares of the differences between forecast sales and actual sales $\Sigma(Y - \hat{Y})^2$ is called the *unexplained variation*. If we look at Figure 10-12, we see brackets around the explained variation $\hat{Y} - \bar{Y}$, around the unexplained variation $\hat{Y} - Y$, and pointing to the total variation $Y - \bar{Y}$ for one value of $X(X = 2000)$.

We are looking for a measure of how good our regression line is for explaining or predicting sales. The measure is the ratio of explained variation to total variation, called the *coefficient of determination* R^2. This coefficient tells us what percentage of the total variation we have been able to explain by using estimates from our least-squares regression line.

R^2 varies between 0 and 1. When $\hat{Y} = \bar{Y}$ for all values of X, $R^2 = 0$; when $Y = Y_i$ (our regression line goes through all data points) for all values of X, $R^2 = 1$. A value of .9 shows that we have been able to explain 90% of the variation in sales by studying the relationship of sales and advertising. R^2 may be expressed in a number of ways.

$$R^2 = \frac{\text{explained variation}}{\text{total variation}} = \frac{\Sigma(\hat{Y} - \bar{Y})^2}{\Sigma(Y - \bar{Y})^2} \qquad (10\text{-}13)$$

Since explained variation added to unexplained variation equals total variation, if we divide both sides of the equation by total variation

$$\frac{\text{Explained variation}}{\text{Total variation}} + \frac{\text{unexplained variation}}{\text{total variation}} = \frac{\text{total variation}}{\text{total variation}} = 1$$

$$R^2 = \frac{\text{explained variation}}{\text{total variation}} = \frac{\text{total variation}}{\text{total variation}} - \frac{\text{unexplained variation}}{\text{total variation}}$$

Therefore,

$$R^2 = 1 - \frac{\text{unexplained variation}}{\text{total variation}} \qquad (10\text{-}14)$$

The unexplained variation is our standard error of estimate squared, $s_{y.x}^2$, which we calculated in the previous section.

Total variation is the squared deviation of the Y values around the mean of Y. Dividing it by $n - 1$, we obtain s_y^2. Thus, if we know $s_{y.x}$ and s_y, we can calculate R^2, the sample coefficient of determination.

$$R^2 = 1 - \frac{s_{y \cdot x}^2}{s_y^2} = \frac{\Sigma(Y - \hat{Y})^2/(n - 2)}{\Sigma(Y - \overline{Y})^2/(n - 1)} \tag{10-15}$$

Computation of R^2 using Equation 10-14 would be very difficult since we would have to estimate the value for Y in the regression equation for every data point. A computational formula has been derived that can be used to compute R^2. It is

$$R^2 = \frac{a\Sigma Y + b\Sigma XY - n\overline{Y}^2}{\Sigma Y^2 - n\overline{Y}^2} \tag{10-16}$$

Computing R^2 for our data we find

$$R^2 = \frac{(-2.633)(340) + 34.537(689.5) - 6(56.667)^2}{23{,}050 - 6(56.667)^2} = \frac{3651.149}{3783.107} = .965$$

This is a very large value for R^2, which indicates that there is a strong relationship between advertising and sales (in the next period) in this mail order gift business. If we continue to find such large R^2 values for our firm over different years, we can conclude that there is a strong relationship between advertising and sales in our gift business.

Use of regression techniques for forecasting is very valuable. Experimentation with available data often leads to useful models. For example, it may be that in certain businesses sales for a given week are related to the previous week's advertising. If this relationship proves to have a larger R^2 value than the relation between a given week's sales and the same week's advertising, use of the *lagged* relationship gives improved forecasting ability.

COEFFICIENT OF CORRELATION

10-9

Sometimes r, the coefficient of correlation, is computed. This measure r is the square root of R^2. The coefficient of correlation can vary from -1 to 0 to $+1$. The prime virtue of this measure is that its sign indicates the direction of the relationship. Thus, a plus sign means a positive (direct) relation, and a minus sign indicates a negative (inverse) relation. The sign really is the sign of the slope of the regression line (the sign of b). For this problem, since $R^2 = .965$, $r = \sqrt{.965} = +.982$. The sign is plus because there is a positive relation showing that as advertising increases, sales increases; in the equation, the term for b is 34.537.

SIGNIFICANCE OF THE COEFFICIENT OF DETERMINATION

10-10

If we obtain an R^2 of .965, we have interpreted it to mean that we effect a 96.5% improvement in our forecast of sales by correlating levels of advertisement with levels of sales. Is this relevant? Is there really a relationship between sales and advertising in the population or is this relationship (R^2) just due to sampling errors? It is possible for sample statistics to differ from population parameters.

First, the larger the sample the more likely the sample statistics (r or R^2) will equal the population parameters. Secondly, the larger the value of R^2, and consequently the absolute value of r, the more likely it is that there is a relationship between the independent and dependent variables in the population.

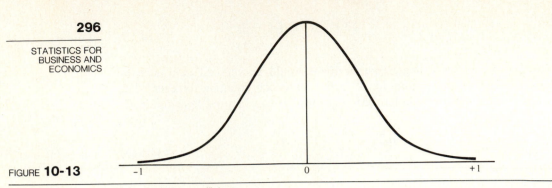

FIGURE **10-13**

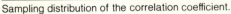

Sampling distribution of the correlation coefficient.

Using the hypothesis testing technique developed in Chapter 6, we set up the following test.

1 $H_0: \rho = 0$

$H_1: \rho \neq 0$

where r is the sample correlation coefficient and ρ is the population correlation coefficient. Since ρ goes from -1 to $+1$, the sampling distribution is symmetrically distributed, as in Figure 10-13, and may be approximated with a t distribution and the estimated standard error of r, s_r. If we hypothesized that there is no correlation in the population, the R^2 values are not symmetrically distributed and it would be more difficult to estimate the sampling distribution $s_r = \sqrt{1 - R^2/n - 2}$. Note that R^2 is what we could explain, so $1 - R^2$ is the error, or what we can't explain. What we are postulating in our null hypothesis is that there is no relationship between sales and advertising in the population. Figure 10-13 shows how r (the relationship between X and Y) may vary in the population.

2 Level of significance $= .05$, t test, df $= 4$.

Since the sample size is small, we should use the t table with $n - 2$ degrees of freedom. We lose 2 degrees of freedom because there are two parameters (a and b) estimated for the regression line. Since there are 6 sets of observations in this problem, $n - 2 = 4$. Using the t table (Table A-4), df $= 4$, and .05 level of significance, we find the following critical points.

3 If $t > 2.776$, reject H_0. Or, if $t < -2.776$, reject H_0.

Since we have 6 sets of observations in our problem, degrees of freedom $= 4$, t value at .05 is equal to 2.776.

The formula for computing the cutoff point is similar to our formula to compute t.

$$t = \frac{\bar{X} - \mu}{\sigma}$$

Instead, we have

$$\frac{r - \rho}{s_r} = \frac{r - \rho}{\sqrt{\dfrac{(1 - R^2)}{n - 2}}}$$

where r is the correlation coefficient for the sample and ρ is the correlation coefficient for the population. (The denominator is the standard error of r.) Since we have assumed that the population ρ is 0, because we are testing to determine if r could be different than 0, $r - \rho$ becomes r. Since we have a small *sample* and must therefore use the t table, the formula becomes

$$t = \frac{r}{\sqrt{(1 - R^2)/n - 2}} \tag{10-17}$$

If the sample were large, we could use z table values. Using our sales advertising example, $R^2 = .965$, $r = .982$, and $t = .982/\sqrt{(1 - .965)/4} = .982/.0935 = 10.503$. Since $10.503 > 2.776$, we cannot accept H_0. Thus, we say that there is reason to believe that there is a relationship between sales and advertising in the population.

Problems

1 Edith Benham, a stock investor, wants to determine how closely a firm's annual net income is related to the dollar value of its assets. Assume that she finds the following data:

COMPANY	ASSETS X ($000)	NET INCOME Y ($000)
A	60	20
B	60	25
C	75	25
D	80	20
E	100	30
F	145	35
G	175	40
H	190	45
I	190	55
J	200	50

(*a*) Plot the data on a scatter diagram.
(*b*) Determine the regression line for this data.
(*c*) What is the standard error of estimate?
(*d*) What is the coefficient of determination?
(*e*) What does this coefficient of determination tell you?

2 Goodwear Tire Company has a large tire distribution center that holds 255,000 tires when it is full. There are 700 different types of tires and, as the warehouse fills, many storage areas are forced to hold several types of tires. Thus, the fuller the warehouse the more difficult it is to get to many types of tires. Use simple regression analysis to study the relationship between the time it takes to pull an average order (3000 pounds, or approximately 122 tires).

Note: To solve this problem, it is necessary to have data on the time it takes to pull an order when the warehouse is filled to different levels. Since there is a difference in speed between workers, the manager averaged 20 order-filling times for each level of capacity and arrived at the following table.

WAREHOUSE LEVEL OF FULLNESS (PERCENT)	AVERAGE ORDER-FILLING TIME (MINUTES)
100	20
95	20
90	19
80	18
70	16
65	15
60	15
50	13
40	9
35	8
30	7
25	6
20	5
10	3

(*a*) Plot these points on a scatter diagram. (Which variable is *Y*?)

(*b*) Fit the least-squares regression line to the points.

(*c*) Plot the least-squares regression line.

(*d*) Calculate the standard error of the regression line.

(*e*) Estimate the time needed to fill an order when the warehouse is at 75% of capacity.

(*f*) On the average, the plant pulls 300 orders each day. Find the difference in worker hours when the plant is 60% full as compared to 100% full. If workers are paid an average of $4 per hour, what is the additional cost per order? How many additional worker hours are required?

3 The popular feeling is that winning teams are likely to have larger attendance figures than losing teams. The following statistics could be used to test this theory for baseball's Eastern Division of the American League. The data represents the actual standings for the 1976 season.

RELATIONSHIP OF ATTENDANCE TO WON-LOST RECORD
(American League Eastern Division, 1976)

TEAM	WINNING PERCENTAGE	AVERAGE HOME ATTENDANCE PER GAME (IN THOUSANDS)	AVERAGE ROAD ATTENDANCE (IN THOUSANDS)
New York	.617	28	27
Baltimore	.602	15	20
Boston	.602	28	25
Detroit	.457	18	20
Cleveland	.441	12	18
Milwaukee	.414	15	17
Toronto	.335	24	14

Source: Sports Information Center, North Quincy, Maine.

(*a*) Plot these points on one scatter diagram for the relation of home attendance and winning percentage and of road attendance and winning percentage. (Use different colors for data points for the two curves.) Does there seem to be a relationship between home attendance and winning percentage, between road attendance and winning percentage?

(*b*)   Fit a least-squares regression line for both home and road attendance.

(*c*)   Plot both the least-squares regression lines.

(*d*)   Which of the two lines shows a higher degree of relationship? What measure could you use to study this? Calculate it.

(*e*)   Outline how this same approach might be used to evaluate the effect of good reviews on theater or movie attendance.

(*f*)   How could this technique be used to decide how much to spend on improving team performance?

(*g*)   Would stadium size affect the results in *d*?

(*h*)   What is the standard error of the regression line that relates average home attendance and winning percentage? Make the same calculation for road attendance and winning percentage?

(*i*)   If the winning percentage were .5, estimate the average home attendance. Make a 95% confidence interval for this estimate.

SIGNIFICANCE OF b, THE REGRESSION COEFFICIENT

10-11

The slope of the regression line b is a very important value for making forecasts. The value of b, computed from sample data, is used to show how much an increase of one unit in the independent variable (such as advertising) leads to an increase or decrease in the dependent variable (such as sales).

The regression coefficient has also become a very important tool for *portfolio analysis*. An equation relating the percentage return for an individual security (Y axis) to percentage returns in the whole market (X axis) is fitted for each stock in the portfolio. The regression coefficient b, which is the slope of this line, is called the *beta (β) coefficient*. It measures the sensitivity of rates of return on the particular security to general market movements. If β is 1.0, a 1 percent increase in the return on the market will lead to an expected 1 percent increase in the return on a particular asset. Similarly, a 1 percent *fall* in the return on the market will lead to a 1 percent decrease in the return on a particular asset. If β is less than 1.0, the asset is *less risky* than the market. An estimate of the beta coefficient, and hence the riskiness of a portfolio of securities, can be made by taking a value-weighted average of the betas of all assets in the portfolio.

While we are determining the value of the regression coefficient, we may also wish to test if two regression coefficients computed at different times are significantly different, or if an individual regression coefficient is significantly different from 0. If the coefficient is significantly different from 0, we can say that the independent variable helps us to predict the dependent variable.

We now set up a test for our sales and advertising example. We wish to determine if, with a given value of b (based on a specific sample size), we can assume that the population coefficient for b is significantly different from 0.

Regression analysis assumes that the dependent variable is normally distributed about the true population regression line; hence, the sampling distribution is normal (see Section 10-5) and z tables may be used. Since we will use a small sample in our next problem and are estimating $s_{y.x}$ to compute these distributions, we will use the t table to test whether b is significantly different from 0. Using the data for our sales and advertising problem (Table 10-2), which yields the regression equation $\overline{Y} = -2.633 + 34.537X$, we will test if our b value (34.537) is significant.

Using the hypothesis testing procedure of Chapter 6, we set up the following three steps. B is the relationship between X and Y for the population, that is, the population regression coefficient. Since we have used β for Type II error and for portfolio risk, we now use B for the population regression coefficient.

1 H_0: $B = 0$. No association of dependent and independent variable in the population.

H_1: $B \neq 0$. Here is a relation of the two variables in the population.

2 t test, degrees of freedom for a regression line is the sample size n minus the number of constants estimated. For this simple regression line we estimate a and b, so we have $n - 2$ degrees of freedom ($6 - 2 = 4$ df).

The stated level of probability (usually .01 or .05) is the possibility of Type I error (α)—rejecting the hypothesis of no population association when there really is a relationship ($B \neq 0$).

3 Using df $= 4$ and $p = .05$, the critical value from our t table is $t = 2.776$. Therefore, if our calculated value of t exceeds 2.776, we reject H_0 and assume that b is significant.

Now that we have set up our hypothesis test to test whether B is significantly different from 0, we must compute the value for t using the formula

$$t = \frac{b - B}{s_b} \tag{10-18}$$

where s_b is the standard error of the regression coefficient b. It is a function of the scatter of the points around the regression line $s_{y.x}$ and the scatter of the X values around their mean (the standard deviation of the X values) s_x. We calculate it by dividing the standard error of the regression line by the standard deviation of our independent variable.

$$s_b = \frac{s_{y.x}}{\sqrt{\Sigma(X - \overline{X})^2 / n}} \tag{10-19}$$

The computation formula is

$$s_b = \frac{s_{y.x}}{\sqrt{\Sigma X^2 - n\overline{X}^2}} \qquad \text{standard deviation of } X \tag{10-20}$$

Now let us test b for our original sales and advertising problem. Reviewing the hypothesis test, we have

1 H_0: $B = 0$.
H_1: $B \neq 0$.
2 $\alpha = .05$, df $= 4$.
3 If $t > 2.776$, reject H_0.

We have computed $s_{y \cdot x}$ previously as 5.744. Now we compute

$$s_x = \sqrt{\Sigma X^2 - n\bar{X}^2} = \sqrt{20.75 - 6(1.717)^2} = \sqrt{20.75 - 17.68} = \sqrt{3.07}$$

$$s_b = \frac{5.744}{\sqrt{3.07}} = \frac{5.744}{1.752} = 3.279$$

Now we calculate our t value. Since we are assuming that the population B is 0, substitute 0 for B. The value for b from our equation is 34.537.

$$t = \frac{34.537 - 0}{3.279} = 10.533 \qquad t > 2.776$$

We reject H_0, and infer that there is reason to believe that an association exists in the population, and that the slope b is significant. Note that this t value is the same (except for round-off errors) as the value we calculated when we tested whether the correlation coefficient was 0 (p. 297). For multiple regression with many independent variables, this value will not be the same. We discuss multiple regression in Section 10-12.

Problems

1 Bess Vick, an insurance salesperson, feels that the size of a home insurance policy is closely related to yearly family income. Based on the following figures (representing her most recent sales):

  (*a*) Graph the points and draw the best-fitting line by eye. Find the equation for the estimating line and fit the line on the same graph. (How do they compare?)

  (*b*) Determine the standard error of estimate.

  (*c*) What is the coefficient of determination for this data?

  (*d*) Is the relationship significant?

YEARLY INCOME X (\$000)	SIZE OF POLICY Y (\$000)
12	15
15	15
17	20
20	25
22	30
30	40
30	30
40	35
40	50
45	70

2 Paul Gray, a director of an Environmental Protection Agency air monitoring station, feels that the parts/million of pollutants in the air should be closely related to the population of the city in which the station is located. If the data from other cities around the country is as follows, do you think the director is correct? (The city in question is number 12 in this chart.)

CITY	POPULATION X (000)	PARTS/MILLION OF POLLUTANTS Y
1	10	20
2	25	25
3	25	40
4	30	40
5	35	35
6	40	30
7	40	45
8	55	50
9	90	120
10	100	130
11	120	100
12	150	200
13	200	300
14	400	350

3 An automotive tire dealer wants a simple linear graph showing how many miles a new tire can be expected to last depending upon its sales price. Assume you are an employee and are given this task to perform using the following data:

n	PRICE OF TIRE ($)	MILEAGE PER TIRE (000)
1	20	10
2	25	20
3	30	25
4	30	30
5	35	30
6	35	35
7	40	35

(*a*) Fit the regression line.
(*b*) If you paid $28 for a tire, how many miles would you expect it to last?
(*c*) Is b significant?

MULTIPLE REGRESSION ANALYSIS

10-12 In the previous sections, we used an independent variable to predict a dependent variable. For example, we used advertising to predict sales. Most social science or business relationships tend to be more complex. Thus, in order to make accurate forecasts of sales volume, we may have to study the relative price of our product, the competing products, and advertising.

Let's look at some examples. If we wish to forecast participation of married women in the labor force, we may have to study the husband's income, family size, age of the youngest child, and the wife's education in order to predict the status of any individual woman. College admissions committees predict the success of prospective college students by using both high school grades and SAT scores. The number of new enrollments in welfare programs (for example, the federal food stamp program) can be predicted using unemployment indexes, rates of inflation, and the number of labor-management disputes as independent variables.

The multiple regression analysis has the following form:

$$\hat{Y} = a + b_1X_1 + b_2X_2 + b_3X_3 + \cdots + b_kX_k \qquad (10\text{-}21)$$

If we were relating sales Y to advertising X_1 and local unemployment X_2, we would have to determine three parameters a_1, b_1, b_2:

$$\hat{Y} = a + b_1X_1(\text{ads}) + b_2X_2(\text{unemployment})$$

Solution of the following three simultaneous equations would provide estimates for a_1, b_1, and b_2.

$$\Sigma Y = na + b_1\Sigma X_1 + b_2\Sigma X_2$$

$$\Sigma X_1 Y = a\Sigma X_1 + b_1\Sigma X_1^2 + b_2\Sigma X_2 X_1$$

$$\Sigma X_2 Y = a\Sigma X_2 + b_1\Sigma X_1 X_2 + b_2\Sigma X_2^2$$

The solution is derived from methods shown in Appendix 10-3A. Let us assume our analysis produced the following values for a_1, b_1, and b_2.

$a = 12.43$

$b_1 = 2.4 \qquad$ in 000

$b_2 = -1.3 \qquad$ in 000

$\hat{Y} = 12.43 + 2.4\ X_1(000)(\text{ads}) - 1.3X_2(000)(\text{unemployment rate})$

The coefficients b_1 and b_2 are called *net regression coefficients*. As a rule, computer packages now estimate net regression coefficients since the calculations are tedious by hand. In Chapter 14, we show a computer output for a multiple regression analysis. Examination of b_1 shows that if we hold employment constant and increase advertising by \$100, then sales rises by \$2400. If we hold advertising constant, a 1 percent increase in unemployment leads to a \$1300 fall in sales.

If we wish to see whether we have improved our forecasting power by moving from a simple regression analysis to a multiple regression analysis, we can compare the values of R^2. Thus, when we related sales and advertising, R^2 was .965. If the addition of unemployment rate to the equation raises R^2 to .975, our ability to forecast has increased. On the average, using advertising and unemployment rates we can now account for 97.5% of the variation in sales. The addition of completely irrelevant variables means that R^2 does not increase.

Another useful feature of multiple regression analysis is that it allows us to examine the effects of one variable while holding other variables in the equation constant. For example, a study was made (Sobol, 1973) to find which married mothers would be most likely to have the longest work careers. By relating the dependent variable, number of years one expects to work (Y), to a number of independent variables using simple regression analysis, it was found that the more children a woman had (# CHILD), the less likely she was to expect to work; the higher the husband's income (H INC), the less likely the wife was to expect to work; and the higher a wife's level of education (WEDUC), the less likely a wife was to plan to work.

The first two findings with respect to the number of children and the husband's income seemed reasonable. The finding that women with higher levels of education were less likely to plan long work careers didn't seem reasonable. Wouldn't a woman with more training be able to have a more interesting job? Upon further reflection, it would seem that a woman who is well-educated would tend to marry a well-educated and well-paid man. Thus, the wife's high education may attract her to the labor market, but the high income of the husband makes it less imperative for her to work. Using all three of these variables in a multiple regression equation, we obtained the following results.

Y (YRS WORK)

$$= 3.465 - 1.129(\text{H INC}) - 1.158(\#\text{ CHILD}) + 2.264(\text{WEDUC})$$

where   YRS WORK = Number of years wife plans to work
              H INC = Husband's income in $10,000 dollar units
          # CHILD = Number of children
            WEDUC = Number of years of wife's education

Now, looking at this equation, we can hold husband's income and number of children constant. Then, a woman who has completed college (16 years of school) would plan to work $(2.264)(4) = 9.056$ more years than her counterpart, with the same number of children and same level of husband's income, who had finished high school (12 years).

However, in using multiple regression analysis, one must be careful not to include in the same equation two independent variables that are highly correlated. This makes it very difficult to disentangle the relative influences of the independent variables, and it also may lead to very large sampling variances for the coefficients. (As a rule of thumb, one should be wary of R^2 values greater than .5 in relating two independent variables.) This leads to a problem called *multicollinearity*. Some information contributed by two or more independent variables may be different, and some may overlap. It is wisest to exclude one of the two highly correlated independent variables. Thus, in this equation, we did not include both husband's income and husband's education since they were highly correlated. Generally, if two independent variables are correlated, it is most effective to use the one that is most highly related to the dependent variable.

SOME LIMITATIONS OF REGRESSION ANALYSIS

10-13   ### Correlation and Causation

In working with the coefficient of determination or the coefficient of correlation, one must be careful not to infer that a strong relationship between two variables means that one *causes* the other. There are several possibilities. First, one variable may cause another; thus, eating a large number of high-calorie foods generally causes a gain in weight. Even here one should be cautious. There is a system of philosophy known as *logical positivism,* founded by Auguste Compte (1798–1857), that suggests we cannot be positive that one thing causes another, that human knowledge of all phenomena is merely relative. Hence, we do not know we have causation; we only know that we have a very high degree of relationship between two variables.

Second, the relationship may arise because a *common cause* offsets each variable in the same way. A very commonly cited case of this type of relationship was the high correlation between storks' nests and births of babies in Sweden during the 1920s. Would this mean that storks really do deliver babies? As you may remember from our discussion of this case in Chapter 1, it was found that storks build nests near chimneys and, during this period, there were many new marriages and hence new homes—thus, the availability of more sites for storks' nests and the possibilities for more babies' births.

Third, the causal relationship may be *interacting*. For example, a high price for a good leads to increased production, but increased production may raise or lower the cost of the commodity.

Finally, the correlation may be due to chance. In a given sample, it may happen that the size of a student's shoe relates to the number of quarters in his or her pocket. It is hard to develop a theory for this relationship, and we have shown how we could test r to tell whether this relationship might be due to sampling error.

Significance versus Ability to Estimate

If r is significant, it may not necessarily mean that we can make a good estimate from our regression equation. The formula to test significance depends solely on the size of n and r; therefore, if the sample is very large, even a small value of r proves significant. For example, if $r = .2$ and $n = 5000$, our t value is

$$t = \frac{.2}{\sqrt{(1 - .04)/4998}} = \frac{.2}{.01386} = 14.43$$

which is significant even though $R^2 = .04$ and we have explained only 4% of the variation in the data. Thus, we can infer that there is a relationship between the two variables in the population. However, if this relationship is very slight, the regression line may not prove to be a very good tool for forecasting since both the standard error (unexplained variation) $s_{y \cdot x}$ and the confidence interval about our estimate will be large.

Curvilinearity

When the original data on sales and advertising was plotted on a scatter diagram, we examined the data to see if the relationship seemed linear. Since the relationship seemed to be a straight line, we fitted a straight line to the data points.

If the relationship does not seem linear, it may still be possible to use regression analysis. This time a more complicated line may be fitted to the data points. Some common curves that might be fitted are a parabola (Figure 10-14)—generally half

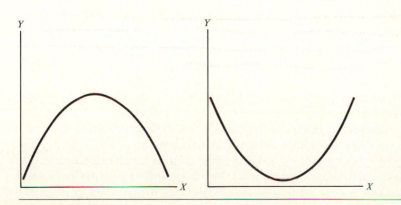

FIGURE **10-14**

Parabolas.

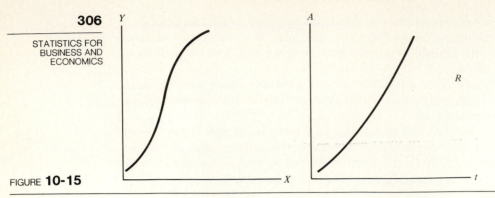

FIGURE **10-15**

Exponential curves.

of the parabola is used—or an exponential curve (Figure 10-15). The form of a parabola is

$$\hat{Y} = a + bX + cX^2 \tag{10-22}$$

The curve could look like either curve in Figure 10-14. Parts of these curves (dotted lines) could be used too. Another possibility is an exponential curve with the form

$$Y = a + b^x \tag{10-23}$$

(Note the special form of b and that x is an exponent.)

The compound interest formula $A_t = P(1 + i)^t$—where P is the original principal, i the interest rate, t the number of periods, and A the amount due—is an example of this curve (see Figure 10-15). If you have plotted your data and the relationship between X and Y seems to be more like a curve, you might try some of these basic curves. Estimating equations for these curves are found in more advanced statistics texts (see the bibliography). Many computer regression programs can fit a number of different kinds of curves to two or more variables. Once you have made a data file, you might try these different types of equations and choose the one for which you have the highest value of R^2. Be careful here, though; if you do not have many data points, you should not fit a complicated line because you will not have enough degrees of freedom. Remember that in an equation like

$$Y = a + bX + cX^2 + dX^3 + eX^4$$

you lose 5 degrees of freedom, one for each of the parameters a, b, c, d, e. You should not fit this type of equation to four observations.

Similarly, for multiple regression analysis, we must be careful not to fit an equation with a large number of independent variables for only a few data points (observations).

Homoscedasticity

When the regression line is plotted on the original scatter diagram, we should examine the data to see if the data points are scattered uniformly about the regression line (homoscedasticity). We considered homoscedasticity in Figure 10-10 when we first introduced the standard error of estimate. If the scatter deviations of the data points about the regression line for each value of X is uniform, the standard error of estimate can be used to form uniform confidence intervals for forecasting purposes. In Figure 10-10(b), we see that the points at the beginning of the curve are closer to the regression line than those at the end. This scatter is termed *heteroscedastic*. The scatter could also be considered heteroscedastic with a high σ^2 at the middle or left end. In Figure 10-10(b), the standard error of estimate is not as useful for forecasting because we are not as sure of forecasts on the right-hand end of the distribution; hence, it is recommended that regression analysis be used only when it can be assumed that the scatter of the data points is homoscedastic. Perhaps a better way to handle the data in Figure 10-10(b) would be to fit a separate regression line to each half of the data.

Extrapolation

The purpose of computing the coefficients of a regression equation is to use this equation for forecasting purposes. If we try to forecast far beyond the range of the data points that we have used to construct this equation, we are likely to have difficulty. For example, in our original problem relating sales to advertising, we used amounts of advertising that varied from $600 to $3000. If we now want to predict what happens when $16,000 is invested in advertising, the results are not likely to be valid. Perhaps at some point there is market saturation so that any advertising beyond $5000 has no additional effect on sales. Often in our analysis we use X as time and predict future values for our Y variable. For example, we could forecast sales over time. However, if we try to predict too far into the future, the variation of sales over time may change. Often our equation has a negative intercept, so that if we forecast sales with no advertising the equation would predict negative sales. It would not be useful to use this equation for very low values of advertising. A likely curve appears in Figure 10-16, which shows that there is a linear relationship between sales and advertising up to point E. Beyond this point, it would seem that there is no relationship. Forecasts for $X = 0$ to $X = E$ would be useful. After that point we cannot use our relationship to make additional forecasts. Thus, forecasting requires the addition of personal judgment to mathematical techniques. In Chapter 11, which discusses the many different ways to make forecasts, we stress the ways in which personal judgment must be used in the process. As a beginning, you can see that if we want to fit a mathematical model (or relationship) to our data points so that we can predict future events, we should try to fit the right type of functions if possible.

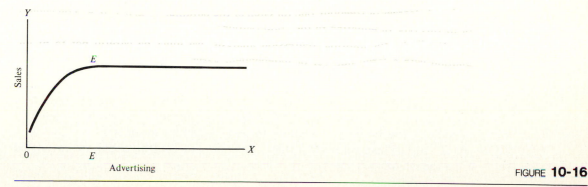

FIGURE **10-16**

Hypothetical curve relating sales and advertising.

Problems

1 Coach Kesner was quite interested in determining whether rushing yard records of running backs related to height, weight, or years as a professional football player. He gathered the following data on running backs for the Dallas Cowboys, Houston Oilers, and New Orleans Saints for 1976.

TEAM	RUNNING BACK	HEIGHT	WEIGHT	YEARS AS A PRO	RUSHING YARDS IN 1976
Dallas Cowboys	Doug Dennison	6-ft	204 lb	4	542
	Scott Laidlaw	6-ft	205 lb	3	424
	Robert Newhouse	5-ft 8-in	205 lb	6	450
	Preston Pearson	6-ft	206 lb	11	233
	Charles Young	6-ft	218 lb	4	208
Houston Oilers	Ronnie Coleman	5-ft 8-in	198 lb	4	684
	Fred Willis	6-ft	205 lb	7	542
	Don Hardemon	6-ft 2-in	235 lb	3	114
	Joe Dawkins	6-ft 2-in	220 lb	8	67
New Orleans Saints	Tony Galbreath	6-ft	220 lb	2	570
	Alvin Maxson	5-ft 9-in	201 lb	4	120
	Chuck Muncie	6-ft 2-in	220 lb	2	652
	Mike Strachen	6-ft	200 lb	3	258

Source: Dallas Cowboys Executive Office, Dallas, Texas.

(*a*)   Plot the relation to rushing yards for height, weight, and years as a pro. (Make three separate scatter diagrams.)

(*b*)   On the basis of your study of these graphs, which of these three variables (height, weight, and years as a pro) seems to show the most relationship to rushing yards?

(*c*)   Use simple regression analysis and relate weight to rushing yards in 1976.

(*d*)   Use multiple regression analysis to relate rushing yards to weight, height, and years as a pro.

SUMMARY

10-14

1 Simple regression analysis provides a means of relating two variables Y (dependent) and X (independent) so that one variable (independent) can be used to help make a prediction for the other variable (dependent). Pairs of data are plotted on a graph called a *scatter diagram*. Study of the scatter diagram reveals whether the relation between the two variables is linear or nonlinear, whether it is positive or negative, or whether no relationship seems to exist. It can be used to study the correlation of a dependent and an independent variable, or the correlation between two independent variables.

2 The best-fitting line for these data points will be the *least-squares regression* line. This is the line about which the sum of the squared deviations is a *minimum*. In addition, the line goes through the mean of X and the mean of Y.

3 To fit this line, values of a (the Y intercept) and b (the slope) are calculated using the following formulas:

$$a = \overline{Y} - b\overline{X}$$

$$b = \frac{\Sigma XY - n\bar{X}\,\bar{Y}}{\Sigma X^2 - \bar{n}X^2}$$

4 The regression line $\hat{Y} = a + bX$ can be used to make estimates of point values by substituting values for X and computing Y.

5 An estimate of the ranges within which a certain percentage of the sample values will fall can be made by using estimates from the regression line $\hat{Y} \pm$ the t value times the standard error of estimate $s_{y.x}$. The range is $\hat{Y} \pm ts_{y.x}$, and the degrees of freedom are $n - 2$. The standard error of estimate measures the deviations of the actual data points from the regression line. The formula used to calculate the standard error of estimate is

$$s_{y.x} = \sqrt{\frac{\Sigma Y^2 - a\Sigma Y - b\Sigma XY}{n - 2}}$$

6 To make estimates of confidence intervals for an individual forecast, we use

$$\hat{Y} \pm ts_{fy}$$

where

$$s_{fy} = s_{y.x}\sqrt{1 + \frac{1}{n} + \frac{(X_f - \bar{X})^2}{\Sigma X^2 - n\bar{X}^2}}$$

and the degrees of freedom are $n - 2$.

7 To make estimates of confidence intervals for a conditional mean, we use

$$\hat{Y} \pm ts_{y.x}\sqrt{\frac{1}{n} + \frac{(X - \bar{X})^2}{\Sigma X^2 - n\bar{X}^2}}$$

where the degrees of freedom are $n - 2$.

8 The coefficient of determination R^2 measures the percentage of total variation (from Y) we have been able to explain using estimates from the least-squares regression line. R^2 varies from 0 to 1 and may be calculated using the formula

$$R^2 = \frac{a\Sigma Y + b\Sigma XY - n\bar{Y}^2}{\Sigma Y^2 - n\bar{Y}^2}$$

9 The coefficient of correlation r is the square root of R^2, and also shows the sign (plus or minus) of the relationship. Thus, it may vary from -1 to $+1$.

10 A test may be performed to see whether r is significantly different from 0 for the population. This test uses the formula

$$t = \frac{r}{\sqrt{(1 - R^2)/(n - 2)}}$$

If the calculated value for t is greater than the t value specified in the hypothesis test, we reject the null hypothesis that the population correlation coefficient is 0 and say that there is a significant relationship between the X and Y variables.

11 Similarly, a test may be performed to see whether the regression coefficient for the sample b indicates that the population regression coefficient B is significantly different from 0.

$$t = \frac{b - B}{s_b}$$

where

$$s_b = \frac{s_{y.x}}{\sqrt{\Sigma X^2 - n\bar{X}^2}}$$

and the degrees of freedom $= n - 2$ for a linear equation.

If the value calculated for t is greater than the t value specified in the hypothesis test, we can reject the null hypothesis that the population correlation coefficient is 0 and say that there is a significant relationship between X and Y. We can also use this method to test whether there have been significant changes in regression coefficients over time.

12 Multiple regression analysis uses two or more independent variables and one dependent variable. The prediction equation for two variables is of the form

$$\hat{Y} = a + b_1 X_1 + b_2 X_2$$

This analysis allows for additional ability to forecast using two variables. Advertising and unemployment rates, for example, may be able to forecast sales better than just advertising. Furthermore, the inclusion of several variables allows examination of the influence of one variable while holding the other constant. Thus, we can observe, for the same levels of unemployment, the influence of different levels of advertising. One must be careful to avoid using two independent variables that are highly correlated *(multicollinearity)*. Choose the independent variable that is most highly related to the dependent variable.

13 Some limitations of linear regression analysis are as follows: (*a*) correlation may not imply causation; (*b*) if the sample size is large a very small value of r may be deemed significant, but the equation may not provide a very effective forecasting tool; (*c*) relationships are often nonlinear and should be fitted using curves, so that an *exponential curve* or a *parabola* may prove useful for fitting business and economic data; (*d*) one condition for using a regression line is that the data points should be scattered normally with a constant variance about the regression line *(homoscedasticity)*—thus, for each value of X, the Y values should have the same variance (σ^2); (*e*) it is unwise to forecast too far beyond the values of the original data points used to establish the least-squares regression line; forecasting beyond these points is called *extrapolation*.

BIBLIOGRAPHY

10-15

The following books offer clear simple explanations of regression analysis.

Hamburg, Morris: *Basic Statistics*, 2d ed., New York: Harcourt, 1979, pp. 243–303.
Plane, Donald R., and Edward Opperman: *Statistics for Management Decisions*, Dallas: Business Publications, 1977, pp. 247–300.
Spurr, William A., and Charles P. Bonini: *Statistical Analysis for Business Decisions*, rev. ed. Homewood Ill.: Irwin, 1973, pp. 448–539.

More advanced techniques are explained in the following texts:

Hamburg, Morris: *Statistical Analysis for Decision Making*, 2d ed., New York: Harcourt, 1977, pp. 356–442.
Kleinbaum, David G., and Lawrence L. Kupper: *Applied Regression Analysis and Other Multivariate Methods*, N. Scituate, Mass.: Duxbury Press, 1978.
Neter, John, and William Wasserman: *Applied Linear Statistical Models*, Homewood, Ill.: Irwin, 1974.

Regression analysis is very widely applied in a number of fields.

Accounting

Bentson, George J.: "Multiple Regression Analysis of Cost Behavior," *The Accounting Review,* Oct. 1966, pp. 657–672.

Dopuch, N., J. G. Burnberg, and Joel Demski: *Cost Accounting,* 2d ed., chapter 3. New York: Harcourt, 1974, pp. 50–89.

Economics

Johnston, J.: *Econometric Methods*, New York: McGraw-Hill, 1972.

Spyros, Makridakris, and Steven Wheelwright: *Forecasting: Methods and Applications*, New York: Wiley, 1978, pp. 146–249.

Finance

Van Horne, James: *Financial Management and Policy,* 4th ed. Englewood Cliffs, N.J.: Prentice-Hall, 1977, pp. 56–65. Good explanation of the use of regression coefficients for portfolio analysis.

Other books in this area are:

Cohen, J. B., E. Zinbarg, and A. Zeikel: *Investment Analysis and Portfolio Management,* 3d ed., Homewood, Ill.: Irwin, 1977, pp. 261–265, 685–686, 689, 701.

Williams, Edward E., and M. Chapman Findlay III: *Investment Analysis*, Englewood Cliffs, N.J.: Prentice-Hall, 1974, pp. 117–119, 419–424.

Marketing

Boyd, Harper W., Jr., and Ralph Westfall: *Marketing Research: Text and Cases,* 3d ed., Homewood, Ill.: Irwin, 1972, pp. 561–563.

Eby, Frank H., Jr., and William J. O'Neill: *The Management of Sales Forecasting*, Lexington, Mass.: D.C. Heath, 1977, pp. 141–169 (simple); pp. 170–186 (multiple).

Real Estate

Pendleton, William: "Statistical Inference in Appraisal and Assessment Procedures," *The Appraisal Journal,* vol. 33, Jan. 1965, pp. 73–82.

Renshaw, Edward F.: "Scientific Appraisal," *National Tax Journal,* vol. 11, Dec. 1958, pp. 314–322.

Stenehjem, Erik J.: "A Scientific Approach to Mass Appraisal of Residential Property," in John B. Rockhemans and Theodore R. Smith (eds.) *Automated Mass Appraisal of Real Property*, Chicago: International Association of Assessing Officers, 1974.

Public Sector

Sobol, Marion G.: "Enrollments and Use of the Federal Food Stamp Program: New Jersey," *Social Science Quarterly*, vol. 57, no. 3, Dec. 1976. Reprinted in Howard Freeman (ed.), *Policy Studies Review Annual*, Beverly Hills, Ca.: Sage, 1978, p. 332.

Sobol, Marion G.: "A Dynamic Analysis of Labor Force Participation of Married Women of Childbearing Age," *Journal of Human Resources,* vol. 8, no. 4., Fall 1973.

Production and Operations Management

Ettlie, John E., and David B. Vellenga: "Adoption Time Period for Some Transportation Innovations," *Management Science,* May 1979, pp. 429–443.

Mayer, Raymond: *Production and Operations Management,* 3d ed., New York: McGraw-Hill, 1975, pp. 21–37.

Starr, Martin: *Operations Management*, Englewood Cliffs, N.J.: Prentice-Hall, 1978, pp. 250–253.

Case 10-1 Lester Real Estate Appraisal

The Lester Realty Company specializes in the sale of homes in a highly transient (high-turnover) residential suburb of Chicago. There are 17 offices throughout the city, each of which specializes in the business in its area.

Realtors are responsible for listing new properties as well as for selling properties. Generally, a real estate agent will be asked for advice by a client who is considering listing a property. Listing is a written contract between an owner and a broker in which the broker attempts to sell the real estate of the owner. When the property is listed, the owner and the broker usually set a price at which the property will be offered. The property may not sell for this price, and the broker who has listed the property will earn a specified commission when a sales contract is signed. The client may want the agent to suggest a selling price. The agent generally tries to advise the client according to the prices for which similar houses in the same neighborhood have sold.

Nora Kay Bilton recently joined the North Chicago office of Lester Realty. She has had quite a bit of difficulty in deciding what features of a house should be used to determine the value of a listing, and she would like to develop a systematic method for evaluation. Information about sales prices and the features of a house are available every week from a local research firm. An example is shown in Figure 1.

Nora chooses a sample of 15 houses from the listings in the neighborhood of the Lester Realty North Branch office. By using only one neighborhood, she has at least partially overcome the problem that the same house may have different values in different areas. She is interested only in the selling prices of houses in this area, since this is her territory. Otherwise, she could do the same analysis— area by area. For each of these properties, she lists sales price, lot size, year built, number of rooms, and living area (Table 1). Now, she ponders which factor or combination of factors would be the best predictor for house price.

TABLE 1

MAP CODE	PROPERTY ADDRESS	SALE PRICE	LOT SIZE (SQUARE FEET)	YEAR BUILT	NUMBER OF ROOMS	LIVING AREA (SQUARE FEET)
2F	Nottingham	$80,900	9,775	1976	11	2,705
2O	Meadow Creek	63,000	10,000	1975	8	2,420
2O	Stonewood Drive	62,500	8,880	1976	7	2,203
2R	Greenhill	69,000	—	1977	9	2,332
2U	Tecumseh	20,000	9,028	1963	5	974
2V	Tecumseh Trail	22,000	8,505	1964	6	1,346
2Y	Terrace Tr.	36,900	7,800	1970	6	1,665
2Z	Sherwood	29,500	7,200	1969	7	1,430
3B	Ash Hill	33,900	7,544	1974	5	1,385
3B	Lymington	30,100	7,500	1973	6	1,433
3F	Christie Lane	44,800	7,350	—	8	2,124
3F	Rayswood Cr.	24,500	8,038	1973	6	1,290
3J	Argonne	30,800	6,600	1970	6	1,415
3J	Grenable	34,200	8,520	1971	5	1,408
3K	Green Valley	41,200	6,100	—	6	1,645
		$623,300	112,841		101	25,775

COUNTY

MAP CODE / CITY / CENSUS TRACT	PROPERTY ADDRESS	$ SALE PRICE	TYPE	CASH DOWN	% 1ST MTG	SALE DATE MO/YR	SALE CLOSED	LOT SIZE OR AREA	LOT ZONE	FLOOD ZONE	SITE INF	OBSOLESCENCE	WATER	SEWER	STYLE	STORIES	FLOOR PLAN	QUALITY	CONDITION	YEAR BUILT	ROOMS	BDRMS	OTHER ROOMS	BATHS FULL	BATHS HALF	SQ. FT. LIVING AREA	BASEMENT % AREA	BASEMENT BEDRMS	BASEMENT BATHS	BASEMENT 1/2 BATH	BASEMENT % FINISH	A/C	PARKING	POOL	FIREPLACE	EQUIPMENT	REMODELED	OTHER IMP	HEATING	FUEL	TYPE CONSTR	EXT WALLS	TYPE ROOF	FLOORING	AMENITIES	LEASEHOLD	TYPE OWNER	TYPE IMP	
39A-Y	1111 MEANDERING WY	61,950	V			1-81	Y	7,000	RN			N	P	P	E	1	G	A	G	80	7	3	$36.53	2		1,696	S					C	A2		1	RDG			A	E	F	X	C	C				S	
	1114 MEANDERING WY	61,050	F			12-80	N	11,845					P	P		1				00	7	3	$36.00	2		1,696	S					C	A2		1	RD					F	B		C				S	T
	1118 MEANDERING WY	63,950	F			7-80	N	10,345					P	P		1				00	7	3	$37.71	2		1,696	S					C	A2		1	RFD					F	B		C				S	T
	1202 MEANDERING WY	62,500	F			7-80	N	7,670					P	P		1				00	6	3	$39.18	2		1,595	S					C	A2		1	RD					F	B		C				S	T
	1203 MEANDERING WY	59,950	V			1-81	Y	65X118	RN			N	P	P	E	1	G	G			5	3	$42.55	2		1,409	S					C	A2		1	RDG			A	E	F	X	C	C				S	
	1206 MEANDERING WY	59,950	V			2-81	Y	65X118	RN			N	P	P	E	1	G	A			6	3	$42.55	2		1,409	S					C	A2		1	RDG			A	E	F	X	C	C				S	
	1210 MEANDERING WY	63,950	F			6-80	N	8,360					P	P		1				00	7	3	$37.71	2		1,696	S					C	A2		1	RD					F	B		C				S	T
	1211 MEANDERING WY	60,950	F			11-80	N	13,234					P	P		1				00	7	3	$35.94	2		1,696	S					C	A2		1	RD					F	B		C				S	T
	1214 MEANDERING WY	60,900	F			12-80	N	9,080					P	P		1				00	6	3	$35.87	2		1,698	S					C	A2		1	RD					F	B		C				S	T
	1122 MEANDERING WI	62,950	F			7-80	N	8,335					P	P		1				00	6	3	$38.48	2		1,636	S					C	A2		1	RD					F	B		C				S	T
	1218 MEANDERING WI	62,950	F			7-80	N	9,980					P	P		1				00	6	3	$38.48	2		1,636	S					C	A2		1	RD					F	B		C				S	T
40 -A	730 MAPLE GLEN	65,000	F			1-81	N	7,440					P	P		1			E	80	6	3	$46.63	2		1,394	S					C	A2		1	RD					F	B		C				S	T
40 -D	4749 KELSO	81,400	C	10%		5-80	Y	100X185	RN				P	P		1	A	G	G	78	7	3	$38.60	2		2,109	S					C	A2			RDG			A	G				C				S	F
40 -H	4214 BLUE CREEK	52,500	F			10-80	N	7,050					P	P		1			E	77	5	3	$38.35	2		1,369	S					C	A2		1	RD					F	B		C				S	T
	6025 HIGHCREST DR	54,450	F			12-80	N	8,930					P	P		1			G	76	5	3	$40.36	2		1,349	S					C	A1		1	RD					F	B		C				S	T
40 -K	2713 DOVE MEADOW	56,500	V			11-80	Y	7,172	RN			N	P	P	D	1	G	A	G	76	5	3	$42.61	2		1,326	S					C	A2		1	RDG		PF	A	G	F	X	C	C				S	
41 -J	2229 MEADOW LAKE CR	75,000	V			2-81	Y	96X130	RN			N	P	P	E	1	G	G	G	80	6	3	$46.38	2		1,617	S					C	A2		1	RDG		L	A	E	F	X	C	C					
	2201 MEADOW LAKE DR	97,600	C	20%	80%	9-80	Y	68X 83	RN		V	N	P	P	E	1	G	A	G	80	7	3	$52.00	2		1,877						C	A2		1	RDG		PF	A	G	F	X	C	C				S	
	2613 MEADOW LAKE DR	99,900	C	47%	53%	9-80	Y	80X120	RN		V	N	P	P	E	1	G	A	G	80	7	3	$51.20	2		1,951						C	A2		1	RDG		PF	A	G	F	X	C	C				S	
41 -N	2321 NOTTINGHAM	71,000	V			1-81	Y	90X125	RN			N	P	P	E	1	A	A	A	67	6	4	$38.42	2		1,848	S					C	A2		1	RDG			A	E	F	X	W	C				S	
	2314 RAVENWOOD	92,500	V			1-81	Y	90X110	RN			N	P	P	E	1	G	G	E	71	8	4	$41.84	2		2,211	S					C	A2		1	RDG	R	PF	A	G	F	X	X	C				S	
41 -S	1830 WILDWOOD	89,500	V			1-81	Y	12,316	RN			Y	P	P	D	1+	A	A	A	77	9	3	$38.59	2	1	2,319	S					C	G2		1	RDG		FS	A	E	F	X	W	C				S	
41 -X	1213 DENMARK	65,000	V			3-81	Y	70X130	RN			Y	P	P	E	1	A	G	A	68	8	4	$35.44	2	1	1,834	S					C	A2		1	RDG		FS	A	E	F	X	X	C				S	
41A-C	1211 BELCLAIRE	48,000	V			12-80	Y	100X120	RN			N	P	P	E	1	G	G	A	59	6	3	$41.20	2		1,165	S					W	A2			RH		F	A	G	F	X	C	C				S	
	2314 NORMANDY	54,000	C	5%		8-80	Y	67X105	RN				P	P	E	1	A	A	A	62	6	3	$39.71	2		1,360	S					C	A2			RDH			N	G			C	C				S	F
41A-G	2708 MARTA	57,900	V			2-81	Y	60X105	RN			N	P	P	E	1	G	G	G	78	6	3	$44.54	2		1,300	S					C	A2		1	RDG		F	A	G	F	X	C	C				S	
	2717 MARTA DR	64,000	F			1-81	N	6,118					P	P		1				79	6	3	$45.01	2		1,422	S					C	A2		1						F	B						S	T
41A-H	1729 MEADOW VALLEY	48,850	F			11-80	N	7,875					P	P		1			G	69	5	3	$44.78	2		1,091	S					C	A1			RD					F	B		C				S	T
41A-Y	1805 MAPLE	27,500	V			11-80	Y	55X130	RN				P	P	B	1	A	A	A	55	4	2	$32.78	1		839							H						F	G	F	L	C	C				S	
	1722 MAPLE AV	32,000	F			1-81	N	11,500					P	P		1			F	50	7	2	$17.55	2		1,823	C					C	H		1						F			C				S	T
41A-Z	2309 SHARLIS CR	27,500	V			12-80	Y	50X125	RN			N	P	P	B	1	A	A	A	55	5	3	$29.38	1		936	S						C1					F	A	G	F	L	C	H				S	
41B-B	817 S IOWA	40,500	V			2-81	Y	60X110	RN			Y	P	P	B	1	A	G	G	50	6	3	$31.15	1		1,300	C					W	G2			RDH	HA	FS	W	G	F	A	C	C				S	
	1507 RINDIE ST	52,000	V			1-81	Y	70X134	RN			N	P	P	E	1	F	G	F	55	6	3	$35.04	1	1	1,484	C					W	A1			RD			W	G	F	L	C	C				S	
41B-C	1119 HIGH SCHOOL	65,600	F			11-80	N	4,987					P	P		1			G	80	5	3	$45.59	2		1,439	S					C	A2			RD					M	B		C				S	T
41B-F	100 POSTWOOD CT	53,850	F			11-80	N	9,760	·				P	P		1			G	00	6	3	$40.04	1	1	1,345	S					C	A2			D					F	B		C				S	T
41B-G	1801 KEATHLEY	64,000	C	5%		5-80	Y	37X 87	RN				P	P		1	A	A	A	78	/7	3	$33.88	2		1,889	S					C		P	1	RDX			A	E			C	C				S	F
42 -A	1517 LINDY LN	35,900	F			12-80	N	11,050					P	P		1			G	65	6	2	$30.19	1		1,189	C						A1								F	B						S	T
43 -Z	1922 OLD ORCHARD	78,000	M			12-80	Y	60X135	RN			N	P	P		2	A	G	A	47	8	3	$44.72	2		1,744	C					W	D2					F	F	G	F	X	C					S	C
44 -J	1720 DENNISON	12,000	C	5%		7-80	Y	40X120	RN				P	P		1	A	A	A	40	5	2	$13.71	1		875	C												N	G			C	H				S	F
	1830 MCBROOM	10,000	C	5%		9-80	Y	50X112	RN				P	P	B	1	A	A	G	40	5	2	$11.30	1		885	C												N	G		Z	C	C				S	F
44 -P	1014 TORONTO	10,000	C	30%		11-80	Y	33X137	RN				P	P		1	A	A	G	40	4	2	$12.69	1		788	C												N	G		L	C					S	F
44 -T	319 N WINNETKA	41,000	C	10%		12-80	Y	60X150	RN				P	P		2	A	A	A	20	9	4	$17.55	2	1	2,336	C					C	D2			F	C		A	G		Z	C	H				S	F
44 -W	1936 W COLORADO	111,000	M			11-80	Y	81X146	RN			N	P	P		1	A	G	G	40	7	3	$57.81	2	1	1,920	C					W	H		1	RX		F	A	G	F	X	C					S	C
	1934 KESSLER PY	112,500	C			12-80	Y	85X170	RN			N	P	P	D	1+	A	G	F	48	5	3	$66.49	2		1,692	S					W	C1			RDG	C		A		F	B	B	O				S	C
44 -X	1306 N EDGEFIELD	155,000	K			1-81	Y	92X195	RN			N	P	P		SF	A	G	G	52	9	3	$52.94	2	1	2,928	C					C	H	H	1		XB	F	A	G	F	X	S	C				S	C
	1000 N WINNETKA	72,500	M			1-81	Y	100X141	RN			N	P	P		1	A	A	G		9	3	$32.84	2		2,208	C					W	D2		1			P	X		F	X	C					S	C
44 -Y	1434 LA SENDA	95,500	M			1-81	Y	74X193	RN		W	N	P	P		1	A	G	A	56	4	2	$77.52	2		1,232	S					C	A2		1	RDG		F	A		F	X	C	C				S	C
45 -H	3207 TREVOLLE PL	128,400	V			2-81	Y	43X 79	RN			N	P	P		1	G	G	G	80	5	2	$71.97	2		1,784	S					C	A2		1	RDG		PF	A	E	F	X	C	C				S	
45 -W	507 SABINE	13,800	A			12-80	Y	50X100	RN			N	P	P		1	A	F	F	25	5	2	$14.60	1	1	945	C					W	D2					F	X	G	F	Z	C					S	C
46 -B	4522 JUNIUS	21,000	C	10%		1-81	Y	50X150	N				P	P		1	F	A	A	26	5	2	$21.11	1		995	C									RF			N	G			C	C				S	F
	4321 SYCAMORE	73,500	C	20%		8-80	Y	50X150	R				P	P	B	1	G	G	G		7	3	$48.39	2		1,519	C					C				RDG	C		A	G			C	H				S	F
	4726 TREMONT	22,900	C	20%		11-80	Y	50X150	RN				P	P		1	A	A	A	40	6	2	$19.00	1		1,205	C						D1						N	G			C	H				S	F
46 -C	5511 WORTH	45,500	C	9%		2-81	Y	45X150	RN				P	P		1	A	A	G	36	7	2	$32.66	1	1	1,393	C						D1						N	G		L	C	H				S	F
46 -D	407 GLASGOW	23,750	C	20%		1-81	Y	50X150	RN				P	P		1	A	A	A	26	5	2	$26.81	1		886	C									X			N	G			C	H				S	F
	523 MARTINIQUE	55,900	V			12-80	Y	50X145	RN			N	P	P	E	1	A	G	G	62	5	3	$34.25	2		1,632	C					C	D2			RH			A	G	F	X	C	W				S	
46 -H	602 S BEACON	46,000	V			1-81	Y	50X150	RN			N	P	P	E	1	A	A	G	47	7	2	$32.28	1		1,425	C						D2				C		W	G	F	L	C	C				S	
46 -M	2005 GORMAN	23,000	F			12-80	N	4,680					P	P		1			G	50	8	4	$14.35	2		1,603	C						H								F	L		C				S	T
46 -X	3819 OCTAVIA	11,000	C	10%		1-81	Y	52X 89	RN				P	P		1	A	A	A	42	6	3	$10.22	1		1,076	C												N	G		L	C	H				S	F
46 -Z	4507 ELECTRA	22,000	C	23%		11-80	Y	50X100	RN				P	P		1	A	A	A	50	5	2	$26.51	1		830	C						D1						N	G			C	C				S	F
	2913 HATCHER	22,900	F			8-80	N	6,060					P	P		1				50	5	3	$26.14	1		876	C						A1								F	L						S	T
47 -D	2505 TELEGRAPH	67,770	C	5%		11-80	Y	11,144	RN				P	P		1	A	A	G	57	6	3	$41.20	2		1,645	C					C	A2			RDG			A	G		X	C	C				S	F
47 -M	7334 HUNNICUT	79,000	C	10%		11-80	Y	90X120	RN				P	P		1	A	A	A	69	8	4	$38.86	2	1	2,033	C					C	A2			RDG			A	E		X	W	C				S	F
47 -R	6050 BELGRADE	37,000	C	32%		5-80	Y	61X150	RN				P	P		1	G	G	G	28	5	2	$40.79	1		907	C						A1						W	G			C	C				S	F
	4713 CHILTON DR	84,000	V			11-80	Y	70X120	RN			N	P	P	E	1	G	G	G	73	7	3	$39.57	2		2,123	C					C	A2		1	RDG		FL	A	G	F	X	W	C				S	
47 -V	6211 HOLLIS	45,000	C	22%		5-80	Y	85X129	RN				P	P		1	G	G	G	50	6	2	$32.14	1		1,400	C						A1			DX			A	G			C	C				S	F
	6509 WOFFORD	29,850	F			1-81	N	9,000					P	P		1			F	50	5	2	$35.71	1		836	C					C	A1			R					F	W		C				S	T
47 -W	3700 HANCOCK	26,000	V			12-80	Y	50X100	RN			N	P	P	E	1	A	A	G	59	6	3	$21.38	2		1,216	C						D2				R		W	G	F	W	C	C				S	
47 -X	5231 BARBER ST	9,000	C	6%		1-81	Y	50X150	N				P	P		1	F	A	A	46	4	2	$11.94	1		754													N	G			C	C				S	F
48 -A	8483 SWIFT	36,150	V			11-80	Y	67X115	RN			N	P	P	D	1	G	G	G	60	9	4	$16.48	2	1	2,193	C					C	A2	P	1	RDH		F	A	G	F	X	C	C				S	
	8142 WOODHUE RD	74,900	F			11-80	N	7,667					P	P		1			G	63	6	3	$39.17	2		1,912	C					C	A2		1	RD					F	B		C				S	T
48 -J	5711 MEADOWICK	68,750	V			1-81	Y	65X110	RN			N	P	P		1	A	A	A	64	7	3	$40.23	2		1,709	C					C	A2		1	RDG		F	A	G	F	X	W	C				S	
48 -N	7110 LOVETTE AV	26,850	C	5%		12-80	Y	60X120	RN				P	P	B	1	A	A	A	50	6	2	$25.77	1		1,042							D1		1	RX			N	G			A	C				S	F
	6411 PETAIN	32,950	F			12-80	N	9,000					P	P		1			G	50	5	2	$37.61	1		876	C					C	A3		1						F	A		C				S	T
48 -S	6828 WOFFORD	32,000	V			12-00	Y	50X142	RN			N	P	P	B	1	A	A	G	50	5	2	$32.19	1		994	C						D1		1	DF	C	PF	X	G	F	A	C	C				S	
48 -T	7049 BATES ST	28,000	C	5%		5-79	Y	54X150	RN				P	P		1	A	A	G	54	4	2	$29.54	1		948	C						A1						N	G			C	H				S	F
48 -W	2724 SANTA CRUZ	43,500	V			1-81	Y	65X155	RN			N	P	P	E	1	G	A	G	60	6	2	$24.86	1		1,750	C					C	D2			RDG	A	F	A	G	F	X	C	C				S	
48 -X	2554 QUINTO	37,750	F			9-80	N	7,500					P	P		1			G	58	5	2	$29.77	1		1,312	C					C	A1								F	B						S	T

**THE ABOVE DATA BELIEVED TO BE RELIABLE BUT ACCURACY IS NOT GUARANTEED

FIGURE 1

(*a*) Single-family residential sales data.

KEY TO ABBREVIATIONS

AIR CONDITIONING
C = Central
L = Wall
E = Evaporative Cooler
W = Window
H = Heat Pump

AMENITIES
C = Club House
G = Golf
H = Health Club
M = Marina
P = Community Pool
S = Security
T = Tennis
+ = Additional Amenities

BASEMENT
AREA ___ Or:
F = Full
S = Slab
C = Crawl Space or Direct Access

FINISH ___ y Or:
C = Completely
U = Unfinished

EQUIPMENT
C = Compactor
D = Dishwasher
E = Energy Efficient Items
G = Disposal
H = Range Hood
M = Microwave
R = Range/Oven
V = Central Vac
W = Washer
X = Washer/Dryer

EXTERIOR WALLS
A = Metal
B = Brick or Stone
C = Block
L = Wood Siding
P = Composition
S = Stucco
V = Vinyl
W = Wood Shingle
X = Brick Veneer
Z = Asbestos Shingle
L = Log

NOTE: CODE OUTSIDE RIGHT MARGIN DENOTES:
T = FHA D.C. Tape Data
P = Public Records Data
C = Class "C" Member
F = FNMA Inputs

FLOOR PLAN
G = Good
A = Average
F = Fair
P = Poor

FLOORING
A = Asphalt Tile
C = Carpeting
H = Hardwood
S = Softwood
T = Cement Tile
V = Vinyl
W = Carpet & Wood
Z = Terrazzo
O = Other

FUEL
C = Coal
E = Electric
G = Gas
O = Oil
S = Solar
L = LPG
W = Wood
X = Other

HEATING
A = Forced Air
E = Electric
B = Baseboard
F = Floor Furnace
G = Gravity
H = Hot Water
K = Solar
N = None
P = Heat Pump
R = Radiant
S = Steam
W = Wall Furnace
X = Space Heater

LOT ZONE
R = Residential
B = Commercial
C = Cluster
I = Industrial
A = Apartments
F = Farm
U = Rural

LOT SIZE
P = Pad Area
C = Condo Site
A = Acres
G = Gross Area

OTHER IMPROVEMENTS
B = Barn
D = Open Deck
F = Fence
G = Guest House
H = Greenhouse
K = Dock
L = Laundry Room
M = Sauna
P = Covered Patio
Q = Servant's Quarters
S = Shed
T = Tennis Court
Z = Breezeway

OTHER ROOMS
AT = Attic
AU = Atrium
BR = Bonus Room
DN = Den
DR = Dining Room
EP = Enclosed Porch
FR = Family Room
FL = Florida Room
FO = Foyer
LA = Lanai
OT = Other
+ = More/other rooms

PARKING
A = Attached
B = Built-in
C = Carport
D = Detached
F = Off-site
G = Open
N = None

POOL
P = Pool
H = Heated
I = Indoor
S = Spa
C = Pool/Spa

QUALITY & CONDITION
P = Poor
F = Fair
A = Average
G = Good
E = Excellent

REMODELED
A = Addition
B = Bath
C = Completely
H = Heat
K = Kitchen
X = Kitchen & Bath
R = Rehabilitated

SALE CLOSED
Y = Yes
N = Committed

SITE INFLUENCE
B = Bay
C = Canal
G = Golf
L = Lake
O = Ocean
R = River
S = Sound
V = View
W = Wooded

STORIES
1+ = 1½
2+ = 2½
SF = Split Foyer
SL = Split or Bi-level
3S = Split (3) Level
4S = Split (4) Level

STYLE
A = Colonial
B = Bungalow
C = Cape
D = Contemporary
E = Ranch
F = Tudor
G = Mediterranean
H = Georgian
I = High Ranch
J = Victorian

TYPE CONSTRUCTION
A = Adobe
B = Brick
C = Concrete
D = Dome
E = Frame
K = Concrete Block
L = Log
M = Masonry
O = Others
P = Manufactured
S = Stone

TYPE IMPROVEMENT
E = End Row
F = Flat
G = Garden
H = High-rise
R = Row
S = Detached S/F
T = Townhouse
Z = Zero Lot Line

TYPE OWNERSHIP
C = Condominium
P = P.U.D.
D = De Minimis P.U.D.
Z = Co-op

TYPE ROOF
A = Asbestos
B = Built-up
C = Composition Shingle
G = Tar & Gravel
R = Rock
S = Slate
T = Tile
W = Wood Shingle
X = Wood Shake
J = Other

TYPE OF SALE
A = Assumption
C = Conventional
F = FHA
G = Agreement of Sale
H = Subsidized Federal Housing
K = Cash Sale
L = Land Contract
R = Mortgage Insurance
E = Real Estate Owned
V = State Vet
VA

UTILITIES/WATER
P = Public
C = Community
I = Individual
K = Co-op
M = M.U.D.

SEWER
P = Public
S = Septic
I = Individual
C = Cesspool

Revised 1/80

FIGURE 1 (b) Key to sales data on p. 313.

Questions

1 How would you choose a random sample of houses from lists such as shown in Figure 1?

2 How should Mrs. Bilton determine which one factor is most closely related to sales price? Perform an analysis using the sample data in Table 1 to determine which factor is most closely related to sales price.

3 What is the estimating equation that can be used to predict the sales price?

4 Would you recommend to management that it make data and computer programs available to old and new sales people? Cite the advantages and disadvantages. Recommend a plan for the introduction of these facilities.

5 What other kind of analysis would you suggest?

Case 10-2 Corporate Research and Development (R&D) and Corporate Success

Dr. John Hughes was director of the research laboratory for Telextronics, a large electronics and calculator firm in Boston. Every year at budget time R&D expenditures were the first to be cut if there were any financial problems in the company. Hughes felt that R&D was essential to company development and profits, and was looking for a way to demonstrate this to management.

Dr. Hughes sought out Tom Sesler, a mechanical engineer, who had recently received an MBA. Sesler was commissioned to find data relating to R&D expenditures and to show that these expenditures led to higher profits and a better market position for the company's stock.

Research and development expenditures were difficult to find, since many companies would not give Sesler this information. He did find the following article and chart in *Physics Today.* The article stated:

> Most technically oriented people believe that research activities within a corporation strengthen its performance by leading to new products and by providing leadership to its intellectual life. However, objective evidence of this influence is not readily available. Certainly, no simple "cause and effect" relationships have been found. Indeed, there is no basis for expecting them to exist, because corporate performance depends on several factors in addition to research, so relationships that might actually exist tend to become obscured from view. Also, research generates embryonic activities that take several years to mature. During the long maturation period, the relationships between the original research and the ensuing products become diffused. . . .
>
> Convenient data are provided by the accompanying list of the 50 manufacturing corporations that did the most spending for research during 1976. This list was first published by *Inside R&D,* vol. 6, no. 22, 1977. The stock price/earnings ratios (P/E) for these 50 companies are shown along with their research spending/sales ratios (R/S), and their income/sales ratios (I/S). . . .

TABLE 1

BIGGEST R&D SPENDING IN US INDUSTRY — 1976

1976 RANK	COMPANY	R&D EXPENDITURES (MILLION $)	R&D/SALES (%)	P/E JAN. 4, 1977	NET 1976 INCOME/SALES (%)
1	General Motors	1257.3	2.7	6.7	6.2
2	IBM	1012.0	6.2	17.4	14.7
3	Ford Motor	924.9	3.2	5.3	3.4
4	AT&T/Bell System	643.0	1.9	10.1	11.7
5	General Electric	411.5	2.6	12.0	5.9
6	DuPont	352.5	4.2	13.6	5.5
7	United Technologies	358.4	6.9	6.9	3.0
8	Eastman Kodak	335.5	6.2	17.1	12.0
9	Chrysler	280.0	1.8	3.4	2.1
10	ITT	246.0	2.1	8.1	4.1
11	Xerox	225.7	5.1	10.7	8.1
12	Exxon	202.0	0.4	8.6	5.4
13	Boeing	191.0	4.9	9.0	2.6
14	Caterpillar Tractor	187.9	3.7	12.4	7.6
15	Dow Chemical	187.5	3.3	11.5	10.8
16	Sperry Rand	168.3	5.1	7.9	4.8
17	3M	157.5	4.5	17.2	9.6
18	Union Carbide	142.4	2.2	8.0	6.9
19	Westinghouse	141.0	2.3	7.3	3.6
20	International Harvester	140.0	2.6	5.6	3.2
21	Procter & Gamble	136.6	2.1	16.2	6.2
22	Merck	136.3	8.2	16.6	15.3
23	Honeywell	125.6	5.0	9.4	4.2
24	Goodyear	113.6	1.9	11.8	2.1
25	Eli Lilly	113.1	8.4	14.9	14.9
26	Johnson & Johnson	112.5	4.4	19.2	8.1
27	RCA	111.9	2.1	12.5	3.3
28	Monsanto	111.2	2.6	7.5	8.6
29	Deere	108.4	3.4	7.6	7.7
30	Burroughs	107.9	5.8	13.3	9.9
31	Hewlett-Packard	107.6	9.6	23.0	8.1
32	General Tel & Electronics	105.64	1.6	9.0	6.7
33	McDonnell Douglas	105.60	3.0	7.2	3.0
34	Motorola	101.5	6.7	15.0	5.7
35	Bendix	100.5	3.4	8.8	3.6
36	NCR	94.2	4.1	10.5	3.9
37	Shell Oil	93.0	1.0	6.9	7.6
38	Upjohn	92.6	9.0	13.3	7.5
39	Pfizer	88.1	4.7	12.3	8.4
40	Signal Companies	83.7	3.4	8.2	2.6
41	American Cyanamid	83.3	4.0	9.2	6.5
42	Warner-Lambert	78.9	3.3	13.1	6.8
43	Polaroid	77.6	8.1	14.2	8.3
44	Standard Oil of California	76.1	0.4	7.7	4.5
45	Mobil Oil	75.0	0.3	7.5	3.6
46	Texas Instruments	72.2	4.3	20.1	5.9
47	Celanese	70.0	3.3	10.4	3.3
48	Bristol-Myers	69.0	3.5	12.7	7.9
49	Standard Oil of Indiana	67.1	0.6	8.6	7.7
50	Gulf Oil	64.0	3.3	6.8	8.6

Source: J. J. Gilman and R. H. Miller, *Physics Today,* Mar. 1978.

The top 10% of the corporations in relative income (IBM, AT&T, Kodak, Merck, Lilly) all have strong research programs. The bottom 10% (UT, Chrysler, Boeing, Goodyear, McDonnell Douglas, Signal) have modest programs. The 10% with the largest relative research expenditures (Merck, Lilly, Hewlett-Packard, Upjohn, Polaroid) have reputations as innovators, so their expenditures have indeed influenced their situations. The 10% with the smallest relative expenditures (Exxon, Shell, Standard of California, Mobil, Standard of Indiana) are uniformly the oil companies and have corresponding reputations as noninnovators. Thus the data appear to have internal consistency.[1]

Using this data, Sesler decided he would make a case for Dr. Hughes to present to the top management of Telextronics. How should he go about this?

Questions

1 Plot the relationship between income/sales and R&D/sales. What do they seem to show? Why are ratios rather than absolute values—profits, sales, research expenditures—used?

2 Now, plot the relationship between P/E ratios and R&D/sales. What does this relationship seem to show? Is there a stronger relation between R&D/sales and income/sales or R&D/sales and P/E ratios? Why do you think this might be?

3 *a.* If you have a computer program, perform a regression analysis to fit a line to the two relationships described in questions 1 and 2. What percentage of the variation do these regression lines explain? What is the standard error of estimate for each of these lines?
b. If you don't have a computer program, use a sampling procedure to pick 10 numbers at random from Table 1. You may use systematic random sampling or simple random sampling. Perform the same analysis described in question 3*a.* What percentage of the variation do these regression lines explain? What is the standard error of estimate for each of these lines? Will the results change according to the sample?

4 What other factors besides research and design expenditures might explain high income/sales ratios?

5 What do you think might be problems of relating current research and design/income ratios to current income/sales ratios? Which causes what?

6 After performing the analyses above, what can you recommend to the management of Telextronics? Or can't you make any recommendations?

---

[1] J. J. Gilman and R. H. Miller, *Physics Today,* Mar. 1978, pp. 9–10.

Case 10-3 Strategies to Achieve Growth Objectives for a Collegiate Basketball Program[1]

Frank Broyles, athletic director at the University of Arkansas, sat in his office one summer day, contemplating some strategies for the growth of the university's basketball program. He had just had a conference with Eddie Sutton, the head basketball coach, and Wilson Matthews, assistant athletic director, regarding the Razorback basketball program.

Frank remembered that a little over a year ago Lanny Van Eman, then basketball coach for the Razorbacks, had resigned. During Van Eman's reign as coach, the team had compiled a 39-65 won-lost record. But during that time Van Eman had made basketball an exciting sport for the fans with his "runnin' Razorback" offensive displays. However, for the past 20 years the basketball program at the University of Arkansas had merely existed. It had never been really promoted like the football program. Its budget was skimpy at best. The facilities for playing were below par. Fan interest was never really high. And, as a result, the Razorbacks had won only one Southwest Conference Championship (tied with SMU in 1958) during the past 25 years.

The day after Lanny Van Eman resigned, Frank Broyles met with the athletic committee of the university board of trustees, which happened to be in town. Together they discussed the future of the basketball program. Frank remembered vividly the commitment he had received from the board of trustees to put the basketball program in full gear. The program was to grow—in fan attendance, in facilities, in budget, in coaching and player talent, and in whatever it would take to field a team that would be competitive on a national scale.

Frank recognized that a winning tradition in basketball, just as it had been in football during the past 20 years, was necessary for growth. His first step was to hire a basketball coach who had a winning tradition. After lengthy interviews with several prospects, Frank finally hired Eddie Sutton, basketball coach at Creighton, an independent school in Omaha.

Eddie Sutton's won-lost record as a college coach was a respectable 73%. The previous 5-year record at Arkansas was 35%. If, somehow or another, Sutton could turn that record around, Frank thought that the first strategy of hiring a quality coach would be instrumental in the growth of the basketball program.

Eddie Sutton was a believer in the Henry Iba school of defensive basketball. However, Sutton was also a strategist himself in developing what he called a patient offense. This strategy had won 23 games for Creighton and gave the team a chance to win the NCAA playoff the year before Sutton was hired at Arkansas as the highest paid coach in the Southwest Conference. Sutton pledged to Frank Broyles that he would turn the basketball program around. Most fans scoffed, some forgot about the team, but a few believed that Sutton could do it.

Sutton hired Gene Keady, who had an 80% won-lost record as head coach of Hutchinson Junior College, as one of the assistant coaches. The other was Pat

---

[1]This case problem was prepared by Robert D. Hay, University of Arkansas. It is intended to be used as a teaching tool in administrative decision making. It is not intended to present correct or incorrect administrative procedures. This case was presented at a Case Workshop and distributed by the Intercollegiate Case Clearing House, Soldiers Field, Boston, Mass.

Foster, assistant coach under Van Eman. Together the three of them, with Tom Skipper, a graduate assistant, performed their recruiting efforts.

After teaching defensive basketball with hard-nosed discipline (something lacking in the Razorback basketball teams during the past years), the first year's team had a 3-4 won-lost record at Christmas time. Then, the Sutton philosophy began to take shape. The Razorbacks filled Barnhill Fieldhouse (capacity 5200) for their opener against Texas Tech, the traditional powerhouse of the SWC. They played Texas A&M with a packed house before regional television and won in overtime. During the first year Sutton's team brought fan interest to its highest peak in several years. The team's 17-9 record represented the most wins by an Arkansas team in 17 years. Their 11-3 record in conference play gave them a second-place tie with the most conference wins since 1943 for an Arkansas team. Eddie Sutton was named SWC basketball coach of the year.

Now that the basketball season was over, some additional plans had to be made to reach the growth objectives laid out by Frank Broyles and the board of trustees. Therefore, an informal three-man strategy committee was formed to discuss and formulate the growth strategies for the basketball program.

The old strategy was summarized by Orville Henry, sportswriter for the *Arkansas Gazette,* as follows: You cannot make any money in basketball. Therefore, just budget so much money, turn your head, and hope that losses can be held to a minimum. The new philosophy was to be: You can have a first-rate basketball program anywhere in the collegiate field if (1) you hire a man who knows what to do, and (2) you provide him with the facilities and support required to win. If you are going to spend money, why not go first class, get the people involved, and make money.

One of the first strategies considered by the three men (Broyles, Sutton, and Matthews) concerned itself with basketball facilities. Barnhill Fieldhouse had a seating capacity of 5200. The court sat on a mounting in a dirt-filled facility that was used for football, baseball, and track during inclement weather. The building was 20 years old but was losing its attractiveness. Somehow or another, a facility was needed to hold larger crowds. How much seating capacity should it have? How much would it cost? How would it be financed? Should it be a multipurpose building? Should Barnhill be renovated or should a new building be proposed? What is the relationship between winning and attendance and seating capacity?

Information was gathered from other schools regarding their won-lost percentage and attendance figures. (See Table 1.)

An estimate was received from local architects and building construction companies that suggested renovation of Barnhill Fieldhouse would cost about $400 a seat. Further information was obtained regarding facilities at other schools (see Table 2).

As far as financing of any new facilities, the three men devised a tentative strategy regarding the sources of capital: (1) raise money from the Razorback Fund, a private source from supporters of the University of Arkansas athletic program; (2) get a "grant" from the state legislature; (3) float a bond issue; (4) if any deficit exists, use money from the football program.

Discussion continued among the three men regarding ticket policies. Should prices be competitive with other schools? Should we price at the market or below

SCHOOL	FIVE-YEAR AVERAGE % OF GAMES WON	FIVE-YEAR AVERAGE YEARLY ATTENDANCE
Oral Roberts	84	102,000
Texas Tech	65	97,000
Hutchinson Junior College	81	85,000
Creighton	64	77,000
Baylor	61	74,000
Texas	50	63,000
Texas A&M	55	55,000
Southern Methodist	48	48,000
Texas Christian	48	44,000
Tulane	40	39,000
Rice	37	39,000
Arkansas	34	39,000
MacMurray	24	5,000
Oklahoma City University	65	22,000
University of Nebraska, Omaha	57	13,000

the market? What about prices for faculty and students? What should we do about selling season tickets?

Information was gathered from different schools concerning ticket policies and prices (see Table 3).

Financial data for the various schools interviewed was difficult to obtain. There were only two schools who made a yearly profit from basketball—Texas Tech and Hutchinson Junior College. The financial data estimates appear in Table 4.

The three men constantly wondered if there was a large enough market area to draw from to increase attendance. Razorback basketball crowds averaged around 3000—$\frac{2}{3}$ students and $\frac{1}{3}$ nonstudents. For 13 home games, the average

TABLE 2

SCHOOL	YEARLY ATTENDANCE	GYMNASIUM SEATING CAPACITY	GYMNASIUM QUALITY*	PARKING FACILITIES
Oral Roberts	102,000	10,750	Good	Good
Texas Tech	97,000	10,000	Good	Good
Hutchinson Junior College	85,000	7,500	Good	Good
Creighton	77,000	9,800	Good	Good
Baylor	74,000	10,000	Good	Good
Texas	63,000	7,800	Poor†	Poor
Texas A&M	55,000	7,500	Fair	Poor
Southern Methodist	48,000	9,000	Good	Good
Texas Christian	44,000	7,200	Good	Good
Tulane	39,000	5,000	Poor	Poor
Rice	39,000	5,000	Fair	Good
Arkansas	39,000	5,200	Poor	Poor
MacMurray	5,000	1,100	Poor	Fair
Oklahoma City University	22,000	3,400	Good	Poor
University of Nebraska, Omaha	13,000	4,000	Good	Fair

*From judgments made by the interviewees.
†A new facility is being built.

TABLE 3

SCHOOL	YEARLY ATTENDANCE	GENERAL ADMISSION	RESERVED SEATS	NUMBER OF SEASON TICKETS SOLD	FACULTY PRICE	STUDENT PRICE
Oral Roberts	102,000	$1.50	$2.00–$3.00	4500	$17.50*	$1.25–1.50
Texas Tech	97,000	2.00	3.50	3500	1.00	1.00
Hutchinson Junior College	85,000	1.50	2.00	2500	Free	Free
Creighton	77,000	2.00	3.50	2000	Half	.50
Baylor	74,000	2.00	3.50	1400	Free	Free
Texas	63,000	2.00	3.00	0	Free	Free
Texas A&M	55,000	2.00	3.00	750	Free	Free
Southern Methodist	48,000	3.00	3.00	1000	Free	Free
Texas Christian	44,000	2.00	3.00	500	Free	Free
Tulane	39,000	2.50	4.00	200	1.00	Free
Rice	39,000	2.00	2.50	100	Nominal	Free
Arkansas	39,000	1.50	3.00	300	Half	Free
MacMurray	5,000	1.00	1.00	25	Free	Free
Oklahoma City University	22,000	2.00	2.50	400	Free	Free
University of Nebraska, Omaha	13,000	2.50	2.50	160	Free	Free

*Season price.

yearly attendance was about 39,000 for the past 5 years. Very few people attended who lived more than 10 miles from the University. However, if the drawing power could be extended to a 50-mile radius, a potential population of 200,000 could be reasonably estimated (a four-county rural area). Further information appears in Table 5.

The University of Arkansas had no major competition from college teams. The closest team was located in Tulsa, 125 miles away. However, the University is located in Fayetteville, which has a population of 35,000.

Promotion of basketball in Razorback country was handled by nine radio stations that were connected into a university-sponsored sports network. The Razorbacks had been on regional TV about 10 times during the past 5 years. No actual promotion was ever made to sell season tickets; about 300 were sold each year to interested fans. The state of Arkansas is really known as a football state. As a result, little coverage was given to basketball in the newspapers. Further information is provided in Table 6.

There was constant discussion among the three men as to whether the Razorbacks should play two or three basketball games in Little Rock, 200 miles

TABLE 4

SCHOOL	NET PROFIT (NET LOSS)	SCHOOL	NET PROFIT (NET LOSS)
Texas Tech	$25,000	Arkansas	($100,000)
Hutchinson Junior College	14,000	Oklahoma City University	(105,000)
Southern Methodist	Break even	Tulane	(150,000)
MacMurray	(21,000)	Texas Christian	(loss)
University of Nebraska, Omaha	(26,000)	Rice	(loss)
Creighton	(30,000)	Texas	?
Baylor	(50,000)	Oral Roberts	?
Texas A&M	(60,000)		

TABLE 5

SCHOOL	YEARLY ATTENDANCE	POPULATION OF MARKET AREA	% OF CUSTOMERS		RADIUS OF DRAWING POWER (MILES)	NUMBER OF COMPETING TEAMS
			STUDENTS	NONSTUDENTS		
Oral Roberts	102,000	350,000	20	80	40	1
Texas Tech	97,000	250,000	50	50	50	0
Hutchinson Junior College	85,000	100,000	20	80	25	0
Creighton	77,000	500,000	20	80	25	3
Baylor	74,000	160,000	60	40	25	0
Texas	63,000	400,000	75	25	30	5
Texas A&M	55,000	75,000	66	34	10	0
Southern Methodist	48,000	1,500,000	50	50	30	5
Texas Christian	44,000	1,500,000	34	66	50	6
Tulane	39,000	1,200,000	60	40	50	3
Rice	39,000	1,200,000	60	40	15	4
Arkansas	39,000	200,000	66	34	50	0
MacMurray	5,000	35,000	90	10	20	1
Oklahoma City University	22,000	500,000	25	75	15	8
University of Nebraska, Omaha	13,000	500,000	80	20	20	3

away. The meetings usually centered around the question of whether the university should try to get the support of central, eastern, and southern Arkansas fans for their basketball program, as well as for their football program. (At least four football games were played in Little Rock each year, three games in Fayetteville). Two years ago, the Razorbacks played two basketball games in Little Rock, but the crowds were very sparse and the project was a financial failure. Last year another attempt was made to play basketball in Little Rock. The results were the same—small crowds and financial losses.

As Frank Broyles pondered the situation, he wondered about what strategies to follow to achieve the growth objectives he had presented to the board of trustees.

TABLE 6

SCHOOL	YEARLY AVERAGE ATTENDANCE	NUMBER OF RADIO OUTLETS	NUMBER OF TIMES ON TV (5 YEARS)	NUMBER OF STARS ON TEAM (5 YEARS)
Oral Roberts	102,000	1	7	2
Texas Tech	97,000	6	10	6
Hutchinson Junior College	85,000	2	0	20
Creighton	77,000	2	10	1
Baylor	74,000	2	10	6
Texas	63,000	1	13	2
Texas A&M	55,000	3	12	3
Southern Methodist	48,000	1	10	1
Texas Christian	44,000	2	11	2
Tulane	39,000	0	1	0
Arkansas	39,000	9	10	1
Rice	39,000	1	10	1
MacMurray	5,000	0	0	0
Oklahoma City University	22,000	0	1	2
University of Nebraska, Omaha	13,000	1	0	0

Sam Stohner graduated from Baylor University School of Business in June 1978 and joined the staff of International Harvester. For his first assignment in management training, Sam was sent to the southwest regional office in Dallas. This office to which he was assigned was studying figures on truck sales for the southwestern region of the United States. The region includes Oklahoma, Louisiana, Arkansas, Texas and New Mexico.

To evaluate performance of the dealerships in this region, International Harvester would estimate *market penetration,* defined as the percentage of the new truck market that its dealers had been able to capture. In order to study market penetration, the company needed figures on new truck sales or new truck registrations. R. L. Polk collects and publishes new car and new truck registrations by counties for all states except Oklahoma, where this type of publication is illegal.

Since Sam was assigned to provide statistical information for the branch reviews and national studies, he determined that he would find a way to estimate new truck sales for Oklahoma. Sam found that the truck market in the 1970s was really booming. In 1970 there were 18 million trucks on the road, and most experts expected this to increase to 24 million by 1980. A boom in truck sales in 1972, 1973, and 1974 caused forecasters to reevaluate their projections. It was expected that by 1980 there would be 30 million trucks on the road (Census of the Motor Fleet Market, *Commercial Car Journal,* Chilton Co., 1978). Sam felt that he couldn't expect constant truck sales from year to year; thus, truck sales for Oklahoma could not be predicted by using previous years sales.

The two largest cities of Oklahoma are Tulsa and Oklahoma City. Sam decided that there seemed to be a relationship between total retail sales and sales of new medium-duty trucks for most cities. Therefore, he collected information on new medium-duty (GVW-6) truck sales and retail sales for 13 southwestern cities to see if there was a relationship between the two (see Table 1).

Questions

1   What technique can be used to tell if there *is* a relationship? Use this method. Which is the independent variable?

2   Plot these points. Does there seem to be a relationship? Plot the line that you have fitted to the data.

3   If retail sales for Tulsa and Oklahoma City are $1,940,763 and $2,451,863, respectively, what sales would you forecast for the two cities?

4   Sam's management was not convinced that statistical analysis could provide the answer. His boss called all medium-duty truck dealers in the two cities to find out the number of trucks sold in 1977. The industry figures were approximately 600 for Oklahoma City, 470 for Tulsa. Do you think that Sam's technique provided a good method of forecasting? What is the coefficient of determination? Is this a strong relationship?

5   After you have estimated sales for each city, compute Harvester's market penetration if they sold 53 trucks in Oklahoma City and 36 trucks in Tulsa.

TABLE 1
RETAIL SALES AND MEDIUM-DUTY TRUCK SALES FOR SELECTED
SOUTHWESTERN CITIES

CITY	RETAIL SALES ($ MILLIONS)	MEDIUM-DUTY TRUCKS (GVW-6)
Dallas	6,089.372	1439
Ft. Worth	3,001.395	603
Houston	10,770.053	2380
Baton Rouge	1,117.307	327
Shreveport	1,092.289	210
San Antonio	3,031.834	765
Austin	1,516.653	300
Amarillo	520.261	149
Midland	340.098	150
Lubbock	809.911	149
Odessa	472.615	191
Longview	470.904	146
Albuquerque	1,345.005	241
	30,577.697	7050

Sources: *1978 Survey of Buying Power* and *1977 R.L. Polk Registrations.*

6 Place yourself in Sam's shoes. Make a report to International Harvester management.

7 What are the limits of this technique for the estimation of sales for the entire state? Suggest some alternatives.

Case 10-5   Lemando Computer Appraisal

Gerardo Lan, director of computer services for the city of Lemando, had been asked to develop a computer system for appraising city property for tax purposes. He found that computerized regression analysis to appraise properties was first adopted by Orange County and San Francisco in 1966–1967. The first computerization of the cost approach also occurred at this time, so the era of computer-assisted mass appraisal systems actually began in 1966. Studies of computer adoptions from 1966 to 1976 indicated that it took about 3 to 5 years for a city to set up this type of system.

Lan knew that the city of Lemando would not pay his salary for 3 to 5 years with no tangible results. It was now 1980, and a new city administration would be elected by 1983. If Lan could show some results by 1982, he could count on reinstatement. As he looked at the problem, he thought he could speed up the appraisal process by copying the regression techniques used in other cities. Nevertheless, the problem of converting all property records in the city books for the computer was very difficult. Further study showed that it would be necessary to have different regression equations for the following classes of properties.

1 Single-family residences
2 Multifamily residences
3 Condominium units
4 Urban land
5 Agricultural land
6 Commercial and industrial properties

He decided to ignore categories 4–6 for the present and consider setting up the system for categories 1, 2, and 3 since these were primarily residential and appeared easier to classify. Lan was especially interested to see if there was any difference in the accuracy of computer forecasts between these three different types of residential property. (Accuracy measures are covered in the next paragraph.) Obviously, he would have to justify the use of computerized techniques by showing data on time saving and accuracy. Thus, if he could pick the relationship that promised the most accuracy, he would have a better case for the computerized system.

The assessment-sales (A/S) ratio is the usual measure of assessment accuracy. Lan called his friend Luis Rincones in the assessment office in Maricopa, Arizona, which used a computerized assessment system for all six categories, and asked him if he would send assessment-sales ratios for about 15 properties in each of the three residential categories that had been sold in the past year.

Assume that an ideal assessment-sales ratio is 1. This means the assessor has exactly predicted the market sales value. For tax appraisal purposes, these assessments are usually lowered by multiplying by some fraction, such as .65, .75, or .85 depending on how much tax revenue the community needs to raise. To simplify matters, Lan decided to assume that A/S = 1, using the assessment figures and not the lowered tax appraisal figures. Thus, 1.05 was just as far off as 0.95 (5% above or below ideal).

Rincones returned a list of properties recently sold in Maricopa County. He used full market value for his assessments, so that A/S = 1 was ideal. The table included houses in each of the three categories (single-family, multifamily, and condominium) with the following assessment-sales ratios based on computer appraisal techniques using regression equations. Thus, the numerator (assessment) is based on the results of a multiple regression equation that takes into account such variables as area, number of rooms, lot size, and so forth. (See Lester Real Estate Appraisal case in this chapter.) The denominator is the actual sales price for these homes. The ideal score is 1, since the computer estimate would then equal the actual sales price.

A/S RATIOS FOR SELECTED PROPERTIES IN MARICOPA COUNTY, 1980

SINGLE-FAMILY RESIDENCES	MULTIFAMILY RESIDENCES	CONDOMINIUMS
.84	1.20	.82
1.10	1.30	.91
1.03	.80	.92
1.00	.67	.93
.99	.55	.87
.69	.32	.54
.87	.48	1.30
.78	.97	1.21
.94	.98	.87
.75	.69	.96
.95	.54	.89
.89	.88	
.56	.76	
	1.00	
	.85	
	.91	
	.31	

Lan looked through the lists and found it difficult to compare them. He looked at the following data on the number of parcels in each of the property classes in Lemando.

Single-family   140,000

Multifamily   20,000

Condominium   500

Most condominiums in Lemando had been built and sold in the last year and were very easy to assess since their market price could be used. But the first two types of residences would be harder to assess. Lan wondered about the simplest way to do the study. Perhaps some comparison of ranks would be simple.

Questions

1 Should Lan include the condominiums in his analysis? Why or why not?

2 Because ratios may not be normally distributed, use a nonparametric test using ranks to determine if regression analysis offers better results for a particular type of property, such as single-family or multifamily residences. *Hint:* First rank each parcel of land in terms of its absolute deviation, ignoring positive or negative signs, from 1.0.

3 What type of property should Lan first try to estimate using regression analysis in order to meet the city administration timing constraint? Why?

4 *Optional:* If you wished to compare the accuracy of all three methods simultaneously, what nonparametric test would you use? What parametric test? Carry out the nonparametric test.

FORECASTING

11

11-1 INTRODUCTION
Three Types of Forecasts
Data Sources

11-2 SIMPLE QUALITATIVE FORECASTS
One-Person Forecasts
Panels
Delphi Method

11-3 PROJECTING TIME TRENDS FROM THE PAST
Short-Range Forecasting
Arithmetic Mean
Moving Average
Exponential Smoothing
Exponential Smoothing—Short-Cut Technique
Problems
Long-Range Forecasts
Decomposition Technique
Isolating and Studying Seasonal Variations
Tier Graph
Problems
Finding Trend Patterns
Problems
Studying Cyclical Patterns
Recomposition and Forecasting
Analysis of Forecasts

11-4 FINDING AND PROJECTING UNDERLYING CAUSES
Regression Analysis
Intention-to-Buy Surveys and Indexes of Consumer Sentiment
Plant and Equipment Expenditure Plans
Consumer Purchase Plans for Durable Goods
Indexes of Consumer Sentiment
Econometric Models
Input-Output Models
Leading Indicators and Diffusion Indexes
Life Cycle Analysis

Consumer Life Cycle
Product Life Cycle

11-5   SUMMARY

11-6   BIBLIOGRAPHY

11-7   CASES
Case 11-1: The Effect of Special Events at the Superdome on Motel Tax
Revenues
Case 11-2: American Brewing Company
Case 11-3: Telephonics, Inc.

INTRODUCTION

11-1

Forecasting is an important part of the decision-making activities of the individual, the profit-making business, the nonprofit enterprise, and the government at all levels. Let us look at a sampling of how each of these groups or individuals might employ a forecast.

Think first of how many implicit or explicit forecasts you use to guide your activities. As the fall approaches you buy a new wardrobe. If you live in a cold climate, perhaps you will choose a fleece-lined jacket. Someone living in a warm climate may estimate that she has little use for this garment. Implicitly, you are predicting next winter's climate on the basis of your experience with previous winters. You have not written down the temperature for all the days during previous winters, but you have an idea of how cold it might be and of the duration of the cold (that is, how many cold days there may be). When you try to decide on a career choice, you are making a number of implicit predictions. First, you are estimating how well you think you can handle the academic work involved in the course of study. You have probably also considered what the job market will be for persons with your training.

The company has to forecast future sales and costs in order to decide upon production, inventory levels, transportation, cash, personnel, borrowing, and advertising. The introduction of new products requires estimates of sales and the effects of the innovation on the sales of other company products. Overall planning for the firm by top corporate management requires forecasts of the need for capital equipment, maintenance of saving and investment levels, research and design investments, and changes in capital structure.

Nonprofit concerns have similar problems. Blue Cross–Blue Shield, for example, must estimate the number of claims and their cost for a given time period. A foundation-endowed art museum needs to know what types of exhibits attract viewers and what viewers might purchase in its gift shop and cafeteria. A religious organization needs to estimate population trends to decide where to place new houses of worship.

Similarly, government organizations at the local, state, and national levels need to make estimates of the future. The local government might predict weather conditions to decide about purchasing a snowplow. Population trends will be considered to determine placement of new schools. State governments must estimate welfare and education needs each year as they decide upon their budgets.

On the national level, the government wants to forecast future unemployment rates to determine marginal tax rates or the level of food stamp subsidies. Forecasts of inflation rates are needed to determine monetary policy. Planning for the economy involves predictions of consumption and investment expenditures to determine monetary and fiscal policy. Population changes and energy, defense, health, education, and welfare needs must also be estimated for adequate planning in the public sector. In all sectors, careful planning for the future requires estimates of the future.

Forecasts are often classified as short range, middle range, and long range depending on how far into the future one looks. This is a very relative concept. For the meteorologist, a short-range forecast predicts today's weather, while a long-range forecast may predict the weather for a week. In business, a short-range forecast might be for the next week, month, or year. An intermediate forecast might be for the next 5 years; a long-range forecast, the next 10–15 years.

Since the distinction between long range and short range varies, we have to specify in each forecasting situation what we consider to be a long-range or a short-range forecast. In addition, we may wish to build a forecasting system so that we can compare different forecasts (for example, sales with inventory with budget) to study how errors in one forecast might affect other estimates of the future.

Generally, it is easier to make a more accurate short-term forecast because we know more about things that affect the short run, since many of today's conditions continue into the near future. However, if we are forecasting averages, a long-term forecast may be more accurate than a short-term one since unusual conditions may tend to balance out. Thus, it may be easier to accurately forecast the average temperature for next July than for July 4 this year.

Three Types of Forecasts

To summarize, certain factors vary over time. When these factors affect achievement of our objectives, we try to forecast their future states. Many methods of making forecasts have been developed and used over the years. To present these methods in an orderly way, we adopt a commonly used breakdown of three categories, which has been summarized by Chambers, Mullick, and Smith in the *Harvard Business Review* (July–August 1971). They divided forecasting techniques into (1) qualitative forecasts, (2) time series analyses and projections, and (3) causal models. For each technique, we will comment on its strengths and weaknesses as well as on its accuracy.

1 Qualitative forecasts use qualitative data, such as experts' opinions. They are used when past history is not available, for example, for a new product. These techniques try to coordinate in an unbiased and systematic way all relevant judgments. Some methods of qualitative forecasting are discussed briefly in Section 11-2. Opinion-based forecasting techniques, which include one person's guess, a group's guesses, panel, or Delphi, are the most popular methods of forecasting; however, most companies use several forecasting techniques. A recent study has advised the use of more sophisticated methods (Rothe, *Industrial Marketing*, 1979).

2 Time series analysis and projection attempt to take data from the past and use it to predict the future. Time is the independent variable in these analyses as we try to predict, for example, how the Gross National Product or our company's product sales will vary over a time period. To do this successfully, several year's data generally must be available and ideally the relationships will be relatively stable. Section 11-3 provides a number of techniques for short-range forecasts (one period into the future). Later in that section, we treat some simple methods for finding seasonal patterns and long-run trends. Using this technique, when seasonal and trend patterns have been eliminated from the data, the business cycle aspects of the remaining data may be studied. If seasonal, cyclical, and trend factors can be estimated separately, a composite forecast using all three estimates can be made. These techniques assume that the same patterns continue over time. Thus, if we find that sales are typically low in February, we continue to predict low sales for that month.

3 There are times when it is not possible to say that the patterns of the past will continue into the future. Perhaps technology or basic economic conditions have changed, and thus a business that has been doing very well may start to founder. A *causal model,* which tries to relate variables other than time to business expectations, may prove useful. For example, a mail order firm may find that its business increases over time because of reorders from its customers. However, regression analysis (see Chapter 10) may show that there is an even stronger relationship between advertising and sales. Thus, predictions for the future should use regression analysis, which estimates sales on the basis of advertising expenditure to help predict demand for this firm. Causal factors are discussed in Section 11-4.

A firm may find that its business is very closely related to the state of the economy. Thus, the forecaster may first wish to make a projection for the economy or look at other forecasters' projections. In Section 11-4, some common forecasts and forecasting techniques for the whole economy and for sectors of the economy are discussed. Results of these regional and/or sector forecasts may be used by an individual business or industry, such as the overall demand for stereos or automobiles. Alternately, business and industry may use these technical methods to provide forecasts for their own special needs, such as the demand for a certain brand of stereo or automobile.

Section 11-4 also discusses intention-to-buy surveys and indexes of consumer sentiment. These business capital investment plans and consumer durable purchase plans can give the businessperson some picture of how nationwide markets will look in the coming quarter, half year, or year. The accuracy of these forecasts is a function of the time interval they attempt to predict; generally the shorter the interval, the more accurate the forecast. The indexes of consumer sentiment seem to relate well to actual purchases and enable us to make forecasts about the economy.

Section 11-4 also discusses econometric models, which are sets of interdependent regression equations. These models provide a sophisticated method of relating many factors (for example, housing starts, consumption expenditures, plant and equipment expenditures) to a forecast of the economy. It is possible to purchase forecasts of some of these models that relate to particular industries. Many nationwide forecasts for the economy are based on models of this type.

We will also study input-output analysis, which shows the interindustry flow of goods and services. A company may draw up its own similar charts for the interdepartmental flow of goods and services. The input-output tables for the national economy are published by the U.S. Department of Commerce (see the Bibliography at the end of this chapter). We will also see how national estimates of flows are set up and how they can be used to estimate changes in an industry's sales. The individual firm must then estimate its market share of industry sales.

In Section 11-4 we will also study leading indicators. Regularly charting trends over time and using them to predict the future usually assumes that "more of the same will continue." Thus, if the sales are rising, we have to predict that they will continue to rise. How can one predict when the "turning point" will be? When will the economy start its downward move? Leading indicators, originated by the National Bureau of Economic Research and published monthly in the *Business Conditions Digest* by the U.S. Bureau of Commerce, is a method of finding turning points (see Chapter 1). The indicators may include building permits, average workweek, and new unemployment insurance claims. There are leading, lagging, and coincident indicators. A leading indicator, such as building permits, starts to rise before the economy as a whole starts to "turn up." Thus, a study of these indicators can provide some forecasts of turning points in the business cycle. When we use a regression equation to forecast, we usually assume that a leading indicator is used as the forecasting variable. Delphi techniques may help us determine what the leading indicators are for our own business.

The last part of Section 11-4 illustrates that various types of cycles may be computed in order to forecast sales demand. Demand for consumer goods depends on the stage in the life cycle of the family: a young family is more likely to buy appliances; an older family is more likely to buy a recreational vehicle. Similarly, the life of a product usually follows a cyclic pattern. Replacement of consumer durables also follows a pattern for most consumers. Thus, the ability to chart these cycles improves forecasting potential.

Data Sources

Now that we have reviewed the areas that this chapter covers, we should recognize that our forecasts are only as accurate as the data we use. A first source of data for business is its own records. Past sales, costs, profits, and inventory are all facts that can be gleaned from these sources. Since we are dealing with the individual firm, this is called *microeconomic* data. The firm may then want to explore data for its industry. Weekly indicators can be obtained from industry associations, such as electric power distribution from the Edison Electric Institute, steel production from the American Iron and Steel Institute, and paperboard production from the National Paperboard Association. For information on the economy of a local area, the local chamber of commerce may be consulted. The *City and Country Data Book,* published every four years as a supplement to the *Statistical Abstract of the United States,* gives important facts as well as sources. In Chapter 1, we listed a wide variety of information sources for *microeconomic* data that deals with the economy as a whole. In addition, the chapter on "Sources of Data" by Justine Rodriquez in *Business Forecasting* (Kavesh and Butler) lists many important data sources as well as a suggestion for a small collection of business research data sources. Chapter 14 of this book outlines some computerized data bases that can be purchased for use in forecasting.

We now describe the commonly used techniques of forecasting. While these scientific techniques are a great improvement over "gazing into the crystal ball," there is still an element of uncertainty in choosing the appropriate forecast for the future, and forecasting remains an art rather than a science.

11-2

One-Person Forecasts

For many firms, forecasting is a one-person task performed by the manager. Its level of sophistication varies from guesses based on previous sales to individual consultation with colleagues or consultants. An extension of this type of process is the panel, which consists of a group of people who meet to forecast the future.

Panels

Frequently, businesses looking to forecast the future will gather together a panel of internal experts and consultants. The panel may be composed of marketing experts or, in the case of technologic forecasts, scientific experts. The group is asked to arrive at some *consensus*. Usually, they are asked to forecast long-run trends. The method is relatively inexpensive and usually yields results rapidly. The results may not be particularly accurate because of inadequate time for research, and each expert may use a different assumption. Usually, the panel leader will try to get the group to agree orally to some estimate. There are some social effects of interaction in small groups that may tend to bias these forecasts. Thus, there may be a tendency for the participants to "go along with" the opinion of the majority or of the highest-status person in the group. The Delphi method overcomes some of these social interaction problems.

Delphi Method

The panel method usually does not involve any systematic form of evaluation. If the panel is very large, only a few participants generally have a chance to express their views. In a smaller group, as we have pointed out above, the views of a high-status person or of the majority often sway the other group members.

In the Delphi system, the panel experts may be known to each other, but their individual opinions are anonymous. Alternatively, the experts are not identified to each other. A questionnaire is given to each member of the panel. It might include such questions as:

1 By what year do you think adequate new energy resources will be developed?
2 What percentage of energy resources in 1990 will be renewable (such as solar energy) versus depletable (such as oil)?

Assume that 16 experts answered question 1. The organizer now arranges their answers in order from lowest to highest: 1984, 1985, 1985, 1986, 1990, 1990, 1990, 1991, 1993, 1995, 1997, 1998, 2000, 2010, 2280, and never. The median is between 1991 and 1993; averaging the two gives 1992 as the median. Another measure frequently computed is the *interquartile range* (IQR). These are the boundaries that cut off the lower 25% and the upper 25% of the data points. This range is the middle 50% of the data points; it omits extreme variations, such as 2280 and never. The cutoff point for the first quartile (lower 25% of the data) is between 1986 and 1990, or 1988. The cutoff point for the top quarter is between 1998 and 2000, or 1999. Each member of the panel is now informed that the median is 1992, the interquartile range 1988–1999. These numbers are tabulated from the questionnaire. Alternatively, interactive computer facilities can be used, where the experts enter their opinions and the results are tabulated.

In the second stage, these results are communicated to the panelists who are asked if they wish to change their opinions. Often, experts reverse their views to approach the median. If they wish to maintain an opinion outside the interquartile range, they are asked to state their reasons. Note that the opinions are still anonymous.

In the third stage, a summary of the numbers in the second stage and reasons for views outside the interquartile range are sent to all panelists. Once more they are asked to provide revised forecasts. Usually, the Delphi method stops after three or four iterations.

The result of these repeated rounds of interviewing and feedback is generally that the interquartile range becomes smaller over the period. Experiments were tried in which a panel was asked to make estimates of value when the *true answers were known*. It was found that respondents changed to move their answers toward the median rather than toward the true value. Thus, if the true value lay outside the IQR, it was usually not approached. It was found that if two panels were used—one with feedback and the other without feedback—the panel receiving feedback about the results on the previous rounds made a better forecast than the one that did not receive feedback. Finally, a Delphi panel is more likely to converge toward the truth than a panel that has engaged in face-to-face discussion.

The Delphi technique was developed at the Rand Corporation in 1963 by Gordon and Helmer.[1] It is named after the famous oracle in Greece that was known to give ambiguous predictions of the future. In light of its ability to narrow the range of a forecast and to avoid some of the "band-wagon" effects of a panel discussion, provided that questions are well-worded and the organizer is skillful, the name "Delphi" technique seems to be a misnomer.

At this point, we should discuss the difference between a forecast and a prediction. In many operations management texts, the terms *prediction* and *forecast* have separate and distinct meanings. A prediction is a choice of one particular state that is most likely to happen. The odds for all the particular states that might occur are the forecast.[2] In this text, since we do not always have probability estimates, we use the two terms interchangeably.

Up to now, we have discussed forecasting techniques that are based on people's opinions and have involved little mathematical computation (Mitroff, North and Pyke, Linstone and Thieroff). Certainly these opinions are based on what happened in the past, but no rigorous uniform methods of analyzing the data from the past are provided. We now proceed to time series analysis, which applies a set of selected replicable methods to the study of past information over a period of time, and eventually generates a forecast for the future. A number of these techniques are available, and part of the art of forecasting is to select the most effective technique or set of techniques for each purpose.

---

[1]See C. W. J. Granger, *Forecasting in Business and Economics*, Academic Press, N. Y., 1980.
[2]See Martin K. Starr, *Operations Management*, Prentice-Hall, Englewood Cliffs, N.J., 1978, p. 243.

11-3 **Short-Range Forecasting**

This section and the following one cover short- and long-range time series forecasts. As we explained earlier, long- and short-range periods may vary. However, we assume that 1 week, 1 month or, at most, 1 quarter are the most common short-range forecasting periods for business. In a time series forecast, time is the variable on the X axis. Often, it is easier to predict next year's (total) aggregate sales level than next month's aggregate sales level, because the longer period generally demonstrates less erratic behavior than the shorter period. In an analogous sense, "It is easier to predict aggregate sales for all floors of a department store than for any one floor, because fluctuations in individual departments tend to cancel each other out. Plots of time series, over long intervals, tend to be smooth; over short intervals, unpredictable."[3]

Arithmetic Mean   If we wish to predict for one period into the future (next month's sales or next quarter's sales), a number of simple methods are available. One simple forecast for the future, called the *historic forecast,* predicts the same figures for this year as for last year. Another simple method uses the mean—an average of what has taken place in the recent past, or in the same months in the past if there is a problem of seasonality. Another simple technique is the moving average forecast.

Let us assume that quarterly sales of optical goods for a small optometry firm, Regal Optometry, are only known for 3 years. We will show data for this firm from 1967 to 1981 so that we can execute long-range analysis later on in this chapter. But now we will analyze the earlier years and have enough data to test our results; see Table 11-1. We wish to make a forecast for quarter 1 in 1970. The easiest forecast would be to take the arithmetic mean of the 12 quarters from 1967 to 1969. Thus, we take the average of the available data.

$$\overline{X}_{q1,1970} = \frac{177.7}{12} = 14.8$$

Our forecast for quarter 1 in 1970 would be 14.8. If we look at column 1 in Table 11-2, we see that quarter 1 sales were actually 15.6. If we were to forecast for quarter

---

[3] *Ibid.* p. 244.

TABLE 11-1

YEAR	QUARTER	SALES ($000)
1967	1	13.1
	2	12.0
	3	15.8
	4	11.4
1968	1	14.0
	2	15.3
	3	17.6
	4	13.0
1969	1	15.2
	2	16.4
	3	19.2
	4	14.7

TABLE 11-2

QUARTERLY SALES OF REGAL OPTOMETRY, 1967–1972

YEAR	QUARTER	SALES ($000) TCSI (1)	4-QUARTER MOVING TOTAL (2)	8-QUARTER MOVING TOTAL (3)	TCI 8-QUARTER MOVING AVERAGE (3)/8 (4)	$\frac{TCSI}{TCI} = S$ SEASONAL AVERAGE (1)/(4) (5)	INDEX (SEE PAGE 346) (6)	DESEASONALIZED DATA [(1)/(6)] × 100 TCI (7)	TREND VALUES $\hat{Y} = a + bX$ T (8)	CYCLICAL (7)/(8) CI (9)
1967	1	13.1					97.9	13.4	13.4	1.00
	2	12.0	52.3				101.6	11.8	13.6	.87
	3	15.8	53.2	105.5	13.19	1.198	113.5	13.9	13.8	1.01
	4	11.4	56.5	109.7	13.71	.832	87.0	13.1	14.0	.94
1968	1	14.0	58.3	114.8	14.35	.976	97.9	14.3	14.3	1.01
	2	15.3	59.9	118.2	14.78	1.035	101.6	15.1	14.5	1.04
	3	17.6	61.1	121.0	15.13	1.163	113.5	15.5	14.7	1.05
	4	13.0	62.2	123.3	15.41	.844	87.0	14.9	14.9	1.00
1969	1	15.2	63.8	126.0	15.75	.965	97.9	15.5	15.1	1.03
	2	16.4	65.5	129.3	16.16	1.015	101.6	16.1	15.3	1.05
	3	19.2	65.9	131.4	16.43	1.169	113.5	16.9	15.5	1.08
	4	14.7	65.0	130.9	16.36	.899	87.0	16.9	15.8	1.06
1970	1	15.6	63.0	128.0	16.00	.975	97.9	15.9	16.0	.99
	2	15.5	65.0	128.0	16.00	.969	101.6	15.3	16.2	.94
	3	17.2	66.2	131.2	16.40	1.049	113.5	15.2	16.4	.93
	4	16.7	67.2	133.4	16.67	1.002	87.0	19.2	16.6	1.16
1971	1	16.8	67.4	134.6	16.83	.998	97.9	17.2	16.8	.98
	2	16.5	65.1	132.5	16.56	.996	101.6	16.2	17.1	.95
	3	17.4	65.3	130.4	16.30	1.067	113.5	15.3	17.3	.88
	4	14.4	68.2	133.5	16.69	.863	87.0	16.6	17.5	.95
1972	1	17.0	70.0	138.2	17.28	.984	97.9	17.4	17.7	.98
	2	19.4	72.3	142.3	17.79	1.091	101.6	19.1	17.9	1.07
	3	19.2					113.5	16.9	18.1	.93
	4	16.7					87.0	19.2	18.3	1.04

2 in 1970, after the figures were in for quarter 1 in 1970, we could again use the average of the 13 known quarters.

$$\overline{X}_{q2,1970} = \frac{177.7 + 15.6}{12 + 1} = \frac{193.3}{13} = 14.9$$

Actually, Table 11-2 shows that sales were 15.5 for this period. Notice that thus far we have not worried about seasonal effects and long-term trends. We assume for the present that they do not exist.

Moving Average   We have been underestimating sales. Possibly, this is because we have included 3 years of data points and have given more recent sales the same weights as early 1967 sales. When the arithmetic mean is used, all data points receive the same weight. A look at the data shows that sales seem to have been rising in more recent years. If this is true, a better way to handle this forecast would be to use a moving average. For a 12-quarter moving average forecast for quarter 1 in 1970, we would add all 12 numbers from 1967 to 1969, as we did above, to get

$$\overline{X}_{q1,1970,MA} = \frac{177.7}{12} = 14.8$$

Now, for a forecast for quarter 2 in 1970, let us drop quarter 1 in 1967 and add quarter 1 in 1970.

$$\overline{X}_{q2,1970,MA} = \frac{177.7 - (13.1) + (15.6)}{12} = \frac{180.2}{12} = 15.0$$

We divide by 12 because we only have 12 quarters in our total since we dropped quarter 1 in 1967 and added quarter 1 in 1970.

The moving average forecast for quarter 2 in 1970 is

$$\overline{X}_{q2,1970,MA} = \frac{180.2}{12} = 15.0$$

Now, we make a forecast for quarter 3 in 1970 using the simple arithmetic mean of the preceding 14 quarters and a 12-quarter moving average (see Table 11-2). The forecast, using the arithmetic mean of 14 quarters, is

$$\overline{X}_{q3,1970} = \frac{177.7 + 15.6 + 15.5}{12 + 1 + 1} = \frac{208.8}{14} = 14.9$$

The forecast, using a 12-quarter moving average, is

$$\overline{X}_{q3,1970,MA} = \frac{177.7 - 13.1 + 15.6 - 12.0 + 15.5}{12} = \frac{183.7}{12} = 15.3$$

Looking at the actual data, we see sales were 17.2 for quarter 3 in 1970. Thus, in a case where a trend seems to exist, the moving average provides a better estimate than the arithmetic mean because it contains more recent data. The simple mean might have been better (more information) if there were no trend. A moving average of the previous 4 quarters only, instead of the 12 we used before, might prove even more useful. Using 4 quarters gives us a quarter in each of the seasons in case there are special seasonal effects in the data. Thus, the high sales of Christmas may be

balanced by low sales during the summer. If we try to forecast quarter 3 in 1970 by
averaging the previous 4 quarters, we get

$$\overline{X}_{q3,1970,4\text{-quarter}} = \frac{19.2 + 14.7 + 15.6 + 15.5}{4} = \frac{65}{4} = 16.3$$

The actual value for third quarter in 1970 is 17.2; thus, the most recent average is
a better forecaster for this information. It accounts for seasons and for the long-run
rise in sales (trend).

We have considered two alternatives. The arithmetic mean uses all of our
information in making a decision, but it gives *equal weight* to all data points. The
moving average, which drops one point from the past as it adds a new point, gives
equal weight to all data points used but keeps *dropping past observations* as it adds
new observations. An alternative system might use all data points but give more
weight to more recent data points.[4] One form of this type of analysis is called *exponential smoothing*.

Exponential Smoothing For exponential smoothing, a single weighting factor is
chosen, usually a number between 0.1 and 0.5. This weighting factor or smoothing
constant is called α. The most recent data point in the past is multiplied by α, the
next most recent by $\alpha(1 - \alpha)$, and the next one by $\alpha(1 - \alpha)^2$, and so forth. All
these weighted numbers are added together to determine the forecast. The formula
is as follows:

$$F_t = \alpha D_t + \alpha(1 - \alpha)D_{t-1} + \alpha(1 - \alpha)^2 D_{t-2} + \ldots + \alpha(1 - \alpha)^k D_{t-k} \quad (11\text{-}1)$$

where F_t = forecast made in period t (for period $t + 1$)
    D_t = data for period t
  D_{t-1} = data for period $t - 1$
    α = smoothing constant
    k = time periods minus 1 (the number of time periods considered minus
        the most recent one)

Before we make our forecasts, we first discuss the problem of choosing a value
for α. If we choose an α of .2, then data for our current period will be multiplied by
.2; data for the previous period will be multiplied by $\alpha(1 - \alpha)$ or $(.2)(.8) = .16$; and
data for the period before that will be multiplied by $\alpha(1 - \alpha)^2 = .2(.64) = .128$.

If we had chosen an α of .5, the current period would be weighted by .5, the
previous period by .5(.5) or .25, and the period before that by $\alpha(1 - \alpha)^2$ or .5(.25)
= .125.

The higher the value of α, the more weight to recent data and the less weight
to past history. Thus, a business experiencing a large amount of change should select
a high smoothing constant; a business with a steady situation should use a low
smoothing constant. Table 11-3 shows the weights given to the data for each time
period, using different smoothing constants ranging from .1 to .5.

---

[4]A simple weighted moving average could be constructed using arbitrarily chosen weights that sum to
1, where there is some logical reason for the weights, for example, $.4X1 + .3X2 + .2X3 + .1X4$, or
$.2X1 + .4X2 + .4X3 + 0X4$.

TABLE 11-3

EFFECTS OF DIFFERENT EXPONENTIAL SMOOTHING CONSTANTS

PERIOD	FORMULA	CONSTANTS				
		.1	.2	.3	.4	.5
t	α	.100	.200	.300	.400	.500
$t-1$	$\alpha(1-\alpha)$	.090	.160	.210	.240	.250
$t-2$	$\alpha(1-\alpha)^2$	.081	.128	.147	.144	.125
$t-3$	$\alpha(1-\alpha)^3$	.073	.102	.103	.086	.063
$t-4$	$\alpha(1-\alpha)^4$	.066	.082	.072	.052	.031
$t-5$	$\alpha(1-\alpha)^5$	.059	.065	.050	.031	.016

As we observe in Table 11-3, if .5 is chosen as the weighting constant, the three most recent periods receive a weight of .5 + .25 + .125, or 87.5%. If .1 is chosen, the three most recent periods are weighted only .1 + .09 + .081, or 27.1%.

Now, using data for the 12 quarters of 1967 through 1969, we generate a forecast for quarter 1 in 1970. The most commonly used smoothing constants are .1, .2, and .3. However, .05, .16, .38, and indeed any number between 0 and .99 are possible smoothing constants. Since, for our example, sales in recent years seem to be higher than that in previous years, let us choose .3 for this forecast instead of .1. A given company should forecast with different constants, compare the forecasts to actual data, and then select the α that makes the most accurate forecast. Choice of a smoothing constant is actually an art within a science. Using Equation 11-1, an α level of .3, and the sales data for Regal Optometry in Table 11-2, we now compute a forecast for quarter 1 in 1970.

$$F_{q1,1970} = (.3)(14.7) + (.21)(19.2) + (.147)(16.4) + (.103)(15.2)$$
$$+ (.072)(13.0) + (.050)(17.6) + (.035)(15.3) + (.025)(14.0)$$
$$+ (.017)(11.4) + (.012)(15.8) + (.008)(12.0) + (.006)(13.1)$$

Therefore:

$$F_{q1,1970} = 4.41 + 4.03 + 2.41 + 1.57 + 0.94 + 0.88 + 0.54 + 0.35$$
$$+ 0.19 + 0.19 + 0.10 + 0.08 = 15.69 = 15.7$$

Now, let us review our three forecasts for quarter 1 in 1970: the arithmetic mean is 14.8; the 12-quarter moving average is 14.8; and the exponential smoothing forecast is 15.7 (constant = .3); the actual value for quarter 1 in 1970 is 15.6. Thus, the smoothing technique provided the best estimate in this case. There was an upward trend that could be estimated best using a relatively large value of α. The forecaster might try out these different techniques on past company data to see which one is the best predictor. (Problem 3(b) on page 341 offers an example of this technique.) Of course, this assumes that the pattern of data remains the same over the years beyond those for which the α level is chosen.

Exponential Smoothing—Short-Cut Technique Although the smoothing technique is good because it uses all data, this method requires very long and cumbersome calculation. A short-cut technique can be used after the first estimate is made. The equation for this forecast, which gives the same results as Equation 11-1, is[5]

$$F_t = \alpha D_t + (1 - \alpha)F_{t-1} \qquad (11\text{-}2)$$

where F_t = latest forecast made at period t (in this case the forecast for quarter 2 in 1970)

D_t = actual data for the latest period (15.6, the data for quarter 1 in 1970)

F_{t-1} = forecast made last period (15.7, where $\alpha = .3$)

Now, forecasting for quarter 2 in 1970, we use the actual data for quarter 1 (15.6 multiplied by α) and then add our quarter 1 forecast, which has already averaged all previous data (15.7 multiplied by $1 - \alpha$).

$$F_{q2,1970} = .3(15.6) + .7(15.7)$$

$$= 4.68 + 10.99$$

$$= 15.67 = 15.7$$

Reviewing our previous forecasts for quarter 2 in 1970 and comparing them to the actual value, we have

$$\text{Arithmetic mean} = 14.9$$

$$\text{Twelve-quarter moving average} = 15.0$$

$$\text{Exponential smoothing } (\alpha = .3) = 15.7$$

$$\text{Actual value} = 15.5$$

It will not always be true that exponential smoothing provides the best forecast. When there is considerable change, exponential smoothing provides a more rapid method of adjustment. Now, let us forecast for quarter 3 in 1970 using exponential smoothing (actual value for quarter 2 = 15.5, forecast = 15.7):

---

[5]Starting with this equation, we can arrive at Eq. 11-1.

$$F_t = \alpha D_t + (1 - \alpha)F_{t-1}$$

$$F_{t-1} = \alpha D_{t-1} + (1 - \alpha)F_{t-2}$$

$$F_{t-2} = \alpha D_{t-2} + (1 - \alpha)F_{t-3}$$

Substituting F_{t-1} in the first equation above, we get

$$F_t = \alpha D_t + (1 - \alpha)\alpha D_{t-1} + (1 - \alpha)(1 - \alpha)F_{t-2}$$

Substituting for F_{t-2}, we get

$$F_t = \alpha D_t + \alpha(1 - \alpha)D_{t-1} + (1 - \alpha)(1 - \alpha)F_{t-2}$$

Substituting for F_{t-3}, we get

$$F_t = \alpha D_t + \alpha(1 - \alpha)D_{t-1} + \alpha(1 - \alpha)(1 - \alpha)D_{t-2} + (1 - \alpha)(1 - \alpha)(1 - \alpha)F_{t-3}$$

which approaches our original equation:

$$F_t = \alpha D_t + \alpha(1 - \alpha)D_{t-1} + \alpha(1 - \alpha)^2 D_{t-2} + \cdots + \alpha(1 - \alpha)^k D_{t-k}$$

$$F_{q3,1970} = .3(15.5) + .7(15.7)$$

$$= 4.65 + 10.99$$

$$= 15.64$$

Reviewing our forecasts for quarter 3 in 1970, we have

Arithmetic mean (for 14 quarters) $= 14.9$

Twelve-quarter moving average $= 15.3$

Exponential smoothing ($\alpha = .3$) $= 15.6$

Actual value $= 17.2$

Thus, we have now developed three easy methods for forecasting one period into the future. The arithmetic mean uses all data and weights it uniformly. The moving average only uses the most recent data and weights it uniformly. The exponential smoothing technique uses all data but gives more weight to recent data. Variation of the smoothing constant allows adjustment for rapidly changing data.

Note that one of the problems arising with our data for Regal Optometry is that quarter 3 is always higher than the other quarters. This is a seasonal effect, which we will isolate and analyze later in this section. These three methods—the mean of all data, the moving average, and the weighted average obtained by exponential smoothing—cannot be used as methods for predicting more than one period into the future. In the next section, we point out and explain methods for making a number of predictions for different periods and for long-range forecasts.

Problems

1 Using data on sales of trucks for the Johnson dealership, make a forecast for quarter 1 in 1981 using the following techniques:

(*a*) Average of all first quarters.

(*b*) Eight-quarter moving average.

(*c*) Exponential smoothing using $\alpha = .2$.

1976	1977	1978	1979	1980
71	80	82	80	78
148	155	160	155	153
100	110	115	100	98
76	87	90	85	82

2 The earnings per share of the ETA Corporation for the period 1973–1979 are given below:

YEAR	ACTUAL EARNINGS/SHARE
1973	$3.69
1974	4.15
1975	4.64
1976	4.73
1977	5.40
1978	5.76
1979	8.36

(*a*)   Suppose the forecast value for 1973 was $4.00. Use exponential smoothing to forecast the earnings per share for 1980, assuming a smoothing constant of .4.

(*b*)   Use 3-year moving averages to forecast the value for 1980.

(*c*)   Plot the following for the data presented: (1) actual results (the actual 1980 result was $6.06 per share); (2) the exponential smoothing forecasts; and (3) the moving average forecasts and discuss the differences observed. Which technique is the better forecaster for this data?

3   (*a*)   Using smoothing constants of .1, .2, and .4, and the sales data in column 1 of Table 11-2, make forecasts for quarters 1–4 in 1969 and 1–4 in 1970. (To do this, use the data for 1967 and 1968 with the long formula to obtain a forecast for each smoothing constant for quarter 1 in 1969. From there on, do the remaining forecasts using the short-cut technique.)

(*b*)   For each of the three constants, make a column in which you subtract the actual value for each of these eight quarters from the predicted value. Ignore plus and minus signs and add the numbers together for each of the three smoothing constants. Now, divide each of the three totals by 8. This gives you the *mean absolute deviation*.

(*c*)   Which of the three constants suggested in part *a* yields the smallest mean absolute deviation? Which would you choose for Regal Optometry? Why?

4   Use exponential smoothing ($\alpha = .1$ and .2) and the moving average method to make a forecast for quarter 3 in 1972 for Regal Optometry. Which gives the best estimate?

Long-Range Forecasts

For example, if one has a list of sales observations over a period of years, or information on production over many months, this type of information is called *time series* data. If we can analyze patterns in order to find certain *regularities* in the past, we may then be able to use these patterns to predict the future. These forecasts could involve predictions of sales, prices, future needs, population growth, expenditures, or almost any other dynamic variable. The visual analysis of a time series chart is usually confusing because a number of patterns are mixed together.

Figure 11-1 shows the quarterly sales (black line) of a small optometry firm over 13 years. This curve contains many "bumps" and turns, and is difficult to interpret. We will try to *decompose* this curve into the various basic kinds of patterns that occur in the data. Then, we will study each pattern and formulate a forecast for the future.

First, if we look at the points, they seem to rise over time. Thus, even though there are highs and lows in the 1970s, the points never seem to fall quite as low as they did during the late 1960s. This pattern is called the *long-run* or *secular* or *trend* pattern. (We use these terms interchangeably.) It could be the result of population change, technologic progress, change in consumer tastes, change in the standard of living, or any of a number of other long-term causes. In the optometry business, long-run changes might result from the stylishness of large glasses, the increased use of contact lenses or perhaps, since this graph is in dollar terms, the general increase in prices. Often, it is wise to deflate all dollar amounts by using a price index before analyzing the data (see Chapter 13). This eliminates the effects of inflation. Usually, secular trends are studied for periods of 15 to 20 years or more, and projected into the future. This analysis could also be applied to other types of variables that are measured over time; the results of an electrocardiogram, for a given patient or a group of patients, might be studied over a period of months. We now fit a regression line to this *long-run* data to show how sales increase over time.

As we noted earlier when we studied this data, it seems that quarter 3 is usually the high quarter every year. A pattern that repeats itself every year is called a *seasonal* pattern. The seasonal pattern could last a week, a month, a quarter, two quarters, or a year; it can result from weather, customs, or perhaps the special features of a business. For example, sales in a supermarket may be highly related to paydays. Obviously, it would not be fair to compare the December sales (Christmas rush) of a department store to February sales. We use an averaging technique to *smooth out* these seasonal fluctuations, then we *calculate the seasonal pattern* for a business or industry. We have seasonal index numbers that tell, for example, how much December sales vary from February sales.

There are still other patterns that recur in the data. Even though our economy moves upward over the years showing a *trend* pattern of growth, every few years there are serious downturns and upswings for the economy as a whole. These are called *business cycles* (see Figure 11-1). An individual firm or an industry may also exhibit this cyclical pattern. Sometimes, the pattern of the firm coincides with the pattern of the economy; sometimes it *lags* behind the economy, or perhaps it *leads* the economy. The machine tool industry, for example, tends to start its downturn before the economy as a whole. Similarly, it rises before the economy as a whole

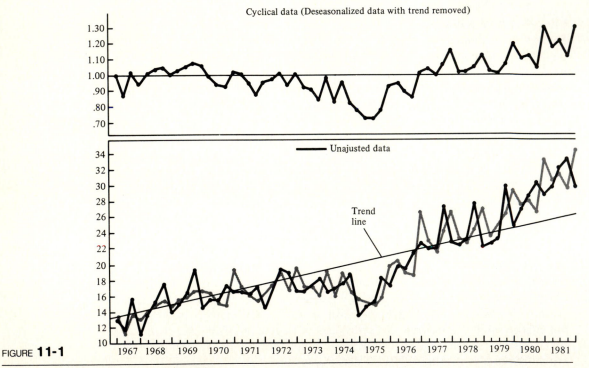

FIGURE **11-1**

Cyclical effects, Regal Optometry, 1967–1981.

rises. The machine tool industry thus *leads* the business cycle. Later on, in the section on leading indicators, we discuss some of the forecasting possibilities involving business cycles.

Karl Marx was one of the first writers to highlight the business cycle. Even though there had been serious "booms and panics" (upturns and downturns) in the economy over the years, classical economists believed in Say's Law—that supply creates its own demand. According to this law, if people didn't offer to buy enough goods, prices would fall until people were willing to buy all that was offered on the market. Thus, even though there might be temporary market problems, there would be no recurrent patterns of economic upturns and downturns in the long run. This system implied that market prices adjusted rapidly, and equilibrium would be reached before any large amount of unemployment could take place.

Using the theory of surplus value, Marx stated that the capitalist would expropriate the worker's share of the product he made. The capitalist would not pay the worker the full value of what the worker produced. Furthermore, the capitalist would not spend all that he earned. Thus, there would be insufficient demand for products. To cope with the lack of demand, the capitalists would seek new markets. They would try to use colonies as markets—hence the term *capitalistic imperialism*. Later on Keynes also pointed to the problem of insufficient demand, although he did not attribute it to surplus value. Keynes showed how government monetary (influence on interest rates) and fiscal (tax and spending) policy could be used to stimulate aggregate demand. In order to use these tools effectively, it became important to predict and to study business cycles. Starting in the 1920s in the United States, extensive studies of the business cycle have been conducted. These studies have led to the development of economic indicators, diffusion indexes, and analysis of industrywide and economywide business cycles. Indicators and diffusion indexes are defined and analyzed later in this chapter. Government economists study these patterns to help set monetary and fiscal policy to stimulate demand.

Decomposition Technique   In this analysis, we assume that our original data contains four influences.

INFLUENCES	METHOD OF STUDY
T = trend (long-run) influences	Fit trend-line regression
S = seasonal influences	Moving averages
C = cyclical influences	Studied as a residual after T and S are removed.
I = irregular influences	Some removed when T, C, and S are calculated; some remain.

We also assume that these elements are contained by the data in multiplicative fashion. Thus, the original data $= T \times S \times C \times I$. We find our data trend, seasonal, and cyclical factors (called the *decomposition technique*). Then, we make forecasts by finding a trend estimate, a seasonal estimate, and a cyclical estimate and by multiplying them together.

Isolating and Studying Seasonal Variations   In order to isolate seasonal variations, we take our original data (Table 11-2, column 1) and make a 4-quarter moving total (column 2). This total of 4 quarters always contains one quarter 1, one quarter 2, one quarter 3, and one quarter 4; thus, when we divide by 4, we average out seasonal fluctuations. One problem is that if we take the average of quarters 1 through 4, the midpoint for the year falls between the months of June and July. Thus, we have placed this total (52.3) on the line between quarters 2 and 3. Later, we use these figures to adjust the corresponding quarter. We need figures centered in the middle of the quarters rather than between the quarters. To center these quarters, we add the totals for the numbers placed between quarters 2 and 3 (q1, 2, 3, 4) and between quarters 3 and 4 (q2, 3, 4, 1); their total is now placed on line 3 of column 3. Note that we have

$$13.1 + 12.0 + 15.8 + 11.4 \qquad = \quad 52.3$$
$$\underline{12.0 + 15.8 + 11.4 + 14.0 = \quad 53.2}$$
$$105.5$$

The 3 middle months are counted twice. This is now a centered moving total of 8 months. Divide these centered moving totals by 8 (column 4) to obtain the quarterly figure. These figures no longer contain seasonal fluctuations. They are year-round averages that cancel out the fluctuations of the various seasons. Column 4, therefore, contains $T \times C \times I$. Note that in column 4, quarter 3 is no longer the high quarter of the year because the seasonal effects have been removed by the moving average. Column 1 contains all four variations: $T \times S \times C \times I$. If we divide each number in column 1 by the corresponding number in column 4, we obtain a number that represents the seasonal effect for that quarter. Therefore, column 5 represents seasonal patterns.

$$\frac{\text{Column 1}}{\text{Column 4}} = \frac{T \times S \times C \times I}{T \times C \times I} = S$$

After we have isolated these seasonal patterns, we begin to refine them in order to build a seasonal index. Now, let us review the steps involved in forming columns 1–5.

1 *Column 1.* This is the original data. We have included sales data from 1967 to 1972 to make the problem simple for computation purposes. We can then use these seasonal and trend-line estimates to study the data from 1972 to 1982 found in Table 11-6. This shows how we can make estimating equations and index numbers and use them to study the future. We must, of course, be alert to test whether these patterns remain stable. In Table 11-6, all the data through 1982 is presented. Since this is the original data, it contains $T \times C \times S \times I$ factors.

2 *Column 2.* In this column, we make 4-quarter moving totals. Thus, if we add the first four numbers (13.1 + 12.0 + 15.8 + 11.4 = 52.3), we put this total in the middle of the 4 quarters we have totaled. (We explain this below.) Now, to *move* the total, drop the first quarter 1 (13.1) and add the second quarter 1 (14.0); our new total is 53.2. Put this total between quarters 3 and 4 in 1967. Then, drop quarter 2 in 1967 (12.0) and add quarter 2 in 1968 (15.3); the new total is 56.5. Continue these moving totals as far as possible.

3 *Column 3.* As we explained above, these totals are not centered in the quarters; rather, they are placed between quarters because we must put the average between the second and third quarters if we average four numbers. When we average the number between the second and third, with the number between the third and fourth, the result is centered just at the third number. In order to center them, we add two 4-quarter moving totals, and put the result on the line opposite quarter 3. Thus, 52.3 + 53.2 = 105.5. To obtain the next moving total, we drop 52.3 and add 56.5; we now have 109.7.

4 *Column 4.* When we divide each of these 8-quarter moving totals by 8, we obtain an average centered on each quarter, from which the seasonal fluctuations have been removed. We have done this to center the data at the middle of the quarter. Thus, 105.5/8 = 13.19, 109.7/8 = 13.71. No longer is quarter 3 higher than the other quarters of that year. Our data now contains $T \times C \times I$. In this problem, we used quarterly data. For monthly data, 12-month moving totals and then 24-month moving totals could be computed; these 24-month moving totals would be divided by 24.

5 *Column 5.* We are interested in isolating seasonal influences and computing a seasonal index. If we divide our original data, column 1, which contains $T \times S \times C \times I$, by column 4, which contains $T \times C \times I$, we are left with only seasonal fluctuations for that period S_t.

$$\frac{\text{Column 1}}{\text{Column 4}} = \frac{T \times S \times C \times I}{T \times C \times I} = S_t$$

There are still some irregularities in this data. You can see in Table 11-1 that quarter 3 in 1967 is 1.198, whereas quarter 3 in 1968 is 1.163. Which should it be? Now, we look at all first, second, third, and fourth quarters and adjust them.

6 *Column 6.* In Table 11-4, we have put all figures for quarters 1, 2, 3, and 4 in columns. We obtain these figures from column 5 in Table 11-1. Sometimes, a figure may be unusually high or low. For example, in quarter 2 in 1970, we have an unusually low number (.969). Perhaps the weather was bad in this quarter, causing

TABLE 11-4

YEAR	QUARTERS 1	2	3	4	
1967			1.198H	.832L	
1968	.976	1.035	1.163	.844	Adjustment
1969	.965L	1.015	1.169	.899	factor:
1970	.975	.969L	1.049L	1.002H	$\dfrac{400}{3.995(100)} =$
1971	.998H	.996	1.067	.863	
1972	.984	1.091H			1.00125
Remaining quarters	2.935	3.046	3.399	2.606	
$\dfrac{}{n}$	3	3	3	3	
Medial average*	.978	1.015	1.133	.869	3.995
Adjusted medial average (Medial average × adjustment factor)	.979	1.016	1.135	.870	Adjusted medial average:
Seasonal index	97.9	101.6	113.5	87.0	× 100 = Seasonal index (see column 6 of Table 11-2)

*We average all numbers except *H* and *L*. If there are only three observations for each quarter, we average the three rather than discarding the highest and lowest numbers and using the middle quarter.

sales to suffer. Since we want a stable seasonal average that we can use from year to year, we wish to ignore any peculiar values that may pull our average up or down. To remedy this, we obtain a *medial* average by crossing out the highest (H) and lowest (L) number in each quarter, and taking the arithmetic mean of the remaining numbers. Thus, we have .978 for quarter 1, 1.018 for quarter 2, 1.133 for quarter 3, and .869 for quarter 4.

In order to convert these numbers to standard index number form where the normal or base period is 100, we multiply by 100. We have

$$\begin{array}{l} \text{Quarter 1} = 97.8 \\ \text{Quarter 2} = 101.5 \\ \text{Quarter 3} = 113.3 \\ \underline{\text{Quarter 4} = 86.9} \\ \phantom{\text{Quarter 4} = }399.5 \end{array}$$

We would like the numbers to average 100 per quarter for a total of 400, so that we can apportion purchases throughout the years. Therefore, we calculate an adjustment factor

$$\frac{400}{399.5} = 1.00125$$

and multiply our index numbers by this factor. Our final adjusted indexes are

$$\begin{array}{l} \text{Quarter 1} = 97.9 \\ \text{Quarter 2} = 101.6 \\ \text{Quarter 3} = 113.5 \\ \underline{\text{Quarter 4} = 87.0} \\ \phantom{\text{Quarter 4} = }400.0 \end{array}$$

Thus, quarter 3 is 13.5% above normal (100), quarter 4 13% below normal. Why is this? In the optometry business, sales are high in quarter 2 for prescription sunglasses. In quarter 3, sales are high for glasses for children returning to school.

Tier Graph   Now that we have calculated our seasonal indexes, we are interested in examining them to see if they look stable. (Does the pattern remain the same over time?) To study this, we prepare a *tier graph,* which compares the spread of the seasonal numbers (column 6) for each of the four quarters. In this graph, we have a base line of 100 for each year. After plotting each of the four quarters above and below 100, we see if the years exhibit similar patterns.

Figure 11-2(*a*) shows the tier graph. We have only two observations for 1967; therefore, we have not charted this year. Similarly, we don't chart 1972. The years 1968, 1969, 1970, and 1971 show similar patterns, with 1970 somewhat different. Its quarter 2 falls instead of rises, and its quarter 4 is higher than usual. Generally, the pattern seems uniform and we can justify using the seasonal index numbers we have calculated for forecasts.

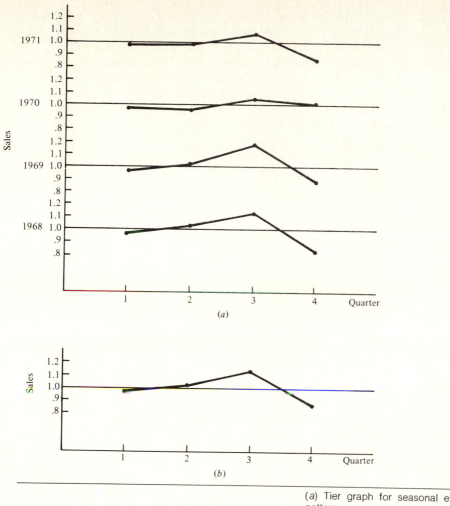

FIGURE **11-2**

(a) Tier graph for seasonal effects. (b) Graph of seasonal patterns.

The tier graph is examined to see if the seasonal pattern has been consistent over time. Note that 1971, 1969, and 1968 look similar, but the 1970 pattern features a sharp dip in quarter 2. Ideally, all patterns should be similar and it would be wise to chart at least 10 tiers. Generally, the pattern seems uniform and we decide to adopt it.

A graphic picture of our seasonal index numbers appears below the tier graph in Figure 11-2(b). We have taken these numbers from our calculation in Table 11-4. Now, in column 6 of Table 11-2, the same type of fixed index number that we have calculated for each quarter is presented. Since our tier chart showed that the seasonality pattern was reasonably uniform, all first quarters are now assigned 97.8; all second quarters, 101.6; all third quarters, 113.5; and all fourth quarters, 87.0.

In column 7, using the newly computed seasonal index, we deseasonalize the original data by dividing the original data (column 1) by the index numbers (column

6) and multiplying by 100. Column 7 now contains deseasonalized data that has been deseasonalized by dividing by our uniform index numbers. This column is preferable to column 4, which was calculated only by use of a moving average.

Seasonal indexes can be used for deseasonalizing data as in column 7. They can also be used for estimating inventory needs and other estimates that take seasonal factors into account. Assume that our optometrist must stock approximately $10,000 a year in frames and lenses and other equipment to service his clients. This equipment can be delivered every quarter. If our optometrist had no idea of the seasonality of sales, he would order $2500 worth of merchandise in each quarter. This might involve costs of borrowing to pay for inventory as well as some storage problems. In addition, in quarter 3, he might run out of inventory and be forced to make his customers wait while he restocked the items. He might also study product mix because in quarter 2 he might need more tinted lenses and colorful frames for sunglasses.

Now, applying the seasonal index numbers, we obtain the following order pattern:

$$\text{Quarter 1} \qquad \$2500 \times .979 = \$ \ 2447.50$$
$$\text{Quarter 2} \qquad \$2500 \times 1.016 = \$ \ 2540.00$$
$$\text{Quarter 3} \qquad \$2500 \times 1.135 = \$ \ 2837.50$$
$$\text{Quarter 4} \qquad \$2500 \times .870 = \$ \ 2175.00$$
$$\overline{\hspace{3cm}}$$
$$\$10,000.00$$

Our optometrist, using index numbers, minimizes the cost of borrowing and helps ensure adequate stock.

Problems

1   Deseasonalize the following quarterly sales figures:

$$\text{Quarter 1} = \$49,800$$
$$\text{Quarter 2} = \ \ 70,000$$
$$\text{Quarter 3} = \ \ 85,000$$
$$\text{Quarter 4} = \ \ 33,000$$

The seasonal indexes computed from previous data are 90 for quarter 1; 120 for quarter 2, 130 for quarter 3, and 60 for quarter 4.

2   (a)   What does a seasonal index of 88 mean?
     (b)   Why is a tier graph used in seasonal analysis?
     (c)   Why is the 8-quarter moving total computed?
     (d)   Why should the quarterly indexes add to 400?

3   For the following data on furniture purchases from the Colonial Furniture Mart, compute the quarterly index numbers using the moving average method.

YEAR	QUARTER	SALES ($)
1973	1	174
	2	274
	3	240
	4	310
1974	1	183
	2	269
	3	230
	4	320
1975	1	170
	2	280
	3	250
	4	330
1976	1	160
	2	270
	3	200
	4	325

4 (*a*) Use exponential smoothing with an α of .2 (use the long method) and moving average techniques to make a forecast for quarter 1 in 1977 for the data in problem 3. For the moving average, use a 12-quarter average. Now, calculate an average of the quarter 1 values.

(*b*) Adjust your moving average (12-quarter) and exponential smoothing estimates using the index number for quarter 1 computed in problem 3.

5 Index numbers for monthly sales of the Spaghetti Store are as follows, starting in January: 80, 90, 100, 100, 110, 90, 85, 70, 110, 125, 145, and 95.

If 2400 pounds of Parmesan cheese and 6000 pounds of super spaghetti are sold annually, how much should be purchased to stock the store each month?

6 Write in outline form the steps you would follow to compute seasonal indexes. (There should be at least 10 steps.)

Finding Trend Patterns As we look at the data in Figure 11-1, there seems to be a general upward movement of sales for Regal Optometry over the 15 years covered. It would be useful if we could fit a straight or even a curved line to this long-run pattern. Then, we could use that line to forecast future sales amounts.

In Chapter 10 we developed a technique to fit a unique line (the least-squares regression line) about which the sum of the squared deviations is a minimum. In this analysis, our independent variable X is time and our dependent variable Y is sales.

We now fit the regression line $\hat{Y} = a + bX$, using our formulas for a and b from Chapter 10.

$$a = \bar{Y} - b\bar{X}$$

$$b = \frac{\Sigma XY - n\bar{X}\bar{Y}}{\Sigma X^2 - n\bar{X}^2}$$

When fitting a regression line to time series data, one must specify the time units (units in which X is measured). In this problem, X is measured in quarters. Also, the origin of the line (the time period for which X is 0), should be specified so that the reader can know where to start computing the forecast values. If we let quarter 1 in 1967 equal 0, quarter 2 will equal 1 and quarter 3 will equal 2. We should remember these assigned values when we make estimates and interpret the results. The computation is shown in Table 11-5. We compute our regression equation on the basis of sales from which we have removed seasonal effects, and estimate long-run effects. Removal of seasonal ups and downs makes it easier to see if there is a long-range pattern. For this equation we should state both origin and time units.

$$\hat{Y} = 13.403 + .215(X)$$

$$\text{Origin} = \text{quarter 1 in 1967}$$

$$\text{Time units} = \text{quarters}$$

If we wish to make a forecast for the quarter 2 in 1973, the value of X that we would substitute in the equation would be 25.

TABLE 11-5

FITTING A LEAST-SQUARES REGRESSION LINE TO THE REGAL OPTOMETRY DATA

YEAR	X	DESEASONALIZED SALES Y*	XY	X²	EQUATION†
1967‡	0	13.4	0	0	$a = \bar{Y} - b\bar{X}$
	1	11.8	11.8	1	
	2	13.9	27.8	4	
	3	13.1	39.3	9	$b = \dfrac{\Sigma XY - n\bar{X}\bar{Y}}{\Sigma X^2 - n\bar{X}^2}$
1968	4	14.3	57.2	16	
	5	15.1	75.5	25	
	6	15.5	93.0	36	$\Sigma X = 276 \quad \bar{X} = \dfrac{276}{24} = 11.5$
	7	14.9	104.3	49	
1969	8	15.5	124.0	64	
	9	16.1	144.9	81	$\Sigma Y = 380.9 \quad \bar{Y} = \dfrac{380.9}{24} = 15.871$
	10	16.9	169.0	100	
	11	16.9	185.9	121	
1970	12	15.9	190.8	144	$a = 15.871 - b(11.5)$
	13	15.3	198.9	169	
	14	15.2	212.8	196	$b = \dfrac{4627.1 - (24)(11.5)(15.871)}{4324 - (24)(132.25)}$
	15	19.2	288.0	225	
1971	16	17.2	275.2	256	
	17	16.2	275.4	289	$= \dfrac{4627.1 - 4380.4}{4324 - 3174}$
	18	15.3	275.4	324	
	19	16.6	315.4	361	
1972	20	17.4	348.0	400	$= \dfrac{246.704}{1150} = .2145$
	21	19.1	401.1	441	
	22	16.9	371.8	484	
	23	19.2	441.6	529	$a = 15.871 - .2145(11.5) = 13.404$
	276	380.9	4627.1	4324	
	ΣX	ΣY	ΣXY	ΣX^2	$\hat{Y} = 13.404 + .215(X)$
					Units = Quarters
					Origin = Q_1 1967

* This data is taken from column 7 in Table 11-2.
† Note that in Chapter 14 we show a computer printout from an SPSS program that obtains this equation. The coefficients in the SPSS program are slightly different because the computer does not round off at three digits, as we have done here.
‡ The origin is the value of Y (sales) at the very beginning ($X = 0$); therefore, let the first time period analyzed, quarter 1 in 1967, be 0.

$$\hat{Y} = 13.403 + .215(25)$$

$$\hat{Y} = 18.778$$

Now, if we wish to adjust this for seasonal factors, our seasonal index for quarter 2 is 1.016. Multiplying our number 18.778 by 1.016, we obtain 19.078.

We now have a forecast that includes long-run time trends, as well as seasonal factors. Using the trend equation, and substituting the X value for each time period, we enter column 8 in Table 11-2; this calculates the trend values for each quarter from 1967 to 1972. For example, if we calculate a value for quarter 4 in 1970, we have $\hat{Y} = 13.402 + .215(15) = 16.6$.

Problems

1 Assume that a trend forecast equation for Dr. Fargo's large liver pills is $\hat{Y} = 300 + 10X$; the origin is January 1980; X is in 1-month intervals; and Y is number of cases sold.

    (*a*) What is the forecast for January 1981?

    (*b*) What is the forecast for June 1981?

    (*c*) What is the forecast for January 1985?

2 You find out that the liver pill business in problem 1 is seasonal. The seasonal index is 175 for January and 90 for June. Adjust your forecasts in problem 1 to account for these seasonal factors.

3 Sales of quart bottles of soda in the United States have shown the following pattern over the decades. Fit a regression line to this data.

YEAR	NUMBER OF BOTTLES (MILLIONS)
1930	20
1940	36
1950	59
1960	80
1970	110
1980	128

    (*a*) Predict sales for 1985 and 1990.

    (*b*) Why is the data expressed in terms of number of bottles rather than in dollar sales?

4 Nipak Fertilizer did a study of the seasonality of its business and found the following quarterly figures after using moving averages. Construct index numbers for these quarters.

    (*a*) Compute the seasonal index numbers for each of the quarters.

YEAR	QUARTER 1	QUARTER 2	QUARTER 3	QUARTER 4
1977	—	—	1.008	1.065
1978	1.001	.929	1.005	1.063
1979	1.015	.933	.991	1.064
1980	1.014	.932	.989	1.062
1981	1.021	.934	.981	1.064

(*b*) If the equation for long-term trend is $\hat{Y} = 15.43 + .2X$, the origin is quarter 1 in 1979, and the units are quarters, make a forecast for quarter 2 in 1984 using trend and seasonal factors.

5 The trend line for sales of Heebie Jeebies Fur Boots is $\hat{Y} = 400 + 72.3X$, the origin is January 1975, and X is the monthly units. The monthly seasonal indexes starting in January are 120, 130, 110, 80, 90, 110, 70, 80, 100, 105, 100, and 105.

(*a*) Estimate sales for May 1982. Justify the forecast by showing all steps.

(*b*) Discuss how this forecast could be improved using the original raw data or other outside data sources.

6 Predict sales for Regal Optometry for quarters 1, 2, 3, and 4 in 1979 (see Table 11-2).

Studying Cyclical Patterns If we divide each of the deseasonalized values in Table 11-2, column 7 ($T \times C \times I$) by the corresponding trend values in column 8, cyclical values with some irregularities will remain. $(T \times C \times I)/T = C \times I$. Column 9, therefore divides column 7 values by column 8 values to arrive at cyclical values. If we wish to study the business cycle, more than these 6 years of data are needed to have a pattern. Table 11-6 presents data for the optical company through 1979. Projecting the trend equation through the end of 1981, and using the quarterly seasonal values already calculated, it is possible to compute column 9—cyclical values through 1981 (see column 5 in Table 11-6).

TABLE 11-6
QUARTERLY SALES OF REGAL OPTOMETRY, 1967–1981 (Rounded to one decimal place)

YEAR	QUARTER	(1) SALES ($TSCI$)	(2) SEASONAL INDEX (S)	(3) DESEASONALIZED SALES [(1)/(2)] 100 (TCI)	(4) TREND ESTIMATES (T)	(5) CYCLICAL (3)/(4) (CI)
1967	1	13.1	97.9	13.4	13.4	1.00
	2	12.0	101.6	11.8	13.6	.87
	3	15.8	113.5	13.9	13.8	1.01
	4	11.4	87.0	13.1	14.0	.94
1968	1	14.0	97.9	14.3	14.3	1.01
	2	15.3	101.6	15.1	14.5	1.04
	3	17.6	113.5	15.5	14.7	1.05
	4	14.0	87.0	14.9	14.9	1.00
1969	1	15.2	97.9	15.5	15.1	1.03
	2	16.4	101.6	16.1	15.3	1.05
	3	19.2	113.5	16.9	15.5	1.08
	4	14.7	87.0	16.9	15.8	1.06
1970	1	15.6	97.9	15.9	16.0	.99
	2	15.5	101.6	15.3	16.2	.94
	3	17.2	113.5	15.2	16.4	.93
	4	16.7	87.0	19.2	16.6	1.16
1971	1	16.8	97.9	17.2	16.8	1.02
	2	16.5	101.6	16.2	17.1	.95
	3	17.4	113.5	15.3	17.3	.88
	4	14.4	87.0	16.6	17.5	.95
1972	1	17.0	97.9	17.4	17.7	.98
	2	19.4	101.6	19.1	17.9	1.07
	3	19.2	113.5	16.9	18.1	.93
	4	16.7	87.0	19.2	18.3	1.04

TABLE 11-6

QUARTERLY SALES OF REGAL OPTOMETRY, 1967–1981 (Rounded to one decimal place) (*Continued*)

YEAR	QUARTER	(1) SALES (TSCI)	(2) SEASONAL INDEX (S)	(3) DESEASONALIZED SALES (1)/(2)100 (*TCI*)	(4) TREND ESTIMATES (*T*)	(5) CYCLICAL (3)/(4) (*C*)
1973	1	16.7	97.9	17.1	18.6	.92
	2	17.4	101.6	17.1	18.8	.91
	3	18.1	113.5	16.0	19.0	.84
	4	16.7	87.0	19.2	19.2	1.00
1974	1	15.7	97.9	16.0	19.4	.82
	2	19.1	101.6	18.8	19.6	.96
	3	18.8	113.5	16.6	19.9	.83
	4	13.5	87.0	15.5	20.1	.77
1975	1	14.4	97.9	14.7	20.3	.72
	2	15.0	101.6	14.8	20.5	.72
	3	18.1	113.5	15.9	20.7	.77
	4	17.1	87.0	19.7	20.9	.94
1976	1	20.0	97.9	20.4	21.1	.96
	2	19.6	101.6	19.3	21.4	.90
	3	21.4	113.5	18.9	21.6	.87
	4	22.9	87.0	26.3	21.8	1.21
1977	1	22.5	97.9	23.0	22.0	1.05
	2	22.6	101.6	22.2	22.2	1.00
	3	27.3	113.5	24.1	22.4	1.07
	4	23.1	87.0	26.6	22.6	1.17
1978	1	22.9	97.9	23.4	22.9	1.02
	2	24.0	101.6	23.6	23.1	1.02
	3	27.8	113.5	24.5	23.3	1.05
	4	23.4	87.0	26.9	23.5	1.14
1979	1	23.9	97.9	24.4	23.7	1.03
	2	24.2	101.6	24.4	23.9	1.01
	3	29.9	113.5	26.3	24.2	1.08
	4	25.6	87.0	29.4	24.4	1.20
1980	1	27.0	97.9	27.6	24.6	1.11
	2	28.9	101.6	28.4	24.8	1.14
	3	30.2	113.5	26.6	25.0	1.06
	4	29.0	87.0	33.3	25.2	1.31
1981	1	30.0	97.9	30.6	25.4	1.19
	2	32.3	101.6	31.8	25.7	1.23
	3	33.4	113.5	29.4	25.9	1.13
	4	30.0	87.0	34.5	26.1	1.32

The low point of the cycle is called a *trough;* the high point is called a *peak.* The length of a cycle is measured by the time it takes to go from peak to peak or from trough to trough (see Figure 11-3). Note that seasonal effects take place within a year, whereas cycles last longer. The length of cycles can vary tremendously. Economists have pointed to short-term cycles (3–7 years), Kuznets cycles (15–25 years), and Kondratieff cycles (45–60 years). The short-term cycle is thought to arise from employment and inventory adjustments in the durables sectors, while the two longer cycles arise from capital equipment and capital investment fluctuations. These cycles run concurrently; thus, it would be useful to trace where the economy is in each of the cycles in order to make a forecast.

In Figure 11-3, interval *A* to *B* is the time from peak to peak; interval *C* to *D,* the time from trough to trough. The time from peak to peak is called the *duration*

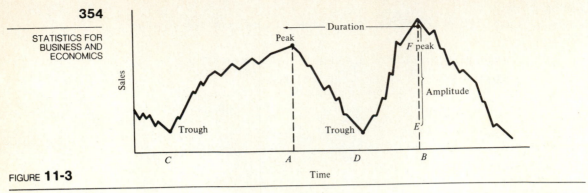

FIGURE **11-3**

Business cycle chart.

of the cycle. The distance on the Y axis from the top of the cycle to the trough is called the *amplitude of the cycle E* to *F.* Often, it is not easy to determine peaks and troughs without 15 to 20 years of data, since some cycles last longer than others. In this example, we have 15 years of information. The peaks seem to be in quarter 3 in 1970 and quarter 3 in 1976. Thus, the *duration* of this cycle might be approximately 6 years from peak to peak. A forecast for 1983 might assume that one was still not too far from the peak, although this data is difficult to analyze. A second measure of the cycle, the *amplitude,* measures the depth of the valleys and the height of the peaks. For Regal Optometry, the variation ranges from .72 to 1.22 over 15 years (see column 5, Table 11-6). Thus, variations are about 20 to 30% above or below normal at the peaks and troughs of the cycle (see Figure 11-3). It would now be valuable to compare the cycle of this business to the overall business cycle. This information can be found in *Business Cycle Indicators,* published by the U.S. Department of Commerce. This comparison enables us to determine if the optometry business is a forerunner of the general business cycle or if it runs parallel to the general cycle. In addition, we may wish to relate the cyclical activities of the optometry business to the apparel business, since glasses are a style-related item. Trade publications often supply this type of data. This relationship may be used to forecast sales in the optometry business.

Recomposition and Forecasting   Putting together our seasonal, cyclical, and trend data, let us attempt a forecast for quarter 2 in 1981. First, the seasonal index number for quarter 2 will be 101.6 (see Figure 11-3). If quarter 1 in 1967 is time period 0, quarter 2 in 1981 will be time period 57, since quarter 2 in 1981 is 57 time periods removed from quarter 1 in 1967, the origin of our equation. Using the regression equation,

$$\hat{Y} = 13.402 + .215X$$

we substitute 57 for X.

$$\hat{Y} = 13.402 + .215(57) = 25.657.$$

Now, looking at the cyclical chart, if we think this might be a 6-year cycle, possibly by quarter 2 in 1981 the cycle will be above normal and the value will be about 1.20. We make this rough esimate by repeating the patterns of previous years on the graph and measuring by eye what the pattern is in 1981. This is only a rough estimate and a demonstration of some of the problems of forecasting. Using the seasonal, trend, and cyclical factors, we obtain

Seasonal index decimal form		Trend forecast		Cyclical forecast	
1.016	×	25.657	×	1.20	= 31.28

as a forecast for quarter 2 in 1981.

This method of analysis of time series data is called *decomposition* (to obtain trend, seasonal, and cyclical factors). The prediction executed above is called *recomposition,* since we have put together three factors to make our forecast. The method is simple and adequate for many purposes.

Analysis of Forecasts   In this problem, we had 15 years of data (1967–1981), yet we based our forecast on the first 6 years. This enables us to test our forecasting ability on known data. For example, our forecast for quarter 2 in 1981 was 31.28; the actual data for the period was 32.3. The error was approximately 1.0 (rounding 31.28 to 31.3), which is 3% of 32.3. Thus, we were able to estimate within 3% of our actual sales. Note that much of our success resulted from choosing a good estimate of the business cycle (1.20). If we assumed that the cycle would turn down to .80, for example, our estimate would have been 20.85, which would have been (32.3 − 20.9)/32.3 = .35, an error of 35%.

Perhaps we would have also noted that our trend equation in this analysis was not rising quickly enough. We could then compute the equation on the basis of 15 years of data or, if there was a change in the last 6 years, for example, we would fit a regression line based on these last 6 years. This is where forecasting becomes an art, and the good forecaster constantly studies the data and watches for shifts. It is very important to plot data points to watch for changes. In studying the trend, a plot of deseasonalized data points might make it easier to observe trend changes. Watch also that seasonality patterns don't change; this can be observed by making the tier charts suggested previously.

Cyclical factors can be plotted after they are isolated from the data (column 5 in Table 11-6). These may reveal a pattern. The good forecaster must try to predict the turning points in these cycles. A study of causal factors and predictors of business cycles used for the economy as a whole (econometric models, leading indicators), as well as forecasts for particular industries (input-output analysis, consumer sentiment indexes, life cycle analysis), may provide useful ways to anticipate future business patterns.

FINDING AND PROJECTING UNDERLYING CAUSES

Regression Analysis

11-4

When we studied regression analysis in Chapter 10, we related sales and advertising for a mail order firm. Using the equation we had computed, it was possible to predict sales for a given level of advertising. This technique can be a powerful forecasting tool, especially for this mail order firm where $R^2 = .96$, signifying a very strong relationship between advertising and sales.

Advertising is not the only variable that can be used to forecast sales; a jewelry firm, for example, might look at the state of the economy. Since jewelry is a luxury item, sales might relate to the regional or national level of employment or to changes in the gross national product.

Multiple regression employing two or more independent variables to predict sales or profits could be used. Thus, the jeweler may wish to forecast sales with a multiple regression equation that uses advertising and expected change in gross national product as independent variables.

Intention-to-Buy Surveys and Indexes of Consumer Sentiment

Plant and Equipment Expenditure Plans   Polling or survey techniques have been used on a nationwide basis to evaluate business plant and equipment expenditure plans. The U.S. Department of Commerce–Securities and Exchange Commission survey is published quarterly in the *Survey of Current Business,* which can be found in most libraries.[6] McGraw-Hill publishes a survey of plant and equipment expenditure intentions twice a year in *Business Week,* which is available on newstands. The McGraw-Hill survey focuses on large firms, while the Department of Commerce survey is somewhat more comprehensive. The Conference Board publishes a survey of capital appropriations (commitment by the board of directors to make a capital outlay in the near future) of 1000 manufacturing firms in the *Conference Board Record Monthly* (available in most libraries) and the *Survey of Current Business.*

Consumer Purchase Plans for Durable Goods   In addition to surveys of capital investments intended by businesses, the intentions of consumers to invest in durable goods (cars, refrigerators, stoves, washing machines, and other large goods having usage lifetimes of more than a year) are charted by a number of organizations. These include the Survey Research Center of the University of Michigan (since 1947), the Conference Board (since 1967), and the Albert Sindlinger Company (since 1959) private survey, which is available in *Business Record,* a publication of The Conference Board. Consumers' Union publishes an annual report on the buying intentions of its members. The U.S. Bureau of the Census also publishes in *Current Population Reports* series P-65 "Consumer Buying Indicators." Since 1976, the Gallup Organization has published an index of consumer attitudes.

Indexes of Consumer Sentiment   Another type of measure that can be made from a consumer survey is an index of consumer sentiment. Consumer responses to questions on their personal finances now and a year from now, business conditions now and during the next 5 years, as well as responses on whether it is a good or bad time to buy durables, are used as the basis for the Survey Research Center's index of consumer sentiment. This data is used to predict the state of the economy and consumer durable spending, or it may be used as input for obtaining forecasts from econometric models. The theory is that discretionary spending (as opposed to rent, basic foods, etc.) increases with favorable consumer attitudes. Durable goods spending is considered discretionary spending since most of these purchases can be post-

---

[6]The bibliography at the end of this chapter furnishes the addresses of the agencies or companies that provide these statistical sources. Most sources can be found in university and public libraries.

poned. The index of consumer sentiment is especially useful because changes in attitude can be used to forecast turning points.

How do these consumer intentions-to-purchase surveys work? How successful are they at forecasting purchases?

In intention-to-buy surveys, a sample of heads of households are asked if they plan to buy selected items (durable goods) in the next 6, 12, 18, or 24 months. A follow-up survey may be used to see if consumers actually purchased what they had stated. Buying expectations can be related to nationwide purchases, and generally they have forecasted purchases fairly well.

Revisions that have been suggested to improve the predictive power of these surveys are evaluation of plans to buy using a probability scale.[7] In this system, the consumer evaluates the probability that he or she will buy a given consumer durable. Thus, the consumer who is 90% sure he or she will buy receives a higher weighting than the consumer who is 60% sure. The forecaster predicts the number of washing machines that will be purchased if one consumer is 90% sure, another 60% sure, and another 50% sure. It might be estimated that for the three people (.9 + .6 + .5), two machines will be purchased. In addition to the use of probabilities, Maynes suggests that different groups of people are more likely to be extremely optimistic or pessimistic regardless of the questions asked. Thus, if high-income people tend to be overly optimistic, an estimate of .9 probability of buying might be reduced to .7. Or, if an ethnic group is very pessimistic about purchase plans and gives a value of .2 for the probability of buying, this might be weighted as .4. In order to add all the responses of different people, it would be useful to find a way to account for and calibrate these interpersonal differences. These suggestions for revision are only in the experimental stage at present.

The predictions from these consumer buying surveys are nationwide. An individual firm might be able to forecast its own demand based on its estimated share of predicted nationwide demand, or it may set up its own market research for its product lines.

Econometric Models

An econometric model draws upon economics, mathematics, statistics, and accounting to set up a system of interdependent regression equations to describe the total economy (changes in consumption, income, housing, investment, plant and equipment expenditures) or a specific business (changes in demand, labor cost, capital costs). Once the equations have been formulated and values for the coefficients (a, b, and c, for example) have been calculated, values are substituted for each of the variables on the right-hand side (independent variables) of the equations; then, solutions are formulated for the left-hand sides of the equations (dependent variables). See Chapter 10.

Some well-known econometric models are the Wharton School model, the Federal Reserve–MIT model, and the Brookings Institution model.[8] These models are composed of from 30 to 600 structural equations and have taken many years to develop. Anyone can buy the results of these models. Some business organizations

[7]T. T. Juster, *Journal of American Statistical Association,* Sept. 1966.
[8]See the bibliography for sources.

develop their own models that relate specifically to the factors influencing their own business.

To show what an econometric model looks like, a small model developed by Friend and Taubman to forecast consumption, income, housing, investment, and plant and equipment expenditure changes for the short run (6 months into the future) will be presented. This model has five behavioral equations and one identity (definitional) equation. Behavioral equations describe the behavior of groups in the economy; they are statements of functional relationships, such as "The quantity of meat demanded is dependent upon the price of meat and the price of fish," or "The change in investment is related to the change in last year's income and the change in interest rates." Definitional equations state the relationships that are set. Thus, $Y = C + S$, where Y is current income, C is current consumption, and S is current savings. The equation states that if we look at current income Y the only choices that households have for current income is to consume or to save. Thus, it defines the ways in which income can be used. This set of equations contains nine variables. Some variables are lagged; thus, we would expect a change in housing units this month to be related to housing starts in a previous period because it would take some time before a house was completed. Lagged variables are shown by subscripts; thus Y_{t-1} is the gross national product of the previous half year in this model. The variables are:

C = consumption expenditures

t_p = average personal tax rate

Y_D = disposable income

Y = gross national product

H = residential construction expenditure

HS = housing starts

PE = plant and equipment expenditures

I = nonfarm inventory investment

S = savings

G^1 = government expenditures and net exports (This number is fixed during the life of our forecast.)

The equations are as follows. Note the following symbols used in the equations: Δ indicates a change; $\sim$ means that the variable must be forecast and inserted in the equation; $t - 1$ is data from previous time period (the time periods are ½ years); and e is the expected value (a weighted probability amount). This is a forecast that must be made and inserted in the equation. It is weighted by the probabilities that the statistician estimates. Thus, ΔY is the change in gross national product over the time period (6 months). $\tilde{Y}$ is a forecast of gross national product for the period.

1
$$\Delta C = .86 + .41(\Delta Y_D + \Delta Y_{D_{t-1}})$$

The change in consumption is a function of the change in disposable income of this period and the previous period.

2 $$\Delta Y_D = \frac{1.7 + .57\,\Delta\tilde{Y} - 10\,\Delta^2\tilde{Y}}{1 + t_p} - \frac{\Delta t_p}{1 + t_p}\,Y_{Dt-1}$$

The change in disposable income ΔY_D depends on the changes in the gross national product, disposable income, and personal tax rates.

$$\Delta H = .35 + .06(\Delta\tilde{Y} - Y_{t-1}) + .58\Delta\,HS_{t-1/2} - .16\,\Delta PE^e$$

The change in housing expenditures ΔH is positively related to income changes and housing starts and negatively related to estimated plant and equipment expenditure.

4 $$\Delta PE = -.82 + .08(\Delta\tilde{Y} + \Delta Y_{t-1}) + .63\,\Delta PE^e$$

The change in plant and equipment expenditure ΔPE is positively related to income change and to estimates of probable changes in plant and equipment spending.

5 $$\Delta I = 1.51 + .025\,\Delta S^e - 1.15\,I_{t-1} + 1.7\,\Delta PE^e$$

The change in investment ΔI is positively related to the expected change in savings and to the expected change in plant and equipment expenditures and negatively related to investment expenditure in the previous period.

6 $$\Delta Y = \Delta C + \Delta H + \Delta PE + \Delta I + \Delta G^1 \text{ (identity)}$$

Income is spent on consumption, housing, plant and equipment, investment, and government expenditure.

 The econometricians who develop these models begin with economic theory (that is, consumption is a function of disposable income) and use mathematics and statistics to obtain quantitative values for the variables in the theory.

 As we can see, there are a number of problems involved in this type of analysis. First, the econometrician must decide which are the most important variables to relate to each other (that is, what should be related to consumption change). These choices are based on economic theory and some experimentation with data over the years. Second, after deciding which variables are important, the econometrician must correlate them with each other using previous years' data to obtain the coefficients. Thus, in the first equation above, the .86 and .41 have been estimated by relating consumption change and disposable income change in previous years. Every few years the analysts change these coefficients. Finally, data must be entered in these six equations and they must be solved simultaneously. In the first equation, for example, we have data to measure the change in disposable income (income minus taxes in the previous time period), but we must make an estimate of what we think the change in disposable income will be in the current time period $\Delta\tilde{Y}_D$. In the second equation, changes in gross national product must be estimated and the forecaster must have an idea of variation in personal tax rates. In the third equation, the change in housing starts over the previous 3 months is used ($.58\Delta HS_{t-1/2}$), and a weighted probability estimate of the change in plant and equipment expenditures ΔPE^e must be inserted.

 The results of the econometric model depend on the reliability of these three types of estimates. Devising good methods for making these estimates is part of the art of being a good forecaster. Lawrence Klein won a Nobel prize in economics in 1980 for his contributions to the art of forecasting changes in the state of the national and world economies by use of econometric models.

Since econometric models require mathematical sophistication and excellent computer facilities, many firms buy specific forecasts that affect their industry. The group that develops the models is often willing to sell the results of special equations to customers. For example, if you were a builder you might want to know what ΔH would be for the next year for the country and for your area. In the end of chapter bibliography, we list the names and addresses of some groups that develop these models.

Input-Output Models

In the previous section we discussed econometric models, which use sets of interdependent regression equations to forecast for the whole economy (macroeconomic forecast) or for an individual firm (microeconomic forecast). Another important tool that can be used for macroeconomic or microeconomic forecasting is the *input-output* tables.

Input-output analysis was developed by Wassily Leontieff in the late 1940s and early 1950s. In 1973, he was awarded the Nobel prize in economics for his contributions. Input-output analysis is a descriptive model of the economy that shows the volume of output of each industry in the economy and the types and amounts of inputs that have gone into the production of this output. Its usefulness for forecasting is based on the assumption that these patterns will remain relatively constant over the years.

The input-output tables, published in the *Survey of Current Business* by the U.S. Department of Commerce, can be obtained in most libraries and show the interrelationships between 85 industries. Tables for 496 industries based on 1972 figures may also be obtained from the U.S. Government Printing Office.

Two types of tables are developed and presented for the 85-industry or the 496-industry groups. These are *direct requirements tables* and *total requirements tables*. The direct requirements tables show inputs from each industry (named in the left-hand stub of the table) required to produce a dollar of the output of the industry at the top of the table. Rows are supplying industries, while columns are producing industries. In Table 11-7, we show a small part of two columns and rows of a direct requirements table for 1972.

Direct requirements do not handle all interactions of the economy. In order to produce enough electric wiring to supply new construction, additional plants or equipment may have to be built, requiring additional electric lighting and wiring equipment. The total requirements table takes into account this interaction as well as the original demand for electric wiring. Now, look at a small part of the total

TABLE 11-7
DIRECT REQUIREMENTS TABLE

	PRODUCERS		
INDUSTRY	NEW CONSTRUCTION	MAINTENANCE AND REPAIR CONSTRUCTION	
Household appliances	.00280	.00500	Suppliers
Electric lighting and wiring equipment	.01715	.00927	

TABLE 11-8
TOTAL REQUIREMENTS TABLE

361

FORECASTING

| | PRODUCERS | |
INDUSTRY	NEW CONSTRUCTION	MAINTENANCE AND REPAIR CONSTRUCTION	
Household appliances	.00468	.00638	Suppliers
Electric lighting and wiring equipment	.01895	.01041	

requirements for electric wiring (Table 11-8). According to this table, for every dollar spent on new construction .00468 of a dollar is spent on household appliances and .01895 of a dollar is spent on electrical wiring and equipment. We see that the total requirements coefficients are larger than the direct requirements coefficients, since they account for all interactions including what an industry consumes of its own output. We now demonstrate how firms and industries can use these total requirements coefficients to forecast.

Assume that we have anticipated new construction of $300 million next year, and we wish to know the effect on the household appliance industry. The coefficient in the direct requirements column is .00280. This figure comes from the 85 industry tables published in the *Survey of Current Business,* by the U.S. Department of Commerce. Since we want the total change in appliances due to new household construction, we look in the total requirements table and find the total coefficient .00468. Now, multiply this by $300 million and find the increase in demand for household appliances due to new construction.

$$\$300,000,000(.00468) = \$1,404,000$$

Thus, the household appliance industry can expect demand of $1.4 million as a result of new construction. An individual appliance manufacturer will now have to determine what its market share of this new demand will be.

Certain businesses, particularly chemical companies, have also developed their own input-output models, although this is a costly procedure. It has been useful to these companies in forecasting demand for their products. In addition 20 countries, half of which are located in Western Europe, have up-to-date input-output tables. These tables can be useful to the firm seeking international markets for information on export expansion, growth areas for investment, and identification of suppliers of raw materials. For controlled economies, these tables are especially useful for planning and regulation. However, when using these tables, there is a time lag between the computation and publication of the coefficients. If the relationships remain *static,* the coefficients will be useful. If the relationships fluctuate, much error can occur. For businesses with demand that comes from the purchases of other businesses rather than from direct consumers (those businesses supplying intermediate rather than final goods), the input-output coefficients are especially effective forecasting tools. Further evaluation of input-output tables as forecasting tools can be found in an article by Platt.[9]

[9]Robert B. Platt, "Input-Output Forecasting in Kavesh and Butler," *Business Forecasting,* Prentice-Hall, Inc., Englewood Cliffs, N. J., 1976.

Leading Indicators and Diffusion Indexes

In 1937–1938, because of a sharp recession in the U.S. economy, Secretary of the Treasury Henry Morgenthau asked the National Bureau of Economic Research, a private, nonprofit research agency, to devise a system of indicators to signal when the recession would be nearing an end. Wesley Mitchell and Arthur F. Burns selected monthly, quarterly, and annual data on prices, employment, production, and other factors that seemed to relate to the turning points of the business cycle. These indicators were classified into three types: leading, lagging, and coincident indicators. The *leading indicators* start to rise before the business cycle itself starts up. The *coincident indicators* reach their *peaks* and *troughs* (highest and lowest points) at approximately the same time that the business cycle does. The *lagging indicators* reach their peak after the general business cycle has peaked, and plummet after the general business cycle has started to turn up. These indicators are now published monthly by the Department of Commerce in *Business Conditions Digest* (BCD). The United Kingdom, Canada, and Japan have also tested similar indicators and found them useful.

There are two lists of these indicators—the long list issued in 1977, which contains 111 indicators (economic series), and the short set of indexes, which is based on 22 indicators. In the short list, there are 12 leading indicators that are said to reach their peaks and troughs before general business conditions reach peaks and troughs. There are four coincident indicators that turn at the same time as aggregate economy measures, such as the GNP. These indicators tend to be time series for which data is released quickly after they have occurred. If many coincident indicators appear to change in one direction, this is considered to mean that a turn has occurred in the economy. There are six lagging indicators that react slowly to changes in the direction of the economy. They are used to confirm what the other series have suggested. If the lagging indicators start to turn down, for example, this is an indication that in the recent past the peak of a business cycle has been reached.

Deciding when a turning point in the economy (peak or trough) has occurred requires some discussion among economists. Comprehensive data on gross national product, a logical criterion of economic change, is difficult and time-consuming to collect. Economists often use the Index of Industrial Production and closely related coincident series to determine the month in which the turn has occurred. The dates of these turning points, called *reference dates,* are used to study the effectiveness of the indicators. Several examples of leading indicators are:

1 Average work week manufacturing leads peaks and troughs by 5 months.
2 Stock market prices (500 common stocks) lead peaks and troughs by 4 to 8 months.
3 New building permits lead peaks and troughs by 6 months.

An increase in the average work week leads an upturn in the business cycle by 5 months because manufacturers, anticipating but not fully certain that business will improve, ask current staff to work overtime instead of hiring additional labor. When the manufacturer is finally convinced that business conditions have improved, new staff will be added.

Building permits must be obtained before new construction is undertaken; therefore, one can use the number of building permits to forecast a future upturn in the construction business. This has secondary effects, similar to those of the input-output model, on other industries. The stock market prices indicator, which uses

Standard and Poor's 500 stocks, is not always reliable. As Samuelson has said, the stock market has predicted "nine of the last five recessions." Of the nine times since 1953 that the stock market has fallen, only five times did a recession result. Thus, one problem with leading indicators is that they don't always work.

Some examples of coincident indicators are:

1 Industrial production (wholesale price index).
2 GNP, in constant dollars.
3 Sales of retail stores.

When these indicators reach their peak, we have reached the peak of the general business cycle. There are four of these indicators in the short list.

Finally, there are six lagging indicators, economic series that reach their peak after the general cycle has peaked. Some examples are:

1 Unemployment rate lags peaks and troughs by 2 months.
2 Labor cost per unit of output lags peaks and troughs by 8 months.
3 Bank rates on short-term business loans lags peaks and troughs by 5 months.

Why does the unemployment rate lag? After the cycle has peaked and business conditions have turned down, it takes about 2 months for employers to lay off the additional workers they have hired. Similarly, at the peak of the cycle, labor costs increase and soon the only labor left is marginal; therefore, labor costs per unit of output increase.

Figure 11-4(*a*) shows how to decipher the samples of leading, lagging, and coincident indicators shown in Figure 11-4(*b*). The vertical darkened stripes show the time period from the peak to the trough of a cycle. Notice that all three leading indexes (average work week, new building permits, and stock prices) started to turn down before the shaded stripe (peak of the cycle). The movement of the industrial production index coincided with the cycle, and the labor cost and prime rate indexes (lagging indicators) started to drop after the trough of the cycle had been reached.

Generally, the leading indicators must rise or fall for 3 consecutive months before analysts predict an economic upturn or downturn. Thus, if the indicators have fallen for 3 consecutive months, a downturn is anticipated. But what if some of the indicators rise while other indicators fall? *Diffusion indexes* are being studied to determine how to interpret mixed signals from the data. A diffusion index of 100 says all of the series have risen and none has fallen. The index represents the percentage of series that have risen; unchanged series are counted as half-risen and half-fallen. A low index number in an expansionary period could indicate that the economy is approaching its cyclical peak. Interpretation of these indexes is quite complex; however, the development of the economic indicators and the diffusion indexes has improved our ability to track and predict the business cycle.

Life Cycle Analysis

Life cycle analysis can be applied in many areas. Family life cycle patterns can be analyzed and used to predict product demand. Thus, as the population age composition changes, changes in consumption can be forecast. In addition, there is a life

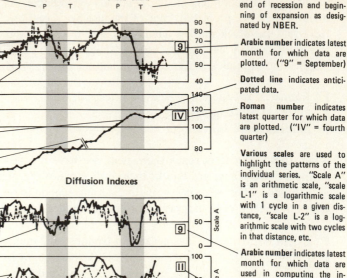

Basic Data

Peak (P) of cycle indicates end of expansion and beginning of recession (shaded area) as designated by NBER.

Solid line indicates monthly data. (Data may be actual monthly figures or moving averages.)

Broken line indicates actual monthly data for series where a moving average is plotted.

Solid line with plotting points indicates quarterly data.

Parallel lines indicates a break in continuity (data not available, extreme value, etc.).

Trough (T) of cycle indicates end of recession and beginning of expansion as designated by NBER.

Arabic number indicates latest month for which data are plotted. ("9" = September)

Dotted line indicates anticipated data.

Roman number indicates latest quarter for which data are plotted. ("IV" = fourth quarter)

Various scales are used to highlight the patterns of the individual series. "Scale A" is an arithmetic scale, "scale L-1" is a logarithmic scale with 1 cycle in a given distance, "scale L-2" is a logarithmic scale with two cycles in that distance, etc.

Diffusion Indexes

Solid line indicates monthly data over 6- or 9-month spans.

Broken line indicates monthly data over 1-month spans.

Broken line with plotting points indicates quarterly data over 1-quarter spans.

Solid line with plotting points indicates quarterly data over various spans.

Diffusion indexes and rates of change are centered within the spans they cover.

Arabic number indicates latest month for which data are used in computing the indexes.

Roman number indicates latest quarter for which data are used in computing the indexes.

Dotted line indicates anticipated quarterly data over various spans.

Rates of Change

Solid line indicates percent changes over 3- or 6-month spans.

Broken line indicates percent changes over 1-month spans.

Solid line with plotting points indicates percent change over 3- or 4-quarter spans.

Arabic number indicates latest month used in computing the changes.

Broken line with plotting points indicates percent changes over 1-quarter spans.

Roman number indicates latest quarter used in computing the changes.

FIGURE **11-4 (a)**

How to read charts. **Source:** *Business Conditions Digest*, May 1980.

cycle for particular products; these patterns of acceptance and use will be analyzed below.

Consumer Life Cycle The consumer life cycle, as defined by Wells and Guber, consists of a series of stages.[10]

1 Bachelor stage: young, single, not living at home.
2 Newly married couples: young, no children.
3 Full nest I: young married couples, youngest child less than 6 years of age.

---

[10]William D. Wells and George Guber, "Life Cycle Concept in Marketing Research," *Journal of Marketing Research*, vol. 3, Nov. 1966, pp. 355–363.

Chart A2. Leading Index Components

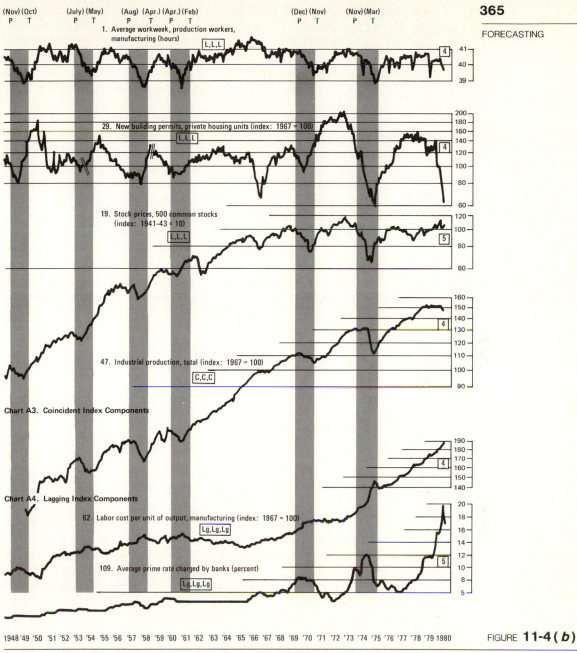

Chart A3. Coincident Index Components

Chart A4. Lagging Index Components

1948 '49 '50 '51 '52 '53 '54 '55 '56 '57 '58 '59 '60 '61 '62 '63 '64 '65 '66 '67 '68 '69 '70 '71 '72 '73 '74 '75 '76 '77 '78 '79 1980

FIGURE **11-4 (b)**

Selected series. **Source:** *Business Conditions Digest*, May 1980.

4   Full nest II: young married couples, youngest child older than 6 years of age.
5   Full nest III: older married couples, dependent children.
6   Empty nest I: older married couples, no children at home, head in labor force.
7   Empty nest II: older married couples, no children at home, head retired.
8   Solitary survivor in labor force.
9   Solitary survivor retired.

Life cycle analysis is very useful for the identification of buyers of a product category. The Census Bureau, *Current Population Reports* P-25, estimates future age distribution and family structure composition of the population. Using knowledge of consumption habits of population groups and future population trends, forecasts of demand for cars, refrigerators, chocolates, or boats can be obtained. Similarly, school districts can use these stages to predict demand for education and health services.

Product Life Cycle Just as the consumers have a life cycle, so does a product. There are six stages in the product life cycle.

1 *Preproduct development.* Before new product ideas emerge and are developed, we need to forecast necessary technologic breakthroughs and social and political issues that affect demand. For example, with increased numbers of married women in the labor force, items that decrease cooking and housekeeping time will be needed. Microwave technology, for example, had to be developed and evaluated in terms of uses and potential health hazards in order to be considered for possible use in home ovens.

2 *Product development.* As the product is being developed, managers wish to forecast potential demand so they can allocate research and development funds. This forecast involves study of similar products to allow better decisions concerning where to enter the market, product differentiation, and future markets.

3 *Testing and introduction.* In this stage, a marketing plan showing where, when, and how much will sell in each market is devised; estimates of manufacturing capacity and research needs must be made. Statistical techniques are used to test products in laboratories and market research is used to estimate product demand.

4 *Rapid growth.* If the product "takes off" (shows a rapid increase in sales), the marketers try to forecast a date when sales will level to steady-state growth. Inventory levels must match growth.

5 *Steady state.* In this stage, facilities planning and expansion have been accomplished. Estimates of steady-state sales level and rates of change are necessary for market planning. This is considered to be a mature product.

6 *Phasing out.* Most products are eventually phased out, or dropped from the market. A firm tries to forecast when the decline will begin and how long it will last in order to arrange production scheduling, inventory control, and facilities planning. Forecasts for phasing out products with short life cycles, like fashion items, are particularly needed. Other items may experience gradual declines in sales, and forecasts will be needed for this process.

Many managers analyze these product life cycles to provide their companies with a set of products in different life cycle stages. Thus, as one product is being phased out, it is replaced by another in the rapid growth or steady-state stage.

Similarly, analyses of the life cycle of products in use allow prediction of replacement sales for durable goods. For example, every 3 years an average car owner may need new tires. Every 5 years the owner may wish to replace the vehicle. Computer hardware may be replaced at certain intervals because of physical breakdowns as well as obsolescence. Many firms try to figure their own product cycles to make sales forecasts.

1 Simple qualitative forecasts can be made by individuals or groups of people. A *panel* of experts can reach consensus; however, there may be some social effects whereby participants "go along with" the opinions of the majority or of the highest-status person in the group. The *Delphi* method allows for consensus without identifying the opinions of the individual participants.

2 *Short-range forecasting* (for one period into the future) can be performed using a number of techniques. The simplest forecast uses the *arithmetic mean* for all previous periods to predict the next period. A *moving average* forecast drops a previous period and adds a new period for each time period that it forecasts. Thus, it leaves off older time periods and only averages the current time periods. Exponential smoothing uses all time periods but assigns higher weights to more recent time periods. The higher the smoothing constant (α), the more weight assigned to more recent time periods. The formula for smoothing is

$$F_t = \alpha D_t + \alpha(1 - \alpha)\, D_{t-1} + \cdots + \alpha(1 - \alpha)^k D_{t-k}$$

Once a forecast is made, the next forecast can be made using the shortcut formula.

$$F_t = \alpha D_t + (1 - \alpha)\, F_{t-1}$$

3 *Long-range forecasting* can be performed by decomposing *time series* data into *secular trends, seasonal influences,* and *cyclical patterns.*

4 Secular trends are long-run patterns that take place over a 15–30 year period for a business cycle analysis. Long-range trends for a business may last for only 5 years. A *regression* line is fitted to the trends in the data.

5 Seasonal patterns are isolated by using a moving average. Seasonal index numbers may then be used to *"deseasonalize"* data or to estimate such factors as seasonal inventory needs or seasonal sales.

6 It is assumed that *trend, seasonal,* and *cyclical* influences are in the data in multiplicative fashion ($T \times S \times C \times I$). When trend and seasonal influences are removed by dividing the original data by these influences, *cyclical* factors remain. It is now possible to graph and study these factors. Some irregularities are smoothed out in the process of studying trend, seasonal, and cyclical effects. Thus, the use of the medial average in calculating seasonal index numbers eliminates some irregular influences.

7 A number of methods for projecting the future can be found by identifying underlying causes and predicting their effects. *Regression analysis,* which relates one variable to another, can be used for forecasting. For example, if sales and advertising are related, an estimate of advertising expenditure can be used to estimate sales. *Multiple regression,* which uses a number of independent variables to predict the dependent variable, may prove even more effective than simple regression analysis.

8 Forecasts of the economy can be made from *intention-to-buy surveys* and *indexes of consumer sentiment.* These forecasts of plant and equipment and durable goods expenditures, when combined with consumers' intentions to buy, are good predictors of market conditions. Using these forecasts, the individual firm can then focus on its own market share.

9 *Econometric models* are systems of interdependent regression equations that

describe the whole economy or a particular industry. Some well-known models are published by the Wharton School, the Federal Reserve, and Brookings Institution. These equations include *lagged variables* and *estimates of the future.* Firms may buy special results of these forecasts for their own industry or for the economy as a whole.

10 *Input-output models* provide *direct* and *total coefficients* that tell how much one industry or sector of the economy purchases from the others. Thus, the effects of a change in demand in one industry can be traced to all other industries.

11 *Leading indicators* are time series that precede (lead) the business cycle. These are used with *coincident* or *lagging indicators,* which help determine the stage of the economy. A study of *diffusion indexes* attempts to predict future business conditions when some indicators rise and others fall.

12 A study of the family *life cycle* is useful for predicting demand based on age and family responsibilities of the population.

13 The *product life cycle* traces the development of a product from its development through market introduction to the phasing-out stage.

BIBLIOGRAPHY

11-6

Books

Butler, W. F., R. A. Kavesh, and R. B. Platt (eds.): *Methods and Techniques of Business Forecasting,* Englewood Cliffs, N.J.: Prentice-Hall, 1976.

Chambers, John C., Satender K. Mullick, and Donald D. Smith: *An Executive Guide to Forecasting,* New York: Wiley, 1974.

Chisholm, Roger K., and Gilbert R. Whitaker, Jr.: *Forecasting Methods,* Homewood, Ill.: Irwin, 1971 (paperback).

Granger, C. W. J.: *Forecasting in Business and Economics,* New York: Academic Press, 1980.

Gross, Charles W., and Robin T. Peterson: *Business Forecasting,* Boston: Houghton Mifflin, 1976.

Linstone, H., and M. Thieroff: *The Delphi Method and Its Applications,* New York: American Elsevier, 1973.

Makridakis, Spyros, and Steven C. Wheelwright: *Forecasting Methods and Applications,* New York: Wiley, 1978.

Silk, Leonard S., and M. Louise Curley: *Business Forecasting,* New York: Random House, 1970 (paperback).

Starr, Martin K.: *Operations Management,* Englewood Cliffs, N.J.: Prentice-Hall, 1978, pp. 243–253.

Articles

Chambers, John C., Satender K. Mullick, and Donald D. Smith: "How to Choose the Right Forecasting Technique," *Harvard Business Review,* July–Aug. 1971, pp. 45–74.

Juster, Thomas: "Consumer Buying Intentions and Purchase Probability: An Experiment in Survey Design," *Journal of American Statistical Association,* Sept. 1966, pp. 658–696.

Maynes, E. Scott: "Attitudes, Behavior and Economics." In *Major Social Issues,* New York: Free Press, 1978, p. 390–411.

Mitroff, Ivan, and Murray Turoff: "The Whys behind the Hows," *IEEE Spectrum,* Mar. 1973, pp. 62–71.

Moore, Geoffrey A.: "The Analysis of Economic Indicators," *Scientific American,* Jan. 1975, pp. 17–24.

North and Pyke: "Probes of the Technological Future," *Harvard Business Review,* May–June 1969, p. 68.

Rothe, James T.: "Effectiveness of Sales Forecasting Methods," *Industrial Marketing,* Fall 1979.

Wells, William D., and George Guber: "Life Cycle Concept in Marketing Research," *Journal of Marketing Research,* vol. 3, Nov. 1966, pp. 355–363.

Government Publications

Updated Input-Output Table of the U.S. Economy: 1972, Washington, D.C.: Bureau of Economic Analysis, Department of Commerce, 1979. Update of 1967 tables. 85 industry tables.

The Detailed Input/Output Structure of the U.S. Economy: 1972, vols. 1 and 2, Washington, D.C.: Bureau of Economic Analysis, Department of Commerce, 1979. 496 industry tables.

Business Conditions Digest, Washington, D.C.: Bureau of Economic Analysis, Department of Commerce. These monthly reports provide data on economic time series found most useful by business analysts and forecasters. The data contains graphs of cyclical indicators and other economic measures.

Economic Statistics Data Finders, 1978, Washington, D.C.: Bureau of the Census, Department of Commerce. A series of eight brochures describing in chart form census and survey data available on the following topics: agriculture, business, construction, economic surveys, energy, foreign trade, governments, and industry.

Private Index Publications

Dow Jones Index. Published daily in *The Wall Street Journal.*

Index of Consumer Sentiment. Published by the Survey Research Center, University of Michigan, Ann Arbor, Mich. 48106.

Case 11-1:   The Effect of Special Events at the Superdome on Motel Tax Revenues

Much of the city of New Orleans' local revenues are derived from the tourist trade and conventions. A direct inflow from out-of-town guests is collected by levying a special tax on hotel and motel rooms in the area. The money collected from this tax is recognized to be seasonal, since there are certain times of the year when people flock to the city.

It was predicted that the construction of the Superdome would increase the number of visitors to the city and thus raise tax revenues to pay for the facility. In addition to issuing bonds, the city also raised the hotel-motel tax from 6% to 7% in January 1977 to provide additional financing.

Opponents of the Dome were unsure about the desirability of the complex, and questioned whether the additional revenues collected with the hotel tax would contribute significantly to the multimillion dollar project. Many people suggested that hotel tax revenues be analyzed to see if they would increase substantially from past trends. The effects of special events at the Superdome, such as Superbowl games, on hotel occupancy could measure some of the extra revenue brought into the city by the Superdome.

Hotel occupancy can be measured by the hotel-motel tax collections. Erroll G. Williams, director of the department of finance, forwarded the figures in Table 1, which can be used for this analysis. In general, taxes reported to the city in a given month represent collections made by the hotels and motels in the previous month. The Superbowl was held in the Superdome in January 1978. The Mardi Gras, an annual festival that takes place in late February and early March, was canceled in 1979 because of a police strike in New Orleans. Once this data is

TABLE 1

MONTHLY COLLECTIONS OF THE HOTEL-MOTEL TAX

(By the city of New Orleans, 1977–1980)

MONTH	1977	1978	1979	1980
January	64,053	82,284	85,468	84,802
February	69,056	104,258	102,873	113,676
March	99,848	127,317	146,690	149,551
April	101,612	130,764	156,571	167,533
May	116,672	134,043	114,146	177,486
June	84,158	105,913	150,686	155,214
July	78,918	98,383	100,131	130,348
August	73,150	86,728	96,509	123,841
September	72,195	92,792	95,904	112,601
October	76,032	127,382	152,006	126,194
November	128,197	123,217	164,808	137,260
December	111,025	115,388	141,498	157,681
Total	1,074,916	1,328,469	1,507,290	1,636,187

Source: New Orleans Department of Finance, Bureau of Revenue.

deseasonalized, it can be used to test the effects of special events and cancellation of events.

Questions

1 Using the data from 1977 to 1980, compute the seasonal indexes for the New Orleans hotel-motel tax receipts. What are the best and worst months for hotels and motels?

2 Deseasonalize the receipts from January 1977 to December 1980.

3 Plot the original data through 1980. Do you see any evidence of a long-run trend?

4 Plot the deseasonalized data from 1977 to 1980. Is the trend clearer? Do the first 6 months of 1978 differ from the others?

5 What factors could cause a rise in hotel tax receipts?

6 Did the Superbowl game affect results?

7 What was the effect of the cancellation of the Mardi Gras?

Case 11-2: American Brewing Company

Lois Jane Harkavy was recently hired by the marketing department of the American Brewing Company to work under the direction of Ted Baker. For a long time, Ted had been interested in forecasting beer sales in relation to average temperature, because he felt that people drank more beer in the summer. He had met with little success. Since Lois seemed extremely bright, he assigned Lois the task of developing a linkage between beer sales and temperature in the north central Texas region. The main brewery was in Dallas, and virtually all beer sales were in this area.

When she first learned of her assignment, Lois quickly gathered the following statistics from local sources and the marketing department:

YEAR	QUARTER	MEAN DALLAS TEMPERATURE, °F	BEER SALES, THOUSANDS OF CASES
1976	3	89.7	47.8
	4	64.3	48.8
1977	1	58.1	33.5
	2	87.4	60.8
	3	96.2	52.7
	4	67.9	51.8
1978	1	57.5	31.0
	2	85.5	63.1
	3	95.1	55.8
	4	54.2	42.1

Questions

1 What is the correlation between beer sales and temperature?

2 Plot the points and establish a regression line.

3 Would this line be very useful for prediction purposes?

Lois was somewhat disappointed with the initial results and knew that her boss was looking for a more substantial link. She began to wonder if seasonal variations besides temperature affected the sales of beer. Lois contacted a friend who worked in the marketing department of a small regional brewery in southern Florida, where there is little temperature variation. When asked about quarterly sales figures, her friend reviewed the past few years and revealed the following seasonal index numbers. The Christmas holidays showed a spurt in liquor and beer sales. Easter time was also good. The index numbers for Florida were:

Quarter 1 sales =   .80

Quarter 2 sales = 1.10

Quarter 3 sales =   .90

Quarter 4 sales = 1.20

Additional Questions

4 Why had Ted Baker met with little success?

5 How could Lois use this information?

6 Is there a significant difference in the correlation achieved?

7 What is the best way to predict beer sales for the American Brewing Company? Predict sales for quarter 1 in 1979.

8 If American Brewing anticipates that it will sell 250,000 cases of beer next year, how many cases should they stock in each quarter?

Case 11-3: Telephonics, Inc.

"I guess the moral of this story is that you are never too old to learn," Jim Ulrich chuckled to himself. "If only I had thought to ask my son earlier!" His son Tom, a business student in a nearby college, had come home from school to spend the weekend. When his father shared a problem currently plaguing him in his new job as a marketing staff member at Telephonics, New York City, Tom offered a suggestion that helped to answer his father's questions. By using an approach that Tom had learned in the time series analysis section of a forecasting course, Jim discovered a viable means of making a needed estimation for his marketing studies.

Part of Jim's responsibility was to develop 10-year forecasts of the demand for company products. These forecasts should be useful in setting up a sales plan. Telephonics was one of a group of new independent companies that had entered the telephone business in the past decade. With such an influx of competition, the corporation felt that as a fairly new enterprise it must secure a better understanding of product demand and company market share of sales. Their two main products, *telephone answering service equipment* and *custom-designed telephones,* were sold throughout the United States.

These products were classified as durable goods because they could be used for more than 1 year, and thus their purchase could be postponed. With such uncertainty as to what the public will buy and when, marketing specialists often rely upon surveys to analyze the quantities of these durable goods the public will buy. The results provide vital data for company sales and production planning.

The Telephonics marketing staff divided product demand into three segments:

1 Replacement demand of previous customers.
2 New demand from regular telephone users who had not yet purchased answering devices or custom phones.
3 New demand from the increasing number of new telephone owners. Surveys were used for the first two types of demand, but were not feasible for the third type. Yet, in order to make a complete forecast, all segments had to be considered, and this is where Tom's suggestion of time series analysis was appreciated. This particular forecasting approach would relate some predictive factor over time, creating a pattern from historical data to arrive at a future estimate.

To find some good predictor that would relate closely to sales of the two product lines, Jim conducted a search of technical magazines and abstracts. In the April 1975 issue of the *IEEE Spectrum,* a journal of the Institute of Electrical and Electronics Engineers, he found an interesting graph (Figure 1). He decided that the number of total U.S. "telephone households" would have a reasonably strong correlation to product demand at Telephonics. Reading the numbers as best as he could from the points on the graph, because he felt he would have difficulty in obtaining the actual numbers, he constructed the information in Table 1.

Searching through past company sales data, Jim concluded that 1 of 10 new telephone households purchased a custom-designed telephone, and Telephonic's market share of this demand was 1%. For telephone answering equipment, 1 of 20 new telephone households made such a purchase, with Telephonics responsible for 3.3% of these sales.

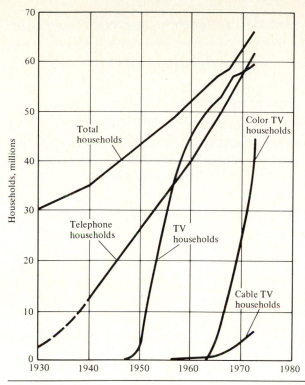

FIGURE **1**

Trends in recent decades show that television and color TV have, with almost incredible speed, been taken into most U.S. households. From the chart it appears that the history of the telephone as a widespread home appliance goes back only about 50 years. Cable TV rates of increase are much lower than those for the other services. (This data was compiled by Joseph G. Wohl and Gope Hingorani of the Mitre Corp., Bedford, Mass.) **Source:** Howard Falk, "Technology Forecasting I, Communications," *IEEE Spectrum*, Apr. 1975, p. 44.

TABLE 1

TELEPHONE HOUSEHOLDS, 1930–1975

(In millions of households)*

YEAR	NO. OF HOUSEHOLDS
1930	5.1
1935	6.8
1940	13.5
1945	18.0
1950	26.7
1955	35.6
1960	41.5
1965	49.2
1970	56.9
1975	68.1

*Estimated from Figure 1.

Questions

1   Derive an equation for a trend line for "telephone households" using time series analysis, and plot it.

2   What would be the forecasted number of telephone households in 1985? What would be the 10-year increase?

3   Using the 1985 forecast number of telephone households found for question 1, what would the prediction be with a 95.5% confidence interval?

4   Using the 1985 point estimate and assuming that Telephonics maintains its current market share of both products sold in the United States, how many unit sales will be realized between 1975 and 1985 from the third type of demand for custom phones and for answering devices?

5   What limitations are there on this type of time series analysis? How else could you possibly forecast sales?

6   What would the effects of different business conditions be on new telephone households?

7   Develop a sales plan for Telephonics.
    (*a*) How much demand will they have?
    (*b*) What do they need to estimate?
    (*c*) What type of strategies must they develop?

DECISION THEORY AND BAYESIAN PROBABILITY

12

12-1   INTRODUCTION

12-2   PAYOFF TABLES

12-3   DECISION TREES

12-4   EXPECTED VALUE OF PERFECT INFORMATION

12-5   SENSITIVITY ANALYSIS
Problems

12-6   BAYESIAN PROBABILITY
Problems

12-7   DECISION MAKING USING SAMPLE INFORMATION (POSTERIOR
PROBABILITY)

12-8   SUMMARY

12-9   BIBLIOGRAPHY

12-10 CASES
12-1 Comfort Furniture Rental Company
12-2 Frozen Convertibles
12-3 Springdale Methodist Church Building Project
12-4 Carolina Canning Company

In Chapter 3 we introduced the concept of expected value—each payoff was weighted by the probability of that event happening and the results were summed. We then calculated the expected value of games. This same technique, as we will show, can be combined with computations about the results of many different kinds of action alternatives to decide what course of action would prove most profitable for a business, or most beneficial for a public sector.

12-1 To set up a model, we must know

1 What the decision maker's possible *actions* are.
2 What external *conditions* (uncontrollable *events*) might occur.
3 What are the *probabilities* that each external event will occur.
4 What are the *payoffs* or costs *for each action* for each event that might occur.

Let us illustrate these decision components with a problem. Assume that Jones Motors Company has purchased time on a large computer system. Using telephone lines, they can gain access to this system with a computer terminal. A terminal, as many of you know, has a typewriterlike keyboard and a mechanism for printing copy or for displaying it on a TV screen; this copy represents what is sent to the computer and what is returned by it. The Jones Motor Company chooses a PIX brand terminal, which prints information on a heat sensitive paper, thereby removing the need for impact printing and its resulting noise. Now, the company must decide whether to *lease* the terminal or to *buy* it.

The cost of renting the terminal is $120 per month (including all necessary repairs); the cost of purchasing it is $2000. The terminal is guaranteed for 1 year, and free monthly service is included in the purchase price. In order to determine whether it would be more profitable to buy or lease, Jones asked for figures on length of life of terminals. The PIX company furnished the following record on *1000 terminals* that had been sold in the past few years. The figures on the life of these terminals could be summarized in five classes: 12, 18, 24, 30, and 36 months, respectively. The Jones Motor Company then set up Table 12-1. Now let us try to analyze this problem.

1 *Actions*. The two possible actions are to *buy* (A_1) or *lease* (A_2) the terminal.
2 *Conditions*. There are five different conditions that might occur. The terminal could wear out in 12, 18, 24, 30, or 36 months. In fact, this is a continuous distri-

TABLE 12-1

(1) EVENTS OR CONDITIONS	TIME INTERVAL	(2) AVERAGE NUMBER OF MONTHS BEFORE SCRAPPED	(3) FREQUENCY COUNT OF NUMBER OF TERMINALS	(4) PROBABILITY OF EACH CONDITION $P(C_i)$
C_1	0–15	12*	100	100/1000 = .100
C_2	15 but less than 21	18	250	250/1000 = .250
C_3	21 but less than 27	24	400	400/1000 = .400
C_4	27 but less than 33	30	150	150/1000 = .150
C_5	33 but less than 39	36	100	100/1000 = .100
			1000	1.000

*Here we use 12 months since the terminal is repaired free if it lasts a shorter time.

bution, but we have converted it to a discrete distribution for ease in computation. (This is a usual procedure.) Thus, a terminal that breaks down in 14 months is put in the shortest interval class, that is, 12 months. The breaking point is 15 months; this is where we start to classify terminals for the group that breaks down in an average of 18 months. Except for the first number (12) each number stands for the midpoint of its class. (Actually for up to 12 months, the terminal is replaced under the guarantee.) Thus, 12 would include 0 but less than 15 months; 18 would include more than 15 months but less than 21 months; 24 would include more than 21 months but less than 27 months. If the computer breaks down between 12 and 24 months, it does matter if we buy the terminal because we must replace it with a rented terminal for the remaining year and pay the rental fee. It is always cheaper to rent for a 1-year period than to buy a new one. If we rent, the company provides a new terminal whenever an old one breaks.

3 *Probabilities*. We are interested in the probabilities of the terminal "wearing out." Using the *past experience* of the terminal company, we can compute these probabilities as in column 4. (For example, the probability that the terminal will wear out in 0–15 months, classified as 12, is 100/1000 or .100. See Table 12-1.) These are called *prior probabilities*.

4 *Payoffs*. Decision theory can apply to a variety of problems that include *maximizing* payoff from sales to *minimizing* cost of buying or producing. In this case, we are trying to *minimize the cost* of using computer terminals over the *next 2 years*, since Jones expects to buy new computer facilities after a 2-year period. This might differ from our costs for a 3-year period. We assume there is no salvage value for the terminals after 2 years.

Now, if we rent the terminal for 2 years at a cost of $120 per month, our total cost will be $2880 under all circumstances, since a rented machine is immediately replaced if it breaks down. If we buy a terminal, it will cost $2000. The probability that it will last 2 or more years is .40 (24 months) + .15 (30 months) + .10 (36 months) = .65. The probability that it will last 18 months is (.25), and the probability that it will last 12 months is .10. We now combine these results in Table 12-2.

If the terminal lasts 18 months, we will spend $2000 to buy it plus $120 a month to rent another one for 6 more months, for a total of $2000 + $720 = $2720. If the terminal lasts 12 months, we will rent another one for 12 months: 12(120) = $1440 + $2000 (original purchase) = $3440.

PAYOFF TABLES

12-2

Table 12-3 is a payoff or cost table that we have developed by using probabilities and expected costs. How do we use the probabilities in this table? To find the

TABLE 12-2

TIME INTERVAL CONDITIONS C_i	$P(C_i)$	COST ($)
C_1: Lasts 2 or more years	.65	2000
C_2: Lasts 18 months	.25	2720 ($2000 + rental for 6 months)
C_3: Lasts 12 months	.10	3440 ($2000 + rental for 12 months)

TABLE 12-3

TIME INTERVAL CONDITIONS C_i	PROBABILITIES $P(C_i)$	COST TO BUY A_1	EXPECTED COST (PAYOFF) $P(C_i)A_1$	COST TO LEASE A_2	EXPECTED COST (PAYOFF) $P(C_i)A_2$
C_1: Lasts 2 or more years	.65	$2000	$1300	$2880	$1872
C_2: Lasts 18 months	.25	2720	680	2880	720
C_3: Lasts 12 months	.10	3440	344	2880	288
			$2324		$2880

expected value for each action (A_1 and A_2), we multiply probabilities by costs (or payoffs), then sum the expected costs for each action. The expected cost for leasing is $2880; the expected cost for buying is $2324. Therefore, the least costly choice, based on the need for a terminal for 2 years, would be to buy.

At this point, you may feel confused or rather upset. You might think, "If I buy a terminal and it turns out to be a lemon that breaks down in 12 months, I could wind up paying $3440." One way to rationalize the purchase is to assume that every 2 years this same kind of decision will occur. Then, on the *average,* the best action will be to buy. Another way to look at this is to consider that this decision rule can be applied to a decision about whether to buy or lease a large number of terminals rather than just one.

DECISION TREES

12-3 We can also set up this decision in the form of a diagram—a *decision tree*. Usually, this tree has a fallen trunk and branches that fan out horizontally. The steps used to construct a decision tree are as follows.

1 Before an action alternative, we place a square box representing a decision fork. From this fork our two decisions, to buy or lease, fan out. If we have three decisions, we would have three branches.

2 Circles are used as branching forks for various events (external conditions) that exist in this problem. These events are (1) the terminal lasts 12 months; (2) the terminal lasts 18 months; and (3) the terminal lasts 24 or more months. For each of these events, place the given probability on the appropriate branch. At the ends of the tree branches, place the dollar amounts of the payoff or cost for each of the action/event scenarios. To solve the decision tree, we work backward from right to left, multiplying the payoffs by the probabilities to derive the expected value. We compute the expected value for each circle by multiplying the probability on each branch by the cost or payoff and adding the results for all branches. Thus,

$$.65 (2000) = 1300$$
$$.25 (2720) = 680$$
$$.10 (3440) = 344$$
$$\overline{\qquad\qquad\qquad \$2324}$$

Place this value near the appropriate branching circle (the top one). On the bottom circle, since the lease costs $120 a month, there is one cost for all ($2880). Probability conditions do not change the value of the bottom branch, in this case. Now use the lines (//) to cross out the branch with the highest cost. The reader knows that the branch chosen is the one that has *not* been crossed out. If we are trying to maximize profits, we cross out the lower profit branches.

Far more extensive trees will be found necessary to describe many decision problems. For example, if the terminal could be purchased or rented from several different companies, we might have the tree shown in Figure 12-1. Here we can buy another terminal, the TX terminal, which has a much longer life expectancy than the PIX terminal (.90 probability of lasting 2 or more years, .08 probability to last 18 months, .02 probability to last 12 months). However the TX terminal costs $2500. If it breaks down, a terminal can be leased at the same rate as above, $120 a month. We see from Figure 12-1(*b*) that the best alternative is still to buy the PIX terminal.

Tree representation is particularly useful when a sequence of actions and events

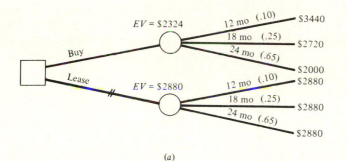

(*a*)

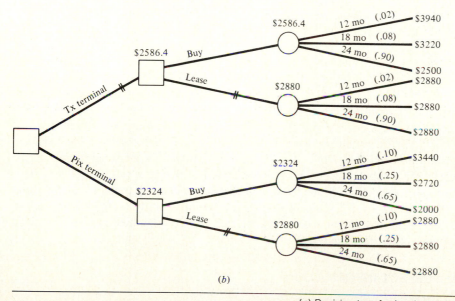

(*b*)

FIGURE **12-1**

(*a*) Decision tree for buy-lease decision for computer terminal. (*b*) Decision tree for buy-lease decision for two competing brands of computer terminals.

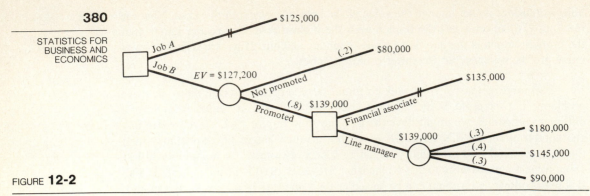

FIGURE **12-2**

Decision tree for job selection.

can take place. Let us illustrate a more complex example of a decision tree for someone choosing two jobs and comparing *5-year potential income*. Assume our applicant
is offered two jobs. Job *A* will not lead to a promotion but will pay $125,000 over a
5-year period. In job *B,* she has an 80% chance of a promotion. If she is not promoted, she will earn a total of $80,000 over 5 years. If she is promoted, she can
choose between a job as a financial associate analyst for the whole company, which
pays $135,000 for 5 years, or one as a line manager (head of the stock option sales
department). In the past, 30% of these department heads have been very successful,
earning $180,000 in salary plus a commission over a 5-year period. She will have a
40% chance of being moderately successful and earning $145,000 over a 5-year
period. If she is not successful, she will earn only the base salary of $18,000 per year
for a total of $90,000 over 5 years. There is a 30% chance of this latter outcome.
First, let us develop the tree; see Figure 12-2. (We will not account for the time value
of money here, although you might want to try this if you know how to handle discounted values.) Then, working from right to left, we calculate the expected value of
choosing the staff associate versus the line manager positions. Since the line manager
position offers a commission, it may prove more lucrative for the successful person.
We find the expected value of the line manager job to be $139,000, as compared to
$135,000 for the staff position. Assuming our candidate makes this choice, move to
the left and calculate the expected returns from job *B*. Remember, there is a 20%
chance that she won't be promoted. Therefore, $80,000(.2) + $139,000(.8) =
$127,200. We know that the returns for job *A* are $125,000; therefore, the expected
value of job *B* is higher. Notice that we have not entered the personal *preference for
risk* into this analysis. If our applicant is afraid of taking a risk, job *A* may be a
better alternative; in job *B*, she has a 20% chance of not being promoted and earning
only $80,000 total for 5 years. We will not attempt to study preference for risk in
this text, but it certainly is a consideration that has been handled in more advanced
treatments of decision analysis.

EXPECTED VALUE OF PERFECT INFORMATION

12-4   Assume that when we considered buying our terminals we could bring a technician
with us who could examine the terminal and tell us whether it would last 12, 18, or
24 months. The technician does this by testing the circuits and examining the equip-

TABLE 12-4

381

DECISION THEORY
AND BAYESIAN
PROBABILITY

$P(C_i)$	COST (PAYOFF)	COST (PAYOFF) $P(C_i)A_i$
.65	$2000	$A_1 = \$1300$
.25	2720	$A_1 = \quad 680$
.10	2880	$A_2 = \quad \underline{288}$
		$2268

ment. If we could determine the life expectancy of a particular terminal, our approach for determining the best course of action would be changed. Also, assume that we must either buy or lease the terminal since we have ordered it.

Looking at the payoff table for the PIX Terminal (Table 12-3), we see that if life expectancy is 12 months it is cheaper to lease: $2880 compared to $3440. If life expectancy is 18 months, it is better to buy: $2720 compared to $2880. If life expectancy is 2 or more years, it is also better to buy: $2000 compared to $2880. In Table 12-4, we combine this information with the probabilities of obtaining machines that will last 12, 18, or 24 months. Thus, if we knew which life would occur with certainty *(perfect information),* the expected cost is $2268. Previously, we would have always chosen action A_1 (buy). However, if we know that a particular terminal will last only 12 months (perhaps as a result of the technician's check), we can choose to lease. The expected value of perfect information (EVPI) is calculated by subtracting the cost when we have perfect information from the cost under risk.

Expected cost under risk	$2324
Expected cost with perfect information	−2268
Expected value of perfect information	$ 56

To reinterpret this result, if the company has no knowledge except the probabilities about the life of the terminals, then it should buy for an expected value of $2324. If the company can tell how long a particular terminal will last, it pays for them to lease *in some cases* (when the terminal will only last 12 months).

If our technician charges $56 or more, it would not be worthwhile to employ his or her services. Later on in this chapter, we study how we can modify decision making under risk conditions by doing market research or other information-gathering activities. We should compute the expected value of perfect information before we seek additional information. The benefits of being able to determine what event will occur does not alter the fact that the occurrence is governed by event probabilities. Also, perfect information is not the same as perfect control, that is, being able to pick the terminal life you want. Then, we would select a terminal with a life of 24 months with a minimum cost of $2000. We discuss a method of handling less than perfect information in terms of Bayesian probability later in this chapter.

SENSITIVITY ANALYSIS

In order to calculate expected cost under uncertainty, as well as under perfect information, we multiplied the costs of our actions by the probability that there would be

PROBABILITY $P(C_i)$ TIME INTERVAL CONDITIONS C_i	PROBABILITY ALTERED	$P(C_i)$ ORIGINAL
C_1: Lasts 2 years or longer	.30	.65 Decreased .35 or 53.8%
C_2: Lasts 18 months	.30	.25 Increased .05 or 20%
C_3: Lasts 12 months	.40	.10 Increased .30 or 300%
	1.00	1.00

different lengths of life for our terminals. In this case, the chance of getting a PIX terminal that would last only 12 months was 10%. The assumption is based on previous experience with this kind of terminal. Often we do not have previous experience to use for estimates. Perhaps the manufacturer could not furnish reliable estimates, or perhaps there is a model change. Sensitivity analysis may be used to assist the decision maker. In sensitivity analysis, we ask such questions as the following: Within what limits can the probability that the terminal will last only 12 months fluctuate without changing the decision to buy rather than to lease? Thus, if the probability of lasting 12 months were 30%, 40%, or 50% and the other probabilities decrease in some proportion such that their sum is 1.00, would it still pay us to buy? When we can develop this analysis of how sensitive the lease-buy decison is to the probability that the terminal will last only 12 months, we can tell how important it will be to have an accurate estimate of this probability. Now, let us alter our set of probabilities, in line with a hypothetical scenario regarding changes in all of the probabilities, and see how it might change outcomes (see Table 12-5). Should we still buy or should we rent?

By redoing the payoff table in Table 12-6, we see that even with these new probabilities and a much higher chance (300% increase) that the terminal will last only 12 months, higher also (by 20%) that it will last only 18 months, it still pays to buy. We have changed the entire original scenario since if there are only three things that can happen, the sum of their probabilities must be 1.00. Continuing with our sensitivity analysis, let us assume a 50/50 chance that it will last 12 months ($C_3 = .50$). Will this change things? Of course, it is important to set reasonable probabilities for C_1 and C_2. We might assume these to be 20% and 30%, respectively. Does it still pay to buy? Table 12-7 provides the answers.

Now, it does pay to lease since the expected cost for leasing is $2880 and the expected cost for buying is $2936. Using such sensitivity analysis, we can build ranges over which any one action will cost the least or be the most profitable. Thus,

TABLE 12-6

TIME INTERVAL CONDITIONS C_i	$P(C_i)$	COST TO BUY A_1	EXPECTED COST $P(C_i)A_1$	COST TO LEASE A_2	EXPECTED COST $P(C_i)A_2$
C_1: Lasts 2 years or longer	.30	$2000	$ 600	$2880	$ 864
C_2: Lasts 18 months	.30	2720	816	2880	864
C_3: Lasts 12 months	.40	3440	1376	2880	1152
			$2792		$2880

TABLE 12-7

TIME INTERVAL CONDITIONS C_i	NEWLY ADJUSTED $P(C_i)$	COST TO BUY A_1	EXPECTED COST $P(C_i)A_1$	COST TO LEASE A_2	EXPECTED COST $P(C_i)A_2$
C_1: Lasts 2 years or longer	.20	$2000	$ 400	$2880	$ 576
C_2: Lasts 18 months	.30	2720	816	2880	864
C_3: Lasts 12 months	.50	3440	1720	2880	1440
			2936		$2880

depending on assumptions about the probabilities of C_1 and C_2, if the chance of the terminals wearing out in 1 year is less than 50%, it pays to lease. We have concentrated in this analysis on $P(C_3)$; however, we could also study the effect of varying the probabilities of the terminals lasting 18 months or 2 or more years. This variation could affect the decision to rent or to buy even when the probability that the terminal would last 12 months was .5. We can work out the conditions where if $P(C_1) = .50$, we would be *indifferent between* renting and buying; that is, we can examine the case in which the expected value of buying equals that of leasing ($2880). Note that since $P(C_3) = .50$, $P(C_1) + P(C_2) = .50$. Let $P(C_1) = X$ and $P(C_2) = .5 - X$.

$$X(\$2000) + (.5 - X)(\$2720) + .5(\$3440) = \$2880$$

$$2000X + 1360 - 2720X + 1720 = 2880$$

$$-720X = -200$$

$$X = .28$$

Thus,

$$P(C_1) = .28$$

$$P(C_2) = .22$$

$$P(C_3) = .50$$

$$\overline{1.00}$$

If $P(C_3)$ stayed at .5 and the probability that the terminal would last 2 years rose to 30%, it would be cheaper to buy:

$$.30(\$2000) + .20(\$2720) + .50(\$3440) = \$600 + \$544 + \$1720 = \$2864$$

$$\$2864 < \$2880 \quad \text{smallest cost preferred}$$

Conversely, if $P(C_1)$ assumed any value below .28 it would be cheaper to lease. We have applied decision analysis to *minimize costs*. It can also be used to maximize profits. Example 12-1 shows such a problem.

EXAMPLE 12-1 Roberto's Real Estate has equity capital of $100,000. In addition, the First National Bank of Baltimore is willing to furnish Roberto with a credit line of $1 million at an interest rate of 8% for 1 year to invest in properties. Roberto is considering three investments. One is a small housing development that will cost $1.1 million. One buyer has promised him one of the following three possibilities.

1 At the end of the year, there is a 50% chance he will buy the property for $1.3 million, or he will ask Roberto to break the property into four smaller parts and sell them for a total of $1.2 million at the end of the year. The prospective buyer estimates there is a 40% chance that this might happen. Thus, there is a 10% chance that he will not buy the property this year.

2 Two other investments also seem promising. The $1.1 million can be invested in a neighborhood shopping center. There is an 80% chance that a prospective customer will invest $1 million after 6 months so that Roberto can pay off the bank loan. At the end of the year, this investor will pay another $300,000. On the other hand, there is a 20% chance that he won't sell the property within the year.

3 The final possibility is the purchase of an industrial park for $1.1 million. Net rentals on this property will yield $50,000, and at the end of the year he has a 90% chance of selling the property for $1.2 million.

Roberto now has three possibilities: (1) to buy the housing development; (2) to buy the neighborhood shopping center; or (3) to buy the industrial park. Which alternative would be more profitable? This is a good example of a complicated decision with many alternatives. Our analysis will help simplify things. Let us first set up a decision tree.

When Roberto borrows $1 million, he must pay interest at 8%, which subtracts $80,000 from the return on any investment. To solve this problem we must first compute the payoffs for each of the events (conditions). Note that the events are different for each alternative. If the housing development is purchased, there are events that could happen at the end of the year.

1 *Purchase housing development.*

Alternative *a* (buyer takes whole property)

$$
\begin{array}{rl}
\$\ 1,300,000 & \text{sales price} \\
-1,100,000 & \text{cost of property} \\
\hline
200,000 & \text{profit} \\
-\quad 80,000 & \text{interest on \$1 million at 8\%} \\
\hline
\$\quad 120,000 & \text{for 1 year}
\end{array}
$$

Alternative *b* (buyer prefers to buy smaller plots for $1.2 million)

$$
\begin{array}{rl}
\$\ 1,200,000 & \text{sales price} \\
-1,100,000 & \text{cost of property} \\
\hline
100,000 & \text{profit} \\
-\quad 80,000 & \text{interest on \$1 million at 8\%} \\
\hline
\$\quad 20,000 & \text{for 1 year}
\end{array}
$$

Alternative *c* (property is not sold this year; must pay interest)

$$
\begin{array}{rl}
-\$\ \ 80,000 & \text{interest on \$1 million at 8\%} \\
& \text{for 1 year}
\end{array}
$$

2 *Purchase shopping center.*

Alternative *a* buyer invests $1 million in 6 months and $300,000 at year end)

$$
\begin{array}{rl}
\$1,300,000 & \text{sales price} \\
-1,100,000 & \text{cost} \\
\hline
200,000 & \text{profit} \\
-\quad 40,000 & \text{interest on \$1 million at 8\%/year} \\
\hline
\$\ 160,000 & \text{for 6 months}
\end{array}
$$

Alternative *b* (no sale)

$$
\begin{array}{rl}
-\$\quad 80,000 & \text{interest on \$1 million at 8\%} \\
& \text{for 1 year}
\end{array}
$$

3 *Purchase industrial park.*

Alternative *a* (rentals of $50,000 and property sells for $1.2 million)	$1,200,000 sales price
	− 1,100,000 cost
	$ 100,000 profit
	+ 50,000 rental income
	$ 150,000
	− 80,000 interest on $1 million at 8% for 1 year
	$ 70,000
Alternative *b* (rentals of $50,000 and property not sold)	−$ 80,000 interest
	+ 50,000 rental income
	−$ 30,000

Now, let us put these values on the tree and combine them with the probabilities of each alternative (see Figure 12-3). Multiplying the profits or losses from each alternative by the probability of each alternative (condition) occurring for the first branch (housing development), we have

$$.5\,(120,000) = \$60,000$$
$$.4\,(20,000) = 8,000$$
$$.1\,(-80,000) = -8,000$$
$$ \$60,000$$

For the second branch (shopping center), we have

$$.8\,(160,000) = \$128,000$$
$$.2\,(-80,000) = -16,000$$
$$ \$112,000$$

For the third branch (industrial park), we have

$$.9\,(70,000) = \$\,63,000$$
$$.1\,(-30,000) = -3,000$$
$$ \$\,60,000$$

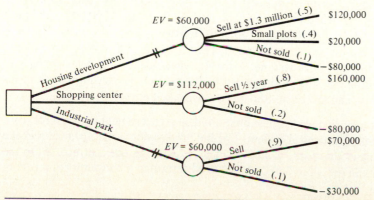

Decision tree for Roberto's Real Estate.

FIGURE **12-3**

Putting the expected value for each decision on the tree at the circular nodes, which show the expected values for all condition branches for a particular decision, we find the shopping center alternative promises maximum profits ($112,000). Therefore, put two lines (//) on each of the decision branches that are rejected. It is now evident that the accepted branch is the shopping center.

Our tree will grow if the second year is added and we would get cascades of squares and circles.

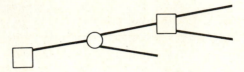

See Figure 12-3 for an example of a cascading decision tree. While a payoff matrix and a decision tree are easily interchanged for simple problems of one square and one circle, the tree becomes essential for lengthy cascades.

Problems

1 Martin Joseph, a plant manager, has $15,000 allocated in his budget to increase productivity. Currently, he is considering choosing one of two projects submitted for approval. The first project is an accelerated maintenance schedule which, according to the manager of engineering, will certainly increase production by 1,550,000 units per year. This accelerated schedule will ensure that parts are repaired or replaced before they wear out. Thus, expensive "down time" (time when the machine is not working) will be avoided. The production manager, on the other hand, proposes a new accessory piece of equipment that will increase production depending on how well the unit can be integrated with present equipment. The plant manager decided that good, fair, and poor levels of integration would increase production 2,310,000 units, 1,640,000 units and 978,000 units, respectively. Further analysis of the use of this accessory in similar plants reveals that chances for good, fair, and poor conditions are .2, .5, and .3, respectively. What action should the manager choose?

2 A young entrepreneur was making a success of her newly formed business when she received an offer to sell out controlling interest in the firm. As part of the contract, the entrepreneur would receive a certain percentage of net income. The business involved a service for highly specialized government contracts that would expire in 1 year. After that time the company would have no salvage value. The offer extended was $125,000 initially for control of the business plus $40,000, $10,000, or $2,000 depending on whether net income was high (over $200,000), medium ($150,000–$200,000), or low (under $150,000). Furthermore, if she did not sell, the owner knew the business could net her $200,000, $150,000, or $90,000, respectively, for high, medium, or low sales volume. After studying business forecasts of the economic climate for the year ahead, the owner assessed the chance for high profit levels at .2, medium at .4, and low at .4. Should the owner sell out?

3 The MGS Corporation wishes to submit a bid on a government contract for work on a defense installation control system. The bid preparation costs $10,000, and the corporation estimates that there is an 8% chance of winning the contract. If the bid is accepted, they can net a predicted $130,000 by installing a conventional mechanical hydraulic control system needed to do the work. New technology has offered the company the option of installing an electrohydraulic system with a potential net profit of $200,000. The new system is only adequate 70% of the time; for the remainder, an additional $120,000 must be spent, reducing profits accordingly. Should the company submit a bid and, if it is accepted, which method should they employ? (Assume net profit figures have already allowed for the $10,000 contract preparation costs.)

4 A recent graduate was considering a choice of three job offers for employment the following month. The first offer was for an annual salary of $15,500 with no chance for review the first year. The second offer entailed a salary of $14,800 and a raise after 6 months. Consultation with the director of personnel indicated that there was a 60% chance of a 10% increase and a 40% chance of a 15% increase for the remaining 6 months. The third offer entailed an annual salary of $15,000, no review the first year, and a bonus according to the year's profit; history had shown that there was a 50% chance of an $800 bonus, a 30% chance of a $400 bonus, and a 20% chance of no bonus. Based strictly on first year's total salary, which offer should a prospective employee accept?

5 A journalist had been studying the various payoffs of a new East Coast casino to determine which game, on the average, gave the best odds to the customer. There were four games. Betting the same amounts at the same intervals, he recorded payoffs for 1000 players and found that the average blackjack player, crap shooter, roulette bettor, and keno player earned or lost the following amounts with the probabilities expressed below:

| GAME | PROBABILITY | | | | |
| | .1 | .2 | .4 | .2 | .1 |
	PAYOFFS				
Blackjack	−1000	−600	−200	+500	+700
Craps	−3000	−1000	−400	+1500	+2000
Roulette	−1500	−800	−100	+700	+1000
Keno	−2500	−1800	−1000	+800	+5000

Which games give the most and the least return to the house? Alternatively, which game offers the player the best chance of success?

6 A student was attempting to plan a housing budget for the coming year. If the student stayed at the same residence the current monthly rent of $180 would increase by $10 every four months. Two other apartments offered different arrangements. Rent for one of these apartments started at $185 per month, and there was a 60% chance that the rent would increase by $15 at the end of 6 months. The other apartment had a rather strange system. Rent started at $175, but at the end of every 4 months the landlord flipped a coin. If the landlord flipped heads, the rent would increase by $25; if the landlord flipped tails, the rent would remain the same. Based on rent price alone, which apartment would you select?

7 A gambler was offered the chance to play one of two games with a friend, who was a mathematician. The friend assured the gambler that one game gave the player an advantage, but that the other did not. The first game cost the gambler $10 to play and consisted of rolling a die *five* times with the following payoffs per roll:

Result of roll	1	2	3	4	5	6
Dollar payoff	−3	−1	+1	+2	+4	+5

The second game cost the gambler $20 to play for *10 rolls* with the following payoffs:

Result of roll	1	2	3	4	5	6
Dollar payoff	−10	−4	+3	+6	+8	+10

Which game should the gambler play?

BAYESIAN PROBABILITY

12-6

In the problem where we decided whether to rent or buy computer terminals, we mentioned that it would be possible to hire a technician to examine each terminal and tell us its life expectancy. This information could possibly save us money in our longer-range decision making.

One of the problems of buying information is that it may not always be correct. Thus, a market researcher can forecast the demand (or market behavior) for us, but seldom with absolute accuracy. If we have recorded this researcher's past forecasting performance, we can develop probabilities for accuracy. Thus, we may be able to revise our prior (or original) probabilities based on additional information, even though the additional information does not guarantee full certainty.

In the early 1700s the Reverend Thomas Bayes, a British minister, developed the concept of inverse probability. From observed events and observed associations with these events, one is able to deduce the probability of what caused the event. By means of Bayes' theorem, we can use a sample of one property to make a prediction about another property. To illustrate this inverse process of reasoning, we now discuss a problem that illustrates the Bayesian method. For example, a personnel director interested in affirmative action is distressed when 65% of applicants for jobs requiring college degrees are men. Library research informs the personnel director that 50% of men and 30% of women in this area of the country are college graduates. This town has 10,000 males and 10,000 females. Thus, the probability of encountering a female $P(\text{female}) = .5$, equals the probability of male $P(\text{male}) = .5$, or $P(F) = .5$ and $P(M) = .5$, if a random drawing is made from the town's population.

If someone is selected at random from those with a college degree, what is the probability that the person will be a woman? We know that fewer women have college degrees; therefore, we would expect that if a person with a college degree is picked, the person is less likely to be a woman than a man. Let us introduce conditional probabilities to help us determine the actual probability.

1 $P(M|D)$: Given a person with a degree (D), $P(M|D)$ is the probability that it will be a male (M).
2 $P(F|D)$: Given that the person has a degree (D), $P(F|D)$ is the probability that it will be a female (F).

3 $P(D|F)$: Given that a person is a female (F), $P(D|F)$ is the probability that she has a degree (D).

4 $P(D|M)$: Given that a person is a male (M), $P(D|M)$ is the probability that he has a degree (D).

In our example, items 3 and 4 are known while 1 and 2 must be found. Of all the people in town, males with a degree have a compound probability of $.5(.5) = .25$, since half the people in town are males and half the males have degrees; this is $P(M) \, P(D|M)$. The compound probability of women with a degree is $.5(.3) = .15$; this is $P(F) \, P(D|F)$. Thus, 40% of the people in town have degrees (the sum of the compound probabilities). The appropriate conditional probabilities for items 1 and 2 are calculated as follows:

$$P(F|D) = \frac{\text{Women having a degree}}{\text{All people having degrees}}$$

$$= \frac{P(F) \, P(D|F)}{P(F) \, P(D|F) + P(M) \, P(D|M)} = \frac{.5(.3)}{(.5)(.3) + (.5)(.5)}$$

Note that the conditional probabilities $P(D|F)$ and $P(D|M)$ are known from library research, and $P(F)$ and $P(M)$ are known from town population records. What we want to determine is the conditional probability that a person with a degree is female (or male). Thus, the denominator includes all degree holders, both male and female. The numerator represents the compound probability previously described.

$$P(F|D) = \frac{.15}{.15 + .25} = \frac{.15}{.40} = 37.5\%$$

This is the probability that if someone has a degree that person will be a female. What is the probability that if someone with a degree responds, that person will be a man?

$$P(M|D) = \frac{P(M) \, P(D|M)}{P(M) \, P(D|M) + P(F) \, P(D|F)}$$

$$P(M|D) = \frac{.5(.5)}{(.5)(.5) + (.5)(.3)} = \frac{.25}{.40} = 62.5\%$$

Forty percent of the people are degree holders (denominator), and 25% of the population are males holding degrees (numerator). Dividing, we obtain the proportion of male degree holders living in town.

Therefore, if someone with a degree walks into the office, there is a 62.5% chance it will be a man. If the personnel director is advertising for people with college degrees and the ads are answered at random, the applicant will be a man 62.5% of the time. Thus, it seems that the personnel director's actual experience (65%) does not differ very much from the expected. Now let us apply this inverse analysis to some other situations.

EXAMPLE 12-2 The Southwood Independent School District is considering the adoption of a special test before students are placed in the honors program. In prior years, acceptance into the honors program was based solely on teacher recommendations. For a period of 4 years, all students who want to enter the program, if they are recommended by teachers, are accepted and given a special test. At the end of 4 years, the results are analyzed in terms of:

F = number who fail test (receive less than 70% score on the test)

P = number who pass test (receive a score of 70% or more on the test)

D = number who drop out of the program (after being accepted)

S = number who stay in the program

We are interested in the ability of the test to identify dropouts since the honors program involves a large investment per student. The results show that of those who dropped out of the program, the percent who failed the test is .95. Of those students who have not dropped out of the program, .03 failed the test. In conditional probability terms, we have

$$P(F|D) = .95$$

$$P(F|S) = .03$$

Thus, 5% of the people who dropped out of the program were not screened by failing the test, and 3% of the people who remained in the program failed the test.

Additional information is available—namely, 20% of all accepted students drop out of the program and 80% remain. What we want to know is if someone has failed the test, what is the probability that he or she will not complete the honors program? In probability notation, we write the conditional statement for $P(D|F)$, which is the probability that a student who has failed the test will drop out of the program.

$$P(D|F) = \frac{P(D)\,P(F|D)}{P(D)\,P(F|D) + P(S)(F|S)}$$

$$P(D|F) = \frac{.20(.95)}{(.20)(.95) + (.80)(.03)} = \frac{.19}{.19 + .024} = .888$$

Thus, 89% of those who fail the test can be expected to drop out of the program, and the test is very useful. (However, the test might be improved since it unfairly "weeds out" 11% who would have succeeded in the program.) In the interest of sensitivity analysis, let us assume the dropout rate for the honors course was much smaller than 20%, say 2%. That is,

$$P(D) = .02 \quad \text{and} \quad P(S) = .98$$

In this case, our use of the test as a predictor will not be as helpful, since

$$P(D|F) = \frac{.02(.95)}{(.02)(.95) + (.98)(.03)} = \frac{.019}{.019 + .0294} = .393$$

In other words, given that someone has failed the test, there is a 39% chance that he or she will drop out. This result indicates a poor test and seems odd. It might be better understood if we translate it into actual numbers. Suppose 500 students sign up for the course and are tested.

1 $P(D) = .20$: Twenty percent of the 500 students, or 100 students, will drop out of the program. Ninety-five of these students would have been identified by the test. In addition, of the 400 students who did not drop out, 3% or 12 of them would have failed the test. Thus, 107 students will fail the test. Of *this group who fail,* 95 will actually drop out, $95/107 = 88.8\%$, as shown above where we have calculated $P(D|F)$.

2 $P(D) = .02$: In this case we assume that only 2% of the students will drop out. Thus, a total of 10 students will drop out. What we are really interested in is the ability of the test to identify dropouts. Of those who dropped out, 95%, or 9.5 students (fractions would not occur if we used 1000 students), would have been identified by the test. Of the 490 students who stayed in the program, 3% or 14.7 would have failed the test. Thus, $9.5 + 14.7$ have failed the test. Of this group, 9.5/24.2, or 39.3%, dropped out. When the dropout rate is low, the test is not as good at predicting dropouts because the results are counterbalanced by the high *number of people* who fail the test and yet do not drop out.

We have set the passing grade at 70%; we can use this data to determine if a different level for passing might prove more effective.

Medical problems, in which the chance of having a disease is very remote, should be analyzed using this technique, since the chance that someone has shown positive results on the test (indicating that he has the disease) may not mean that there is a substantial probability that one actually does have the disease. Example 12-3 illustrates this situation.

EXAMPLE 12-3   In Puritania, 1 person in 10,000 (.01%) has Minzies disease. The test that identifies this disease gives a positive indication 99% of the time when an individual has the disease. However, 2% of the time it gives a positive indication when a person doesn't have the disease.

Assume that a person is selected at random by a medical school class for this test, and that the test turns out positive. This does not mean that there is a 99% chance that the person has the disease. What is the probability?

We are examining a typical health-related problem. Given a positive test result, what is the probability that the individual has the disease? We set up the appropriate conditional probability model. Note that Equation 12-1 is *a general formula for computing Bayesian probabilities.*

$$P(A|B) = \frac{P(A_1)\, P(B_1|A_1)}{P(A_1)\, P(B_1|A_1) + P(A_2)\, P(B_1|A_2)} \qquad (12\text{-}1)$$

where A_1 = person has the disease
A_2 = person does not have the disease
B_1 = positive test result
B_2 = negative test result

Using a matrix we have

Test	State	
	A_1 (.0001)	A_2 (.9999)
B_1	.99	.02
B_2	.01	.98

$$P(A_1 | B_1) = \frac{.0001 \,(.99)}{.0001\,(.99) + .9999\,(.02)} = .0049$$

Thus, there is a .49% chance (about 5 chances in 1000) that a person with a positive test actually has the disease. This may be an unacceptable test; it is likely to worry people who do not have the disease (and will involve them in further medical expenses). The doctor might use this test in conjunction with others before making the final diagnosis.

Another computation of interest would be $P(A_1 | B_2)$ because if we do not identify the disease, no treatment will be given. This probability is

$$P(A_1 | B_2) = \frac{P(A_1)\, P(B_2 | A_1)}{P(A_1)\, P(B_2 | A_1) + P(A_2)\, P(B_2 | A_2)}$$

$$= \frac{.0001\,(.01)}{(.0001)(.01) + (.9999)(.98)} = \frac{.000001}{.979903} = .000001$$

Thus, the chance of missing someone who actually has the disease is very unlikely. If the disease is deadly, the test might be used.

Personnel departments use a wide variety of testing procedures in the selection of employees for hiring, training, and promotion. A study of their success rates combined with Bayesian analysis would help them to identify the testing procedures that are not good at identifying people who might be successful or, conversely, people who might fail. In the next section, we use Bayesian analysis to study the value of forecasts that can be combined with decision trees in order to make more accurate estimates of expected values of different managerial decisions.

Problems

1 Sue Rosenstock, director of special events in Ann Harbour, is trying to set up a rock concert for July 4. If it rains, it will be a disaster since the concert will be held at an open-air stadium. Carlos "Guru" Sesler, the local KFIV weatherman, says that it will rain; Carlos has accurately predicted rain 80% of the time. He has forecast rain when it didn't rain 10% of the time. The chance of rain on July 4 is 30% according to weather statistics. Given that Guru has predicted rain, what is the probability that it will rain?

2 Using the data in problem 1, what would happen if Guru made perfect forecast predictions? If you were running the concerts, what would you do as a result of evaluating Guru's forecast? What would you do in this situation when Guru makes perfect forecasts?

3 Using the data in problem 1, what would happen if Guru made random forecast predictions (50% chance of being right)? What action should Sue take?

DECISION MAKING USING SAMPLE INFORMATION (POSTERIOR PROBABILITY)

When we were selecting computer terminals earlier in this chapter, we mentioned that we could consult a technician to determine the life of particular terminals. In the example, we assumed that the technician could supply *perfect information* about the future state of each terminal. Most often it is very difficult to purchase such perfect information. Even when we buy market research results from the best market research companies, there is the real possibility that the companies will not be able to forecast the market accurately. The same can be said about medical diagnoses.

Let us assume that we hire a technician who forecasts that a particular terminal will last 18 months. (C_2 will apply; see Table 12-5.) We should now obtain some figures from the technician about the accuracy of previous predictions (C_2) that terminals would last for 18 months. Our technician tells us that past predictions when terminals turned out to last 18 months were 75% accurate. When terminals lasted 24 months or more, 30% of the time the technician had predicted they would last only 18 months. Finally, when terminals had lasted 12 months, the technician predicted 5% of the time that they would last 18 months.

$$F_{24} = \text{forecast to last 24 or more months}$$

$$F_{18} = \text{forecast to last 18 months}$$

$$F_{12} = \text{forecast to last 12 months}$$

First, let us put this in the form of a payoff table (Table 12-8). If we combine Table 12-8 and Table 12-1, we have Table 12-9. This table shows us for all the cases where the technician predicted 18 months what the chances would have been of this forecast (a forecast of 18 months life) when the terminals actually lasted 2 or more years, 18 months, or 12 months. Using column 4, we compute the probability that the terminals will last for each of these three time periods, given that we have a prediction that they will last for 18 months, given the previous accuracy of our forecaster, and given the previous experience of the company with these terminals, that is, $P(C_1) = .65$, $P(C_2) = .25$, $P(C_3) = .10$. Conditional probability (column 3) states three probabilities. The first is the probability that given the true state (length of life) was 24 months, our expert would have predicted 18 months, $P(F_{18}|C_1) =$

TABLE 12-8

	TRUE STATE		
PREDICTION	C_1 LASTS 2 OR MORE YEARS (.65)	C_2 LASTS 18 MONTHS (.25)	C_3 LASTS 12 MONTHS (.10)
F_{12}	—	—	—
F_{18}	.30	.75	.05
F_{24}	—	—	—

TABLE 12-9

PROBABILITIES OF COMPUTER TERMINAL LIFE

(1) TIME INTERVAL CONDITIONS C_i	(2) PRIOR PROBABILITY $P(C_i)$	(3) CONDITIONAL PROBABILITY $P(F_{18} \mid C_i)$	(4) JOINT PROBABILITY $P(C_i) \, P(F_{18} \mid C_i)$
C_1: Lasts 2 or more years	.65	$P(F_{18} \mid C_1) = .30$	.1950
C_2: Lasts 18 months	.25	$P(F_{18} \mid C_2) = .75$	.1875
C_3: Lasts 12 months	.10	$P(F_{18} \mid C_3) = .05$	.0050
			.3875

.30. Similarly, $P(F_{18} \mid C_2) = .75$ is the probability that the true state was 18 months and the expert forecast 18 months. Finally, $P(F_{18} \mid C_3) = .05$ is the probability that, given the true state was 12 months, the forecaster predicted 18 months. These probabilities do not add to 1 because each one is the probability of forecasting 18 months given *different* true states. Thus, we are adding probabilities estimated on different bases. The joint probability (column 4) is the compound probability. We obtain this probability by multiplying the prior probability $P(C_i)$ in column 2 by the conditional probability $P(C_i) \, P(F_{18} \mid C_i)$, or column 2 multiplied by column 3. If we have a forecast of 18 and given the probabilities of making this forecast under the three different conditions, then weighting by the probability, this shows us that the three conditions will occur. To find our posterior probability, since we know prior probability and chance of our forecast error, we can use Bayes' theorem.

$$P(C_1 \mid F_{18}) = \frac{P(C_1) \, P(F_{18} \mid C_1)}{P(C_1)P(F_{18} \mid C_1) + P(C_2)P(F_{18} \mid C_2) + P(C_3)P(F_{18} \mid C_3)}$$

This is the probability that the terminal will last 2 or more years given that the technician predicted that it will last 18 months. Notice that the denominator is the sum of the probabilities in the joint probability column (4). The numerator appears in the first row of the same column.

$$P(C_1 \mid F_{18}) = \frac{.1950}{.3875} = .5032$$

This is the probability that terminal life is 24 or more months when the forecast is 18 months. Now, given that the technician forecasts that the terminals would last 18 months, what is the probability that they will actually last 18 months?

$$P(C_2 \mid F_{18}) = \frac{P(C_2)P(F_{18} \mid C_2)}{P(C_1)P(F_{18} \mid C_1) + P(C_2)P(F_{18} \mid C_2) + P(C_3)P(F_{18} \mid C_3)}$$

$$P(C_2 \mid F_{18}) = \frac{.1875}{.3875} = .4839$$

Finally, we compute the probability that the technician predicted 18 months and the terminals actually last 12 months.

$$P(C_3 \mid F_{18}) = \frac{P(C_3)P(F_{18} \mid C_3)}{P(C_1)P(F_{18} \mid C_1) + P(C_2)P(F_{18} \mid C_2) + P(C_3)P(F_{18} \mid C_3)}$$

$$P(C_3 \mid F_{18}) = \frac{.0050}{.3875} = .0129$$

TABLE 12-10

395

DECISION THEORY
AND BAYESIAN
PROBABILITY

TIME INTERVAL CONDITIONS C_i	$P(C_i\|F_{18})$	BUY A_1	$P(C_i\|F_{18})A_1$	LEASE A_2	$P(C_i\|F_{18})A_2$
C_1: Lasts 2 or more years	.5032	$2000	$1006.4	$2880	$1449.2
C_2: Lasts 18 months	.4839	2720	1316.2	2880	1393.6
C_3: Lasts 24 months	.0129	3440	44.4	2880	37.2
			$2367.0		$2880.0

Using these revised probabilities in our original payoff table, let us see if we would still advocate this decision given that our technician has predicted that the terminal will last 18 months. We substitute the Bayesian probabilities for our original probabilities of $P(C_1) = .65$, $P(C_2) = .25$, and $P(C_3) = .10$. Then, we multiply these probabilities by the costs of each option when we are buying (A_1) or leasing (A_2) (see Table 12-10). The best decision is *still* to buy. Look at the case we presented in Section 12-5 dealing with sensitivity analysis. When we changed our probabilities in Table 12-7 to a .20 chance that it will last 2 or more years, a .30 chance that it will last 18 months, and a .2 chance that it will last 12 months, the best decision was to lease (see Table 12-11).

Now weighting these new prior probabilities (column 2) by the conditional probabilities, because our expert predicted 18 months (column 3), we obtain new revised probabilites (see Table 12-12).

$$P(C_1|F_{18}) = \frac{.06}{.310} = .1935$$

$$P(C_2|F_{18}) = \frac{.225}{.310} = .7258$$

$$P(C_3|F_{18}) = \frac{.025}{.310} = .0807$$

The total is 1.000, as we know it must be.

TABLE 12-11

(1) TIME INTERVAL CONDITIONS C_i	(2) PRIOR PROBABILITY $P(C_i)$	(3) CONDITIONAL PROBABILITY $P(F_{18}\|C_i)$	(4) JOINT PROBABILITY $P(C_i)P(F_{18}\|C_i)$
C_1: Lasts 2 or more years	.20	.30	.060
C_2: Lasts 18 months	.30	.75	.225
C_3: Lasts 12 months	.50	.05	.025
			.310

TABLE 12-12

TIME INTERVAL CONDITIONS C_i	$P(C_i\|F_{18})$	BUY A_1	$P(C_i\|F_{18})A_1$	LEASE A_2	$P(C_i\|F_{18})A_2$
C_1: Lasts 2 or more years	.1935	$2000	$ 387.0	$2880	$ 551.3
C_2: Lasts 18 months	.7258	2720	1974.2	2880	2090.3
C_3: Lasts 24 months	.0807	3440	277.6	2880	232.4
			$2638.8		$2880.0

From these calculations, we develop Table 12-12. In our problem in Table 12-7, the best decision was to lease. The technician has said the terminal will last 18 months, so the best action has changed to *buy*. Thus, use of forecast information and its probability of success, sometimes called *posterior* information because it is a result of previous forecast experience, in this case *has changed the original decision*, which was based only on prior probabilities.

SUMMARY

12-8

1 To set up a decision model, we must know at least 4 things: What are the decision maker's possible *actions?* What external *conditions* or *events* might occur? What are *probabilities* of each event or condition occurring? What are the *payoffs* or *costs* for each action?

2 A *payoff table* can be developed where for each action j the probability of each event occurring $P(C_i)$ is multiplied by its costs A_{ij} and summed $\Sigma P(C_i)A_{ij}$. For event 1, we obtain $\Sigma P(C_1)A_{1j}$. This sum is compared to the sum for alternate events [for example, $\Sigma P(C_2)A_{2j}$], and the cost-minimizing (or profit-maximizing) alternative chosen.

3 A *decision tree* may be used to portray the data found in a payoff table. For complex multiple-sequenced decisions, the decision tree may be superior to the payoff table. Decision facts are preceded by a box. For each of these decisions, various conditions or events may occur. These are designated by circles. From these circles, the conditional branches radiate. The payoff is written at the end of each branch.

For each branch, work from right to left multiplying payoff by probability. At the circle from which the branches radiate, place the *sum* for all the payoffs multiplied by the probabilities. Now, compare the figures at each of the circles and choose the best alternative. Cross out the branches that do not represent optimal solutions, using two lines (//).

4 In some situations it will be possible to obtain information to make decisions. The *expected value with perfect information* can be calculated. Perfect information tells us if each event will occur. Thus, for each event, we can choose the best course of action if that event were to occur; for example, in the computer terminal problem, renting is the best choice if the terminal will last only 12 months. By multiplying the payoffs for the best actions chosen for each event by the probability of each event occurring and summing, we obtain the *cost with perfect information* (EVPI).

5 *Sensitivity analysis* varies the values of parameters in a problem to determine those conditions that require a change in the best course of action. In the computer problem, we estimated the probabilities that the terminals would last 12, 18, or 24 months. More optimistic or more pessimistic estimates might lead to different payoffs and decisions. Other problems might call for probability estimates of economic conditions. If a small change in the probabilities of an economic upturn will make a change in the actions we take, it becomes very important to forecast economic conditions accurately. Costs might also be varied. We might not be certain about the costs of terminals and, hence, might want to see how variations in terminal prices might affect our favored action. If the problem entailed maximizing profits, profits from different actions might also be varied. We are interested in the likelihood of changes that would cause us to alter our decisions.

6 *Bayesian probability* is often referred to as *inverse probability*. If we know the percentage of men and women who have college degrees and draw a person from our population who has a college degree, we can infer the probability that the person is a woman. The equation for the probability that a person with a degree is a female is

$$P(F|D) = \frac{P(F)\ P(D|F)}{P(F)\ P(D|F) + P(M)\ P(D|M)}$$

where F = female, D = degree, and M = male. We restructure this equation to fit similar situations.

7 Additional information using this type of posterior probability may be used together with our decision-tree analysis. Thus, we may obtain a forecast from an expert (perhaps an engineer, a market analyst, or an economist). This prediction tells us what the conditions might be. For example, in the computer terminal problem, we might have the expert predict how long our terminal will last. If we have some record of the accuracy of the experts previous forecasts, we can then infer, given that the expert predicts an event, the probability that the event will actually take place. Combining this *posterior probability* with our past experience (*prior probability,* the probability in the past that the terminals last 12, 18, or 24 months), we can formulate an improved forecast of future events. The costs of these tests or experts' opinions should be compared to expected savings for both perfect and imperfect information to see if the use of such tests is warranted. These forecasts, which use Bayesian probabilities, may lead to a different course of action than our prior probabilities suggest, but they may not.

BIBLIOGRAPHY

12-9

Boot, John C., and Edwin B. Cox: *Statistical Analysis for Managerial Decisions,* 2d ed., New York: McGraw-Hill, 1974. See chapter 12 for an easy-to-understand explanation of decision theory.

Hamburg, Morris: *Basic Statistics,* New York: Harcourt Brace, 2d ed., 1979. See chapter 12 for an excellent simplified explanation of elementary decision theory.

Miller, David W., and Martin K. Starr: *Executive Decisions and Operations Research,* 2d ed., Englewood Cliffs, N.J.: Prentice Hall, 1969. One of the first texts relating quantitative methods and decision theory. Chapter 9 deals with Bayesian analysis.

Raiffa, Howard: *Decision Analysis,* Reading Mass.: Addison-Wesley, 1968. One of the earliest expositions of decision theory. Raiffa's early expository lectures.

Schaifer, Robert: *Analysis of Decisions under Uncertainty,* New York: McGraw-Hill, 1969. Outstanding exposition of decision theory.

Marketing

Brown, Rex. V.: "Do Managers Find Decision Theory Useful?" *Harvard Business Review,* May–June 1970, pp. 78–89.

Green, Paul E.: "Bayesian Decision Theory in Pricing Strategy." In Enis and Cox, (eds.), *Marketing Classics,* 3d ed., pp. 434–450.

Finance

Hespos, Richard F., and Paul A. Strassman: "Stochastic Decision Trees for the Analysis of Investment Decisions," *Management Science,* Aug. 1965, pp. 244–259.

Accounting

Knoblett, James A.: "The Application of Bayesian Statistics in Auditing," *Decision Science,* vol. 1, 1970, pp. 423–440.

Reinmuth, James E.: "On the Application of Bayesian Statistics in Auditing," *Decision Science,* vol. 3, 1972, pp. 139–141.

Production and Finance
Ulvila, J. W., Rex V. Brown, and Karle Packard: "A Case in On-Line Decision Analysis for Product Planning," *Decision Science,* vol. 8, July 1977, pp. 598–615.

CASES

12-10

Case 12-1   Comfort Furniture Rental Company

Don Howard, a recent college graduate, was moving to Columbus to attend a 2-year graduate program at Ohio State University. Having lived in a dorm during his 4 years as an undergrad, Don decided it was time to start living "on his own" in an apartment. After an exhaustive search, he finally located an apartment in his price bracket that was fairly close to the main campus. The major drawback in the new-found home was that the apartment was unfurnished. After a brief discussion with the prospective landlord, Don found that a local furniture rental company offered college students two options for buying new furniture. He had only $500 at the moment to spend on furniture.

During a visit to the Comfort Furniture Rental Company, Don collected as much information as possible about the ways he could furnish his apartment. The basic rental plan supplied an apartment full of new furniture for $30 per month, with an option to buy the furniture at the end of any 1-year contract. Thus, he could rent for 1 year and buy at that time, or rent for 2 years and then exercise his prerogative of buying the furniture or returning it. The option allowed for two-thirds of the total paid to be applied to the purchase price of $850, with the balance due when the choice to purchase is made.

Comfort Furniture Rental also had a warehouse of previously rented furniture for sale. Although the furniture was not of as good a quality as the new rental furniture, Don judged it adequate for the next 2 years. After touring the warehouse, Don decided he could furnish his apartment for $450.

Later that night Don was still considering the options. He thought that the previously rented furniture would have only 2 years life left, and could then be sold for only $150. He also realized that he would certainly be leaving Columbus in 2 years, and there was only a 60% chance that anything he might buy would be suitable in a new location. If he had bought the new furniture and found it unsuitable, he determined that he could sell or trade it in at the end of 2 years for $450. Don also esitmated that a new set of furniture at the end of two years would cost $1000, allowing for the cost of inflation.

Questions

1 In straight dollar terms, what is the least-expensive option in order to have furniture when he moves into a new apartment in 2 years? (*Hint:* Use decision-tree analysis.)

2 Besides the dollar difference in options, what qualitative aspects should Don examine?

3 What do you recommend that Don should do?

4 *Optional question—for students who can calculate discounted values:* With money valued at 12% per year, compounded annually, what is the least-expensive path that Don could choose in order to have furniture when he moves into a new apartment in 2 years.

Case 12-2 Frozen Convertibles

Rita Hamilton had recently joined Data Analysis Corporation as a financial analyst. Rita's first assignment was to determine the best way to raise capital over the next 2 years. The controller stated that $1 million was going to be needed each year. However, the controller did not think it would be easy to raise additional capital by selling stock, because the company had experienced difficulty raising money by doing so in the previous year and the experts now predicted a recession.

There were two types of debt equity that the company could sell: a straight debt issue (bond) or a convertible debenture. Rita's task, with the help of the financial staff at Data Analysis, was to determine which type of debt to use in raising the essential capital.

A straight debt issue is simply a bank note with a fixed interest payment. Interest is paid on the amount of the note in installments set up in the terms of the note. The lower the interest rate at the time of issuance, the cheaper it is to borrow money. On the other hand, a convertible debenture is similar to straight debt except that the investors, or holders of the note, can trade their claim on the company for common stock if the stock rises to a certain level stated in the debenture. For example, Data Analysis Corporation is currently selling for $22½ per share. An investor holds a $1000 convertible debenture paying 8% and convertible at $25 per share. The investor holds the note and recieves $80 (.08 × $1000) per year in interest. When the stock price rises above $26, the investor finds it advantageous to convert the debenture into 40 ($1000 ÷ $25) shares of stock and forego the interest receipts because the stock can be sold for $26 or more immediately.

Many companies find convertible debentures a good way to raise money, which they hope will be converted to equity at prices higher than current levels. Companies prefer equity capital because when times are bad it is not necessary to distribute a dividend, whereas interest on bonds is a fixed claim on the company.

There is a danger with convertibles: If the stock price does not exceed $25 (in this case), the investor would never trade in for stock. This would leave the company paying interest for the entire term of the issue, which they had really hoped to avoid. A situation like this is called a *frozen convertible.*

The first thing Rita decided to consider for the coming period was earnings of the company, commonly measured as earnings per share of common stock (EPS). This is a major determinant of stock price, since investors view an increase in earnings as a strong sign of future improvements. After reviewing the financial records and consulting with others in the department, Rita determined that there was a 90% chance that the EPS would rise over the next 2 years and a 10% chance that it would fall or stay the same.

Interest rates are closely linked to the economy. This is the second variable related to stock prices that Rita decided to consider. Interest rate changes tend to push stock prices in the opposite direction from which they move. (Thus, as interest rates go up, stock prices tend to go down.) Naturally, if interest rates were rising, Data Analysis Corporation would prefer to issue straight debt now. On the other hand, falling interest rates would make it advisable that debt be issued in the second year. As mentioned earlier, convertibles should be issued in a rising stock market. In a falling or stable market, the signals would be too confusing to make a sound judgment about whether to issue convertibles.

Economists for the company predicted an 80% chance that interest rates would rise over the next 2 years and a 20% chance that they would fall. The combination of rising or falling EPS and rising or falling interest rates produces four basic conditions under which the stock prices would either rise or fall. From studying several econometric models and reading various financial theorists, Rita determined that if EPS and interest rates move in the same direction—both up or both down—meaning conflicting signals to the market (assume down includes remain the same), there would be a 50/50 chance that the stock price would move up or down. If interest rates and EPS move in opposite directions (reinforcing signals) there would be a 90% chance that the stock price would move in the same direction as EPS and a 10% chance it would move in the opposite direction.

This decision model produces eight potential scenarios for EPS, interest rates, and stock prices; see Table 1. We assume that if the stock price rises, the owner *will convert.*

Rita now determined that for each of the actions [selling convertible debentures (1) and selling straight debt (2)] she should estimate the expected cost to the company and then pick the lowest-cost alternative.

Straight bonds can be sold at 10% interest while convertible debentures can be sold at 9% because of the conversion feature, but it will cost the company another 3% to cover the clerical cost of conversion. However, if the bonds are converted, the company analysts estimate that it will save about $60,000 a year on $1 million of bonds because people who have equity capital expect to take profits in terms of equity appreciation, and dividends payments can be lower than interest would have been.

TABLE 1

A EARNINGS PER SHARE	B INTEREST RATE	C STOCK PRICE	
Rising	Rising	Rising (Convert)	(1)
		Falling	(2)
	Falling	Rising (Convert)	(3)
		Falling	(4)
Falling (some)	Rising	Rising (Convert)	(5)
		Falling	(6)
	Falling	Rising (Convert)	(7)
		Falling	(8)

Questions

1   For each of the eight possibilities, compute the joint probabilities.

2   Set up a decision tree for this problem. What is the expected cost of straight debentures? What is the expected cost of convertibles?

3   What is the probability of a frozen convertible?

4   What other factors should Rita consider in making this type of decision?

5   What should Rita recommend?

Case 12-3   Springdale Methodist Church Building Project

"Well, gentlemen, we have to reach a financing decision soon or lose our favorable contract bid on the new addition; therefore, we have to build immediately." Reverend Taylor made these candid remarks as he stood before the stewardship committee of Springdale Methodist Church. This particular committee meeting was called by the minister to resolve the question of how the church could pay for the construction of its new educational building. The church was a medium-size institution (550 members) located in the Midwest. Due to growth beyond that anticipated when the main church building was completed in 1954, the congregation had recently voted to build an education addition that would provide much needed space for offices, classrooms, a library, and a day-care center. But, as sometimes occurs in nonprofit institutions, the group had not planned for financing such a venture.

The contract stipulated that the $225,000 cost of the building would be due at the beginning of construction. The building would be completed in 1 year. At that time, the church would name the building after a prospective donor who would pay off the mortgage debt once the donor had seen and approved the new structure. The church decided it was crucial that they evaluate the financing alternatives before the final signing of the contract or face the possibility of impairing annual operating funds in order to cover the debt. The future years' operating budgets were projected to be strained even without the construction financing problems, so the church leaders agreed that they would prefer to owe no debt for the project after this 1-year time limit.

With this in mind, the stewardship committee began to evaluate the church's alternatives. The most obvious and common fund-raising method was through an appeal to the church congregation, a fund drive that would cost the church $5000 immediately. Money could be raised with church pledges or special events known as *fund raisers*. However, church pledges had been increasing slowly or not at all during the past few years, and the stewardship committee believed that there was only a 20% chance that the entire amount could be derived from this source. The group guessed that for the remaining options (80% of the possible occurrences), the probability of raising total gift packages of any amount from $25,000 to $150,000 were equally likely (thus forming a uniform distribution), due to the unpredictability of major individual donations. One benefit from fund raising was that total pledges would be known within 6 weeks. If the church did not meet its goal, a local bank promised to provide an 8% loan for the remainder.

Two alternatives relied upon outside sources for funds. Through the bank, the church could immediately borrow the entire $225,000 at the current 8% interest rate. Or another frequently used approach was to apply for a grant or loan from the Methodist Church at the national level through the Board of Global Ministries, which provided assistance for mission and building projects. The church leaders knew that on the average 80% of all local church requests for funds were somehow met. If approved, they felt their chances were 70% for a totally free grant and 30% to receive a full loan at the extremely low interest rate of 3%.

Yet a drawback was that the application and reviewing processes were lengthy and usually took anywhere from 0 to 12 months (following a uniform distribution) before the local church would know if the funds were granted. The church leaders did not know if they should apply because they were afraid the risk might be too high and, if their proposal was rejected, they would not have sufficient time to conduct a fund drive to meet the cutoff date. Then, the group would be forced by the time constraint to immediately take out a bank loan. Because of rapid inflation, the local bank could not promise the church an 8% interest rate in 12 months. National economists were predicting interest rates to rise to 12% by year's end. The church could take out a loan at 1% a month to pay the immediate total expense of the addition and then repay this loan as soon as the Global funds were approved.

Questions

1 What alternative should the stewardship committee pursue to obtain funds for the new education building?

2 Is there any difference between this problem and those for the profit sector?

3 If the church could wait a year to construct its building, draw a tree depicting the best alternative.

Case 12-4   Carolina Canning Company

As operations manager of a production facility of the Carolina Canning Company, Jim Hamilton was faced with a problem. Profits were slipping due to intense competition from the major canners in the Southeast. Carolina, operating on a profit-center basis, placed this responsibility for improving margins on Jim for his plant. Before taking any actions, he first decided to summarize the alternatives.

Jim Hamilton had recently been told that the canning operations were to be centralized in about 2 years so that he should be concerned only with profitability for that duration; if Jim does well, he has a good chance of running the centralized operations. Since the disposition of the present plant and equipment (which might range from moving some machinery to the new plant or scrapping it altogether) was unknown, any salvage values were eliminated from the calculations.

Jim Hamilton's plant was somewhat outdated and the equipment required frequent repairs. This led to extra costs for repair crews and overtime runs to maintain schedules. Currently, it costs about *$.018* to fill, close, label, and package a can. A complete maintenance overhaul would cost *$25,000,* but Jim believed it would reduce these costs per can to *$.017.* If the maintenance project were undertaken, there were several accessory items, such as updated automatic loaders, feeders, and packers that could be purchased to increase canning speeds. Working with a vendor for the accessory equipment, Jim decided that immediate purchases of *$75,000* in accessory equipment plus maintenance in both years could

reduce costs to *$.016* per can. Finally, Jim was considering the sequential reno-
vation of all canning production lines with the most up-to-date equipment available.
The cost for the new production lines would be *$200,000,* but it would reduce the
average cost per can to an industry minimum of *$.014.* Due to interchangeability
requirements of the system, if one production line is replaced the remaining lines
must also be replaced, resulting in little flexibility in the $200,000 cost of the final
option.

Jim Hamilton then went to visit Daniel Medrano, head of marketing, to acquire
additional information. Medrano told Jim that the selling price for cans was not
likely to deviate from $.020 for the next several years. Medrano also presented
sales volume forecasts in units for the next 2 years for Carolina Canning's particular lines of cans.

DEMAND	1981	1982	PROBABILITY OF SITUATION
Pessimistic (small)	23,000,000	21,500,000	.25
Average	28,000,000	26,500,000	.50
Optimistic (large)	35,000,000	34,000,000	.25

Demand for cans would be expected to decrease in 1982 because one important
customer was going to employ microwave packaging, which cannot use metal.
Jim Hamilton's budget is approved at the beginning of the year and cannot be
substantially changed until the next year. Therefore, he must anticipate demand
for the whole year when he sets his budget.

There were now four possibilities. Equipment could be left as is for the first
year, but it would require $25,000 in maintenance during the second year. These
lines could produce at a cost of $.018 per can. Another alternative was to overhaul
in both year 1 and year 2 at a cost of $25,000 each time. These lines could pro-
duce at a cost of $.017 per can. Another possibility was to buy the $75,000 of
accessory equipment and overhaul in both year 1 and 2. Finally, new canning lines
could be bought in year 1 and the overhaul done in year 2. If new lines were not
installed in the first year, Jim felt that it would be foolish to install them later
because he was unsure of their scrap value. Similarly, the $75,000 of accessory
equipment should only be purchased in year 1.

After examining all options, Jim Hamilton realized that a quantitative study
was required to decide upon the best course of action. A member of the Carolina
Canning Operations research department, headquartered in Winston-Salem, North
Carolina, suggested that Jim try a decision tree to help him organize the
alternatives.

Since there was quite a bit of variation in terms of the different returns, Jim
considered paying $2000 to Linda Snowden, an independent market research
analyst, who felt that she could perform a series of studies of expected gross
national product and input-output tables and apply Carolina Canning's expected
market share to these national estimates to forecast if demand for Carolina Canning for 1981 and 1982 would be high (69 million cans), average (54.5 million) or
low (44.5 million). Jim hired Linda, who predicted that demand will be high because
expected exports of canned food will be very large due to droughts in many foreign

countries. In the past, Linda had been quite accurate in her predictions of high demand. When demand was high, she predicted it correctly 90% of the time. When demand was average, she predicted it would be large 10% of the time. When demand turned out to be low, she had predicted large 5% of the time.

Questions

1 Which course of action promises the largest profit over the 2-year period?

2 What other factors should Jim Hamilton consider? What final decision would you make in this situation? Why?

3 What is the most one should pay for market research?

4 Using Linda's forecasts, what action should Jim Hamilton take?

5 *Optional—for students who can calculate discounted values:* We have not used discounting in this problem even though expenditures have been made over a 2-year period. If you have learned discounting in a finance course, assume that the interest rate is 12% and adjust for the discounting effects. Would this change the decision in the simple case (where market research is not used)? Assume that sales of cans in year 2 are made at the beginning of year 2 (1982), and that costs of maintenance in year 2 and equipment purchased in year 2 are paid at the beginning of year 2. Similarly, assume that all year 1 (1981) purchases and sales are made at the beginning of 1981. Thus, you will not need to discount 1981 figures.

INDEX NUMBERS

13-1   USES AND CHARACTERISTICS OF INDEX NUMBERS

13-2   HISTORY OF INDEX NUMBERS

13-3   UNWEIGHTED AGGREGATIVE INDEX NUMBERS
        Computation
        Dow Jones Index

13-4   UNWEIGHTED INDEX OF PRICE RELATIVES
        Computation
        Problems

13-5   WEIGHTED AGGREGATIVE INDEX NUMBERS
        Base-Year Weights: Laspeyres' Index
        Given-Year Weights: Paasche's Index

13-6   WEIGHTED INDEX OF PRICE RELATIVES
        Base-Year Weights: Laspeyres' Index
        Given-Year Weights: Paasche's Index
        Problems

13-7   PROBLEMS OF INDEX NUMBER CONSTRUCTION
        Choice of Base Period
        Choice of Items to Include in an Index
        Choice of Base-Year or Given-Year Weights

13-8   LINK RELATIVES
        Construction
        Consumer Price Index

13-9   COMPUTATION WITH INDEX NUMBERS
        Shifting the Base Year
        Using an Index to Adjust for Price Changes
        Consumer Price Index
        Gross National Product (Implicit) Deflator
        Splicing Two Indexes
        Producer (Wholesale) Price Index
        Problems

13-10   QUANTITY INDEXES
Computation
The Index of Industrial Production

13-11   SUMMARY

13-12   BIBLIOGRAPHY

13-13   CASES
Case 13-1: Bilko Commercial Realty
Case 13-2: Lomans Department Store
Case 13-3: Braniff Airways

Of all measures and tests discussed in statistics courses, index numbers are probably the most frequently used. Index numbers do not rely upon probability theory. Rather, they are forms of weighted averages, and thus they could have been placed in the descriptive statistics sections of this book. However, index numbers are often based upon sample results that are used to make estimates for the entire population. Thus, a knowledge of sampling techniques and theory is important in helping us study the results. Many conventional applied statistics books do not discuss index number formulation; however, since these techniques are used so frequently by business people and economists, we include a section describing how different types of index numbers are computed. We also give information on some major indexes used in this country.

Daily news programs and newspapers report the Dow Jones average and the Index of Industrial Production; monthly reports are available in the media on the latest rise in the Consumer Price Index and the Producer (Wholesale) Price Index. Unions watch the Consumer Price Index, since it is a key determinant of escalator clauses in wage contracts. About 8.5 million workers are covered by collective bargaining contracts that provide for increases in wage rates based on increases in the Consumer Price Index. In addition, 31 million Social Security beneficiaries, 2.5 million retired military and civil service employees and their survivors, and 20 million food stamp recipients are affected by the Consumer Price Index.

USES AND CHARACTERISTICS OF INDEX NUMBERS

13-1

An index number is a ratio relating a price or a quantity in one period to a price in another (base) period. Thus, we can use an index number to trace the movement of important economic variables through time. The price or value in the base period is considered to be 100, and index numbers are expressed to the nearest tenth. Thus, if we paid $50 for a dress in 1970 and $70.55 for a comparable dress in 1980, the index number is $(70.55/50)100 = 141.1$.

Index numbers are used for many reasons. First, they enable us to compare changes in unlike series. Thus, we can compare changes in production with changes in prices. Secondly, index numbers reduce large numbers to small manageable quantities. If production was $295,932,456 in 1979 and $296,044,529 in 1980, it would be easier to say that production rose from 100 to 100.04, or increased .04%. Thirdly, index numbers enable us to compare changes in *groups* of items. Thus, the Consumer Price Index handles increases and decreases for a "market basket" of goods, including housing, food, clothing, and many other costs incurred by the average consumer. Similarly, the Index of Industrial Production includes changes in prices of steel, autos, television, and many other items. Finally, index numbers can also be used to remove influences (such as seasonality) or to make estimates of real income or the purchasing power of money (actual income divided by the cost of living index).

HISTORY OF INDEX NUMBERS

Actually, the concept of index numbers is at least two centuries old. In 1764, Carli, an Italian statistician, used index numbers to compare the Italian price level in 1750 to that in 1500. Included in this index were wine, grain, and oil.

In 1780, in Massachusetts, a law was passed to protect lenders against a change in the purchasing power of money. The law set out a market basket that contained the following items:

5 bushels of corn

68⅘ pounds of beef

10 pounds of wine

16 pounds of leather

The cost of this market basket was 130 pounds. (The monetary unit was pounds sterling, like the English currency.)

If this package cost 130 pounds in current prices (1780), when a loan of say 26 pounds is repaid 5 years later (when the same market basket costs 155 pounds), the lender must repay $(155/130)26 = 31$ pounds in 1785. It is not quite clear what happened to this piece of legislation! However, in recent years, a number of countries have adopted a similar system, called *indexing.* Brazil and Israel are among the countries using this system.

The publication of government index numbers in this country began in 1890 when the Wholesale Price Index was published by the Bureau of Labor Statistics (BLS). The first Consumer Price Index (CPI), called a *cost-of-living index,* was used by the Shipbuilding Labor Adjustment Board to arrive at a fair wage scale in November 1917. Prices for a family market basket of goods purchased by wage earners and clerical-worker families were published in 1919 at semiannual intervals for 32 large shipbuilding and industrial centers. On the private scene, Dow's first stock average was published in 1884. This index was an average of 11 stock prices (9 of which were railroads). In 1896, *The Wall Street Journal* began daily publication of the Dow Jones industrial average. This average was an unweighted average of the prices of industrial stocks. Since these early statistical averages were published, there has been much work in devising systems of computing index numbers. From a mathematical standpoint, there are aggregative indexes and indexes of price relatives. These two methods of index number construction are covered in the next two sections. While the computation of index numbers is relatively straightforward, the problems remain as to how well they model changes in the cost of living or producing, for example, and how they should be interpreted.

13-3

An *aggregative index number* is one that compares the total of prices in a given year to the total of prices in another year. If we wish to compare a set of prices of commodities in 1980 to a set in 1970, we add the prices for these commodities in 1980 and divide by their prices in 1970.

Computation

Suppose we are trying to determine the degree to which the cost of snack food covered by college students' allowances has risen in the last decade. Assume students buy the commodities listed in Table 13-1. We have listed the prices for each of the items in the 2 years. First, add the prices in the base year (1970) Σp_0. Then, add the prices in the given year (1980), called Σp_n.

$$I = \frac{\Sigma p_n}{\Sigma p_0}(100) \tag{13-1}$$

The index number is $I = 158.3$. This means that the aggregate price of these commodities has risen 58.3% from 1970 to 1980. We assume the value of the base year (1970) is 100.

Dow Jones Index

The Dow Jones Index is a simple aggregative index of a somewhat different type. The industrial average represents the prices of 30 stocks; these are added together and divided by the number of stocks. The base year, when the price index for these stocks was 100, was 1906. In 1928 the number was 300, and in October 1975 it was 837. Since then the index has fluctuated between 750 and 1100.

Since there have been many stock splits, the divisor for the 30 stocks is no longer 30; currently, it fluctuates about 1.443. How did this come about? Let us assume we have 3 stocks A, B, and C at the following prices:

$$A = 80$$
$$B = 60$$
$$C = \underline{60} \qquad \frac{200}{3} = 66.7$$
$$\ 200$$

TABLE 13-1

COMMODITY	PRICE, 1970	PRICE, 1980
Coffee	.10	.25
Hamburgers	.50	.65
French fries	.20	.40
Ice cream (cone)	.25	.40
Chocolate bars	.15	.20
	$\Sigma p_0 = \$1.20$	$\Sigma p_n = \$1.90$

Now, assume stock A splits so that two shares are offered for one. On the next day, the price of A falls since more shares are outstanding. Assume it falls to 40. Now, we have

$$A = 40$$

$$B = 60$$

$$C = \frac{60}{160} \qquad \frac{160}{3} = 53.3$$

From this new average, one would assume that there has been a serious drop in stock prices. In reality nothing has happened except that the market has adjusted for the additional shares of stock outstanding.

To convey the idea that the market is in the same place, we must find a new denominator (divisor) that allows our index number to be the same (66.7).

Therefore,

$$\frac{160}{X} = 66.7$$

$$66.7X = 160$$

$$X = 2.4$$

Now, we see that even though there are still three types of stocks, the divisor has fallen from 3 to 2.4. The adjustment for stock splits explains why the divisor for 30 industrial stocks is 1.443.

UNWEIGHTED INDEX OF PRICE RELATIVES

13-4

Computation

Another way of calculating a price index is to find the relative changes in each of the prices and average them. We use our students' example in Table 13-2. We find the ratios of the prices p_n in the given year (1980) to the prices p_0 in the base year (1970). Add all the ratios and divide by the number of items we have included in the index. Now, multiply by 100 to get the index number.

$$I = \frac{\Sigma(p_n/p_0)}{n}(100) = \frac{8.7}{5}(100) = 174 \qquad (13\text{-}2)$$

TABLE 13-2

COMMODITY	(1) 1970	(2) 1980	(3) p_n/p_0
Coffee	.10	.25	2.5
Hamburgers	.50	.65	1.3
French fries	.20	.40	2.0
Ice cream (cone)	.25	.40	1.6
Chocolate bars	.15	.20	1.3
		$\Sigma(p_n/p_0) =$	8.7

Thus, using the index of price relatives, the index number is $I = 174$. We see that the index number using the average of price relatives is higher than the one adding the prices in the 2 years ($I = 158.3$). If we examine our figures, we find that the chief increase arises because coffee (a relatively cheap item in 1980 that has little weight in the aggregative index as compared to the more expensive items) has more than doubled in price over a 10-year period. Since the price relatives take account only of percentage changes, the change in coffee price has a greater weight here than in the aggregate index.

Being truly interested in a student's cost of living, neither index is very useful until we can determine how many units of each item a student buys in a given time period. Thus, if a student buys 20 cups of coffee and 1 candy bar each week, we should pay more attention to increases in coffee prices than to increases in candy prices. In order to do this, most index procedures use a system of weights. We explain various techniques of weighting in the next section of this chapter.

Problems

1 The National Association of Homebuilders (NAH) claims that "Grandma paid more for housing" than we do. The association presented the data below in the October 1976 issue of *Real Estate Today*. Compute index numbers for 1975 with 1890 as a base year. Some claim that World War II was responsible for the inflation in housing values. Use 1930 as a base year and compute index numbers for 1950. Compare these index numbers for annual family income and median sales price. Do you agree with the NAH? Did housing prices rise faster than income as a result of World War II? *Hint:* House prices and family incomes both show evidence of inflation. The question is which one has risen more?

YEAR	MEDIAN SALES PRICE OF HOUSE	ANNUAL FAMILY INCOME
1890	$ 4,422	$ 455
1900	4,881	490
1910	5,377	630
1920	6,296	1,489
1930	7,146	1,360
1940	6,558	1,300
1950	9,446	3,319
1960	16,652	5,620
1970	23,400	9,867
1975	39,300	13,991

2 The Juniper Jelly Company is considering raising prices in the coming year because of the increased cost of fruit and sugar. The jelly is made from three fruits (1 pound each and 1 pound of sugar). Compute index numbers for material costs of the jelly in 1981 as compared to 1976.

FOOD	1976 PRICE/POUND	1981 PRICE/POUND
Plums	.20	.55
Apples	.15	.49
Peaches	.25	.60
Sugar	.30	.25

(a) Compute the simple aggregative price index.

(b) Compute the simple average of price relatives.

WEIGHTED AGGREGATIVE INDEX NUMBERS

Base-Year Weights: Laspeyres' Index

To compute how much students' costs for snack food have risen, it is necessary to find how much an average student purchases of each commodity. Suppose that in the base year (1970) our survey showed that the average student purchased 20 cups of coffee, 5 hamburgers, 5 orders of french fries, 3 ice cream cones, and 1 chocolate bar each week. We now weight our prices by the base-year quantities q_0 and compute the change in our cost of living using the formula

$$I = \frac{\Sigma p_n q_0}{\Sigma p_0 q_0} (100)$$

$$= \frac{11.65}{6.40} (100) = 182.0$$

(13-3)

The Laspeyres index, named after E. Laspeyres who first used the formula in 1864, shows us that the average cost of food for our student has increased 82%. Our unweighted aggregative index was $I = 158.3$. The weighted index is much higher because coffee, a relatively inexpensive item with a very large change in price, is very important in the student budget. We can see that 182.0 is almost twice as much as 100. Thus, because of inflation, the student needs 82% more allowance to buy the same snack food. (See Table 13-3).

Given-Year Weights: Paasche's Index

In the course of time, eating habits may change. For example, emphasis on diet may lead to less consumption of french fries. Similarly, because coffee has become relatively expensive, there may be a substitution effect: less coffee is consumed and water is drunk instead. A survey in 1980 gives us the following average consumption figures: coffee, 15 cups; hamburgers, 6; french fries, 4; ice cream cones, 3; and chocolate bars, 2. The survey may also find that new items (tea, pizza) are now part of the budget; see Section 13-7. To account for changes in taste, let us compute the index using given-year (current-year) weights. We now compute the index numbers using given-year (current year) purchase quantity weights using the following formula:

TABLE 13-3

COMMODITY	1970 PRICE p_0	1980 PRICE p_n	QUANTITY PURCHASED IN 1970 q_0	$p_0 q_0$	$p_n q_0$
Coffee	.10	.25	20	2.00	5.00
Hamburgers	.50	.65	5	2.50	3.25
French fries	.20	.40	5	1.00	2.00
Ice cream cones	.25	.40	3	.75	1.20
Chocolate bars	.15	.20	1	.15	.20
				$\Sigma p_0 q_0 = 6.40$	$\Sigma p_n q_0 = 11.65$

$$I = \frac{\Sigma p_n q_n}{\Sigma p_0 q_n}(100) = \frac{10.85}{6.35}(100) = 170.9 \qquad (13\text{-}4)$$

This formula is called a *Paasche's aggregative index,* named after H. Paasche who developed it in 1874. Using current-year consumption weights and an aggregative index, we find that the cost of living has risen only 70.9%. Using base-year consumption weights, our aggregative index number was 182.0, or an increase of 82%. Indexes using base-year weights may tend to overestimate cost of living changes because they don't allow for substitution effects. Thus, if beef became particularly expensive, you might include more chocolate bars, tea, and pizza in your diet and fewer hamburgers. Thus, you would be changing your style of living. Current-year weights would be more likely to reflect your new living style. (See Table 13-4.)

TABLE 13-4

COMMODITY	1970 PRICE p_0	1980 PRICE p_n	QUANTITY PURCHASED IN 1980 q_n	$p_0 q_n$	$p_n q_n$
Coffee	.10	.25	15	1.50	3.75
Hamburgers	.50	.65	6	3.00	3.90
French fries	.20	.40	4	.80	1.60
Ice cream cones	.25	.40	3	.75	1.20
Chocolate bars	.15	.20	2	.30	.40
				$\Sigma p_0 q_n = 6.35$	$\Sigma p_n q_n = 100.85$

WEIGHTED INDEX OF PRICE RELATIVES

13-6

Base-Year Weights: Laspeyres' Index

Using our index of price relatives, we will use *value weights. Value* is price times quantity so that each price change is weighted in terms of the value of the commodity purchased in the base year, $p_0 q_0$ (see Table 13-5).

$$I = \frac{\Sigma[(p_n/p_0)(p_0 q_0)]}{\Sigma p_0 q_0}(100) = \frac{11.65}{6.40} = 182.0 \qquad (13\text{-}5)^1$$

---

[1]This $(p_n/p_0)(p_0 q_0)$ will simplify to $p_n q_0$; however, in many cases, the analysts wish to use the price relatives for the study of individual commodity changes. The Consumer Price Index uses price relatives in this way.

TABLE 13-5

COMMODITY	1970 p_0	1980 p_n	q_0	$p_0 q_0$	p_n/p_0	$(p_0 q_0)(p_n/p_0)$
Coffee	.10	.25	20	2.00	2.5	5.00
Hamburgers	.50	.65	5	2.50	1.3	3.25
French fries	.20	.40	5	1.00	2.0	2.00
Ice cream cones	.25	.40	3	.75	1.6	1.20
Chocolate bars	.15	.20	1	.15	1.3	.20
				$\Sigma p_0 q_0 = 6.40$		11.65

TABLE 13-6

COMMODITY	1970 PRICE p_0	1980 PRICE p_n	QUANTITY PURCHASED IN 1980 q_n	$p_n q_n$	(p_n/p_0)	$(p_n/p_0)(p_n q_n)$
Coffee	.10	.25	15	3.75	2.5	9.38
Hamburgers	.50	.65	6	3.90	1.3	5.07
French fries	.20	.40	4	1.60	2.0	3.20
Ice cream cones	.25	.40	3	1.20	1.6	1.92
Chocolate bars	.15	.20	2	.40	1.3	.52
				$\Sigma p_n q_n = 10.85$		20.09

Note that this is the same result we obtained with the weighted aggregate Laspeyres' index.

We see that the weighted index of price relatives using base-year value weights produces the same results as the weighted aggregative index using base-year weights (Equation 13-3). The relatives index is usually preferred since it also gives an index number for the change in each item $(p_n/p_0)(100)$.

Given-Year Weights: Paasche's Index

We now compute the index of price relatives using given-year value weights $(p_n q_n)$.

$$I = \frac{\Sigma[(p_n/p_0)(p_n q_n)]}{\Sigma p_n q_n}(100) = \frac{20.09(100)}{10.85} = 185.2$$

Thus, the price increase due to inflation from 1970 to 1980 is 85.2%. This might be preferred to a Laspeyres index, except for the difficulties in finding new quantity weights each time we compute the index. (See Section 13-7.)

Problems

1 Food prices in the United States have shown great variation. The following table shows prices for selected representative foods in 1965, 1970, and 1980.

	PRICES			QUANTITIES		
	1965	1970	1980	1965	1970	1980
Flour, 5 pounds	.58	.59	1.00	1	.8	.5
Pork chops, 1 pound	.97	1.16	1.86	5	5	3
Milk, 1/2 gallon	.53	.66	.77	3	4	4
Potatoes, 10 pounds	.94	.90	1.34	1	2	1

Weekly quantities purchased by a family of four are listed under quantities.

(*a*) Using 1970 quantity weights, construct aggregative indexes comparing 1965 and 1980 prices with those in 1970.

(*b*) Using 1970 value weights, construct a weighted index of price relatives for 1980 compared to 1970.

(*c*) Using 1980 value weights, construct weighted indexes of price relatives comparing 1980 to 1965 and 1970.

(*d*) Use 1980 quantity weights to compute aggregative indexes for 1965, 1970, and 1980.

(*e*) Using 1965 quantity weights, construct aggregative indexes comparing 1970 and 1980 prices. (Note that the base year is 1970, yet quantity weights are for 1965. The Consumer Price Index uses reference period weights for 1972–1973 with a base year $I = 100$ of 1967. The reference period is the years when the surveys of consumer purchases were made.)

PROBLEMS OF INDEX NUMBER CONSTRUCTION

13-7 ### Choice of Base Period

A base period may be a year or a set of years that is treated as the period when the index number is 100; for example, the old Consumer Price Index used 1957–1959 = 100 as the base period. For this period, the prices and the quantities that people consume of each commodity are computed. Usually, the base year should be a normal year (for example, not a wartime period) although it is difficult to define a normal period. Generally, a year that is at a peak or a trough of the business cycle should be avoided. A year in which things are stable is ideal. A base year should not be too far away from the given year, since the comparison would lose meaning. In the 1940s, there were no television sets, TV dinners, or jet travel, and few frozen or already prepared foods. Thus, it would be difficult to compare costs of living in 1940 and 1960, because "living" has a different meaning. Most index numbers are constructed so that there is a change in the base year every decade. This allows for changes in the consumption patterns. When a new index is published, the old index is also published at the same time. In this way, it is possible to continue comparisons for a long time, even though the two groups don't use the same variety of commodities in their base. This technique of splicing together two index numbers is explained in Section 13-9. The Dow Jones average, for example, no longer includes IBM and as many railroads as it did in the 1940s. Since aviation has risen in importance, a number of airlines are now included in the Dow Jones average.

Choice of Items to Include in an Index

The choice of items for inclusion in an index is based upon how important these items are for measuring whatever the index portrays. The Consumer Price Index, for example, includes goods and services purchased for consumption, including both luxuries and necessities. About 265 major categories are priced from a total of more than 2000 items that an urban consumer purchases. These items are chosen by studying what goods and services a random sample of urban consumers purchases.

The sample groups are a cross section of consumers living in a representative selection of urban places, such as large, medium-size, and small cities. The Consumer Price Index (CPI) differs from a cost of living index in a number of ways. It does not immediately account for the fact that if prices rise the consumer will substitute other items; for example, if beef becomes more expensive, the consumer will use pork instead. The items included in the index remain constant for at least a decade to allow comparisons of changes in costs of the same market basket of goods over a 10-year period. The CPI doesn't include income and social security taxes since, unlike sales taxes, these costs are not directly related to the retail prices of goods and services. The CPI is based on expenditures and does not reflect noncash consumption, such as fringe benefits and government benefits. The index excludes personal life

insurance, income and personal property tax, but it includes real estate taxes and
excise taxes. (See Table 13-8.) If we chose an item for pricing in 1967, it may not
be as important in the budget in 1980, yet it is still included in the same proportion
in the 1980 budget. In order to make comparisons of prices between the years comparable, we must keep the quantities of each good purchased constant because our
index is a composite of many goods and services. Thus, it is advisable at some regular
interval to revise the list and weights of items included in the index to adjust for
changes in the style of living. Usually, this has been done approximately every 10
years. Despite these difficulties, the CPI has been used in this country to study cost
of living changes. A recent study by Triplett has shown that if the effects of substitution were taken into account, and new market baskets of goods were priced when
consumption habits shifted, there would be very little difference from the present
index numbers (less than one tenth of an index point each year). Thus, if the current
index number were 256.7, it might change to 256.8.

Once items have been chosen for the index, a new problem arises—*quality*
change. For example, with each automobile model change, the Bureau of Labor Statistics (BLS) has to separate the rise in price due to inflation from the price rise due
to quality change. Adjustments for quality change in the CPI new car index include
structural and engineering changes that affect safety, environment, reliability, performance, durability, economy, carrying capacity, maneuverability, comfort, and
convenience. Only quality changes that lead to additional costs for the automobile
manufacturer are counted. Moreover, the Bureau of Labor Statistics does not consider changes in style and appearance as improvements in quality. Many economists
have pointed out that changes in quality are not adequately covered by the CPI and,
therefore, the CPI overestimates inflation. They feel that when we compare the price
of a car this year to that last year, we may be comparing the price of a better car to
that of an inferior car, hence our price index is higher than it should be. A 1978
Department of Labor study (USDL 78-921) found that 1979 model cars had
improved $46.35 (retail value) in quality over the previous year. Research on quality
changes have widely divergent findings. Some economists see considerable unaccounted changes while others find very few unaccounted differences.

Choice of Base-Year or Given-Year Weights

Most indexes are computed with base-year weights (Laspeyres). Using base-year
quantity weights, it is easy to compute index numbers for subsequent years because
we know the relative quantities of each good consumed. If given-year or current
weights are used (Paasche's index), we must perform a survey of consumer expenditures each year to determine the relative amount of the budget spent on each item.
All previous years used in the comparison must be reweighted using current values.

The Consumer Price Index uses *fixed-year weights*. These are derived from a
survey of urban expenditures for 1972–1973 adjusted for price change between the
survey date and December 1977. At the same time, the base year for the index is
1967. We have seen in the previous section that the use of base-year weights may
give the index a slight upward bias in inflationary times, since the weighting system
does not change when people substitute cheaper items for items with rising prices.
The extent to which this substitution occurs depends on elasticity of demand for
particular products. The elasticity of demand refers to the relation between the

change in price and the change in the quantity of a particular good that the consumer will demand. On the other hand, if one uses given-year weights, it is necessary to make constant weight revisions and recalculate all previous index numbers. Generally, most series of index numbers are base-year or fixed-year weights and try to revise the weights at relatively frequent intervals.

LINK RELATIVES

13-8

Frequently, we are primarily interested in comparing this year to the previous year. If 1980 prices were set at 100, what would 1981 prices be? If the index number for 1981 were 120, we could say that prices had risen 20%. Link relatives provide a method to evaluate the current time period on the basis of the previous time period. At the same time, we may also wish to see how 1981 prices compare to 1978 prices. It is possible to *chain* these *individual link relatives* together to find the 1981 prices in terms of 1978 prices (chain relatives). The CPI uses this technique to enable us to compare each year to the previous year as well as to prices for several previous years. In the next section, we show how these index numbers are constructed.

Construction

It is possible to link together indexes of price relatives from a series of years to arrive at new index numbers. This system allows us to compare the percentage change each year to the previous year as well as to the base year. For example,

*Link
index number*

$$\text{1979 link relative} = \frac{\text{1979 price}}{\text{1978 price}} = \frac{3.00}{2.50} = 1.20 \qquad 120$$

$$\text{1980 link relative} = \frac{\text{1980 price}}{\text{1979 price}} = \frac{4.00}{3.00} = 1.33 \qquad 133$$

$$\text{1981 link relative} = \frac{\text{1981 price}}{\text{1980 price}} = \frac{5.00}{4.00} = 1.25 \qquad 125$$

$$\text{1981 } chain\ relative = \frac{\text{1979 price}}{\text{1978 price}} \times \frac{\text{1980 price}}{\text{1979 price}} \times \frac{\text{1981 price}}{\text{1980 price}} = \frac{\text{1981}}{\text{1978}}$$

$$1.20 \quad \times \quad 1.33 \quad \times \quad 1.25 \quad = 1.995$$

To form an index number, we multiple by 100: $1.995 \times 100 = 199.5$. Thus, prices have almost doubled from 1978 to 1981.

We would have obtained the same result for 1981 with base year 1978 by dividing 1981 price ($5.00) by the 1978 price ($2.50): $I = 199.5$. The advantage of links is that they show the percentage change of each year over the previous year. Thus the 1979 price is 20% higher than the 1978 price. The CPI is constructed with reference-year weights (fixed-year weights) using price relatives for each item and a system of link relatives. Thus, for each area of the country and for the country as a whole, a comparison can be made for each item to the previous year as well as to the base year. In Table 13-7, we show the areas of the country for which CPI information is avilable on a monthly basis.

TABLE 13-7

CONSUMER PRICE INDEX FOR ALL URBAN CONSUMERS: SELECTED AREAS, ALL ITEMS INDEX

1967 = 100 unless otherwise noted

| AREA* | PRICING SCHEDULE† | OTHER INDEX BASE | INDEXES | | | | PERCENT CHANGE TO APR. 1980 FROM: | | | PERCENT CHANGE TO MAR. 1980 FROM: | | |
			JAN. 1980	FEB. 1980	MAR. 1980	APR. 1980	APR. 1979	FEB. 1980	MAR. 1980	MAR. 1979	JAN. 1980	FEB. 1980
U.S. city average			233.2	236.4	239.8	242.5	14.7	2.6	1.1	14.7	2.8	1.4
Chicago, Ill.– northwestern Ind.	M		230.3	232.7	235.5	240.1	15.0	3.2	2.0	14.0	2.3	1.2
Detroit Mich.	M		237.2	240.4	242.9	248.2	16.4	3.2	2.2	14.8	2.4	1.0
L.A.–Long Beach, Anaheim, Calif.	M		232.6	237.6	241.3	244.6	17.7	2.9	1.4	18.4	3.7	1.6
New York City– northeastern N.J.	M		226.1	228.0	231.2	233.1	11.9	2.2	.8	12.0	2.3	1.4
Philadelphia, Pa.–N.J.	M		227.2	231.1	234.6	237.4	14.3	2.7	1.2	14.6	3.3	1.5
Anchorage, Alas.	1	10/67	218.2	—	223.5	—	—	—	—	11.2	2.4	—
Baltimore, Md.	1		234.4	—	245.0	—	—	—	—	17.2	4.5	—
Boston, Mass.	1		227.3	—	234.2	—	—	—	—	14.2	3.0	—
Cincinnati, Ohio–Ky.–Ind.	1		239.5	—	247.8	—	—	—	—	14.9	3.5	—
Denver–Boulder, Colo.	1		247.3	—	255.2	—	—	—	—	14.4	3.2	—
Miami, Fla.	1	11/77	123.3	—	127.7	—	—	—	—	14.8	3.6	—
Milwaukee, Wis.	1		236.4	—	242.7	—	—	—	—	16.9	2.7	—
Northeast Pennsylvania	1		224.4	—	229.0	—	—	—	—	12.5	2.0	—
Portland, Oreg.–Wash.	1		244.6	—	253.6	—	—	—	—	17.7	3.7	—
St. Louis, Mo.–Ill.	1		232.7	—	238.1	—	—	—	—	14.3	2.3	—
San Diego, Calif.	1		254.0	—	258.3	—	—	—	—	16.7	1.7	—
Seattle–Everett, Wash.	1		236.0	—	243.8	—	—	—	—	17.8	3.3	—
Washington, D.C.–Md.– Va.	1		231.9	—	238.8	—	—	—	—	12.3	3.0	—
Atlanta, Ga.	2		—	230.3	—	235.3	13.8	2.2	—	—	—	—
Buffalo, N.Y.	2		—	227.9	—	233.7	13.1	2.5	—	—	—	—
Cleveland, Ohio	2		—	243.5	—	247.3	15.0	1.6	—	—	—	—
Dallas–Fort Worth, Tex.	2		—	241.7	—	251.4	19.1	4.0	—	—	—	—
Honolulu, Hawaii	2		—	220.9	—	227.4	13.3	2.9	—	—	—	—
Houston, Tex.	2		—	255.9	—	260.8	14.3	1.9	—	—	—	—
Kansas City, Mo.–Kans.	2		—	238.7	—	243.8	15.3	2.1	—	—	—	—
Minneapolis–St. Paul, Minn.–Wis.	2		—	237.9	—	244.3	13.2	2.7	—	—	—	—
Pittsburgh, Pa.	2		—	235.5	—	240.9	13.6	2.3	—	—	—	—
San Francisco–Oakland, Calif.	2		—	240.7	—	243.5	16.6	1.2	—	—	—	—
Region‡												
Northeast	2	12/77	—	123.7	—	126.8	13.3	2.5	—	—	—	—
North central	2	12/77	—	128.0	—	131.3	14.2	2.6	—	—	—	—
South	2	12/77	—	127.4	—	130.8	14.6	2.7	—	—	—	—
West	2	12/77	—	129.4	—	132.7	16.6	2.6	—	—	—	—
Population size class‡												
A-1	2	12/77	—	125.4	—	128.9	14.6	2.8	—	—	—	—
A-2	2	12/77	—	128.1	—	131.1	15.1	2.3	—	—	—	—
B	2	12/77	—	128.0	—	131.6	14.9	2.8	—	—	—	—
C	2	12/77	—	127.7	—	130.9	14.3	2.5	—	—	—	—
D	2	12/77	—	125.8	—	128.6	13.5	2.2	—	—	—	—

TABLE 13-7
CONSUMER PRICE INDEX FOR ALL URBAN CONSUMERS: SELECTED AREAS, ALL ITEMS INDEX (Continued)

AREA*	PRICING SCHEDULE†	OTHER INDEX BASE	INDEXES				PERCENT CHANGE TO APR. 1980 FROM:			PERCENT CHANGE TO MAR. 1980 FROM:		
			JAN. 1980	FEB. 1980	MAR. 1980	APR. 1980	APR. 1979	FEB. 1980	MAR. 1980	MAR. 1979	JAN. 1980	FEB. 1980
Region/population size class cross classification‡												
Northeast/A	2	12/77	—	122.1	—	125.0	12.8	2.4	—	—	—	—
North central/A	2	12/77	—	129.6	—	133.2	15.1	2.8	—	—	—	—
South/A	2	12/77	—	127.1	—	130.7	15.2	2.8	—	—	—	—
West/A	2	12/77	—	129.6	—	132.8	17.2	2.5	—	—	—	—
Northeast/B	2	12/77	—	125.6	—	129.0	14.1	2.7	—	—	—	—
North central/B	2	12/77	—	127.2	—	130.9	13.7	2.9	—	—	—	—
South/B	2	12/77	—	128.0	—	131.7	15.1	2.9	—	—	—	—
West/B	2	12/77	—	130.6	—	134.1	16.4	2.7	—	—	—	—
Northeast/C	2	12/77	—	129.1	—	132.7	15.6	2.8	—	—	—	—
North central/C	2	12/77	—	126.4	—	128.9	13.1	2.0	—	—	—	—
South/C	2	12/77	—	127.9	—	131.3	14.3	2.7	—	—	—	—
West/C	2	12/77	—	128.1	—	131.4	15.2	2.6	—	—	—	—
Northeast/D	2	12/77	—	124.2	—	127.4	12.8	2.6	—	—	—	—
North central/D	2	12/77	—	125.8	—	128.7	12.8	2.3	—	—	—	—
South/D	2	12/77	—	125.9	—	128.3	13.5	1.9	—	—	—	—
West/D	2	12/77	—	127.1	—	130.4	15.7	2.6	—	—	—	—

*Area is generally the Standard Metropolitan Statistical Area (SMSA), exclusive of farms. L.A.–Long Beach, Anaheim, Calif. is a combination of two SMSAs, and New York City–northeastern N.J. and Chicago, Ill.–northwestern Ind. are the more extensive Standard Consolidated Areas. Area definitions are those established by the Office of Management and Budget in 1973, except for Denver–Boulder, Colo., which does not include Douglas County. Defintions do not include revisions made since 1973.

†Foods, fuels, and several other items priced every month in all areas; most other goods and services priced as indicated: M, every month; 1, January, March, May, July, September, and November; 2, February, April, June, August, October, and December.

‡Regions are defined as the four Census regions. The population-size classes are aggregations of areas that have urban population as defined below: A-1, more than 4,000,000; A-2, 1,250,000 to 4,000,000; B, 385,000 to 1,250,000; C, 75,000 to 385,000; D, Less than 75,000. Population size class A is the aggregation of population size classes A-1 and A-2.

Note: Price changes within areas are found in the Consumer Price Index; differences in living costs among areas are found in Family Budgets.

Source: U.S. Department of Labor, Bureau of Labor Statistics, *News*, May 23, 1980, USDL-80-326.

Consumer Price Index

As stated at the beginning of this chapter, it has been estimated that about one-half of the incomes in the United States today are tied to the Consumer Price Index. Roughly 8.5 million workers are covered by "escalator clauses" in union contracts; 31 million Social Security beneficiaries, 2.5 million retired military and federal Civil Service employees and survivors, and 20 million food stamp recipients have their incomes related to the index. The payment rate to schools for the 25 million children in the subsidized National School Lunch program is also adjusted semiannually by the Department of Agriculture on the basis of the CPI series.

The CPI tells what changes are taking place in the cost of a market basket of goods and services. Up to 1978, the market basket of goods and services represented the buying habits of urban wage earners and clerical workers, a low-income or low-to-medium income group. Beginning with the January 1978 index, the Bureau of Labor Statistics published a revised CPI for urban wage earners and clerical workers *as well as a new CPI* for all urban consumers. The index for urban consumers represents the buying habits of a wider group, representing 80 percent of the noninstitutional, civilian population of the United States. This index covers self-employed, professional, white collar, and other salaried workers and retired persons, others not in the labor force, and the unemployed. The 85 primary sampling units for this index include central cities, suburbs, and urbanized places with 2500 or more inhabitants.

The items included in the market baskets of goods since 1935 have been weighted in the following ways; see Table 13-8. Note that eight major types of expenditures have been included in this index.

We can see that the three top items in both the all urban consumer index and the wage earners and clerical workers index are housing, food, and transportation. These three account for about 80% of expenditures. How do they compare to your family's budget? Note the growth in transportation over the years and the decrease in food and alcoholic beverages. Would you imagine that this trend will continue in the 1980s?

The new index provides for expanded city coverage so that monthly or bimonthly cost of living figures can be obtained for 28 cities. The other areas are broken down by four regions—Northeast, North Central, South, and West—and five population classes—major metropolitan areas (more than 4 million people), large metropolitan areas (1.25–4 million people), medium metropolitan areas (385,000–1,250,000 people), small metropolitan areas (75,000–385,000 people), and urban areas outside of metropolitan areas (less than 75,000 people). Cities that do not have specifically reported indexes can use the appropriate population-size class for their region to approximate an index. Table 13-7 shows examples of the different index numbers and index number changes in the regions and cities for which monthly information is published. Note the variation in the percent changes in the first quarter of 1980. Thus, prices in Baltimore increased 4.5%, while prices in San Diego increased only 1.7%. *Monthly Labor Review,* published by the Bureau of Labor Statistics, publishes this information every month.

The CPI has been used for (1) the formulation and evaluation of economic policy measures, (2) an escalator of income payments, (3) a deflator of earnings to

TABLE 13-8

PERCENT DISTRIBUTION OF THE CPI MARKET BASKET BY MAJOR EXPENDITURE GROUP, BENCHMARK YEAR
(Fixed-year weights)

| MAJOR GROUP | WAGE AND CLERICAL WORKERS (OLD) | | | | ALL URBAN CONSUMERS (NEW) |
	1935–1939	1952	1963	1972–1973	1972–1973*
Food and alcoholic beverages	35.4	32.2	25.2	20.4	18.8
Housing	33.7	33.6	34.9	39.8	42.9
Apparel	11.0	9.0	10.6	7.0	7.0
Transportation	8.1	11.3	14.0	19.8	17.0
Medical care	4.1	4.8	5.7	4.2	4.6
Entertainment	2.8	4.3	3.9	4.3	4.5
Personal care	2.5	2.1	2.8	1.8	1.7
Other goods and services	2.4	2.7	2.9	2.7	2.8

*This is the new weighting system established in 1978.
Source: *The Consumer Price Index: Concepts and Content Over the Years.* U.S. Department of Labor, Bureau of Labor Statistics, Report 517, 1977.

provide measures of real earnings, and (4) a measure of the purchasing power of the consumer dollar. We now give examples of these uses.

COMPUTATION WITH INDEX NUMBERS

13-9

Shifting the Base Year

Frequently, we wish to compare changes in index numbers that have two different base years. It is not correct to compare the *percentage points* of increase for the two such series. For example, in Table 13-9, we can compare November 1977 to August 1977 for Japan and the United States (columns 1 and 3) to determine if prices rose more in Japan than they did in the United States. We can resolve this problem by shifting the base for both series to August 1977 (100). We cannot really compare Japanese and American price changes unless we start from numbers that have the same time base. The base year for the Japanese Commodities Index is 1969; for the U.S. Consumer Price Index, 1967. Since we have monthly data from both for August 1977 to November 1977, we make the base year August for both countries. First, let August 1977 = 100. Now for the United States, using ratios, we enter these values in column 2.

$$\frac{176.3 \text{ (September 1977)}}{176.0 \text{ (August) 1977}} = \frac{X_1 \text{ (September 1977 − new index)}}{100 \text{ (August 1977 − new index)}} \qquad X_1 = 100.2$$

$$\frac{176.7 \text{ (October 1977)}}{176.0 \text{ (August 1977)}} = \frac{X_2 \text{ (October 1977 − new index)}}{100 \text{ (August 1977 − new index)}} \qquad X_2 = 100.4$$

$$\frac{177.6 \text{ (November 1977)}}{176.0 \text{ (August 1977)}} = \frac{X_3 \text{ (November 1977 − new index)}}{100 \text{ (August 1977 − new index)}} \qquad X_3 = 100.9$$

Now, performing a similar operation with the Japanese commodities, let August 1977 = 100. We enter these values in column 4.

$$\frac{278.8 \text{ (September 1977)}}{278.4 \text{ (August 1977)}} = \frac{X_1 \text{ (September 1977 − new index)}}{100 \text{ (August 1977 − new index)}} \qquad X_1 = 100.1$$

$$\frac{279.3 \text{ (October 1977)}}{278.4 \text{ (August 1977)}} = \frac{X_2 \text{ (October 1977 − new index)}}{100 \text{ (August 1977 − new index)}} \qquad X_2 = 100.3$$

$$\frac{280.2 \text{ (November 1977)}}{278.4 \text{ (August 1977)}} = \frac{X_3 \text{ (November 1977 − new index)}}{100 \text{ (August 1977 − new index)}} \qquad X_3 = 100.6$$

TABLE 13-9

COMPARISON OF U.S. AND JAPANESE PRICE CHANGES, AUGUST 1977 TO NOVEMBER 1977

	(1) U.S. CONSUMER PRICE INDEX (BASE 1967)	(2) BASE AUGUST 1977	(3) JAPANESE COMMODITIES PRICE INDEX (BASE 1969)	(4) BASE AUGUST 1977
August 1977	176.0	100	278.4	100
September 1977	176.3	100.2	278.8	100.1
October 1977	176.7	100.4	279.3	100.3
November 1977	177.6	100.9	280.2	100.6

Although the original Japanese index rose by more percentage points than the U.S. CPI (1.8 in column 3 compared to 1.6 in column 1) we see that because of the different bases the U.S. inflation actually increased at a higher rate—.9 percent (column 2) compared to .6 percent (column 4). In order to compare changes in index numbers, it is important that they both start in the same base year.

Using an Index to Adjust for Price Changes

Consumer Price Index   Workers entering labor agreements are increasingly aware of the change in their wages in real terms. *Real* refers to the purchasing power of the dollar. For example, if a worker in Chicago earned $200 a week in 1967 and $300 a week in 1979, the worker might at first say that in monetary terms salary has increased by $100, or 50%. A look at the price index for Chicago (with June 1967 = 100) reveals that the current price index (June 1978) is 195.3. To find *real income,* we divide monetary income $300 by this index: ($300/195.3) × 100 = $153.61. Actually, our worker is in a worse position because although monetary income increased by 50% the cost of living rose 95.3%. Therefore, $300 today is worth $153.61 in terms of 1967 purchasing power of the dollar. We encountered the same kind of problem in the cost of snack food for our college student. Thus, using base-year weights and an aggregate index computation, our index number was $I = 182$. In order to buy what a student had been able to purchase for $6.40 a week in 1970, the student would need by 1980

$$\frac{6.40(182)}{100} = \$11.65$$

Alternatively, the *real value* of $10 in 1980 in terms of 1970 purchasing power is

$$\frac{10}{182}(100) = 5.4945 = \$5.49$$

This *real value* of the dollar indicates the *purchasing power* of the dollar.

Purchasing power of a dollar is found by finding the reciprocal of the price index. For example, if the index is 179.4, then (1/179.4)(100) = .557, or 56 cents. If prices go up 50%, our index number is 150; then, we have (1/150)(100), or the dollar is worth two-thirds of a dollar, or 67 cents. If prices increase 25%, the purchasing power of the dollar is (1/125)(100) or .80, or 80 cents. A dollar will buy what 80 cents used to buy. This decline in the purchasing power of the dollar shows the real effect of inflation. On the other hand, if prices were to fall, purchasing power of the dollar would increase.

Gross National Product (Implicit) Deflator   In the previous section, we have estimated the real value (the value in terms of goods and services) of personal incomes. Now, we are interested in studying the output of the economy as a whole. Each year the U.S. government issues dollar figures on the Gross National Product (GNP). In order to measure the *real* growth in goods and services produced by this country, it is important to adjust for the effects of inflation or deflation. The GNP must be deflated by a price index just as we adjusted personal income, but the CPI includes only consumer goods. A GNP deflator, which also includes investment goods, is used by the government to find the real value of goods and services. To properly deflate the GNP, each component of the GNP is deflated for a given quarter or year by the appropriate indexes. Consumer spending components are deflated by the CPIs; gross private domestic investments are deflated by different Producer (Wholesale) Price Indexes; construction costs are deflated by special construction cost indexes prepared by the Bureau of the Census. Once the components have been deflated, they are added to obtain real GNP (GNP in constant dollars). If we want to know the overall (implicit) GNP deflator, we can divide the current dollar GNP by the constant dollar GNP. It is said to be implicit because it is not calculated directly but may be derived by comparing the current GNP in current prices and the base-year cost of the current GNP for the total of all goods. In many years, the CPI and the GNP implicit price deflator have risen at different rates; in 1974 the GNP deflator rose 11.5% while the CPI rose *11%*, and in 1977 the GNP deflator rose 5.8% while the CPI rose *6.5%*.

Although the GNP deflator is not published, it can be found by comparing GNP figures for a given year to deflated GNP figures for the same year.[2] The deflated GNP allows for price changes. For example, in 1975 the GNP was estimated to be $1499 billion in current dollars. In 1972 dollars, it was $1186 billion; $1499/X = 1186$. Therefore, X, our deflator, is $1499/1186 = 1.264$ or, in index number terms, 126.4. Now, let us compare the *GNP deflator,* which adds investment goods to consumption goods reflected by the CPI. The CPI for 1975 with base year 1967 = 100 was 161.2; for 1972 with 1967 = 100, it was 125.3. If we change the base year of the CPI to 1972 by dividing 1975 by 1972, we find that $(161.2/125.3)(100) = 128.7$. Thus, consumer prices in this 3-year period had risen slightly more than the GNP implicit deflator (126.4), which contained both consumption and investment goods.

Splicing Two Indexes

In June 1978, a *new* Consumer Price Index was published by the Bureau of Labor Statistics: the *Consumer Price Index for All Urban Consumers.* The Consumer Price Index for Urban Wage Earners and Clerical Workers is similar to the CPI that has been used since 1935. However, there have been revisions in the urban wage earners and clerical workers index in terms of expanded city coverage, improved item selection, new statistical techniques, and new ways of collecting price information. From November 1977 to June 1978, the old and the new indexes were published; thus, we can connect the two to form a series from the early 1970s to the present.

For April 1978, the all urban consumers index was 191.5 and the unrevised index was 191.3. For May 1978, the all urban consumers index was 193.3. If we wish to continue the unrevised series for July 1980, for example, a simple algebraic technique of splicing could be applied.

$$\frac{\text{April 1978 revised}}{\text{April 1978 unrevised}} = \frac{\text{July 1980 revised}}{\text{July 1980 unrevised}}$$

$$\frac{191.5}{191.3} = \frac{247.8}{X}$$

$$X = 247.5$$

[2]See William H. Wallace and William E. Cullison, *Measuring Price Changes: A Study of the Price Indexes,* 4th ed., Federal Reserve Bank of Richmond, 1979, pp. 14–15, 46–49.

Thus, 247.5 is what the old CPI would have been if we had computed it in July 1980. The ability to make these links enables us to compare 1980 prices to 1970 prices, even though the market basket of goods has changed.

Producer (Wholesale) Price Index   This index has been calculated since 1902, when it was developed to measure the effect of tariff laws. The index measures the price level of goods, including imports at their first level of transaction in the United States. The index originally was an unweighted relative index of 250 commodities. It was revised in 1914 and 1952, and is currently a weighted index consisting of some 2800 commodities. The index is divided into three groups: farm products, processed foods and feeds, and industrial commodities. A revision is scheduled for completion in 1984.[3] Just as the CPI is used to adjust workers' wages, sellers may protect themselves against cost increases by having their contracts specify one or more producer price indexes as a "materials escalator." Thus, if materials costs rise 10%, the contractor may increase material costs charges 10%. At the end of 1976, contracts escalated by producer price indexes were valued at a minimum of $100 billion.

Producer price indexes are also used for evaluating replacement costs of existing plant and equipment. Currently, four industries are being surveyed by the Bureau of Labor Statistics as a pilot project to produce new indexes that will most accurately reflect price changes. The revisions are designed to eliminate multiple counting of price changes, to expand coverage of production, to try to use actual transactions prices rather than list prices for commodities, and to improve sampling techniques. After the revision program is completed, the Producer Price Index will include industry output price indexes, industry input price indexes, detailed commodity indexes, and stage of processing indexes (crude materials, intermediate goods, and consumer finished goods at the wholesale level). The All Commodities Index will be phased out.[4] Since the information is obtained by industry or sectors, there are no area breakdowns as in the CPI. Table 13-10 shows the industries and stages of processing that are included.

The Producer Price Index (PPI) and the CPI may often exhibit different degrees of movement. In June 1980 the CPI rose 1.1%, while the PPI rose .8%. For the year prior to June 1980, the CPI rose 14.3%, while the PPI rose 13.5%.

Producer price indexes formerly were computed on a base of 1957–1959 = 100. In 1969, a new index based on 1967 prices and 1972 commodity distributions was issued. We can now connect these indexes as we did for the CPI.

	1957–1959 = 100	**1967 = 100**
1969	113.0	106.5
1970	X	110.4

The 1970 index, using 1967 as the base year, is 110.4. What would this 1970 index number have been in terms of 1957–1959 prices? We allow 1970 with the base 1957–1959 to be X. Form an equation and solve for X.

$$\frac{106.5 \text{ (1969 new base)}}{113.0 \text{ (1969 old base)}} = \frac{110.4 \text{ (1970 new base)}}{X \text{ (1970 old base)}}$$

---

[3]See John F. Early, "Improving the Measurement of Producer Price Change," *Monthly Labor Review,* Apr. 1978, pp. 7–15.
[4]*Ibid.*

TABLE 13-10

RELATIVE IMPORTANCE OF COMMODITIES INCLUDED IN THE PRODUCER PRICE INDEX, DECEMBER 1975

INDUSTRY	1963 WEIGHTS	1972 WEIGHTS
Farm products	11.28	8.40
Processed foods and feeds	16.55	14.37
Textile products and apparel	5.76	5.78
Hides, skins, leather, and related products	1.08	.76
Fuels and related products, and power	10.39	10.34
Chemicals and allied products	6.55	7.17
Rubber and plastic products	2.02	2.80
Lumber and wood products	2.54	2.23
Pulp, paper, and allied products	4.75	5.28
Metals and metal products	13.45	13.00
Machinery and equipment	11.32	11.84
Furniture and household durables	2.86	3.44
Nonmetallic mineral products	3.05	2.82
Transportation equipment	6.26	8.61
Miscellaneous products	2.14	3.19
Stage of processing		
Crude materials for further processing	12.31	11.33
Foodstuffs and feedstuffs	7.84	6.97
Nonfood materials except fuel	3.18	3.15
Crude fuel	1.29	1.21
Intermediate materials, supplies, and components	47.28	47.11
Materials and components for manufacturing	25.62	25.59
Materials and components for construction	8.45	7.94
Processed fuels and lubricants	4.53	4.85
Containers	1.58	1.39
Supplies	7.09	7.35
Finished goods (including raw foods and fuel)	40.41	41.56
Consumer goods	31.47	29.71
Producer finished goods	8.94	11.85

Source: William H. Wallace and William E. Cullison, *Measuring Price Changes: A Study of the Price Indexes*, 4th ed., Federal Reserve Bank of Richmond, 1979, p. 44.

The index number for the old base is 117.14. Using this technique, we can put together index numbers over a long period of time with any base year. In July 1980 the CPI for all consumers was 247.8 (1967 = 100). Let us estimate what the old index number would have been:

$$\frac{106.5 \text{ (1969 new)}}{113.0 \text{ (1969 old)}} = \frac{247.8 \text{ (1980 new)}}{X \text{ (1980 old)}} \qquad X = 262.9$$

Problems

1 In May 1978, the CPI for wage and clerical workers (base 1967 = 100) was 193.2.

(*a*) What was the purchasing power of a dollar in terms of 1967 prices?

(*b*) The CPI (base 1957–1959 = 100) was 224.7. What was the purchasing power of the dollar in terms of 1957–1959 prices?

2 If the CPI rises from 120 to 173, should we conclude that the cost of living has risen 53%?

3 Clarence Durrell, a realtor, wanted to study if apartment rentals have increased more than house rentals in order to advise investment clients. From the Chicago Board of Realtors, Clarence obtains the following figures:

YEAR	APARTMENT PRICES, BASE YEAR 1967 = 100	HOUSE RENTALS, BASE YEAR 1970
1970	120	100
1972	124	115
1975	138	130
1978	156	140

Have apartment prices increased more than house rentals?

4 The CPI for wage and clerical workers (base year 1967 = 100) is 205.3. What was the purchasing power of a dollar in terms of 1967 prices?

5 In 1979 a particular index series was reset to 100. The following table shows the values of the old index and the new index.

YEAR	OLD INDEX	NEW INDEX
1975	100	
1976	95	
1977	101	
1978	110	
1979	115	100
1980		110

(*a*) What is the value of the old index in 1980?

(*b*) What would have been the value of the new index in 1976?

6 Below are world cotton production figures from the U.S. Department of Agriculture. Compute and compare index numbers for 1979–1980 using 1977–1978 as a base year. Which region showed the largest increase? Which showed the largest decrease? Which increased the most in absolute terms?

WORLD COTTON PRODUCTION
(480-pound bales in hundreds of thousands)

REGION	1977–1978	1978–1979	1979–1980 FORECAST
North America	14.4	13.9	14.5
Latin America and Caribbean	5.5	5.8	5.4
USSR	12.7	12.3	13.0
China	9.4	10.0	9.8
Middle East and Africa	4.4	4.2	4.4
South Asia	8.1	8.4	8.7
Other regions and countries	9.3	8.3	8.4

Source: U.S. Department of Agriculture, *Foreign Agricultural Service*, December 1979.

7 In December 1977, the executive council of the AFL-CIO, at the Los Angeles Convention, reported the following figures on average weekly earnings.

STATISTICS FOR
BUSINESS AND
ECONOMICS

YEAR	GROSS WEEKLY EARNINGS	TAKE-HOME PAY AFTER FEDERAL TAXES FOR WORKER WITH THREE DEPENDENTS	
		CURRENT DOLLARS	CPI
1960	$80.67	72.96	88.7
1965	95.06	86.30	—
1966	98.82	88.66	94.5
1967	101.84	90.86	100.0
1968	107.73	95.28	104.2
1969	114.61	99.99	109.8
1970	119.46	104.61	116.3
1971	127.28	112.41	121.0
1972	136.16	121.09	125.3
1973	145.43	127.41	133.1
1974	154.45	134.37	147.7
1975	163.89	145.93	161.2
1976	176.29	156.50	170.5
June 1977	189.28	172.93	181.8

Source: *The National Economy 1977*, American Federation of Labor and Congress of Industrial Organizations, 1978.

(*a*)   Compute workers' real net income for 1960 and 1977.

(*b*)   What has happened to gross earnings from 1960 to 1977?

(*c*)   What happened to gross earnings between 1972 and 1977?

(*d*)   Has the change in income from 1960 to 1977 been greater for gross pay or net pay? What does this seem to indicate about tax structure?

8   In the index above, change the CPI to a 1972 base. Compute 1973–1977.

9   Figures, in billions of dollars, for U.S. imports and exports from 1968 to 1976 are given below. Make index numbers for exports and imports using 1972 as the base year.

	1968	1969	1970	1971	1972	1973	1974	1975	1976
Exports	34	36	42	43	49	71	98	107	115
Imports	33	36	40	46	56	70	104	98	124

10   Compare the index numbers for exports and imports that you developed in problem 9. Using the index number for consumer prices developed in question 8, compare the indexes of consumer prices and imports and exports.

QUANTITY INDEXES

13-10

Computation

A *quantity index number* compares the change in quantities produced or consumed (holding prices constant). Table 13-11 compares production of farm crops in 1975 to production in 1970. Now, if we wish to compute an index number for 1975 using 1970 price weights see Table 13-12. And, using 1975 price weights, we have Table 13-13. Separate index numbers may be computed for each commodity over the years. The prices are needed in the index numbers because without value it would be difficult to sum unlike items, such as bales of cotton, pounds of tobacco, and number of cattle.

TABLE 13-11

IMPORTANT FARM OUTPUTS IN THE UNITED STATES FOR 1970 and 1975

(In millions)

	1970		1975	
OUTPUTS	QUANTITY q_0	PRICE p_0	QUANTITY q_n	PRICE p_n
Corn, bushels	4152	$100	5767	$120
Cotton, bales	10	25	8	35
Tobacco, pounds	1906	10	2184	8
Cattle, head	112.4	300	131.8	320
Hogs, head	56.7	200	49.6	250

$$I_Q = \frac{\Sigma q_n p_0}{\Sigma q_0 p_0}(100) \qquad \text{using base-year price weights}$$

$$I_Q = \frac{\Sigma q_n p_n}{\Sigma q_0 p_n}(100) \qquad \text{using given-year price weights}$$

TABLE 13-12

	1970		1980		
	q_0	$q_0 p_0$	q_n	$q_n p_0$	p_0
Corn	4,152	415,200	5,767	576,700	$100
Cotton	10	250	8	200	25
Tobacco	1,906	19,060	2,184	21,849	10
Cattle	112.4	33,720	131.8	39,540	300
Hogs	56.7	11,340	49.6	9,920	200
		$\Sigma q_0 p_0 = 479,570$		$\Sigma q_n p_0 = 648,200$	

$$I_Q = \frac{\Sigma q_n p_0}{\Sigma q_0 p_0}(100) = \frac{648,200}{479,570}(100) = 1.3516(100) = 135.2$$

TABLE 13-13

	1970		1975		
	q_0	$q_0 p_n$	q_n	$q_n p_n$	p_n
Corn	4,152	498,240	5,767	692,040	$120
Cotton	10	350	8	280	35
Tobacco	1,906	15,248	2,184	17,472	8
Cattle	112.4	35,968	131.8	42,176	320
Hogs	56.7	14,175	49.6	12,400	250
		563,981		764,368	

$$I_Q = \frac{\Sigma q_n p_n}{\Sigma q_0 p_n}(100) = \frac{764,368}{563,981}(100) = 1.3553(100) = 135.5$$

The Index of Industrial Production

Measurement of price-level changes or of real income is not the only use of index numbers. The well-being of a country is often measured by its industrial productivity. The Board of Governors of the Federal Reserve System compiles a monthly index of industrial production, published continuously since 1927; it is based on more than 200 separate series collected by government agencies and trade associations. These indexes measure quantities of output in manufacturing, mining, and utilities. Only value added in each stage of production is considered on each item to avoid double counting. For example, if coal is used to manufacture electric power the value of the coal used is counted under mining, and only the additional value added by the conversion of coal to electricity is counted under utilities.

The formula used takes the relative change in quantity (quantity relatives) and multiplies it by base-year value weights $p_0 q_0$. Note that although we could simplify the numerator to $q_n p_0$, we wish to find the quantity relatives separately for each commodity to study commodity changes separately.

$$I = \frac{\Sigma[(q_n/q_0)p_0 q_0]}{\Sigma p_0 q_0} (100)$$

The Index of Industrial Production (IIP) can be found in monthly issues of the Federal Reserve Bulletin or the Survey of Current Business. These indexes are arranged by major markets (consumer goods, equipment, intermediate products, materials, and supplementary goods) or by industry (mining and utilities and manufacturing—nondurable and durable). The indexes show how production has changed. Thus, using 1967 as the base year (100), the 1977 average for industrial production was 137.1, showing a 37.1% increase in industrial production.

SUMMARY

13-11

1 An index number is a ratio that relates a price or quantity in one period to a price or quantity in another *(base)* period.

2 Index numbers have been published since the 1700s. The *Wholesale Price Index* was introduced in the United States in 1890. The *Consumer Price Index* was introduced in 1917 to help arrive at a fair scale for shipbuilders' wages. The *Dow Jones average* for stock market performance was introduced in 1884.

3 Unweighted index numbers can be constructed using an aggregative approach or a price relatives approach.

$$I = \frac{\Sigma p_n}{\Sigma p_0} (100) \qquad \text{aggregative index}$$

$$I = \frac{\Sigma(p_n/p_0)}{n} (100) \qquad \text{price relatives index}$$

4 Weighted index numbers may be calculated using *base-year* weights. These are called *Laspeyres' indexes*.

$$I = \frac{\Sigma p_n q_0}{\Sigma p_0 q_0} (100) \qquad \text{Laspeyres' aggregative index}$$

$$I = \frac{\Sigma[(p_n/p_0)(p_0 q_0)]}{\Sigma p_0 q_0} (100) \qquad \text{Laspeyres' index of price relatives}$$

These indexes sometimes overestimate increases because they do not allow for substitution effects. Note that we do not simplify the price relatives formula, since we are interested in computing and studying the price relatives for each commodity.

5 Weighted index numbers may also be calculated using *given-year* weights. These are called Paasche's indexes.

$$I = \frac{\Sigma p_n q_n}{\Sigma p_0 q_n}(100) \qquad \text{Paasche's aggregative index}$$

$$I = \frac{\Sigma[(p_n/p_0)(p_n q_n)]}{\Sigma p_n q_n}(100) \qquad \text{Paasche's index of price relatives}$$

These indexes involve current weights that lead to continuous changes in quantity weights and recalculation of index numbers.

6 Some problems of index number construction are choice of a base year, items to include in the index, and base-year, given-year, or reference-year weights.

7 *Link relatives* provide a way to find index numbers for each year using the previous year as base. In addition, *chaining* these links together (by multiplying them by each other) provides an index number based on the base year of the first link as long as the chain is continuous.

8 *The Consumer Price Index* shows changes in the prices of a market basket of goods representing the buying habits of 80% of the noninstitutional civilian population of the United States. The three most important items in the index are housing, food, and transportation. The index uses reference-year (fixed-year) quantity weights. This index has been used for the formulation and evaluation of economic policy measures, as an *escalator* for income payments, as a *deflator* to measure *real earnings,* and as a measure of the purchasing power of the dollar.

9 *Shifting the base* of an index number enables us to compare changes of indexes with different bases. A system of ratios may be used to compute this shift. To find current *real income,* we divide current income by the index number and multiply by 100. This gives the monetary value of current income in terms of base-year prices.

10 *Purchasing power of the dollar* is computed by finding the reciprocal of the price index. Thus, if the current index number is 179.4, the purchasing power of the dollar is $(1/179.4)100 = .557$.

11 In order to *splice two indexes,* it is necessary to have data for the same time period for both indexes. Thus, we can compute the old May 1980 index if we have the new and old April 1980 index number as well as the new May 1980 data. Simply solve the following equation for X:

$$\frac{\text{Old April 1980}}{\text{New April 1980}} = \frac{X(\text{Old May 1980})}{\text{New May 1980}}$$

12 The *Gross National Product implicit price deflator* contains both consumption and investment goods, and is the result of deflating the current price of each type of commodity by an index for that commodity. The overall index number is found by comparing the total cost of all commodities at current prices with the total cost of deflated prices. Since this index number uses current-year quantity weights, it is not generally used as an inflator for future years. Rather, it is used to find the real change in GNP. It is used to express Gross National Product from year to year in terms of constant prices.

13 The *Producer Price Index,* previously called the *Wholesale Price Index,* is calculated by the Bureau of Labor Statistics on a 1967 base. It currently covers 2800 commodities and uses commodity weights from 1972. The index has stage-of-processing categories in which separate indexes are calculated for crude materials, intermediate materials, consumer finished goods at the wholesale level, and producer finished goods. These indexes enable one to look at price changes by stage of production. There are also detailed commodity indexes that enable one to explore price changes for different types of commodities.

14 *Quantity indexes* compare changes in quantitites produced while holding prices constant. They enable one to combine several commodities in one price index.

15 The *Index of Industrial Production,* published by the Federal Reserve Board, is a quantity index used to measure the well-being of the country. Output changes in mining, manufacturing, and utilities are measured by this index of *quantity relatives:*

$$I = \frac{\Sigma[(q_n/q_0)p_0q_0]}{\Sigma p_0 q_0}$$

The computation involves taking relative changes in the quantities of each of the 200 series included and weighting them by base-year value weights p_0q_0.

BIBLIOGRAPHY

13-12

Books

Allen, R. G. D.: *Index Numbers in Theory and Practice*, Chicago: Aldine, 1975.

Banerjee, Kali S.: *Cost of Living Index Numbers, Practice, Precision and Theory*, New York: Marcel Dekker, 1975.

Jedamus, Paul, Robert Frame, and Robert Taylor: *Statistical Analyses for Business Decisions*, New York: McGraw-Hill, 1976, pp. 68–111.

Mason, Robert D.: *Statistical Techniques in Business and Economics,* 4th ed, Homewood, Ill.: Irwin, 1978, pp. 115–143.

Mendenhall, William, and James Reinmuth: *Statistics for Management and Economics,* 3d ed, North Scituate, Mass.: Duxbury Press, 1978, pp. 522–533.

Shao, Stephen: *Statistics for Business and Economics,* 2d ed, Columbus, Ohio: Merrill, 1972, pp. 541–561. Contains a table of important price, value, and quantity indexes.

Wallace, William H., and William E. Cullison: *Measuring Price Changes: A Study of the Price Indexes,* 4th ed, Federal Reserve Bank of Richmond, 1979.

Articles

"Adjusting Wages to Living Costs: A Historical Note," *Monthly Labor Review,* July 1974, pp. 21–26.

Early, John F: "Improving the Measurement of Producer Price Change," *Monthly Labor Review,* Apr. 1978, pp. 7–15. Describes revisions in the Wholesale Price Index scheduled for completion in 1984.

Kipnis, Gregory: "Implicit Price Index." In *Inflation and the Price Indexes* (Appendix C), Subcommittee on Economic Statistics, Joint Economic Committee, Washington, D.C., 1966.

Meadows, Edward: "Our Flawed Inflation Indexes," *Fortune,* Apr. 24, 1978, pp. 66–70.

Moss, Bennett: "Industry and Sector Price Indexes," *Monthly Labor Review,* Aug. 1965, pp. 974–982.

Triplett, Jack E.: "Determining the Effect of Quality Change on the CPI," *Monthly Labor Review,* May 1971, pp. 27–38.

Government Publications

Industrial Production— 1976 Revision. Washington, D.C.: Board of Governors of the Federal Reserve System, Dec. 1977.

For information on how to purchase government documents, write to the U.S. Government Printing Office, Washington, D.C. 20402; or telephone 202-783-3238. In Chapter 14, information on securing important data bases for research work is given.

Case 13-1: Bilko Commercial Realty

Bilko Commercial Realty has been purchasing undeveloped (raw) land zoned for commercial use for investors who are interested in setting up small shopping centers and office complexes. The properties Bilko considered were located in Michigan, Ohio, and Iowa. Generally, Bilko would purchase a plot of approximately 500 to 600 acres and advertise it in commercial newspapers. Usually, Bilko was able to sell a property within an average of 2 years. Between the time of purchase and sale, Bilko financed its activities by obtaining loans at the current rate of interest from the Ames National Bank of Commerce (Iowa).

Over the years, property prices rose at differing rates in the various states covered by Bilko. This meant that the costs of property or the liabilities of Bilko increased. In the period from 1974 to 1976, Bilko had spent an average of $2 million each year on properties in Michigan, $3 million each year on properties in Ohio, and $5 million each year on properties in Iowa. Company policy had been established to continue to distribute purchases among the states in the same way, buying approximately the same amount of acreage per state.

Daniel Gross, the accountant for Bilko Commercial Realty, felt that the computation of index numbers for land-price changes in each state would provide a good measure of average annual change in land prices in each state. If one assumed that land prices would continue to change in the same way, these indexes would provide a way to estimate future land price changes for each state. In addition, the index numbers could provide estimates of statewide, and hence total, increases in mortgage borrowing necessary for Bilko's business. This could lead to revised policies about investment distribution.

Using average property prices Bilko paid per acre in each of the three states, Daniel Gross drew up Table 1. Then using 1974 as the base year, Gross calculated the following index numbers for each state in Table 2.

Questions

1 For each of the three states, estimate the amount of land purchased in 1974.

2 How can these state index numbers be combined with the amount of land pur-

TABLE 1

AVERAGE RAW LAND PRICE PER ACRE

YEAR	MICHIGAN	OHIO	IOWA
1974	$500	$615	$550
1975	521	622	558
1976	524	623	594
1977	540	640	603
1978	545	642	613
1979	555	645	625

TABLE 2

INDEX FOR RAW LAND PRICE (1974 = 100)

YEAR	MICHIGAN	OHIO	IOWA
1974	$100	$100	$100
1975	104.2	101.1	101.5
1976	104.8	101.3	108.0
1977	108.0	104.1	109.6
1978	109.0	104.4	111.5
1979	111.0	104.9	113.6

chased to form a composite index for the three states? This number would give Bilko an idea of how its overall borrowing needs would rise. Compute composite index numbers for 1974–1979. What does this composite index number show about the increase in cost of the same amount of land?

3 (a) In 1974, the value of Bilko accounts payable was $10 million. How much would Bilko have to pay in 1979 to acquire the same amount of land?

(b) If interest rates were 11.5%, what would the expected additional annual interest cost be? If rates were 17%, what would the additional interest cost be?

4 Can this information be used to change policies? If you were in Daniel Gross's position, what would you recommend to management?

Case 13-2:   Lomans Department Store

In many departments of a large department store, it is customary for salespeople to work on a commission basis. Under this system, the salesperson receives a base wage and then receives a commission based on superior sales. Thus, the salesperson who really "sells" rather than takes orders will earn more than the apathetic salesperson.

At Lomans Department Store, it was customary to offer commissions in the shoe, fine jewelry, cosmetics, men's furnishings, and appliance departments. Lomans, a large midwestern department store with a relatively expensive line of merchandise, has annual sales of $110 million. The main store was located downtown in a large midwestern city, and seven branch stores were scattered in shopping centers throughout the metropolitan area. The president, Celia Sapp, had an MBA degree from Indiana University and 14 years of retail experience as a buyer and divisional merchandise manager at Lazarus Department Store in Columbus, Ohio.

In early 1980, a delegation of female salesclerks approached the personnel department and Celia Sapp with the complaint that, except for the cosmetics department, all departments offering commissions were primarily staffed by men. The delegation felt that the store should hire women in the "high-paid" incentive departments or else offer commissions in all store departments. Since there were

many men in the commission departments who had been with the store for years, Celia Sapp felt that she might have difficulty shifting salespeople around. Therefore, she asked Jeanette Myers, the director of personnel, to see if she could work out an incentive pay system.

Jeanette, who had majored in statistics as an undergraduate and had an MBA degree with a strong emphasis on personnel management, began to reflect upon an equitable system. In most departments of Lomans, an average salesperson sold about $250 worth of merchandise a day. In an average month, sales should be 20 (which represents the number of sales days worked by each employee) times $250, or $5000.

As Jeanette prepared the figures for this work, it became evident to her that there was a decided seasonal variation in sales for Lomans. As expected, in November and December sales were very high due to the Christmas rush. Sales were generally low in the summer. Before Easter there was some increase in sales, and in May there was another spurt as people purchased summer clothing, furniture, and outdoor equipment. Using store data for the past 10 years, Jeanette was able to compute the following index numbers. (See Chapter 11 for this technique.)

MONTH	SEASONAL INDEX NUMBERS
January	75
February	90
March	100
April	80
May	130
June	110
July	65
August	70
September	80
October	100
November	140
December	160

Looking at these numbers, Jeanette speculated that if salaries were strongly tied to sales, workers would have highly fluctuating incomes. Thus, if salaries were completely dependent on sales, the average worker would earn twice as much in December as he or she did in April. Therefore, Jeanette decided to consider a bonus wage that would include a flat hourly amount ($3.25), a bonus for years of seniority of 10¢ per hour per year up to 10 years, and 10% of the sales above the seasonally adjusted average for that month. If a salesperson fell below the monthly estimated sales, there would be no penalty; the salesperson would receive $3.25 per hour and the seniority bonus.

Georgia Golden, a fairly typical salesclerk with a good record of sales, had worked in the women's handbag departments for 7 years. Her sales in 1978 were as follows:

MONTH	SALES
January	$4203
February	4955
March	4700
April	4390
May	4930
June	5300
July	4398
August	4837
September	5838
October	5970
November	6302
December	6800

Georgia earned $4.15 an hour, or $166 a week; her annual pay before taxes was $8632. Jeanette Myers decided to use Georgia's sales record to see how she would be paid under the new incentive system. She assumed that the average salesperson would work 4.33 weeks a month (52/12) and that the average work-week was 40 hours.

First, Jeanette assumed that average sales per salesperson for each month would be $5000, since sales in the handbag department were close in value to the storewide average. Then, multiplying by the seasonal index number and dividing by 100, she computed seasonally adjusted estimated sales. For example, the index number for January is 75; therefore, $5000(75)/100 = $3750 estimated January sales. Jeanette then compared estimated sales to actual sales and computed regular pay and the bonus.

Questions

1 How do you compute the seasonally adjusted monthly base sales upon which incentives will be based? Compute base sales for each month for Georgia Golden.

2 Compute the wage for Georgia Golden for each month in 1978.

3 Will she ever fall below her monthly wage of 1978? Does her total annual pay change by very much?

4 What if the store kept the base pay for each individual the same ($4.15 per hour), and added the incentive bonus to it? How much more would Georgia earn? Can you suggest some alternate incentive wage systems? What other objectives might be used?

5 In your opinion, what should Jeanette Myers recommend?

Case 13-3: Braniff Airways

Braniff Airways negotiated a contract on April 21, 1976, with the International Brotherhood of Teamsters. A feature of the contract was article 44, an unlimited cost of living increase that was to become effective the first pay period beginning on or after July 1, 1978. This article is quoted below:

All employees covered by this agreement shall be entitled to a cost-of-living increase as prescribed below. The first cost-of-living increase shall be effective the first pay period beginning on or after July 1, 1978.

The first cost-of-living allowance shall be based on the change in the Consumer Price Index, U.S. All items of the Bureau of Labor Statistics, U.S. Department of Labor (1967 = 100) for urban wage earners, etc., between October 15, 1977 and April 15, 1978. The next cost-of-living shall be granted on the first pay period beginning on or after December 1, 1978 and shall be based on the change in the CPI between April 15, 1978 and October 15, 1978, using the October 15, 1977 index figure as the base. The cost-of-living increases shall be calculated on the basis of: for every .3 increase in the CPI there shall be a one cent (.01) per hour increase in wages. The cost-of-living adjustments shall become a part of the base rate for all pay purpose calculations.

In the event the CPI for October or April has not been issued in time for the effective date, then any adjustments that are required will be made at the beginning of the first pay period after receipt of the CPI and will be made retroactive to the effective date.

In the event the urban wage earners index shall be revised or discontinued and in the event the Bureau of Labor Statistics, U.S. Department of Labor, does not issue information that would enable the company and the union to know what the index would have been had it not been revised or discontinued, then the company and the union will meet, negotiate and agree upon an appropriate substitute for the Index, pursuant to Section 6, of the Railway Labor Act as amended.

The labor-management department was assigned to study the cost implications of the new provision. There were 25 seniority groups involved. To begin with, the rising costs for stewards and stewardesses (flight attendants) were to be explored.

Attendants were paid according to seniority by the pay scale below, which

MONTHLY WAGES: SENIORITY GROUP 15

NUMBER OF ATTENDANTS, NOV. 1, 1977	PROGRESSION	FLIGHT SERVICE ATTENDANT			FIRST PAY PERIOD, JULY 1, 1978
		AUG. 1, 1975	OCT. 1, 1976	NOV. 1, 1977	
6	0–6 months	$ 874	$ 880	$ 931	
20	6–12 months	880	890	945	
12	12–18 months	907	924	955	
5	18–24 months	917	934	977	
4	24–30 months	937	954	1029	
3	30–36 months	957	984	1040	
0	36–42 months	977	994	1061	
2	42–48 months	1007	1024	1097	
1	48–54 months	1037	1054	1132	
0	54–60 months	1077	1086	1207	
0	60–72 months		1147	1300	
1	72 months and over		1210	1350	
54					

is copied from page 14 of the contract. A random sample of attendants in each category is supplied for easy computation purposes (column 1). The number of attendants chosen in each category is proportional to the number actually in each category. Later, the company would weight its answers to obtain the total costs of the escalator clause.

The labor-management department was trying to estimate the future cost of the escalator clause for changes based on changes in the CPI from October 15, 1977 to April 1978. For the period from November 1976 to April 1977, the CPI for all items rose as follows:

PERIOD	INDEX POINT INCREASE FROM PRECEDING MONTH
October–November 1976	.3
November–December 1976	.3
December–January 1977	.6
January–February 1977	1.0
February–March 1977	.6
March–April 1977	.8
	3.6

Questions

1 In 1977, what would the labor-management department have to assume to compute the expected total wage cost and wage increases for flight service attendants for July 1, 1978? *Hint:* Examine the CPI, the hours, and the distribution of attendants in time categories.

2 What is the total wage increase based on the change in the index number for the 6-month period? (Assume a 40-hour week and 4.33 weeks per month.) If the sample is one-sixth of the population of flight attendants, what would the total cost be?

3 How does this type of escalator clause affect wage differentials (the percentage relation between the lowest and the highest wages) of the seniority classes?

4 How does this type of escalator clause affect absolute wage differences?

5 Would it cost the company more if it gave a 1% wage increase for every 1 percentage point increase in the CPI for the same 6-month period? *Optional:* What percentage of wage increase for each percentage point increase in CPI would give the same monetary results as the 1 cent for every .3 index point increase for this category?

6 What would this type of escalator (percentage) do to wage differentials? Would it make for a narrower or a wider spread in percentage terms between the highest- and lowest-income categories?

7 What type of escalator clause should the company fight for in future labor-management negotiations? Why?

8 Some companies have negotiated contracts so that if the index rises by less

than 1 point (1.0), the escalator is not used. Should the company try to employ this clause? Would such a clause be worthwhile in light of current index number trends?

9 As the head of the labor-management department, what would you report to management on the cost implications of the new provision?

MULTIVARIATE TECHNIQUES, DATA BASES, AND COMPUTER SOFTWARE

14

14-1   INTRODUCTION

14-2   MULTIVARIATE ANALYSIS
       Multiple Regression Analysis
       Discriminant Analysis
       Factor Analysis
       Multiple Analysis of Variance

14-3   DATA BASES AVAILABLE FOR BUSINESS AND SOCIAL SCIENCE
       RESEARCH
       Inter-University Consortium for Political and Social Research (ICPSR)
       National Longitudinal Studies (NLS)
       Census Tapes (1980, 1970)
       Compustat Tapes

14-4   COMPUTER SOFTWARE STATISTICS PACKAGES
       Biomedical Computer Programs (BMD and BMDP)
       Statistical Package for the Social Sciences (SPSS)
       Other Programs

14-5   INTERPRETATION OF COMPUTER PRINTOUTS
       Scattergram and Simple Regression Program
       Multiple Regression Program

14-6   STATISTICAL PROGRAMS FOR HANDHELD CALCULATORS

14-7   REVIEW QUESTIONS

14-8   BIBLIOGRAPHY

INTRODUCTION

14-1

Thus far we have studied one variable at a time using descriptive statistical techniques, such as the mean, median, and standard deviation, or inferential techniques, such as estimates of means, proportions, confidence intervals. We have also looked at the relationship of two variables, such as advertising and sales, education and political preference, using tests of the difference between means and between proportions and nonparametric tests, such as the chi-square test. These tests look at the nature and degree of association between two variables. In addition, we have found formulas for estimating the value of one variable (dependent) if we know another (independent) using regression analysis. Basically, we have either summarized data (descriptive statistics) or used a sample to try to estimate what the population looks like (inferential statistics) with respect to a particular phenomenon.

Advanced statistics courses introduce more complex multivariate techniques. These techniques use a number of variables to make estimates of one or more population characteristics, hence the name *multivariate*. The use of these techniques has increased greatly in recent years because new computers have raised significantly the speed at which these measures can be calculated. In the not so distant past, one could obtain a doctorate in many fields if he or she could compute and present a multiple regression analysis to study some issue in the field. The hand computation involved could take many months. Today, with a proper computer program, one can turn out several hundred multiple regression equations and error terms in several minutes. In the first part of this chapter, we discuss several important multivariate techniques. We do not focus on how to compute these measures but rather on what they mean and when they might be used. Thus, if you hear about these techniques in other classes or read about them in journal articles, you will have an idea of the basic nature of these tests. If you need to employ these methods, you can consult more advanced statistics texts for the methods of computation. There are a number of computer programs (software) that can be used to do these computations and print out results. In Section 14-4 we briefly discuss two very important sets of programs that are available at most universities and can be purchased by private individuals or companies. These two sets are the Biomedical Computer Program (BMD and BMDP) and the Statistical Package for the Social Sciences (SPSS). In Section 14-5, we show typical computer printouts from two of these programs and discuss how to read and interpret them.

In order to use more complicated multivariate analysis where we study many variables at the same time, we must have observations from a relatively large number of individuals to make a reliable estimate. Now that the use of these techniques is possible, we can make good estimates about the populations of states, cities, countries, and customer markets. In order to make estimates, we must collect some data. Data collection for nationwide estimates is expensive and time-consuming. Fortunately, there are groups that have collected nationwide data and stored it on magnetic computer tapes. This information has been obtained from surveys of random samples of the population. The National Longitudinal Studies (NLS) and the Inter-University Consortium for Political and Social Research (ICPSR), which can be obtained from Ohio State University and from the University of Michigan, respectively (see the bibliography for addresses), provide nationwide sample survey data. United States Census data contains information from a survey of the entire population as well as special information from selected samples of the population (U.S. Census). These sources are called *data bases*. It is possible to purchase copies of data bases from many academic groups and government agencies. The fees for these bases are usually far less expensive than the costs of collecting this information on one's own. Some private groups also offer data bases. In Section 14-3, we briefly discuss some available data bases.

First, we briefly describe the purpose and nature of some multivariate techniques that you might meet in more demanding situations or in your reading of journals or books on business, economic, sociologic, and psychologic topics. Then, we briefly discuss available data bases. Following this discussion we briefly cover statistical software packages and give an example of how to interpret computer printouts from some of these programs.

441

MULTIVARIATE
TECHNIQUES
DATA BASES, AND
COMPUTER
SOFTWARE

MULTIVARIATE ANALYSIS

Multivariate analysis describes a family of analytical methods. There has been some controversy over what should be classified as multivariate analysis. Some people say that the term should apply only to analyses in which *both* multiple *independent* and *dependent* variables are studied simultaneously. Others use it for types of measures in which there is more than one independent variable or more than one dependent variable or both. We use the latter definition. Thus, multiple regression analysis having one dependent variable and more than one independent variable is included here. This analysis is most useful, since it can handle a large number of independent variables that are either continuous (divisible into an infinite number of categories) or categorical.

Multivariate techniques have usually used interval- or ratio-scaled (divisible into only a few categories) variables or binary variables that can be coded 0 or 1. Thus, we may use a variable like working or not working, male or female, or married or not married. These categorical variables can be coded as either 0 or 1. Interval-scaled variables that are relatively continuous within a given range, such as height, age, weight, grade point average, years of education, and prices, can easily be used in most types of multivariate analyses. Notice that we have not discussed ordinal variables, where order is important but the distance between categories is not necessarily the same. Currently, statisticians are devising multivariate techniques to handle these ordinally scaled variables. We do not present these methods here, but will now briefly discuss several of the more widely used multivariate techniques. These are:

1 Multiple regression analysis
2 Discriminant analysis
3 Factor analysis
4 Multiple analysis of variance

Multiple Regression Analysis

In Chapter 10, we described multiple regression analysis and found it useful when we are trying to predict a given dependent variable using two or more independent variables. For example, if we have two independent variables, we can study variations in the dependent variable when we hold one independent variable constant and vary the other independent variable. Thus, we can study the effect of a wife's education on labor force participation of married women when the husband's income is held constant. In Section 14-5, we interpret a computer printout of the results of a multiple regression analysis that attempts to predict rushing yardage if we know the height, weight, and number of years as a professional football player for running backs (problem 1*d*, p. 308, Chapter 10).

The variables used in multiple regression analyses are usually interval or ratio scales. Categorical variables can be used as independent variables by employing what are called *dummy variables*. Thus, if we wish to learn the effects of marital status on our independent variable, we would enter married as (1) and not married as (0). If we wish to examine the effects of housing status and had three categories (for example, single-family housing, two-family housing, and multifamily housing), we would enter two dummy variables. The first variable could be single-family housing (1) versus other (0), and the second variable could be two-family housing (1) versus other (0). We would not need a third variable for multifamily since, if the respondent were 0 on single-family housing and 0 on two family, we would infer that our respondent occupied multifamily housing.

Discriminant Analysis

Discriminant analysis is a variation of regression analysis that allows us to predict the membership of people or objects in groups. We have two or more dependent variables, or groups, instead of the one continuous dependent variable we usually have in multiple regression analysis. *Two-way* discriminant analysis is typical where we are trying to find variables that help distinguish between two groups. If we were trying to classify a group of nonvoters as to whether they would vote Republican or Democratic, we might ask a series of questions on how they felt about the regulation of business, the level of armaments, social welfare, foreign policy, and a balanced budget. Or we may wish to predict which firms will finance expansion using internal sources versus those firms that will use regular capital markets. Such independent variables as credit rating, return on investment, return on assets, and capital intensity may affect the financing decision. We could find the issues that would distinguish between our groups, but no *single* variable might perfectly distinguish between internal financers and capital market financers, or between Democrats and Republicans. By taking several issues and weighting and combining them, we would hope to find dimensions that would clearly separate one group from another. This is what discriminant analysis does; it discriminates groups from one another on the basis of linear combinations or *sets* of variables. Discriminant analysis determines which of these variables are most important in predicting whether or not the respondents will vote Democratic or Republican. We can then use the results of this analysis to predict how additional people will vote if we know their attitudes about these issues. It may also be used to assign individuals to one of the two financing types on the basis of their scores on different variables, such as credit rating, capital intensity, return on investment, and return on assets.

The result of a discriminant analysis is one or more discriminant functions ($n - 1$ discriminant functions, where n is the number of groups). The discriminant function in a two-group analysis is a multiple regression equation with a dichotomous (coded 0,1) dependent variable representing membership in one group or another. Usually, in discriminant analysis, the dependent variable is categorical, while the independent variables are interval- or ratio-scaled, although dummy variables may be used for the independent variables. Multiple discriminant analysis distinguishes between three or more groups.

To use discriminant analysis, we assume normality of the underlying distributions and equal dispersions for the groups. Assume we have two groups, Republicans (0) and Democrats (+), and wish to be able to classify them on two opinion variables—X_2 (amount of social welfare payments desired) and X_1 (amount of government control of business desired). We can plot these points using crosses for Democrats and circles for Republicans; we can also fit a regression equation that gives us weights for each variable. This is called a *discriminant function;* see Figure 14-1.

443

MULTIVARIATE
TECHNIQUES
DATA BASES, AND
COMPUTER
SOFTWARE

The general form is

$$Z = W_1 X_1 + W_2 X_2 + \cdots + W_n X_n$$

where Z is the discriminant score, W_i the discriminant weights, and X_i the independent variables. For this problem, the equation is $Z = W_1 X_1 + W_2 X_2$. Note that there is some overlap, but that the groups tend to be quite different on the two issues. We can weight these characteristics to get Z scores that will enable us to classify people as Republican or Democrat.

For each group, we can multiply the weight (the regression coefficient) by the value for each individual on a particular variable and obtain an average of the scores for all people in the group (Republican or Democrat). The mean value for these scores in each group on each variable is called the *centroid*. Somewhere between the centroids the *optimum cutting score* will be set. People above this score will be classified in one group (say, Republican), and people with scores below this will be classified in another group (say, Democrat).

A group of respondents that have not been previously used to build the discriminant function(s) is called the *holdout sample*. This sample is now used to check the predictive value of the analysis. A *hit ratio* is calculated, which is the percentage of statistical units correctly classified by the discriminant function. The hit ratio is compared to the ratio of those who would have been placed in each category by chance. Thus, the higher the hit ratio, the better the discriminant function.

In summary, discriminant analysis is useful for determining where the differences exist between groups, and the relative importance of different variables in predicting group membership.

Factor Analysis

Factor analysis is a name for a family of multivariate statistical methods that can be used to represent a set of variables in terms of a *smaller* number of variables. A

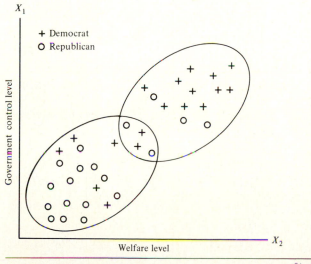

FIGURE **14-1**

Classification of voters on level of government control desired and level of welfare payments desired.

large number of variables are analyzed to find their common underlying dimensions or *factors*. Thus, many observed variables can be condensed into a smaller set of components. For example, assume we are giving tests to entering college students, and we administer vocabulary (V), reading (R), arithmetic problem solving (P), and computation (C) tests. After the tests are scored, we can correlate the results of each test with every other test, and we have the matrix of correlation coefficients shown in Table 14-1. Note that the values on the diagonal are one since this would be the relation of each variable to itself. Also, note that the correlation between V and C is the same as that between C and V. We now try to find the number of underlying variables or factors. Circling V and R we find factor 1, which may represent some type of verbal ability. In the lower right-hand part of this matrix, we circle the other high relation, that of P and C, which is factor 2. Verbal (V) and reading (R) seem to measure some underlying ability—perhaps language ability; problem solving (P) and computation (C) seem to measure some type of mathematical ability. We have identified to two *factors*. Most factor analyses have many more variables and identify a number of factors. These factors may be *orthogonal* (not related to each other) or *oblique* (related to each other).

This type of analysis which reduces the number of variables into a smaller number of factors that can help explain behavior or performance, has a number of important types of uses in business and social science situations. The factor analyses may be used to discover the *basic structure* underlying many measures. Thus, Kinnear and Taylor give an example in which 50 attributes of coffee were studied that might in the end lead to two factors, (1) sweetness/bitterness and (2) degree of freshness, as the important underlying dimensions.

Factor analysis is also useful in the development of *scales*. In a scale, we combine a number of measures to find a way to compare people or products. For example, a graduate school may wish to obtain a scale to rate recommendations, work experience, and extracurricular activities of prospective students. Using factor analysis, the important independent variables could be identified. Each factor would measure some underlying dimension. The analysis also provides *weights*. Thus, we could tell if the number of offices held in campus organizations should be given more weight than the number of years of work experience.

Factors, once identified, can also be used in other types of analysis. We have shown earlier in this chapter that multiple regression analysis requires that the independent variables are not correlated with each other. Factor analysis can be used to identify the factors that are uncorrelated, and these factors can then be used in multiple regression analysis.

Computation of factor analysis generally requires use of a computer program. SPSS, BMD, and OSIRIS—discussed in Section 14-4—all have programs of this

TABLE 14-1

COEFFICIENTS OF CORRELATION AMONG FOUR TESTS

	VOCABULARY	READING	PROBLEM SOLVING	COMPUTATION
Vocabulary	1.00	.78	.10	.05
Reading	.78	1.00	.15	.08
Problem solving	.10	.15	1.00	.82
Computation	.05	.08	.82	1.00

type. There are three basic computation steps in this type of analysis. First, we compute the correlations between all variables of interest, as we have done in Table 14-1. Since we are using correlation analysis, we should have variables that are at least interval scaled. In the second step, we extract a set of initial factors from the correlation analysis. In the third step, we adjust these initial factors by "rotation" to find a final solution.

445

MULTIVARIATE
TECHNIQUES
DATA BASES, AND
COMPUTER
SOFTWARE

There are many ways to extract the initial factors from the correlation matrix. We will briefly discuss the *principal factors method* (sometimes called the *principal components method*).

The basic method of extracting factors is to try to find the *minimum* number of factors necessary to reproduce the observed correlations. In factor extraction, we find a set of factors that are a linear combination of variables in the correlation matrix. If variables X_1, X_2, X_3, X_4, X_5, and X_6 were highly correlated with each other, they could be combined to form one factor F_1. Thus, $F_1 = b_1X_1 + b_2X_2 + b_3X_3 + b_4X_4 + b_5X_5 + b_6X_6$. F_1 would be called a *principal component* or *principal factor*. In this method, the computer program would search for the values of each b_i (regression coefficient) in the equation above that explains more variance in the correlation matrix than any other set of b_i's. Factor F_1 would now be our first principal factor. The variance explained by this factor is subtracted from the original input matrix to yield a residual matrix. Then, a second principal factor that explains further variation in the residual matrix is extracted. This procedure is repeated until there is very little variance left to be explained.

A third procedure, called *rotation,* is then used to obtain simpler and more readily interpretable results. Using a graph, we will demonstrate how rotation can improve interpretation of results. If we look at variables X_1, X_2, X_3, X_4, X_5, and X_6 in Figure 14-2 and see their weights or loadings (*b* values) for factor 1 and factor 2, we read these points from the graph to obtain columns 1 and 2 in Table 14-2. When we look at variables X_1, X_2, and X_3, we are not sure if they should be included in factor 1 or factor 2. By rotating our axis, keeping the axes at 90° angles (orthogonal rotation), we now read a new set of factor values for X_1, X_2, X_3, X_4, X_5, and X_6 from the new axes and record them in columns 3 and 4 of Table 14-2. In this second set, it is quite clear that variables 4, 5, and 6 should be included in factor 1, and variables 1, 2, and 3 should be included in factor 2. Other more complex kinds of rotations are available, called *oblique rotations,* where the axes are not kept at right angles. There are many forms of orthogonal and oblique rotations. These techniques are covered in the more advanced texts listed in the bibliography.

Multiple Analysis of Variance

Remember that in Chapter 7, in our discussion of one-way analysis of variance, we assumed that group variances were equal and examined means of groups to determine if all groups could have come from the same population. Our first variable (statistics books) was nominal and our second variable (test scores) was interval. We compared the variation between groups V_B to the variation within groups V_W. This ratio was called an *F ratio,* and we determined its significance by comparing it to F critical values at either the .05 or .01 significance level (Type I error) in our table.

When we studied whether the four texts were equally good in determining students' test performance, we assumed that all other conditions were held constant. Frequently, this is difficult to do. Even if the classes were picked at random to ensure

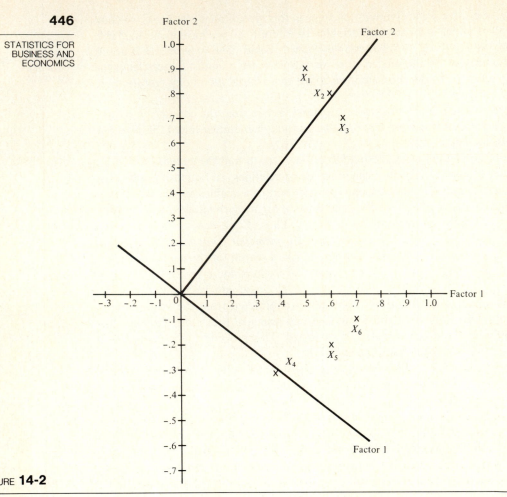

FIGURE **14-2**

Graph of variables used in two factors showing improvement in
interpretation resulting from rotation of axes.

TABLE 14-2

COMPARISON OF ROTATED AND UNROTATED FACTOR LOADINGS

VARIABLE	UNROTATED FACTOR LOADINGS		ROTATED FACTOR LOADINGS	
	1	2	1	2
X_1	.50	.90	−.20	.99
X_2	.60	.80	−.04	.97
X_3	.65	.70	.10	.90
X_4	.40	−.30	.50	−.05
X_5	.60	−.20	.60	.20
X_6	.70	−.10	.70	.30

equal ability in each class, and the teachers were kept constant to ensure the same class lectures, it might be that the previous math training of the students might vary in each of the classes and might tend to affect the grades of the classes. If we divide math training into two groups, we have a 2 (groups) × 4 (books) research design. This makes a 2 × 4 matrix, or eight different groups to study.

447

MULTIVARIATE
TECHNIQUES
DATA BASES, AND
COMPUTER
SOFTWARE

Previous math training	Book 1	Book 2	Book 3	Book 4
No previous math training	Book 1	Book 2	Book 3	Book 4

We can study the test grades for each of the eight groups. This is a two-way analysis of variance, and there are four types of variance present in this data.

We will study (1) the effect of factor 1 (book) on the dependent variable (test score); (2) the effect of factor 2 (previous math training) on the dependent variable; and (3) the combined or joint effects of factors 1 and 2 on the dependent variable. This combined effect is called the *interaction effect*. These three effects will be compared to the variance within groups (error), which will be used as the denominator of the F ratio.

In order to study the variances, three F tests are computed. They are:

$$\frac{\text{Between column variance}}{\text{Within groups variance}} = F_B \quad \text{effects of book}$$

$$\frac{\text{Between row variance}}{\text{Within groups variance}} = F_M \quad \text{effects of math training}$$

$$\frac{\text{Combined effects of book and training}}{\text{Within groups variance}} = F_{MB} \quad \text{interaction effect}$$

The degrees of freedom for the numerator of the first F ratio is the number of columns minus 1 ($c - 1$). The number of degrees of freedom for the denominator is the number of observations minus the number of columns. The degrees of freedom for the second F ratio is the number of rows minus 1 ($r - 1$). The same number of degrees of freedom is used for the denominator as in the first ratio. The degrees of freedom for the third ratio is equal to the number of rows minus 1, multiplied by the number of columns minus 1 ($r - 1$)($c - 1$). The same degrees of freedom for the denominator is used as in the first two ratios. The calculated F ratios are now compared to the F ratios for the given degrees of freedom and level of significance to tell if there are significant effects.

Thus far we have studied the effectiveness of the books in terms of test scores. In Chapter 7, we saw that finding the measures needed for a one-way analysis of variance involved considerable computation, even for a very small sample of 20 students. If we add another variable in this case (mathematical training) and increase our sample size, the computation becomes very long and involved. Computer programs have been designed to handle this size problem and have facilitated the development and use of even more complex techniques. For example, multivariate analysis of variance (MANOVA) allows simultaneous testing of all variables and the interrelationships among them. This technique is used when there are two or more dependent variables. Computer programs designed to do complex statistical computation will be discussed in Section 14-4.

In order to perform statistical analyses, we will need to collect our own data by sample surveys (see Chapters 4 and 5) or to use data that others have collected. In the next section, we discuss some widely used data bases that are currently available.

DATA BASES AVAILABLE FOR BUSINESS AND SOCIAL SCIENCE RESEARCH

14-3

A large number of data bases are available to universities, individuals, and business establishments. It often pays to obtain this data since, as we pointed out in Chapters 4 and 5, the cost of interviewing is very high. In this section, we mention four important sources and briefly describe the type of data each contains. The bibliography at the end of this chapter gives the addresses of the groups providing this data. These data sources are especially good for multivariate analyses, since they supply information on many variables for each respondent or each firm studied. The four sources are:

1 The Inter-University Consortium for Political and Social Research (ICPSR)
2 National Longitudinal Studies (NLS)
3 Census Tapes, Summary Tape Files (STF), and Public Use Sample (PUS)
4 Compustat tapes

Inter-University Consortium for Political and Social Research (ICPSR)

Sharing data provides an excellent way to reduce the cost of research and to improve the quality of research by allowing for duplication or *replication* of statistical investigations. In 1954, at the Survey Research Center of the University of Michigan, a group of political scientists met to share and make use of data on voting behavior of the national electorate in the 1952 election. The need to collect, archive, and disseminate this data evolved into a consortium that came into existence in 1962. In 1974, the consortium changed its name to include both political and *social* research. It is now the Inter-University Consortium for Political and Social Research (ICPSR). Today, the ICPSR has a file of more than 5000 data bases relevant to political science, history, sociology, economics, social psychology, public health, public policy, education, and international studies. The ICPSR also serves as a buyers' cooperative to acquire expensive commercial and government data and send it to its members. Large parts of the 1980 Census and a large amount of International Monetary Fund data is available to member colleges and universities. More than 200 member institutions today have access to this data. Some examples of relevant data are:

International Financial Statistics, 1948–1978

Panel Study of Income Dynamics, 1968–1977

Surveys of Consumer Attitudes and Behavior, 1953–1976

World Handbook of Social and Political Indicators, 1950–1975

Macroeconomic Time Series for United States, United Kingdom, Germany, and France

If your university is a member of this consortium, you may be able to have access to this data for class projects. If not, you might suggest that your institution contact the consortium (see the bibliography for its address). You may be able to find other universities in your area that will allow you to use these data bases.

449

MULTIVARIATE
TECHNIQUES
DATA BASES, AND
COMPUTER
SOFTWARE

National Longitudinal Studies (NLS)

Another useful source of economic and labor force data is the National Longitudinal Studies. These studies, conducted by the Ohio State University Center for Human Resource Research and the U.S. Bureau of the Census for the last 15 years, represent a number of surveys on nationwide panels of 5000 respondents. Four subsets of the U.S. civilian population have been studied in panels that have been reinterviewed at specific intervals.

1 Middle-aged men, ages 45–59 in 1966 at the beginning of the study
2 Women, ages 30–44 at the beginning of the study
3 Young men, ages 14–24 at the beginning of the study
4 Young women, ages 14–24 at the beginning of the study

The surveys focus on labor force behavior and work attitudes, but they contain a wealth of financial information over a long period for each of the persons studied.

Census Tapes (1980, 1970)

The Bureau of the Census, U.S. Department of Commerce, provides extensive Census information in the form of printed reports, computer tapes, and microfiche. The computer tapes enable people to manipulate data to make studies suited to their individual needs. In addition, the Census Bureau will prepare, on a cost-reimbursable basis, special tabulations of data from the 1980 Census based on consumer specifications. The types of information contained in the 1980 Census are detailed in Table 14-3.

The 1980 Census information will be issued on Summary Tape Files (STF), which will present extensive cross-tabulations of data summarized for geographic areas of the country. Two of these tapes will be based on complete count (100% data). The other three will be based on sample data and will either have extensive geographic detail or extensive subject matter detail.

Public Use Sample Data (PUS) tape files will contain a sample of unidentified household records for large geographic areas. Each household sample record will contain all Census data collected about each person, as well as the housing unit characteristics. Users can tabulate and summarize data in any way they wish. For example, one could find average incomes for families with 6 or more children.

To improve access to and use of Census data on computer tape, the Bureau of the Census has developed a software package—the Census Software Package (CENSPAC). This system can be used to extract a subset of data from files, to merge data in two or more files, to compute data, and to present data in different formats. For information on costs and methods of obtaining this data, you can write to the address mentioned in the bibliography at the end of this chapter.

Vincent Barabba, director of the Bureau of the Census, in a speech in Phoenix, Arizona, in October 1979, pointed out some interesting uses of Census data by the business community.

1 A furniture store owner used data on home values, rent levels and incomes in deciding what price merchandise to stock.

TABLE 14-3

1980 CENSUS DATA

100% population items
Household relationship*
Sex
Race
Age
Marital status
Spanish/Hispanic origin or descent*

100% housing items
Number of housing units at address
Complete plumbing facilities*
Number of rooms in unit
Tenure (whether the unit is owned or rented)
Condominium identification*
Value of home (for owner-occupied units and condominiums)
Rent (for renter-occupied units)
Vacant for rent, for sale, etc.; and period of vacancy

Sample population items
School enrollment
Educational attainment
State or foreign country of birth
Citizenship and year of immigration
Current language and English proficiency†
Ancestry†
Place of residence 5 years ago

Activity 5 years ago
Veteran status and period of service
Presence of disability or handicap*
Children ever born
Marital history
Employment status last week
Hours worked last week
Place of work
Travel time to work†
Means of transportation to work*
Persons in carpool†
Year last worked
Industry
Occupation
Class of worker
Work in 1979 and weeks looking for work in 1979*
Amount of income by source in 1979*
Total income in 1979†

Sample housing items
Number of units in structure
Stories in building and presence of elevator
Year unit built
Year moved into this house*
Source of water

Sewage disposal
Heating equipment
Fuels used for house heating, water heating, and cooking
Costs of utilities and fuels*
Complete kitchen facilities
Number of bedrooms and bathrooms
Telephone
Air conditioning
Number of automobiles
Number of light trucks and vans†
Homeowner shelter costs for mortgage, real estate taxes, and hazard insurance†

Derived items (illustrative examples)
Families
Family type, size, and income
Poverty status
Population density
Persons per room (overcrowding)
Household size
Institutions and other group quarters
Gross rent
Farm residence

*Changed relative to 1970.
†New item.
Source: *Census 1980, Introduction to Products and Services.* U.S. Department of Commerce, Bureau of the Census.

---

2 ... Hardware stores have done well ... in areas with heavy concentration of homeowners. Sales have been especially good where many houses are more than 15 years old, since they are prime candidates for fit-it-yourself projects, storm windows and roofing products.
3 A highly successful women's home-permanent manufacturer forecasts production for 5 year periods by the number of girls turning 16 years old in those years, and products are distributed according to the number of these girls in each area where there is an outlet.

The last data source to be discussed provides financial information on a large number of firms. These tapes are called the *Compustat Tapes.*

Compustat Tapes

A good source of data on over 3800 industrial companies and nonindustrial companies (banks and utilities) is provided by Standard and Poors Compustat Services, Inc. in the form of tapes. These tapes provide annual data for up to 20 years and quarterly data for up to 10 years. Half of the companies included have sales under $100 million. Compustat tapes were introduced in 1962 and have proven useful for many types of business analysis. Table 14-4 shows the types of items included. These tapes have been used for securities analysis, investment portfolio management, corporate planning, competitive analysis, marketing-screening customers and marketing strategy, credit analysis, potential merger or acquisition (offense and defense against

TABLE 14-4

BREAKDOWN OF COMPUSTAT FILES

451

MULTIVARIATE
TECHNIQUES
DATA BASES, AND
COMPUTER
SOFTWARE

INDUSTRIAL FILES*	NONINDUSTRIAL FILES	SPECIAL FILE
Annual data is provided for up to 20 years, and quarterly data for up to 10 years.	Annual data is provided for up to 20 years, and quarterly data for up to 12 years.	*Price-dividends-earnings (PDE)* Data as early as 1962.

INDUSTRIAL FILES*

Annual data is provided for up to 20 years, and quarterly data for up to 10 years.

Primary
171 annual data items
65 quarterly data items
Some 900 major New York
Stock Exchange (NYSE),
American Stock Exchange
(ASE), and Over-the-Counter
(OTC) companies
All companies in the Standard &
Poor's 400 Index

Supplementary
171 annual data items
65 quarterly data items
Some 900 NYSE and ASE
companies

Tertiary
171 annual data items
65 quarterly data items
Some 900 companies which
complete the NYSE and ASE
industrials in conjunction with
the Primary and
Supplementary files
Groups of nonindustrial
companies which complete
coverage of the Standard &
Poor's 500 in conjunction with
Primary

Over-the-counter
171 annual data items
Some 900 companies from the
NASDAQ list

Canadian
75 annual data items
Some 325 of the leading
Canadian industrial companies

NONINDUSTRIAL FILES

Annual data is provided for up to 20 years, and quarterly data for up to 12 years.

Bank
221 annual data items
141 quarterly data items
Some 125 leading U.S. banks
and bank holding
companies

Utilities
90 annual data items
98 quarterly data items
Some 185 Class A gas and
electric utilities and
subsidiaries

SPECIAL FILE

Price-dividends-earnings (PDE)
Data as early as 1962.
Available on a monthly
basis, this file duplicates
company coverage of the
Primary, Supplementary,
Tertiary, OTC, Bank and
Utility Files.
10 data items
3600 industrial and
nonindustrial companies
Some 120 indices including
the S&P 400, the S&P 500,
the Dow Jones 30
industrials, the ASE and the
NYSE Indices, and 115 S&P
industry indices

*The Industrial File offers 171 distinct annual and 65 district quarterly data items as follows:

Compustat II Data Series	Number of data items	Compustat II Data Series	Number of data items
	Annual data		Quarterly data
Income-statement-related	28	Income-statement-related	24
Supplementary income statement	6	Balance-sheet-related	27
Balance-sheet-related	51	Market-related and other data	8
Supplementary balance sheet	17		
Retained earnings statement	6		
Statement of changes in financial position (sources and applications of funds)	18		
Reconciliation of property, plant, and equipment	4 5		
Reconciliation of accumulated depreciation	7		
Market-related	22		
Restated data	12		
Other data			

Source: Compustat Services, New York.

potential mergers or takeovers), and divestiture studies. Companies and universities may purchase these tapes, manuals, and the services of applications consultants.

COMPUTER SOFTWARE STATISTICS PACKAGES

14-4   Statistical programs that use data from tapes or punch cards provide an excellent method for analysis as compared to hand computation. Using these systems the analyst does not have to write a computer program, but merely has to provide the labels for all tables and the instructions to the computer on the statistical technique used, the appearance of data, and the boundaries (that is, number of observations, number of variables) for the problem. The computer then provides many kinds of printouts showing the results of the statistical analyses. In this section, we briefly discuss two very widely used computer software packages that offer programs for statistical computation. They are the Biomedical Computer Programs (BMD and BMDP) and the Statistical Package for the Social Sciences (SPSS). Most university computer systems have purchased one or more of these packages, and many private research companies have access to these programs. In the bibliography, we list the references for these and other programs, such as OSIRIS.

Biomedical Computer Programs (BMD and BMDP)

This system of biomedical computer programs was first published in 1961 by the University of California Press. The programs were developed at the University of California, Los Angeles. A more recent edition was published in 1979. Programs are available for (1) description and tabulation, (2) regression analysis, (3) time series analysis, (4) variance analysis, (5) multivariate analysis, and (6) special programs (for example, life tables, Guttman scales, probit analysis).

The user of these programs prepares program control cards that tell the computer which programs are to be used, where the information needed for the program is located in the data file, and what parts of the program are to be used. Another set of control cards sets up labels for the tables that will be used in the printout and notifies the computer when all data cards or entries have been read.

Statistical Package for the Social Sciences (SPSS)

This system contains programs for the following procedures:

1   Descriptive statistics
2   Cross-tabulations
3   Tests of differences
4   Correlation analyses
5   Multiple regression analyses
6   Analyses of variance and covariance
7   Discriminant analyses
8   Factor analyses
9   Canonical correlation analyses
10   Scalogram analyses

The 1979 revision contains facilities for report generation, survival tests, 14 nonparametric tests, reliability analysis, multiple response variables, and creation of data files on interactive terminals. This last procedure means that the student does not need to use punch cards to enter data. Instead, the student can sit at a computer terminal and type in the data; see Figure 14-4(a).

453

MULTIVARIATE
TECHNIQUES
DATA BASES, AND
COMPUTER
SOFTWARE

This system also uses control cards and label cards similar to those described in the biomedical programs.

Other Programs

Other well-known statistical software packages are OSIRIS, available from the Survey Research Center, University of Michigan, and packages that have been developed for specific computers. For example, there have been a number of statistical packages developed at Dartmouth University for the DEC computers (Digital Equipment Corporation). Hewlett-Packard computers also feature a list of programs that do regression analysis, nonparametric tests, and other simple statistical analyses. Almost every computer company has a statistical package that can be used on its system. The chief difference between these packages and such specific packages as SPSS and BMDP is that the latter can handle much larger amounts of data and more complex types of analysis. There are frequent improvements in computer software and it is advisable to watch for new programs. Most classroom and simple business analyses use the statistical packages designed for specific computers, which are adequate for most analyses. For people wishing to buy computer software, a newsletter listing new packages and where they can be obtained is published by Daniel Couger at the University of Colorado (see the bibliography at the end of this chapter). In the next section, we show a simple printout from a SPSS program and discuss its interpretation.

INTERPRETATION OF COMPUTER PRINTOUTS

Scattergram and Simple Regression Program
14-5

Figure 14-3 shows a computer printout from a SPSS program that performs simple regression analysis and plots a scatter diagram of the points. We used the deseasonalized data in Table 11-2, column 7. The dependent variable is *sales* of Regal Optometry (p. 335), and the independent variable is time expressed in quarters. Quarter 1 in 1967 is set at 0. The data was entered using 24 punched cards (one for each quarter). The instructions to the computer were entered using 9 control cards. We have placed a checkmark near each control card.[1]

Let us read the output on page 2 (the bottom half of Figure 14-3). First, the plot of the data points has quarters on the X axis and sales (in thousands) on the Y axis. Each asterisk is a unique data point. The lowest and highest points on each axis determine the first and last numbers on the axis in this illustration, although other scale possibilities are available. In its X and Y columns, Table 11-2 presents the data points used in this analysis.

In the lines below the scattergram are the statistics calculated for this relationship. Reading across row 1, we have the coefficient of correlation $R = .81008$, the coefficient of determination $r^2 = .65623$. The probability level for the significance test of r is the next value; the lower this value, the more significant the results.

---

[1]Instructions for making data cards, as well as control cards, can be found on pp. 293–298 of the **SPSS** manual (see the bibliography at end of this chapter).

SMU COMPUTING CENTER
SOUTHERN METHODIST UNIVERSITY

S P S S - - STATISTICAL PACKAGE FOR THE SOCIAL SCIENCES

VERSION 8.0 - - JUNE 18, 1979
SCATTERGRAM AND SIMPLE REGRESSION PROGRAM
  ✓ FILE NAME   STUDY 1
  ✓ VARIABLE LIST   QTR, SALES
  ✓ INPUT MEDIUM   CARDS
  ✓ N OF CASES   24
  ✓ INPUT FORMAT   FIXED (F2.0, X, F3.1)

       ACCORDING TO YOUR INPUT FORMAT, VARIABLES ARE TO BE READ AS FOLLOWS
       VARIABLE FORMAT RECORD COLUMNS

       QTR   F 2.0   1   1- 2
       SALES   F 3.1   1   4- 6

THE INPUT FORMAT PROVIDES FOR 2 VARIABLES. 2 WILL BE READ.
IT PROVIDES FOR 1 RECORDS (*CARDS*) PER CASE.
A MAXIMUM OF   6 *COLUMNS* ARE USED ON A RECORD.
  ✓ VAR LABELS   QTR, YEARLY QUATERS 0 = QTR 1 1967/SALES, DESEASONALIZED SALES
  ✓ SCATTERGRAM   SALES WITH QTR
  ✓ OPTIONS   ALL
  ✓ STATISTICS   ALL

    GIVEN 2 VARIABLES, INITIAL CM ALLOWS FOR 4233 CASES
                      MAXIMUM CM ALLOWS FOR 16521 CASES

    OPTION - 1
    IGNORE MISSING VALUE INDICATORS
    (NO MISSING VALUES DEFINED . . . OPTION 1 WAS FORCED)

- -

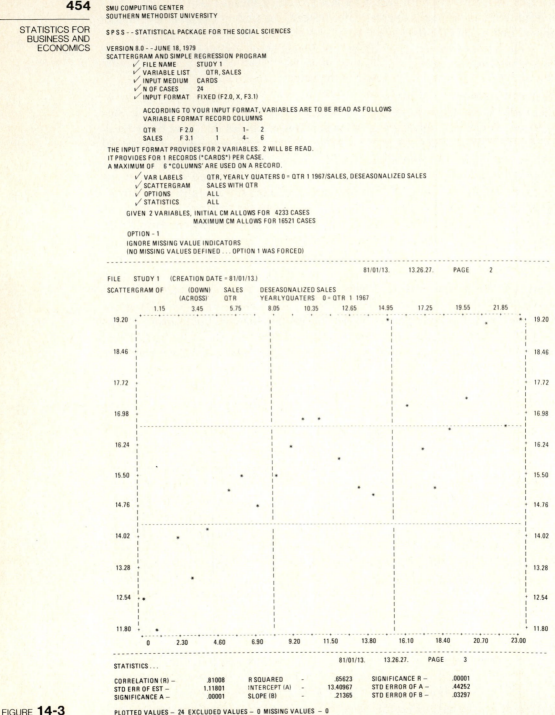

FIGURE **14-3**

SPSS printout for scattergram and simple regression analysis.

Row 2 presents the standard error of estimate $s_{y.x}$ (p. 288), the value of a (the Y intercept). Note that it is similar to the value computed in Table 11-4. Small differences are due to rounding errors. The next value is the standard error of a, which we have not learned to calculate in this text but which can be found in more advanced texts. On line 3, we find the significance of a, which can also be found in more advanced texts. In the middle of row 3 is the value of the slope b, which is .21365. Note that in the text this was calculated to be .215. Once again the small differences are due to different rounding techniques. The standard error for b (s_b) is the last value calculated in this line (p. 301). The significance of b is presented in line 4. To do this computation, the t value was calculated and then the level of significance for a t value of this size was estimated. The lower this value, the more likely it is that b is significantly different from 0.

The final line tells how many values are plotted and if any values are missing (this would be a quarter for which there is no data) or excluded. We have the option of calculating information for any number of data points. Thus, we could omit the first year (1967) and use the remaining 20 observations.

Multiple Regression Program

Another very important SPSS program is the *multiple regression program,* where we are trying to relate several independent variables to a dependent variable. For this example, we have tried to forecast rushing yards for professional football running backs in 1976. We use the data in problem 1(d) Chapter 10, where we have 13 sets of observations (height, weight, years as a professional, and rushing yardage in 1976 for each player). We now reproduce part of the printout in Figure 14-4(a) (see pp. 456–457) along with an explanation. Further explanation of the results and entries for this multiple regression program can be found in the SPSS manual.

Page 1 describes the variables to be used and the amount of space they take, the number of cases, and the program regression. It also tells the computer "regression equals yards with height, weight, years," which means that yards is the dependent variable and the other three are independent variables. This data can be entered on cards or at the terminal. A copy of the data file used from the terminal is shown at the end of our explanation [Figure 14-4(b), p. 458]. As we have mentioned, the data can be found on page 308.

On page 2, the mean and standard deviation for each variable is presented. Then, the correlation coefficients that relate each variable using simple regression analysis to every other variable are shown. Note the high correlation between height and weight (.68158). If two independent variables are highly correlated, we generally choose only one of them for use in our final multiple regression equation to avoid problems of *multicollinearity.* Note also the negative relationship between all the other variables.

On page 3, we have the multiple regression analysis. Note that $R = .48533$ and the coefficient of determination $r^2 = .23555$. Thus, we have explained relatively little of rushing yardage by studying height, weight, and years as a professional.

The second column presents the results of an analysis of variance for the multiple regression equation. The *variation explained* by the regression equation is 132,798.30240. To obtain the mean square, we divide by 3 degrees of freedom to obtain values of 44,266.10080. To obtain the mean square for *values not explained,* we divide 430,983.38991 by 9, which gives 47,887.04332. Now, dividing these mean

455

MULTIVARIATE
TECHNIQUES
DATA BASES, AND
COMPUTER
SOFTWARE

SMU COMPUTING CENTER
SOUTHERN METHODIST UNIVERSITY

S P S S - - STATISTICAL PACKAGE FOR THE SOCIAL SCIENCES

VERSION 8.0 -- JUNE 18, 1979

```
     FILE NAME      FOOTI
     VARIABLE LIST  YARDS,HEIGHT,WEIGHT,YEARS
     VAR LABELS     YARDS;RUSHING YARDS IN 1976/HEIGHT,PLAYER HEIGHT IN INCHES/
                    WEIGHT;PLAYER WEIGHT IN LBS./YEARS,YEARS AS A PRO
     INPUT FORMAT   FIXED(F3.0,X,F4.1,X,F3.0,X,F2.0)
```

ACCORDING TO YOUR INPUT FORMAT, VARIABLES ARE TO BE READ AS FOLLOWS

```
     VARIABLE    FORMAT    RECORD    COLUMNS

     YARDS       F  3.0       1        1-  3
     HEIGHT      FF 4.1       1        5-  8
     WEIGHT      FF 3.0       1       10- 12
     YEARS       FF 2.0       1       14- 15
```

THE INPUT FORMAT PROVIDES FOR   4 VARIABLES.   4 WILL BE READ.
IT PROVIDES FOR 1 RECORDS (*CARDS*) PER CASE.
A MAXIMUM OF 15 *COLUMNS* ARE USED ON A RECORD.

```
     N OF CASES     13
     REGRESSION     VARIABLES=YARDS,HEIGHT,WEIGHT,YEARS
                    REGRESSION=YARDS WITH HEIGHT,WEIGHT,YEARS
     STATISTICS     ALL
```

00053000 CM NEEDED FOR REGRESSION

OPTION - 1
IGNORE MISSING VALUE INDICATORS
(NO MISSING VALUES DEFINED..OPTION 1 WAS FORCED)

- -

FILE   FOOTI   (CREATION DATE = 81/01/21.)

* * * * * * * * * * * * * * * * * *   M U L T I P L E   R E G R E S S I O N   *

VARIABLE	MEAN	STANDARD DEV	CASES
YARDS	374.1538	216.7529	13
HEIGHT	71.5846	1.9574	13
WEIGHT	210.5385	10.9439	13
YEARS	4.6923	2.6263	13

CORRELATION COEFFICIENTS.

A VALUE OF 99.00000 IS PRINTED
IF A COEFFICIENT CANNOT BE COMPUTED.

	YARDS	HEIGHT	WEIGHT
HEIGHT	-.19955		
WEIGHT	-.29323	.68158	
YEARS	-.31948	-.06098	-.19671

```
FILE   FOOT1   (CREATION DATE = 81/01/21.)                          81/01/21.    14.25.37.      PAGE    3

* * * * * * * * * * * * * * * * *   M U L T I P L E   R E G R E S S I O N   * * * * * * * * * * * * * * * * * *

DEPENDENT VARIABLE..    YARDS      RUSHING YARDS IN 1976

MEAN RESPONSE    374.15385      STD. DEV.      216.75287

VARIABLE(S) ENTERED ON STEP NUMBER   1..    HEIGHT      PLAYER HEIGHT IN INCHES
                                            YEARS       YEARS AS A PRO
                                            WEIGHT      PLAYER WEIGHT IN LBS.

MULTIPLE R            .48533       ANALYSIS OF VARIANCE      DF      SUM OF SQUARES      MEAN SQUARE          F       SIGNIFICANCE
R SQUARE             .23555       REGRESSION                 3.      132798.30240       44266.10080        .92439        .463
ADJUSTED R SQUARE                 RESIDUAL                   9.      430983.38991       47887.04332
STD DEVIATION   218.83108         COEFF OF VARIABILITY     58.5 PCT

------------- VARIABLES IN THE EQUATION -------------              ----------- VARIABLES NOT IN THE EQUATION -----------
                                                F           BETA
VARIABLE        B           STD ERROR B    SIGNIFICANCE   ELASTICITY      VARIABLE    PARTIAL    TOLERANCE        F
                                                                                                             SIGNIFICANCE

HEIGHT       6.0588814        44.335218    .18676144E-01    .0547151
YEARS      -32.724080         24.660960   1.76082040      -.16508063
WEIGHT      -8.0911450         8.0726490   1.00453876      -.39650030
(CONSTANT) 1796.8739        2371.3656       .57416696      -.40852042
                                            .468            -4.55243

ALL VARIABLES ARE IN THE EQUATION.

COEFFICIENTS AND CONFIDENCE INTERVALS.
VARIABLE        B           STD ERROR B         T          95.0 PCT CONFIDENCE INTERVAL

HEIGHT       6.0588814        44.335218    .13666069      -94.234299      106.35206
YEARS      -32.724080         24.660960   -1.32692589     -88.511018       23.062857
WEIGHT      -8.0911450         8.0726490   -1.00022912     -26.352736       10.170446
CONSTANT   1796.8739        2371.3656       .75773805    -3567.5249       7161.2728
```

FIGURE **14-4**

(a) SPSS printout for multiple regression analysis.

```
RECOVER/SYSTEM:  BATCH
$RFL, 20000.
/GET, FOOTI
/EDIT, FOOTI
 BEGIN TEXT EDITING.
? 10L
FILE NAME          FOOTI
VARIABLE LIST      YARDS, HEIGHT, WEIGHT, YEARS
VAR LABELS         YARDS, RUSHING YARDS IN 1976/HEIGHT, PLAYER HEIGHT IN INCHES/
                   WEIGHT, PLAYER WEIGHT IN LBS./YEARS, YEARS AS A PRO
INPUT FORMAT       FIXED (F3.0, X, F3.1, X, F3.0, X, F2.0)
N OF CASES         13
REGRESSION         VARIABLES = YARDS, HEIGHT, WEIGHT, YEARS
                   REGRESSION = YARDS WITH HEIGHT, WEIGHT, YEARS
STATISTICS         ALL
–END OF FILE–
? END
 END TEXT EDITING.
$EDIT, FOOTI.
/GET, FOOTD
/EDIT, FOOTD
 BEGIN TEXT EDITING.
? 19L


542 72.0  204   4
424 72.0  205   3
450 68.3  205   6
233 72.1  206  11
208 72.1  218   4
684 68.3  198   4
542 72.0  205   7
114 73.7  235   3
 67 73.7  220   8
570 72.0  220   2
120 69.2  201   4
652 74.5  220   2
258 72.0  200   3
–END OF FILE–
? END
  END TEXT EDITING.
$EDIT, FOOTD.
/BYE


B3KI015   LOG   OFF    12.07.46.
B3KI015   SRU          1.000 UNTS.
```

FIGURE **14-4**

(*b*) Edited data file entered from a terminal for SPSS multiple
regression analysis program.

square values for the F ratio of explained to unexplained, we have .92439. To be
significant at the .05 level with 3 degrees of freedom in the numerator and 9 in the
denominator, our F ratio should be at least 3.86. (This value was obtained from the
F table at the back of this book.) The computer has estimated that our actual level
of significance is .468, or 46.8%; thus, the multiple regression equation for this data
is *not* significant at either the 5 or 10% level.

Looking below these figures to the section titled variables in the equation, we
see, for example, that the printout says:

	B	STANDARD ERROR B
Height	6.058814	44.335
Years	−32.72080	
Weight	− 8.0911450	
Constant	1796.873	

B (referred to as "*b*" in Chapter 10) is the value of the coefficients for each variable. The constant, which we have called *a* in our equation, is given last. In the next column, the standard error for each coefficient is given. We have computed these for simple regression analysis in Chapter 10. The *F* table tells us the level of significance. For example, height is .894. If this is .05 or less, we generally consider the variable to be important enough to include in our study. Note in this problem that the highest level of significance is for years as a professional (which bears a negative relationship, meaning that the more years one has played, the lower the rushing yardage), and even this has a significance level of only .217. We might have expected this since the r^2 value was relatively low (.236). Thus, these measures do not offer a good explanation of rushing yardage.

In the next section of the printout, coefficients and confidence intervals, the values of *B* and the standard error of *B* are followed by *t* values, which we have calculated on pp. 299–301. These are the ratios of the *B* values to their standard errors. Since there are 13 sets of observations and we have estimated 4 coefficients, our degrees of freedom are 9. For a 95% confidence interval, our *t* value would be 2.262 (see the *t* table at end of this book). Multiplying this by our standard error and adding and subtracting it from our *B* value, we obtain the 95% confidence intervals shown in the last column. More advanced statistics texts offer further explanations of multiple regression analysis and useful computer analyses.

As you can see, these programs perform a tremendous amount of computation in a short time. If you are doing repeated or complicated computation, it would be well worth your while to investigate the possibility of using statistical computer software packages. Such packages are available at many universities. In addition, many handheld calculators now have regression programs and other statistical packages. This capability will increase in the coming decades.

459

MULTIVARIATE
TECHNIQUES
DATA BASES, AND
COMPUTER
SOFTWARE

STATISTICAL PROGRAMS FOR HANDHELD CALCULATORS

14-6

Financial calculators manufactured by such companies as Hewlett-Packard and Texas Instruments often feature *built-in-programs* that allow computation of means, standard deviations, regression equations, and areas under the normal curve. One can also purchase "computer chips" designed to calculate such measures as linear regression, one- and two-way analysis of variance, rank-sum tests, multiple linear regression, probabilities for the binomial chi square, and *t* and *F* distributions. These programs can also generate random numbers. Programmable calculators can be used to write programs to calculate statistical measures. These programs are often available in manuals furnished free of charge with the computer and in other books.[2] The handheld calculator is a useful device because it is readily available and transportable. Calculators like the TI-58 and 59 also offer printers that can be used to record programs as well as statistical calculations. Let us now show how regression analyses can be performed on a handheld calculator. If we use the illustration from Chapter 10 (p. 279), where we related sales and advertising, we have the following.

---

[2]For example, see *Sourcebook for Programmable Calculators,* Texas Instruments, 1978, chapter 4, pp. 1–36, and chapter 7, pp. 1–22.

AMOUNT SPENT ON ADVERTISING X ($000)	DOLLAR AMOUNT OF SALES Y ($000)
1.7	50
3.0	100
2.0	75
1.5	45
.6	20
1.5	50

Using the Texas Instruments TI-59 (master module), we perform the following steps:

1 To clear the calculator and find program, we press

$\boxed{\text{2nd}}$ $\boxed{\text{Pgm}}$ $\boxed{1}$ $\boxed{\text{SBR}}$ $\boxed{\text{CLR}}$ calculator shows 0

2 Now, enter the data:

Press 1.7 Press $\boxed{\text{x t}}$ Press 50 Press $\boxed{\text{2nd}}$ $\Sigma+$ calculator shows 1

Press 3.0 Press $\boxed{\text{x t}}$ Press 100 Press $\boxed{\text{2nd}}$ $\Sigma+$ calculator shows 2

Press 2.0 Press $\boxed{\text{x t}}$ Press 75 Press $\boxed{\text{2nd}}$ $\Sigma+$ calculator shows 3

Press 1.5 Press $\boxed{\text{x t}}$ Press 45 Press $\boxed{\text{2nd}}$ $\Sigma+$ calculator shows 4

Press .6 Press $\boxed{\text{x t}}$ Press 20 Press $\boxed{\text{2nd}}$ $\Sigma+$ calculator shows 5

Press 1.5 Press $\boxed{\text{x t}}$ Press 50 Press $\boxed{\text{2nd}}$ $\Sigma+$ calculator shows 6

3 To find the Y intercept,

Press $\boxed{\text{2nd}}$ $\boxed{\text{op}}$ 12   calculator shows -2.544812602

4 To find the slope,

Press $\boxed{\text{x t}}$ calculator shows 34.49212385

5 To find the correlation coefficient,

Press $\boxed{\text{2nd}}$ $\boxed{\text{op}}$ 13   calculator shows .9822768355

6 To find the coefficient of determination, leave the correlation coefficient in the calculator, then,

Press $\boxed{X^2}$ calculator shows .9648677816

If we round this to three places, as we have done in Chapter 10, we have

$$\hat{Y} = -2.545 + 34.492X$$

$$r = .982$$

$$R^2 = .964$$

Refer to p. 279 to see that our answers were

$$\hat{Y} = -2.633 + 34.537X$$

On p. 295, we see that $R^2 = .965$ and $r = .982$. The slight differences are due to the way the numbers were rounded, since the calculator programs use all decimal places and we rounded off to three places in our hand computation.

Note how much easier it was to calculate the regression line using the calculator program. Many calculators offer these programs. Before you buy a calculator, ask about these programs and examine the instruction books. These handheld calculators are especially good for computations based on small data bases. For larger data bases, it is more advantageous to use a statistical program available on a computer.

461

MULTIVARIATE
TECHNIQUES,
DATA BASES, AND
COMPUTER
SOFTWARE

REVIEW QUESTIONS

1 What are multivariate techniques?

2 Why are they superior to univariate techniques?

3 What types of assumptions must be made to use these techniques?

4 When would one need to use dummy variables for regression analysis?

5 In what sort of situation is discriminant analysis particularly useful?

6 In what sort of situation is factor analysis particularly useful?

7 Why are the axes rotated in factor analysis?

8 Under what circumstances is multiple analysis of variance needed?

9 In constructing F ratios for analysis of variance, what are the three types of variance that are studied?

10 What is a data base?

11 What are the advantages of purchasing data bases?

12 What types of difficulties may arise when one is using a data base prepared by someone else?

13 Name four important sources of data bases.

14 What data base would you use for studies of the sales of large firms?

15 What data base would you use to study market areas for consumer products?

16 What data base could be used to study unemployment of urban workers?

17 If you wanted to study voting behavior, which source could you write to for data?

18 What are computer statistical packages?

19 Under what circumstances is the use of computer statistical packages ideal? When would it be more preferable to use a program on a handheld calculator?

BIBLIOGRAPHY

14-8

Multivariate Analysis

Dixon, W. J.: *Biomedical Computer Programs (BMDP), 1975*, Health Sciences Computing Facility, Department of Biomathematics, School of Medicine, University of California, Los Angeles, 1975.

Hair, J. F., Jr., R. E. Anderson, R. L. Tathom, and B. J. Groblowsky: *Multivariate Data Analyses with Readings*, Tulsa: PennWell, 1979. An excellent, clearly written, non-mathematical explanation of a number of multivariate techniques.

Hays, William L.: *Statistics for the Social Sciences*, New York: Holt, 1973. Chapters 12 and 13 provide a very thorough explanation of analysis of variance.

Hull, C. H., and N. H. Nie: *SPSS Update: New Procedures and Facilities for Releases 7 and 8*, New York: McGraw-Hill, 1979.

Kerlinger, F. N.: *Foundations of Behavioral Research,* 2d ed, New York: Holt, 1973. Chapter 35 thoroughly discusses multiple regression analysis.

Kim, J. O., and C. W. Mueller: *Introduction to Factor Analysis*, (University Paper Ser. No: 13), Beverly Hills, Calif.: Sage Publications, 1978. Short monograph with nonmathematical exposition of factor analysis.

Kim, J. O., and C. W. Mueller: *Factor Analysis*, (University Paper Ser. No: 14), Beverly Hills, Calif.: Sage Publications, 1978. Short monograph following up paper 13 explanations. Also a nonmathematical exposition.

Kinnear, T. C., and J. R. Taylor: *Marketing Research: An Applied Approach*, New York: McGraw-Hill, 1979. Excellent simple explanation of factor analysis and other multivariate techniques.

Nie, N. H., et al.: *Statistical Package for the Social Sciences (SPSS),* 2d ed, New York: McGraw-Hill, 1975. This book contains excellent discussions of all the multivariate techniques covered in this chapter, as well as descriptions of the SPSS programs and how they are used.

Nie, N. H., et al.: *SCSS: A Users Guide to the SCSS Conversational System*, New York: McGraw-Hill, 1980.

Data Bases

Bureau of the Census, Data User Services Division, Washington, D.C. 20233; telephone 301-763-2400. Will give information on Census tapes and regional office contacts.

Inter-University Consortium for Political and Social Research, P.O. Box 1248, Ann Arbor, Mich. 48106. Guide to Resources and Services, 1980–1981.

Longitudinal Data Banks on Labor Force Behavior and Work Attitudes, NLS User's Office, Center for Human Resource Research, 215 W. 11 Ave., Columbus, Ohio 43201.

Standard and Poor's Compustat Services, 1221 Ave. of the Americas, New York, N.Y. 10020; telephone 212-997-4900.

Statistical Computer Software

Aronofsky, J., E. Greynolds, and R. J. Frame: *Programmable Calculators: Business Applications*, New York: McGraw-Hill, 1978.

Computer Support Group: *OSIRIS IV: Statistical Analysis and Data Management Software System, 1979*, System tape available.

Couger, Daniel J., ed.: *Computing Newsletter* (for Schools of Business), College of Business Administration, University of Colorado, Colorado Springs.

Dixon, W. J.: *Biomedical Computer Programs*, University of California, Berkeley and Los Angeles, 1968. Description of programs and how to use them.

Nie, N. H., et al.: *Statistical Package for the Social Sciences (SPSS)*, 2d ed, New York: McGraw-Hill, 1975. Gives information on how to use the programs and where to purchase them.

Publication Sales, Institute for Social Research, University of Michigan, P.O. Box 1248, Ann Arbor, Mich. 48106. Information on purchasing OSIRIS.

Rattenbury, J. and P. Pelletier: *Data Processing in the Social Sciences with OSIRIS*, Survey Research Center, University of Michigan, 1974.

Texas Instruments: *Sourcebook for Programmable Calculators*, Dallas, 1978.

ANSWERS
TO EVEN-NUMBERED
PROBLEMS

CHAPTER 2

Section 2-9 (p. 34)

2 (*a*)
$$\bar{X} = \frac{\Sigma f(x)}{n} = \frac{8080}{40} = \$202$$

$$S = \sqrt{\frac{17,840}{(40 - 1)}} = 21.39$$

$$\text{Median} = 200 + \frac{(40/2) - 19}{3}(10) = 203.33$$

4 (*a*)
$$\bar{X}_A = \frac{\Sigma WX}{\Sigma W} = \frac{25.8}{105} = .25$$

$$\bar{X}_B = \frac{40.59}{110} = .37$$

$$\bar{X}_C = \frac{40.11}{93} = .43$$

$$\bar{X}_D = \frac{43.99}{91} = .48$$

(*b*) $(.25)(105) + .37(10) + .43(93) + .48(91) = \$150.62$

(*c*) $(\$150.62)(512)(12) = \$925,409.28$

6 (*a*)
$$\bar{X}_W = \frac{337,650}{8952} = 37.72$$

$$S_W = \sqrt{\frac{1,845,289.6}{8951}} = 14.36$$

$$Md_W = 35 + \frac{4476 - 4410}{1694}(10) = 35.39$$

$$\cdots$$

$$\bar{X}_B = \frac{370,950}{10,147} = 36.56$$

$$S_B = \sqrt{\frac{1,966,420.6}{10,146}} = 13.92$$

$$Md_B = 25 + \frac{5073.5 - 2513}{2818}(10) = 34.09$$

$$\bar{X}_H = \frac{276,810}{7574} = 36.55$$

$$S_H = \sqrt{\frac{1,795,814.3}{7573}} = 15.40$$

$$Md_H = 25 + \frac{3787 - 2207}{1926}(10) = 33.2$$

(b) $W: P_{70} = 45 + \dfrac{7/10(8952) - 6104}{1509}(10) = 46.08$

$B: P_{70} = 35 + \dfrac{7/10(10,147) - 5331}{1983}(10) = 43.94$

$H: P_{70} = 35 + \dfrac{7/10(7574) - 4133}{1368}(10) = 43.54$

(c) Hispanics show the most variation in age, since the standard deviation is largest.

(d) Hispanics are the youngest.

Section 2-10 (p. 38)

2 (a) $\dfrac{-112 + 52}{12} = -5 \qquad \pm 5 = K \qquad \dfrac{25}{25} = \dfrac{K^2}{25} \qquad K^2 = 25$

$\dfrac{172 - 112}{12} = 5 \qquad\qquad\qquad -1 = -.04K^2$

$$1 - \frac{1}{K^2} = .96$$

There is at least a .96 probability of serving between 52 and 172 customers.

Section 2-12 (p. 40)

2 (a) $\bar{X} = 71.2 \qquad Md = 75.5 \qquad s = \sqrt{\dfrac{1482.4}{14}} = 10.29$

(b) $C = 71.2 \pm 10.29 = 60.91 \leftrightarrow 81.49 \qquad$ 10 students

$B = 81.5 \pm 10.29 = 81.50 \leftrightarrow 91.79 \qquad$ 2 students

$$A = 91.8 \text{ to } 100 = 91.8 \rightarrow 100 \qquad \text{0 students}$$

$$D = 71.2 \pm 2(10.29) = 50.61 \leftrightarrow 60.90 \qquad \text{3 students}$$

$$F = \text{below } 50.61 \qquad \text{0 students}$$

Skewed to left.

(c) Allow students to offer any logical scheme provided they offer a set of reasons for their decisions.

CHAPTER 3

Section 3-3 (p. 63)

2 No. If the state takes money for tax purposes, the players don't get back as much as they invested.

4 (a) $(40,000)(.6) - 10,000(.4) = 24,000 - 4000 = \$20,000$

(b) $(30,000)(.8) - 10,500(.2) = 24,000 - 2100 = \$21,900$

Choose the second offer.

Section 3-5 (p. 73)

2 (a) $P(3) = \dfrac{6!}{3!(3!)} \left(\dfrac{3}{5}\right)^3 \left(\dfrac{2}{5}\right)^3 = .2760$

$P(4) = \dfrac{6!}{4!(2!)} \left(\dfrac{3}{5}\right)^4 \left(\dfrac{2}{5}\right)^2 = .3105$

$P(5) = \dfrac{6!}{5!(1!)} \left(\dfrac{3}{5}\right)^5 \left(\dfrac{2}{5}\right)^1 = .1866$

$P(6) = \dfrac{6!}{6!(0!)} \left(\dfrac{3}{5}\right)^6 \left(\dfrac{2}{5}\right)^0 = \underline{.0467}$

$.8198$

(b) $P(4) = \dfrac{6!}{4!(2!)} \left(\dfrac{3}{5}\right)^4 \left(\dfrac{2}{5}\right)^2 = .33104$

4 (a) $P(4) = \dfrac{8!}{4!(4!)} (.40)^4(.60)^4 = .2322$ probability of exactly 4

(b) More than $5 = P(6) + P(7) + P(8)$

$P(6) = .0413$

$P(7) = .0079$

$P(8) = \underline{.0007}$

$.0499$

2 $p(X) = \dfrac{1}{250} = .004$ $150(.004) = .6 = \mu$ $p(0) = .5488$

4 $.004 = .004(100) = .4$ $p(1) = .2681$ $p = .0072$

6 $\mu = 6$ $p(0 - 5) = .4457$

$1 - .4457 = .5543$

8 $\dfrac{60}{5} = \mu = 12$ $x = 26, 27$

$P(26) = .0002$. $P(27) = .0001$. $P(28$ and more) is so low that we can ignore it. Since the probability is so low that too many planes will arrive at once, you would have to vote no.

10 $\mu = 700(.02) = 14$

(a) $\Sigma P(x > 15) = .3307$ (b) $\Sigma P(x < 8) = .0316$ (c)   0

Section 3-6 (p. 84)

2 $\mu = 7000$

$\sigma = 700$

8000 or 10,500

$\dfrac{8000 - 7000}{700} = 1.4286$ .4236   Reserve 8000 at only 1.4σ away instead of 5σ away.

$\dfrac{10,500 - 7000}{700} = 5$?   There will be many empty seats.

4 $\mu = 1200$

$\sigma = 35$

$\dfrac{1300 - 1200}{35} = 2.86$ $.4979; .5000 - .4979 = .0021$

$\dfrac{1000 - 1200}{35} = -5.71$ off the table

$\dfrac{1100 - 1200}{35} = -2.86$ $|.4979|$

$\dfrac{1250 - 1200}{35} = 1.43$ $\dfrac{.4236}{.9215, \text{ or } 92.15\%}$

6 $\mu = 150$

$\sigma = 25$

(a) $z = \dfrac{170 - 150}{25} = .8$ .2281; .5000 − .2281 = .2119, or 21.19%

(b) $z = \dfrac{100 - 150}{25} = -2$ $p = .4772$; .5000 − .4772 = .0228

8 (a) $\dfrac{1,000,000 - \mu}{\sigma} = 1.645$

$\dfrac{70,000 - \mu}{\sigma} = 1.28$

$\sigma = \$10,256$ $\mu = \$83,129$

(b) $P(X > 90,000) = \dfrac{90,000 - 83,129}{10,256} = z = .67$; .5000 − .2486 = .2514

$P(X < 80,000) = \dfrac{80,000 - 83,129}{10,256} = z = -.305$; .5000 − .1179 = 3821

$P(90,000 - 100,000) = \dfrac{100,000 - 83,129}{10,256} = z = .164$; .4495

$\dfrac{90,000 - 83,129}{10,256} = z = .67$; $\dfrac{.2486}{.2009}$

CHAPTER 4

Section 4-7 (p. 108)

2 $\$10,000 \pm 1.96\left(\dfrac{760}{\sqrt{196}}\right)$

$\$10,000 \pm 106.4 = 9893.6 \leftrightarrow 10,106.4$

Section 4-8 (p. 109)

2 50% of the time they would not have enough wine if they stock only 800 bottles.
To reduce the chance to 3 in 100, for area = .4700,

$z = 1.88$

$\sigma_{\bar{p}} = \sqrt{\dfrac{.2(.8)}{100}} = \sqrt{\dfrac{.16}{100}} = .04$

$\begin{array}{ll} 1.88 & .0752 \\ \underline{\times .04} & \underline{\times 4000} \text{ number customers} \\ .0752 & 300.800 \end{array}$

$800 + 300.8 = 1101$ bottles they should stock

4 (*a*) $56.82 - 59.18$

(*b*) We can assert with a probability of .99 that our error is less than 1.18.

Section 4-9 (p. 112)

2 $n = \dfrac{2^2(12)^2}{5^2} = 23.04$ or 24 (rounding up)

4 $n = \dfrac{2^2(.40)(60)}{(.04)^2} = \dfrac{.96}{.0016} = 600$

CHAPTER 5

Section 5-1 (p. 127)

2 $450 \pm 1.96 \dfrac{160}{\sqrt{162}} \sqrt{1 - \dfrac{162}{900}} = 450 \pm 1.96 \dfrac{160}{12.7} (.91) = \$450 \pm \$22.47$

Section 5-2 (p. 129)

2 $n_0 = \dfrac{1.96^2(.75)(.25)}{.10^2} = 72.03 = 73$

$n = \dfrac{n_0}{1 + (n_0/N)} = \dfrac{73}{1 + (73/300)} = 58.7 = 59$

Section 5-4 (p. 134)

2 $24 \pm 2.896 \dfrac{.5}{\sqrt{9}}$

$24 \pm .483(60)$

Converting to minutes: $.483 \times 60 = 28.98 = 29$ min

23 hr, 31 min $\leftrightarrow$ 24 hr, 29 min

4 $n = 196$ $\bar{X} \pm z\sigma_{\bar{x}}cf$

$N = 625$ $12,000 \pm 1.96 \left(\dfrac{760}{\sqrt{196}} \right) \sqrt{1 - \dfrac{196}{625}}$

$\bar{X} = 12,000$ $12,000 \pm \dfrac{1234.123}{\sqrt{196}}$

$\sigma = 760$ $12,000 \pm 88.15$

$z = 1.96$ $\$11,911.85 \leftrightarrow \$12,088.15$

The 95% confidence interval is between \$11,911.85 and \$12,088.15.

2 (*a*) $\left(\dfrac{40}{160}\right)\left(\dfrac{40,000}{700,000}\right) + \left(\dfrac{100}{300}\right)\left(\dfrac{240,000}{700,000}\right) +$

$$\left(\dfrac{250}{500}\right)\left(\dfrac{420,000}{700,000}\right) = .42857$$

(*b*) $\bar{p} = 42.9\% = .429$

$$\sigma_{\bar{p}} = \sqrt{\dfrac{pq}{n}}$$

$.429 \pm 1.96\sigma_{\bar{p}_s}$

$$.429 \pm 1.96 \ \sqrt{\Sigma\dfrac{N_i^2}{N^2}\left(\dfrac{p_i q_i}{n_i}\right)\left(1 - \dfrac{n_i}{N_i}\right)}$$

$.429 \pm 1.96 = \left[\dfrac{40,000^2}{700,000^2}\dfrac{(40/160)(120/160)}{160}\left(1 - \dfrac{160}{40,000}\right) + \dfrac{240,000^2}{700,000^2}\dfrac{(100/300)(200/300)}{300}\right.$

$\left. \left(1 - \dfrac{300}{240,000}\right) + \dfrac{420,000^2}{700,000^2}\dfrac{(250/500)(250/500)}{500}\left(1 - \dfrac{500}{420,000}\right)\right]^{1/2}$

$= .429 \pm 1.96(.016) = .429 \pm .0322 = .3968 \leftrightarrow .4612$

(*c*) Preference for jewelry appears to be related to income class. There seems to be an inverse relationship between income class and preference for jewelry.

(*d*) Equal

	Over $35,000	233
	$20,000–34,999	233
	Under 20,000	234
		700

Proportional

$\dfrac{40}{700}(700) = \quad 40$

$\dfrac{240}{700}(700) = \quad 240$

$\dfrac{420}{700}(700) = \quad 420$

$\phantom{\dfrac{420}{700}(700) = } \quad \overline{700}$

Optimal

$s_i = \sqrt{.25(.75)} = .433 \qquad \dfrac{40,000(.433)}{341,800}(700) = 35.47 = 35$

$s_i = \sqrt{.33(.67)} = .477 \qquad \dfrac{240,000(.477)}{341,800}(700) = 234.45 = 235$

$$s_i = \sqrt{.5(.5)} = .500 \qquad \frac{420,000(.500)}{341,800}(700) = 430.08 = 430$$

We cannot calculate least-cost allocation.

CHAPTER 6

Section 6-4 (p. 172)

2 Accepting a false hypothesis (car is good when it isn't) is a problem here. Try to decrease the Type II error.

4 (1) Null hypothesis: H_0: $\mu \geq 200$
Alternate hypothesis: H_1: $\mu < 200$

(2) z test, one-tailed test, $\alpha = .05$

(3) Decision rule: If $z < -1.65$, reject H_0.

(a) $\dfrac{190 - 200}{\dfrac{20}{\sqrt{64}}} = \dfrac{-10}{20/8} = -4$

Reject H_0; send back shipment or use detailing.

(b) $\sigma = \dfrac{20}{\sqrt{64}} = 2.5$

$200 - (1.65)(2.5) = 200 - 4.125 = 195.875 \qquad$ minimum level for $\bar{X}$

6 (1) Null hypothesis: H_0: $p = .4$
Alternate hypothesis: H_1: $p \neq .4$

(2) z test, two-tailed test, $\alpha = .05$

(3) Decision rule: If $z < -1.96$ or > 1.96, reject H_0.

$$\sigma_{\bar{p}} = \sqrt{\frac{.40(.60)}{600}} = \sqrt{\frac{.2400}{600}} = .02$$

Now, the proportion over 25 in the sample is $\bar{p} = 300/600 = .5$.

$$z = \frac{.5 - .4}{.02} = \frac{.1}{.02} = 5.0 \qquad \text{ad campaign should be changed}$$

8 (1) Null hypothesis—average sales remain the same.
H_0: $\mu \leq \$35$
Alternate hypothesis—average sales have increased.
H_1: $\mu > \$35$

(2) $\alpha = .05$, one-tailed z test
$n = 40$

(3)   If $z > 1.65$, reject H_0.

$$\sigma_X = \sigma/\sqrt{n} = 8/\sqrt{40} = 1.26$$

Decision rule: If $\bar{X} > 35 + [1.26(1.65)] = 37.07$, reject H_0. Since 37 < 37.07, we must accept H_0; the average sale has remained constant. Note how close this result is. In a case like this, it would be wise to redo the experiment using a larger sample.

10 (1)   Null hypothesis—mean average equals 1 in.
H_0: $\mu = 1$
Alternate hypothesis—mean average does not equal 1 in.
H_1: $\mu \neq 1$

(2) $\alpha = .05$, two-tailed z test, $n = 50$

(3)   Decision rule: If $z > 1.96$ or < -1.96, reject H_0.

$$\sigma_{\bar{X}} = \frac{\sigma}{\sqrt{n}} = \frac{.005}{\sqrt{50}} = .0071$$

Or, if $\bar{X} > [1 + .0007(1.96)] = 1.0014$; if $\bar{X} < [1 - .0071(1.96)] = 0.9986$ in. Thus, if $\bar{X}$ lies between .9986 in and 1.0014 in, accept the shipment.

12 (1)   Null hypothesis—50% of consumers are age 28 or less.
H_0: $p = .5$ drinkers are of age 28 or less
Alternate hypothesis—50% of consumers are *not* age 28 or less.
H_1: $p \neq .5$ drinkers of age 28 or less

(2) $\alpha = .05$, two-tailed test, z test
$z = 1.96$ $n = 500$

$$\sigma_{\bar{p}} = \sqrt{pq/n} = \sqrt{(.50)(.50)/500} = .0224$$

(3)   Critical range: $p + 1.96\sigma_{\bar{p}} = .5 + (1.96)(.0224) = .544$

$$p - 1.96\sigma_{\bar{p}} = .5 - (1.96)(.0224) = .456$$

Decision rule: If $.456 \leq \bar{p} \leq .544$, accept H_0. If $\bar{p} < .456$ or $\bar{p} > .544$, reject H_0. If $z > +1.96$ or $z < -1.96$ reject H_0.

$$\bar{p} = \frac{238}{500} = .476$$

Therefore, accept H_0; 50% cannot be disproved.

14 (1)   Null hypothesis—at least 75% of Americans think they can cut gasoline consumption by 10% next year.

H_0: $p \geq .75$

Alternate hypothesis—less than 75% of Americans think they can cut gasoline consumption by 10% next year.

H_1: $p \leq .75$

(2) $\alpha = .01$, one-tailed test, z test

$z = 2.33$ $n = 1000$

$$\sigma_{\bar{p}} = \sqrt{(.75)(.25)/1000} = .0137$$

(3) Critical value: $.75 - (2.33)(.0137) = .718$

Decision rule: If $\bar{p} < .718$, reject H_0. If $\bar{p} \geq .718$, accept H_0. Or, if $z < -2.33$ reject H_0.

$$\bar{p} = \frac{705}{1000} = .705$$

Therefore, reject H_0. The program is unrealistic at present. A test at the .01 level will be easier to pass because the cutoff point for a .05 level of significance is $.75 - (1.65)(.0137) = .727$. Thus, the higher the level of α, the more difficult it is for a sample value to lead to acceptance of the null hypothesis.

Section 6-5 (p. 178)

2 (a) (1) H_0: $\mu \leq \$200$ H_1: $\mu > \$200$

(2) $\alpha = .05$, one-tailed test, df = 19

$$s_{\bar{X}} = \frac{25}{\sqrt{20}} = 5.590$$

Critical value: $\$200 + 1.729(5.590) = \$209.67$

(3)   Decision rules: If $\bar{X} > 209.67$, reject H_0. Or, if $t > 1.729$, reject H_0; $\bar{X} = 210$, reject H_0.

$$t = \frac{210 - 200}{5.590} = 1.789$$

Therefore, reject H_0. The banker's statement is not justified.

(b) (1) H_0: $\mu \leq 200$ H_1: $\mu > 200$

(2) $\alpha = .05$, z test, one-tailed test

$$s_{\bar{X}} = \frac{25}{\sqrt{200}} = 1.768$$

Critical value: $200 + (1.65)(1.768) = \$202.92$

(3)   Decision rule: If $\bar{X} > 202.92$, reject H_0. Or, if $z > 1.65$, reject $\bar{X} = 210$: $210 > 202.92$, so reject H_0.

or $\qquad t = \dfrac{210 - 200}{1.768} = 5.656$

Reject H_0. The banker's statement is not justified.

CHAPTER 7

Section 7-1 (p. 184)

2 (1) Null hypothesis—batteries are of equal life.
$H_0: \mu_1 - \mu_2 = 0$
Alternate hypothesis—batteries are not of equal life.
$H_1: \mu_1 - \mu_2 \neq 0$

(2) $\alpha = .04$, two-tailed z test, $z = 2.05$

$$s_{\bar{X}_1 - \bar{X}_2} = \sqrt{\dfrac{s_1^2}{n_1} + \dfrac{s_2^2}{n_2}} = \sqrt{\dfrac{12^2}{100} + \dfrac{15^2}{100}} = 1.92$$

(3) Critical value difference: $1.92(2.05) = 3.94$

Decision rule: If $\bar{X}_1 - \bar{X}_2 > \$3.94$, reject H_0; if $\bar{X}_1 - \bar{X}_2 < -3.94$, reject H_0. Or, if $z > 2.05$, reject H_0; if $z < -2.05$, reject H_0.

$$|\bar{X}_1 - \bar{X}_2| = |107 - 112| = 5$$

Therefore, reject H_0.

$$z = \dfrac{107 - 112}{1.92} = -2.6$$

Therefore, reject H_0. Turning to the data, select battery 2.

Section 7-1 (p. 186)

2 (1) Null hypothesis—attitude of the voters is the same.
$H_0: p_1 - p_2 = 0$
Alternate hypothesis—attitude of the voters has changed.
$H_1: p_1 - p_2 \neq 0$

(2) Two-tailed z test, $\alpha = .05$, $z = 1.96$, $n_1 = 1100$, $n_2 = 950$

$$\bar{p} = \dfrac{553 + 451}{1100 + 950} = .490$$

$$s_{\bar{p}_1 - \bar{p}_2} = \sqrt{\bar{p}\bar{q}\left(\dfrac{1}{n_1} + \dfrac{1}{n_2}\right)} = \sqrt{(.49)(.51)\left(\dfrac{1}{1100} + \dfrac{1}{950}\right)}$$
$$= .022$$

Critical value: $.022(1.96) = .043$

(3) Decision rule: If $\bar{p}_1 - \bar{p}_2 > .043$ or $< -.043$, reject H_0. Or, if $z > 1.96$ or < -1.96, reject H_0.

$$|\bar{p}_1 - \bar{p}_2| = \left|\frac{451}{950} - \frac{553}{1100}\right| = |.475 - .503| = -.028$$

We cannot find a statistical difference; do not reject H_0. Or, using z,

$$z = \frac{.475 - .503}{.022} = -1.27$$

We cannot reject H_0. No reason to think there is a significant change in voter preferences. The pollster cannot really make a good forecast of the winner in the election.

Section 7-1 (p. 189)

2 (1) Null hypothesis—short women are at least as positive as tall women.
$H_0: p_t \le p_s \qquad H_1: p_t > p_s$

(2) One-tailed z test, $\sigma = .05$, $z = 1.65$

$$\bar{p}_t = \frac{143}{215} = .665 \qquad \bar{p}_s = \frac{70}{145} = .483 \qquad \bar{p} = \frac{143 + 70}{215 + 145} = .592$$

$$s_{\bar{p}1-\bar{p}2} = \sqrt{(.592)(.408)\left(\frac{1}{215} + \frac{1}{145}\right)} = \sqrt{.592(.408)(.01155)}$$

$$= \sqrt{.0028} = .0528$$

Critical value: $(.0528)(1.65) = .08712$

(3) Decision rule: If $\bar{p}_t - \bar{p}_s > .087$, reject H_0; or, if $z > 1.65$, reject H_0. If $\bar{p}_t - \bar{p}_s = .665 - .483 = .182$, reject H_0; or $(.665 - .483)/.0528 = 3.446$, so reject H_0 since $3.446 > 1.65$.

Decision rule at .01 level: If $\bar{p}_t - \bar{p}_s > .0528(2.33) = .123$, reject H_0; or, if $z > 2.33$, reject H_0. If $\bar{p}_t - \bar{p}_s = .172$, reject H_0; $(.655 - .483)/.0528 = 3.446$; $3.446 > 2.33$, so reject H_0. Reject H_0 at the .01 significance level.

Section 7-2 (p.191)

2 (1) Null hypothesis—there was no rise in settlement claims between 1970 and 1980.
$H_0: \mu_2 - \mu_1 \le 0$
Alternate hypothesis—there was a significant rise in settlement claims between the two sets of years.
$H_1: \mu_2 - \mu_1 > 0$

(2) $\alpha = .05$; $n_1 = 14$, $n_2 = 12$; one-tailed t test
Degrees of freedom $n_1 + n_2 - 2 = 24$; $t = 1.711$

$$s = \sqrt{\frac{(n_1 - 1)s_1^2 + (n_2 - 1)s_2^2}{n_1 + n_2 - 2}}$$

$$= \sqrt{\frac{(14 - 1)(1050)^2 + (12 - 1)(875)^2}{14 + 12 - 2}}$$

$$= 973.70$$

$$s_{\bar{X}_1 - \bar{X}_2} = s\sqrt{\frac{1}{n_1} + \frac{1}{n_2}} = 973.70\sqrt{\frac{1}{14} + \frac{1}{12}} = 383.05$$

Critical value: $383.05(1.711) = 655.40$

(3) Decision rule: If $\bar{X}_2 - \bar{X}_1 > 655.40$, reject H_0; or, if $t > +1.711$, reject H_0. Since $\bar{X}_2 - \bar{X}_1 = 13,000 - 12,050 = 950$, reject H_0 since $950 > 655.40$.

$$t = \frac{13,000 - 12,050}{383.05} = 2.48$$

Reject H_0 since $2.48 > 1.711$. We infer that there has been a significant rise in claim size.

Section 7-3 (p. 199)

2 (1) $H_0: \mu_1 = \mu_2 = \mu_3 = \mu_4$
$H_1: \mu_1 \neq \mu_1 \neq \mu_3 \neq \mu_4$

(2) $\alpha = .05$, analysis of variance, df $= 3/16$

(3) If $F > 3.24$, reject H_0

4.5	4.7	3.9	5.4
3.7	5.1	4.2	3.3
4.6	4.8	4.3	4.0
4.1	4.3	3.8	3.8
4.6	4.1	3.4	4.6
21.5	23.0	19.6	21.1

$n = 5$ 5   5   5

$\bar{X} = 4.30$ 4.60   3.92   4.22 $\bar{\bar{X}} = 4.26$

$\bar{X}_i - \bar{\bar{X}}$	$(\bar{X}_i - \bar{\bar{X}})^2$	$n(\bar{X}_i - \bar{\bar{X}})^2$
$4.30 - 4.26 = .04$	.0016	.0080
$4.60 - 4.26 = .34$	.1156	.5780
$3.92 - 4.26 = -.34$	.1156	.5780
$4.22 - 4.26 = -.04$	.0016	.0080
		1.1720

$$V_B = \frac{1.1720}{3} = .3907 \text{ between group variance}$$

STICKUM

$X_i - \bar{X}_i$	$X_i - \bar{X}_i$	$(X_i - \bar{X}_i)^2$
4.5 − 4.3	.2	.04
3.7 − 4.3	−.6	.36
4.6 − 4.3	.3	.09
4.1 − 4.3	−.2	.04
4.6 − 4.3	.3	.09
		.62

QWIKSTICK

$X_i - \bar{X}_i$	$X_i - \bar{X}_i$	$(X_i - \bar{X}_i)^2$
4.7 − 4.6	.1	.01
5.1 − 4.6	.5	.25
4.8 − 4.6	.2	.04
4.3 − 4.6	−.3	.09
4.1 − 4.6	−.5	.25
		.64

TITEBOND

$X_i - \bar{X}_i$	$X_i - \bar{X}_i$	$(X_i - \bar{X}_i)^2$
3.9 − 3.92	−.02	.0004
4.2 − 3.92	.28	.0784
4.3 − 3.92	.38	.1444
3.8 − 3.92	−.12	.0144
3.4 − 3.92	−.52	.2704
		.5080

STICKWIKET

$X_i - \bar{X}_i$	$X_i - \bar{X}_i$	$(X_i - \bar{X}_i)^2$
5.4 − 4.22	1.18	1.3924
3.3 − 4.22	−.92	.8464
4.0 − 4.22	−.22	.0484
3.8 − 4.22	−.42	.1764
4.6 − 4.22	.38	.1444
		2.6080

$$.62 + .64 + .5080 + 2.6080 = 4.3760$$

$$V_W = \frac{\Sigma(X_{ij} - \bar{X}_j)^2}{n - c} = \frac{4.3760}{16} = .2735$$

$$F = \frac{.3907}{.2735} = 1.4285$$

$1.4285 < 3.24$; do not reject H_0. The epoxies do not seem to differ.

CHAPTER 8

Section 8-4 (p. 225)

2 To compute each theoretical number for the table in the problem use a process like this. Thus the first number will be
$$\frac{40}{145} = \frac{X}{47}$$
$X = 12.96$ (round to 13).

E	$O - E$	$(O - E)^2$	$\dfrac{(O - E)^2}{E}$
13	−1	1	.08
19.4	5.6	31.2	1.62
14.6	−4.6	21.2	1.45
13.8	6.2	38.4	2.78
20.7	−5.7	32.5	1.57
15.5	− .5	.25	.02
13.2	−5.2	27.0	2.05
19.9	.1	.01	0
14.9	5.1	26.0	1.74
		$\Sigma \dfrac{(O - E)^2}{E}$	= 11.31

(1) H_0: Purchases of accessories are independent of age.
   H_1: Purchases of accessories are not independent of age

(2) Chi square test, $\alpha = .05$
   df $= (3 - 1)(3 - 1) = 4$

(3) If $\chi^2 > 9.488$, reject H_0. Since $\chi^2 = 11.31$, reject H_0. Therefore, we say we have reason to believe that amount spent on accessories is related to age.

4 To calculate the theoretical distribution using past year's sales percentages, we multiply each percentage by the total trucks sold this year (200). The first number will be $.20(200) = 40$.

REGION	PAST YEAR'S SALES, %	ACTUAL DISTRIBUTION OF TRUCKS SOLD THIS YEAR	THEORETICAL DISTRIBUTION
Far East	20	50	40
Europe	40	75	80
South America	20	40	40
Canada	10	10	20
United States	10	25	20
	100	200	200

(1) H_0: This year's sales follow the same distribution as last year's sales.
   H_1: This year's sales do not follow the same distribution as last year's sales.

(2) Chi-square test, $\alpha = .01$, df $= 4$ (number of categories minus 1, since we are holding totals constant

(3) If $\chi^2 > 13.277$, reject H_0

$$\frac{(50 - 40)^2}{40} + \frac{(75 - 80)^2}{80} + \frac{(40 - 40)^2}{40} + \frac{(10 - 20)^2}{20} + \frac{(25 - 20)^2}{20}$$

$$2.5 \quad + \quad .312 \quad + \quad 0 \quad + \quad 5.0 \quad + \quad 1.25$$

$$\chi^2 = 9.062$$

since $9.062 < 13,277$, we cannot reject H_0; there is not sufficient reason to believe that this year's sales are distributed differently than last year's sales.

Section 8-5 (p. 230)

2 (1) H_0: The percentage tipped is the same for all sizes of parties.
   H_1: The percentage tipped differs for different-sized parties.

(2) Kruskal-Wallis test, $\alpha = .10$, df $= 3$

(3) If $H > 6.251$, reject H_0.

PARTIES OF 1		PARTIES OF 2		PARTIES OF 3 OR 4		PARTIES OF 5 OR MORE	
% TIP	RANK	% TIP	RANK	% TIP	RANK	% TIP	RANK
25	20	20	16.5	15	11.5	4	4
20	16.5	16	13.5	16	13.5	13	9
15	11.5	22	19	8	7	17	15
14	10	21	18	7	6	0	2
10	8	5	5	0	2	0	2
$\bar{p}$ = 16.8%	66	$\bar{p}$ = 16.8%	72	$\bar{p}$ = 9.2%	40	$\bar{p}$ = 6.8%	32

Ranking from lowest to highest,

$$H = \frac{12}{20(21)}(871.200 + 1036.800 + 320.000 + 204.800) - 3\,(21)$$

$$.029(2432.800) - 63$$

$$70.5512 - 63.000 = 7.5512$$

Since $7.5512 > 6.251$, reject H_0. There seems to be a difference in propensity to tip between large and small parties. A further examination of the data shows a higher percentage is tipped by the smaller parties, so the waiter *seems* to be right.

CHAPTER 9

Section 9-1 (p. 245)

2

NUMBER	GRADE POINT RANK	STARTING SALARY RANK	d	d^2
1	6	7	−1	1
2	2	3	−1	1
3	8	6	+2	4
4	9	9	0	0
5	3	2	1	1
6	1	1	0	0
7	7	4	3	9
8	4	5	−1	1
9	10	10	0	0
10	5	8	3	9

$$r_r = 1 - \frac{6\Sigma d^2}{n(n^2 - 1)} = 1 - \frac{6(26)}{10(99)} = .8424$$

4 October 7: $r_r = 1 - \dfrac{6\Sigma d^2}{n(n^2 - 1)} = 1 - \dfrac{6(30)}{20(399)} = .9774$

October 14: $r_r = 1 - \dfrac{6\Sigma d^2}{n(n^2 - 1)} = 1 - \dfrac{6(68)}{20(399)} = .9489$

The rankings were most consistent on October 7.

2

	MIDTERM	R_1	FINAL	R_2
1	78	22.5	85	11.5
2	84	13	88	8.5
3	87	10	83	15
4	65	29	79	21
5	94	2	92	3
6	72	27	80	20
7	76	25	82	17.5
8	90	5.5	90	5.5
9	88	8.5	81	19
10	75	26	77	24
11	78	22.5	83	15
12	91	4	97	1
13	85	11.5	89	7
14	82	17.5	83	15
15	69	30	70	28

(1) $H_0: \mu_1 \leq \mu_2$. Midterm grades are less than or equal to final grades.
$H_1: \mu_1 > \mu_2$. Midterm grades are higher than final grades.

(2) .05 level of significance, one-tailed test, z table, Mann-Whitney test

(3) If $z < 1.65$, reject H_0.

$n_1 = 15$, $n_2 = 15$; $R_1 = 254$, $R_2 = 211$

$$\mu_U = \frac{15(15)}{2} = 112.5$$

$$\sigma_U = \sqrt{\frac{15(15)(31)}{12}} = 24.109$$

$$U_1 = n_1 n_2 + \frac{n_1(n_1 + 1)}{2} - R_1 = 91$$

$$U_2 = 134$$

$$z_1 = \frac{U_1 - \mu_U}{\sigma_U} = -.89 \qquad \text{Accept } H_0 \text{ since } -.89 > -1.65.$$

4

	OLD MAINTENANCE PLAN		NEW MAINTENANCE PLAN	
	NUMBER	RANK*	NUMBER	RANK
A	2	10.5	1	5
B	4	19	0	1.5
C	7	28	5	22.5
D	5	22.5	6	16
E	0	1.5	2	10.5
F	3	15.5	1	5
G	4	19	1	5
H	1	5	2	10.5
I	2	10.5	5	22.5
J	6	26	2	10.5
K	9	30	4	19

	OLD MAINTENANCE PLAN		NEW MAINTENANCE PLAN	
	NUMBER	RANK*	NUMBER	RANK
L	3	15.5	3	15.5
M	5	22.5	1	5
N	6	26	3	15.5
O	8	29	2	10.5

*Ranking system: 0 breakdowns = 1. As the number of breakdowns increases, rank increases. Thus, for 9 breakdowns, the rank is 30. Since there are many tied ranks in this problem, the correction for ties in Appendix A should be used.

(1) $H_0: \mu_1 \leq \mu_2$. There are the same or more breakdowns before the plan.
$H_1: \mu_1 > \mu_2$. There are fewer breakdowns after the plan.

(2) .05 level of significance, one-tailed test, z table

(3) If $z > 1.65$, reject H_0.

$$n_1 = 15, \ n_2 = 15; \ R_1 = 280.5, \ R_2 = 184.5$$

$$\mu_U = \frac{15(15)}{2} = 112.5$$

$$\sigma_U = \sqrt{\frac{15(15)(31)}{12}} = 24.109$$

$$U_2 = (15)(15) + \frac{15(16)}{2} - 184.5 = 160.5$$

$$z = \frac{160.5 - 112.5}{24.109} = 1.99 \qquad \text{reject } H_0 \text{ since } z > 1.65$$

The new maintenance schedule is effective. There seems to be fewer breakdowns after the plan. Since there are many tied ranks here, see Appendix A.

Section 9-4 (p. 259)

2 Use the chi-square test (nonparametric).

THEORETICAL	ACTUAL
21	50
63	50
84	70
42	40
210	210

$$\chi^2 = \frac{(50 - 21)^2}{21} + \frac{(50 - 63)^2}{63} + \frac{(70 - 84)^2}{84} + \frac{(40 - 42)^2}{42}$$

$$40.05 + 2.68 + 2.33 + .09 = 45.15$$

χ^2 for 3 df, $\alpha = .05 = 7.82$. Since $45.15 > 7.82$, reject H_0. Note how large the calculated χ^2 is. This is frequently true for large-sample sizes. The Kolmogorov-Smirnov tests, which use proportions only, avoid this problem.

A test of proportion (parametric test) could have been used. For example, is .238 significantly different from .100?

$$\sigma_{\bar{p}} = \sqrt{\frac{pq}{n}} = \sqrt{\frac{(.10)(90)}{210}} = .02$$

If $z > 1.96$ or < -1.96, reject H_0. Since $(.238 - .100)/.02 = .138/.02 = 6.9$, reject H_0. There is a significant difference. Since we are not sure of the nature of the distribution, it is safer to use a nonparametric test.

4

			CUMULATIVE FREQUENCIES				
CHOICE	GOVERNMENT/ NONPROFIT	PROFIT	GOVERNMENT/ NONPROFIT		PROFIT		ABSOLUTE DIFFERENCES
1	20	10	20/50	.40	10/100	.10	.30
2	20	20	40/50	.80	35/100	.35	.45
3	8	50	48/50	.96	85/100	.85	.11
4	2	15	50/50	1.00	95/100	.95	.05
5	0	5	50/50	1.00	100/100	1.00	.00
	50	100					

(1) H_0: Government and nonprofit offer equal or more promotions for women.
H_1: Government and nonprofit offer less promotions for women.

(2) Kolmogorov-Smirnov test, chi-square table, one-tailed test, 2 df, $\alpha = .01$

(3) If $\chi^2 > 9.21$, reject H_0.

$$\chi^2 = 4D_C^2 \frac{n_1 n_2}{n_1 + n_2} = 4(.45)^2 \frac{100(50)}{150} = \frac{.81(5000)}{150} = 27$$

Since $27 > 9.21$, we cannot accept H_0. Advancement seems to have been less rapid for women in the nonprofit and government sectors than in the profit-making area.

Section 9-5 (p. 265)

2 First discard the N's: $n = 47$ minus 8 N's, so $n = 39$; $n_1 = 16(P)$, $n_2 = 23$ (C), and $r = 7$. First, compute μ_r and σ_r.

$$\mu_r = \frac{2n_1 n_2}{n_1 + n_2} + 1 = \frac{2(16 + 23)}{16 + 23} + 1 = 19.87$$

$$\sigma_r = \sqrt{\frac{2n_1 n_2(2n_1 n_2 - n_1 - n_2)}{(n_1 + n_2)^2(n_1 + n_2 - 1)}}$$

$$= \sqrt{\frac{2(16)(23)[\,2(16)(23) - 16 - 23]}{(16 + 23)^2(16 + 23 - 1)}}$$

$$= \sqrt{\frac{736[697]}{(1521)(38)}} = \sqrt{\frac{512{,}992}{57{,}798}} = \sqrt{8.8756} = 2.98$$

(1) H_0: The interview results are randomly mixed.
   H_1: The interview results are not randomly mixed.

(2) $\alpha = .05$, two-tailed test, runs test, z table

(3) Critical value: If $z > 1.96$ or < -1.96, reject H_0.

$$z = \frac{r - \mu_r}{\sigma_r} = \frac{7 - 19.87}{2.98} = -4.319$$

Since $-4.319 < -1.96$, reject H_0. Therefore, assume responses are not randomly mixed.

4 $\mu_r = \dfrac{2n_1 n_2}{n_1 + n_2} + 1 = \dfrac{2(13)(15)}{13 + 15} + 1 = 14.93;$

$n_1 = 13(D),\ n_2 = 15(U),\ r = 18$

$$\sigma_r = \sqrt{\frac{2n_1 n_2(2n_1 n_2 - n_1 - n_2)}{(n_1 + n_2)^2(n_1 + n_2 - 1)}}$$

$$= \sqrt{\frac{2(13)(15)[\,2(13)(15) - 13 - 15]}{(13 + 15)^2(13 + 15 - 1)}}$$

$$= \sqrt{\frac{390(362)}{28^2(27)}} = \sqrt{\frac{141{,}180}{21{,}168}} = 2.58$$

(1) H_0: Ups and downs follow a random pattern.
   H_1: Ups and downs do not follow a random pattern.

(2) $\alpha = .05$, two-tailed test, runs test, z table

(3) Critical value: If $z > 1.96$ or < -1.96, reject H_0.

$$z = \frac{r - \mu_r}{\sigma_r} = \frac{18 - 14.93}{2.58} = 1.19$$

Since $1.19 < 1.96$, the randomness hypothesis H_0 cannot be rejected; the number of runs is what one might have expected.

6 The median for Dallas is 70. The median for Chicago is 117. For Dallas, we have:

$\overset{\cdot}{76}, \overset{\cdot}{72}, 69, \overset{\cdot}{77}, 68, 49, \overset{\cdot}{80}, \overset{\cdot}{75}, \overset{\cdot}{70}, 58, 63, 67, \overset{\cdot}{72}, \overset{\cdot}{76}$

$68, 65, \overset{\cdot}{70}, 66, 69, \overset{\cdot}{73}, \overset{\cdot}{74}, 59, 64, \overset{\cdot}{75}, \overset{\cdot}{78}$

$$\mu_r = \frac{2n_1 n_2}{n_1 + n_2} + 1 \qquad\qquad r = 12$$

$$n_1 = 11 \text{ (above median)}$$

$$n_2 = 12 \text{ (below median)}$$

$$\mu_r = \frac{2(11)(12)}{23} + 1 = 12.48 \qquad 2 \text{ are at the median}$$

$$\sigma_r = \sqrt{\frac{2n_1 n_2 (2n_1 n_2 - n_1 - n_2)}{(n_1 - n_2)^2 (n_1 - n_2 - 1)}}$$

$$= \sqrt{\frac{264(264 - 23)}{(529)(22)}} = \sqrt{\frac{63624}{11638}} = 2.34$$

(1) H_0: There is a random relationship between seasons and repairs.
H_1: There isn't a random relationship between seasons and repairs.

(2) $\alpha = .20$, two-tailed test, runs test, z table

(3) Critical value: If $z > 1.28$ or < -1.28, reject H_0.

$$z = \frac{11 - 12.48}{2.34} = -.63$$

Since $-.63 > -1.28$, we cannot reject H_0. For Dallas, there seems to be no relationship between seasons and repairs.

For Chicago, the median is 117. Charting the numbers for Chicago, we have double dots indicate the median and a single dot means a number above the median; ignore the median in counting runs

$113, 94, 1\overset{\cdot\cdot}{1}8, 1\overset{\cdot\cdot}{1}8, 1\overset{\cdot}{2}2, 90, 1\overset{\cdot\cdot}{1}7, 116, 115, 85, 116, 1\overset{\cdot\cdot}{1}7, 1\overset{\cdot\cdot}{1}7, 86, 1\overset{\cdot}{2}0, 1\overset{\cdot}{1}9, 1\overset{\cdot}{2}2,$
$80, 1\overset{\cdot}{2}4, 1\overset{\cdot}{2}3, 1\overset{\cdot}{2}5, 81, 1\overset{\cdot}{2}5, 1\overset{\cdot}{2}6, 1\overset{\cdot}{3}0$

$r = 9 \qquad n_1 = 12 \text{ (above median)} \qquad n_2 = 10 \text{ (below median)}$
At median $= 3$

$$\mu_r = \frac{2(10)(12)}{10 + 12} + 1$$

$$= 11.91$$

$$\sigma_r = \sqrt{\frac{240(240 - 22)}{484(21)}} = \sqrt{\frac{52,320}{10,164}} = 2.27$$

(1) H_0: There is a random relationship between seasons and repairs.

H_1: There isn't a random relationship between seasons and repairs.

(2) $\alpha = .20$, two-tailed test, runs test, z table

(3) Critical value: If $z > 1.28$ or < -1.28, reject H_0.

$$z = \frac{9 - 11.91}{2.27} = -1.282$$

Since $-1.282 > -1.28$, there may be some reason to believe that there is a nonrandom pattern for Chicago, and we can reject H_0. Thus, in Chicago, where there are more dramatic climate changes than in Dallas, season may affect the number of repairs needed.

Section 9-6 (p. 269)

2 (1) H_0: $p = .5$. There is no preference for museums.
        H_1: $p \neq .5$. There is a preference for museums.

(2)   .05, two-tailed z test

(3)   If $z > 1.96$ or $z < -1.96$, reject H_0.

$$n = 80 - 5 = 75$$

$$\sigma_{\bar{p}} = \sqrt{\frac{pq}{n}} = \sqrt{\frac{.5(.5)}{75}} = .058$$

$$z = \frac{45/75 - .5}{.057} = 1.72$$

Don't reject H_0: $1.72 < 1.96$.

CHAPTER 10

Section 10-10 (p. 297)

2

	WAREHOUSE LEVEL OF FULLNESS X	X^2	AVERAGE ORDER FILLING TIME (MINUTES) Y	XY	Y^2
$n = 14$	100	10,000	20	2,000	400
	95	9,025	20	1,900	400
$\bar{X} = \dfrac{\Sigma X}{14} = \dfrac{770}{14}$	90	8,100	19	1,710	361
	80	6,400	18	1,440	324
	70	4,900	16	1,120	256
$\bar{X} = 55$	65	4,225	15	975	225
	60	3,600	15	900	225
$\bar{Y} = \dfrac{\Sigma Y}{14} = \dfrac{174}{14}$	50	2,500	13	650	169
	40	1,600	9	360	81
	35	1,225	8	280	64
$\bar{Y} = 12.4285$	30	900	7	210	49
	25	625	6	150	36
$\bar{Y} = 12.4$	20	400	5	100	25
	10	100	3	30	9
	$\Sigma X = 770$	$\Sigma X^2 = 53,600$	$\Sigma Y = 174$	$\Sigma XY = 11,825$	$\Sigma Y^2 = 2,624$

(a)

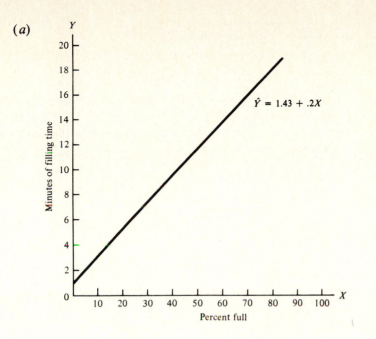

(b) $\hat{Y} = a + bX$

$$\hat{Y} = \frac{\Sigma XY - n\bar{X}\bar{Y}}{\Sigma X^2 - n\bar{X}^2} = \frac{11825 - 14(55)(12.43)}{53,600 - 14(55^2)}$$

$$= \frac{11,825 - 9571.1}{53,600 - 42,350} = \frac{2253.9}{11,250}$$

$b = .2$

$a = \bar{Y} - b\bar{X} = 12.43 - .2(55) = 12.43 - 11$

$a = 1.43$

(c) $\hat{Y} = 1.43 + .2X$

X	Y	
0	1.43	
5	2.43	1.43 + 1 = 2.4
10	3.43	1.43 + 2 = 3.4

(d) $s_{y.x} = \sqrt{\dfrac{\Sigma Y^2 - a\Sigma Y - b\Sigma xy}{n - 2}}$

$$s_{y.x} = \sqrt{\frac{2624 - 1.43(174) - .2(11,825)}{14 - 2}}$$

$$= \sqrt{\frac{2624 - 248.82 - 2365}{12}}$$

$$s_{y.x} = \sqrt{\frac{10.18}{12}} = \sqrt{.84833}$$

$$s_{y.x} = .921$$

(e) $X = 75, Y = ?$

$\hat{Y} = 1.43 + .2(75)$

$\hat{Y} = 1.54 + 15$

$\hat{Y} = 16.43$ minutes

(f)   Given:

$X = 60\%$ $\qquad\qquad$ $X = 100\%$

$Y = 1.43 + .20(60)$ $\qquad$ $Y = 1.43 + .20(100)$

$Y = 13.43$ min/order $\qquad$ $Y = 21.43$ min/order

13.43 min/order (300 order/day) ($4.00/60 min)

$/day = $268.60/day   21.43 min/order (300 orders/day ($4.00/60 min) = $428.6/day

$$\begin{array}{r} 428.60 \\ -268.60 \\ \hline 160.00 \end{array}$$ $\dfrac{\$160.00}{300 \text{ orders}} = \$.53/\text{order}$

Section 10-11 (p. 301)

2

CITY	POPULATION X(000)	PARTS/MILLION OF POLLUTANTS Y	X^2	Y^2	XY
1	10	20	100	400	200
2	25	25	625	625	625
3	25	40	625	1,600	1,000
4	30	40	900	1,600	1,200
5	35	35	1,225	1,225	1,225
6	40	30	1,600	900	1,200
7	40	45	1,600	2,025	1,800
8	55	50	3,025	2,500	2,750
9	90	120	8,100	14,400	10,800
10	100	130	10,000	16,900	13,000
11	120	100	14,400	10,000	12,000
12	150	200	22,500	40,000	30,000
13	200	300	40,000	90,000	60,000
14	400	350	160,000	122,500	140,000

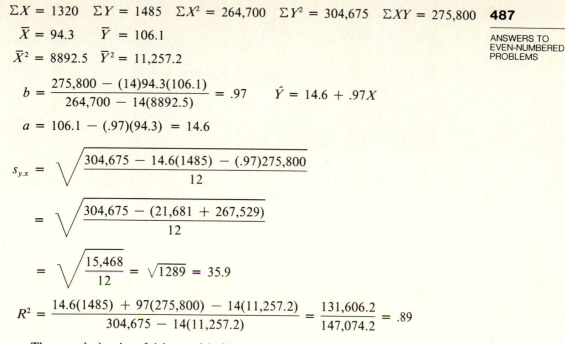

$$\Sigma X = 1320 \quad \Sigma Y = 1485 \quad \Sigma X^2 = 264{,}700 \quad \Sigma Y^2 = 304{,}675 \quad \Sigma XY = 275{,}800$$

$$\bar{X} = 94.3 \qquad \bar{Y} = 106.1$$

$$\bar{X}^2 = 8892.5 \quad \bar{Y}^2 = 11{,}257.2$$

$$b = \frac{275{,}800 - (14)94.3(106.1)}{264{,}700 - 14(8892.5)} = .97 \qquad \hat{Y} = 14.6 + .97X$$

$$a = 106.1 - (.97)(94.3) = 14.6$$

$$s_{y.x} = \sqrt{\frac{304{,}675 - 14.6(1485) - (.97)275{,}800}{12}}$$

$$= \sqrt{\frac{304{,}675 - (21{,}681 + 267{,}529)}{12}}$$

$$= \sqrt{\frac{15{,}468}{12}} = \sqrt{1289} = 35.9$$

$$R^2 = \frac{14.6(1485) + 97(275{,}800) - 14(11{,}257.2)}{304{,}675 - 14(11{,}257.2)} = \frac{131{,}606.2}{147{,}074.2} = .89$$

The population is a fairly good indicator, since 89% of the pollutants in the air have been explained by it.

CHAPTER 11

Section 11-3 (p. 340)

2 (*a*) and (*b*)

YEAR	MOVING-AVERAGE FORECAST	ACTUAL EARNINGS/SHARE	PROJECTED ($\alpha = .4$)
1973		$3.69	4.000
1974		4.15	3.876*
1975		4.64	3.986
1976	4.160	4.73	4.427
1977	4.507	5.40	4.440
1978	4.923	5.76	4.824
1979	5.297	8.36	5.198
1980	6.507†		6.463†

*.4(3.69) + .6(4.00) = 3.876
†Exponential smoothing forecast.

(*c*) For these years, exponential smoothing provides a slightly better fit, since 6.463 is a closer fit to $6.06 than is $6.507.

4 $F_t = 14.8$, $\alpha = .1$ $\qquad$ $F_t = 17.2$, $\alpha = .3$. (19.2 is the actual value; $\alpha = .3$ is the better estimator.)

2 (*a*) That the period for which the index applies is 12% below the normal or base.

(*b*) A tier graph provides a graphic picture of seasonal index numbers and is used to see if our indexes are stable. If the pattern is uniform, the indexes calculated for forecasts can be justified.

(*c*) To center or arrange the data so it will be centered on each quarter rather than fall between two quarters.

(*d*) We want quarterly indexes to add to 400, so that each individual quarter is 100 in order to have a standard index number form where the normal or base period is 100. Then if we compute monthly or quarterly inventory orders, for example, it will add to the total annual amount.

4 (*a*) Exponential smoothing ($\alpha = .2$)

YEAR	(1) QUARTER	(2) SALE ($)	(3) VALUE OF α	(4) (2) × (3)
1973	1	174	.007	1.218
	2	274	.009	2.466
	3	240	.011	2.640
	4	310	.014	4.340
1974	1	183	.017	3.111
	2	269	.021	5.649
	3	230	.027	6.210
	4	320	.034	10.880
1975	1	170	.042	7.140
	2	280	.052	14.560
	3	250	.065	16.250
	4	330	.082	27.060
1976	1	160	.102	16.320
	2	270	.128	34.560
	3	200	.160	32.000
	4	325	.200	65.000
Total				249.404

Writing this out,

$$F_{q1,1977} = .2(325) + .16(200) + .128(270) + .102(160)$$

$$+ .082(330) + .065(250) + .052(280) + .042(170)$$

$$+ .034(320) + .027(230) + .021(269) +$$

$$.017(183) + .014(310) + .011(240) +$$

$$.009(274) + .007(174)$$

$$= 65 + 32 + 34.6 + 16.3 + 27.1 + 16.3 + 14.6$$

$$+ 7.1 + 10.9 + 6.2 + 5.6 + 3.1 +$$
$$4.3 + 2.6 + 2.5 + 1.2$$
$$= 249.4$$

Moving average:

$$F_{q1,1977} = \frac{325 + 200 + 270 + 160 + 330 + 250 + 280 + 170 + 320 + 230 + 269 + 183}{12}$$

$$= 248.9 \text{ (12-quarter average)}$$

$$F_{q1,1977} = \frac{174 + 183 + 170 + 160}{4} = 171.75 \qquad \text{4-quarter average, average of quarter 1 values}$$

(b) Adjusting exponential smoothing forecast, we have 249.404(.683) = 170.34. Adjusting the 12-quarter moving average by the seasonal first quarter equals 248.9(.683) = 170. These more closely approximate the average quarter 1 values.

6 Original data—*TCSI*.
Four-quarter moving total.
Eight-quarter moving total.
Divide by 8.
Divide original data by data in step 4.
Form table by quarters or months.
Drop lowest and highest observations.
Average remaining numbers in each column.
Total averages.
Compute "fudge factor" and multiply by each average.
Multiply each average by 100.

Section 11-3 (p. 351)

2 (a) 420(1.75) = 735
(b) 470(.90) = 423
(c) 900(1.75) = 1575

4 (a) 1.0145   .9325   .9950   .1.0637

$$\frac{4.0000}{4.0057} = .99859 \qquad \text{(fudge factor)}$$

1.013   .931   .994   1.062

Multiply by 100:

101.3 = q1   93.1 = q2   99.4 = q3   106.2 = q4

(b) $Y = 15.43 + .2(21) = 19.63$

$$19.63(.931) = 18.2755$$

Forecast: q2,1984 = 18.28

6 *Trend × Seasonal*
Trend 1   23.7(.979)   = 23.2
Trend 2   23.9(1.016) = 24.3
Trend 3   24.2(1.135) = 27.5
Trend 4   24.4(.87)   = 21.2

CHAPTER 12

Section 12-5 (p. 386)

2

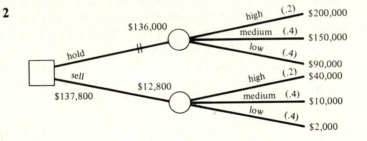

Sell out since expected receipts = 125,000 + 12,800 = 137,800

4

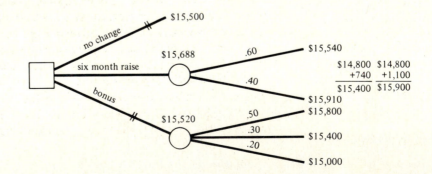

Offer with six month raise is best

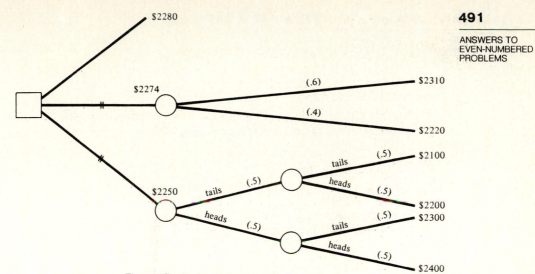

The coin-flipping landlord provided the best deal.

Section 12-6 (p. 392)

2 RP = rain predicted R = actually rained
NRP = fair predicted (won't rain) NR = actually didn't rain

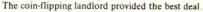

	.3 R	.7 NR
RP	1	0
NRP	0	1

$$P(R|RP) = \frac{P(R)P(RP|R)}{P(R)P(RP|R) + P(NR)P(RP|NR)}$$

$$= \frac{.30(1)}{(.30)(1) + (.70)(0)} = 1$$

Note that the previous forecasts of 30% chance for rain would not be sufficient to call off the concert. The 77.4% chance in Example 12-1 should mean that we might make provisions for rain shelters. Certainly, if we could believe the results where the guru is always correct, she should make provisions for rain shelters or an indoor concert.

CHAPTER 13

Section 13-4 (p. 410)

2 (*a*) $\dfrac{\Sigma p_n}{\Sigma p_0}(100) = \dfrac{1.89}{.90}(100) = 210.0$

(*b*) $= 2.75 + 3.27 + 2.40 + 0.83 = 9.25$

$$\frac{9.25}{4} = 231.3$$

Section 13-9 (p. 424)

2 No; 53/120, or 44%. Even though the index number increased 53 *points*, the base was 120 so the percentage increase is 44%.

4 $\dfrac{100}{205.3} = .487$, or 49 cents

6

North America	100.7
Latin America	98.1
USSR	102.4
China	104.3
Middle East	100.0
South Asia	107.4
Other regions	90.3

The greatest index increase is South Asia. The largest index decrease is other regions. The largest absolute increase is South Asia.

8 72 = 100
73 = 106.2 = (133.1/125.3) (100)
74 = 117.9
75 = 128.7
76 = 136.1
77 = 145.1

10 Exports seem to be rising more quickly than imports. Imports and exports have both been rising more rapidly than consumer prices.

APPENDIX: STATISTICAL TABLES

TABLE A-1

SELECTED VALUES OF THE BINOMIAL PROBABILITY DISTRIBUTION

$$P(X) = \frac{n!}{x!(n-x)!} p^x q^{n-x}$$

How to use: If $p = .10$, $n = 6$, and $x = 2$, look under .10 across the top column and $n = 6$, $x = 2$ down the left-hand column: $p(2) = .0984$. For values of p greater than .50, use $1 - p$ for p, $n - x$ for x and look under the same n value. Thus if $p = .70$, $n = 6$, $x = 2$, look under $p = .30$, $n = 6$, $x = 4$, and the answer will be .0595.

n	x	.05	.10	.15	.20	.25	.30	.35	.40	.45	.50
1	0	.9500	.9000	.8500	.8000	.7500	.7000	.6500	.6000	.5500	.5000
	1	.0500	.1000	.1500	.2000	.2500	.3000	.3500	.4000	.4500	.5000
2	0	.9025	.8100	.7225	.6400	.5625	.4900	.4225	.3600	.3025	.2500
	1	.0950	.1800	.2550	.3200	.3750	.4200	.4550	.4800	.4950	.5000
	2	.0025	.0100	.0225	.0400	.0625	.0900	.1225	.1600	.2025	.2500
3	0	.8574	.7290	.6141	.5120	.4219	.3430	.2746	.2160	.1664	.1250
	1	.1354	.2430	.3251	.3840	.4219	.4410	.4436	.4320	.4084	.3750
	2	.0071	.0270	.0574	.0960	.1406	.1890	.2389	.2880	.3341	.3750
	3	.0001	.0010	.0034	.0080	.0156	.0270	.0429	.0640	.0911	.1250
4	0	.8145	.6561	.5220	.4096	.3164	.2401	.1785	.1296	.0915	.0625
	1	.1715	.2916	.3685	.4096	.4219	.4116	.3845	.3456	.2995	.2500
	2	.0135	.0486	.0975	.1536	.2109	.2646	.3105	.3456	.3675	.3750
	3	.0005	.0036	.0115	.0256	.0469	.0756	.1115	.1536	.2005	.2500
	4	.0000	.0001	.0005	.0016	.0039	.0081	.0150	.0256	.0410	.0625
5	0	.7738	.5905	.4437	.3277	.2373	.1681	.1160	.0778	.0503	.0312
	1	.2036	.3280	.3915	.4096	.3955	.3602	.3124	.2592	.2059	.1562
	2	.0214	.0729	.1382	.2048	.2637	.3087	.3364	.3456	.3369	.3125
	3	.0011	.0081	.0244	.0512	.0879	.1323	.1811	.2304	.2757	.3125
	4	.0000	.0004	.0022	.0064	.0146	.0284	.0488	.0768	.1128	.1562
	5	.0000	.0000	.0001	.0003	.0010	.0024	.0053	.0102	.0185	.0312
6	0	.7351	.5314	.3771	.2621	.1780	.1176	.0754	.0467	.0277	.0156
	1	.2321	.3543	.3993	.3932	.3560	.3025	.2437	.1866	.1359	.0938
	2	.0305	.0984	.1762	.2458	.2966	.3241	.3280	.3110	.2780	.2344
	3	.0021	.0146	.0415	.0819	.1318	.1852	.2355	.2765	.3032	.3125
	4	.0001	.0012	.0055	.0154	.0330	.0595	.0951	.1382	.1861	.2344
	5	.0000	.0001	.0004	.0015	.0044	.0102	.0205	.0369	.0609	.0938
	6	.0000	.0000	.0000	.0001	.0002	.0007	.0018	.0041	.0083	.0156
7	0	.6983	.4783	.3206	.2097	.1335	.0824	.0490	.0280	.0152	.0078
	1	.2573	.3720	.3960	.3670	.3115	.2471	.1848	.1306	.0872	.0547
	2	.0406	.1240	.2097	.2753	.3115	.3177	.2985	.2613	.2140	.1641
	3	.0036	.0230	.0617	.1147	.1730	.2269	.2679	.2903	.2918	.2734
	4	.0002	.0026	.0109	.0287	.0577	.0972	.1442	.1935	.2388	.2734
	5	.0000	.0002	.0012	.0043	.0115	.0250	.0466	.0774	.1172	.1641
	6	.0000	.0000	.0001	.0004	.0013	.0036	.0084	.0172	.0320	.0547
	7	.0000	.0000	.0000	.0000	.0001	.0002	.0006	.0016	.0037	.0078
8	0	.6634	.4305	.2725	.1678	.1001	.0576	.0319	.0168	.0084	.0039
	1	.2793	.3826	.3847	.3355	.2670	.1977	.1373	.0896	.0548	.0312
	2	.0515	.1488	.2376	.2936	.3115	.2965	.2587	.2090	.1569	.1094
	3	.0054	.0331	.0839	.1468	.2076	.2541	.2786	.2787	.2568	.2188
	4	.0004	.0046	.0185	.0459	.0865	.1361	.1875	.2322	.2627	.2734
	5	.0000	.0004	.0026	.0092	.0231	.0467	.0808	.1239	.1719	.2188
	6	.0000	.0000	.0002	.0011	.0038	.0100	.0217	.0413	.0703	.1094
	7	.0000	.0000	.0000	.0001	.0004	.0012	.0033	.0079	.0164	.0312
	8	.0000	.0000	.0000	.0000	.0000	.0001	.0002	.0007	.0017	.0039

Source: R. S. Burington and D. C. May, *Handbook of Probability and Statistics with Tables*, 2d ed., McGraw-Hill, New York, 1970, pp. 347–50. Reprinted with permission.

n	x	.05	.10	.15	.20	.25	.30	.35	.40	.45	.50
9	0	.6302	.3874	.2316	.1342	.0751	.0404	.0207	.0101	.0046	.0020
	1	.2985	.3874	.3679	.3020	.2253	.1556	.1004	.0605	.0339	.0176
	2	.0629	.1722	.2597	.3020	.3003	.2668	.2162	.1612	.1110	.0703
	3	.0077	.0446	.1069	.1762	.2336	.2668	.2716	.2508	.2119	.1641
	4	.0006	.0074	.0283	.0661	.1168	.1715	.2194	.2508	.2600	.2461
	5	.0000	.0008	.0050	.0165	.0389	.0735	.1181	.1672	.2128	.2461
	6	.0000	.0001	.0006	.0028	.0087	.0210	.0424	.0743	.1160	.1641
	7	.0000	.0000	.0000	.0003	.0012	.0039	.0098	.0212	.0407	.0703
	8	.0000	.0000	.0000	.0000	.0001	.0004	.0013	.0035	.0083	.0176
	9	.0000	.0000	.0000	.0000	.0000	.0000	.0001	.0003	.0008	.0020
10	0	.5987	.3487	.1969	.1074	.0563	.0282	.0135	.0060	.0025	.0010
	1	.3151	.3874	.3474	.2684	.1877	.1211	.0725	.0403	.0207	.0098
	2	.0746	.1937	.2759	.3020	.2816	.2335	.1757	.1209	.0763	.0439
	3	.0105	.0574	.1298	.2013	.2503	.2668	.2522	.2150	.1665	.1172
	4	.0010	.0112	.0401	.0881	.1460	.2001	.2377	.2508	.2384	.2051
	5	.0001	.0015	.0085	.0264	.0584	.1029	.1536	.2007	.2340	.2461
	6	.0000	.0001	.0012	.0055	.0162	.0368	.0689	.1115	.1596	.2051
	7	.0000	.0000	.0001	.0008	.0031	.0090	.0212	.0425	.0746	.1172
	8	.0000	.0000	.0000	.0001	.0004	.0014	.0043	.0106	.0229	.0439
	9	.0000	.0000	.0000	.0000	.0000	.0001	.0005	.0016	.0042	.0098
	10	.0000	.0000	.0000	.0000	.0000	.0000	.0000	.0001	.0003	.0010
11	0	.5688	.3138	.1673	.0859	.0422	.0198	.0088	.0036	.0014	.0005
	1	.3293	.3835	.3248	.2362	.1549	.0932	.0518	.0266	.0125	.0054
	2	.0867	.2131	.2866	.2953	.2581	.1998	.1395	.0887	.0513	.0269
	3	.0137	.0710	.1517	.2215	.2581	.2568	.2254	.1774	.1259	.0806
	4	.0014	.0158	.0536	.1107	.1721	.2201	.2428	.2365	.2060	.1611
	5	.0001	.0025	.0132	.0388	.0803	.1321	.1830	.2207	.2360	.2256
	6	.0000	.0003	.0023	.0097	.0268	.0566	.0985	.1471	.1931	.2256
	7	.0000	.0000	.0003	.0017	.0064	.0173	.0379	.0701	.1128	.1611
	8	.0000	.0000	.0000	.0002	.0011	.0037	.0102	.0234	.0462	.0806
	9	.0000	.0000	.0000	.0000	.0001	.0005	.0018	.0052	.0126	.0269
	10	.0000	.0000	.0000	.0000	.0000	.0000	.0002	.0007	.0021	.0054
	11	.0000	.0000	.0000	.0000	.0000	.0000	.0000	.0000	.0002	.0005
12	0	.5404	.2824	.1422	.0687	.0317	.0138	.0057	.0022	.0008	.0002
	1	.3413	.3766	.3012	.2062	.1267	.0712	.0368	.0174	.0075	.0029
	2	.0988	.2301	.2924	.2835	.2323	.1678	.1088	.0639	.0339	.0161
	3	.0173	.0852	.1720	.2362	.2581	.2397	.1954	.1419	.0923	.0537
	4	.0021	.0213	.0683	.1329	.1936	.2311	.2367	.2128	.1700	.1208
	5	.0002	.0038	.0193	.0532	.1032	.1585	.2039	.2270	.2225	.1934
	6	.0000	.0005	.0040	.0155	.0401	.0792	.1281	.1766	.2124	.2256
	7	.0000	.0000	.0006	.0033	.0115	.0291	.0591	.1009	.1489	.1934
	8	.0000	.0000	.0001	.0005	.0024	.0078	.0199	.0420	.0762	.1208
	9	.0000	.0000	.0000	.0001	.0004	.0015	.0048	.0125	.0277	.0537
	10	.0000	.0000	.0000	.0000	.0000	.0002	.0008	.0025	.0068	.0161
	11	.0000	.0000	.0000	.0000	.0000	.0000	.0001	.0003	.0010	.0029
	12	.0000	.0000	.0000	.0000	.0000	.0000	.0000	.0000	.0001	.0002
13	0	.5133	.2542	.1209	.0550	.0238	.0097	.0037	.0013	.0004	.0001
	1	.3512	.3672	.2774	.1787	.1029	.0540	.0259	.0113	.0045	.0016
	2	.1109	.2448	.2937	.2680	.2059	.1388	.0836	.0453	.0220	.0095
	3	.0214	.0997	.1900	.2457	.2517	.2181	.1651	.1107	.0660	.0349
	4	.0028	.0277	.0838	.1535	.2097	.2337	.2222	.1845	.1350	.0873
	5	.0003	.0055	.0266	.0691	.1258	.1803	.2154	.2214	.1989	.1571
	6	.0000	.0008	.0063	.0230	.0559	.1030	.1546	.1968	.2169	.2095
	7	.0000	.0001	.0011	.0058	.0186	.0442	.0833	.1312	.1775	.2095
	8	.0000	.0000	.0001	.0011	.0047	.0142	.0336	.0656	.1089	.1571
	9	.0000	.0000	.0000	.0001	.0009	.0034	.0101	.0243	.0495	.0873
	10	.0000	.0000	.0000	.0000	.0001	.0006	.0022	.0065	.0162	.0349
	11	.0000	.0000	.0000	.0000	.0000	.0001	.0003	.0012	.0036	.0095
	12	.0000	.0000	.0000	.0000	.0000	.0000	.0000	.0001	.0005	.0016
	13	.0000	.0000	.0000	.0000	.0000	.0000	.0000	.0000	.0000	.0001

TABLE A-1

continued

495

APPENDIX:
STATISTICAL
TABLES

						p					
n	*x*	.05	.10	.15	.20	.25	.30	.35	.40	.45	.50
14	0	.4877	.2288	.1028	.0440	.0178	.0068	.0024	.0008	.0002	.0001
	1	.3593	.3559	.2539	.1539	.0832	.0407	.0181	.0073	.0027	.0009
	2	.1229	.2570	.2912	.2501	.1802	.1134	.0634	.0317	.0141	.0056
	3	.0259	.1142	.2056	.2501	.2402	.1943	.1366	.0845	.0462	.0222
	4	.0037	.0349	.0998	.1720	.2202	.2290	.2022	.1549	.1040	.0611
	5	.0004	.0078	.0352	.0860	.1468	.1963	.2178	.2066	.1701	.1222
	6	.0000	.0013	.0093	.0322	.0734	.1262	.1759	.2066	.2088	.1833
	7	.0000	.0002	.0019	.0092	.0280	.0618	.1082	.1574	.1952	.2095
	8	.0000	.0000	.0003	.0020	.0082	.0232	.0510	.0918	.1398	.1833
	9	.0000	.0000	.0000	.0003	.0018	.0066	.0183	.0408	.0762	.1222
	10	.0000	.0000	.0000	.0000	.0003	.0014	.0049	.0136	.0312	.0611
	11	.0000	.0000	.0000	.0000	.0000	.0002	.0010	.0033	.0093	.0222
	12	.0000	.0000	.0000	.0000	.0000	.0000	.0001	.0005	.0019	.0056
	13	.0000	.0000	.0000	.0000	.0000	.0000	.0000	.0001	.0002	.0009
	14	.0000	.0000	.0000	.0000	.0000	.0000	.0000	.0000	.0000	.0001
15	0	.4633	.2059	.0874	.0352	.0134	.0047	.0016	.0005	.0001	.0000
	1	.3658	.3432	.2312	.1319	.0668	.0305	.0126	.0047	.0016	.0005
	2	.1348	.2669	.2856	.2309	.1559	.0916	.0476	.0219	.0090	.0032
	3	.0307	.1285	.2184	.2501	.2252	.1700	.1110	.0634	.0318	.0139
	4	.0049	.0428	.1156	.1876	.2252	.2186	.1792	.1268	.0780	.0417
	5	.0006	.0105	.0449	.1032	.1651	.2061	.2123	.1859	.1404	.0916
	6	.0000	.0019	.0132	.0430	.0917	.1472	.1906	.2066	.1914	.1527
	7	.0000	.0003	.0030	.0138	.0393	.0811	.1319	.1771	.2013	.1964
	8	.0000	.0000	.0005	.0035	.0131	.0348	.0710	.1181	.1647	.1964
	9	.0000	.0000	.0001	.0007	.0034	.0116	.0298	.0612	.1048	.1527
	10	.0000	.0000	.0000	.0001	.0007	.0030	.0096	.0245	.0515	.0916
	11	.0000	.0000	.0000	.0000	.0001	.0006	.0024	.0074	.0191	.0417
	12	.0000	.0000	.0000	.0000	.0000	.0001	.0004	.0016	.0052	.0139
	13	.0000	.0000	.0000	.0000	.0000	.0000	.0001	.0003	.0010	.0032
	14	.0000	.0000	.0000	.0000	.0000	.0000	.0000	.0000	.0001	.0005
	15	.0000	.0000	.0000	.0000	.0000	.0000	.0000	.0000	.0000	.0000
16	0	.4401	.1853	.0743	.0281	.0100	.0033	.0010	.0003	.0001	.0000
	1	.3706	.3294	.2097	.1126	.0535	.0228	.0087	.0030	.0009	.0002
	2	.1463	.2745	.2775	.2111	.1336	.0732	.0353	.0150	.0056	.0018
	3	.0359	.1423	.2285	.2463	.2079	.1465	.0888	.0468	.0215	.0085
	4	.0061	.0514	.1311	.2001	.2252	.2040	.1553	.1014	.0572	.0278
	5	.0008	.0137	.0555	.1201	.1802	.2099	.2008	.1623	.1123	.0667
	6	.0001	.0028	.0180	.0550	.1101	.1649	.1982	.1983	.1684	.1222
	7	.0000	.0004	.0045	.0197	.0524	.1010	.1524	.1889	.1969	.1746
	8	.0000	.0001	.0009	.0055	.0197	.0487	.0923	.1417	.1812	.1964
	9	.0000	.0000	.0001	.0012	.0058	.0185	.0442	.0840	.1318	.1746
	10	.0000	.0000	.0000	.0002	.0014	.0056	.0167	.0392	.0755	.1222
	11	.0000	.0000	.0000	.0000	.0002	.0013	.0049	.0142	.0337	.0667
	12	.0000	.0000	.0000	.0000	.0000	.0002	.0011	.0040	.0115	.0278
	13	.0000	.0000	.0000	.0000	.0000	.0000	.0002	.0008	.0029	.0085
	14	.0000	.0000	.0000	.0000	.0000	.0000	.0000	.0001	.0005	.0018
	15	.0000	.0000	.0000	.0000	.0000	.0000	.0000	.0000	.0001	.0002
	16	.0000	.0000	.0000	.0000	.0000	.0000	.0000	.0000	.0000	.0000
17	0	.4181	.1668	.0631	.0225	.0075	.0023	.0007	.0002	.0000	.0000
	1	.3741	.3150	.1893	.0957	.0426	.0169	.0060	.0019	.0005	.0001
	2	.1575	.2800	.2673	.1914	.1136	.0581	.0260	.0102	.0035	.0010
	3	.0415	.1556	.2359	.2393	.1893	.1245	.0701	.0341	.0144	.0052
	4	.0076	.0605	.1457	.2093	.2209	.1868	.1320	.0796	.0411	.0182
	5	.0010	.0175	.0668	.1361	.1914	.2081	.1849	.1379	.0875	.0472
	6	.0001	.0039	.0236	.0680	.1276	.1784	.1991	.1839	.1432	.0944
	7	.0000	.0007	.0065	.0267	.0668	.1201	.1685	.1927	.1841	.1484
	8	.0000	.0001	.0014	.0084	.0279	.0644	.1134	.1606	.1883	.1855
	9	.0000	.0000	.0003	.0021	.0093	.0276	.0611	.1070	.1540	.1855
	10	.0000	.0000	.0000	.0004	.0025	.0095	.0263	.0571	.1008	.1484
	11	.0000	.0000	.0000	.0001	.0005	.0026	.0090	.0242	.0525	.0944
	12	.0000	.0000	.0000	.0000	.0001	.0006	.0024	.0081	.0215	.0472
	13	.0000	.0000	.0000	.0000	.0000	.0001	.0005	.0021	.0068	.0182
	14	.0000	.0000	.0000	.0000	.0000	.0000	.0001	.0004	.0016	.0052

TABLE A-1

concluded

n	x	.05	.10	.15	.20	.25	.30	.35	.40	.45	.50
17	15	.0000	.0000	.0000	.0000	.0000	.0000	.0000	.0001	.0003	.0010
	16	.0000	.0000	.0000	.0000	.0000	.0000	.0000	.0000	.0000	.0001
	17	.0000	.0000	.0000	.0000	.0000	.0000	.0000	.0000	.0000	.0000
18	0	.3972	.1501	.0536	.0180	.0056	.0016	.0004	.0001	.0000	.0000
	1	.3763	.3002	.1704	.0811	.0338	.0126	.0042	.0012	.0003	.0001
	2	.1683	.2835	.2556	.1723	.0958	.0458	.0190	.0069	.0022	.0006
	3	.0473	.1680	.2406	.2297	.1704	.1046	.0547	.0246	.0095	.0031
	4	.0093	.0700	.1592	.2153	.2130	.1681	.1104	.0614	.0291	.0117
	5	.0014	.0218	.0787	.1507	.1988	.2017	.1664	.1146	.0666	.0327
	6	.0002	.0052	.0301	.0816	.1436	.1873	.1941	.1655	.1181	.0708
	7	.0000	.0010	.0091	.0350	.0820	.1376	.1792	.1892	.1657	.1214
	8	.0000	.0002	.0022	.0120	.0376	.0811	.1327	.1734	.1864	.1669
	9	.0000	.0000	.0004	.0033	.0139	.0386	.0794	.1284	.1694	.1855
	10	.0000	.0000	.0001	.0008	.0042	.0149	.0385	.0771	.1248	.1669
	11	.0000	.0000	.0000	.0001	.0010	.0046	.0151	.0374	.0742	.1214
	12	.0000	.0000	.0000	.0000	.0002	.0012	.0047	.0145	.0354	.0708
	13	.0000	.0000	.0000	.0000	.0000	.0002	.0012	.0045	.0134	.0327
	14	.0000	.0000	.0000	.0000	.0000	.0000	.0002	.0011	.0039	.0117
	15	.0000	.0000	.0000	.0000	.0000	.0000	.0000	.0002	.0009	.0031
	16	.0000	.0000	.0000	.0000	.0000	.0000	.0000	.0000	.0001	.0006
	17	.0000	.0000	.0000	.0000	.0000	.0000	.0000	.0000	.0000	.0001
	18	.0000	.0000	.0000	.0000	.0000	.0000	.0000	.0000	.0000	.0000
19	0	.3774	.1351	.0456	.0144	.0042	.0011	.0003	.0001	.0000	.0000
	1	.3774	.2852	.1529	.0685	.0268	.0093	.0029	.0008	.0002	.0000
	2	.1787	.2852	.2428	.1540	.0803	.0358	.0138	.0046	.0013	.0003
	3	.0533	.1796	.2428	.2182	.1517	.0869	.0422	.0175	.0062	.0018
	4	.0112	.0798	.1714	.2182	.2023	.1491	.0909	.0467	.0203	.0074
	5	.0018	.0266	.0907	.1636	.2023	.1916	.1468	.0933	.0497	.0222
	6	.0002	.0069	.0374	.0955	.1574	.1916	.1844	.1451	.0949	.0518
	7	.0000	.0014	.0122	.0443	.0974	.1525	.1844	.1797	.1443	.0961
	8	.0000	.0002	.0032	.0166	.0487	.0981	.1489	.1797	.1771	.1442
	9	.0000	.0000	.0007	.0051	.0198	.0514	.0980	.1464	.1771	.1762
	10	.0000	.0000	.0001	.0013	.0066	.0220	.0528	.0976	.1449	.1762
	11	.0000	.0000	.0000	.0003	.0018	.0077	.0233	.0532	.0970	.1442
	12	.0000	.0000	.0000	.0000	.0004	.0022	.0083	.0237	.0529	.0961
	13	.0000	.0000	.0000	.0000	.0001	.0005	.0024	.0085	.0233	.0518
	14	.0000	.0000	.0000	.0000	.0000	.0001	.0006	.0024	.0082	.0222
	15	.0000	.0000	.0000	.0000	.0000	.0000	.0001	.0005	.0022	.0074
	16	.0000	.0000	.0000	.0000	.0000	.0000	.0000	.0001	.0005	.0018
	17	.0000	.0000	.0000	.0000	.0000	.0000	.0000	.0000	.0001	.0003
	18	.0000	.0000	.0000	.0000	.0000	.0000	.0000	.0000	.0000	.0000
	19	.0000	.0000	.0000	.0000	.0000	.0000	.0000	.0000	.0000	.0000
20	0	.3585	.1216	.0388	.0115	.0032	.0008	.0002	.0000	.0000	.0000
	1	.3774	.2702	.1368	.0576	.0211	.0068	.0020	.0005	.0001	.0000
	2	.1887	.2852	.2293	.1369	.0669	.0278	.0100	.0031	.0008	.0002
	3	.0596	.1901	.2428	.2054	.1339	.0716	.0323	.0123	.0040	.0011
	4	.0133	.0898	.1821	.2182	.1897	.1304	.0738	.0350	.0139	.0046
	5	.0022	.0319	.1028	.1746	.2023	.1789	.1272	.0746	.0365	.0148
	6	.0003	.0089	.0454	.1091	.1686	.1916	.1712	.1244	.0746	.0370
	7	.0000	.0020	.0160	.0545	.1124	.1643	.1844	.1659	.1221	.0739
	8	.0000	.0004	.0046	.0222	.0609	.1144	.1614	.1797	.1623	.1201
	9	.0000	.0001	.0011	.0074	.0271	.0654	.1158	.1597	.1771	.1602
	10	.0000	.0000	.0002	.0020	.0099	.0308	.0686	.1171	.1593	.1762
	11	.0000	.0000	.0000	.0005	.0030	.0120	.0336	.0710	.1185	.1602
	12	.0000	.0000	.0000	.0001	.0008	.0039	.0136	.0355	.0727	.1201
	13	.0000	.0000	.0000	.0000	.0002	.0010	.0045	.0146	.0366	.0739
	14	.0000	.0000	.0000	.0000	.0000	.0002	.0012	.0049	.0150	.0370
	15	.0000	.0000	.0000	.0000	.0000	.0000	.0003	.0013	.0049	.0148
	16	.0000	.0000	.0000	.0000	.0000	.0000	.0000	.0003	.0013	.0046
	17	.0000	.0000	.0000	.0000	.0000	.0000	.0000	.0000	.0002	.0011
	18	.0000	.0000	.0000	.0000	.0000	.0000	.0000	.0000	.0000	.0002
	19	.0000	.0000	.0000	.0000	.0000	.0000	.0000	.0000	.0000	.0000
	20	.0000	.0000	.0000	.0000	.0000	.0000	.0000	.0000	.0000	.0000

TABLE A-2

SELECTED VALUES OF THE POISSON PROBABILITY DISTRIBUTION

$$P(X) = \frac{\mu^x e^{-\mu}}{x!}$$

How to use: If $\mu = 4$, $x = 3$ look across the top column for μ value, then down the side column for x value. $p(3) = .1954$.

x	0.1	0.2	0.3	0.4	0.5	0.6	0.7	0.8	0.9	1.0
0	.9048	.8187	.7408	.6703	.6065	.5488	.4966	.4493	.4066	.3679
1	.0905	.1637	.2222	.2681	.3033	.3293	.3476	.3595	.3659	.3679
2	.0045	.0164	.0333	.0536	.0758	.0988	.1217	.1438	.1647	.1839
3	.0002	.0011	.0033	.0072	.0126	.0198	.0284	.0383	.0494	.0613
4	.0000	.0001	.0002	.0007	.0016	.0030	.0050	.0077	.0111	.0153
5	.0000	.0000	.0000	.0001	.0002	.0004	.0007	.0012	.0020	.0031
6	.0000	.0000	.0000	.0000	.0000	.0000	.0001	.0002	.0003	.0005
7	.0000	.0000	.0000	.0000	.0000	.0000	.0000	.0000	.0000	.0001

x	1.1	1.2	1.3	1.4	1.5	1.6	1.7	1.8	1.9	2.0
0	.3329	.3012	.2725	.2466	.2231	.2019	.1827	.1653	.1496	.1353
1	.3662	.3614	.3543	.3452	.3347	.3230	.3106	.2975	.2842	.2707
2	.2014	.2169	.2303	.2417	.2510	.2584	.2640	.2678	.2700	.2707
3	.0738	.0867	.0998	.1128	.1255	.1378	.1496	.1607	.1710	.1804
4	.0203	.0260	.0324	.0395	.0471	.0551	.0636	.0723	.0812	.0902
5	.0045	.0062	.0084	.0111	.0141	.0176	.0216	.0260	.0309	.0361
6	.0008	.0012	.0018	.0026	.0035	.0047	.0061	.0078	.0098	.0120
7	.0001	.0002	.0003	.0005	.0008	.0011	.0015	.0020	.0027	.0034
8	.0000	.0000	.0001	.0001	.0001	.0002	.0003	.0005	.0006	.0009
9	.0000	.0000	.0000	.0000	.0000	.0000	.0001	.0001	.0001	.0002

x	2.1	2.2	2.3	2.4	2.5	2.6	2.7	2.8	2.9	3.0
0	.1225	.1108	.1003	.0907	.0821	.0743	.0672	.0608	.0550	.0498
1	.2572	.2438	.2306	.2177	.2052	.1931	.1815	.1703	.1596	.1494
2	.2700	.2681	.2652	.2613	.2565	.2510	.2450	.2384	.2314	.2240
3	.1890	.1966	.2033	.2090	.2138	.2176	.2205	.2225	.2237	.2240
4	.0992	.1082	.1169	.1254	.1336	.1414	.1488	.1557	.1622	.1680
5	.0417	.0476	.0538	.0602	.0668	.0735	.0804	.0872	.0940	.1008
6	.0146	.0174	.0206	.0241	.0278	.0319	.0362	.0407	.0455	.0504
7	.0044	.0055	.0068	.0083	.0099	.0118	.0139	.0163	.0188	.0216
8	.0011	.0015	.0019	.0025	.0031	.0038	.0047	.0057	.0068	.0081
9	.0003	.0004	.0005	.0007	.0009	.0011	.0014	.0018	.0022	.0027
10	.0001	.0001	.0001	.0002	.0002	.0003	.0004	.0005	.0006	.0008
11	.0000	.0000	.0000	.0000	.0000	.0001	.0001	.0001	.0002	.0002
12	.0000	.0000	.0000	.0000	.0000	.0000	.0000	.0000	.0000	.0001

x	3.1	3.2	3.3	3.4	3.5	3.6	3.7	3.8	3.9	4.0
0	.0450	.0408	.0369	.0334	.0302	.0273	.0247	.0224	.0202	.0183
1	.1397	.1304	.1217	.1135	.1057	.0984	.0915	.0850	.0789	.0733
2	.2165	.2087	.2008	.1929	.1850	.1771	.1692	.1615	.1539	.1465
3	.2237	.2226	.2209	.2186	.2158	.2125	.2087	.2046	.2001	.1954
4	.1734	.1781	.1823	.1858	.1888	.1912	.1931	.1944	.1951	.1954
5	.1075	.1140	.1203	.1264	.1322	.1377	.1429	.1477	.1522	.1563
6	.0555	.0608	.0662	.0716	.0771	.0826	.0881	.0936	.0989	.1042
7	.0246	.0278	.0312	.0348	.0385	.0425	.0466	.0508	.0551	.0595
8	.0095	.0111	.0129	.0148	.0169	.0191	.0215	.0241	.0269	.0298
9	.0033	.0040	.0047	.0056	.0066	.0076	.0089	.0102	.0116	.0132
10	.0010	.0013	.0016	.0019	.0023	.0028	.0033	.0039	.0045	.0053
11	.0003	.0004	.0005	.0006	.0007	.0009	.0011	.0013	.0016	.0019
12	.0001	.0001	.0001	.0002	.0002	.0003	.0003	.0004	.0005	.0006
13	.0000	.0000	.0000	.0000	.0001	.0001	.0001	.0001	.0002	.0002
14	.0000	.0000	.0000	.0000	.0000	.0000	.0000	.0000	.0000	.0001

Source: R. S. Burington and D. C. May, *Handbook of Probability and Statistics with Tables,* 2d ed., McGraw-Hill, New York, 1970, pp. 359–362. Reprinted with permission.

continued

x	μ 4.1	4.2	4.3	4.4	4.5	4.6	4.7	4.8	4.9	5.0
0	.0166	.0150	.0136	.0123	.0111	.0101	.0091	.0082	.0074	.0067
1	.0679	.0630	.0583	.0540	.0500	.0462	.0427	.0395	.0365	.0337
2	.1393	.1323	.1254	.1188	.1125	.1063	.1005	.0948	.0894	.0842
3	.1904	.1852	.1798	.1743	.1687	.1631	.1574	.1517	.1460	.1404
4	.1951	.1944	.1933	.1917	.1898	.1875	.1849	.1820	.1789	.1755
5	.1600	.1633	.1662	.1687	.1708	.1725	.1738	.1747	.1753	.1755
6	.1093	.1143	.1191	.1237	.1281	.1323	.1362	.1398	.1432	.1462
7	.0640	.0686	.0732	.0778	.0824	.0869	.0914	.0959	.1002	.1044
8	.0328	.0360	.0393	.0428	.0463	.0500	.0537	.0575	.0614	.0653
9	.0150	.0168	.0188	.0209	.0232	.0255	.0280	.0307	.0334	.0363
10	.0061	.0071	.0081	.0092	.0104	.0118	.0132	.0147	.0164	.0181
11	.0023	.0027	.0032	.0037	.0043	.0049	.0056	.0064	.0073	.0082
12	.0008	.0009	.0011	.0014	.0016	.0019	.0022	.0026	.0030	.0034
13	.0002	.0003	.0004	.0005	.0006	.0007	.0008	.0009	.0011	.0013
14	.0001	.0001	.0001	.0001	.0002	.0002	.0003	.0003	.0004	.0005
15	.0000	.0000	.0000	.0000	.0001	.0001	.0001	.0001	.0001	.0002

x	μ 5.1	5.2	5.3	5.4	5.5	5.6	5.7	5.8	5.9	6.0
0	.0061	.0055	.0050	.0045	.0041	.0037	.0033	.0030	.0027	.0025
1	.0311	.0287	.0265	.0244	.0225	.0207	.0191	.0176	.0162	.0149
2	.0793	.0746	.0701	.0659	.0618	.0580	.0544	.0509	.0477	.0446
3	.1348	.1293	.1239	.1185	.1133	.1082	.1033	.0985	.0938	.0892
4	.1719	.1681	.1641	.1600	.1558	.1515	.1472	.1428	.1383	.1339
5	.1753	.1748	.1740	.1728	.1714	.1697	.1678	.1656	.1632	.1606
6	.1490	.1515	.1537	.1555	.1571	.1584	.1594	.1601	.1605	.1606
7	.1086	.1125	.1163	.1200	.1234	.1267	.1298	.1326	.1353	.1377
8	.0692	.0731	.0771	.0810	.0849	.0887	.0925	.0962	.0998	.1033
9	.0392	.0423	.0454	.0486	.0519	.0552	.0586	.0620	.0654	.0688
10	.0200	.0220	.0241	.0262	.0285	.0309	.0334	.0359	.0386	.0413
11	.0093	.0104	.0116	.0129	.0143	.0157	.0173	.0190	.0207	.0225
12	.0039	.0045	.0051	.0058	.0065	.0073	.0082	.0092	.0102	.0113
13	.0015	.0018	.0021	.0024	.0028	.0032	.0036	.0041	.0046	.0052
14	.0006	.0007	.0008	.0009	.0011	.0013	.0015	.0017	.0019	.0022
15	.0002	.0002	.0003	.0003	.0004	.0005	.0006	.0007	.0008	.0009
16	.0001	.0001	.0001	.0001	.0001	.0002	.0002	.0002	.0003	.0003
17	.0000	.0000	.0000	.0000	.0000	.0001	.0001	.0001	.0001	.0001

x	μ 6.1	6.2	6.3	6.4	6.5	6.6	6.7	6 8	6.9	7.0
0	.0022	.0020	.0018	.0017	.0015	.0014	.0012	.0011	.0010	.0009
1	.0137	.0126	.0116	.0106	.0098	.0090	.0082	.0076	.0070	.0064
2	.0417	.0390	.0364	.0340	.0318	.0296	.0276	.0258	.0240	.0223
3	.0848	.0806	.0765	.0726	.0688	.0652	.0617	.0584	.0552	.0521
4	.1294	.1249	.1205	.1162	.1118	.1076	.1034	.0992	.0952	.0912
5	.1579	.1549	.1519	.1487	.1454	.1420	.1385	.1349	.1314	.1277
6	.1605	.1601	.1595	.1586	.1575	.1562	.1546	.1529	.1511	.1490
7	.1399	.1418	.1435	.1450	.1462	.1472	.1480	.1486	.1489	.1490
8	.1066	.1099	.1130	.1160	.1188	.1215	.1240	.1263	.1284	.1304
9	.0723	.0757	.0791	.0825	.0858	.0891	.0923	.0954	.0985	.1014
10	.0441	.0469	.0498	.0528	.0558	.0588	.0618	.0649	.0679	.0710
11	.0245	.0265	.0285	.0307	.0330	.0353	.0377	.0401	.0426	.0452
12	.0124	.0137	.0150	.0164	.0179	.0194	.0210	.0227	.0245	.0264
13	.0058	.0065	.0073	.0081	.0089	.0098	.0108	.0119	.0130	.0142
14	.0025	.0029	.0033	.0037	.0041	.0046	.0052	.0058	.0064	.0071
15	.0010	.0012	.0014	.0016	.0018	.0020	.0023	.0026	.0029	.0033
16	.0004	.0005	.0005	.0006	.0007	.0008	.0010	.0011	.0013	.0014
17	.0001	.0002	.0002	.0002	.0003	.0003	.0004	.0004	.0005	.0006
18	.0000	.0001	.0001	.0001	.0001	.0001	.0001	.0002	.0002	.0002
19	.0000	.0000	.0000	.0000	.0000	.0000	.0000	.0001	.0001	.0001

continued

x	7.1	7.2	7.3	7.4	7.5	7.6	7.7	7.8	7.9	8.0
0	.0008	.0007	.0007	.0006	.0006	.0005	.0005	.0004	.0004	.0003
1	.0059	.0054	.0049	.0045	.0041	.0038	.0035	.0032	.0029	.0027
2	.0208	.0194	.0180	.0167	.0156	.0145	.0134	.0125	.0116	.0107
3	.0492	.0464	.0438	.0413	.0389	.0366	.0345	.0324	.0305	.0286
4	.0874	.0836	.0799	.0764	.0729	.0696	.0663	.0632	.0602	.0573
5	.1241	.1204	.1167	.1130	.1094	.1057	.1021	.0986	.0951	.0916
6	.1468	.1445	.1420	.1394	.1367	.1339	.1311	.1282	.1252	.1221
7	.1489	.1486	.1481	.1474	.1465	.1454	.1442	.1428	.1413	.1396
8	.1321	.1337	.1351	.1363	.1373	.1382	.1388	.1392	.1395	.1396
9	.1042	.1070	.1096	.1121	.1144	.1167	.1187	.1207	.1224	.1241
10	.0740	.0770	.0800	.0829	.0858	.0887	.0914	.0941	.0967	.0993
11	.0478	.0504	.0531	.0558	.0585	.0613	.0640	.0667	.0695	.0722
12	.0283	.0303	.0323	.0344	.0366	.0388	.0411	.0434	.0457	.0481
13	.0154	.0168	.0181	.0196	.0211	.0227	.0243	.0260	.0278	.0296
14	.0078	.0086	.0095	.0104	.0113	.0123	.0134	.0145	.0157	.0169
15	.0037	.0041	.0046	.0051	.0057	.0062	.0069	.0075	.0083	.0090
16	.0016	.0019	.0021	.0024	.0026	.0030	.0033	.0037	.0041	.0045
17	.0007	.0008	.0009	.0010	.0012	.0013	.0015	.0017	.0019	.0021
18	.0003	.0003	.0004	.0004	.0005	.0006	.0006	.0007	.0008	.0009
19	.0001	.0001	.0001	.0002	.0002	.0002	.0003	.0003	.0003	.0004
20	.0000	.0000	.0001	.0001	.0001	.0001	.0001	.0001	.0001	.0002
21	.0000	.0000	.0000	.0000	.0000	.0000	.0000	.0000	.0001	.0001

μ

x	8.1	8.2	8.3	8.4	8.5	8.6	8.7	8.8	8.9	9.0
0	.0003	.0003	.0002	.0002	.0002	.0002	.0002	.0002	.0001	.0001
1	.0025	.0023	.0021	.0019	.0017	.0016	.0014	.0013	.0012	.0011
2	.0100	.0092	.0086	.0079	.0074	.0068	.0063	.0058	.0054	.0050
3	.0269	.0252	.0237	.0222	.0208	.0195	.0183	.0171	.0160	.0150
4	.0544	.0517	.0491	.0466	.0443	.0420	.0398	.0377	.0357	.0337
5	.0882	.0849	.0816	.0784	.0752	.0722	.0692	.0663	.0635	.0607
6	.1191	.1160	.1128	.1097	.1066	.1034	.1003	.0972	.0941	.0911
7	.1378	.1358	.1338	.1317	.1294	.1271	.1247	.1222	.1197	.1171
8	.1395	.1392	.1388	.1382	.1375	.1366	.1356	.1344	.1332	.1318
9	.1256	.1269	.1280	.1290	.1299	.1306	.1311	.1315	.1317	.1318
10	.1017	.1040	.1063	.1084	.1104	.1123	.1140	.1157	.1172	.1186
11	.0749	.0776	.0802	.0828	.0853	.0878	.0902	.0925	.0948	.0970
12	.0505	.0530	.0555	.0579	.0604	.0629	.0654	.0679	.0703	.0728
13	.0315	.0334	.0354	.0374	.0395	.0416	.0438	.0459	.0481	.0504
14	.0182	.0196	.0210	.0225	.0240	.0256	.0272	.0289	.0306	.0324
15	.0098	.0107	.0116	.0126	.0136	.0147	.0158	.0169	.0182	.0194
16	.0050	.0055	.0060	.0066	.0072	.0079	.0086	.0093	.0101	.0109
17	.0024	.0026	.0029	.0033	.0036	.0040	.0044	.0048	.0053	.0058
18	.0011	.0012	.0014	.0015	.0017	.0019	.0021	.0024	.0026	.0029
19	.0005	.0005	.0006	.0007	.0008	.0009	.0010	.0011	.0012	.0014
20	.0002	.0002	.0002	.0003	.0003	.0004	.0004	.0005	.0005	.0006
21	.0001	.0001	.0001	.0001	.0001	.0002	.0002	.0002	.0002	.0003
22	.0000	.0000	.0000	.0000	.0001	.0001	.0001	.0001	.0001	.0001

μ

x	9.1	9.2	9.3	9.4	9.5	9.6	9.7	9.8	9.9	10
0	.0001	.0001	.0001	.0001	.0001	.0001	.0001	.0001	.0001	.0000
1	.0010	.0009	.0009	.0008	.0007	.0007	.0006	.0005	.0005	.0005
2	.0046	.0043	.0040	.0037	.0034	.0031	.0029	.0027	.0025	.0023
3	.0140	.0131	.0123	.0115	.0107	.0100	.0093	.0087	.0081	.0076
4	.0319	.0302	.0285	.0269	.0254	.0240	.0226	.0213	.0201	.0189
5	.0581	.0555	.0530	.0506	.0483	.0460	.0439	.0418	.0398	.0378
6	.0881	.0851	.0822	.0793	.0764	.0736	.0709	.0682	.0656	.0631
7	.1145	.1118	.1091	.1064	.1037	.1010	.0982	.0955	.0928	.0901
8	.1302	.1286	.1269	.1251	.1232	.1212	.1191	.1170	.1148	.1126
9	.1317	.1315	.1311	.1306	.1300	.1293	.1284	.1274	.1263	.1251

concluded

x	9.1	9.2	9.3	9.4	9.5 μ	9.6	9.7	9.8	9.9	10
10	.1198	.1210	.1219	.1228	.1235	.1241	.1245	.1249	.1250	.1251
11	.0991	.1012	.1031	.1049	.1067	.1083	.1098	.1112	.1125	.1137
12	.0752	.0776	.0799	.0822	.0844	.0866	.0888	.0908	.0928	.0948
13	.0526	.0549	.0572	.0594	.0617	.0640	.0662	.0685	.0707	.0729
14	.0342	.0361	.0380	.0399	.0419	.0439	.0459	.0479	.0500	.0521
15	.0208	.0221	.0235	.0250	.0265	.0281	.0297	.0313	.0330	.0347
16	.0118	.0127	.0137	.0147	.0157	.0168	.0180	.0192	.0204	.0217
17	.0063	.0069	.0075	.0081	.0088	.0095	.0103	.0111	.0119	.0128
18	.0032	.0035	.0039	.0042	.0046	.0051	.0055	.0060	.0065	.0071
19	.0015	.0017	.0019	.0021	.0023	.0026	.0028	.0031	.0034	.0037
20	.0007	.0008	.0009	.0010	.0011	.0012	.0014	.0015	.0017	.0019
21	.0003	.0003	.0004	.0004	.0005	.0006	.0006	.0007	.0008	.0009
22	.0001	.0001	.0002	.0002	.0002	.0002	.0003	.0003	.0004	.0004
23	.0000	.0001	.0001	.0001	.0001	.0001	.0001	.0001	.0002	.0002
24	.0000	.0000	.0000	.0000	.0000	.0000	.0000	.0001	.0001	.0001

x	11	12	13	14	15 μ	16	17	18	19	20
0	.0000	.0000	.0000	.0000	.0000	.0000	.0000	.0000	.0000	.0000
1	.0002	.0001	.0000	.0000	.0000	.0000	.0000	.0000	.0000	.0000
2	.0010	.0004	.0002	.0001	.0000	.0000	.0000	.0000	.0000	.0000
3	.0037	.0018	.0008	.0004	.0002	.0001	.0000	.0000	.0000	.0000
4	.0102	.0053	.0027	.0013	.0006	.0003	.0001	.0001	.0000	.0000
5	.0224	.0127	.0070	.0037	.0019	.0010	.0005	.0002	.0001	.0001
6	.0411	.0255	.0152	.0087	.0048	.0026	.0014	.0007	.0004	.0002
7	.0646	.0437	.0281	.0174	.0104	.0060	.0034	.0018	.0010	.0005
8	.0888	.0655	.0457	.0304	.0194	.0120	.0072	.0042	.0024	.0013
9	.1085	.0874	.0661	.0473	.0324	.0213	.0135	.0083	.0050	.0029
10	.1194	.1048	.0859	.0663	.0486	.0341	.0230	.0150	.0095	.0058
11	.1194	.1144	.1015	.0844	.0663	.0496	.0355	.0245	.0164	.0106
12	.1094	.1144	.1099	.0984	.0829	.0661	.0504	.0368	.0259	.0176
13	.0926	.1056	.1099	.1060	.0956	.0814	.0658	.0509	.0378	.0271
14	.0728	.0905	.1021	.1060	.1024	.0930	.0800	.0655	.0514	.0387
15	.0534	.0724	.0885	.0989	.1024	.0992	.0906	.0786	.0650	.0516
16	.0367	.0543	.0719	.0866	.0960	.0992	.0963	.0884	.0772	.0646
17	.0237	.0383	.0550	.0713	.0847	.0934	.0963	.0936	.0863	.0760
18	.0145	.0256	.0397	.0554	.0706	.0830	.0909	.0936	.0911	.0844
19	.0084	.0161	.0272	.0409	.0557	.0699	.0814	.0887	.0911	.0888
20	.0046	.0097	.0177	.0286	.0418	.0559	.0692	.0798	.0866	.0888
21	.0024	.0055	.0109	.0191	.0299	.0426	.0560	.0684	.0783	.0846
22	.0012	.0030	.0065	.0121	.0204	.0310	.0433	.0560	.0676	.0769
23	.0006	.0016	.0037	.0074	.0133	.0216	.0320	.0438	.0559	.0669
24	.0003	.0008	.0020	.0043	.0083	.0144	.0226	.0328	.0442	.0557
25	.0001	.0004	.0010	.0024	.0050	.0092	.0154	.0237	.0336	.0446
26	.0000	.0002	.0005	.0013	.0029	.0057	.0101	.0164	.0246	.0343
27	.0000	.0001	.0002	.0007	.0016	.0034	.0063	.0109	.0173	.0254
28	.0000	.0000	.0001	.0003	.0009	.0019	.0038	.0070	.0117	.0181
29	.0000	.0000	.0001	.0002	.0004	.0011	.0023	.0044	.0077	.0125
30	.0000	.0000	.0000	.0001	.0002	.0006	.0013	.0026	.0049	.0083
31	.0000	.0000	.0000	.0000	.0001	.0003	.0007	.0015	.0030	.0054
32	.0000	.0000	.0000	.0000	.0001	.0001	.0004	.0009	.0018	.0034
33	.0000	.0000	.0000	.0000	.0000	.0001	.0002	.0005	.0010	.0020
34	.0000	.0000	.0000	.0000	.0000	.0000	.0001	.0002	.0006	.0012
35	.0000	.0000	.0000	.0000	.0000	.0000	.0000	.0001	.0003	.0007
36	.0000	.0000	.0000	.0000	.0000	.0000	.0000	.0001	.0002	.0004
37	.0000	.0000	.0000	.0000	.0000	.0000	.0000	.0000	.0001	.0002
38	.0000	.0000	.0000	.0000	.0000	.0000	.0000	.0000	.0000	.0001
39	.0000	.0000	.0000	.0000	.0000	.0000	.0000	.0000	.0000	.0001

AREAS UNDER THE NORMAL CURVE BETWEEN THE MEAN AND VARIOUS Z-SCORES

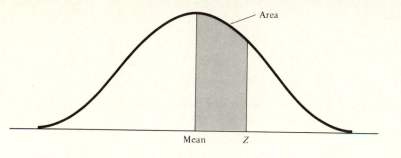

Z	.00	.01	.02	.03	.04	.05	.06	.07	.08	.09
.0	.0000	.0004	.0080	.0120	.0160	.0199	.0239	.0279	.0319	.0359
.1	.0398	.0438	.0478	.0517	.0557	.0596	.0636	.0675	.0714	.0753
.2	.0793	.0832	.0871	.0910	.0948	.0987	.1026	.1064	.1103	.1141
.3	.1179	.1217	.1255	.1293	.1331	.1368	.1406	.1443	.1480	.1517
.4	.1554	.1591	.1628	.1664	.1700	.1736	.1772	.1808	.1844	.1879
.5	.1915	.1950	.1985	.2019	.2054	.2088	.2123	.2157	.2190	.2224
.6	.2257	.2291	.2324	.2357	.2389	.2422	.2454	.2486	.2517	.2549
.7	.2580	.2611	.2642	.2673	.2704	.2734	.2764	.2794	.2823	.2852
.8	.2881	.2910	.2939	.2967	.2995	.3023	.3051	.3078	.3106	.3133
.9	.3159	.3186	.3212	.3238	.3264	.3289	.3315	.3340	.3365	.3389
1.0	.3413	.3438	.3461	.3485	.3508	.3531	.3554	.3577	.3599	.3621
1.1	.3643	.3665	.3686	.3708	.3729	.3749	.3770	.3790	.3810	.3830
1.2	.3849	.3869	.3888	.3907	.3925	.3944	.3962	.3980	.3997	.4015
1.3	.4032	.4049	.4066	.4082	.4099	.4115	.4131	.4147	.4162	.4177
1.4	.4192	.4207	.4222	.4236	.4251	.4265	.4279	.4292	.4306	.4319
1.5	.4332	.4345	.4357	.4370	.4382	.4394	.4406	.4418	.4429	.4441
1.6	.4452	.4463	.4474	.4484	.4495	.4505	.4515	.4525	.4535	.4545
1.7	.4554	.4564	.4573	.4582	.4591	.4599	.4608	.4616	.4625	.4633
1.8	.4641	.4649	.4656	.4664	.4671	.4678	.4686	.4693	.4699	.4706
1.9	.4713	.4719	.4726	.4732	.4738	.4744	.4750	.4756	.4761	.4767
2.0	.4772	.4778	.4783	.4788	.4793	.4798	.4803	.4808	.4812	.4817
2.1	.4821	.4826	.4830	.4834	.4838	.4842	.4846	.4850	.4854	.4857
2.2	.4861	.4864	.4868	.4871	.4875	.4878	.4881	.4884	.4887	.4890
2.3	.4893	.4896	.4898	.4901	.4904	.4906	.4909	.4911	.4913	.4916
2.4	.4918	.4920	.4922	.4924	.4927	.4929	.4930	.4932	.4934	.4936
2.5	.4938	.4940	.4941	.4943	.4945	.4946	.4948	.4949	.4951	.4952
2.6	.4953	.4955	.4956	.4957	.4958	.4960	.4961	.4962	.4963	.4964
2.7	.4965	.4966	.4967	.4968	.4969	.4970	.4971	.4972	.4973	.4974
2.8	.4974	.4975	.4976	.4977	.4977	.4978	.4979	.4979	.4980	.4981
2.9	.4981	.4982	.4982	.4983	.4984	.4984	.4985	.4985	.4986	.4986
3.0	.4987	.4987	.4987	.4988	.4988	.4989	.4989	.4989	.4990	.4990

Source: D. G. Dannenbring and M. K. Starr, *Management Science: An Introduction,* McGraw-Hill: New York, 1981, p. 582. Reprinted with permission.

TABLE A-4

CRITICAL VALUES OF STUDENT'S-t DISTRIBUTION

df is the parameter (degrees of freedom); P is the probability that t exceeds the critical value k.

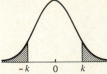

How to use: If you have 12 degrees of freedom and are interested in 95% confidence interval, you will need a t value of 2.179 to have an area of .05 in both tails of the curve combined.

df \ P	0.1	0.05	0.02	0.01	0.001
1	6.314	12.706	31.821	63.657	636.619
2	2.920	4.303	6.965	9.925	31.599
3	2.353	3.182	4.541	5.841	12.924
4	2.132	2.777	3.747	4.604	8.610
5	2.015	2.571	3.365	4.032	6.869
6	1.943	2.447	3.143	3.708	5.959
7	1.895	2.365	2.998	3.500	5.408
8	1.860	2.306	2.896	3.355	5.041
9	1.833	2.262	2.821	3.250	4.781
10	1.812	2.228	2.764	3.169	4.587
11	1.796	2.201	2.718	3.106	4.437
12	1.782	2.179	2.681	3.055	4.318
13	1.771	2.160	2.650	3.012	4.221
14	1.761	2.145	2.624	2.977	4.140
15	1.753	2.131	2.602	2.947	4.073
16	1.746	2.120	2.583	2.921	4.015
17	1.740	2.110	2.567	2.898	3.965
18	1.734	2.101	2.552	2.878	3.922
19	1.729	2.093	2.539	2.861	3.883
20	1.725	2.086	2.528	2.845	3.850
21	1.721	2.080	2.510	2.831	3.819
22	1.717	2.074	2.508	2.819	3.792
23	1.714	2.069	2.500	2.807	3.768
24	1.711	2.064	2.492	2.797	3.745
25	1.708	2.060	2.485	2.787	3.725
26	1.706	2.056	2.479	2.779	3.707
27	1.703	2.052	2.473	2.771	3.690
28	1.701	2.048	2.467	2.763	3.674
29	1.699	2.045	2.462	2.756	3.659
30	1.697	2.042	2.457	2.750	3.646
31	1.696	2.040	2.453	2.744	3.633
32	1.694	2.037	2.449	2.738	3.622
33	1.692	2.035	2.445	2.733	3.611
34	1.691	2.032	2.441	2.728	3.601
35	1.690	2.030	2.438	2.724	3.591
36	1.688	2.028	2.434	2.719	3.582
37	1.687	2.026	2.431	2.715	3.574
38	1.686	2.024	2.429	2.712	3.566
39	1.685	2.023	2.426	2.708	3.558
40	1.684	2.021	2.423	2.704	3.551
Normal Distribution	1.645	1.960	2.326	2.576	3.291

Source: Adapted from a table computed by Dr. Edward L. Spitznagel, Washington University, St. Louis, MO. Reprinted with permission.

TABLE A-5
F DISTRIBUTION

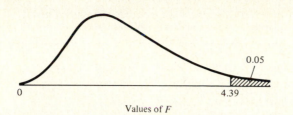

Values of F

How to use: Numbers in boldface represent values to the right of which can be found .01 of the area under the curve. Numbers in light type represent values to the right of which can be found .05 of the area under the curve. df_1, along the top column, represents degress of freedom for the numerator. df_2, going down the side columns, represents degrees of freedom for the denominator.

df_2 \ df_1	1	2	3	4	5	6	7	8	9	10	20	30	40	50	100	200	∞	df_2
1	161	200	216	225	230	234	237	239	241	242	248	250	251	252	253	254	254	1
	4,052	**4,999**	**5,403**	**5,625**	**5,764**	**5,859**	**5,928**	**5,981**	**6,022**	**6,056**	**6,208**	**6,261**	**6,286**	**6,302**	**6,334**	**6,352**	**6,366**	
2	18.51	19.00	19.16	19.25	19.30	19.33	19.36	19.37	19.38	19.39	19.44	19.46	19.47	19.47	19.49	19.49	19.50	2
	98.49	**99.00**	**99.17**	**99.25**	**99.30**	**99.33**	**99.36**	**99.37**	**99.39**	**99.40**	**99.45**	**99.47**	**99.48**	**99.48**	**99.49**	**99.49**	**99.50**	
3	10.13	9.55	9.28	9.12	9.01	8.94	8.88	8.84	8.81	8.78	8.66	8.62	8.60	8.58	8.56	8.54	8.53	3
	34.12	**30.82**	**29.46**	**28.71**	**28.24**	**27.91**	**27.67**	**27.49**	**27.34**	**27.23**	**26.69**	**26.50**	**26.41**	**26.35**	**26.23**	**26.18**	**26.12**	
4	7.71	6.94	6.59	6.39	6.26	6.16	6.09	6.04	6.00	5.96	5.80	5.74	5.71	5.70	5.66	5.65	5.63	4
	21.20	**18.00**	**16.69**	**15.98**	**15.52**	**15.21**	**14.98**	**14.80**	**14.66**	**14.54**	**14.02**	**13.83**	**13.74**	**13.69**	**13.57**	**13.52**	**13.46**	
5	6.61	5.79	5.41	5.19	5.05	4.95	4.88	4.82	4.78	4.74	4.56	4.50	4.46	4.44	4.40	4.38	4.36	5
	16.26	**13.27**	**12.06**	**11.39**	**10.97**	**10.67**	**10.45**	**10.29**	**10.15**	**10.05**	**9.55**	**9.38**	**9.29**	**9.24**	**9.13**	**9.07**	**9.02**	
6	5.99	5.14	4.76	4.53	4.39	4.28	4.21	4.15	4.10	4.06	3.87	3.81	3.77	3.75	3.71	3.69	3.67	6
	13.74	**10.92**	**9.78**	**9.15**	**8.75**	**8.47**	**8.26**	**8.10**	**7.98**	**7.87**	**7.39**	**7.23**	**7.14**	**7.09**	**6.99**	**6.94**	**6.88**	
7	5.59	4.74	4.35	4.12	3.97	3.87	3.79	3.73	3.68	3.63	3.44	3.38	3.34	3.32	3.28	3.25	3.23	7
	12.25	**9.55**	**8.45**	**7.85**	**7.46**	**7.19**	**7.00**	**6.84**	**6.71**	**6.62**	**6.15**	**5.98**	**5.90**	**5.85**	**5.75**	**5.70**	**5.65**	
8	5.32	4.46	4.07	3.84	3.69	3.58	3.50	3.44	3.39	3.34	3.15	3.08	3.05	3.03	2.98	2.96	2.93	8
	11.26	**8.65**	**7.59**	**7.01**	**6.63**	**6.37**	**6.19**	**6.03**	**5.91**	**5.82**	**5.36**	**5.20**	**5.11**	**5.06**	**4.96**	**4.91**	**4.86**	
9	5.12	4.26	3.86	3.63	3.48	3.37	3.29	3.23	3.18	3.13	2.93	2.86	2.82	2.80	2.76	2.73	2.71	9
	10.56	**8.02**	**6.99**	**6.42**	**6.06**	**5.80**	**5.62**	**5.47**	**5.35**	**5.26**	**4.80**	**4.64**	**4.56**	**4.51**	**4.41**	**4.36**	**4.31**	
10	4.96	4.10	3.71	3.48	3.33	3.22	3.14	3.07	3.02	2.97	2.77	2.70	2.67	2.64	2.59	2.56	2.54	10
	10.04	**7.56**	**6.55**	**5.99**	**5.64**	**5.39**	**5.21**	**5.06**	**4.95**	**4.85**	**4.41**	**4.25**	**4.17**	**4.12**	**4.01**	**3.96**	**3.91**	
20	4.35	3.49	3.10	2.87	2.71	2.60	2.52	2.45	2.40	2.35	2.12	2.04	1.99	1.96	1.90	1.87	1.84	20
	8.10	**5.85**	**4.94**	**4.43**	**4.10**	**3.87**	**3.71**	**3.56**	**3.45**	**3.37**	**2.94**	**2.77**	**2.69**	**2.63**	**2.53**	**2.47**	**2.42**	
30	4.17	3.32	2.92	2.69	2.53	2.42	2.34	2.27	2.21	2.16	1.93	1.84	1.79	1.76	1.69	1.66	1.62	30
	7.56	**5.39**	**4.51**	**4.02**	**3.70**	**3.47**	**3.30**	**3.17**	**3.06**	**2.98**	**2.55**	**2.38**	**2.29**	**2.24**	**2.13**	**2.07**	**2.01**	
40	4.08	3.23	2.84	2.61	2.45	2.34	2.25	2.18	2.12	2.07	1.84	1.74	1.69	1.66	1.59	1.55	1.51	40
	7.31	**5.18**	**4.31**	**3.83**	**3.51**	**3.29**	**3.12**	**2.99**	**2.88**	**2.80**	**2.37**	**2.20**	**2.11**	**2.05**	**1.94**	**1.88**	**1.81**	
50	4.03	3.18	2.79	2.56	2.40	2.29	2.20	2.13	2.07	2.02	1.78	1.69	1.63	1.60	1.52	1.48	1.44	50
	7.17	**5.06**	**4.20**	**3.72**	**3.41**	**3.18**	**3.02**	**2.88**	**2.78**	**2.70**	**2.26**	**2.10**	**2.00**	**1.94**	**1.82**	**1.76**	**1.68**	
100	3.94	3.09	2.70	2.46	2.30	2.19	2.10	2.03	1.97	1.92	1.68	1.57	1.51	1.48	1.39	1.34	1.28	100
	6.90	**4.82**	**3.98**	**3.51**	**3.20**	**2.99**	**2.82**	**2.69**	**2.59**	**2.51**	**2.06**	**1.89**	**1.79**	**1.73**	**1.59**	**1.51**	**1.43**	
200	3.89	3.04	2.65	2.41	2.26	2.14	2.05	1.98	1.92	1.87	1.62	1.52	1.45	1.42	1.32	1.26	1.19	200
	6.76	**4.71**	**3.88**	**3.41**	**3.11**	**2.90**	**2.73**	**2.60**	**2.50**	**2.41**	**1.97**	**1.79**	**1.69**	**1.62**	**1.48**	**1.39**	**1.28**	
∞	3.84	2.99	2.60	2.37	2.21	2.09	2.01	1.94	1.88	1.83	1.57	1.46	1.40	1.35	1.24	1.17	1.00	∞
	6.64	**4.60**	**3.78**	**3.32**	**3.02**	**2.80**	**2.64**	**2.51**	**2.41**	**2.32**	**1.87**	**1.69**	**1.59**	**1.52**	**1.36**	**1.25**	**1.00**	

Source: George W. Snedercor and William G. Cochran, *Statistical Methods,* 6th ed., The Iowa State University Press, Ames, Iowa, 1967. Reprinted with permission.

TABLE A-6

SELECTED CRITICAL VALUES OF THE χ^2 DISTRIBUTION

How to use: If $df = 4$ and the α value is .05, look under .05 across the top and at 4 going down the side column. The χ^2 value is 9.488.

v \ P	0.05	0.025	0.01	0.001
1	3.841	5.024	6.635	10.828
2	5.991	7.378	9.210	13.816
3	7.815	9.348	11.345	16.266
4	9.488	11.143	13.277	18.467
5	11.070	12.833	15.086	20.515
6	12.592	14.449	16.812	22.458
7	14.067	16.013	18.475	24.322
8	15.507	17.535	20.090	26.124
9	16.919	19.023	21.666	27.877
10	18.307	20.483	23.209	29.588
11	19.675	21.920	24.725	31.264
12	21.026	23.337	26.217	32.909
13	22.362	24.736	27.688	34.528
14	23.685	26.119	29.141	36.123
15	24.996	27.488	30.578	37.697
16	26.296	28.845	32.000	39.252
17	27.587	30.191	33.409	40.790
18	28.869	31.526	34.805	42.312
19	30.144	32.852	36.191	43.820
20	31.410	34.170	37.566	45.315
21	32.671	35.479	38.932	46.797
22	33.924	36.781	40.289	48.268
23	35.172	38.076	41.638	49.728
24	36.415	39.364	42.980	51.179
25	37.652	40.646	44.314	52.620
26	38.885	41.923	45.642	54.052
27	40.113	43.195	46.963	55.476
28	41.337	44.461	48.278	56.892
29	42.557	45.722	49.580	58.301
30	43.773	46.979	50.892	59.703
31	44.985	48.232	52.191	61.098
32	46.194	49.480	53.486	62.487
33	47.400	50.725	54.776	63.870
34	48.602	51.966	56.061	65.247
35	49.802	53.203	57.342	66.619
36	50.998	54.437	58.619	67.985
37	52.192	55.668	59.893	69.346
38	53.384	56.896	61.162	70.703
39	54.572	58.120	62.428	72.055
40	55.758	59.342	63.691	73.402
41	56.942	60.561	64.950	74.745
42	58.124	61.777	66.206	76.084

Source: Table computed by Dr. Edward L. Spitznagel, Washington University, St. Louis, MO. Reproduced by permission.

INDEXES

NAME INDEX

Allen, R. G. D., 430
Anderson, R. L., 462
Andrews, John E., 147*n*.
Armstrong, Charles P., 146
Aronofsky, J., 462

Banerjee, Kali S., 430
Barabba, Vincent, 449
Barry, Thomas, 234*n*.
Bayes, Thomas, 388
Benson, P. George, 201
Bentson, George J., 311
Bonini, Charles P., 146, 201, 232, 310
Boot, John C., 397
Borg, W. R., 149
Boyd, Harper W., Jr., 311
Brown, Rex V., 397, 398
Burnberg, J. G., 311
Burns, Arthur F., 362
Butler, William F., 12, 331, 368

Cardano, Girolamo, 56
Carli, G. R., 407
Chambers, John C., 329, 368
Chapman, M., 311
Chisholm, Roger K., 368
Cochran, William G., 114, 143*n*., 146
Cohen, J. B., 311
Coman, E. T., 11
Compte, Auguste, 304
Cougar, Daniel J., 462
Cox, Edwin B., 397
Cullison, William E., 422*n*., 430
Curly, M. Louise, 12, 360

Demski, Joel, 311
Dixon, W. J., 461, 462

Dopuch, N., 311

Early, John F., 423*n*. 430
Eby, Frank H., Jr., 311
Ettlie, John E., 311

Falk, Howard, 373
Farley, William B., 92*n*.
Federer, Walter T., 2, 11
Feller, William, 87
Ferber, Robert, 146
Finkelstein, Michael O., 92*n*.
Fisher, R. A., 195
Fortenberry, Jane, 234*n*.
Frame, Robert, 430, 462
Freund, John E., 45, 86, 358

Gall, M. D., 149
Galton, Francis, 284
Gauss, Karl Fredrick, 78
Gilman, J. J., 316, 317*n*.
Gordon, 333
Gosset, 130
Granger, C. W. J., 333*n*., 368
Green, Paul, 232, 397
Greynolds, E., 460
Groblowsky, B. J., 462
Gross, Charles W., 368
Groves, Robert M., 114
Guber, George, 364*n*., 369

Hair, J. F., Jr., 462
Hamburg, Morris, 45, 271, 310, 397
Hansen, Morris, 143*n*., 146
Hay, Robert D., 318*n*.
Hays, William L., 149, 201, 462

Helmer, C., 333
Hespos, Richard F., 397
Huff, Darrel, 45
Hull, C. H., 462
Hunt, Pearson, 6, 11
Hurwitz, William, 146*n.*

Isaac, S., 149
Iverson, Gudmund R., 201

Jedamus, Paul, 430
Johnston, J., 292*n.*, 311
Juster, Thomas, 357*n.*, 360

Kahn, Robert L., 114
Kavesh, Robert A., 12, 331, 368
Kerlinger, F. N., 462
Kim, J. O., 462
King, Amy C., 56*n.*, 86
Kinnear, T. C., 462
Kipnis, Gregory, 430
Kish, Leslie, 143*n.*, 146
Klein, Lawrence, 359
Kleinbaum, David G., 310
Knoblett, James A., 397
Kupper, Lawrence L., 310

LaCava, Jerry J., 179
Laspeyres, E., 411
Lefcourt, H. M., 87*n.*
Leontieff, Wassily, 360
Levin, Richard I., 179, 271
Levinson, Horace C., 86
Likert, Rensis, 256
Lininger, Charles, 146
Linstone, H., 333, 368
Loebbecke, James K., 146

McCarthy, Phillip, 114
McClave, James T., 201
Madow, William, 143*n.*, 146
Makridakis, Spyros, 311, 368
Mason, Robert D., 430
Mayer, Raymond, 311
Maynes, E. Scott, 368
Meadows, Edward, 430
Mendenhall, William, 114, 271, 430
Miller, David W., 397
Miller, R. H., 316, 317*n.*
Mitchell, Wesley, 362
Mitroff, Ivan, 333, 368
Moore, Geoffrey A., 368

Morganthau, Henry, 362
Morton, J. E., 12
Moss, Bennett, 430
Mosteller, Fredrick, 232, 249*n.*
Mueller, C. W., 460
Mullick, Satender K., 329, 368

Neter, John, 86, 146, 201, 310
Neyman, J., 136, 137, 139
Nie, N. H., 460
Norpoth, Helmut, 201
North, Harper Q., 333, 368

O'Brien, J., 12
O'Neill, William J., 311
Opperman, Edward B., 179, 310

Paasche, H., 411
Packard, Karle, 398
Pearson, Karl, 215
Pelletier, P., 462
Pendleton, William, 311
Peters, William S., 146
Peterson, Robin T., 368
Plane, Donald R., 179, 310
Platt, Robert B., 12, 361*n.*, 368
Poisson, Simeon Denis, 75
Potts, Terrell, 234*n.*
Pyke, Donald L., 333, 368

Raiffa, Howard, 397
Rattenbury, J., 462
Read, Cecil B., 56*n.*, 86
Reinmuth, James E., 271, 398, 430
Renshaw, Edward F., 311
Reynolds, F. D., 256*n.*
Richards, Larry E., 179
Robertson, Jack C., 146
Rodriguez, Justine, 331
Roecks, Alan L., 147*n.*
Rothe, James T., 329, 368
Rowke, Robert E. K., 232, 249*n.*
Runyon, Richard, 45

Samuelson, Paul, 363
Schaifer, Robert, 397
Senter, R. J., 232
Shao, Stephen, 430
Sheehy, E. P., 12
Siegel, S., 232, 255*n.*, 257*n.*
Silk, Leonard S., 12, 368
Slonem, Mark, 96*n.*, 114

Smith, Donald D., 268, 329
Sobol, Marion G., 202*n*., 234*n*., 303, 311
Spurr, William A., 146, 201, 232, 310
Starr, Martin K., 311, 333*n*., 368, 397
Stenehjem, Erik J., 311
Stephan, Fredrick F., 114
Strassman, Paul A., 397
Stuart, Alan, 114
Sudman, S., 137*n*., 146
Summers, George W., 146
Swanson, Carl, 202*n*.

Tathom, R. L., 462
Taubman, R., 358
Taylor, J. R., 462
Taylor, Robert, 430
Thieroff, M., 333, 368
Torgerson, Warren S., 232
Trike, Lawrence H., 92*n*.
Triplett, Jack E., 415, 430
Tull, Donald S., 232
Turoff, Murray, 368

Ulvila, J. W., 398

Van Horne, James, 311
Vellenga, David B., 311
Verdoorn, P. J., 146
Von Bortkewitsch, Ladislaus, 77

Wallace, William H., 422*n*., 430
Warwick, Donald, 146
Wasserman, P., 12
Wasserman, William, 86, 201, 310
Weaver, Warren, 77*n*., 86, 220
Wells, William D., 256*n*., 364*n*., 369
Westfall, Ralph, 311
Wheelwright, Steven, 311, 368
Whitaker, Gilbert R., Jr., 368
Whitmore, G. A., 86, 201
Williams, Edward E., 311
Williams, F. J., 86

Yamane, Taro, 146

Zeikel, Arthur, 311
Zinbarg, Edward, 311

SUBJECT INDEX

α (alpha) error, 158
a, normal equations and formulas for, 286–287
a, value of (Y intercept), 284, 308
ABI/INFORM (data base), 7
Absolute deviation of the mean, 27
Absolute values of the deviations, 282
Accept a false hypothesis (*see* Type II errors)
Accuracy of data in sampling, 96, 98
Action learning, 2
Actions, 376, 396
Adjustment factor, 346
Aerospace Industries Association, 6
AFL-CIO, 425
Aggregative index:
    Laspeyres, 411, 428
    Paasche's, 411, 415, 429
Aggregative index numbers, 408
    unweighted, 408–409
    weighted, 411–412
Albert Bell vs. Robert S. Rippy, 115
All Commodities Index, 423
Allocation formula, 136
Allocation of sample, 134–135
Almanacs, 4
Alternative hypothesis, 161, 178
Alternate mean, specific value of the, 162
American Institute of Certified Public
        Accountants, 131
American Iron and Steel Association, 6
American Iron and Steel Institute, 331
American Statistics Index, 4, 5
Amplitude of the cycle, 354
Analysis:
    Bayesian, 392
    discriminant, 441, 442–443
    factor, 441, 443–445
    input-output, 355, 360
    life cycle, 355, 363–368
    linear regression: conditions for using, 292
        limitations of, 310

Analysis (*Cont.*):
    multiple analysis of variance, 441, 445
    multiple regression, 272, 277, 287, 302, 310,
        356, 367, 440
    multivariate, 441–448
    portfolio, 299
    regression (*see* Regression analysis)
    sensitivity, 381–386, 396
Analysis of variance (ANOVA), 178, 182,
        192–197, 200, 230
Area sampling, 101, 118, 141
Arithmetic mean, 20, 334
Array, 22
ASI (data base), 7
Asymptotic in normal distribution, 29, 78
Autocorrelation, 292
Average, 20, 75, 86
    (*See also* Arithmetic mean)
Average deviation, 27
Average personal tax rate (t_p), 358
Average work week, 362

β (beta) coefficient, 299
β (beta) error, 158
b, normal equations and formulas for, 286–287
b, value of (slope), 284, 308
Bank rates, 363
Bar chart (histogram), 16, 43
Base period, choice of, 414
Base-year, shifting the, 429
Base-year weights:
    choice of, 415–416
    Laspeyres' index, 411, 412, 415, 428
Bayesian analysis, 392
Bayesian (inverse) probability, 388–392,
        396–397
Bell-shaped curve, 29, 78
Best-fitting line, 282
Between column variation (V_B), 195

STATISTICS FOR
BUSINESS AND
ECONOMICS

Bimodal distribution, 22
Binomial distribution, 67, 68–74, 86, 217
    discrete, 80
    mean of, 72
    normal distribution, relation to, 79
    Poisson distribution, relation to, 74, 75
    probabilities using, 83
    standard deviation of, 72–73
Binomial probabilities, computation of, 68
Binomial tables, use of, 71–72
Biomedical Computer Programs (BMD or
        BMDP), 439, 440, 444, 452
Book on Games of Chance, 56
Box, 396
Brookings Institution, 5, 357, 368
    econometric model, 357
Building permits, 362
Built-in programs, 459
Bureau of the Census (*see* U.S. Census
        Bureau)
Bureau of Housing and Urban Development
        (*see* U.S. Department of Housing and
        Urban Development)
Bureau of Labor Statistics (*see* U.S. Bureau of
        Labor Statistics)
Business Conditions Digest, 5, 331, 362, 363
Business Cycle Indicators, 354
Business cycles, 342
Business Forecasting, 331
Business Periodicals Index, 6
Business Record, 356
Business Week, 5, 244n., 245, 356

Capitalistic imperialism, 343
Card catalogue, 4, 7
Cardinal scales, 215
Cases, 2, 9–10
Category, 15
Causal factors, 355–366
Causal models, 329, 330
Causality, 8–9
Causation and correlation, 304–305
Census Reports, 4
Census Software Package (CENSPAC), 449
Census tapes:
    1970, 449
    1980, 449
        Public Use Sample (PUS), 448, 449
        Summary Tape Files (STF), 448, 449
Census tracts, 118–122
Central Limit Theorem, 102–105, 108, 113,
        130, 154, 182
Central tendency, 20–22
Centroid, 443
Chaining of link relatives, 416, 429
Chance, correlation due to, 305
Chebycheff's inequality, 37–38, 44, 214

Chi-square curves, 215
Chi-square distribution, 215, 216, 219
Chi-square table, 217
Chi-square test(s):
    of goodness of fit, 215–217, 224–225, 231,
        240, 271
    of independence, 211, 221–222, 224–225,
        231, 240, 271
Choice in index construction:
    of base period, 414
    of base-year weights, 415
    of given-year weights, 415
    of items to include in an index, 414–415
Circles, 396
City and Country Data Book, 331
Civil Rights Act, 115
Civil Service, 418
Class boundaries, 43
Class mark, 24, 43, 72
    (*See also* Midpoint)
Classical (objective) probability, 56, 85
Clustered samples, 113, 141–146
    standard error of, 142, 146
Clustering, 100–101
Clusters, variability between and within, 141
Coefficient of correlation (r), 240, 295, 309
    sampling distribution of, 296
Coefficient of determination (R^2), 293–295, 309
    significance of, 295–297
Coefficient of variation, 38–39, 44
Coefficients:
    direct, 368
    regression (*see* Regression coefficients)
    total, 368
Coincident indicators, 362, 363, 368
Column mean, 197
Combinations, 68
Combined or joint effects of factors 1 and 2,
        447
Commercial Car Journal, 323
Common cause, 304
Comparison of sampling error, 140
Compustat tapes, 448, 450
Computation:
    of binomial probabilities, 68–71
    with index numbers, 420
Computation formulation, 287
Computer printouts, interpretation of, 453–461
Computer Software Statistics Packages, 439
Computer tape, 147
Computerized data bases, 6–7
Computing the mean, 72–73
Conditional mean:
    confidence interval for a, 309
    estimating a, 291
Conditional probabilities, 395
Conditions, 376, 396
Conference Board, 356

Conference Board Record Monthly, 356
Confidence interval(s), 105–107, 108, 113,
    289, 290
  for conditional mean, 309
  finite population correction factor (*cf*) and,
    126–127
  forecast for, 290, 309
  for a proportion, 108–109
  standard deviation not known, 107–108
  width of, 126
Construction, 416
"Consumer Buying Indicators," 356
Consumer life cycle, 364–366
Consumer Price Index (CPI), 7, 406, 407, 414,
    418–420, 421, 428
  for All Urban Consumers (Selected Areas),
    417–419
  for Urban Wage Earners and Clerical
    Workers, 422
Consumer purchase plans for durable goods,
    356
Consumer's risk, 154, 178
Consumers' Union, 356
Consumption expenditures (*C*), 358
Continuity correction, 225, 227
Continuous interval, 241
Continuous normal distribution, 80, 86
Continuous probability distribution, 78, 86
Continuous random variable, 67
Convenience samples, 101, 113
Correction formula, 242*n.*, 254
Correlation and causation, 304–305
Correlation coefficient (*see* Coefficient of
    correlation)
Cost comparison for different sample
    allocations, 140
Cost-of-living index, 407
  (*See also* Consumer Price Index)
Cost of sample survey, 96, 98
Costs, 376, 396
CPI (*see* Consumer Price Index)
Critical value, 160, 161, 177, 183, 219
Cumulative frequency distribution, 16–17
Current Population Reports:
  P-25, 366
  P-65 Series, 356
Current Population Surveys, 141
Curve(s):
  bell-shaped, 29, 78
  exponential, 306
  F distribution, 193*n.*
  normal, 214
    standard deviation of, 79, 86
  ogive, 17, 43
  power, 164–167, 179
Curvilinear (curved line), 279
  direct, 280
  inverse, 280

Curvilinearity, 305
Cyclical influences (*C*), 343, 367
Cyclical patterns, 352–354

d (given percent of population proportion),
    133
Dallas Morning News, 45, 46*n.*, 90*n.*
Data:
  accuracy of, in sampling, 96, 98
  grouped (*see* Grouped data)
  methods of classification of, 214
  microeconomic, 331
  nominal, 240, 271
  ordinal, 214, 228, 231, 271
  primary, 4
  ranked, 240
  secondary, 4
  sources of, 331
  ungrouped, 20
    standard deviation of, 28, 44
Data bases, 439, 440
  business and social science research,
    448
  computerized, 6–7
DEC (Digital Equipment Corporation)
    computers, 453
Deciles, 26, 44
Decision making using sample information,
    376–386
Decision trees, 8, 378–380, 396
Decompose a curve, 341
Decomposition, 355
Decomposition technique, 343
Definitional formula, 288
Deflator, 429
Degrees of freedom, 132, 194, 217, 288
  determining number of, 217
  (*See also* Independence)
Delphi method, 332–333, 367
Demand, elasticity of, 415–416
Denominator (V_2), 195
Dependent variable, 278, 442
Deriving the normal equations for *a* and *b*,
    286–287
Descriptive statistics, 7
Descriptive techniques, 14
"Deseasonalize," 367
Destructive testing, 96
Determination of sample size for different
    allocation methods, 140, 141
Determining number of degrees of freedom,
    217, 222
Deviation(s):
  absolute values of, 282
  average, 27
  mean absolute, 27
  standard (*see* Standard deviation)

Dichotomous dependent variable, 442
Difference:
   test of differences between means, 190,
      197, 199, 200
      one-tailed, 187–188
      two-tailed, 182–184
   test of differences between means and
      proportions, 186
   test of differences between proportions, 199
      one-tailed, 189
      two-tailed, 185
   test of differences between sample means,
      182
   test of differences between two means,
      197, 199
      standard error of, 183, 190
   test of differences between two proportions,
      197, 200
Diffusion indexes, 343, 362, 363, 368
*Digest of Education Statistics and Projections
   of Education Statistics*, 5
Direct coefficients, 368
Direct curvilinear, 280
Direct linear, 280
Direct requirements tables, 360
Discrete binomial distribution, 80
Discrete distribution, 67, 72, 74
Discrete probability distributions, 67, 85
Discrete random variable, 67
Discriminant analysis, 441, 442–443
Discriminant functions, 442, 443
Dispersion, 29
   around regression line, 288
Disposable income (Y_D), 358
Distorted graphs, 17
Distribution(s):
   bimodal, 22
   binomial (*see* Binomial distribution)
   continuous probability, 78, 86
   discrete, 67, 72, 74
   discrete probability, 67, 85
   frequency (*see* Frequency distribution)
   normal (*see* Normal distribution)
   Poisson (*see* Poisson distribution)
   probability (*see* Probability distribution)
   of sample means, 103
   student's *t*, 130
   uniform, 217, 218
Distribution-free (nonparametric) tests, 214,
     231, 240
Divisor, 408
Dollars & Cents of Shopping Centers: 1975, 90
Dow Jones average, 406, 407, 414, 428
Dow Jones Index, 408–409
Dummy variables, 442
Dun's Market Identifiers, 5
Duration of the cycle, 353–354
Durbin-Watson test, 292

e (constant), 75
E (expected frequency), 216
Econometric models, 330, 355, 357–360,
     367–368
Economic Almanac, 4
Edison Electric Institute, 331
Effect of factor:
   1, 447
   1 and 2, 447
   2, 447
Elasticity of demand, 415–416
Electronics Industries Association, 6
Encyclopedia of Associations, 6
Equal allocation, 134, 135, 137, 138, 140, 141,
     145
Equal Rights Amendment, 61–62
Equations and formulas for *a* and *b*, 287
Errors:
   Type I (*see* Type I errors)
   Type II (*see* Type II errors)
Escalator, 429
Estimate:
   ability to, 305
   interval, 153
   point, 105, 113, 153, 285–286
   standard error of (*see* Standard error, of
     estimate)
Estimates of the future, 368
Estimating a conditional mean, 291
Estimating a mean, 110
Events, 396
   independent, 59, 85
   non-mutually exclusive, 58, 85
   nonindependent, 59, 85
Expected frequency (*E*), 216
Expected value, 375
   of perfect information, 380–381, 396
Explained variation, 293, 294, 455
Exponential curve, 306
Exponential smoothing, 337–338
   constants, 338
   short-cut technique for, 327, 339
External control, 87
Extrapolation, 286, 307, 310

F distribution, 193*n.*
F distribution curves, 196
F ratio, 193, 458
F statistic, 195
*F & S Index of Corporations and Industries,
   The*, 5
FAA Statistical Handbook, 4
Factor analysis, 441, 443–445
Factors, 444
   causal, 355
False hypothesis, 178
   acceptance of (*see* Type II errors)

False hypothesis (*Cont.*):
　power of the test to reject, 165, 166
Family life cycle patterns, 363, 368
Federal Aviation Agency (FAA), 4
Federal Housing Authority (FHA), 5
Federal Reserve Board of Governors, 4, 368,
　427
Federal Reserve Bulletin, 4, 428
Federal Reserve–MIT model, 357
Federal Trade Commission, 202
Final adjusted indexes, 346
Financial firms, 5
Finding and projecting underlying causes,
　355–366
Finite population correction factor (*cf*),
　126–130, 145
　confidence intervals and, 126–127
　sample size with, 127–130
Fitting a line, 281–284
Fixed-year weights, 415
Forecast for confidence intervals, 290, 309
Forecast interval for an individual forecast,
　290
Forecasting, 327–374
　causal models technique of, 329, 330
　long-range forecasts, 8, 329, 341, 367
　middle range forecasts, 329
　one-person forecasts, 332
　one-time forecasts, 289
　qualitative forecasts, 329
　regional and/or sector forecasts, 330
　short-range forecasts, 8, 329, 330, 334, 367
　standard error of estimate for a forecast,
　　289–291
　time series analysis and projection
　　technique of, 329–330
　(*See also* Recomposition and forecasting)
Frame, 98, 113
Frequency, 15
　expected (*E*), 216
　observed (*O*), 216
Frequency distribution, 43, 72
　cumulative, 16–17
Frequency distribution table, 14–16
Frequency of occurrence, relative, 56, 85
Frequency polygon, 16, 43

Gallup Organization, 356
"Gee-whiz" graph, 17
Given-year weights, Paasche's index, 411,
　413, 415, 429
GNP (*see* Gross national product)
Goodness of fit, tests of, 218, 231
　chi-square, 215–217, 224–225, 231, 240,
　　271
　Kolmogorov-Smirnov, 240, 255–257, 271
Government agencies, 5

Government expenditures and net exports (*G¹*),
　358
Grand mean $\overline{\overline{X}}$, 194, 197
Gross national product (*Y*), 358, 363
Gross national product (implicit) deflator,
　421–422, 429
Grouped data:
　computation of mean for, 24–25
　computation of median for, 25–26
　standard deviation of, 33

H (test statistic), 229, 232
Handbook of Labor Statistics, 4
Heteroscedastic, 292, 307
Hewlett-Packard computers, 453
Histogram (bar chart), 16, 43
Historic forecast, 334
History of index numbers, 407–408
Hit ratio, 443
Holdout sample, 443
Homogeneity within clusters, 141
Homoscedasticity, 192*n.*, 292, 306
Housing and Urban Development Trends, 5
Housing starts (*HS*), 358
Housing Statistics, 5
HUD Statistical Yearbook, 4
Hypothesis:
　alternate, 161, 178
　false (*see* False hypothesis)
　null (*see* Null hypothesis)
　true, 154, 178
Hypothesis tests, 8
　procedure for, 161
Hypothesized mean, 162, 164

IEEE Spectrum, 372
Implicit function, 286
Independence, 222
　statistical, 60–63
　tests of, 222, 231
　　chi-square, 211, 221–222, 224–225, 231,
　　　240, 271
　　Kolmogorov-Smirnov, 240, 257–259
Independent events, 59, 85
Independent variable, 278, 441–442
Index(es), 8
　to adjust for price changes, 421–422
　consumer sentiment, 330, 355, 356–357,
　　367
　diffusion, 343, 362, 363, 368
　final adjusted, 346
　items to include in, 414–415
　Laspeyres (*see* Laspeyres' indexes)
　Paasche's (*see* Paasche's indexes)
　of price relatives (*see* Price relatives, index
　　of)

Index(es) (*Cont.*):
  quantity, 426–428, 430
  quantity relatives, 430
  splicing two, 422, 429
Index of Industrial Production, 406, 427–428, 430
Index numbers:
  base period and, 414
  base-year weights and, 415
  computation with, 420
  given-year weights and, 415
  history of, 407–408
  problems of construction, 414–416
  unweighted aggregative, 408–409
  weighted aggregative, 411–412
Indexing, 407
Indicators:
  coincident, 362, 363, 368
  lagging, 362, 363, 368
  leading, 331, 343, 355, 362, 363, 368
Indifferent between renting and buying, 383
Individual value of *Y*, 289–291
Inductive accounting, 96
Industrial production, 363
Inferences about the population, 8
Inferential statistics, 7
Information in study of statistics, 1–4
Information Please Almanac, 4
Input-output analysis, 355, 360
Input-output models, 330, 360–361, 368
Institute of Social Research, 256
Intention-to-buy surveys, 330, 356, 357, 367
Inter-University Consortium for Political and
    Social Research (ICPSR), 440, 448–449
Interacting, 305
Interaction effect, 447
Intercorrelation between samples, 143
Interest groups, 6
Internal control, 87
Internal structure, 261
International Harvester, 323
Interpretation of computer printouts, 453–461
Interquartile range (IQR), 332
Interval data, 271
Interval estimate, 153
Interval scale, 214, 215, 231, 240
Interview(s):
  bias of interviewer in, 98
  length of, 98
  personal, 98, 113
  selection diagram for interviewer, 123
  telephone, 98, 113
Inverse curvilinear, 280
Inverse linear, 280
Inverse (Bayesian) probability, 388–392, 396–397
Inverse process of reasoning, 388

IQR (interquartile range), 332
Irregular influences (*I*), 343

Journal of American Statistical Association, 357*n*.
Judgment samples, 102, 113

Kolmogorov-Smirnov tests:
  D statistic, 256–257, 270
  goodness of fit for ordinal data, 240, 255–257, 271
  independence, 240, 257–259
Kondratieff cycles, 353
Kruskal-Wallis test, 192, 228–230, 231–232, 240, 255, 271
Kurtosis, 40, 45
Kuznets cycles, 353

Labor cost, 363
Lagged variables, 368
Lagging indicators, 362, 363, 368
Lags, 342
Large samples:
  one-tailed test, 258
  two-tailed test, 258
Laspeyres' indexes:
  aggregative, 411, 428
  price relatives, 412, 415, 428
Law of Small Numbers, The, 77
Leading indicators, 331, 343, 355, 362, 363, 368
Leads, 343
Least-cost allocation, 134, 137–141, 146
Least-squares, method of, 284–287
Least-squares criterion, 283
Least-squares regression line, 284, 308
  computation of, 284–285, 308–309
Length of interview, 98
Leptokurtic, 40, 45
Level of significance, 158, 161
Lichten Foundation for Human Rights, 117
Life cycle analysis, 355, 363–368
Likert scales, 256
Limitations of regression analysis, 304–308, 310
Line, best-fitting, 282
Linear:
  direct, 280
  inverse, 280
Linear regression analysis:
  conditions for using, 292
  limitations of, 310
Link relatives, 416, 429
List in sampling, 98

Literary Digest, 8, 9
Local almanacs, 4
Logical positivism, 304
Long-range forecasts, 8, 329, 341, 367
Long-run patterns, 341, 342
    finding, 349–351
Long-run trends, 330
Lowering type II error, 163–164

McGraw-Hill survey of plant and equipment
    expenditure intentions, 356
Mail questionnaire, 98, 113
Mann-Whitney test, 240, 247, 248, 251, 254,
    271
    one-tailed, 251–252
    two-tailed, 247–251
MANOVA (multivariate analysis of variance),
    447
"Market basket," 407, 418–419
Market penetration, 323
Market research agencies, 262
Marketing strategy, 212
Matched pairs, 267
Mathematicial expectation, 63
Maximum deviation D, 256
Mean, 43, 289
    alternate, specific value of, 162
    arithmetic, 20, 334
        weighted, 23
    of binomial distribution, 72
    column, 197
    computing, 72–73
        for grouped data, 24–25
    conditional, 291, 309
    difference between: means and proportions,
        186, 199
        sample means, 182
        several means, 197
        two means, 197, 199
    estimating a, 110
    hypothesized, 162, 164
    population, 20, 21, 75
    sample [*see* Sample mean(s)]
    standard error of (*see* Standard error, of the
        mean)
    tests: of differences between means, 190,
        197, 199, 200
        one-tailed, 187–188
        two-tailed, 182–184
        of differences between means and
            proportions, 186
        of a mean, small sample, 174, 200
        one-tailed, 168–169, 176
        two-tailed, 169–170, 175
    theoretical, 247
Mean absolute deviation, 27

Mean sales at a given level, 291
Meaningful units of measurement to use a
    scattergram, 281
Measuring error, 138–140, 141–143
    standard error of estimate, 287
    type II, 162
Medial average, 346
Median, 21, 22, 25, 43, 332
    above the, 263–265
    below the, 263–265
    for grouped data, 25–26
Mesokurtic, 40, 214*n*.
Method of least-squares, 284–287
Methods of data classification, 214
Microeconomic data, 331
Middle range forecasts, 329
Midpoint, 15, 24, 72
Minimizing costs, decision analysis for, 383
Minimum, 308
Modal class, 22
Mode, 22, 43
Monthly Business Failures, 5
Monthly Catalogue, 6
Monthly Labor Review, 4, 419
Monthly New Business Incorporations, 5
Moving average, 336–337, 367
Multicollinearity, 304, 310, 455
Multiple analysis of variance, 441, 445
Multiple regression analysis, 272, 277, 287,
    302, 310, 356, 357, 440
Multiple regression program, 455–459
Multisample test, 177
Multistage sampling technique, 141
Multivariate analysis, 441–448
Multivariate analysis of variance (MANOVA),
    447
Multivariate techniques, 440
Mutually exclusive bounds, 14
Mutually exclusive events, 57, 85

National Association of Homebuilders (NAH),
    410
National Bureau of Economic Research, 5, 331
National Industrial Conference Board, 4, 5
National Longitudinal Studies (NLS), 440, 448,
    449
National Paperboard Association, 331
National School Lunch program, 418
Net regression coefficients, 303
New sample size formula, 128
New York Times Index, 6
Nominal data, 240, 271
Nominal variable, 214, 231, 240
Non-mutually exclusive events, 58, 85
Nonfarm inventory investment (*I*), 358
Nonindependent events, 59, 85

Nonparametric (distribution-free) tests, 214, 231, 240

Nonprobability samples, 101–102

Normal curve(s), 214
of error, 78
standard deviation of, 79, 86

Normal distribution, 29, 78–79, 102, 113, 217
binomial distribution, relation to, 79
continuous, 80, 86
probabilities using, 83

Normal equations for a and b, 286–287

Null hypothesis, 158, 161, 178, 199
reject a, 165, 166

Numerator (V_1), 195

Objective (classical) probability, 56, 85

Oblique factors, 444

Oblique rotations, 445

Observed frequency (O), 216

Odds, 66

Ogive curve, 17, 43

One-person forecasts, 332

One-sample runs test, 261–263

One-sample tests, 167–172, 177, 181

One-tailed test, 160–161
of the difference between means, 187–188
of the difference between proportions, 189
of a large sample, 258
of a mean, 168–169, 176
of a proportion, 170–171
of a small sample, 176, 258

One-time forecasts, 289

"Open-ended" category, 15

Optimum allocation (Neyman), 134, 136–141, 146

Optimum cutting score, 443

Ordinal data, 214, 228, 231, 271

Ordinal scales, 240

Origin, 350

Orthogonal, 444, 445

OSIRIS, 444, 453

Overlapping boundaries, 14

Paasche's indexes:
aggregative, 411, 415, 429
price relatives, 413, 415, 429

Panels, 332, 367

Parabolas, 305

Parameter, 20, 79

Partial derivatives, 286

PATS (data base), 7

Payoff tables, 377–378, 396

Payoffs, 376, 396

P/E NEWS (data base), 7

Peak, 353, 362

Peakedness, 40, 214n.

Percentage points, 420

Percentiles, 26, 44

Perfect information, 381, 393
expected value of, 380–381, 396

Permutations, 68

Personal interview, 98, 113

Personal tax rate, 358

Phasing out, 366

Physics Today, 315

Plant and equipment expenditures (*PE*), 358
plans for, 356

Platykurtic, 40, 45

Point estimate, 105, 113, 153, 285–286

Poisson distribution, 67, 74–75, 217, 220
binomial distribution, relation to, 74–75

Poisson statistics, 214

Poisson table, use of, 75–77

Polk, R. L., Registrations, 1977, 324

Pompeii, A. D. 79, 10

Pooling, 190

Population, 103
inferences about, 8
parameters of, 213–214
relation of sample size to population size, 126

Population mean, 20, 21, 75

Population regression coefficient, 300

Population standard deviation, 28

Population variance, 28

Portfolio analysis, 299

Positively skewed, 215

Posterior information, 396

Posterior probability, 393–396, 397

Pounds per square inch (psi), 237

Power curve, 164–167, 179

Power of the test to reject a false hypothesis, 165, 166

Predicasts, Inc., 5

Prediction, 333

Preproduct development, 366

Price relatives, index of, 413, 428, 429
Laspeyres', 412, 415, 428
Paasche's, 413, 415, 429
unweighted, 409–410
weighted, 412

Primary data, 4

Principal components method, 445

Principal factors method, 445

Prior probabilities, 395, 397

Probability(ies), 376, 396
Bayesian (inverse), 388–392, 396–397
of a failure, 70
game of chance, 64
objective (classical), 56, 85
posterior, 393–396, 397
prior, 395, 397
simple rules of, 57–60, 85
standard normal, 156

Probability (ies) (*Cont.*):
  subjective, 56, 85
  of successes, 70
  using binomial distribution, 83
  using normal distribution, 83
Probability distribution, 66, 67, 79
  continuous, 78, 86
  discrete, 67, 85
Probability samples, 97–101
Probability theory, 8, 56
Problems of index number construction,
    414–416
Producer Price Index, 406, 423, 428, 429
  formerly called Wholesale Price Index, 429
Producer's risk, 154, 178
Product development, 366
Product life cycle, 328, 366, 368
Profit maximization, 383
Profitability, 211
Projecting and finding underlying causes,
    355–366
Proportion(s):
  confidence interval for, 108–109
  sample size for, using correction factor,
    128, 145
  standard error of, 104, 108, 113
  standard error of difference between, 185
  test(s), 177
    of difference between proportions, 199
      one-tailed, 189
      two-tailed, 185
    of differences between means and
      proportions, 186
    of differences between sample
      proportions, 182
    of differences between two proportions,
      197, 200
    one-tailed, 170–171
    two-tailed, 171–172
Proportional allocation, 134, 135, 137, 138,
    140, 141, 145
Public Affairs Information Services Index, 6
Purchasing power of the dollar, 421, 429

Qualitative forecasts, 329
Quality, 415
Quantity indexes, 426–428, 430
Quantity relatives index, 430
Quartiles, 26, 44
Questionnaire, 98, 113
Quota samples, 101, 113

r (coefficient of correlation), 295, 309
  sampling distribution of the, 296
R² (coefficient of determination), 293–295, 309
  significance of the, 295–297

Rand Corporation, 333
Random numbers, 98
Random sampling, 98, 141
  stratified, 100
  systematic, 100, 113
Random variable:
  continuous, 67
  discrete, 67
Range, 27, 44, 309
Rank-order correlation, 240–245, 255, 271
Rank-sum test, 240, 247, 267
  Mann-Whitney (*see* Mann-Whitney test)
  Wilcoxon, 240, 248
Ranked data, 240
Rapid growth, 366
Rare events, 75
Ratio data, 241, 271
Ratio scales, 215
Reader's Guide to Periodical Literature, 6
Real Estate Today, 410
Real growth, 421
"Real-life" situation, 2
Recomposition, 355
Recomposition and forecasting, 354–355
Reference dates, 362
Regional and/or sector forecasts, 330
Regression analysis, 355–366, 367
  assumptions of, 299–300
  limitations of, 304–308, 310
Regression coefficient(s), 286, 288, 299,
    309
  net, 303
  population, 300
  significance of *b* for, 299
  standard error of, 300
Regression line, 367
  dispersion around, 288
  least-squares (*see* Least-squares regression
    line)
  slope of, 299
  standard error of, 288, 300
Reject a null hypothesis, 165, 166
Reject a true hypothesis (*see* Type I errors)
Relative frequency of occurrence, 56, 85
Relative Importance of Commodities (included
    in the Producer Price Index), 424
Replace, 60
Representativeness, 9
Research organizations, 5
Residential construction expenditure, 358
Response rate, 98
Retain type I error, 163–164
Rotation, 445
Rotter's test for internal and external control,
    87
Rounding, 14
Rule of thumb, 84
Run, 261

Runs test, 261, 271
  one-sample, 261–263

Sales Management, 46, 47
Sales of retail stores, 363
Sample(s), 20
  clustered, 113, 141–146
    standard error of, 142, 146
  convenience, 101, 113
  decision making using, 376–386
  intercorrelation between, 143
  judgment, 102, 113
  nonprobability, 101–102
  probability, 97–101
  quota, 101, 113
  self-weighting, 135, 146
  standard deviation of, 28–29, 107
Sample allocation(s), 134–135
  cost comparison for different, 140
Sample correlation coefficient, 296
Sample mean(s), 20, 21, 197
  distribution of, 103
  test of difference between sample
    proportions and, 182
Sample proportion(s), 197
  test of difference between sample means
    and, 182
Sample size, 110–111, 133–134, 140, 145,
    182–184
  determination of, 140, 141
  with finite population correction factor (*cf*),
    127–130
  new, formula for, 128
  for a proportion using correction factor,
    128, 145
  relation of population size to, 126
Sample survey, 3
  cost of, 96, 98
  methods of, 97, 98
  time required for, 96, 98
Sample test(s):
  one-tailed, 176, 258
  two-tailed, 258
Sample units, 113
Sampling, 96
  accuracy of data in, 96, 98
  area, 101, 118, 141
  multistage technique of, 141
  random, 98, 141
  simple random, 100, 113
  stratified, 134–141
  stratified random, 100
  systematic random, 100, 113
Sampling error, 146
  comparison of, 140
Sampling fraction, 126, 135
SAT scores, 79

Savings (*S*), 358
Say's Law, 343
Scales, 444
  cardinal, 215
  ordinal, 240
Scatter, 29
Scatter diagrams, 278–281, 308
Scattergram, 453
Scientific test, 161
Seasonal influences (*S*), 343, 367
Seasonal patterns, 330
Seasonal variations, isolating and studying,
    343–346
Second derivatives, 287
Secondary data, 4
Sector forecasts, 330
Secular trends, 341, 367
Securities and Exchange Commission (SEC), 5,
    291, 356
Self-weighting sample, 135, 146
Sensitivity analysis, 381–386, 396
Shifting the base-year, 429
Shipbuilding Labor Adjustment Board, 407
Short-cut computation methods, 225, 227
Short-cut formula, 288
Short-range forecasts, 8, 329, 330, 334, 367
Short-term cycles, 353
Sign test, 239, 266, 271
Significance:
  versus ability to estimate, 305
  level of, 158, 161
Simple random sampling, 100, 113
Simple regression program, 453
Simple rules of probability, 57–60, 85
Simultaneous equations, 303
Skewness, 40, 45, 214*n*.
  positively skewed, 215
Slope:
  b, 284, 308
  regression line, 299
  straight line, 283, 284, 308
Small sample, 125
  one-tailed test, 176, 258
  two-tailed test, 258
SMSA (Standard Metropolitan Statistical Area),
    45, 48, 101
SOCIAL SCI SEARCH (data base), 7
Specific value of the alternate mean, 162
Splicing two indexes, 422, 429
SPSS (Statistical Package for the Social
    Sciences), 440, 444, 452
"Stairstep plan," 115
Standard Corporation Descriptions, 5
Standard deviation, 247
  of binomial distribution, 72–73
  of grouped data, 33
  of normal curve, 79, 86
  population, 28

Standard deviation (*Cont.*):
  of sample, 28–29, 107
  of ungrouped data, 28, 44
Standard error:
  of clustered samples, 142, 146
  of difference between proportions, 185
  of difference between two means, 183, 190
  of estimate, 287, 293, 309
    meaning of, 288–289
    measuring, 287
    use of, for a forecast, 289–291
  of mean, 104, 105, 107, 113, 155
    all strata combined, 138, 146
  of proportions, 104, 108, 113
  of regression coefficient b, 300
  of regression line, 288, 300
Standard Metropolitan Statistical Area (SMSA),
  45, 48, 101
Standard normal probabilities, 156
Standard normal table, 80
Standard and Poor's Corporation, 5, 363
Statistic(s), 20, 231
  descriptive, 7
  inferential, 7
Statistical Abstract of the United States, 4, 331
Statistical experiments, 3, 9–11
Statistical independence, 60–63
Statistical investigations, 9–11
Statistical Package for the Social Sciences
  (SPSS), 440, 444, 452
Statistical programs for hand-held calculators,
  459
Statistical Yearbook of the United Nations, 4
Steady state, 366
Stock market prices, 362
Stock split, 408
Stratified random sampling, 100
Stratified sampling, 134–141
Student's t distribution, 130
Subjective probability, 56, 85
Substitution, 415
Successes, probability of, 70
Sum or errors, 282
Survey (*see* Sample survey)
Survey of Buying Power, 1978, 324
Survey of Consumer Finances, 141
Survey of Current Business, 4, 356, 360, 361,
  428
Survey Research Center, 5, 356
Surveys, intention-to-buy, 330, 356, 357, 367
Symmetric, 40, 78, 214*n.*, 215
Systematic random sampling, 100, 113

t distribution, 131–133, 215
t statistic, 131
t tables, 167, 179
t test, 161, 190, 271

Telephone interview, 98, 113
Test(s):
  chi-square [*see* Chi-square test(s)]
  Durbin-Watson, 292
  goodness of fit (*see* Goodness of fit, tests of)
  independence (*see* Independence, tests of)
  Kolmogorov-Smirnov (*see* Kolmogorov-
    Smirnov tests)
  Kruskal-Wallis (*see* Kruskal-Wallis test)
  Mann-Whitney (*see* Mann-Whitney test)
  mean (*see* Mean, tests)
  multisample, 177
  nonparametric (distribution-free), 214, 231,
    240
  one-sample, 167–172, 177, 181
  one-sample runs, 261–263
  one-tailed (*see* One-tailed test)
  proportion [*see* Proportion(s), test(s)]
  rank-sum (*see* Rank-sum test)
  Rotter's, for internal and external control, 87
  runs, 261, 271
  sign, 266–269, 271
  small sample, 176, 258
  t, 161, 190, 271
  two-sample, 181
  two-tailed (*see* Two-tailed test)
  Wilcoxon, 240, 248
  z, 161, 271
Test statistic (H), 229, 232
Testing, destructive, 96
Testing and introduction of product, 366
Texas Almanac, 4, 46
Tied ranks, 242*n.*, 255
Tier graph, 346–348
Time series, 341, 367
Time series analysis and projection technique
  of forecasting, 329–330
Time survey, 96, 98
Time units, 350
Total coefficients, 368
Total requirements tables, 360
Total variance for all strata, 138
Total variation, 293, 294
Trade associations, 6
Traffic, 211
Trend, 341, 367
Trend influences (T), 343, 367
Trend patterns, 330, 341
  finding, 349–351
Trials, 70
Trough, 353, 362
True hypothesis, 154, 178
Two-sample tests, 181
Two-tailed test, 160, 247–251, 258
  of differences between means, 182–184
  of differences between proportions, 185
  of a large sample, 258
  of a mean, 169–170, 175

Two-tailed test (*Cont.*):
  of a proportion, 171–172
  of a small sample, 258
Type I errors, 154, 156–159, 163, 164, 179
  retaining, 163–164
Type II errors, 154, 157–159, 163, 164, 178, 179
  lowering, 163–164
  measuring, 162

U statistic, 247
U test, 247
Unbiased estimator, 28*n.*
Uncontrollable events, 376
Underlying causes, finding and projecting, 355–366
Unemployment rate, 363
Unexplained variation, 293, 294
Ungrouped data, 20
  standard deviation of, 28, 44
Uniform distribution, 217, 218
Unimodal, 40
U.S. Bureau of Labor Statistics, 4, 407, 415, 418, 423
U.S. Census Bureau, 5, 118, 356, 366
U.S. Department of Agriculture, 425
U.S. Department of Commerce, 4, 5, 330, 331, 354, 356, 360, 361
U.S. Department of Health, Education, & Welfare, 5
U.S. Department of Housing and Urban Development, 4, 5
U.S. Department of Labor, 4
U.S. Department of the Treasury, 5
U.S. government documents, 4–5
U.S. Government Printing Office, 360
Unweighted aggregative index numbers, 408–409
Unweighted index of price relatives, 409–410
Use of binomial tables, 71–72
Use of Poisson table, 75–77
Using an index to adjust for price changes, 421–422

V_B (between column variation), 195
Value of *a*, (*Y* intercept), 284, 308
Value of *b*, (slope), 284, 308
Value weights, 412

Values not explained, 455
Variability between and within clusters, 141
Variable(s):
  continuous random, 67
  dependent, 278, 442
  discrete random, 67
  dummy, 442
  independent, 278
  lagged, 368
Variance, 44, 138, 182
  analysis of (ANOVA), 178, 182, 192–197, 200, 230
  multiple analysis of, 441, 445
  multivariate analysis of (MANOVA), 447
  nominal, 214, 231, 240
  population, 28
  total, for all strata, 138
Variation(s):
  between column (V_B), 195
  between groups, 192, 193
  coefficient of, 38–39, 44
  explained, 293, 294, 455
  of sample means, 107
  seasonal, 343–346
  total, 293, 294
  unexplained, 293, 294
  within each group, 192, 193

Wall Street Journal, 5, 202*n.*, 245*n.*, 407
Weighted aggregative index numbers, 411–412
Weighted arithmetic mean, 23
Weighted index of price relatives, 412
Wharton School, 368
  econometric model of, 357
Wholesale Price Index (*see* Producer Price Index)
Width of a confidence interval, 126
Wilcoxon test, 240, 248
World Almanac, 4

Y, individual value of, 289–291
Y intercept, 283, 284, 308

z score, 80
z table, 132, 167
z test, 161, 271
z values, 156, 183, 185

$$N = n_1 + n_2$$

$$T = \frac{t^3 - t}{12} \qquad \text{(p. 255)}$$

Kolmogorov-Smirnov one-sample test

$$D_c = \max |cF_E(X) - cF_O(X)| \qquad \text{(9-10)}$$

Kolmogorov-Smirnov two-sample test

$$\chi^2 = 4D_c^2 \frac{n_1 n_2}{n_1 + n_2} \qquad \text{(9-12)}$$

Runs test one sample

$$\mu_r = \frac{2n_1 n_2}{n_1 + n_2} + 1 \qquad \text{(9-14)}$$

$$\sigma_r = \sqrt{\frac{2n_1 n_2 (2n_1 n_2 - n_1 - n_2)}{(n_1 + n_2)^2 (n_1 + n_2 - 1)}} \qquad \text{(9-15)}$$

$$z = \frac{r - \mu_r}{\sigma_r} \qquad \text{(p. 252)}$$

Least-squares regression line $\hat{Y} = a + bX$ (10-4)

$$a = \bar{Y} - b\bar{X} \qquad \text{(10-5)}$$

$$b = \frac{\Sigma XY - n\overline{XY}}{\Sigma X^2 - \bar{n}X^2} \qquad \text{(10-6)}$$

Standard error of estimate

$$s_{y.x} = \sqrt{\frac{\Sigma Y^2 - a\Sigma Y - b\Sigma XY}{n - 2}} \qquad \text{(10-8)}$$

Confidence interval for an individual forecast

$$\hat{Y} \pm ts_{fy} \qquad \text{(10-9)}$$

$$\text{where} \quad s_{fy} = s_{y.x} \sqrt{1 + \frac{1}{n} + \frac{(X_f - \bar{X})^2}{\Sigma X^2 - n\bar{X}^2}} \qquad \text{(10-10)}$$

Confidence intervals for a conditional mean

$$\hat{Y} \pm ts_{y.x} \sqrt{\frac{1}{n} + \frac{(X - \bar{X})^2}{\Sigma X^2 - n\bar{X}^2}} \qquad \text{(10-12)}$$

Coefficient of determination

$$R^2 = \frac{a\Sigma Y + b\Sigma XY - n\bar{Y}^2}{\Sigma Y^2 - n\bar{Y}^2} \qquad \text{(10-16)}$$

Test r is significantly different from 0

$$t = \frac{r}{\sqrt{(1 - R^2)/n - 2}} \qquad \text{(10-17)}$$

Test regression coefficient B is significantly different from 0.

$$t = \frac{b - B}{s_b} \qquad \text{(10-18)}$$

$$\text{where} \quad s_b = \frac{s_{y.x}}{\sqrt{\Sigma X^2 - n\bar{X}^2}} \qquad \text{(10-19)}$$

Multiple regression analysis

$$\hat{Y} = a + b_1 X_1 + b_2 X_2 \qquad \text{(10-21)}$$

Exponential smoothing

$$F_t = \alpha D_t + \alpha(1 - \alpha)D_{t-1} + \\ \dots + \alpha(1 - \alpha)^k D_{t-k} \qquad \text{(11-1)}$$

Once a forecast is made, the next forecast can be made using

$$F_t = \alpha D_t + (1 - \alpha)F_{t-1} \qquad \text{(11-2)}$$

Bayesian probability

$$P(A_1|B_1) = \frac{P(A_1)P(B_1|A_1)}{P(A_1)P(B_1|A_1) + P(A_2)P(B_1|A_2)} \qquad \text{(12-1)}$$

Unweighted index numbers

$$I = \frac{\Sigma p_n}{\Sigma p_0}(100) \quad \text{aggregative index} \qquad \text{(13-1)}$$

$$I = \frac{\Sigma(p_n/p_0)}{n}(100) \quad \text{price relatives index} \qquad \text{(13-2)}$$

Weighted index numbers using base-year *weights*

$$I = \frac{\Sigma p_n q_0}{\Sigma p_0 q_0}(100) \quad \begin{array}{l}\text{Laspeyres'}\\\text{aggregative index}\end{array} \qquad \text{(13-3)}$$

$$I = \frac{\Sigma[p_n/p_0(p_0 q_0)]}{\Sigma p_0 q_0}(100) \quad \begin{array}{l}\text{Laspeyres' index}\\\text{of price relatives}\end{array} \qquad \text{(13-5)}$$

Weighted index numbers using given-year *weights*

$$I = \frac{\Sigma p_n q_n}{\Sigma p_0 q_n}(100) \quad \begin{array}{l}\text{Paasche's}\\\text{aggregative index}\end{array} \qquad \text{(13-4)}$$

$$I = \frac{\Sigma[p_n/p_0(p_n q_n)]}{\Sigma p_n q_n}(100) \quad \begin{array}{l}\text{Paasche's index}\\\text{of price relatives}\end{array} \qquad \text{(p. 413)}$$

Index of quantity relatives

$$I = \frac{\Sigma[(q_n/q_0)p_0 q_0]}{\Sigma p_0 q_0} \qquad \text{(p. 428)}$$